Other Kaplan Books for College-Bound Students

College Admissions and Financial Aid

Straight Talk on Paying for College

Parent's Guide to College Admissions

The Unofficial, Unbiased Guide to the 328 Most Interesting Colleges

Test Preparation

SAT 1600

Ring of McAllister: A Score-Raising Mystery Featuring 1,046 Must Know SAT Vocabulary Words

What Smart Girls Know About the SAT

SAT for Super Busy Students

SAT Vocabulary Flashcards Flip-O-Matic

SAT Vocab Velocity

SAT Math Mania

SAT II: Biology E/M

SAT II: Chemistry

SAT II: Literature

SAT II: Mathematics Levels IC and IIC

SAT II: Physics

SAT II: Spanish

SAT II: U.S. History

SAT II: World History

SAT II: Writing

SAT Verbal Workbook

SAT Math Workbook

ACT

SAT* 2005

BY THE STAFF OF KAPLAN, INC.

Simon & Schuster

NEW YORK · LONDON · SYDNEY · TORONTO

Kaplan Publishing
Published by Simon & Schuster
1230 Avenue of the Americas
New York, NY 10020

Contributing Editors: Seppy Basili and Jon Zeitlin

Project Editor: Charli Engelhorn

Cover Design: Cheung Tai

Interior Page Layout: Evan Smith Rakoff

Production Manager: Michael Shevlin

Managing Editor: Déa E. Alessandro

Executive Editor: Jennifer Farthing

Thanks to: Renée Mitchell, Laurel Douglas, Grace Begany, Michael Bitz, Joanna Cohen, and Darcy Galane

July 2004

10 9 8 7 6 5 4 3 2 1

Manufactured in the United States of America

Published simultaneously in Canada

ISBN 0-7432-4132-0

ISSN 1093-3395

Table of Contents

Section 5: Practice Tests and Explanations

Section 6: SAT Study Aids

www.kaptest.com/booksonline

Want more help preparing for the SAT? Log on to
www.kaptest.com/booksonline to access a wide selection of
additional practice questions. Prepare for all parts of the SAT
online, or focus on those sections where you feel weakest.

Access to this selection of Kaplan's online SAT practice questions is free of charge to purchasers of this book. When you
log on, you'll be asked to input the ISBN number of the book
you purchased (see the bar code on the back cover). And
you'll be asked for a specific password derived from a passage
in this book, so have your book handy when you log on.

www.kaptest.com/publishing

The material in this book is up-to-date at the time of publication. However, the College Entrance Examination Board may
have instituted changes in the test or test registration process
after this book was published. Be sure to carefully read the
materials you receive when you register for the test.

If there are any important late-breaking developments—or any
changes or corrections to the Kaplan test preparation materials
in this book—we will post that information online at
www.kaptest.com/publishing. Check to see if there is any
information posted there for readers of this book.

SAT 2004 Update

SAT COMPETITION

Getting into college has never been more competitive. More students are applying to more colleges with some predictable results: more rejection letters going out, and significantly more wait-list notices. Here's a snapshot of what you're up against when it comes to the SAT:

- In 2003, the mean score on the Verbal section was 507, a 3 point increase from 2002. On the Math section, the mean score was 519 in 2003—a 35-year high.

- In 2003, 1,406,324 high school graduates took the SAT (a 5 percent rise over 2002). Twenty-two percent of SAT I test takers attained a combined (Verbal and Math) score of 1200 or higher. Twenty-eight percent of test takers had GPAs that placed them in the top 10 percent of their high school class.

SAT TEST DATES

The competitive college admissions landscape has changed testing patterns: more students are taking the SAT earlier. To some degree, this trend is the result of an increased number of students applying to early decision programs. Another factor is that more students are taking the SAT more than once. In general, the shift to taking the SAT earlier reflects the importance of getting your SAT scores under your belt by the end of your junior year so that you know where you stand and can plan accordingly.

Here are the SAT dates for the remaining part of 2004. In March 2005, the New SAT will make its debut.

2004 Saturday Administrations			
National Test Dates	**Tests Offered**	**Registration Deadlines**	
		U.S. and International	**U.S. Late**
Ocotber 9, 2004	SAT I, SAT II	September 7, 2004	September 11, 2004
November 6, 2004	SAT I, SAT II and ELPT	October 1, 2004	October 13, 2004
December 4, 2004	SAT I & SAT II	October 29, 2004	November 10, 2004
January 22, 2005	SAT I, SAT II and ELPT	December 20, 2004	December 29, 2004
March 12, 2005 New SAT	SAT I only	February 7, 2005	February 16, 2005

A New SAT in 2005

The SAT is getting a major overhaul. A new version of the SAT will replace the current test beginning in March 12, 2005. The changes are designed to align the test more closely to high school curricula and college skills, thus making the test a more accurate predictor of college performance. There will be changes not only in the content tested but also in the types of questions used. Here are the most important changes.

The New Writing Section

The biggest change in the SAT will be the addition of a writing test. The SAT Writing Section will include multiple choice questions and a written essay. The multiple choice questions will test the students ability to identify sentence errors and to make improvements in sentences and paragraphs. The essay section will assess the student's writing ability. Plans call for the student to be asked to write a persuasive essay taking a position on a particular issue given them in the test and support their position with reasons and evidence. The Writing Section of the SAT will be 50 minutes in length.

Changes to the Verbal Section

First, the Verbal section is getting a new name to reflect its new focus: Critical Reading. The Analogies questions, which required test takers to understand the meanings of specific words and analyze the relationship between them (see chapter 5 for examples) are being dropped. In their place there will be short reading passages added with one to two multiple-choice questions following each passage. The new Critical Reading section will be 70 minutes instead of the 75 minutes currently allocated for the Verbal section.

Changes to the Math Section

Some questions of greater difficulty will be added to the SAT Mathematical section; these will cover the topics usually taught in algebra II in U.S. high schools. In addition, the Quantitative Comparison questions, which require a comparison of a quantity in column A to a quantity in column B to determine which is larger, are being eliminated entirely (see chapter 12 for examples). They will be replaced by additional regular multiple choice questions and Grid-in questions. The Math section in the new SAT will be 70 minutes—five minutes shorter than it currently is.

Scoring the New Test

The new writing test will be scored on a scale 200-800, the same scale currently used for the Mathematical and Verbal sections of the SAT. The composite scores on the new test will be between 600-2400, instead of the 400-1600 now used.

Frequently Asked Questions

Which test should I take?

Students in the class entering college in 2005 will take the current SAT, and students in the class of 2007 will take the new test. However, if you are in the class of 2006, most colleges plan to accept the higher of the scores from the current SAT and the new SAT. Check with the colleges you're considering to find out their policies. Kaplan recommends that students in the class of 2006 take both tests.

Will the new test be harder?

Yes, most students will find the new test to be harder. The new writing section will test students' knowledge of grammar and require them to write an essay in 20–25 minutes. The new SAT math section will include more advanced algebra. The test itself will be longer and require more stamina. However, keep in mind that your score is based on how well you did compared with other students. Therefore, even though it's harder, your score on the new SAT may be better than your score on the current test.

How will the essays on the new SAT be graded?

Essay graders hired by the test makers will assign a score of 1 to 6 to each essay based on a rubric, or scoring scale. Each essay will be graded by two readers. If the essay readers' scores differ by more than two points, the essay will be graded by a third reader and all the readers' scores averaged together.

Will many colleges still require the SAT II: Writing test?

No. Since writing will be tested on the new SAT, there is no reason for colleges to require the SAT II: Writing test. In fact, the College Board has announced plans to discontinue this test.

For More Information

The latest information about the new SAT is available at kaptest.com/newsat.

SAT Changes in a Nutshell

	Current SAT	Changes for New SAT
Verbal	Critical Reading (long passages), Sentence Completion, Analogies	Analogies eliminated, Short Critical Reading passages added
Math	5-Answer Multiple Choice, Quantitative Comparisons, Grid-Ins	Quantitative Comparisons eliminated, Advanced Algebra added
Writing	Does not exist	Multiple-Choice Grammar, 20–25 minute essay
Time	3 hours	Now 3 hours and 35 minutes
Scoring	Math: 200-800 Verbal 200-800	Math: 200-800 Critical Reading 200-800 Writing: 200-800

KAPLAN

The SAT Emergency Plan

You can make the best use of this book by starting several months before the test and giving yourself plenty time to practice the strategies, work through the review chapters, and take all the practice tests. If you wish, you can take one of the practice tests first so that you get a sense of what it is you are facing.

However, if you have only two or three weeks—or even less time than that—you'll need a different plan.

Maybe you have only two or three weeks—or even less time than that. Don't freak! *SAT* has been designed to work for students in your situation, too. If you go through a chapter or two every day, you can finish this book in a couple of weeks. If you have limited time to prepare for the SAT (fewer than two weeks), we suggest you do the following:

1. If you feel totally stressed out, take a slow, deep breath. Read chapter 16, "Stress Management," to maximize your study and testing time.

2. Read the "SAT Mastery" chapter.

3. Read the "SAT Emergency" sidebar at the beginning of each chapter. The suggestions in these sidebars can really streamline your study strategy as well as ensure that you cover the vital concepts before Test Day.

4. Take as many of the Practice Tests as you can—in the book or on the CD-ROM, depending on your preference—*under timed conditions*.

5. Review your results, with special attention to the questions you missed.

6. Give yourself the day before the test off.

Scattered throughout the text you'll find "hints"—special points that we feel deserve emphasis and amplification. Pay special attention to these hints, which spotlight some very important test prep information. Sidebars also highlight key concepts and strategies, fun facts, and real-world stories.

SAT Emergency FAQs

Q. It's two days before the SAT and I'm clueless. What should I do?

A. First of all, don't panic. If you only have a day or two to prepare for the test, then you don't have time to prepare thoroughly. But that doesn't mean you should just give up. There's still a lot you can do to improve your potential score. First and foremost, you should become familiar with the test. Read chapter 1, "SAT Mastery." And if you don't do anything else, take one of the full-length practice tests at the back of this book under reasonably testlike conditions. When you finish the practice test, check your answers and look at the explanations to the questions you didn't get right.

Q. Math is my weak spot. What can I do to get better at math in a big hurry?

A. Review the "SAT Math in a Nutshell" chapter, which highlights the 100 Key Math Concepts for the SAT. Then do as many of the sample problems in chapter 13, "Classic Problem-Solving Techniques," as you have time for. If you don't have time to do the sample problems, just read the sidebars in the math chapters. They contain really helpful facts and tips.

Q. I'm great at Math, but Verbal scares me. How can I improve my Verbal score right away?

A. Go straight to the section called "Decoding Strange Words on the Test" in chapter 4. Much of the SAT Verbal depends on your ability to work with unfamiliar words. It's also a good idea to check out the SAT Word Families, as well as the SAT Root List. Then do as many of the sample problems in the Verbal chapters as you have time for. If you don't have time to do the sample problems, just read the sidebars in those chapters. These strategies can help boost your score.

Q. I get to use a calculator on the SAT! Does that mean I don't have to worry about learning math?

A. Not exactly. You ARE allowed to bring a calculator to the SAT, but that's actually a mixed blessing. If you don't use your calculator wisely, you could actually end up wasting time or, even worse, generating wrong answers. Make sure to read the chapter on "Calculators and the SAT," particularly the pages on Common Calculator Mistakes, before you take the test. Knowing when and how to use your calculator will help you immeasurably. And remember, your calculator won't think for you!

Q. My parents are upset with me for waiting till the last minute to study, and now I can't concentrate. Help!

A. Take a deep breath! Anxiety and stress are the enemies of all test takers—no matter how much time they have to prepare. Turn to chapter 16 and read through Kaplan's suggestions for managing stress. Do the suggested exercises. And don't forget to think positively!

Q: The SAT is tomorrow. Should I stay up all night studying geometry formulas?

A: The best thing to do right now is to try to stay calm. Read the "What Do I Do Now?" chapter to find out the best way to survive, and thrive, on Test Day. And get a good night's sleep.

Q: I don't feel confident. Should I just guess?

A: You should always guess if you can do so intelligently. The SAT does have a wrong-answer penalty for most question types, but that doesn't mean you should never guess. If you can rule out even ONE answer choice, you should guess, because you have significantly increased your chances of guessing correctly. Also, on questions that appear early in a section, more obvious answers will tend to be correct, so you can guess more confidently on those questions. Finally, always guess on Grid-ins, since there is no wrong-answer penalty on that question type.

Q: What's the most important thing I can do to get ready for the SAT quickly?

A. In addition to basic Math and Verbal skills, the SAT mainly tests your ability to take the SAT. Therefore, the most important thing you can do is to familiarize yourself with the directions, the question types, the answer grid, and the overall structure of the test. Make sure you feel comfortable with the logistics—how to get to your test center, how to fill in Grid-ins, how (and when) to use your calculator. Read every question carefully—many mistakes are the result of simply not reading thoroughly.

Q. So it's a good idea to panic, right? RIGHT?

A. No! No matter how prepared you are for the SAT, stress will hurt your performance, and it's really no fun. Stay confident, and don't cram. So . . . breathe. Stay calm, and remember, it's just a test.

How to Team Up for a Better Score on the SAT

Being a loner has a certain mystique, it's true. Loners seem cool and aloof, which has some benefits when it comes to cultivating a rock star image. But when it comes to preparing for the SAT, there is safety in numbers. Even if the term "group work" makes you cringe, you should think about setting up an SAT study team—what we call an **SAT Power Pack**.

Why Join an SAT Power Pack?

- *An SAT Power Pack keeps you committed.* You are far less likely to blow off studying if your friends are depending on you to show up at meetings and be useful.

- *An SAT Power Pack points out the error of your ways.* It is sometimes hard to see your own weaknesses. Your SAT Power Pack will help you recognize and correct your trouble spots.

- *An SAT Power Pack calms you down.* Preparing for the SAT is stressful. With so much riding on your score, it's no wonder some students get a bit frayed around the edges as test day approaches. Your SAT Power Pack is there to give you the support you need. It is always comforting to know that you are not alone.

How to Get Started

Having a successful study group takes a lot more than a box of doughnuts and a dining room table. It takes careful planning and a little negotiation. Use the list below to get off to the right start.

- *Choose your Power Pack wisely.* This doesn't mean you can only team up with straight-A students. But you should steer clear of people who are not as serious as you are about preparing well for the SAT. They will only waste your time. The right number of partners is important, too: we recommend limiting your group to three to six members. That way you have all the benefits of teaming up, but no one gets overshadowed or left behind.

- *Set realistic goals from the outset.* Everyone in your Power Pack needs to take a practice test from section 6 of this book before the first meeting. Once you know what your strengths and weaknesses are, you should have a discussion with your partners about what you hope to gain from the SAT Power Pack. A 100-point score improvement? Better math skills? Reduced anxiety? You can certainly have individual goals, but your pack needs to be heading in the same general direction for you to work together well.

- *Find the right meeting place.* You need a place where you can all sit comfortably for a couple of hours free from distraction. You need room to spread out your materials. Some access to food and drinks is a nice bonus.

- *Make an ironclad schedule.* Get out your calendars and mark down every meeting in advance. Commit to those times. We recommend at least four meetings of at least one hour each; two hours is better. It's hard to get anything accomplished in less time than this. Decide in advance what material you will cover at each meeting.

General Guidelines

OK, you've got the members, you've got the place, you've got the time. But exactly what are you all supposed to do for two hours?

The Best Way to Learn Is to Teach

To make every minute count, you need to agree on a procedure for learning. One effective way to use your meeting time is to pick a "teacher" from the group for each chunk of material you want to cover.

For example, Bianca takes chapter 8, "Critical Reading Skills." Everyone reads chapter 8 in advance, but it is Bianca's job to set up a lesson on Critical Reading for the rest of the group. It is up to her to set the agenda. This takes a lot of preparation and extra planning, but the advantage is that by the time Bianca has taught the session, she will be an expert on critical reading.

Warning: *Do* Attempt This at Home

To make your SAT Power Pack meetings more productive, you will all have to do some preparation on your own. This means reading chapters in advance, taking practice tests, and bringing in whatever extra materials your pack thinks are necessary.

Practice, Practice, Practice

Take at least two of the three practice tests in this book. You should take the first before your initial meeting so you have an idea of your skill level. Take another test after a couple of meetingsm and discuss your results in a Power Pack meeting. This will help you pinpoint trouble areas, gauge your progress, and build your familiarity with the test format. If you like, you can take a final practice test after your last meeting to measure your improvement.

I'm a Tutor, You're a Tutor

The children of millionaires aren't the only ones who can get one-on-one SAT tutoring. Your SAT Power Pack can provide that, too. Just have every member of your group pair up with a partner. Partners should evaluate one another's practice tests to locate weaknesses and give some focused help in those areas.

Get Hooked on Mnemonics

Performing well on the SAT Verbal section does take more than a good vocabulary . . . but a good vocabulary sure will help a lot. It makes sense to spend some time studying the SAT Word List in section 7. There are several tried-and-true memorization techniques you can use on your own, like making flashcards with the vocabulary word on one side and the definition on another.

But in an SAT Power Pack, you can get more creative and have a little more fun. One activity you can try is having each member select ten words from the SAT Word List and come up with a mnemonic device for each one to share with the pack. A mnemonic (pronounced "nuh-MON-ik") device is just a memory aid—something catchy that helps you remember a piece of information.

For example, take the word *florid*, which means "ruddy" or "flushed." You might remember this definition by thinking of the state of Florida, which sounds like *florid*. Florida has lots of sunny beaches where tourists get badly sunburned. Imagine the red-faced tourists of Florida, and you will probably remember *florid*. Mnemonic devices can be as weird or creative as you want. In fact, you may find you can remember weird ones better than straightforward ones.

Run a Math Guess-a-Thon

As you'll learn, there's a so-called "guessing penalty" on most sections of the SAT. That means that on everything but Math Grid-In questions, you lose part of a point for every wrong answer, while leaving a question blank costs you nothing. This spooks a lot of students into skipping questions they find tough. Wrong strategy! If you can cross out even one answer choice using the process of elimination, it is in your best interest to take a good guess. The odds are that over the course of the whole test, you will wind up with a better score. Aggressive guessing takes some guts, so you'd better practice. Try this exercise during your SAT Power Pack meetings:

- Throughout this book, you'll find tons of practice questions. Review the chapter on "Math Guessing," then try any of the practice questions in the Math section without actually working the problems. Eliminate answers you think seem unlikely, then guess. (You can also try this on the Critical Reading practice questions in chapters 7 and 8 by answering the questions without reading the passages and sentences associated with the questions.) See which one of your Power Pack members is the best guesser. Then talk about some of the reasons you used for eliminating answer choices. You may even develop some guessing strategies of your own!

Above All: Don't Panic

To quote the science fiction classic *Dune*, "Fear is the mind killer." If you are super-stressed during the test, you won't think clearly and you won't perform well. Chapters 16 and 17 contain some very effective tips for handling stress. Here are some of the ways you can put these tips into action with your pack:

- *Work out with your SAT Power Pack:* Exercise is an ideal stress reducer. Take an SAT Power Pack partner—or your whole group—and do a quick walk around the block. Get together and go jogging or play basketball. Anything that gets your heart pounding for a little while will take the edge off your anxiety.

- *Get into group meditation:* You might want to close each of your meetings with a short meditation period. We're not talking about chanting and incense here, don't worry. Just have everyone close their books, close their eyes, breathe in and out slowly and deeply, and empty their minds of all worry.

- *Compliment each other:* Sometimes it's hard to focus on the positive when you're stressed out. Make it an SAT Power Pack activity for each group member to point out the strengths of other members (like "Bianca is an ace on Critical Reading passages"). Do this regularly. You will see that new strengths will develop as you continue studying.

- *Celebrate together:* Don't forget to get together one last time after the test to celebrate a job well done!

A Special Note for
International Students

If you are an international student considering attending an American university, you are not alone. Over 582,000 international students pursued academic degrees at the undergraduate, graduate, or professional school level at U.S. universities during the 2001–2002 academic year, according to the Institute of International Education's Open Doors report. Almost 50 percent of these students were studying for a bachelor's or first university degree. This number of international students pursuing higher education in the United States is expected to continue to grow. Business, management, engineering, and the physical and life sciences are particularly popular majors for students coming to the United States from other countries.

If you are not a U.S. citizen and you are interested in attending college or university in the United States, here is what you'll need to get started.

- If English is not your first language, you'll probably need to take the TOEFL* (Test of English as a Foreign Language) or provide some other evidence that you are proficient in English. Colleges and universities in the United States will differ on what they consider to be an acceptable TOEFL score. A minimum TOEFL score of 213 (550 on the paper-based TOEFL) or better is often required by more prestigious and competitive institutions. Because American undergraduate programs require all students to take a certain number of general education courses, all students—even math and computer science students—need to be able to communicate well in spoken and written English.

- You may also need to take the SAT* or the ACT*. Many undergraduate institutions in the United States require both the SAT and TOEFL of international students.

- There are over 3,400 accredited colleges and universities in the United States, so selecting the correct undergraduate school can be a confusing task for anyone. You will need to get help from a good advisor or at least a good college guide that gives you detailed information on the different schools available. Since admission to many undergraduate programs is quite competitive, you may want to select three or four colleges and complete applications for each school.

- You should begin the application process at least a year in advance. An increasing number of schools accept applications year round. In any case, find out the application deadlines and plan accordingly. Although September (the fall semester) is the traditional time to begin university study in the United States, you can begin your studies at many schools in January (the spring semester).

- In addition, you will need to obtain an I-20 Certificate of Eligibility from the school you plan to attend if you intend to apply for an F-1 Student Visa to study in the United States.

Kaplan English Programs

If you need more help with the complex process of university admissions, assistance preparing for the SAT, ACT, or TOEFL, or help building your English language skills in general, you may be interested in Kaplan's programs for international students.

Kaplan English Programs were designed to help students and professionals from outside the United States meet their educational and career goals. At locations throughout the United States, international students take advantage of Kaplan's programs to help them improve their academic and conversational English skills, raise their scores on the TOEFL, SAT, ACT, and other standardized exams, and gain admission to the schools of their choice. Our staff and instructors give international students the individualized attention they need to succeed. Here is a brief description of some of Kaplan's programs for international students:

General Intensive English

Kaplan's General Intensive English classes are designed to help you improve your skills in all areas of English and to increase your fluency in spoken and written English. Classes are available for beginning to advanced students, and the average class size is 12 students.

TOEFL and Academic English

This course provides you with the skills you need to improve your TOEFL score and succeed in an American university or graduate program. It includes advanced reading, writing, listening, grammar, and conversational English. You will also receive training for the TOEFL using Kaplan's exclusive computer-based practice materials.

SAT Test Preparation Course

The SAT is an important admission criterion for American colleges and universities. A high score can help you stand out from other applicants. This course includes the skills you need to succeed on each section of the SAT, as well as access to Kaplan's exclusive practice materials.

Other Kaplan Programs

Since 1938, more than 3 million students have come to Kaplan to advance their studies, prepare for entry to American universities, and further their careers. In addition to the above programs, Kaplan offers courses to prepare for the ACT, GMAT*, GRE*, MCAT*, DAT*, USMLE*, NCLEX*, and other standardized exams at locations throughout the United States.

*All test names used in this section are registered trademarks of their respective owners.

KAPLAN

Applying to Kaplan English Programs

To get more information, or to apply for admission to any of Kaplan's programs for international students and professionals, contact us at:

Kaplan English Programs
700 South Flower, Suite 2900
Los Angeles, CA 90017, USA
Phone (if calling from within the United States): 800-818-9128
Phone (if calling from outside the United States): 213-452-5800
Fax: 213-892-1364
Website: www.kaplanenglish.com
Email: world@kaplan.com

FREE Services for International Students

Kaplan now offers international students many services online—*free of charge*!
Students may assess their TOEFL skills and gain valuable feedback on their English
language proficiency in just a few hours with Kaplan's TOEFL Skills Assessment.
Log onto www.kaplanenglish.com today.

Kaplan is authorized under federal law to enroll nonimmigrant alien students.

Kaplan is accredited by ACCET (Accrediting Council for Continuing Education and Training).

The Basics

1

SAT Mastery

HIGHLIGHTS

- Learn how to use the structure of the SAT to your advantage
- Formulate a plan for attacking the questions

To perform well on the SAT, you need to draw on a set of skills that the College Board does not mention in any of their materials. You need to be a good SAT test taker.

Acquiring this ability, and the confidence it produces, is what this book is about.

There are three simple things you need to master the SAT:

- You need to have a basic understanding of SAT content.
- You need to hone the thinking and testing skills that underlie the SAT.
- You need to know the nature of the SAT.

Content and skills are obviously important. You can't do well without them. But understanding the nature of the SAT, its setup, its structure, and the traps it often sets for you will allow you to gain points on the test that you might not otherwise have earned.

USING THE STRUCTURE OF THE SAT TO YOUR ADVANTAGE

The SAT is different from the tests that you're used to taking. On a school test, you probably go through the problems in order. You spend more time on the hard questions than on easy ones, since this is where you get more points. And

SAT Emergency

If you have just a few weeks to prep for the SAT, don't panic. The first thing you should do is become familiar with the test. This chapter is the place to start.

you often show your work since the teacher tells you that how you approach a problem is as important as getting the answer right.

None of this works on the SAT. You can benefit from moving around within a section, the hard questions are worth the same as the easy ones, and it doesn't matter how you answer the question—only what your answer is.

To succeed in this peculiar context, you need to know some fundamentals about the overall structure of the SAT.

The SAT Is Highly Predictable

Because the format and directions of the SAT remain unchanged from test to test, you can learn the setup in advance. On the day of the test, Analogies, QCs, Grid-ins— or the setup of any other question type or section—shouldn't be new to you.

One of the easiest things you can do to help your performance on the SAT is to understand the directions before taking the test. Since the instructions are always exactly the same, there's no reason to waste your time on the day of the test reading them. Learn them beforehand, as you go through this book, and skip them during the test.

Most SAT Questions Are Arranged by Order of Difficulty

You've probably noticed that not all the questions on the SAT are equally difficult. Except for the Critical Reading problems, the questions are designed to get tougher as you work through a set.

Here's how to use this pattern to your advantage. As you work, you should always be aware of where you are in the set. When working on the easy problems, you can generally trust your first impulse—the obvious answer is likely to be right.

As you get to the end of the set, you need to become more suspicious. Now the answers probably won't come easy. If they do, look at the problem again, because the obvious answer is likely to be wrong. Watch out for the answer that just "looks right." It may be a *distractor*—a wrong answer choice meant to entice you.

There's No Mandatory Order to the Questions

You're allowed to skip around within each section of the SAT. High scorers know this. They move through the test efficiently. They don't dwell on any one question, even a hard one, until they've tried every question at least once.

When you run into questions that look tough, circle them in your test booklet and skip them for the time being. Go back and try again after you have answered the easier ones if you have time. On a second look, troublesome questions can turn out to be amazingly simple.

If you've started answering a question and get confused, quit and go on to the next question. Persistence may pay off in school, but it usually hurts your SAT score. Don't spend so much

SAT Myth

Some people believe that the SAT is an absolute predictor of college performance. Not true— despite the fact that female students score about 43 points lower than male students on the SAT, females tend to earn higher grades in both high school and college!

A Different Kind of Test

The SAT is not like the tests you take in school. In school, you might need to get about 85 or 90 percent of the questions right to get a decent score. On the SAT, you sometimes need little more than 75 percent of the questions right to get a 1300— a very solid combined score.

time answering one tough question that you use up three or four questions' worth of time. That costs you points, especially if you don't get the hard question right.

There's a Guessing Penalty That Can Work in Your Favor

The test makers like to talk about the guessing penalty on the SAT. This is a misnomer. It's really a *wrong answer* penalty. If you guess wrong you get penalized. If you guess right, you're in great shape.

The fact is, if you can eliminate one or more answers as definitely wrong, you'll turn the odds in your favor and *actually come out ahead* by guessing.

Here's how the penalty works:

- If you get an answer wrong on a Quantitative Comparison, which has four answer choices, you lose 1/3 point.

- If you get an answer wrong on other multiple-choice questions, which have five answer choices, you lose 1/4 point.

- If you get an answer wrong on a Grid-in math question, for which you write in your own answers, you lose nothing.

Kaplan Rules

DON'T GUESS, unless you can eliminate at least one answer choice.

DON'T SKIP IT, unless you have absolutely no idea.

The fractional points you lose are meant to offset the points you might get "accidentally" by guessing the correct answer. With practice, however, you'll learn that it's often easy to eliminate several answer choices on some of the problems that you see. By learning the techniques for eliminating wrong answer choices, you can actually turn the guessing "penalty" to your advantage.

The Answer Grid Has No Heart

It sounds simple but it's extremely important: Don't make mistakes filling out your answer grid. When time is short, it's easy to get confused going back and forth between your test book and your grid. If you know the answer, but misgrid, you won't get the points. To avoid mistakes on the answer grid:

Always Circle the Questions You Skip

Put a big circle in your test book around any question numbers you skip. When you go back, these questions will be easy to locate. Also, if you accidentally skip a box on the grid, you can check your grid against your book to see where you went wrong.

Always Circle the Answers You Choose

Circling your answers in the test book makes it easier to check your grid against your book.

Circle Before You Skip

A common cause of major SAT disasters is filling in all of the questions with the right answers—in the wrong spots.

Every time you skip a question, circle it in your test book and make doubly sure that you skip it on the answer grid as well.

Grid Five or More Answers at Once

Don't transfer your answers to the grid after every question. Transfer your answers after every five questions, or at the end of each reading passage. That way, you won't keep breaking your concentration to mark the grid. You'll save time and you'll gain accuracy.

These fundamentals apply to every section of the test. But each question type also has its own structural peculiarities that make them easy to prep for. Some examples: On Grid-ins, the grid cannot accommodate five-digit answers, negatives, or variables. If you get such an answer, you know you've made a mistake and need to redo the problem.

Analogy answer choices are always ordered with the same parts of speech; this helps you determine if you're building an appropriate bridge.

Critical Reading questions with line references, "Little Picture" questions, can often be done quickly and don't require you to read the entire passage. You can do these first in a later reading passage if you're running out of time.

We'll show you lots of these structural elements, and the strategies you can use to take advantage of them, throughout this book.

APPROACHING SAT QUESTIONS

Apart from knowing the setup of the SAT, you've got to have a system for attacking the questions. You wouldn't travel around a foreign city without a map and you shouldn't approach the SAT without a plan. Now that you know some basics about how the test is set up, you can approach each section a little more strategically. What follows is the best method for approaching SAT questions systematically.

Think about the Question Before You Look at the Answer

The people who make the test love to put distractors among the answer choices. Distractors are answer choices that look like the right answer, but aren't. If you jump right into the answer choices without thinking first about what you're looking for, you're much more likely to fall for one of these traps.

Use Backdoor Strategies If the Answer Doesn't Come to You

There are usually a number of ways to get to the right answer on an SAT question. Most of the questions on the SAT are multiple-choice. That means the answer is right in front of you—you just have to find it. This makes SAT questions open to a lot of ways of finding the answer. If you can't figure out the answer in a straightforward way, try other techniques. We'll talk about specific Kaplan methods such as backsolving, picking numbers, and eliminating weak Analogy bridges in later chapters.

Guess Only When You Can Eliminate One Answer Choice

You already know that the wrong answer "penalty" can work in your favor. Don't simply skip questions that you can't answer. Spend some time with them to see if you can eliminate any of the answer choices. If you can, it pays for you to guess.

Pace Yourself

The SAT gives you a lot of questions in a short period of time. To get through a whole section, you can't spend too much time on any one question. Keep moving through the test at a good speed; if you run into a hard question, circle it in your test booklet, skip it, and come back to it later if you have time.

In the sidebar to the right are recommended average times per question. This doesn't mean that you should spend exactly 40 seconds on every Analogy. It's a guide. Remember, the questions get harder as you move through a problem set. Ideally, you can work through the easy problems at a brisk, steady clip, and use a little more of your time for the harder ones that come at the end of the set.

One caution: Don't completely rush through the easy problems just to save time for the harder ones. These early problems are points in your pocket, and you're better off not getting to the last couple of problems than losing these easy points.

Recommended Timing

Section	On Average
Analogies	40 seconds
Sentence Completions	40 seconds
Critical Reading*	75 seconds
Regular Math	70 seconds
QCs	45 seconds
Grid-ins	90 seconds

* Average time for Critical Reading includes time to read the passage. Spend about 30 secs. per question.

Locate Quick Points If You're Running Out of Time

Some questions can be done quickly; for instance, some reading questions will ask you to identify the meaning of a particular word in the passage. These can be done at the last minute, even if you haven't read the passage. On most Quantitative Comparisons, even the hardest ones, you can quickly eliminate at least one answer, improving your chances of guessing correctly. When you start to run out of time, locate and answer any of the quick points that remain.

When you take the SAT, you have one clear objective in mind—to score as many points as you can. It's that simple. The rest of this book will help you do it.

2

Inside the SAT

HIGHLIGHTS

- Familiarize yourself with the breakdown of questions

- Learn how the test is timed and scored

Because it's a standardized test, you can feel safe in knowing that the structure, contents, and questions on the SAT will be pretty much what you should expect after working your way through this book. In this chapter, we will walk you through the structure of the SAT. When you sit down to take the test, you should already know what kind of questions you'll find, what the instructions say, how the test will be scored, and how you will be timed.

STRUCTURE OF THE TEST

There are six types of questions on the SAT, three Verbal and three Math. The likely number of questions you'll see of each type is shown below.

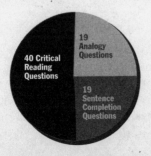

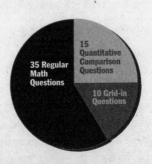

SAT Emergency

If you have only a week or two to prep for the SAT, you should spend time getting familiar with the test. Be sure to read this chapter.

Verbal

On the Verbal section of the SAT you'll find:

- 19 *Analogies*—Analogies test your ability to see relationships between words.

- 19 *Sentence Completions*—These test your ability to see how the parts of a sentence relate. About half will have one word missing from a sentence; the rest will have two words missing. Both types test vocabulary knowledge and reasoning ability.

- *40 Critical Reading questions*, in four separate sets—Critical Reading tests your ability to read and understand a passage. The passages are long (400–850 words), and at least one passage contains two related readings. Some reading questions test your understanding of the content of the passage; others will require you to draw conclusions. Some will also explicitly test vocabulary in context.

Math

On the Math section you'll find:

- 15 *Quantitative Comparisons*—QCs, as they're called, give you two quantities and ask you to compare them. You have to determine if one quantity is larger, if they're equal, or if you don't have enough information to decide. They test your knowledge of math, your ability to apply that knowledge, and your reasoning ability. They're also designed to be done quickly, making them a good source of quick points.

- 35 *Regular Math* questions—These are straightforward multiple-choice math questions, with five answer choices.

- 10 *Grid-ins*—These questions are open-ended, with no answer choices. Instead, you enter your response into a small grid. These questions test the same math concepts as the other types of questions.

SECTION BREAKDOWN

The SAT is divided into seven sections, which can appear in any order:

- Two 30-minute Verbal sections with Analogies, Sentence Completions, and Critical Reading

- One 15-minute Verbal section with Critical Reading

- One 30-minute section with QCs and Grid-ins

- One 30-minute section with Regular Math

- One 15-minute section with Regular Math

There is also one 30-minute Experimental section. This section does not affect your score and is used to try out new questions. It can show up anyplace and it will look like any other Verbal or Math section. Don't try to figure out which section is experimental so you can nap during that period. First of all, you'll lose your momentum in the middle of the test. Second, and more important, you might be wrong.

KAPLAN

SCORING

You get one point added to your score for each correct answer on the SAT, and lose a fraction of a point for each wrong answer (except for Grid-ins—but we'll go into that later). If you leave a question blank, you neither gain nor lose points. The totals are added up for all the Verbal and Math questions, and that produces two raw scores.

These numbers aren't your SAT scores. The raw scores are converted into scaled scores, each on a scale of 200 to 800, and these are the scores that are reported to you and the colleges you choose. (The reports include subscores as well, but most colleges focus on the two main scores.)

In April of 1995, the College Board adjusted or "recentered" the scoring of the SAT. The average scaled score (on a 200- to 800-point scale) for either Math or Verbal is now 500, for an average combined score of 1,000 points. This is almost 100 points higher than the old combined averages. The test isn't any easier or harder; only the scoring has changed.

Bottom line: If you compared your SAT score with that of someone who took the test before 1995 (someone who got the exact number of questions right as you did), your score would probably be higher. Sounds great, right?

Well, it's not so cut-and-dried. Remember, everyone's score is adjusted, so you'll fall in the same percentile range using this new scale as you would using the old. The percentile is the percentage of SAT takers scoring at or below a given score.

> **Did You Know . . .**
>
> . . . that a little bit of improvement on the SAT can go a long way? Getting just one extra question right every ten minutes on the SAT translates to 15 more questions right over the entire test. This improvement could boost your scaled score by close to 150 points.

SAT TIMING

The SAT:

- Is three hours long
- Includes two ten-minute breaks (after Sections 2 and 4)

There are some rules about how you can and cannot allocate this time:

- You are not allowed to jump back and forth between sections.
- You are not allowed to return to earlier sections to change answers.
- You are not allowed to spend more than the allotted time on any section.
- You can move around within a section.
- You can flip through your section at the beginning to see what type of questions you have.

You'll get more familiar with the format and setup of the SAT as you work your way through this book. For now, just remember the basics we covered in chapter 1: The SAT is predictable, there are elements built right into the test that allow you to prep for it, and you need to develop an approach to answering the questions.

SAT Registration Overview

- Check the College Board website at www.collegeboard.com for complete information about registering for the SAT.

- To register for the SAT by mail, you'll need to get a Registration Bulletin from your high school guidance counselor.

- You can also register online at www.collegeboard.com/sat/html/satform.html. The website contains easy, step-by-step instructions for electronically submitting your registration. Not all students are eligible to register online; read the instructions and requirements carefully.

- You may register by telephone, for a fee of $10, only if you've previously registered for the SAT and you require no special forms (like a fee waiver). If you have a touch-tone phone and a major credit card, you can reregister by calling (800) SAT-SCORE. If you need assistance, you can reach a customer service representative at (609) 771-7600.

- Register early to secure the time you want at the test center of your choice and to avoid late registration fees.

- Students with Disabilities can call (609) 771-7137 (TTY: (609) 882-4118) for more information.

- The basic fee at press time is $26 in the United States. This price includes reports for you, your high school, and up to four colleges and scholarship programs. There are additional fees for late registration, standby testing, international processing, changing test centers or test dates, rush reporting, and for additional services and products.

- The SAT is administered on select Saturdays during the school year. Sunday testing is available for students who cannot take the Saturday test because of religious observances.

- You will receive an admission ticket at least a week before the test. The ticket confirms your registration at a specified date, at a specified test center. Make sure to bring it, and proper identification, with you to the test center. Some acceptable forms of identification include photo IDs such as a driver's license, a school identification card, or a valid passport. Unacceptable forms of identification include a social security card, credit card, or birth certificate.

- Check with the College Board for all the latest information on the test. Every effort is made to keep the information in this book up to date, but changes may occur after the book is published.

- You might be considering whether to take the SAT, ACT, or both. For more information on the ACT, go to the ACT website at www.act.org/aap/.

- SAT scores will be available online approximately three weeks after the test. If you can't wait that long, you can get your scores eight days earlier with Scores by Web or Scores by Phone. Both services are $13. Please visit www.collegeboard.com for more information.

Verbal Skills Workout

Introducing SAT Verbal

- Understand the breakdown and setup of the Verbal section
- Tap into existing Verbal skills such as paraphrasing and making inferences

Imagine yourself driving through Paris, France. As you approach an intersection, you see a red octagonal sign with the word *arrêtez* on it. Even if you don't speak a word of French, you come to a stop and look down the crossroads before driving on through the city.

If you didn't know the language, you probably took the information given to you—the shape, color, and location of the sign—and related it to what you already know. You may also have noticed, maybe subconsciously, that *arrêtez* sounds something like *arrest*, which means "stop."

The skills you displayed by making this deduction are skills of inference. To do well on the SAT Verbal section, you need to apply these same skills. The SAT does not test spelling or grammar. It does not test your knowledge of English literature or literary terms. It will never ask you to interpret a poem. SAT Verbal questions cover a fairly predictable, fairly limited body of skills and knowledge: vocabulary, verbal reasoning, and reading skills.

There are three scored Verbal sections on the SAT. The breakdown of the questions will go something like this:

SAT Emergency

This chapter will help you get a handle on the SAT Verbal section. You should read this chapter even if you have two weeks or fewer to prep.

- One 30-minute section with nine Sentence Completions, 13 Analogies, and 13 Critical Reading questions

- One 30-minute section with 10 Sentence Completions, six Analogies, and 14 Critical Reading questions

- One 15-minute section with 13 Critical Reading questions

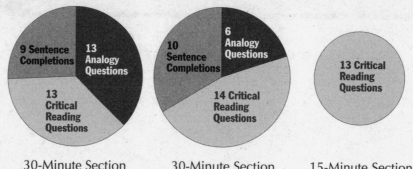

30-Minute Section   30-Minute Section   15-Minute Section

The Sentence Completions and Analogy sets are arranged by order of difficulty. The first few questions in a set are meant to be fairly straightforward and manageable. The middle few questions will be a little harder and the last few are the most difficult. Keep this in mind as you work and move through the early questions a little more quickly to leave yourself more time for the difficult ones. Work through the Sentence Completions and Analogies quickly and efficiently. Make sure you get all the points you can there, and then move on to Reading.

Critical Reading is not arranged by difficulty. Any time you find yourself beginning to spend too much time on a question, you should skip it and return to it later.

What Matters

Your score on the Verbal section is based on your ability to do the following:

- Solve analogies by finding two words that are related in the same way as the two words they give you.

- Fill in the blanks in sentences that are missing one or two words.

- Read a passage and answer a bunch of questions about it.

HOW TO APPROACH SAT VERBAL

To do well on SAT Verbal, you need to be systematic in your approach to each question type and each of the three Verbal sections. Sentence Completions and Analogies are designed to be done relatively quickly. That means you can earn points fast, so you should do these first. Critical Reading takes a lot longer, so you can't just leave yourself five minutes to do a passage. Remember, you earn just as many points for an easy question as you do for a hard one.

Tapping Your Verbal Skills

Although the test materials never explain this, a big key to doing well on the verbal part of the SAT is sharpening your verbal critical thinking skills—skills that you already use every day.

If you get to a movie ten minutes late, do you give up and walk out, deciding you'll never understand what's going on? Probably not. Instead, you use your inference skills—the ability to draw valid conclusions from limited information—to catch up and enjoy the rest of the film.

If you have a sudden urge for a tub of popcorn, do you leave during the climactic scene? More likely, you use your ability to distinguish important concepts from minor details to pick a dull moment to make your move.

When your younger brother asks you what the movie was about, do you take two hours to explain it to him? You probably use your paraphrasing skills—the ability to condense complex ideas into a few words—to give him the highlights in a few minutes before you go back to ignoring him.

Know What to Expect

Doing your best on SAT Verbal comes from knowing what to expect, and knowing that you have the skills to handle it. You use words every day. You make your own ideas clear and you understand and respond to those of others. In all of these cases—talking with friends or talking with teachers, reading a textbook or reading a billboard, listening to lyrics or listening to your SAT proctor's instructions—you take limited information, process it through your own intellect and experience, and make sense of it. If you can learn to make the most of these skills on the test, you'll be well on the road to a great Verbal score.

What Doesn't Matter

You don't need to know pronunciation, antonyms, foreign languages, creative writing, spelling, or anything about literature.

Teacher Tip

"Write all over your test booklet. Crossing out wrong answers eliminates confusion and helps you to see clearly which answer is correct. Underlining key points when reading passages helps you to determine the main idea, and underlining key words in Sentence Completions helps you to predict which word fits correctly in the blank."

—Jennifer Killmer
  Kaplan Teacher
  Coral Gables, FL

4

Vocabulary

HIGHLIGHTS

- Practice working with unfamiliar words and familiar words with secondary meanings

- Improve your vocabulary by studying word roots and families

- Find out how to decode strange words

You know how to read. You can explain the relationship between *kitten* and *cat* to a three-year-old. You can finish a friend's sentence when she sneezes in the middle. So what makes the Verbal section such a challenge? Vocabulary. You may have a solid understanding of a Critical Reading passage but then get thrown by one tough vocabulary word. You may know the relationship between the original pair of words in an Analogy, but have a tough time finding the answer because all the choices have words you've never seen before. You may know precisely what kind of word to fill in on a Sentence Completion, and then find that all the answer choices look like they're in a foreign language.

All three Verbal question types—Analogies, Sentence Completions, and Critical Reading—depend upon your ability to work with unfamiliar words. You won't be asked to define words on the SAT. But you'll need to have a sense of their meaning in order to answer the questions.

SAT Emergency

If you have only a week or two to prep for the SAT, go straight to the section called "Decoding Strange Words on the Test" and try to master those skills.

TWO TYPES OF HARD WORDS

There are two types of hard SAT words:

- Unfamiliar words
- Familiar words with secondary meanings

Some words are hard because you haven't seen them before. The words *scintilla* or *circumlocution*, for instance, are probably not part of your everyday vocabulary. But they might pop up on your SAT.

Easy words, such as *recognize* or *appreciation*, may also trip you up on the test because they have secondary meanings that you aren't used to. Analogies and Critical Reading in particular will throw you familiar words with unfamiliar meanings.

To get a sense of your vocabulary strength, we've provided a representative list of words you might find on the SAT. Take a couple of minutes to look through it and see how many you know. Write your answer right in the book. Give yourself one point for each word you know. (Answers follow the quiz.)

Who Cares?

Somewhere in the process of studying for the Verbal section, you may decide that learning the difference between *taciturn* and *tenacious, obdurate,* and *obloquy,* and even *plaudit* and *pusillanimous* is among the silliest things you've ever done. After all, no one on TV talks that way.

Your vocabulary says a lot about your ability to express yourself, as well as giving some valuable hints as to how well read you are. Colleges like students with big vocabularies, so humor them. Learn some new words.

The single best way to do well on SAT verbal is to read as much as possible. Read newspapers and magazines to see words in use. Underline the ones you need to look up. If you recognize the words you see on the exam, you'll be on your way to acing the SAT.

irritate _____

truthful _____

conquer _____

passionate _____

inactive _____

eliminate _____

benevolent _____

elocution _____

irk _____

pragmatic _____

breadth _____

KAPLAN

rectify _____

duplicity _____

impartial _____

abandon (n.) _____

vie _____

overt _____

august (adj.) _____

laud _____

voluble _____

flag (v.) _____

perspicacity _____

maladroit _____

sonorous _____

doleful _____

serpentine _____

rail (v.) _____

quiescence _____

idiosyncrasy _____

kudos _____

Strange Word Origins

Learning the derivation of words can often help you remember the meaning of words. Did you know . . .

- *Jovial* (joyful) comes from the Roman deity Jove, who was known for his pleasant disposition.

- *Sardonic* (characterized by bitter mockery) comes from sardinia, a mythical plant from the island of the same name. Ingestion of the plant caused convulsive laughter followed by death.

- *Maudlin* (overly sentimental) comes from Mary Magdalene, a follower of Christ who is shown weeping in many paintings. *Maudlin* is an alternate pronunciation of Magdalene.

Here are the definitions of the words in the list on the previous page:

irritate	to annoy, bother
truthful	honest, straightforward, trustworthy
conquer	to defeat, overthrow
passionate	emotional, ardent, enthusiastic
inactive	not active, not moving
eliminate	to get rid of
benevolent	generous, kind
elocution	the study and practice of public speaking
irk	to irritate, anger, annoy
pragmatic	practical; moved by facts rather than abstract ideal
breadth	broadness, wideness
rectify	to correct
duplicity	deception, dishonesty, double-dealing
impartial	fair, just, unbiased, unprejudiced
abandon (n.)	total lack of inhibition
vie	to compete, contend
overt	apparent, unconcealed
august (adj.)	dignified, awe-inspiring, venerable
laud	to praise, applaud, honor
voluble	speaking much and easily, talkative; glib
flag (v.)	to droop, lose energy; to signal, to mark
perspicacity	shrewdness, astuteness, keenness of wit
maladroit	clumsy, tactless
sonorous	producing a full, rich sound
doleful	sad, mournful
serpentine	serpentlike; twisting, winding
rail (v.)	to scold with bitter or abusive language
quiescence	inactivity, stillness
idiosyncrasy	peculiarity of temperament, eccentricity
kudos	fame, glory, honor

If you got ten definitions or fewer right, you should probably work on building your vocabulary. The techniques and tools in this chapter will help you improve your vocabulary and make the most out of what you do know about words.

If you got between 10 and 20 right, your vocabulary is average. If you're willing to put in the time, using these techniques and tools can help you do better.

If you got 20 definitions or more right, your vocabulary is in great shape. You can polish it further, but you don't have to. If time is short, learn the strategies in the "Decoding Strange Words" section and concentrate on other aspects of the SAT that you find difficult.

A VOCABULARY-BUILDING PLAN

A great vocabulary can't be built overnight, but you can develop a better SAT vocabulary with a minimum of pain. Here's a plan:

Learn Words Strategically

The best words to learn are words that have appeared often on the SAT. The test makers are not very creative in their choice of words for each test; words that have appeared frequently are likely bets to show up again.

The word lists in the "SAT Study Aids" section of this book give you a jump on some common SAT words. Learn a few words a day from these lists, spreading them over the time remaining before the SAT. Keep reviewing those you've already studied.

The Word Families list groups words into common meaning families. For example, *loquacious, verbose,* and *garrulous* all mean "wordy, talkative." *Taciturn, laconic, terse, concise,* and *pithy* all mean "not talkative, not wordy." Instead of learning just one of these words, learn them all together—you get eight words for the price of one definition.

Be strategic. How well you use your time between now and the day of the test is just as important as how much time you spend prepping.

Work with Word Roots

Most SAT words are made up of prefixes and roots that can get you at least partway to a definition. Often, that's all you need to get a right answer.

Use the Root List in the "SAT Study Aids" section to pick up the most valuable SAT roots. Target these words in your vocabulary prep. Learn a few new roots a day, familiarizing yourself with the meaning.

Personalize Your Vocabulary Study

Figure out a study method that works best for you, and stick to it.

Teacher Tip

"Take five vocabulary flashcards a day and learn them thoroughly—flip through them at least three times. Each day take on five more, adding them to the cards from the previous day. Review your collection as it grows. Vocabulary skills will build dramatically if this is kept up until Test Day!"

—Jennifer Killmer
Kaplan Teacher
Coral Gables, FL

- Use flashcards: Write down new words or word groups and run through them whenever you have a few spare minutes. Put one new word or word group on one side of a 3 × 5 index card and a short definition on the back.

Personalize Your Home Study

- Use flashcards.
- Make a vocabulary notebook.
- Make a vocabulary tape.
- Look for hooks or phrases that will lodge a new word in your mind.

- Make a vocabulary notebook: List words in one column and their meaning in another. Test yourself. Cover up the meanings, and see which words you can define from memory. Make a sample sentence using each word in context.

- Make a vocabulary tape: Record unknown words and their definitions. Pause for a moment before you read the definition. This will give you time to define the word in your head when you play the tape back. Quiz yourself. Listen to your tape in your portable cassette player. Play it in the car, on the bus, or whenever you have a few spare moments.

- Think of hooks that lodge a new word in your mind: Create visual images of words.

- Use rhymes and other devices that help you remember the words.

It doesn't matter which techniques you use, as long as you learn words steadily and methodically. Doing so over several months is ideal.

DECODING STRANGE WORDS ON THE TEST

Trying to learn every word that could possibly appear on the SAT is like trying to memorize the license plate number of every car on the freeway. It's not much fun, it'll give you a headache, and you probably won't pull it off.

No matter how much time you spend with flashcards, vocabulary tapes, or word lists, you're bound to face some mystery words on your SAT. No big deal. Just as you can use your basic multiplication skills to find the product of even the largest numbers, you can use what you know about words to focus on likely meanings of tough vocabulary words.

Go with Your Hunches

When you look at an unfamiliar word, your first reaction may be to say, "Don't know it. Gotta skip it." Not so fast. Vocabulary knowledge on the SAT is not an all-or-nothing proposition.

- Some words you know so well you can rattle off a dictionary definition of them.

- Some words you "sort of" know. You understand them when you see them in context, but don't feel confident using them yourself.

- Some words are vaguely familiar. You know you've heard them somewhere before.

If you think you recognize a word, go with your hunch!

Try to Recall Where You've Heard the Word Before

If you can recall a phrase in which the word appears, that may be enough to eliminate some answer choices, or even zero in on the right answer.

Between the two villages was a ---- through
which passage was difficult and hazardous.

(A) precipice

(B) beachhead

(C) quagmire

(D) market

(E) prairie

To answer this question, it helps to know the word *quagmire*. You may remember *quagmire* from news reports referring to "a foreign policy *quagmire*" or "a *quagmire* of financial indebtedness." If you can remember how *quagmire* was used, you'll have a rough idea of what it means, and you'll see it fits. You may also be reminded of the word *mire*, as in "We got *mired* in the small details and never got to the larger issue." Sounds something like stuck, right? You don't need an exact definition. A *quagmire* is a situation that's difficult to get out of, so (C) is correct. Literally, a *quagmire* is a bog or swamp.

Decide If the Word Has a Positive or Negative "Charge"

Simply knowing that you're dealing with a positive or negative word can earn you points on the SAT. For example, look at the word *cantankerous*. Say it to yourself. Can you guess whether it's positive or negative? Often words that sound harsh have a negative meaning, while smooth-sounding words tend to have positive meanings. If *cantankerous* sounded negative to you, you were right. It means "difficult to handle."

You can also use prefixes and roots to help determine a word's charge. *Mal, de, dis, un, in, im, a,* and *mis* often indicate a negative, while *pro, ben,* and *magn* are often positives.

Not all SAT words sound positive or negative; some sound neutral. But if you can define the charge, you can probably eliminate some answer choices on that basis alone.

EXAMPLE

He seemed at first to be honest and loyal, but
before long it was necessary to ---- him for his
---- behavior.

(A) admonish . . steadfast

(B) extol . . conniving

(C) reprimand . . scrupulous

(D) exalt . . insidious

(E) castigate . . perfidious

All you need to know to answer this question is that **negative words are needed in both blanks.** Then you can scan the answer choices for a choice that contains two clearly **negative words.** Choice (E) is right. *Castigate* means "punish or scold harshly," and *perfidious* means "treacherous."

Use Your Foreign Language Skills

Many of the roots you'll encounter in SAT words come from Latin. Spanish, French, and Italian also come from Latin, and have retained much of it in their modern forms. English is also a cousin to German and Greek. That means that if you don't recognize a word, try to remember if you know a similar word in another language.

Look at the word *carnal*. Unfamiliar? What about *carne*, as in *chili con carne*? *Carn* means "meat" or "flesh," which leads you straight to the meaning of *carnal*—pertaining to the flesh. You could decode *carnivorous* ("meat eating") in the same way.

You can almost always figure out something about strange words on the test because SAT words are never all that strange. Chances are that few words on the SAT will be totally new to you, even if your recollection is more subliminal than vivid.

When All Else Fails

Eliminate choices that are clearly wrong and make an educated guess from the remaining choices. A wrong answer won't hurt you much; a right answer will help you a lot.

Don't forget to study the word lists in the "SAT Study Aids" section!

Checklist

Once you've mastered a concept, check it off.
Vocabulary:
❏ A vocabulary-building plan
❏ Decoding strange words

5

Analogies

HIGHLIGHTS

- Become proficient in building bridges

- Study the Kaplan Three-Step Method for Analogies

- Review the nine classic bridges

- Use process of elimination as a backup strategy

- Complete the Analogies Practice Set

Analogies may seem frightening at first because they don't look like anything you've ever done before. But you'll feel better about them as soon as you realize that you speak and think in analogies all the time. Any time you say "my sister is like a slug," you're drawing an analogy between your sister and slugs—perhaps your sister is as gross as a slug. That may not be the kind of relationship that will appear on your SAT, but the way of thinking is the same.

Once you get familiar with the Analogy format, you'll find there's a simple method for mastering this question type. In fact, prepping often gains you more points on Analogies than on any other Verbal question type. With practice, you can even learn to get the Analogy right when you don't know all of the vocabulary words involved.

SAT Emergency

If you don't have much time to prep for the SAT, here's the best way to spend your time:

- Learn the Kaplan Three-Step Method for Analogies.

- Do the practice set in this chapter.

- If you miss an answer, review the tips in this chapter.

THE FORMAT

There are 19 Analogies in all on the SAT. You'll probably see one set of 13 and one set of six. Each 30-minute Verbal section contains a set of Analogies. A question looks like this:

| EXAMPLE |

FLAKE : SNOW ::

(A) storm : hail

(B) drop : rain

(C) field : wheat

(D) stack : hay

(E) cloud : fog

The two words in capital letters are called the *stem words*. The instructions will tell you to choose the pair of words from the five answer choices that is related in the same way as this pair. In this example, the answer above is (B). A flake is a small unit of snow, just as a drop is a small unit of rain.

BUILDING BRIDGES

In every Analogy question, there exists a strong, definite connection between the two stem words. Your task is to identify this relationship, and then to look for a similar relationship among the answer pairs.

What's a strong, definite relationship?

- The words *library* and *book* have a strong, definite connection. A library is defined as a place where books are kept. LIBRARY : BOOK could be a question stem.

- The words *library* and *child* do not have a strong, definite connection. A child may or may not have anything to do with a library. LIBRARY : CHILD would never be a question stem.

Teacher Tip

"Analogies are not just about knowing the words, they are also about knowing how to spot a strong bridge. Right answers are chosen based on good elimination strategies."

—Suzanne Riskin
   Kaplan Teacher
   Miami, FL

The best way to pinpoint the relationship between the stem words is to build a bridge. A bridge is a short sentence that relates the two words. Often, a bridge reads like a definition of one of the two words. For instance: "A *library* is a place where BOOKS are kept."

The ability to find bridges is fundamental to Analogy success. Your bridge needs to capture the strong, definite connection between the words.

KAPLAN'S THREE-STEP METHOD

The Kaplan Method for solving Analogies has three simple steps:

1. Build a bridge between the stem words.
2. Plug in the answer choices.
3. Adjust your bridge, if you need to.

Here's an Analogy stem. We've left out the answer choices because you need to focus first on the stem.

EXAMPLE

LILY : FLOWER ::

1. Build a Bridge

The best bridge here is, "A LILY is, by definition, a type of FLOWER."

2. Plug in the Answer Choices

Here is the complete question.

EXAMPLE

LILY : FLOWER ::

(A) rose : thorn

(B) cocoon : butterfly

(C) brick : building

(D) maple : tree

(E) sky : airplane

> ### What Makes a Strong Bridge?
>
> You might be lured into thinking the words *trumpet* and *jazz* have a strong bridge. They don't.
>
> You can play lots of things on trumpets other than jazz—fanfares, taps, whatever. You can also play jazz on things other than trumpets.
>
> *Trumpet* and *instrument* do have a strong bridge. A trumpet is, by definition, a type of instrument. This is always true—it's a strong, definite relationship.

Take the bridge you have built and plug in answer choices (A) through (E). If only one pair fits, it's the answer.

HINT: *Be sure to try all five choices.*

Here's how plugging in the answer choices works:

(A)   A *rose* is a type of *thorn*? No.

(B)   A *cocoon* is a type of *butterfly*? No.

(C)   A *brick* is a type of *building*? No.

(D)   A *maple* is a type of *tree*? Yes.

(E)   A *sky* is a type of *airplane*? No.

We've got four nos and only one yes, so the answer is (D).

3. Adjust Your Bridge If You Need To

If no answer choice seems to fit, your bridge is too specific and you should go back and adjust it. If more than one answer choice fits, your bridge is not specific enough. Look at this example:

EXAMPLE

SNAKE : SLITHER ::

(A) egg : hatch

(B) wolf : howl

(C) rabbit : hop

(D) turtle : snap

(E) tarantula : bite

With a simple bridge, such as "a snake slithers," you'd have a hard time finding the answer. All the answer choices make sense: an *egg hatches*, a *wolf howls*, a *rabbit hops*, a *turtle snaps*, and a *tarantula bites*. Don't worry. Go back to step one and build another bridge, this time making it more specific. Think about what *slither* means.

New bridge: "Slithering is how a snake gets around."

(A)   *Hatching* is how an *egg* gets around? No.

(B)   *Howling* is how a *wolf* gets around? No.

(C)   *Hopping* is how a *rabbit* gets around? Yes.

(D)   *Snapping* is how a *turtle* gets around? No.

(E)   *Biting* is how a *tarantula* gets around? No.

Four nos and one yes; the answer is (C).

HINT: *If no answer fits, or too many answers fit, build a new bridge and plug in again.*

WHAT PART OF SPEECH IS A STEM WORD?

Occasionally with an Analogy you might have to take a quick peek at the answer choices before you can build a bridge for the stem. The part of speech of a stem word may be ambiguous. When you're not sure whether a stem word is a noun, verb, adjective, or adverb, look at the words directly beneath that stem word. As a rule, the words in a vertical row are all the same part of speech.

For example, you might see this:

> VERB : NOUN ::
>
> (A) verb : noun
>
> (B) verb : noun
>
> (C) verb : noun
>
> (D) verb : noun
>
> (E) verb : noun

or this:

> ADJECTIVE : NOUN ::
>
> (A) adjective : noun
>
> (B) adjective : noun
>
> (C) adjective : noun
>
> (D) adjective : noun
>
> (E) adjective : noun

but you'll *never* see this on an SAT Analogy:

> NOUN : NOUN ::
>
> (A) verb : noun
>
> (B) noun : noun
>
> (C) verb : verb
>
> (D) verb : noun
>
> (E) verb : noun

To establish the part of speech of a stem word, you don't usually have to look at more than choice (A).

How would you think through the following example?

> EXAMPLE
>
> PINE : DESIRE ::
>
> (A) laugh : sorrow
>
> (B) drink : thirst
>
> (C) watch : interest
>
> (D) listen : awe
>
> (E) starve : hunger

The word *pine* can be a noun, but that's not likely here. You can't build a bridge between a tree with needlelike leaves and *desire*. Try another part of speech. A glance at the answer choices below *pine* (*laugh, drink, watch, listen,* and *starve*) tells you *pine* is being used as a verb.

What about *desire*? It could be a noun or a verb, but the answer choices beneath it (*sorrow, thirst, interest, awe,* and *hunger*) tell you it's used as a noun.

You've probably heard of someone pining away from unrequited love. As a verb, *pine* means "to yearn or suffer from longing." A good bridge would be: "By definition, to pine is to suffer from extreme desire." Plugging in the answer choices, you get:

(A)   To *laugh* is to suffer from extreme *sorrow*? No.

(B)   To *drink* is to suffer from extreme *thirst*? No.

(C)   To *watch* is to suffer from extreme *interest*? No.

(D)   To *listen* is to suffer from extreme *awe*? No.

(E)   To *starve* is to suffer from extreme *hunger*? Yes.

Once again, four nos and one yes; the answer is (E).

TEST YOUR ANALOGY SMARTS

Try out what you've learned on these Analogies. (Answers on p. 34.)

1. SWEEP : BROOM ::

    (A) cut : scissors
    (B) soil : cloth
    (C) dry : bucket
    (D) thread : needle
    (E) wash : dish   Ⓐ Ⓑ Ⓒ Ⓓ Ⓔ

2. MAP : ATLAS ::

    (A) lock : key
    (B) road : highway
    (C) recipe : cookbook
    (D) concept : encyclopedia
    (E) theory : hypothesis   Ⓐ Ⓑ Ⓒ Ⓓ Ⓔ

3. HUNGRY : FAMINE ::

    (A) thirsty : rainfall
    (B) sick : plague
    (C) sated : dinner
    (D) dry : flood
    (E) sore : injury   Ⓐ Ⓑ Ⓒ Ⓓ Ⓔ

NINE CLASSIC BRIDGES

It's easier to build bridges when you know the types of bridges that have appeared on the SAT in the past. While no one can give you a list of the words that will appear on SAT Analogies, you can learn what types of relationships to expect. The following classic bridges appear over and over again on the SAT. Don't memorize these bridges, or lists of words that fit these bridges. Instead, learn which types of bridges can lead you to the right answer on SAT Analogies and which cannot.

HINT: *Become familiar with the types of bridges that connect stem words on the SAT. They can lead you to the right answer.*

Classic bridges may take different forms, depending on what parts of speech are used. But the underlying concepts are what matter. Here are examples of nine classic types:

Bridge Type #1: Description

In many Analogies, one stem word is a person, place, or thing, and the other word is a characteristic of that person, place, or thing.

Look at these examples:

PAUPER : POOR—A PAUPER is always POOR.

GENIUS : INTELLIGENT—A GENIUS is always INTELLIGENT.

TRAGEDY : SAD—A TRAGEDY is always SAD.

This classic bridge can also describe a person, place, or thing by what it is *not*.

PAUPER : WEALTHY—A PAUPER is never WEALTHY.

GENIUS : STUPID—A GENIUS is never STUPID.

TRAGEDY : HAPPY—A TRAGEDY is never HAPPY.

Here are more types of classic bridges. Fill in each blank with a stem word that will complete the bridge. There is more than one way to fill in each blank. The important thing is to get the right idea. Suggested answers follow.

Bridge Type #2: Characteristic Actions

An INSOMNIAC can't ----.

A GLUTTON likes to ----.

A PROCRASTINATOR tends to ----.

Bridge Type #3: Lack

Something MURKY lacks ----.

A PESSIMIST lacks ----.

A PAUPER lacks ----.

Do It Yourself

One way to see the inner workings of Analogies is to put some together yourself. Make sure you include five answer choices. This exercise will give you a good feel for the structure of SAT Analogies and may help you spot and avoid bad answer choices.

Bridge Type #4: Categories

MEASLES is a type of ----.

A MOTORCYCLE is a type of ----.

A POLKA is a type of ----.

Bridge Type #5: Size/Degree

To SPEAK very quietly is to ----.

To LIKE strongly is to ----.

To BRUSH is to ---- lightly.

Bridge Type #6: Causing/Stopping

A REMEDY stops or cures an ----.

An OBSTACLE prevents ----.

Something INCENDIARY causes ----.

Bridge Type #7: Places

A JUDGE works in a ----.

A PLAY is performed on a ----.

BREAD is made in a ----.

Bridge Type #8: Function

GILLS are used for ----.

A PAINTBRUSH is used to ----.

A HELICOPTER is used for ----.

Bridge Type #9: Part/Whole

An ARMY is made up of ----.

A CROWD is made up of many ----.

An arrangement of FLOWERS is a ----.

Suggested Answers to Bridge Types

Your answers may vary from our suggested answers. As long as you've got the basic idea, that's okay.

Characteristic Actions:

An INSOMNIAC can't SLEEP.

A GLUTTON likes to EAT.

A PROCRASTINATOR tends to DELAY.

KAPLAN

Lack:

Something MURKY lacks CLARITY.

A PESSIMIST lacks OPTIMISM.

A PAUPER lacks MONEY.

Categories:

MEASLES is a type of ILLNESS.

A MOTORCYCLE is a type of VEHICLE.

A POLKA is a type of DANCE.

Size/Degree:

To SPEAK very quietly is to WHISPER.

To LIKE strongly is to LOVE (or ADORE).

To BRUSH is to TOUCH lightly.

Causing/Stopping:

A REMEDY stops or cures an ILLNESS.

An OBSTACLE prevents PROGRESS (or MOVEMENT).

Something INCENDIARY causes FIRE.

Places:

A JUDGE works in a COURTROOM.

A PLAY is performed on a STAGE (or in a THEATER).

BREAD is made in a BAKERY.

Function:

GILLS are used for BREATHING.

A PAINTBRUSH is used to PAINT.

A HELICOPTER is used for FLYING.

Part/Whole:

An ARMY is made up of SOLDIERS.

A CROWD is made up of many PEOPLE.

An arrangement of FLOWERS is a BOUQUET.

HOW TO FILL VOCABULARY GAPS

Sometimes on an SAT Analogy, you simply don't know one of the stem words. When this happens, the basic three-step process won't do much good. You can't even do step one; you can't build a bridge using a word you don't know. You need another plan.

The best backup strategy is not to focus on the stem pair. Instead, try looking at the answer pairs and eliminate those that simply can't be right. If you can knock out even one, guessing from the remaining choices is to your advantage. You may be surprised at how far this strategy can take you.

Before you guess, take these three steps to eliminate some answer choices. (And remember, even if you can eliminate only one answer choice, guessing comes out in your favor.)

1. Eliminate answer choices with weak bridges.

2. Eliminate any two answer choices with identical bridges.

3. Eliminate answer choices with bridges that couldn't work with the stem pair no matter what that unknown word means.

Here's how you do it.

Eliminate Answer Choices with Weak Bridges

You learned earlier that a strong, definite relationship always exists between the pair of stem words. The answer pairs, however, don't always have a good bridge—and any choice without a good bridge can't be right. In other words, you can eliminate certain answer choices without looking at the stem at all.

Try this exercise. Here is a list of six answer pairs without any stem pairs—answers without questions. Try to make a bridge for each pair. If no strong bridge is possible, mark the pair with an *X*. (Answers on p. 38.)

1. DOG : HOUSE

2. AQUATIC : WATER

3. NOCTURNAL : ANIMAL

4. INFANTILE : TOY

5. STEAK : POTATOES

6. RAISIN : GRAPE

In many cases, this method alone will allow you to eliminate one, two, or even three answer choices.

Eliminate Answer Choices with Identical Bridges

There's another way of eliminating some wrong choices that's so obvious you might not think of it. If two choices have the same bridge, it follows that neither one can be more right than the other. And since they can't both be right, they must both be wrong. For example, look at the following question:

EXAMPLE

LEGERDEMAIN : MAGICIAN ::

(A) baggage : immigrant

(B) justice : pragmatist

(C) sluggishness : racer

(D) diplomacy : diplomat

(E) indifference : fanatic

Don't Fall for Same-Subject Traps

Same-Subject Traps are wrong answer choices that lure you in by providing words that remind you of stem words. The same subject doesn't make it right.

Remember, you're looking for an answer choice that has the same relationship as the stem, not an answer choice that reminds you of the stem.

What if you don't know what *legerdemain* means? (C) seems like a possible answer because this pair of words has a strong bridge: "Sluggishness is the opposite of what you'd expect from a racer." But choice (E) has a very similar bridge: "Indifference is the opposite of what you'd expect from a fanatic."

Since a question can't have two right answers, and both (C) and (E) have the same bridge, both must be wrong. The correct answer is (D).

Eliminate Answer Choices with Bridges That Can't Fit the Stem

What do you do with answer pairs that can't be eliminated by either of the first two methods? The next step is to find bridges for the remaining answers, and then to plug in the stem word pair. It's true that you don't even know what one of the stem words means. But in some cases you'll see that the stem word pair can't fit the answer bridge no matter what that unknown word means. Here's an example:

EXAMPLE

GENUFLECT : KNEE ::

(A) pierce : ear

(B) hold : hand

(C) nod : neck

(D) stub : toe

(E) pick : tooth

You may not know what *genuflect* means. Since you can't work directly with this stem, take a look at the answer choices instead.

Answer pair (A) has a strong bridge: To *pierce* an *ear* is to put a hole in it. Now try plugging *genuflect* and *knee* into this same bridge: To *genuflect* a *knee* is to put a hole in it. Hmmm. Can you really imagine that there exists a verb in the English language that means "to put a hole in a knee"? No way. The concept doesn't even make sense. So GENUFLECT : KNEE and pierce : ear can't possibly have the same bridge. (A) can't be the right answer.

Answers to Weak Bridges Exercise on p. 36

1. A dog may or may not live in a house.—Weak bridge

2. Aquatic means "having to do with water."—Strong bridge

3. Not all animals are nocturnal, or active at night.—Weak bridge

4. You don't have to be infantile, or immature, to play with a toy.—Weak bridge

5. You can eat steak and potatoes, but you don't have to.—Weak bridge

6. A raisin is, by definition, a dried-up grape.—Strong bridge

The same technique can be used to eliminate choice (E). *Picking* your *teeth* is a way of cleaning between them. Is there a comparable way of cleaning between your knees? Not likely.

So you've been able to eliminate two of the answer choices—without knowing what *genuflect* means. Sometimes, of course, this technique demands a bit more intuition. Without knowing for sure, you might just have a feeling that there wouldn't be a word for a very large telephone or for a group of hammers. If you're guessing anyway, go with these hunches. The correct answer is (C).

Putting It Together

Now apply all three answer-eliminating techniques to one question. (Pretend that you don't know the word *scimitar* even if you do.)

EXAMPLE

SCIMITAR : SWORD ::

(A) diamond : ring

(B) greyhound : dog

(C) saddle : horse

(D) lance : shield

(E) forest : tree

(A) A *diamond* may adorn a *ring*, but plenty of rings don't have diamonds, and plenty of diamonds don't have rings. Choice (A) has a weak bridge. Eliminate.

(B) A *greyhound* is a kind of *dog*. Could a *scimitar* be a kind of *sword*? It sounds possible.

(C) A *saddle* is used for riding a *horse*. A *scimitar* is used for *riding* a sword? That can't make sense. Eliminate.

(D) A *lance* and a *shield* are both part of the traditional gear of a knight, but that's all we can say to connect them. Again, a weak bridge. Eliminate.

(E) A *forest* is a group of *trees*. Could a *scimitar* be a group of *swords*? Maybe.

Without knowing a stem word, you've gotten down to two answer choices—(B) and (E). Is there more likely to be a word for a kind of sword or for a group of swords? Take your best guess.

(B) is, in fact, the answer.

A DOUBLE VOCABULARY GAP

What if you don't know either of the stem words? You can still eliminate weak bridges and identical bridges. For example:

EXAMPLE

MANUMISSION : THRALL ::

(A) submission : employee

(B) prediction : artist

(C) promotion : rank

(D) tip : waiter

(E) parole : prisoner

Kaplan Rules

Not all bridges are classic bridges, but there is always a strong and definite relationship between the stem words.

Promotion is the act of raising an employee in rank. A *tip* is a type of gratuity or reward given to a waiter. *Parole* is the act of freeing a prisoner. These are all good bridges, and none of them repeat, so (C), (D), and (E) are all possible answers. But *submission* is not a characteristic of every *employee*, and there's no particular connection between *prediction* and *artist*. So eliminate (A) and (B).

To make your final decision, of course, you still have to guess. But now that you've eliminated answer choices, guessing works in your favor. The answer here happens to be (E), since *manumission* is, by definition, the act of freeing a *thrall*, or slave.

Now test your Analogy skills on the questions in the Analogies Practice Set that starts on the next page.

ANALOGIES PRACTICE SET

1. COPPER : METAL ::

   (A) grain : sand
   (B) helium : gas
   (C) stem : flower
   (D) tree : trunk
   (E) stone : clay ⒶⒷⒸⒹⒺ

2. BROOM : DIRT ::

   (A) brush : bristles
   (B) fork : plate
   (C) rake : leaves
   (D) mirror : face
   (E) scissors : blades ⒶⒷⒸⒹⒺ

3. COWARD : BRAVERY ::

   (A) eccentric : conformity
   (B) hero : fortitude
   (C) prophet : vision
   (D) sage : wisdom
   (E) comedian : humor ⒶⒷⒸⒹⒺ

4. REVERE : ADMIRE ::

   (A) cherish : conceive
   (B) release : reject
   (C) guess : solve
   (D) propose : change
   (E) despise : disdain ⒶⒷⒸⒹⒺ

5. PERPLEXING : CONFUSION ::

   (A) appalling : dismay
   (B) static : change
   (C) unpleasant : chaos
   (D) dignified : pride
   (E) grave : regret ⒶⒷⒸⒹⒺ

6. AMUSING : MIRTH ::

   (A) ailing : health
   (B) painful : sympathy
   (C) optimistic : objectivity
   (D) protective : insecurity
   (E) terrifying : fear

   Ⓐ Ⓑ Ⓒ Ⓓ Ⓔ

7. FOOD : MENU ::

   (A) accounting : inventory
   (B) index : foreword
   (C) silverware : spoon
   (D) merchandise : catalog
   (E) films : credits

   Ⓐ Ⓑ Ⓒ Ⓓ Ⓔ

8. IMPERCEPTIBLE : DETECT ::

   (A) fundamental : begin
   (B) inconceivable : imagine
   (C) rugged : seize
   (D) costly : overcharge
   (E) immense : notice

   Ⓐ Ⓑ Ⓒ Ⓓ Ⓔ

9. PERSEVERE : DOGGED ::

   (A) comply : obedient
   (B) inspire : pompous
   (C) hesitate : reckless
   (D) speak : laconic
   (E) retard : expeditious

   Ⓐ Ⓑ Ⓒ Ⓓ Ⓔ

10. ENTHRALLING : TEDIUM ::

   (A) witty : frivolity
   (B) insipid : appetite
   (C) glaring : illumination
   (D) wearisome : redundancy
   (E) trite : originality

   Ⓐ Ⓑ Ⓒ Ⓓ Ⓔ

Answers and Explanations for Analogies Practice Set

1.   (B) (Copper is a kind of metal.)

2.   (C) (A broom is used to clear away dirt.)

3.   (A) (A coward does not display bravery.)

4.   (E) (By definition, to revere is to admire very much.)

5.   (A) (Something that is perplexing causes confusion.)

6.   (E) (Something that is amusing causes mirth.)

7.   (D) (A menu is, by definition, a list of available food.)

8.   (B) (If something is imperceptible, you cannot detect it.)

9.   (A) (A dogged person is one who perseveres.)

10.   (E) (Something that is enthralling lacks tedium.)

Checklist

Once you've mastered a concept, check it off.

Analogies:

❏ The format

❏ Building bridges

❏ Kaplan's Three-Step Method

❏ Test your analogy smarts

❏ Nine classic bridges

❏ How to fill vocabulary gaps

❏ Analogy practice set

6

Sentence Completions

HIGHLIGHTS

- Master the Kaplan Four-Step Method for Sentence Completions

- Learn to pick up on clues and predict answers

- Practice special techniques for tackling hard or tricky questions

- Complete the Sentence Completions Practice Set

Of all the Verbal question types, Sentence Completions are probably the most student-friendly. Unlike Analogies, they give you some context in which to think about vocabulary words, and unlike Critical Reading, they only require you to pay attention to a single sentence at a time. The 19 Sentence Completions count for about one-fourth of your verbal score.

THE FORMAT

There are 19 Sentence Completions in all on the SAT. You'll probably see one set of nine and one set of ten. They appear in both 30-minute Verbal Sections. The instructions for Sentence Completions look something like this:

Select the lettered word or set of words that best completes the sentence.

SAT Emergency

If you have only a week or two to prep for the SAT, here's the best way to spend your time:

- Learn the Kaplan Four-Step Method for Sentence Completions (pp. 46–47).

- Do the practice set starting on p. 56. If you miss an answer, skim through the chapter and look at the examples.

EXAMPLE

Today's small, portable computers contrast markedly with the earliest electronic computers, which were ----.

(A) effective

(B) invented

(C) useful

(D) destructive

(E) enormous

In the example, the new computers, which are small and portable, are contrasted with old computers. You can infer that the old computers must be the opposite of small and portable, so (E), *enormous*, is right.

KAPLAN'S FOUR-STEP METHOD

Here's the basic method for Sentence Completions:

1. Read the Sentence for Clue Words

Think about the sentence before looking at the answer choices. Figure out what the sentence means, taking special note of clue words.

HINT: *Clue words such as* and, but, such as, *and* although *tell you where a sentence is heading.*

2. Anticipate the Answer

You can see the direction some sentences are headed in from a mile away. Consider these examples:

"I still want to be your friend . . . ."

"Despite your impressive qualifications . . . ."

"If I ever get my hands on you, you little . . . ."

You could probably finish off these sentences on your own with pretty much the same language that the speaker would use. That's because the tone and structure of a sentence often clue you in to the meaning of the sentence.

On SAT Sentence Completions, you need to fill in missing pieces. Predict the word that goes in the blanks before looking at the answer choices. Do this by using the sentence's clue words (e.g., *despite, although*) and structural clues (construction and punctuation) to determine where the sentence is headed.

Kaplan Rules

To solve a Sentence Completion question:

1. Read the sentence for clue words.

2. Anticipate the answer.

3. Compare your prediction with each answer choice, and pick the best match.

4. Read the sentence with your answer choice in the blank or blanks.

You don't have to make an exact prediction. A rough idea of the kind of word you'll need will do. Often enough, it's simple to predict whether the missing word is positive or negative.

3. Compare Your Prediction with Each Answer Choice, and Pick the Best Match

Scan every answer choice before deciding.

4. Read the Sentence with Your Answer Choice in the Blank or Blanks

Keep in mind that only one choice will make sense.

If you've gone through the four steps and more than one choice seems possible, don't get stuck on the sentence. If you can eliminate at least one answer as wrong, guess and move on. If a question really stumps you, skip it and come back when you're done with the section.

Let's take a look at how the Four-Step Method works on some examples.

EXAMPLE

Alligators, who bask in the sun for hours, appear to be ---- creatures, yet they are quite capable of sudden movement.

(A) active

(B) violent

(C) stern

(D) content

(E) sluggish

Kaplan Rules

Timing Tip: Spend no more than 40 seconds per Sentence Completion question. Don't read the sentence five times, plugging in every answer choice. That method takes too much time and makes you vulnerable to traps. Think about the question before you look for the answer.

Read the sentence carefully, looking for clue words. *Yet* is a major clue. It tells you that the sentence switches direction midstream. The word in the blank must be the opposite of *sudden*.

Predict the word that goes in the blank. You can guess that alligators seem like lazy or idle creatures.

Compare your prediction with each answer choice, and pick the best match. (A), *active*, has nothing to do with being lazy or idle. Neither does (B), *violent*. Neither does (C), *stern*. Neither does (D), *content*. But (E), *sluggish*, means inactive or slow moving, so pick (E).

Check your answer by plugging it into the sentence. Let's check: "Alligators, who bask in the sun for hours, appear to be sluggish creatures, yet they are quite capable of sudden movement." Sounds okay. Finally, scan the other choices to make sure this is the best choice. None of the other choices works in the sentence, so (E) is correct.

EXAMPLE

The king's ---- decisions as a diplomat and administrator led to his legendary reputation as a just and ---- ruler.

(A) quick . . capricious

(B) equitable . . wise

(C) immoral . . perceptive

(D) generous . . witty

(E) clever . . uneducated

Read the sentence carefully, looking for clue words. A big clue here is the phrase *led to*. You know that the kind of decisions the king made led to his reputation as a just and ---- ruler. So whatever goes in both blanks must be consistent with *just*.

Predict the word that goes in the blank. Notice that both blanks must be similar in meaning. Because of his ---- decisions, the king is viewed a certain way, as a just and ---- ruler. So if the king's decisions were good, he'd be remembered as a good ruler, and if his decisions were bad, he'd be remembered as a bad ruler. *Just*, which means "fair," is a positive-sounding word; you can predict that both blanks will be similar in meaning, and that both will be positive words. Write a "+" in the blanks or over the columns of answer choices to remind you.

Compare your prediction with each answer choice, and pick the best match. One way to do this is to determine which answers are positive and which are negative.

In (A), *quick* and *capricious* aren't similar. (*Capricious* means "erratic or fickle.")

In (B), *equitable* means "fair." *Equitable* and *wise* are similar and they're both positive. When you plug them in, they make sense, so (B)'s right.

In (C), *immoral* and *perceptive* aren't similar at all. *Perceptive* is positive but *immoral* isn't.

In (D), *generous* and *witty* are both positive qualities, but they aren't really similar and they don't make sense in the sentence.

In (E), *clever* and *uneducated* aren't similar. *Clever* is positive but *uneducated* isn't.

Check your answer by plugging it into the sentence. "The king's equitable decisions as a diplomat and administrator led to his legendary reputation as a just and wise ruler." (B) makes sense in the sentence. Finally, a scan of the other choices reveals that none works as well. So (B) is our answer.

EXAMPLE

Charlie Parker was ---- artist, inspiring a generation of modern jazz musicians with his brilliant improvisations and experiments in bebop style.

(A) an arbitrary

(B) a benign

(C) a seminal

(D) an emphatic

(E) a candid

Read the sentence carefully, looking for clue words. The big clue is: Whatever goes in the blank must fit with the phrase *inspiring a generation*.

Predict the word that goes in the blank. The sentence tells you Parker inspired a generation of musicians, so you can predict that he was an influential artist.

Compare your prediction with each answer choice, and pick the best match.

(A) *arbitrary:* Too negative—you need a positive word.

(B) *benign:* Benign means "mild or gentle"—again, not what you want.

(C) *seminal:* Most closely matches your prediction—it means "containing the seeds of later development."

(D) *emphatic:* Might sound reasonable at first, but it means "expressive or forceful," which is not the same as "major or important."

(E) *candid:* Candid means "frank or open," which doesn't adequately describe how Parker influenced a generation.

Choice (C), *seminal*, is the answer. Notice that you could have found this answer by elimination, without actually knowing what the word means. Check your answer by plugging it into the sentence. "Charlie Parker was a seminal, or influential, artist inspiring a generation with his brilliant improvisations." Sounds fine.

Impulse Answer Buyer

Don't be an "impulse answer buyer." It's hard to know what to buy when you don't know what you're shopping for. The same thing is true of Sentence Completions. You should make a prediction of the answer you're looking for before you go to the answer choices. This way, you won't fall for a distractor. You'll find the answer you want rather than the answer the test maker wants you to find.

PICKING UP ON CLUES

To do well on Sentence Completions, you need to see how a sentence fits together. Clue words help you do that. The more clues you get, the clearer the sentence becomes, and the better you can predict what goes in the blanks.

What do we mean by clue words? Take a look at this example:

Get a Clue

Clue words help you get to the right answer. Look for the following types of words:

Contrasts:

- but
- however
- although

Continuations:

- ; (a semicolon)
- also
- and
- because
- due to
- notably

EXAMPLE

Though some have derided it as ----, the search for extraterrestrial intelligence has actually become a respectable scientific endeavor.

Here, *though* is an important clue. *Though* contrasts the way some have derided, belittled, or ridiculed the search for extraterrestrial intelligence with the fact that that search has become respectable. Another clue is *actually*. *Actually* completes the contrast—though some see the search one way, it has actually become respectable.

You know that whatever goes in the blank must complete the contrast implied by the word *though*. So for the blank, you need something that describes the opposite of a *respectable scientific endeavor*. A word such as *useless* or *trivial* would be a good prediction for the blank.

Try using clue words to predict the answers to the questions below. First, look at the sentences without the answer choices and:

- Circle clue words.
- Think of a word or phrase that might go in each blank.
- Write your prediction below each sentence.

1. One striking aspect of Caribbean music is its ---- of many African musical ----, such as call-and-response singing and polyrhythms.

    _____   _____

2. Although Cézanne was inspired by the Impressionists, he ---- their emphasis on the effects of light and ---- an independent approach to painting that emphasized form.

    _____   _____

3. They ---- until there was no recourse but to ---- a desperate, last-minute solution to the problem.

    _____   _____

4. Her normally ---- complexion lost its usual glow when she heard the news of her brother's accident.

    _____

Here are the same questions with their answer choices. Now find the right answer to each question, referring to the predictions you just made. See page 52 for the answers.

1. One striking aspect of Caribbean music is its ---- of many African musical ----, such as call-and-response singing and polyrhythms.

   (A) recruitment . . groups
   (B) proficiency . . events
   (C) expectation . . ideas
   (D) absorption . . forms
   (E) condescension . . priorities   Ⓐ Ⓑ Ⓒ Ⓓ Ⓔ

2. Although Cézanne was inspired by the Impressionists, he ---- their emphasis on the effects of light and ---- an independent approach to painting that emphasized form.

   (A) accepted . . developed
   (B) rejected . . evolved
   (C) encouraged . . submerged
   (D dismissed . . aborted
   (E) nurtured . . founded   Ⓐ Ⓑ Ⓒ Ⓓ Ⓔ

3. They ---- until there was no recourse but to ---- a desperate, last-minute solution to the problem.

   (A) compromised . . try
   (B) delayed . . envision
   (C) procrastinated . . implement
   (D debated . . maintain
   (E) filibustered . . reject   Ⓐ Ⓑ Ⓒ Ⓓ Ⓔ

4. Her normally ---- complexion lost its usual glow when she heard the news of her brother's accident.

   (A) wan
   (B) pallid
   (C) sallow
   (D) ashen
   (E) sanguine   Ⓐ Ⓑ Ⓒ Ⓓ Ⓔ

Answers and Explanations to Picking Up On Clues Exercises

1. (D) Clue: *aspect*. The only choice that could logically complete a description of Caribbean music is (D): Caribbean music is characterized by its *absorption* of many African musical *forms*.

2. (B) Clue: *Although*. *Although* indicates that Cézanne must have somehow differed from the Impressionists. So he must have (B) *rejected* or (D) *dismissed* their emphasis on the effects of light. For the second blank, there's no reason to say that Cézanne *aborted* an independent approach to painting. Only (B) works for both blanks.

3. (C) Clues: *until, desperate*. For the first blank, you can predict that they must have waited until only a "desperate solution" was possible. (C) and (D) fit this prediction. (C)'s *implement*, or carry out, makes more sense in the second blank.

4. (E) Clue: *usual glow*. If her complexion had a "usual glow" it must have been normally rosy. The only choice that means rosy is (E), *sanguine*.

TACKLING HARD QUESTIONS

The last few Sentence Completions in a set are usually difficult. If you're getting stuck, here are a few special techniques to pull you through:

- Avoid tricky wrong answers.
- Take apart tough sentences.
- Work around tough vocabulary.

Kaplan Rules

Don't pick tough words just because they're tough—pick them because they work in the sentence.

Avoiding Tricky Wrong Answers

Towards the end of a set, watch out for tricky answer choices. Avoid:

- Opposites of the correct answer
- Words that sound right because they're hard
- Two-blankers in which one word fits but the other doesn't

HINT: *Questions go from easiest to hardest—the higher the question number, the harder the question.*

The following example would be the seventh question out of a ten-problem set.

EXAMPLE

Granted that Joyce is extremely ----, it is still
difficult to imagine her as a professional
comedian.

(A) dull

(B) garrulous

(C) effusive

(D) conservative

(E) witty

A Sentence Like This Might Show up Towards the End of a Set

Read this sentence carefully or you may get tricked. If you read too quickly, you might think,
"If Joyce is hard to imagine as a comedian, she's probably extremely dull or conservative. So
I'll pick either (A) or (D)." But the sentence is saying something else.

Pick Up the Clues

The key is the clue word *granted*. It's another way of saying *although*. So the sentence means,
"Sure Joyce is funny, but she's no professional comedian." Therefore, the word in the blank
must resemble funny. That means (E), *witty*, is correct.

Don't Pick an Answer Just Because It Sounds Hard

Garrulous means "talkative" and *effusive* means "overly expressive." You might be tempted to
pick one of these simply because they sound impressive. But they're put there to trick you.
Don't choose them without good reason.

Now let's look at a two-blank sentence. The following example is another seventh question
out of a ten-problem set.

Two-Blankers

Two-blank sentences can be
easier than one-blankers.

- Try the easier blank first.

- Eliminate all choices that
  won't work for that blank.

EXAMPLE

When the state government discovered that
thermal pollution was killing valuable fish,
legislation was passed to ---- the dumping of hot
liquid wastes into rivers and to ---- the fish
population.

(A) discourage . . decimate

(B) regulate . . quantify

(C) facilitate . . appease

(D) discontinue . . devastate

(E) prohibit . . protect

Look at All the Choices

Check out the first blank first. Legislation was not passed to *facilitate* dumping, so that eliminates choice (C). The other four are all possible.

Now check the second blanks. The legislature wouldn't pass a law to *decimate*, or *quantify*, or *devastate* the fish population, so (A), (B), and (D) are wrong. Only choice (E), *prohibit . . protect*, fits for both blanks. The legislature might well pass a law to *prohibit* dumping hot liquids and to *protect* fish.

HINT: *Don't jump at an answer choice because one blank fits. Check both blanks.*

Taking Apart Tough Sentences

Look at the following example, the seventh question of a nine-problem set.

Weird Words Don't Work

Listen to the part of the sentence around the blank. Rule out funny-sounding answer choices.

If you can rule out even one or two weird-sounding choices, you can profit by making an educated guess.

EXAMPLE

Although this small and selective publishing house is famous for its ---- standards, several of its recent novels have a mainly popular appeal.

(A) proletarian

(B) naturalistic

(C) discriminating

(D) imitative

(E) precarious

What if you were stumped, and had no idea which word to pick? Try this strategy.

The process might go like this:

(A) *Proletarian* standards? Hmmm . . . sounds funny.

(B) *Naturalistic* standards? Not great.

(C) *Discriminating* standards? That's got a familiar ring.

(D) *Imitative* standards? Weird-sounding

(E) *Precarious* standards? Nope.

(C) sounds best and, as it turns out, is correct. Although the small publishing house has *discriminating*, or picky, standards, several of its recent novels appeal to a general audience.

Now try a complex sentence with two blanks. Remember our rules:

- Try the easier blank first.

- Save time by eliminating all choices that won't work for one blank.

The following example is the fifth question out of a nine-problem set.

EXAMPLE

These latest employment statistics from the
present administration are so loosely
documented, carelessly explained, and
potentially misleading that even the most loyal
Senators will ---- the ---- of the presidential
appointees who produced them.

(A) perceive . . intelligence

(B) understand . . tenacity

(C) recognize . . incompetence

(D) praise . . rigor

(E) denounce . . loyalty

It's not so easy to see what goes in the first blank, so try the second blank. You need a word to describe presidential appointees who produced the "loosely documented," "carelessly explained," and "misleading" statistics. So it's got to be negative. The only second-word answer choice that's definitely negative is (C), *incompetence*, or inability to perform a task. Now try *recognize* in the first blank. It fits, too. (C) must be correct.

Working Around Tough Vocabulary

The following example is the second question out of a nine-problem set.

EXAMPLE

Despite her ---- of public speaking experience,
the student council member was surprisingly
cogent, and expressed the concerns of her
classmates persuasively.

(A) hope

(B) depth

(C) method

(D) lack

(E) union

> **Kaplan Rules**
>
> If you find a word you don't understand, look in the sentence for its definition.

If you don't know what *cogent* means, work around it.

From the sentence, especially the clue word *and*, you know that cogent goes with "expressed the concerns of her classmates persuasively." So you don't have to worry about what *cogent* means. All you need to know is that the student council member was persuasive despite a ---- of speaking experience. Only (D), *lack*, fits. "Despite her lack of public speaking experience, the student council member expressed the concerns of her classmates persuasively." (By the way, *cogent* means "convincing, believable," roughly the same as "expressing concern persuasively.")

Let's look at this Sentence Completion problem. This time the tough vocabulary is in the answer choices. This example is the sixth question out of nine questions.

A Valuable Resource

To help yourself earn extra points, study the vocabulary lists in the "SAT Study Aids" section.

EXAMPLE

Advances in technology occur at such a fast pace that dictionaries have difficulty incorporating the ---- that emerge as names for new inventions.

(A) colloquialisms

(B) euphemisms

(C) compensations

(D) neologisms

(E) clichés

Again, look at the sentence. Whatever goes in the blank has to describe "names for new inventions." If you don't know what the word *colloquialisms* or *euphemisms* means, don't give up. Rule out as many choices as you can, and guess among the remaining ones.

You can eliminate (C) and (E) right off the bat. They don't describe names for new inventions. Now you can make an educated guess. Again, educated guessing will help your score more than guessing blindly or skipping the question.

Or, if you studied your word roots, you might know that *neo-* means "new," so the word *neologisms* might be the best choice for names of new inventions. In fact, it's the right answer. *Neologisms* are newly coined words.

If All Else Fails

If you're really stumped, don't be afraid to guess. Eliminate all answer choices that seem wrong and guess from the remaining choices.

SENTENCE COMPLETIONS PRACTICE SET

1. In the years following World War II, almost all Canadian Inuits ---- their previously nomadic lifestyle; they now live in fixed settlements.

   (A) abandoned

   (B) continued

   (C) fashioned

   (D) preserved

   (E) rebuilt

   Ⓐ Ⓑ Ⓒ Ⓓ Ⓔ

2. A newborn infant's ---- skills are not fully ----, for it cannot discern images more than ten inches from its face.

   (A) perceptual . . stimulated
   (B) visual . . developed
   (C) descriptive . . ripened
   (D) olfactory . . shared
   (E) average . . familiar

   Ⓐ Ⓑ Ⓒ Ⓓ Ⓔ

3. Some geysers erupt regularly while others do so ----.

   (A) consistently
   (B) copiously
   (C) perennially
   (D) sporadically
   (E) violently

   Ⓐ Ⓑ Ⓒ Ⓓ Ⓔ

4. Because of the lead actor's ---- performance, the play received poor reviews from influential theater critics, and was canceled only one week after it opened.

   (A) erudite
   (B) corporeal
   (C) overwrought
   (D) fractious
   (E) resplendent

   Ⓐ Ⓑ Ⓒ Ⓓ Ⓔ

5. Sociologists have found that, paradoxically, many children of unorthodox, creative parents grow up to be rather tame ----.

   (A) idealists
   (B) conformists
   (C) individualists
   (D) alarmists
   (E) elitists

   Ⓐ Ⓑ Ⓒ Ⓓ Ⓔ

6. In Han mortuary art, the ---- and the ---- are combined; one tomb may contain eerie supernatural figures placed next to ordinary likenesses of government administrators at work.

   (A) fantastic . . mundane
   (B) inventive . . remorseful
   (C) illusory . . derivative
   (D) enlightened . . conservative
   (E) unique . . historical

   Ⓐ Ⓑ Ⓒ Ⓓ Ⓔ

Turn to the next page for answers and explanations.

Answers and Explanations to the Sentence Completions Practice Set

1. (A) *Nomadic* means "wandering, transient." If Inuit people now live in fixed settlements, we can predict that they rejected, or *abandoned*, "their previously nomadic lifestyle."

2. (B) If a newborn infant "cannot discern (or perceive) images more than 10 inches from its face," then the infant's ability to see things has not fully evolved. In other words, its visual skills are not fully developed. The word *olfactory*, choice (D), means "relating to sense of smell."

3. (D) The clue words *while others* indicate contrast. If some geysers "erupt regularly," we can predict that others do so irregularly. The best choice is (D), since *sporadically* means "infrequently or irregularly."

4. (C) If the play "received poor reviews" and was canceled because of something about the lead actor's performance, that performance must have been quite bad. The word *overwrought*, choice (C), means "overdone" or "excessively agitated." It is one of two negative words in the answer choices, and the only one that could logically describe a performance.

5. (B) Paradoxically (or contrary to what one would expect), children of creative and unorthodox parents grow up to be something other than creative and unorthodox. We need a word that contrasts with *creative* and *unorthodox* and goes along with *tame*. (B) is the best choice; *conformists* are people who follow established norms and customs without challenging anything or anyone.

6. (A) If "one tomb contains eerie supernatural figures" and "ordinary likenesses of government administrators," it's likely that Han mortuary art combines the unearthly or bizarre with the ordinary or mundane. The best answer is (A). In Han art, the *fantastic* (eerie supernatural figures) and the *mundane* (administrators) are combined.

Checklist

Once you've mastered a concept, check it off.

Sentence Completions:

❑ The format

❑ Kaplan's Four-Step Method

❑ Picking up on clues

❑ Tackling hard questions

❑ Practice set

Critical Reading: The Basics

- Practice reading actively

- Apply the Kaplan Five-Step Method for Critical Reading questions

- Review Big Picture, Little Picture, and Vocabulary-in-Context question types

Improving your Critical Reading score means building the skills you have and applying them to the SAT. You don't need outside knowledge to answer the Critical Reading questions. And you don't need an amazing vocabulary, since unfamiliar words will be defined for you.

Doing well on the Critical Reading section isn't really that hard. Take this everyday situation as an example. If you bought a new VCR, as soon as you unpacked it you'd read the instruction manual to figure out how to hook it up and get it working. You probably wouldn't sit down and read the whole book, though. You'd skip the pages that contain step-by-step instructions on how to record programs from the TV until you'd gotten the VCR connected and plugged in. If the manual said, "connect the xygupts to terminal c," you'd probably figure out how to do that, even though you don't know the word *xygupts*.

In setting up your VCR, you'd have demonstrated that you know how to read with a purpose; know how and when to deal with details; and can figure out the meaning of unfamiliar words from context—all skills you'll be using in the Critical Reading section. .

SAT Emergency

If you have two weeks or fewer to prep for the SAT, here's the best way to spend your time:

- Since Critical Reading makes up half of the Verbal section of the SAT, it's important that you read the whole chapter.

- Pay special attention to the practice questions beginning on pp. 63 and 68.

Critical Reading passages and questions are very predictable, since the test makers use a formula to write them. You'll be given four reading passages, 400 to 850 words each, drawn from the arts, humanities, social sciences, sciences, and fiction. One of these is a "paired passage" consisting of two related excerpts. You'll be asked about the overall tone and content of a passage, the details, and what the passage suggests. You'll also be asked to compare and contrast the related passages.

THE FORMAT

Critical Reading instructions tell you to answer questions based on what is stated or implied in the accompanying passage or passages. As with other question types, you should get familiar enough with the Critical Reading format that you don't waste time reading the directions again on the day of the test.

Each reading passage begins with a brief introduction. Related questions follow the passage. Don't skip the brief introductions. They'll help you focus your reading.

Critical Reading questions have a specific order: The first few questions ask about the beginning of the passage, the last few about the end.

Questions following "paired passages" are generally ordered. The first few questions relate to the first passage, the next few to the second passage, and the final questions ask about the passages as a pair—generally, but not always. You'll learn more about this on p. 70.

Critical Reading questions are not ordered by difficulty. Unlike the other kinds of questions on the SAT, the location of a Critical Reading question tells you nothing about its potential difficulty. So don't get bogged down on a hard Critical Reading question. The next one might be a lot easier.

How NOT to Read

DON'T wait for important information to jump out and hit you in the face. Search for important points.

DON'T read the passage thoroughly. It's a waste of time. Skim the passage to get the drift.

DON'T skim so quickly that you miss the passage's main point.

DON'T get caught up in details.

HOW TO READ A PASSAGE

Some students find Critical Reading passages dull or intimidating. Remember that each passage is written for a purpose: The author wants to make a point, describe a situation, or convince you of his or her ideas. As you're reading, ask yourself, "What's the point of this? What's this all about?" This is active reading, and it's the key to staying focused on the page.

Active reading doesn't mean reading the passage word-for-word. It means reading lightly, but with a focus—in other words, skimming. The questions will help you fill in the details by directing you back to important information in the passage.

Getting hung up on details is a major Critical Reading pitfall. You need to grasp the outline, but you don't need to get all the fine features.

The less time you spend on reading the passages, the more time you'll have to answer the questions—and that's where you score points.

Test Your Critical Reading Smarts

Test your reading skills on the following sample passage, keeping our tips in mind. Remember that active reading will make this difficult passage—and every passage—more doable.

EXAMPLE

In this essay, the author writes about her childhood on a Caribbean island that was an English colony for many years.

When I saw England for the first time, I was a child in school sitting at a desk. The England I was looking at was laid out on a map gently, beautifully, delicately, a very special jewel; it lay on a bed of sky blue, its yellow form

Line mysterious, because though it looked like a leg of mutton*, it could not
(5) really look like anything so familiar as a leg of mutton because it was England. England was a special jewel all right, and only special people got to wear it. The people who got to wear England were English people. They wore it well and they wore it everywhere: in jungles, in deserts, on plains, in places where they were not welcome, in places they should not have been. When my teacher had
(10) pinned this map up on the blackboard, she said, "This is England"—and she said it with authority, seriousness, and adoration, and we all sat up. We understood then—we were meant to understand then—that England was to be our source of myth and the source from which we got our sense of reality, our sense of what was meaningful, our sense of what was meaningless—and much
(15) about our own lives and much about the very idea of us headed that last list.

At the time I was a child sitting at my desk seeing England for the first time, I was already very familiar with the greatness of it. Each morning before I left for school, I ate a breakfast of half a grapefruit, a bowl of oat porridge, bread and butter and a slice of cheese, and a cup of cocoa. The can of cocoa was
(20) often left on the table in front of me. It had written on it the name of the company, the year the company was established, and the words "Made in England." Those words, "Made in England," were written on the box the oats came in too. The shoes I wore were made in England; so were my socks and cotton undergarments and the satin ribbons I wore tied at the end of two plaits of my hair. My father, who might have sat next to me at breakfast, was a
(25) carpenter and cabinet maker. The shoes he wore to work would have been made in England, as were his khaki shirt and trousers, his underpants and undershirt, his socks and brown felt hat. Felt was not the proper material from which a hat that was expected to provide shade from the hot sun should be made, but my father must have seen and admired a picture of an Englishman wearing such a hat in England. As we sat at breakfast a car might go by. The car, a Hillman or a
(30) Zephyr, was made in England. The very conception of the meal itself, breakfast, and its substantial quality and quantity was an idea from England; we somehow knew that in England they began the day with this meal called breakfast and a proper breakfast was a big breakfast.

At the time I saw this map—seeing England for the first time—I did not say to myself, "Ah, so that's what it looks like," because there was no longing in me to put a shape to those three
(35) words that ran through every part of my life, no matter how small; for me to have had such a longing would have meant that I lived in a certain atmosphere, an atmosphere in which those three words were felt as a burden. But I did not live in such an atmosphere. My father's brown felt hat would develop a hole in its crown, the lining would separate from the hat itself, and six weeks before he thought that he could not be seen wearing it—he was a very vain man—he
(40) would order another hat from England. And my mother taught me to eat my food in the English way: the knife in the right hand, the fork in the left, my elbows held still close to my side. When I had finally mastered it, I overheard her saying to a friend, "Did you see how nicely she can eat?" But I knew then that I enjoyed my food more when I ate it with my bare hands, and I continued to do so when she wasn't looking. And when my teacher showed us the map, she

Kaplan Rules

As you read the passage, ask yourself:

- What's this passage about?
- What's the point of this?
- Why did someone write this?
- What's the author trying to say?
- What are the two or three most important things in this passage?

(45) asked us to study it carefully, because no test we would ever take would be complete without this statement: "Draw a map of England."

I did not know then that the statement "Draw a map of England" was something far worse than a declaration of war. I did not know then that this statement was part of a process that would result in my erasure, not my physical erasure, but my erasure all the same. I did not know

(50) then that this statement was meant to make me feel in awe and small whenever I heard the word "England": awe at its existence, small because I was not from it. I did not know very much of anything then—certainly not what a blessing it was that I was unable to draw a map of England correctly.

*the flesh of a sheep

It's important to learn how to read the passage quickly and efficiently. Remember, though, that reading the passage won't earn you points—it's the questions that count.

KAPLAN'S FIVE-STEP METHOD

Here's Kaplan's proven approach to Critical Reading questions:

1. Read the question stem.
2. Locate the material you need.
3. Come up with an idea of the right answer.
4. Scan the answer choices.
5. Select your answer.

1. Read the Question Stem

This is the place to really read carefully. Take a second to make sure you understand what the question is asking.

Critical Reading Is Critical

The 38 to 40 Critical Reading questions count for about half your Verbal score. You need to do well on these questions.

2. Locate the Material You Need

If you are given a line reference, read the material surrounding the line mentioned. It will clarify exactly what the question is asking.

If you're not given a line reference, scan the text to find the place where the question applies, and quickly reread those few sentences. Keep the main point of the passage in mind.

3. Come up with an Idea of the Right Answer

Don't spend time making up a precise answer. You need only a general sense of what you're after, so you can recognize the correct answer quickly when you read the choices.

4. Scan the Answer Choices

Scan the choices, looking for one that fits your idea of the right answer. If you don't find an ideal answer, quickly eliminate wrong choices by checking back to the passage. Rule out choices that are too extreme or go against common sense. And get rid of answers that sound reasonable, but don't make sense in the context of the passage.

5. Select Your Answer

You've eliminated the obvious wrong answers. One of the remaining should fit your ideal. If you're left with more than one contender, consider the passage's main idea, and make an educated guess.

Now try the following Critical Reading practice questions. (Answers on p. 66.)

Having Trouble?

Unlike the other Verbal question types, Critical Reading questions are not ordered by difficulty. If you're having trouble answering a question, the next one might be easier.

1. According to the author, England could not really look like a leg of mutton (lines 4–5) because

    (A) maps generally don't give an accurate impression of what a place looks like
    (B) England was too grand and exotic a place for such a mundane image
    (C) England was an island not very different in appearance from her own island
    (D) the usual metaphor used to describe England was a precious jewel
    (E) mutton was one of the few foods familiar to her that did not come from England

2. The author's reference to felt as "not the proper material" (line 27) for her father's hat chiefly serves to emphasize her point about the

    (A) extremity of the local weather
    (B) arrogance of island laborers
    (C) informality of dress on the island
    (D) weakness of local industries
    (E) predominance of English culture

    Ⓐ Ⓑ Ⓒ Ⓓ Ⓔ

3. The word *conception* as used in line 30 means
    (A) beginning
    (B) image
    (C) origination
    (D) notion
    (E) plan

    Ⓐ Ⓑ Ⓒ Ⓓ Ⓔ

4. The word *substantial* in line 31 means

   (A) important
   (B) abundant
   (C) firm
   (D) down-to-earth
   (E) materialistic

   Ⓐ Ⓑ Ⓒ Ⓓ Ⓔ

5. In the third paragraph, the author implies that any longing to put a shape to the words *made in England* would have indicated

   (A) a resentment of England's predominance
   (B) an unhealthy desire to become English
   (C) an inability to understand England's authority
   (D) an excessive curiosity about England
   (E) an unfamiliarity with English customs

   Ⓐ Ⓑ Ⓒ Ⓓ Ⓔ

6. The author cites the anecdotes about her father and mother in lines 37–43 primarily to convey their

   (A) love for their children
   (B) belief in strict discipline
   (C) distaste for anything foreign
   (D) reverence for England
   (E) overemphasis on formal manners

   Ⓐ Ⓑ Ⓒ Ⓓ Ⓔ

7. The word *erasure* (line 49) as used by the author most nearly means

   (A) total annihilation
   (B) physical disappearance
   (C) sense of insignificance
   (D) enforced censorship
   (E) loss of freedom

   Ⓐ Ⓑ Ⓒ Ⓓ Ⓔ

8. The main purpose of the passage is to

   (A) advocate a change in the way a subject is taught in school
   (B) convey the personality of certain figures from the author's childhood
   (C) describe an overwhelming influence on the author's early life
   (D) analyze the importance of a sense of place to early education
   (E) relate a single formative episode in the author's life

   Ⓐ Ⓑ Ⓒ Ⓓ Ⓔ

9. For the author, the requirement to "Draw a map of England" (line 46) represented an attempt to

   (A) force students to put their studies to practical use
   (B) glorify one culture at the expense of another
   (C) promote an understanding of world affairs
   (D) encourage students to value their own heritage
   (E) impart outmoded and inappropriate knowledge

   Ⓐ Ⓑ Ⓒ Ⓓ Ⓔ

10. At the end of the passage, the author suggests that her inability "to draw a map of England correctly" indicated a

   (A) heartfelt desire to see the country in person rather than through maps
   (B) serious failure of the education she received
   (C) conscious rejection of the prestige of a foreign power
   (D) harmful preoccupation with local affairs and customs
   (E) beneficial ignorance of her own supposed inferiority

Applying the Five-Step Method

Try Kaplan's Five-Step Method on question one from the sample reading passage above.

1. Read the Question Stem

In this case, the question is straightforward: Why couldn't England really look like a leg of mutton? (Notice that *mutton* is defined for you at the end of the passage—you aren't expected to know the meaning of unfamiliar terms.)

2. Locate the Material You Need

You're given a clue: The answer lies somewhere near the fourth or fifth line. But don't read just those lines—read the line or two before and after as well. By doing so, you learn that England was mysterious and special, so it couldn't look like something as familiar (to the author) as a leg of mutton.

3. Come up with an Idea of the Right Answer

After reading those couple of lines, you'd expect the answer to be something like, "England was too special to look like a familiar leg of mutton."

4. Scan the Answer Choices

Choice (B) comes close to the ideal—it should have popped out. But if you weren't sure, you could have quickly eliminated the other choices. Thinking of the main idea would have helped you eliminate (A) and (C). England was precious—like a jewel—but the author doesn't imply that England was usually compared to a jewel (D). And you never learn where mutton comes from (E).

5. Select Your Answer

Choice (B) is the only one that works here. By reading the material surrounding the line reference and putting an answer into your own words, you should have been able to choose (B) with confidence.

Now try the Five-Step Method on the remaining questions for the passage.

HINT: *From the questions, you can "fill in" the information you don't get in a quick reading. It's a way of working backwards, to reconstruct the passage.*

> **What's *Mutton*?**
>
> When a word is too obscure for the SAT, they'll define it at the bottom of the reading passage.

> **Teacher Tip**
>
> "Mark up the passages! Have a system worked out where you use different symbols to mean different things. For example, circle names, box numbers and dates, underline key sentences, and draw arrows to lists of details. Once you know your system, you can find the facts you are looking for faster."
>
> —Laura Cunnington
>   Kaplan Teacher
>   Reno, NV

BIG PICTURE, LITTLE PICTURE, AND VOCABULARY-IN-CONTEXT QUESTIONS

Most SAT Critical Reading questions fall into three basic types. "Big Picture" questions test your overall understanding of the passage's biggest points. "Little Picture" questions ask about localized bits of information. About 70 percent of Critical Reading questions are "Little Picture." Vocabulary-in-Context questions ask for the meaning of a single word.

In the passage above, question eight is an example of a Big Picture question. Question two is an example of a Little Picture question. Question three is a Vocabulary-in-Context question.

HINT: *Remember to skip around if you need to. You can tackle whichever passages you like in any order you like within the same section. But once you've read through the passage, try all the questions that go with it.*

Big Picture Questions

Big Picture questions test your overall understanding of a passage. They might ask about:

- The main point or purpose of a passage

- The author's attitude or tone

- The logic underlying the author's argument

- How ideas relate to each other

One way to see the Big Picture is to read actively. As you read, ask yourself, "What's this all about? What's the point of this?"

HINT: *Still stumped after reading the passage? Do the Little Picture questions first. They can help you fill in the Big Picture.*

Turn back to the passage you tried above. What did you get out of the first reading? Something like, "England was a profound influence on the author's early life, but not a completely positive influence"? That would have been enough.

Now look at question eight. It's a Big Picture question, asking for the main point of the passage. Use the Five-Step Method to find your answer.

1. Read the Question Stem

Simple enough: What's the main point of the passage?

2. Locate the Material You Need

In this case, you're asked about the overall point. You should have grasped a sense of that from reading the passage.

3. Get an Idea of the Right Answer

Again, you need just a rough statement. Here, something like this would do: "The purpose is to describe how England was a huge influence, but maybe not a completely positive one, in the author's young life."

Answers to Critical Reading Questions, pp. 63–65

1. (B)
2. (E)
3. (D)
4. (B)
5. (B)
6. (D)
7. (C)
8. (C)
9. (B)
10. (E)

4. Scan the Answer Choices

(C) should have popped out. But (D) might have looked good, too, if you focused on the words "sense of place." So put those two aside as contenders. How a subject was taught in school (A), figures in the author's childhood (B), and a single formative episode (E) are too narrow.

5. Select Your Answer

You've crossed off the poor choices, and you're down to two possibilities. Which matches your ideal? (C) comes closer. Look closely at (D) and you'll see that it's too general. Go with the best choice.

Little Picture Questions

More than two-thirds of Critical Reading questions ask about the Little Picture. Little Picture questions usually give you a line reference or refer you to a particular paragraph—a strong clue to where in the passage you'll find your answer.

Little Picture questions might:

- Test whether you understand significant information that's stated in the passage

- Ask you to make inferences or draw conclusions based on a part of the passage

- Ask you to relate parts of the passage to one another

Question two is a Little Picture question. You're asked about the felt hat of the author's father—what does this point emphasize? Applying Kaplan's Step Two, locate the material you'll need. You're given a clue—a line reference—to help you here. Reread that, and the lines before and after it as well.

So why did the father wear a felt hat, which was probably quite hot in the tropical sun? Because it was English. That's what correct choice (E) says. Rereading that bit of the passage should have led you right to that answer. (A) comes close, but doesn't fit the main point of the passage. Even with Little Picture questions, grasping the main point of the passage can help you find the correct answer.

HINT: *Beware of answer choices that provide a reasonable answer to the stem, but don't make sense in the context of the passage.*

Vocabulary-in-Context Questions

Vocabulary-in-Context questions ask about an even smaller part of the passage than other Little Picture questions do. They ask about the usage of a single word. These questions do not test your ability to define hard words such as *archipelago* and *garrulous*. They do test your ability to infer the meaning of a word from context.

In fact, the words tested in these questions will probably be familiar to you—they are usually fairly common words with more than one definition. Many of the answer choices will be definitions of the tested word, but only one will work in context. Vocabulary-in-Context questions always have a line reference, and you should always use it!

Avoid the Farfetched

Don't pick farfetched inferences. SAT inferences tend to be strongly implied in the passage.

Kaplan Rules

Once you find the tested word in the passage, you can treat a Vocabulary-in-Context question like a Sentence Completion.

Pretend the word is a blank in the sentence. Read a line or two around the "blank," if you need to. Then predict a word for the "blank." Check the answer choices for a word that comes close to your prediction.

Teacher Tip

"Read for the moment, not for memory. Unlike in a school class, you're not going to be tested on details two weeks from now. Don't try to remember them, pronounce them, even totally understand them. If there's a question about a particular detail, then you'll go back and figure it out. If there's no question, forget it!"

—Marilyn Engle
  Kaplan Teacher
  Encino, CA

HINT: *CONTEXT is the most important part of Vocabulary-in-CONTEXT questions.*

Sometimes one of the answer choices will jump out at you. It'll be the most common meaning of the word in question—but it's rarely right! We call this the "obvious" choice. For example, say *curious* is the word being tested. The obvious choice is *inquisitive*. But *curious* also means "odd," and that's more likely to be the answer. Using context to find the answer will help prevent you from falling for this trap. You can use these choices to your advantage, though. If you get stuck on a Vocabulary-in-Context question, you can eliminate the "obvious" choice and guess.

HINT: *If a question has an "obvious" choice, steer clear of it.*

Vocabulary-in-Context Practice

(Answers on p. 70.)

1. Embodied and given life in the social realities of her own period, Jane Austen's satire still has currency in ours.

   In the lines above, *currency* most nearly means
   (A) usualness
   (B) stylishness
   (C) prevalence
   (D) funds
   (E) relevance

2. A perpetual doubting and a perpetual questioning of the truth of what we have learned is not the temper of science.

   In the lines above, *temper* most nearly means
   (A) disposition
   (B) nature
   (C) anger
   (D) mood
   (E) mixture

   Ⓐ Ⓑ Ⓒ Ⓓ Ⓔ

3. Captain Wentworth had no fortune. He had been lucky in his profession, but, spending freely what had come freely, had realized nothing.

   Which most nearly captures the meaning of the word *realized* in the sentence above?
   (A) understood
   (B) accomplished
   (C) learned
   (D) accumulated
   (E) fulfilled

4. Anyone with more than a superficial knowledge of Shakespeare's plays must necessarily entertain some doubt concerning their true authorship.

   In the lines above, *entertain* most nearly means
   (A) amuse
   (B) harbor
   (C) occupy
   (D) cherish
   (E) engage   Ⓐ Ⓑ Ⓒ Ⓓ Ⓔ

5. Many people who invested in the booming art market of the 1980s were disappointed; few of the works appreciated in value.

   In the lines above, *appreciated* most nearly means
   (A) admired
   (B) applauded
   (C) spiraled
   (D) increased
   (E) acknowledged   Ⓐ Ⓑ Ⓒ Ⓓ Ⓔ

6. Charles de Gaulle's independence of mind can be seen by the fact that he negotiated with Algerian nationalists, although he was pressed by his advisors, French colonists, and the army itself to continue the war.

   Which most nearly captures the meaning of the word *pressed* in the sentence above?
   (A) squeezed
   (B) urged
   (C) troubled
   (D) required
   (E) compelled   Ⓐ Ⓑ Ⓒ Ⓓ Ⓔ

7. Today some would say that those struggles are all over—that all the horizons have been explored—that all the battles have been won—that there is no longer an American frontier. But I trust that no one in this vast assemblage will agree with those sentiments.

   In the lines above, *sentiments* most nearly means
   (A) beliefs
   (B) results
   (C) loyalties
   (D) challenges
   (E) emotions   Ⓐ Ⓑ Ⓒ Ⓓ Ⓔ

8. The convicts made their escape by scaling the prison walls and stealing away under the cover of darkness.

   Which most nearly captures the meaning of the word *stealing* in the line above?
   (A) seizing
   (B) taking
   (C) slipping
   (D) grabbing
   (E) abducting   Ⓐ Ⓑ Ⓒ Ⓓ Ⓔ

PAIRED PASSAGES—A (NOT-SO) SPECIAL CASE

Don't let the paired passages worry you—they're not twice as hard as the single reading selections. In fact, students often find the paired passages the most interesting on the test. With paired passages, focus as you read on the relationship between the two passages. Just as with single passages, the questions following paired passages can help fill in the picture.

Questions following paired passages tend to be ordered, with the first few questions relating to the first passage, the next few to the second passage, and the final questions asking about the passages as a pair. This is the best way to tackle the questions in any case, even if the test makers mix in a question about both passages amidst questions on the first passage (it's been known to happen).

To do paired passages:

1. Skim the first passage, looking for the drift (as you would with a single passage).

2. Do the questions that relate to the first passage.

3. Skim the second passage, looking for the drift and thinking about how the second passage relates to the first.

4. Do the questions that relate to the second passage.

5. Now you're ready to do the questions that ask about the relationship between the two passages.

Alternately skimming passages and answering questions is especially important if you're short of time. You'll be able to answer at least some of the questions before time runs out. By the time you've looked at both passages and answered the questions about each passage, you'll have a firm sense of the relationship between the pair. That will help you to answer the last group of questions.

Active reading can help you answer these questions, too. Remember to ask yourself, "What are these passages about? What is each author's point? What is similar about the two passages? What is different?"

Answers to Vocabulary-in-Context Questions, pp. 68–69

1. (E)
2. (B)
3. (D)
4. (B)
5. (D)
6. (B)
7. (A)
8. (C)

WHAT TO DO WHEN TIME IS RUNNING OUT

It's always best to skim the passage before you hit the questions. But if you only have a few minutes left, here's how to score points even while time is running out.

You can answer Vocabulary-in-Context questions and many Little Picture questions without reading the passage. If the question has a line reference, locate the material you need to find your answer and follow the five-step method as usual. You won't have the overall picture to guide you, but you might be able to reach the correct answer just by understanding the "little picture."

Checklist

Once you've mastered a concept, check it off.

The Basics of Critical Reading:

❑ How to read a passage

❑ Kaplan's Five-Step Method for Critical Reading questions

❑ Paired passages—a (not-so) special case

❑ What to do when time is running out

How to Do Specific Question Types:

❑ Big picture questions

❑ Little picture questions

❑ Vocabulary-in-context questions

Critical Reading Skills

- Learn to skim passages effectively and efficiently

- Use the Kaplan Four-Step Paraphrasing Method

- Strengthen your ability to draw inferences

In the previous chapter, you learned the basics of Critical Reading—what it looks like, what to expect, how to read the passages, how to tackle the questions. This chapter will help you improve the Critical Reading skills tested on the SAT—skimming, paraphrasing, and drawing inferences. You already have these skills.

- *Skimming* means reading quickly and lightly. You do this when you look information up in a phone book, or glance at a newspaper article only long enough to get the gist of the story.

- When you restate something in your own words, that's *paraphrasing*. You do it all the time in daily life—when you give a phone message, or retell a story.

- When you deduce information from a statement or situation, you're *making inferences*. You do it every day. If your best friend stopped talking to you, you'd probably infer that your friend was mad at you, even if your friend didn't actually say so.

SAT Emergency

If you have just a few weeks to prep for the SAT, here's the best way to spend your time:

- Read the section on skimming.

- Hold off on the rest of the chapter until you've covered all the basics in this book. If you have time to come back, work on the paraphrasing and inference sections.

SKIMMING

Skimming is a specific reading style in which you read quickly and in less detail than usual. These two characteristics are what make skimming the best way to read SAT passages. You want to read quickly because time is limited, and you want to read lightly because the questions direct you to the details you need. Spending a lot of time with the passage before you see the questions just doesn't make sense. So skimming works well—as long as you read with three things in mind:

- The content of the passage
- The organization of the passage
- The author's purpose or point of view

If you have a general idea of these three things when you're done skimming, then you're ready for the questions.

Read This Quickly

Joe stood at the edge of town, a cigarette in his left hand, a bottle of bourbon in his right. He'd had tough ones before, but this was gonna be the end of him. He looked back towards the light of the city below him. "If only I could get Martinez to talk," he thought to himself. In a flash, Joe was back in the Mustang racing towards town. . . .

What was this little story about? Chances are, even with a quick read, you took away some information that helped you piece it together. That's because you've already developed your reading skills (you're reading this, right?).

Your challenge on the SAT is to apply these skills in a peculiar context and not to be intimidated by the passages they throw at you.

In order to be an effective skimmer, you need to practice. Treat your practice sessions as an opportunity to learn. In time, you'll notice improvement.

- Practice frequently, in short sessions.
- Use these methods every time you read.

How to Skim

To improve your reading speed, get your eyes to move quickly and lightly along each line of type. Think about the way you usually read. Do you dwell on each word, as if you were plodding through a field of mud? Or do your eyes move quickly over the page, as if you were walking on hard, dry ground?

The way your eyes habitually move across each line of type and return to the beginning of the next line is your tracking style. That's what you'll work on here. The object is to make it light and swift, rather than heavy and deliberate. Don't read each word separately. Move your eyes lightly over the page, grouping words. Improving your tracking style will help you perform your best when under pressure.

Here are some skimming tips:

Don't Subvocalize

Subvocalizing is "sounding out" words as you read. Even if you don't move your lips, you're probably subvocalizing if you read one word at a time. Subvocalizing costs you time—because you can't read faster than you speak. If you group words, you won't subvocalize.

Keep Asking Yourself Where the Author's Going

Stay alert for the author's signals. Each SAT passage takes you on a journey, and every passage contains phrases or paragraph breaks that signal the next phase of this journey. As you skim, notice where each passage changes course.

Keep Your "Footsteps" Light

Don't read a passage slowly and deliberately. On the other hand, don't race as fast as you can. The idea is to increase your reading rate slightly while remaining comfortable.

Skimming Exercises

Now try a few exercises to see how skimming works. Read the following paragraph word by word.

> The prohibitive prices of some exhibits, as well as the continued depression of the local economy, prevented the 1939 World's Fair from being a great financial success. In a cultural sense, however, the Fair was enormously successful, and a landmark event of the era. As one historian noted, the Fair became "a cultural document of American values and aspirations at a crucial crossroads." After a decade of hardship, many Americans were ready to embrace a vision of social harmony, prosperity, and a bright future.

Now read the same paragraph, concentrating phrase by phrase.

> The prohibitive prices/ of some exhibits, /as well as/ the continued depression/ of the local economy, /prevented/ the 1939 World's Fair/ from being/ a great financial success. /In a /cultural sense,/ however,/ the Fair/ was enormously successful,/ and a landmark event/ of the era./ As one historian noted,/ the Fair became / "a cultural document/ of American values and aspirations/ at a crucial crossroads." /After a decade /of hardship,/ many Americans/ were ready to embrace/ a vision of social harmony,/ prosperity,/ and a bright future.

Here's another paragraph. Put in the slash marks yourself, phrase by phrase.

> The theme of the 1939 World's Fair was "Building the World of Tomorrow." Indeed, the modern and the futuristic were everywhere apparent. The main symbols of the Fair were the Trylon and the Perisphere, a huge pyramid and orb which were lit up at night in a dazzling display. The most popular exhibit, sponsored by General Motors, was the Futurama, which claimed to provide visitors with a glimpse of

Kaplan Rules

Don't put slash marks in your test booklet on the real SAT. You're allowed to, but it's a waste of time.

The point is to make "mental" slash marks so that you get in the habit of moving briskly through the passage.

automotive America in 1960. Patrons were carried by individual moving chairs on a simulated cross-country voyage, along a superhighway which would allow drivers to reach speeds up to 100 miles an hour.

No two readers will mark up this paragraph the same way, because each person sees phrases differently. That's okay. What's important is to begin working phrase-by-phrase, instead of word-by-word.

Now try another method. Read the following paragraphs, letting your eyes move down the page, and coming to rest at only two places per line:

The *Catcher in the Rye*, published in 1951, is the only novel written by J.D. Salinger in a career that lasted less than twenty years. It is the story of Holden Caulfield, a sensitive, rebellious New York City teen-ager taking his first hesitant steps into adulthood. Holden flees the confines of his snobbish Eastern prep school, searching for innocence and truth, but finds only "phoniness." Filled with humor and pathos, *The Catcher in the Rye* won wide critical acclaim at the time of its publication. In the four decades since then, however, it has become a true phenomenon, selling hundreds of thousands of copies each year, and Holden Caulfield has gained the status of a cultural icon. What accounts for this book's remarkable hold on generation after generation of American youth?

Holden Caulfield is the narrator of *The Catcher in the Rye*, and his narration is a stylistic tour de force, revealing Salinger's masterful ear for the linguistic idioms and rhythms of adolescent speech. Slang evolves continuously, of course, and yesterday's "in" expressions are usually passé by tomorrow. But Holden's characteristic means of expression—the vernacular of a teen-age social misfit, desperately trying to find his niche—transcends the particulars of time and place. Like another 1950s icon, James Dean in *Rebel Without a Cause*, Holden Caulfield has "outlived" his era and become an enduring symbol of sensitive youth, threatened by an indifferent society.

Teacher Tip

"Ordinary reading is too slow to find things and too fast to analyze text. Good test takers scan quickly to find what they need and then analyze intensely."

—Eirik Johnson
Kaplan Teacher
Chicago, IL

See how your eye takes in whole phrases, though you haven't read every word? That's another skimming method.

Remember, skim the passage before you turn to the questions. When you tackle the questions, you'll focus more tightly on parts of the passage. Many questions will direct you back to specific lines or paragraphs, so you won't be desperately searching for relevant information.

PARAPHRASING

What happens when your best friend misses a day of school? You probably tell her or him what went on that night on the phone, or the next day before class. If you did, you'd be para-phrasing—condensing a day's worth of events into a few minutes, highlighting the most important things. Critical Reading questions often ask you to do a similar thing. They ask what a passage, or part of it, says. The right answer accurately paraphrases the meaning of the passage or excerpt, that is, it restates the meaning without losing any important points. Let's see how this works. Here are a few sentences from a Critical Reading passage:

EXAMPLE

No doubt because it painted a less than flattering picture of American life in America for Asian immigrants, *East Goes West* was not well received by contemporary literary critics. According to them, Kang's book displayed a curious lack of insight regarding the American effort to accommodate those who had come over from Korea. The facet of the novel reviewers did find praiseworthy was Han's perseverance and sustained optimism in the face of adversity.

The passage indicates that the response of critics to *East Goes West* was one of

(A) irony regarding the difference between Han's expectations and reality

(B) admiration of the courage and creativity Kang showed in breaking from literary tradition

(C) confusion about the motivation of the protagonist

(D) qualified disapproval of Kang's perception of his adopted homeland

(E) anger that Kang had so viciously attacked American society

A Good Paraphrase

A good paraphrase accurately restates the meaning of the original, without adding or losing important points.

There's a lot going on in the passage, but don't let it confuse you. Follow our advice:

Kaplan's Four-Step Paraphrasing Method

1. Read the question stem. That's the partial sentence leading into the answer choices.
2. Read the lines you're referred to, searching for the relevant phrases. (If a question gives you a line reference, be sure to read a line or two before and after the keyed line.)
3. Predict a good paraphrase for what's being asked.
4. Find a similar answer choice.

Now apply Kaplan's method to the reading question above:

1–2.   After reading the stem and relevant lines of the passage (in this case, we found them for you), the key phrases should have popped out: *not well received, a curious lack of insight,* and *the facet reviewers did find praiseworthy.*

3.   Predicted paraphrase: The critics were displeased with Kang's view of the immigrant's experience, but approved of the hero's persistence.

4.   Look for the answer choice that means the same as your paraphrase.

Choice (D) comes closest. *Qualified* means "modified" or "limited," so *qualified disapproval* captures both the negative and the positive reaction the reviewers had.

Notice that Choice (E) is too negative, and choice (B) is too positive. Choices (A) and (C) don't reflect what the excerpt says. So (D) is the answer.

Paraphrasing Practice

The excerpts on the following page will help you recognize a good paraphrase quickly. Follow the method you've just learned. Notice as you go if your paraphrase includes too much or too little information, or if it has the wrong focus. If so, adjust it.

Each excerpt is followed by a space in which you can write your own paraphrase. Compare your paraphrase with the answer choices and pick the best approximation. You'll find the answers on page 84.

1.   He was not in love with Margaret, and he believed, though one could never be sure, that she was not in love with him—that her preference was for the handsome young clergyman who read Browning with her every Tuesday afternoon. But he was aware also that she would marry him if he asked her; he knew that the hearts of four formidable parents were set on the match; and in his past experience his mother's heart had invariably triumphed over his less intrepid resolves.

The protagonist believes that Margaret will marry him because (give the reason in your own words):

_____

_____

Now find the best paraphrase:

(A) she wouldn't have the resolve to refuse him
(B) they are in love with each other
(C) they both feel parental pressure
(D) she knows the clergyman won't marry her
(E) his mother will talk her into accepting him

2. Only with effort can the camera be forced to lie: basically it is an honest medium; so the photographer is much more likely to approach nature in a spirit of inquiry, of communion, instead of with the saucy swagger of self-dubbed "artists."

The distinction made in the passage between a photographer and an "artist" can best be summarized as which of the following (summarize the distinction in your own words):

_____

_____

Now find the best paraphrase:

(A) The photographer's job is to record the world, and the artist's is to embellish it.
(B) The photographer's work is realistic, while the artist's is impressionistic.
(C) The artist finds his inspiration in the urban environment, the photographer in nature.
(D) The photographer has a more open and unassuming attitude toward the natural world than the artist does.
(E) Photographers are more pretentious than artists are.   Ⓐ Ⓑ Ⓒ Ⓓ Ⓔ

3. The following excerpt is from a speech given by Frederick Douglass.

"What to the American slave is your Fourth of July? I answer, a day that reveals more to him than all other days of the year, the gross injustice and cruelty to which he is the constant victim. To him your celebration is a sham; your boasted liberty an unholy license; your national greatness, swelling vanity , . . ."

According to Douglass, for slaves, the Fourth of July (complete the sentence in your own words):

_____

_____

Now find the best paraphrase:

(A) highlights the hypocrisy of stated American ideals
(B) reveals the injustice of not being invited to participate
(C) is a reminder of the greatness of their homeland
(D) shows the depravity of the celebrants
(E) is a completely meaningless day   Ⓐ Ⓑ Ⓒ Ⓓ Ⓔ

MAKING INFERENCES

Inferences are conclusions you reach that are hinted at, but not directly stated, in the reading passage. When you infer, you're "reading between the lines." In Critical Reading:

- If you're given a line reference, be sure to read a line or two around it.

- Always look for evidence in the passage to support an inference.

Many SAT questions test your power to make accurate inferences.

EXAMPLE

My father was a justice of the peace, and I supposed that he possessed the power of life and death over all men and could hang anybody that offended him. This distinction was enough for me as a general thing; but the desire to become a steamboat man kept intruding, nevertheless. I first wanted to be a cabin boy, so that I could come out with a white apron on and shake a tablecloth over the side, where all my old comrades could see me. Later I thought I would rather be the deck hand who stood on the end of the stage plank with a coil of rope in his hand, because he was particularly conspicuous.

The author makes the statement that "I supposed he possessed the power of life and death over all men and could hang anybody that offended him" primarily to suggest the

(A) power held by a justice of the peace in a frontier town

(B) naive view that he held of his father's importance

(C) respect that the townspeople had for his father

(D) possibility of miscarriages of justice on the American frontier

(E) harsh environment in which he was brought up

The answer is implied here. The author doesn't say "my view of my father's importance at the time was naive." But the idea is implicit in the excerpt.

As the author explains it, he supposed at the time that his father was all powerful and that he could kill almost anyone. On a first reading, that probably struck you as odd. You also probably wondered why the son was proud of it. But read the passage carefully and you'll realize the tone is ironic. The author is making fun of his youthful ideas. So the correct answer has to be (B).

Don't Go Too Far with Inferences

SAT inferences tend to be straightforward and consistent with the overall idea of the passage. They are not extreme, complex, or subtle. In fact, they're incredibly predictable. (You can use this to your advantage.) That's why choices (A) and (E) go too far.

- Is it realistic that the author's father could hang anyone he wanted? Even if he could, would the author be proud of it? Very unlikely.

- Do the boy's early assumptions about his father's power indicate anything about the environment he grew up in? Not a thing.

Look at another question about the same excerpt:

> EXAMPLE
>
> The author decides that he would rather become a deck hand than a cabin boy because
>
> (A) the job offers higher wages
>
> (B) he believes that the work is easier
>
> (C) he wants to avoid seeing his older friends
>
> (D) deck hands often go on to become pilots
>
> (E) the job is more visible to passersby

The author never says, "I decided to become a deck hand because the job was more visible to passersby." He does say he wanted to become a cabin boy so his old comrades could see him. And he adds the deck hand job would make him conspicuous. Between the lines, the correct answer, (E), is strongly implied.

Teacher Tip

"Once you've finished a reading passage or question, put it out of your mind. There's no connection at all between passages, so don't carry your stress or doubt to the next. Approach each passage as if it were the only one. Stay active and confident!"

—Marilyn Engle
Kaplan Teacher
Encino, CA

Inference Practice

To sharpen your ability to deal with all kinds of inferences, do the following exercise. (Answers on p. 84.)

1. The graduating classes were the nobility of the school. Like travelers with exotic destinations on their minds, the graduates were remarkably forgetful. They came to school without their books, or tablets, or even pencils. Volunteers fell over themselves to secure replacements for the missing equipment. Even the teachers were respectful of the now quiet and aging seniors, and tended to speak to them, if not as equals, as beings only slightly lower than themselves.

   In the lines above, the author most likely mentions the eagerness of the "volunteers" in order to

   (A) indicate the ambition of younger school members
   (B) explain a double standard in teachers' attitudes
   (C) underline the respect with which seniors were treated
   (D) emphasize how careless seniors were with their equipment
   (E) point out a shortage in school supplies

2. Without knowing exactly what he'd done, Marc realized that he'd really done it now, and he felt the silence incriminating him. "Now wait just a minute. Hold on there," he said, producing a laugh from somewhere. Marc was the statesman of the class. People joked about how much money he was going to make coming out of law school. But he was groping for his words now, his eyes flickering over the countertop as if the words he was looking for were visible there.

   In the lines above, Marc's reputation as "the statesman of the class" is most likely mentioned in order to indicate that

   (A) he is noted for his diplomacy
   (B) many people resent his success
   (C) he is generally an articulate speaker
   (D) he is a popular student on campus
   (E) his ambitions are not realistic

3. Everyone seems to agree that there is something wrong with the way science is being taught these days. But no one is at all clear about what went wrong or what is to be done about it. The term "scientific illiteracy" has become almost a cliché in educational circles. Graduate schools blame the colleges, colleges blame the high schools, the high schools blame the elementary schools, which, in turn, blame the family. I suggest that the scientific community is partly, perhaps largely, to blame.

   In the lines above, the phrase "almost a cliché in educational circles" is used to indicate

   (A) the lack of unity between different sectors of education
   (B) the widespread concern about the way science is being taught
   (C) the inability of many scientists to communicate effectively
   (D) the ignorance displayed by the scientific community about literature
   (E) the extent of agreement over specific educational reforms

Checklist

Once you've mastered a concept, check it off.

Building Reading Skills:

❏ Skimming

❏ Paraphrasing

❏ Making inferences

Answers to Paraphrasing and Inference Questions

Paraphrasing:

1. (C) Their parents want them to get married.

2. (D) A photographer is more open to nature and less pretentious than an "artist" is.

3. (A) The Fourth of July is a sham because the holiday celebrates freedom and they are not free.

Inferences:

1. (C)

2. (C)

3. (B)

KAPLAN

Math Skills Workout

Introducing SAT Math

- Understand the breakdown and setup of the Math section
- Study traditional Math strategies as well as picking numbers and backsolving

Mathematics is many things. It is linear algebra and complex analysis. It is topology and trigonometry. It is number theory and multivariable calculus. Mathematics is a huge and daunting field, which requires years of study to master. But SAT Math is different. To ace the SAT, you need only a small body of mathematical knowledge covering basic concepts in arithmetic, algebra, and geometry. These concepts have been distilled into 100 principles that you'll find in the "SAT Study Aids" section of this book.

A solid grasp of these principles will get you a good SAT score. Understanding the ways in which these principles are tested—the twists and turns that the test makers throw into many SAT problems—can get you a great score.

This chapter explains:

- The SAT Math sections
- The SAT Math question types
- How to approach SAT Math problems
- Picking numbers
- Backsolving

SAT Emergency

This chapter will help you get a handle on the SAT Math section. You should read this chapter even if you have two weeks or fewer to prepare.

Then, in chapters 10 through 15, you'll learn:

- When to use your calculator
- Specific strategies for solving Regular Math questions, Quantitative Comparisons (QCs), and Grid-ins
- How to avoid math traps the test makers have set
- How to make educated guesses on difficult math problems

HOW SAT MATH IS SET UP

There are three scored Math sections on the SAT:

- One 30-minute section with 25 Regular Math questions
- One 30-minute section with a set of 15 QCs and a set of ten Grid-ins
- One 15-minute section with ten Regular Math questions

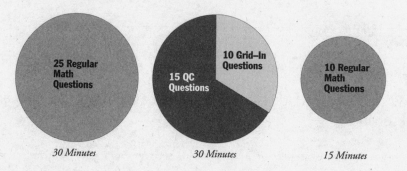

Difficulty Level

All sets of SAT Math questions are designed to start off basic and gradually increase in difficulty.

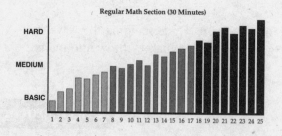

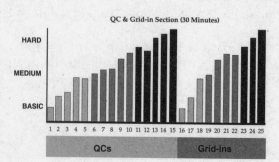

The ten Regular Math questions in the 15-minute section also get more difficult.

Always be aware of the difficulty level as you go through a question set. Easy problems call for different strategies. The harder the questions, the more traps you will encounter. If you know you're dealing with a hard question (even though it may look easy), you'll be prepared.

Know What to Expect

You'll save a lot of time on the SAT Math by knowing the directions. They take a fair amount of time to plow through and are the same for every test. With just a little prior experience, you'll know what to do with each question type so that you can skip the directions and go straight to the first question.

At the start of each Math section you will find the following information:

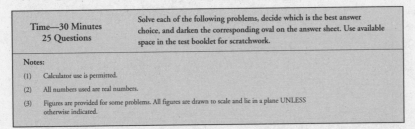

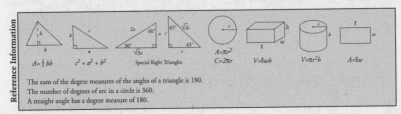

Note (2) means you won't have to deal with imaginary numbers, such as i (the square root of –1).

Note (3) tells you diagrams are drawn to scale, which means you can use these diagrams to estimate measurements. However, if the diagrams are labeled "Figure not drawn to scale," you can't do this.

Saying the figures "lie in a plane" simply means you are dealing with flat figures, like rectangles or circles, unless the question says otherwise.

The math information you're given includes many basic geometry formulas. By the day of the test you should know all these formulas by heart. But if you forget one at the last minute, you'll find them in the directions.

The Grid-ins and QCs have slightly different instructions, which we'll discuss in detail in chapter 11 and chapter 12.

HOW TO APPROACH SAT MATH

To maximize your Math score, you need to learn to use your time efficiently. Then you won't get bogged down on a single hard question and miss other problems you could have solved if you'd had more time.

The key to working systematically is: Think about the question before you look for the answer. A few seconds spent up front looking for traps, thinking about your approach, and deciding whether to tackle the problem now or come back to it later will pay off in SAT points. On basic problems, you may know what to do right away. But on hard problems, the few extra seconds are time well spent.

Now apply it to the problem below:

EXAMPLE

12. At a certain diner, Joe orders three doughnuts and a cup of coffee and is charged $2.25. Stella ordered two doughnuts and a cup of coffee and is charged $1.70. What is the price of two doughnuts?

(A) $0.55

(B) $0.60

(C) $1.10

(D) $1.30

(E) $1.80

Read Through the Question

This means the whole question. If you try to start solving the problem before reading it all the way through, you may end up doing unnecessary work.

Decide whether the question is basic, medium, or hard. All SAT Math questions are arranged in order of difficulty. Within a set, the first questions are basic, the middle ones moderately difficult, and the last ones are hard. Question 12 above is a moderately difficult word problem.

On difficult questions, watch out for Math Traps. Hard questions are often misleadingly worded to trip up careless readers. (For more on Math Traps, see chapter 14, Top Ten SAT Math Traps.)

Make sure you know what's being asked. Question 12 looks straightforward, but read through it carefully and you'll see a slight twist. You're asked to find the cost of two doughnuts, not one. Many people will find the price of a single doughnut and forget to double it.

Decide Whether to Do the Problem or Skip It for Now

- If you have no idea what to do, skip the problem and circle it in your test booklet. Spend your time on the problems you can solve.

- If you think you can solve it, but it will take a lot of time, circle the question number in your test booklet and make a note to come back to it later if you have time.

- If you can eliminate one or more answer choices, do so and make an educated guess. Mark that you guessed in your test booklet, and try solving later if time permits. (For details on educated guessing, see the Math Guessing chapter.)

If You Do Tackle the Problem, Look for the Fastest Approach

Look for hidden information. On an easy question, all the information you need to solve the problem may be given up front, in the stem, or in a diagram. But in a harder question, you may need to look for hidden information that will help you solve the problem. Since questions are arranged in order of difficulty, you should be a little wary of question 12. If you get the answer too easily, you may have missed something. In this case, you're asked to find the price of two doughnuts, not one. For more on Hidden Instructions, see chapter 14, Top Ten SAT Math Traps.

Helpful Hint

When you skip a question, make a note in your test booklet to come back to it later, if you have time.

Look for shortcuts. Sometimes the obvious way of doing a problem is the long way. If the method you choose involves lots of calculating, look for another route. There's usually a shortcut you can use that won't involve tons of arithmetic.

In question 12, for example, the cost of doughnuts and coffee could be translated into two distinct equations using the variables d and c. You could find c in terms of d, then plug this into the other equation. But if you think carefully, you'll see there's a quicker way: The difference in price between three doughnuts and a cup of coffee and two doughnuts and a cup of coffee is the price of one doughnut. So one doughnut costs $2.25 - $1.70 = $0.55. (Remember, you have to find the price of *two* doughnuts. Twice $0.55 is $1.10.)

Use a variety of strategies. Chapter 13, Classic Problem-Solving Techniques, reviews many strategies for specific problem types that will help you get to the answer faster. You can also use special Kaplan methods, such as Picking Numbers and Backsolving. (For more on these methods, see pp. 92–96 in this chapter.)

Make an Educated Guess

If you're not sure what to do, or if you've tried solving a problem but got stuck, cut your losses. Eliminate any answer choices you can, and make an educated guess.

Let's say it's taking too long to solve the doughnut problem. Can you eliminate any answer choices? The price of two doughnuts and a cup of coffee is $1.70. That means the cost of two doughnuts alone can't be $1.80, which eliminates choice (E). Now you can choose between the remaining choices, and your odds of guessing correctly have improved. (See chapter 15, Math Guessing.)

If you practice using this approach to the Math problems on the SAT, you will save time and avoid mistakes on the day of the test.

WHEN YOU'RE STUCK

The great thing about math, even if you hate it, is that there are usually a lot of different ways to get to the right answer. On the SAT, there are two methods in particular that are really useful when you don't see the straightforward way to solve the problem—picking numbers and backsolving. These strategies can take longer than traditional methods, but they're worth trying if you have enough time.

Picking Numbers

Sometimes you can get stuck on a math question just because it's too general or abstract. A good way to get a handle on such a question is to bring it down to earth and make it more explicit by temporarily substituting particular numbers. This "picking numbers" strategy works especially well with even/odd questions.

EXAMPLE

If a is an odd integer and b is an even integer, which of the following must be odd?

(A) $2a + b$

(B) $a + 2b$

(C) ab

(D) a^2b

(E) ab^2

Rather than try to think this one through abstractly, it's easier for most people simply to pick numbers for a and b. There are rules that predict the evenness or oddness of sums, differences, and products, but there's no need to memorize these rules. When it comes to adding, subtracting, and multiplying evens and odds, what happens with one pair of numbers generally happens with all similar pairs.

Just say, for the time being, that $a = 3$ and $b = 2$. Plug those values into the answer choices, and there's a good chance that only one choice will be odd:

(A) $2a + b = 2(3) + 2 = 8$

(B) $a + 2b = 3 + 2(2) = 7$

(C) $ab = (3)(2) = 6$

(D) $a^2b = (3^2)(2) = 18$

(E) $ab^2 = (3)(2^2) = 12$

Choice (B) is the only odd one for $a = 3$ and $b = 2$, so it must be the one that's odd no matter what odd number a and even number b actually stand for. The answer is (B).

Another good situation for using the "picking numbers" strategy is when the answer choices to a percent problem are all percents.

EXAMPLE

From 1985 to 1990, the population of City X increased by 20 percent. From 1990 to 1995, the population increased by 30 percent. What was the percent increase in the population over the entire ten-year period 1985–1995?

(A) 10%

(B) 25%

(C) 50%

(D) 56%

(E) 60%

Kaplan Rules

On percents, 100 is an easy number to work with.

Instead of trying to solve this problem in the abstract, pick a number for the original 1985 population and see what happens. There's no need to pick a realistic number. You're better off picking a number that's easy to work with. And in percent problems the number that's easiest to work with is almost always 100. Say the 1985 population was 100, then what would the 1990 population be? Twenty percent more than 100 is 120. Now, if the 1990 population was 120, what would the 1995 population be? What's 30 percent more than 120? Be careful. Don't just add 30 to 120. You need to find 30 percent of 120 and add that on. Thirty percent of 120 is $(.30)(120) = 36$. Add 36 to 120 and you get a 1995 population of 156. What percent greater is 156 than 100? That's easy—that's why we picked 100 to start with. It's a 56 percent increase. The answer is (D).

A third good situation for using the "picking numbers" strategy is when the answer choices to a word problem are not numbers, but algebraic expressions.

EXAMPLE

If n apples cost p dollars, then how many dollars would q apples cost?

(A) $\dfrac{np}{q}$

(B) $\dfrac{nq}{p}$

(C) $\dfrac{pq}{n}$

(D) $\dfrac{n}{pq}$

(E) $\dfrac{p}{nq}$

SAT Math: The Warning Signs

- If your answer depends on calculating the weight of the moon, in kilograms, you've read something wrong.

- "One potato, two potato" is not a useful guessing technique.

Kaplan Rules

Avoid picking weird numbers like 0 and 1, as these often give several "possibly correct" answers.

The only thing that's hard about this question is that it uses variables instead of numbers. So, make it real. Pick numbers for the variables. Pick numbers that are easy to work with. Say $n = 2$, $p = 4$, and $q = 3$. Then the question becomes: "If two apples cost $4.00, how many dollars would three apples cost?" That's easy—$6.00. When $n = 2$, $p = 4$, and $q = 3$, the correct answer should equal 6. Plug those values into the answer choices and see which ones yield 6:

(A) $\dfrac{np}{q} = \dfrac{(2)(4)}{3} = \dfrac{8}{3}$

(B) $\dfrac{nq}{p} = \dfrac{(2)(3)}{4} = \dfrac{6}{4} = \dfrac{3}{2} = 1\dfrac{1}{3}$

(C) $\dfrac{pq}{n} = \dfrac{(4)(3)}{2} = \dfrac{12}{2} = 6$

(D) $\dfrac{n}{pq} = \dfrac{2}{(4)(3)} = \dfrac{2}{12} = \dfrac{1}{6}$

(E) $\dfrac{p}{nq} = \dfrac{4}{(2)(3)} = \dfrac{4}{6} = \dfrac{2}{3}$

Choice (C) is the only one that yields 6, so it must be the correct answer.

When picking numbers for an abstract word problem like this one, it's important to try all five answer choices. Sometimes more than one choice will yield the correct result, in which case one or more choices work coincidentally with the numbers you picked. When that happens, pick another set of numbers to weed out the coincidences. Avoid picking weird numbers such as 0 and 1, as these often give several "possibly correct" answers.

Backsolving

On some Math questions, when you can't figure out the question, you can try working backwards from the answer choices. Plug the choices back into the question until you find the one that works.

Backsolving works best:

- When the question is a complex word problem and the answer choices are numbers
- When the alternative is setting up multiple algebraic equations

Don't backsolve:

- If the answer choices include variables
- On algebra questions or word problems that have ugly answer choices such as radicals and fractions (plugging them in takes too much time)

Complex Question, Simple Answer Choices

EXAMPLE

An office has 27 employees. If there are seven more women than men in the office, how many employees are women?

(A) 8

(B) 10

(C) 14

(D) 17

(E) 20

Sometimes backsolving is faster than setting up an equation.

The five answer choices represent the possible number of women in the office, so try them in the question stem. The choice that gives a total of 27 employees, with seven more women than men, will be the correct answer.

Plugging in choice (C) gives you 14 women in the office. Since there are seven more women than men, there are seven men in the office. But $14 + 7 < 27$. The sum is too small, so there must be more than 14 women. Eliminate answer choices (A), (B), and (C).

Either (D) or (E) will be correct. Plugging in (D) gives you 17 women in the office and $17 - 7$, or 10 men. $17 + 10 = 27$ employees total. Answer choice (D) is correct.

Algebra Problems for Which You Need to Solve Multiple Equations

EXAMPLE

If $a + b + c = 110$, $a = 4b$, and $3a = 2c$, then $b =$

(A) 6

(B) 8

(C) 9

(D) 10

(E) 14

You're looking for b, so plug in the answer choices for b in the question and see what happens. The choice that gives us 110 for the sum $a + b + c$ must be correct.

Start with the midrange number, 9, choice (C):

If $b = 9$, then $a = 4 \times 9 = 36$.

$2c = 3a = 3 \times 36 = 108$

$c = 54$

$a + b + c = 36 + 9 + 54 = 99$

Since this is a smaller sum than 110, the correct value for b must be greater. Therefore, eliminate answer choices (A), (B), and (C).

Now plug in either (D) or (E) and see if it works. If it doesn't, the remaining choice must be correct.

Short of time? Try guessing between (D) and (E). But guess intelligently. Since (C) wasn't far wrong, you want a number just slightly bigger. That's choice (D).

Now work through the remaining chapters in the Math Skills Workout section to master other strategies that will help you to ace your test.

10

Calculators and the SAT

- Practice with the calculator you'll bring to the test

- Use your calculator selectively

- Know the most common calculator mistakes and how to avoid them

You are allowed to use a calculator on the SAT. That's a mixed blessing. The good news is you can do computation faster. The bad news is you may be tempted to waste time using a calculator on questions that shouldn't involve lengthy computation.

Remember, you never *need* a calculator to solve an SAT problem. If you ever find yourself doing extensive calculation on the SAT—elaborate long division or long, drawn-out multiplication—stop and look again, because you probably missed a shortcut.

SHOULD I BRING A CALCULATOR?

You definitely want to bring your calculator on the day of the test. The fact is, there are some problems for which using the calculator will really come in handy. By using your calculator on particular problem types and by zeroing in on the parts of problems that need calculation, you can increase your score and save yourself time on the SAT.

SAT Emergency

If you have a week or two to prep for the SAT, be sure to read the section on common calculator mistakes.

WHAT KIND OF CALCULATOR SHOULD I BRING?

The best calculator to bring is one you're comfortable with. The most important thing is not how fancy your calculator is, but how good you are at using it. Remember, you won't be doing logs, trig functions, or preprogrammed formulas on the SAT. Most of the time you'll be multiplying and dividing.

You can use the following calculators on the SAT:

- A four-function calculator (that adds, subtracts, multiplies, divides)

- A scientific calculator (that also does radicals, exponents, etc.)

- A graphing calculator (that displays the graph of an equation in a coordinate plane)

But the following are not allowed:

- A calculator that prints out your calculations

- A hand-held minicomputer or a laptop computer

- Any calculator with a typewriter keypad

- A calculator that "speaks," makes strange noises, or requires an electrical outlet for use

The More You Know about the SAT . . .

. . . the less you'll use your calculator.

Using a calculator too much could actually hurt your score. The better you are at the SAT, the less you'll need your calculator.

WHEN SHOULD I USE A CALCULATOR?

Calculators help the most on Grid-ins and the least on QCs.

The reason for this is that QCs are designed to be done very quickly, and rarely involve much computation—if you think you need a calculator on them, then you're probably missing something. Both Grid-ins and Regular Math will sometimes involve computation—never as the most important part of the question, but often as a final step.

Since Grid-ins don't give you answer choices to choose from, it's especially important to be sure of your work. Calculators can help you avoid careless errors.

Remember, a calculator can be useful when used selectively. Not all parts of a problem are necessarily easier on a calculator. Consider this problem:

EXAMPLE

If four grams of cadmium yellow pigment can make 3 kilograms of cadmium yellow oil paint, how many kilograms of paint could be produced from 86 grams of pigment?

KAPLAN

This word problem has two steps. Step one is to set up the following proportion:

$$\frac{4 \text{ gms}}{3 \text{ kgs}} = \frac{86 \text{ gms}}{x \text{ kgs}}$$

A little algebraic engineering tells you that:

$$x \text{ kgs} = \frac{3 \text{ kgs} \times 86 \text{ gms}}{4 \text{ gms}}$$

Here's where you whip out that calculator. This problem has now been reduced down to pure calculation: $(3 \times 86) \div 4 = 64.5$.

Your calculator will also be especially useful for picking numbers and backsolving.

When You Pick Numbers

When you plug in real numbers to replace variables in complex equations, your calculator can speed things up. (See Picking Numbers in chapter 9, Introducing SAT Math.)

When You Backsolve

When you plug multiple-choice answers into a problem to see which answer is right, your calculator can speed up the process. (See Backsolving, in chapter 9.)

WHEN SHOULDN'T I USE A CALCULATOR?

Don't be fooled. On most SAT problems you may be tempted to use your calculator, but many questions will be easier without a calculator. That's particularly true on QCs.

Consider this problem:

EXAMPLE

Column A	Column B

The ratio of b to 7 is equal to the ratio of 143 to 188.

$$b \qquad\qquad 7$$

Check Your Batteries

The best calculator in the world won't help if the batteries are dead or if you forget to put them in. Make sure you have fresh batteries in your machine on the day of the test.

Sure, you could set up the proportion $\frac{b}{7} = \frac{143}{188}$, grab your calculator, and cross multiply to find that $b = 5.324468085$. But why bother doing the calculation? Once you've set up the proportion, you can make a quick comparison without any further calculation. Your task is to compare b to 7. If $b = 7$, then $\frac{b}{7} = 1$. However, $\frac{b}{7}$ must be less than 1 since $\frac{143}{188} < 1$. Therefore, $b < 7$. Column B must be greater.

Be careful on non-QC questions, too. Consider this:

EXAMPLE

If $x^2 \times 8^2 = 49 \times 64 \times 81$, $x^2 =$

(A) 49^2

(B) 56^2

(C) 63^2

(D) 72^2

(E) 81^2

Now if you punch in $49 \times 64 \times 81$ you'll get 254,016. But that won't be too helpful. Look at the answer choices! Instead realize that:

$$(x^2) \times 8^2 = (49 \times 81) \times 64$$

8^2 is the same as 64, so get rid of the 64s on both sides. You get:

$$x^2 = 49 \times 81$$

So that's $x^2 = 7^2 \times 9^2$ or $x^2 = 7 \times 7 \times 9 \times 9$, which is 63×63 or 63^2.

No calculator required.

COMMON MISTAKE #1: CALCULATING BEFORE YOU THINK

On the Grid-in problem below, how should you use your calculator?

Calculator Abuse: The Warning Signs

- Punching in numbers before you've read the question.

- Hand cramps from punching in too many numbers.

- Repeatedly spelling *hello* or *Shell Oil* on your calculator rather than answering the question.

EXAMPLE

The sum of all the integers from 1 to 44, inclusive, is subtracted from the sum of all the integers from 7 to 50, inclusive. What is the result?

The Wrong Approach:

- Grab calculator.

- Punch in all the numbers.

- Put down an answer and hope you didn't hit any wrong buttons.

The wrong approach is to punch in all the numbers from 1 to 44, find their sum, then do the same for numbers 7 through 50, and subtract the first sum from the second. Doing that means punching 252 keys. The odds are you'll slip up somewhere, hit the wrong key, and get the wrong answer. Even if you don't, punching in all those numbers takes too much time.

The Kaplan Method

- Think first.

- Decide on the best way to solve it.

- Only then, use your calculator.

The right approach is to *think first*. The amount of computation involved in solving this directly tells you that there *must* be an easier way. You'll see this if you realize that both sums are of the same number of consecutive integers. Each integer in the first sum has a corresponding integer six units greater than it in the second sum, like so:

$$
\begin{array}{cc}
1 & 7 \\
+2 & +8 \\
+3 & +9 \\
\cdot & \cdot \\
\cdot & \cdot \\
\cdot & \cdot \\
+42 & +48 \\
+43 & +49 \\
+44 & +50 \\
= & =
\end{array}
$$

Teacher Tip

"I often tell students not to rely on their calculators too much. They are excellent tools, but when we begin to use them to do every operation, they are no longer tools that we are using to augment our abilities, but tools we are using to replace them."

—Jaelithe Russ
  Kaplan Teacher
  Akron, OH

There are 44 pairs of integers that are six units apart. So the total difference between the two sums will be the difference between each pair of integers times the number of pairs.

Now take out your calculator, multiply 6 by 44, and get the correct answer of 264, with little or no time wasted.

HINT: *If you're punching buttons for long stretches at a time, you're approaching the problem the wrong way.*

COMMON MISTAKE #2: FORGETTING THE ORDER OF OPERATIONS

Watch out. Even when you use your calculator, you can't just enter numbers in the order they appear on the page—you've got to follow the order of operations. This is a very simple error but it can cost you lots of points.

The order of operations, or PEMDAS, means you do whatever is in:

Kaplan Rules

Different calculators do chain calculations different ways. Make sure you know how your calculator does chains so you don't miscalculate.

Parentheses first, then deal with

Exponents, then

Multiplication and

Division, and finally

Addition and

Subtraction

For example, say you want to find the value of the expression:

$$\frac{x^2 + 1}{x + 3} \quad \text{when } x = 7$$

If you just punched in "$7 \times 7 + 1 \div 7 + 3 =$" you would get the wrong answer. The correct way to work it out is:

$$(7^2 + 1) \div (7 + 3) = (7 \times 7 + 1) \div (7 + 3) = (49 + 1) \div 10 = 50 \div 10 = 5$$

Combining a calculator with an understanding of when and how to use it can help you boost your score.

Checklist

Once you've mastered a concept, check it off.

Calculators and the SAT:

❏ What kind of calculator should I bring?

❏ When should I use a calculator?

❏ When shouldn't I use a calculator?

❏ Common mistakes

11

Grid-Ins

HIGHLIGHTS

- Familiarize yourself with grid formats, techniques, and rules
- Practice gridding in answers with fractions, mixed numbers, and decimals

In high school math class, you usually don't get five answer choices to choose from on a test. And you don't lose a quarter of a point for a wrong answer. Instead, you're given a problem and asked to find the answer.

The Grid-in section on the SAT is a lot like the math tests you're already used to taking. Unlike other questions on the SAT, Grid-ins have no multiple-choice answers and there's no penalty for wrong answers. You have to figure out your own answer and fill it in on a special grid. Note that some Grid-ins have only one correct answer, while others have several, or even a range of correct answers.

SAT Emergency

If you have two weeks or fewer to prep for the SAT, here's the best way to spend your time:

- Read this entire chapter. It's pretty short and the gridding tips that we discuss can help prevent you from making careless mistakes that can make a big difference in your score.

- Do the gridding drills at the end of the chapter.

THE FORMAT

You'll get ten Grid-ins, following the QCs, in one of the Math sections. To get an idea of what the instructions will look like on the day of the test, check out the example below.

For each question, you'll see a grid with four boxes and a column of ovals beneath each. First write your numerical answer in the boxes, one digit, decimal point, or fraction bar per box. Then fill in the corresponding ovals below.

Warning:

- The computer cannot scan the numerical answer in the boxes; you must fill in the corresponding ovals.

- Fill in no more than one oval per column.

- Make the oval you grid match your number above that oval.

For each of the questions below (16–25), solve the problem and indicate your answer by darkening the ovals in the special grid. For example:

Answer: 1.25 or $\frac{5}{4}$ or 5/4

Write answer in boxes. → Grid in result →

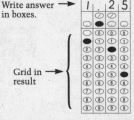

Fraction line ← Decimal point

You may start your answers in any column, space permitting. Columns not needed should be left blank.

Either position is correct.

- It is recommended, though not required, that you write your answer in the boxes at the top of the columns. However, you will receive credit only for darkening the ovals correctly.

- Grid only one answer to a question, even though some problems have more than one correct answer.

- Darken no more than one oval in a column.

- No answers are negative.

- Mixed numbers cannot be gridded. For example: the number $1\frac{1}{4}$ must be gridded as 1.25 or 5/4.

(If is gridded, it will be interpreted as $\frac{11}{4}$ not $1\frac{1}{4}$.)

- Decimal Accuracy: Decimal answers must be entered as accurately as possible. For example, if you obtain an answer such as 0.1666. . ., you should record the result as .166 or .167. **Less accurate values such as .16 or .17 are not acceptable.**

Acceptable ways to grid $\frac{1}{6}$ =.1666. . .

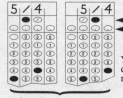

Grid instructions

KAPLAN

FILLING IN THE GRID

The grid cannot accommodate:

- Negative answers

- Answers with variables

- Answers greater than 9,999

- Answers with commas

- Mixed numbers

Recommendation: Start your answer in the first column box. Do this even if your answer has only one or two figures. If you always start with the first column, your answers will always fit. Since there is no oval for 0 in the first column, grid an answer of 0 in any other column. (Technically, you can start in any column, but follow this rule to avoid mistakes.)

In a fractional answer, grid (/) in the correct column. The sign (/) separates the numerator from the denominator. It appears only in columns two and three.

Example: If you get an answer of $\frac{5}{8}$. Grid (/) in col. two.

Example: If you get an answer of $\frac{11}{9}$. Grid (/) in col. three.

WARNING: *A fractional answer with four digits won't fit.*

Change mixed numbers to decimals or fractions before you grid. If you try to grid a mixed number, it will be read as a fraction, and be counted wrong. For example, $4\frac{1}{2}$ will be read as the fraction $\frac{41}{2}$, which is $20\frac{1}{2}$.

Two Grid-in Tips

1. Always start from the left.

2. Guess when you can. Skip it when you haven't a clue. Be sure to circle the question number in your test booklet if you skip it.

There's no wrong-answer penalty for Grid-ins. So if you have time, take an educated guess. It can't hurt.

Kaplan Rules

Bubble trouble: The computer scores only the numbers that are bubbled in, not what you've written on top of the grid. The only reason to write your answers out is to help you bubble in.

Kaplan Rules

Always use the most accurate answer that fits. For example, 1.4 is not a substitute for 1.43.

So first change mixed numbers to fractions or decimals, then grid in. In this case:

- Change $4\frac{1}{2}$ to $\frac{9}{2}$ and grid in as shown below.

- Or change $4\frac{1}{2}$ to 4.5 and grid in the decimal.

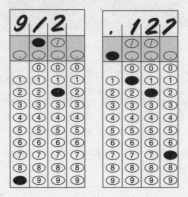

HINT: *Watch where you put your decimal points.*

- For a decimal less than 1, such as .127, enter the decimal point in the first box as shown in the figure above.

- Put a zero before the decimal point only if it's part of the answer—don't just put one there to make your answer look more accurate.

- Never grid a decimal point in the last column.

With long or repeating decimals, grid the first three digits only and plug in the decimal point where it belongs. Say three answers are .45454545, 82.452312, and 1.428743. Grid .454, 82.4, and 1.42, respectively.

You could round 1.428743 up to the nearest hundredth (1.43), but it's not required. So don't bother, since you could make a mistake. Shorter, less accurate answers—such as 1.4—are wrong.

On Grid-ins with more than one right answer, choose one, and enter it. Say you're asked for a two-digit integer that is a multiple of 2, 3, and 5. You might answer 30, 60, or 90. Whichever you grid would be right.

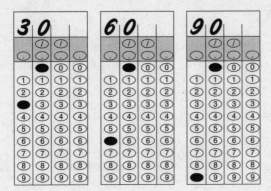

Some Grid-ins have a range of possible answers. Suppose you're asked to grid a value of m, given that $1 - 2m < m$ and $5m - 2 < m$. Solving for m in the first inequality, you find that $\frac{1}{3} < m$. Solving for m in the second inequality, you find that $m < \frac{1}{2}$. So $\frac{1}{3} < m < \frac{1}{2}$. Grid in any value between $\frac{1}{3}$ and $\frac{1}{2}$. (Gridding in $\frac{1}{3}$ or $\frac{1}{2}$ would be wrong.) When the answer is a range of values, it's often easier to work with decimals: $.333 < m < .5$. Then you can quickly grid .4 (or .35 or .45, etc.) as your answer.

Write your answers in the number boxes. You will make fewer mistakes if you write your answers in the number boxes. You may think that gridding directly will save time, but writing first and then gridding ensures accuracy, which means more points.

Top Grid-in Screw-Ups

- Gridding in mixed numbers
- Making rounding errors
- Writing your answer and forgetting to grid it in
- Double bubble gridding two numbers in the same column (the computer reads this as an omission)
- Filling the wrong bubble under the right number—it's still considered a wrong answer

PRACTICE GRIDDING

With just a little practice, you can master the gridding-in process. Complete the Grid-ins below, following our instructions. After you finish, check your work against the grids on p. 110.

126	$\dfrac{3}{8}$	85.9	2,143	$5\dfrac{1}{2}$

0	.141414	$\dfrac{14}{5}$	$1\dfrac{2}{3}$	8.175

Checklist

Once you've mastered a concept, check it off.

Grid-Ins:

❏ The format

❏ Filling in the grid

❏ Practice gridding

Gridding Answers

126       $\frac{3}{8}$ 85.9   2,143 $5\frac{1}{2}$

Or .375   Omit the comma.   Convert $5\frac{1}{2}$ to $\frac{11}{2}$ (or 5.5); "5 1/2" is incorrect.

0   .141414 $\frac{14}{5}$ $1\frac{2}{3}$ 8.175

 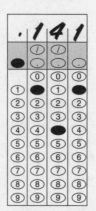

Place the decimal point in the first column and grid as many digits as possible.

Convert $1\frac{2}{3}$ to $\frac{5}{3}$ (or 1.66 or 1.67); "12/3" is incorrect.

Or 8.18. Start in the left column and grid as many digits as possible.

12

Quantitative Comparisons

HIGHLIGHTS

- Understand the answer choices and the rules for choice (D)

- Master Kaplan's six strategies for tackling QCs

- Complete the Quantitative Comparisons Practice Set

In Quantitative Comparisons, instead of solving for a particular value, you need to compare two quantities. At first, QCs may appear really difficult because of their unfamiliar format. However, once you become used to them, they can be quicker and easier than the other types of math questions.

THE FORMAT

Where They Appear

The 15 QCs appear in the Math section that also contains the ten Grid-in questions. They are arranged in order of increasing difficulty.

The Questions

In each question, you'll see two mathematical expressions. They are boxed, one in Column A, the other in Column B. Your job is to compare them.

SAT Emergency

If you don't have much time to prep for the SAT, here's the best way to spend your time:

- Read p. 112.

- Learn the two rules for choice (D) on p. 112.

- Do the practice problems on pp. 121–122. If you miss an answer, review the strategy before continuing.

Some questions include additional information about one or both quantities. This information is centered, unboxed, and essential to making the comparison.

HINT: *To score high on QCs, learn what the answer choices stand for.*

The Directions

The directions you'll see will look something like this. Familiarize yourself with them now.

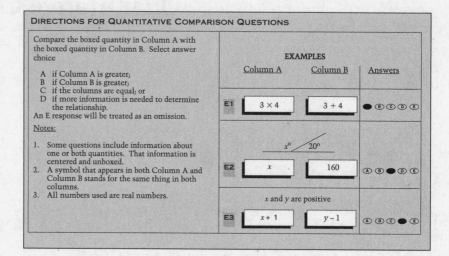

WARNING: *Never pick choice (E) as the answer to a QC.*

Two Rules for Answer Choice (D)

Choices (A), (B), and (C) all represent definite relationships between the quantities in Column A and Column B. But choice (D) represents a relationship that cannot be determined. Here are two things to remember about choice (D) that will help you decide when to pick it:

1. Choice (D) is never correct if both columns contain only numbers. The relationship between numbers is unchanging, but choice (D) means more than one relationship is possible.

2. Choice (D) is correct if you can demonstrate two different relationships between the columns. Suppose you ran across the following QC:

Column A	Column B
$2x$	$3x$

If x is a positive number, Column B is greater than Column A. If $x = 0$, the columns are equal. If x equals any negative number, Column B is less than Column A. Since more than one relationship is possible, the answer is (D). In fact, as soon as you find a second possibility, stop work and pick choice (D).

COMPARE, DON'T CALCULATE: KAPLAN'S SIX STRATEGIES

Here are six Kaplan strategies that will enable you to make quick comparisons. In the rest of this chapter you'll learn how they work and you'll try them on practice problems.

Strategy 1: Compare Piece by Piece

This works on QCs that compare two sums or two products.

Strategy 2: Make One Column Look Like the Other

This is a great approach when the columns look so different that you can't compare them directly.

Strategy 3: Do the Same Thing to Both Columns

Change both columns by adding, subtracting, multiplying, or dividing by the same amount on both sides in order to make the comparison more apparent.

Strategy 4: Pick Numbers

Use this to get a handle on abstract algebra QCs.

Strategy 5: Redraw the Diagram

Redrawing a diagram can clarify the relationships between measurements.

Strategy 6: Avoid QC Traps

Stay alert for questions designed to fool you by leading you to the obvious, wrong answer.

Now learn how these strategies work.

STRATEGY 1: COMPARE PIECE BY PIECE

EXAMPLE

Column A	Column B
$w > x > 0 > y > z$	
$w + y$	$x + z$

In the problem above, there are four variables—w, x, y, and z. Compare the value of each "piece" in each column. If every "piece" in one column is greater than a corresponding "piece" in the other column and the only operation involved is addition, the column with the greater individual values will have the greater total value.

From the given information we know that $w > x$ and $y > z$. Therefore, the first term in Column A, w, is greater than the first term in Column B, x. Similarly, the second term in Column A, y, is greater than the second term in Column B, z. Since each piece in Column A is greater than the corresponding piece in Column B, Column A must be greater; the answer is (A).

STRATEGY 2: MAKE ONE COLUMN LOOK LIKE THE OTHER

When the quantities in Columns A and B are expressed differently, you can often make the comparison easier by changing one column to look like the other. For example, if one column is a percent and the other a fraction, try converting the percent to a fraction.

EXAMPLE

Column A	Column B
$x(x-1)$	$x^2 - x$

Here Column A has parentheses, and Column B doesn't. So make Column A look more like Column B: Get rid of those parentheses. You end up with $x^2 - x$ in both columns, which means they are equal and the answer is (C).

Try another example, this time involving geometry.

EXAMPLE

Column A	Column B

The diameter of circle O is d and the area is a.

Column A	Column B
$\dfrac{\pi d^2}{2}$	a

Make Column B look more like Column A by rewriting a, the area of the circle, in terms of the diameter, d. The area of any circle equals πr^2, with r as the radius.

Since the radius is half the diameter, we can plug in $\dfrac{d}{2}$ for r in the area formula to get $\pi\left(\dfrac{d}{2}\right)^2$ in Column B. Simplifying, we get $\dfrac{\pi d^2}{4}$. Since both columns contain π, we can simply compare $\dfrac{d^2}{2}$ with $\dfrac{d^2}{4}$. Since $\dfrac{d^2}{4}$ is half as much as $\dfrac{d^2}{2}$, and d^2 must be positive, Column A is greater.

Choice (A) is correct.

STRATEGY 3: DO THE SAME THING TO BOTH COLUMNS

Some QC questions become much clearer if you change not just the appearances, but the values of both columns. Treat them like two sides of an inequality, with the sign temporarily hidden.

You can add or subtract the same amount from both columns and multiply or divide by the same positive amount without altering the relationship. You can also square both columns if you're sure they're both positive. But watch out. Multiplying or dividing an inequality by a negative number reverses the direction of the inequality sign. Since it alters the relationship between the columns, avoid multiplying or dividing by a negative number.

HINT: *Don't multiply or divide both QC columns by a negative number.*

In the QC below, what could you do to both columns?

| EXAMPLE |

Column A	Column B
	$4a + 3 = 7b$
$20a + 10$	$35b - 5$

All the terms in the two columns are multiples of 5, so divide both columns by 5 to simplify. You're left with $4a + 2$ in Column A and $7b - 1$ in Column B. This resembles the equation given in the centered information. In fact, if you add 1 to both columns, you have $4a + 3$ in Column A and $7b$ in Column B. The centered equation tells us they are equal. Thus choice (C) is correct.

In the next QC, what could you do to both columns?

| EXAMPLE |

Column A	Column B
	$y > 0$
$1 + \dfrac{y}{(y + 1)}$	$1 + \dfrac{1}{(1 + y)}$

Solution: First subtract 1 from both sides. That gives you $\dfrac{y}{(1 + y)}$ in Column A, and $\dfrac{1}{(1 + y)}$ in Column B. Then multiply both sides by $(1 + y)$, which must be positive since y is positive.

You're left comparing y with 1.

Kaplan Rules

Some surprising things can happen when you play around with negative numbers and fractions. Keep things like this in mind:

- When you square a positive fraction less than 1, the result is smaller than the original fraction.

- When you square a negative number, the result is a positive number.

- When you square 0 and 1, they stay the same.

You know y is greater than 0, but it could be a fraction less than 1, so it could be greater or less than 1. Since you can't say for sure which column is greater, the answer is (D).

STRATEGY 4: PICK NUMBERS

If a QC involves variables, try picking numbers to make the relationship clearer. Here's what you do:

- Pick numbers that are easy to work with.

- Plug in the numbers and calculate the values. Note the relationship between the columns.

- Pick another number for each variable and calculate the values again.

EXAMPLE

Column A	Column B

$$r > s > t > w > 0$$

Column A	Column B
$\dfrac{r}{t}$	$\dfrac{s}{w}$

Try $r = 4$, $s = 3$, $t = 2$, and $w = 1$. Then Column A $= \dfrac{r}{t} = \dfrac{4}{2} = 2$. And Column B $= \dfrac{s}{w} = \dfrac{3}{1} = 3$.

So in this case Column B is greater than Column A.

Always Pick Another Number and Calculate Again

In the example above, we first found Column B was bigger. But that doesn't mean Column B is always bigger and that the answer is (B). It *does* mean the answer is not (A) or (C). But the answer could still be (D)—not enough information to decide.

If time is short, guess between (B) and (D). But whenever you can, pick another set of numbers and calculate again.

As best you can, make a special effort to find a second set of numbers that will alter the relationship. Here for example, try making r a lot larger. Pick $r = 30$ and keep the other variables as they were. Now Column A $= \dfrac{30}{2} = 15$. This time, Column A is greater than Column B, so answer choice (D) is correct.

HINT: *If the relationship between Columns A and B changes when you pick other numbers, (D) must be the answer.*

Pick Different Kinds of Numbers

Don't assume all variables represent positive integers. Unless you're told otherwise, variables can represent zero, negative numbers, or fractions. Since different kinds of numbers behave differently, always pick a different kind of number the second time around. In the example above, we plugged in a small positive number the first time and a larger number the second.

In the next three examples, we pick different numbers and get different results. Since we can't find constant relationships between Columns A and B, in all these cases the answer is (D).

EXAMPLE

Column A	Column B
w	$-w$

If $w = 5$, Column A = 5 and Column B = -5, so Column A is greater.

If $w = -5$, Column A = -5 and Column B = 5, so Column B is greater.

EXAMPLE

$$x \neq 0$$

Column A	Column B
x	$\dfrac{1}{x}$

If $x = 3$, Column A = 3 and Column B = $\dfrac{1}{3}$, so Column A is greater.

If $x = \dfrac{1}{3}$, Column A = $\dfrac{1}{3}$ and Column B = $\dfrac{1}{\frac{1}{3}} = 3$, so Column B is greater.

EXAMPLE

Column A	Column B
x	x^2

If $x = \dfrac{1}{2}$, Column A = $\dfrac{1}{2}$ and Column B = $\dfrac{1}{4}$, so Column A is greater.

If $x = 2$, Column A = 2 and Column B = 4, so Column B is greater.

STRATEGY 5: REDRAW THE DIAGRAM

- Redraw a diagram if the one that's given misleads you.

- Redraw scale diagrams to exaggerate crucial differences.

Kaplan Rules

Remember:

- Not all numbers are positive.
- Not all numbers are integers.

Some geometry diagrams may be misleading. Two angles or lengths may look equal as drawn in the diagram, but the given information tells you that there is a slight difference in their measures. The best strategy is to redraw the diagram so that their relationship can be clearly seen.

EXAMPLE

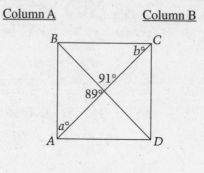

ABCD is a rectangle

    a   b

Redraw this diagram to exaggerate the difference between the 89-degree angle and the 91-degree angle. In other words, make the larger angle much larger, and the smaller angle much smaller. The new rectangle that results is much wider than it is tall.

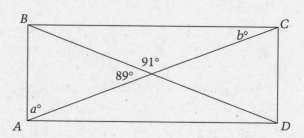

In the new diagram, where the crucial difference jumps out, *a* is clearly greater than *b*.

STRATEGY 6: AVOID QC TRAPS

To avoid QC traps, always be alert. Don't assume anything. Be especially cautious near the end of the question set.

Don't Be Tricked by Misleading Information

EXAMPLE

Column A   Column B

John is taller than Bob.

John's weight in pounds   Bob's weight in pounds

The test makers hope you think, "If John is taller, he must weigh more." But there's no guaranteed relationship between height and weight, so you don't have enough information. The answer is (D). Fortunately, problems like this are easy to spot if you stay alert.

Don't Assume

A common QC mistake is to assume that variables represent positive integers. As we saw in using the Picking Numbers strategy, fractions or negative numbers often show another relationship between the columns.

EXAMPLE

Column A	Column B

When 1 is added to the square of x the result is 37.

x	6

It is easy to assume that x must be 6, since the square of x is 36. That would make choice (C) correct. However, it is possible that $x = -6$. Since x could be either 6 or -6, the answer is (D).

HINT: *Be aware of negative numbers!*

Don't Forget to Consider Other Possibilities

The following question appears at the end of the QC section.

EXAMPLE

Column A	Column B

$$\begin{array}{r} R \\ S \\ \underline{T} \\ 1W \end{array}$$

In the addition problem above, R, S, and T are different digits that are multiples of 3, and W is a digit.

W	8

Since you're told that R, S, and T are digits and different multiples of 3, most people will think of 3, 6, and 9, which add up to 18. That makes W equal to 8, and Columns A and B equal. But that's too obvious for a QC at the end of the section.

There's another possibility. Zero is also a multiple of 3. So the three digits could be 0, 3, and 9, or 0, 6, and 9, which give totals of 12 and 15, respectively. That means W could be 8, 2, or 5. Since the columns could be equal, or Column B could be greater, answer choice (D) must be correct.

Don't Fall for Look-Alikes

EXAMPLE

<u>Column A</u>

$\sqrt{5} + \sqrt{5}$

<u>Column B</u>

$\sqrt{10}$

At first glance, forgetting the rules of radicals, you might think these quantities are equal and that the answer is (C). But use some common sense to see this isn't the case. Each $\sqrt{5}$ in Column A is bigger than $\sqrt{4}$, so Column A is more than 4. The $\sqrt{10}$ in Column B is less than another familiar number, $\sqrt{16}$, so Column B is less than 4. The answer is (A).

Now use Kaplan's six strategies to solve nine typical QC questions. Then check your work against our solutions on page 123.

TEST YOUR QC SMARTS

Column A   Column B

1. $x^2 + 2x - 2$ $x^2 + 2x - 1$ Ⓐ Ⓑ Ⓒ Ⓓ Ⓔ

$x = 2y$
$y > 0$

2. 4^{2y} 2^x Ⓐ Ⓑ Ⓒ Ⓓ Ⓔ

$\frac{x}{y} = \frac{z}{4}$

x, y, and z are positive

3. $6x$ $2yz$ Ⓐ Ⓑ Ⓒ Ⓓ Ⓔ

q, r, and s are positive integers
$qrs > 12$

4. $\frac{qr}{5}$ $\frac{3}{s}$ Ⓐ Ⓑ Ⓒ Ⓓ Ⓔ

$x > 1$
$y > 0$

5. y^x $y^{(x+1)}$ Ⓐ Ⓑ Ⓒ Ⓓ Ⓔ

$7p + 3 = r$
$3p + 7 = s$

6. r s Ⓐ Ⓑ Ⓒ Ⓓ Ⓔ

Column A   Column B

In triangle *XYZ*, the measure of angle *X* equals the measure of angle *Y*.

7. The degree measure   The degree measure
   of angle *Z*   of angle *X* plus the
                            degree measure of
                            angle *Y*   Ⓐ Ⓑ Ⓒ Ⓓ Ⓔ

....

$$h > 1$$

8. The number of $\dfrac{60}{h}$
   minutes in *h*
   hours   Ⓐ Ⓑ Ⓒ Ⓓ Ⓔ

....

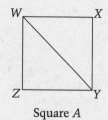

Square *A*   Square *B*

Note: Figures not drawn to scale.

9. $\dfrac{\text{Perimeter of square } A}{\text{Perimeter of square } B}$ $\dfrac{\text{Length of } WY}{\text{Length of } PR}$ Ⓐ Ⓑ Ⓒ Ⓓ Ⓔ

Answers to QC Practice Set

1. (B) Comparing the respective pieces of the two columns, the only difference is the third piece: -2 in Column A and -1 in Column B. We don't know the value of x, but whatever it is, x^2 in Column A must have the same value as x^2 in Column B, and $2x$ in Column A must have the same value as $2x$ in Column B. Since any quantity minus 2 must be less than that quantity minus 1, Column B is greater than Column A.

2. (A) Replacing the x exponent in Column B with the equivalent value given in the problem, we're comparing 4^{2y} to 2^{2y}. Since y is greater than 0, raising 4 to the $2y$ power will result in a greater value than raising 2 to the $2y$ power.

3. (B) Do the same thing to both columns until they resemble the centered information. When we divide both columns by $6y$ we get $\frac{6x}{6y}$, or $\frac{x}{y}$ in Column A, and $\frac{2yz}{6y}$, or $\frac{z}{3}$ in Column B. Since $\frac{x}{y} = \frac{z}{4}$, and $\frac{z}{3} > \frac{z}{4}$ (because z is positive), $\frac{z}{3} > \frac{x}{y}$.

4. (D) Do the same thing to both columns to make them look like the centered information. When we multiply both columns by $5s$ we get qrs in Column A and 15 in Column B. Since qrs could be any integer greater than 12, it could be greater than, equal to, or less than 15.

5. (D) Try $x = y = 2$. Then Column A $= y^x = 2^2 = 4$. Column B $= y^{x+1} = 2^3 = 8$, making Column B greater. But if $x = 2$ and $y = \frac{1}{2}$, Column A $= \left(\frac{1}{2}\right)^2 = \frac{1}{4}$ and Column B $= \left(\frac{1}{2}\right)^3 = \frac{1}{8}$. In this case, Column A is greater than Column B, so the answer is (D).

6. (D) Pick a value for p, and see what effect this has on r and s. If $p = 1$, $r = (7 \times 1) + 3 = 10$, and $s = (3 \times 1) + 7 = 10$, and the two columns are equal. But if $p = 0$, $r = (7 \times 0) + 3 = 3$, and $s = (3 \times 0) + 7 = 7$, and Column A is smaller than Column B. Since there are at least two different possible relationships, the answer is choice (D).

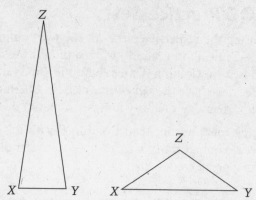

7. (D) Since angle X = angle Y, this is an isosceles triangle. We can draw two diagrams with X and Y as the base angles of an isosceles triangle. In one diagram, make the triangle tall and narrow, so that angle X and angle Y are very large, and angle Z is very small. In this case, column B is greater. In the second diagram, make the triangle short and wide, so that angle Z is much larger than angle X and angle Y. In this case, Column A is greater. Since more than one relationship between the columns is possible, the correct answer is choice (D).

8. (A) The "obvious" answer here is choice (C), because there are 60 minutes in an hour, and 60 appears in Column B. But the number of minutes in h hours would equal 60 times h, not 60 divided by h. Since h is greater than 1, the number in Column B will be less than the actual number of minutes in h hours, so Column A is greater. (A) is correct.

9. (C) We don't know the exact relationship between Square A and Square B, but it doesn't matter. The problem is actually just comparing the ratios of corresponding parts of two squares. Whatever the relationship between them is for one specific length in both squares, the same relationship will exist between them for any other corresponding length. If a side of one square is twice the length of a side of the second square, the diagonal will also be twice as long. The ratio of the perimeters of the two squares is the same as the ratio of the sides. Therefore, the columns are equal. (C) is correct.

Checklist

Once you've mastered a concept, check it off.

Quantitative Comparisons:

❏ Compare piece by piece

❏ Make one column look like the other

❏ Do the same thing to both columns

❏ Pick numbers

❏ Redraw the diagram

❏ Avoid QC traps

13

Classic Problem-Solving Techniques

Review ten popular question types and methods to solve each:

- Remainders

- Averages

- Ratios

- Rates

- Percents

- Combinations

- Simultaneous equations

- Symbolism

- Special triangles

- Multiple and oddball figures

SAT Emergency

If you have just a few weeks to prep for the SAT, here's how you should spend your time:

- In each of the ten sections, try the sample problems.

- Review any section where you have trouble.

The test makers are not paid to be creative. In fact, there are certain types of problems that they like to use again and again on the SAT. This chapter gives you ten of their favorite problem types, along with Kaplan's classic techniques for solving them.

REMAINDERS

Remainder questions can be easier than they look. You might think you have to solve for a certain value, but often you don't.

EXAMPLE

When n is divided by 7, the remainder is 4.
What is the remainder when $2n$ is divided by 7?

(A) 0

(B) 1

(C) 2

(D) 3

(E) 4

The question above doesn't depend on knowing the value of n. In fact, n has an infinite number of possible values.

HINT: *Pick a number for* n.

Which number should you pick? Since the remainder when n is divided by 7 is 4, pick any multiple of 7 and add 4. The easiest multiple to work with is 7. So, 7 + 4 = 11. Use 11 for n.

Plug 11 into the question and see what happens.

What is the remainder when $2n$ is divided by 7?

$$2(11) \div 7 =$$

$$22 \div 7 =$$

$$\frac{22}{7} = 3 \text{ remainder } 1$$

The remainder is 1 when $n = 11$. So the answer is (B). The remainder will also be 1 when $n = 18, 25$, or 46.

QC Remainders

Speed Tip

EXAMPLE

When picking a number for a remainder problem, add the remainder to the number you're dividing by.

<u>Column A</u>   <u>Column B</u>

When p is divided by 5, the remainder is 3.

When q is divided by 5, the remainder is 4.

p q

The centered information tells you that p can be any of the integers 3, 8, 13, 18, 23, . . . ; and that q can be any of the integers 4, 9, 14, 19, 24, and so forth. So how do p and q compare? You can't tell; p could be small and q big, or the other way around. The answer is (D), not enough information to decide.

Practice Problems: Remainders

REGULAR MATH

1. When z is divided by 8, the remainder is 5. What is the remainder when $4z$ is divided by 8?

   (A) 1
   (B) 3
   (C) 4
   (D) 5
   (E) 7   Ⓐ Ⓑ Ⓒ Ⓓ Ⓔ

....

QC

<u>Column A</u>   <u>Column B</u>

When x is divided by 6 the remainder is 3.
When y is divided by 6 the remainder is 4.

2. x y Ⓐ Ⓑ Ⓒ Ⓓ Ⓔ

....

When m is divided by 5 the remainder is 2.
When n is divided by 5 the remainder is 1.

3.   The remainder   The remainder when
     when $m + n$ is mn is divided by 5
     divided by 5   Ⓐ Ⓑ Ⓒ Ⓓ Ⓔ

Answers to Remainders Problems

1. (C) Let $z = 13$ and plug in $4z = 4(13) = 52$, which leaves a remainder of 4 when divided by 8.

2. (D) We determine that x can be any of the integers 3, 9, 15, 21, . . . , and y can be any of the integers 4, 10, 16, 22, ... Since x could be greater than or less than y, the correct answer must be choice (D).

3. (A) The variable m can be any integer that ends in either a 2 or a 7; n can be any integer that ends in either a 1 or a 6. Plugging in will show that in any case, $m + n$ will leave a remainder of 3 when divided by 5, and mn will leave a remainder of 2 when divided by 5, so Column A is greater.

Use Your Head

Use common sense to learn about the size of the value you're asked to find. If all the terms listed are less than the given average, then the unknown term must be greater than the average to balance it out.

Likewise, if adding a new value, x, to a group of numbers raises the average value of the group, then x must be greater than the average of the original numbers.

AVERAGES

EXAMPLE

The average weight of five dogs in a certain kennel is 32 pounds. If four of the dogs weigh 25, 27, 19, and 35 pounds, what is the weight of the fifth dog?

(A) 28
(B) 32
(C) 49
(D) 54
(E) 69

Instead of giving you a list of values to plug into the average formula, SAT average questions often put a slight spin on the problem. They tell you the average of a group of terms and ask you to find the value of the missing term.

HINT: *Work with the sum.*

Let x = the weight of the fifth dog. Plug this into the average formula:

$$32 = \frac{25 + 27 + 19 + 35 + x}{5}$$

$$32 \times 5 = 25 + 27 + 19 + 35 + x$$

So the average weight of the dogs, times the number of dogs, equals the total weight of the dogs, or, mathematically:

$$\text{Average} \times \text{Number of Terms} = \text{Sum of Terms}$$

Remember this manipulation of the average formula so that whenever you know the average of a group of terms and the number of terms, you can find the total sum.

Now you can solve for the weight of the fifth dog:

$$32 \times 5 = 25 + 27 + 19 + 35 + x$$
$$160 = 106 + x$$
$$54 = x$$

So the weight of the fifth dog is 54 pounds, choice (D).

Practice Problems: Averages

REGULAR MATH

1. The average (arithmetic mean) of six numbers is 16. If five of the numbers are 15, 37, 16, 9, and 23, what is the sixth number?

   (A) −20
   (B) −4
   (C) 0
   (D) 6
   (E) 16

2. Bart needs to buy five gifts with $80. If two of the gifts cost a total of $35, what is the average (arithmetic mean) amount Bart can spend on each of the remaining three gifts?

   (A) $45
   (B) $17
   (C) $16
   (D) $15
   (E) $10

3. The average (arithmetic mean) of five numbers is 8. If the average of two of these numbers is −6, what is the sum of the other three numbers?

   (A) 28
   (B) 34
   (C) 46
   (D) 52
   (E) 60

Answers to Averages Problems

1. (B) Average × Number of Terms = Sum of Terms

   $$16 \times 6 = 15 + 37 + 16 + 9 + 23 + x$$

   $$96 = 100 + x$$

   $$-4 = x$$

2. (D) Bart has \$80 and spent \$35 on two gifts; therefore he has \$45 left to spend on the remaining three. So,

   $$x = \frac{\$45}{3}$$

   $$x = \$15$$

3. (D) Average × Number of Terms = Sum of Terms

   The sum of all five numbers is

   $$8 \times 5 = 40$$

   The sum of two of these numbers is

   $$(-6) \times 2 = -12$$

   So, the difference of these two sums, $40 - (-12) = 52$, is the sum of the other numbers.

RATIOS

Train Your Brain

Use common sense to check your math on this example to the right. Most of the chips are nondefective, so the ratio must be greater than 1. If you reversed the terms and thought (C) was the answer, that would tell you that you did something wrong.

EXAMPLE

Out of every 50 chips produced in a certain factory, 20 are defective. What is the ratio of nondefective chips produced to defective chips produced?

(A) 2:5

(B) 3:5

(C) 2:3

(D) 3:2

(E) 5:2

HINT: *Identify the parts and the whole in the problem.*

Find the parts and the whole in the problem. In this case the total number of chips is the whole, and the number of nondefective chips and the number of defective chips are the parts that make up this whole.

You're given a part-to-whole ratio—the ratio of defective chips to all chips, and asked to find a part-to-part ratio—the ratio of nondefective chips to defective chips.

If 20 chips out of every 50 are defective, the remaining 30 chips must be non-defective. So the part-to-part ratio of nondefective to defective chips is 30/20, or 3/2, which is equivalent to 3:2—answer choice (D).

If you hadn't identified the part and the whole first, it would be easy to get confused and compare a part to the whole, like the ratios in answer choices (A) and (B).

This approach also works for ratio questions that ask you to find actual quantities. For example:

> Out of every five chips produced in a certain factory, two are defective. If 2,200 chips were produced, how many were defective?

Here you need to find a quantity—the number of defective chips.

HINT: *If you're looking for the actual quantities in a ratio, set up and solve a proportion.*

You're given a part-to-whole ratio (the ratio of defective chips to all chips), and the total number of chips produced. You can find the answer by setting up and solving a proportion.

$$\frac{\text{Number of defective chips}}{\text{Total number of chips}} = \frac{2}{5} = \frac{x}{2,200}$$

$$x = \text{Number of defective chips}$$

$$5x = 4,400$$

$$x = 880$$

HINT: *Remember that ratios compare only relative size—they don't tell you the actual quantities involved.*

Kaplan Rules

When you look at a ratio, make sure you know if you're dealing with *parts* to *parts* or *parts* to *whole*.

You also need to see if the parts that you're given add up to the whole. For example, the number of male and female students in a classroom must add up to the whole. The number of students with blond hair and the number of students with brown hair are parts, but do not necessarily add up to the whole.

Practice Problems: Ratios

REGULAR MATH

1. The ratio of right-handed pitchers to left-handed pitchers in a certain baseball league is 11:7. What fractional part of the pitchers in the league are left-handed?

   (A) $\dfrac{6}{7}$

   (B) $\dfrac{6}{11}$

   (C) $\dfrac{7}{11}$

   (D) $\dfrac{7}{18}$

   (E) $\dfrac{11}{18}$

   Ⓐ Ⓑ Ⓒ Ⓓ Ⓔ

....

2. In a group of 24 people who are either homeowners or renters, the ratio of homeowners to renters is 5:3. How many homeowners are in the group?

   (A) 15
   (B) 14
   (C) 12
   (D) 9
   (E) 8

   Ⓐ Ⓑ Ⓒ Ⓓ Ⓔ

....

3. Magazine *A* has a total of 28 pages, 16 of which are advertisements and 12 of which are articles. Magazine *B* has a total of 35 pages, all of them either advertisements or articles. If the ratio of the number of pages of advertisements to the number of pages of articles is the same for both magazines, then Magazine *B* has how many more pages of advertisements than Magazine *A*?

   (A) 2
   (B) 3
   (C) 4
   (D) 5
   (E) 6

   Ⓐ Ⓑ Ⓒ Ⓓ Ⓔ

Answers to Ratios Problems

1. (D) The parts are the number of right-handed (11) and the number of left-handed pitchers (7). The whole is the total number of pitchers (right-handed + left-handed), which is 11 + 7, or 18. So:

$$\frac{\text{part}}{\text{whole}} = \frac{\text{left-handed}}{\text{total}} = \frac{7}{11 + 7} = \frac{7}{18}$$

2. (A) The parts are the number of homeowners (5) and the number of renters (3). The whole is the total (homeowners + renters). So:

$$\frac{\text{part}}{\text{whole}} = \frac{\text{homeowners}}{\text{homeowners} + \text{renters}} = \frac{5}{5 + 3} = \frac{5}{8}$$

Since we are trying to find an actual quantity, set up a proportion.

$$\frac{\text{Homeowners}}{\text{Total people}} = \frac{5}{8} = \frac{x}{24}$$

$$8x = 120$$

$$x = 15$$

Time Trouble

Use logic to narrow your choices. Most are homeowners, so the answer must be more than half of 24, or 12. Either (A) or (B) is the right answer.

3. (C) The $\frac{\text{part}}{\text{whole}}$ ratio of advertisements (16) to total pages (28) in Magazine A is $\frac{16}{28}$, or $\frac{4}{7}$. Magazine B has the same ratio, so if there are 35 pages in Magazine B, $\frac{4}{7} \times 35$—or 20 pages—are advertisements. Therefore, there are four more pages of advertisements in Magazine B than in Magazine A.

RATES

EXAMPLE

If eight oranges cost *a* dollars, *b* oranges would cost how many dollars?

(A) $8ab$

(B) $\dfrac{8a}{b}$

(C) $\dfrac{8}{ab}$

(D) $\dfrac{a}{8b}$

(E) $\dfrac{ab}{8}$

A rate is a ratio that compares quantities that are measured in different units. In the problem above the units are oranges and dollars.

What makes the rate problem above difficult is the presence of variables. It's hard to get a clear picture of the relationship between the units.

HINT: *Pick numbers for the variables to make the relationship between the units clearer.*

Pick numbers for *a* and *b* that are easy to work with in the problem. Let *a* = 16. Then eight oranges cost $16.00. So the cost per orange at this rate is $\dfrac{16 \text{ dollars}}{8 \text{ oranges}}$ = $2 per orange. Let *b* = 5. So the cost of five oranges at this rate is five oranges × $2.00 per orange = $10.00.

Now plug in *a* = 16 and *b* = 5 into the answer choices to see which one gives you a value of 10.

Choice (A): $8 \times 16 \times 5 = 640$. Eliminate.

Choice (B): $\dfrac{8 \times 16}{5} = \dfrac{128}{5}$. Eliminate.

Choice (C): $\dfrac{8}{16 \times 5} = \dfrac{1}{10}$. Eliminate.

Choice (D): $\dfrac{16}{8 \times 5} = \dfrac{2}{5}$. Eliminate.

Choice (E): $\dfrac{16 \times 5}{8} = 10$.

Since (E) is the only one that gives the correct value, it is correct.

Practice Problems: Rates

REGULAR MATH

1. If David paints at the rate of h houses per day, how many houses does he paint in d days, in terms of h and d ?

   (A) $\dfrac{h}{d}$

   (B) hd

   (C) $h + \dfrac{d}{2}$

   (D) $h - d$

   (E) $\dfrac{d}{h}$ Ⓐ Ⓑ Ⓒ Ⓓ Ⓔ

2. Bill has to type a paper that is p pages long, with each page containing w words. If Bill types an average of x words per minute, how many hours will it take him to finish the paper?

   (A) $60\,wpx$

   (B) $\dfrac{wx}{60p}$

   (C) $\dfrac{60wp}{x}$

   (D) $\dfrac{wpx}{60}$

   (E) $\dfrac{wp}{60x}$ Ⓐ Ⓑ Ⓒ Ⓓ Ⓔ

3. If Seymour drove 120 miles in x hours at constant speed, how many miles did he travel in the first 20 minutes of his trip?

   (A) $60x$

   (B) $3x$

   (C) $\dfrac{120}{x}$

   (D) $\dfrac{40}{x}$

   (E) $\dfrac{6}{x}$ Ⓐ Ⓑ Ⓒ Ⓓ Ⓔ

Answers to Rates Problems

1. (B) Pick numbers for h and d. Let $h = 2$ and $d = 3$; that is, suppose he paints two houses per day and he paints for three days, so in three days he can paint six houses. You multiply the rate (h) by the number of days (d). The only answer choice that equals 6 when $h = 2$ and $d = 3$ is choice (B).

2. (E) Pick numbers for p, w, and x that work well in the problem. Let $p = 3$ and let $w = 100$. So there are three pages with 100 words per page, or 300 words total. Say he types five words a minute, so $x = 5$. So he types 5×60, or 300 words an hour. Therefore, it takes him one hour to type the paper. The only answer choice that equals 1 when $p = 3$, $w = 100$, and $x = 5$ is choice (E).

3. (D) Let $x = 4$. That means that he drove 120 miles in four hours, so his speed was $\frac{120 \text{ miles}}{4 \text{ hours}}$, or 30 miles per hour. Since 20 minutes $= \frac{1}{3}$ of an hour, the distance he traveled in the first 20 minutes is $\frac{1}{3}$ hours $\times$ 30 miles per hour = 10 miles. The only answer choice that equals 10 when $x = 4$ is choice (D).

PERCENTS

Memorize These

When you need to, you can figure out a percent equivalent on your calculator by dividing the numerator by the denominator. You'll save time by knowing some common percent equivalents.

$\frac{1}{5} = 20\%$

$\frac{1}{4} = 25\%$

$\frac{1}{3} = 33\frac{1}{3}\%$

$\frac{1}{2} = 50\%$

$\frac{2}{3} = 66\frac{2}{3}\%$

$\frac{3}{4} = 75\%$

EXAMPLE

Last year Julie's annual salary was $20,000. This year's raise brings her to an annual salary of $25,000. If she gets the same percent raise every year, what will her salary be next year?

(A) $27,500

(B) $30,000

(C) $31,250

(D) $32,500

(E) $35,000

In percent problems, you're usually given two pieces of information and asked to find the third. When you see a percent problem, remember:

• If you are solving for a percent:

$$\text{Percent} = \frac{\text{Part}}{\text{Whole}}$$

• If you need to solve for a part:

$$\text{Percent} \times \text{Whole} = \text{Part}$$

This problem asks for Julie's projected salary for next year—that is, her current salary plus her next raise.

You know last year's salary ($20,000) and you know this year's salary ($25,000), so you can find the difference between the two salaries:

$$\$25,000 - \$20,000 = \$5,000 = \text{her raise}$$

Now find the percent of her raise, by using the formula

$$\text{Percent} = \frac{\text{Part}}{\text{Whole}}$$

Since Julie's raise was calculated on last year's salary, divide by $20,000.

HINT: *Be sure you know which Whole to plug in. Here you're looking for a percent of $20,000, not $25,000.*

$$\text{Percent raise} = \frac{\$5,000}{\$20,000} = \frac{1}{4} = 25\%$$

You know she will get the same percent raise next year, so solve for the part. Use the formula Percent × Whole = Part. Her raise next year will be

$$25\% \times \$25,000 = \frac{1}{4} \times 25,000 = \$6,250$$

Add that sum to this year's salary and you have her projected salary: $25,000 + $6,250 = $31,250, or answer choice (C).

Make sure that you change the percent to either a fraction or a decimal before beginning calculations.

Mirror Image

x percent of y = y percent of x

20% of 50 = 50% of 20

$$\frac{1}{5} \times 50 = \frac{1}{2} \times 20$$

$$10 = 10$$

Practice Problems: Percents

QC

Column A	Column B
1. 5% of 3% of 45	6.75

Ⓐ Ⓑ Ⓒ Ⓓ Ⓔ

....

GRID-IN

2. Eighty-five percent of the members of a student organization registered to attend a certain field trip. If 16 of the members who registered were unable to attend, resulting in only 65 percent of the members making the trip, how many members are in the organization?

....

REGULAR MATH

3. If a sweater sells for $48 after a 25 percent markdown, what was its original price?

(A) $56
(B) $60
(C) $64
(D) $68
(E) $72

Ⓐ Ⓑ Ⓒ Ⓓ Ⓔ

Answers to Percents Problems

1. (B) Percent × Whole = Part. Five percent of (3 percent of 45) = .05 × (.03 × 45) = .05 × 1.35 = .0675, which is less than 6.75 in Column B.

2. (80) You need to solve for the Whole, so identify the Part and the Percent. If 85 percent planned to attend and only 65 percent did, 20 percent failed to attend, and you know that 16 students failed to attend.

   Percent × Whole = Part

   $$\frac{20}{100} \times \text{Whole} = 16$$

   $$\text{Whole} = 16 \times \frac{100}{20}$$

   $$\text{Whole} = 80$$

3. (C) We want to solve for the original price, the Whole. The percent markdown is 25 percent, so $48 is 75 percent of the whole.

   Percent × Whole = Part

   75 percent × Original Price = $48

   $$\text{Original Price} = \frac{\$48}{0.75} = \$64$$

COMBINATIONS

EXAMPLE

If Alice, Betty, and Carlos sit in three adjacent empty seats in a movie house, how many different seating arrangements are possible?

(A) 3

(B) 4

(C) 5

(D) 6

(E) 8

Combination problems ask you to find the different possibilities that can occur in a given situation.

HINT: *Simply count the number of possibilities by listing them in a quick but systematic way.*

To solve this problem, let the first letter of each name stand for that person. First, find all the combinations with Alice in the first seat:

ABC

ACB

Using the same system, try Betty in the first seat, and then Carlos:

BAC

BCA

CAB

CBA

At this point we've exhausted every possibility. So there are six possible arrangements, and that's answer choice (D).

Some problems set up conditions that limit the possibilities somewhat. Some may ask for the number of distinct possibilities, meaning that if the same combination shows up twice in different forms, you should count it only once. Consider the following problem.

EXAMPLE

Set I: {2, 3, 4, 5}

Set II: {1, 2, 3}

If x is a number generated by multiplying a number from Set I by a number from Set II, how many possible values of x are greater than 5?

(A) 3

(B) 4

(C) 5

(D) 6

(E) 7

Warning

Don't use complex formulas to solve combinations problems. SAT combinations questions are simple enough that you can write down the possibilities and count them.

Again, list the possibilities in a systematic way, pairing off each number in the first set with each number in the second set, so every combination is included:

$2 \times 1 = 2$	$4 \times 1 = 4$
$2 \times 2 = 4$	$4 \times 2 = 8$
$2 \times 3 = 6$	$4 \times 3 = 12$
$3 \times 1 = 3$	$5 \times 1 = 5$
$3 \times 2 = 6$	$5 \times 2 = 10$
$3 \times 3 = 9$	$5 \times 3 = 15$

How many of these values are greater than 5? Going down the list: 6, 6, 9, 8, 12, 10, and 15. Although there are seven answers for x that are greater than 5, two of them are the same. So there are six different values of x greater than 5, not seven. The answer is (D).

HINT: *Always write down the possibilities as you organize them, so you can count them accurately, and so you don't count the same combination twice.*

Practice Problems: Combinations

REGULAR MATH

1. A three-digit code is made up of three different digits from the set {2,4,6,8}. If 2 is always the first digit in the code, how many three-digit codes can be formed?

   (A) 16
   (B) 12
   (C) 10
   (D) 8
   (E) 6

   Ⓐ Ⓑ Ⓒ Ⓓ Ⓔ

....

QC

Column A	Column B

Five people attend a meeting. Each person shakes hands once with every other person at the meeting.

2.   The total number   15
      of handshakes that
         take place

   Ⓐ Ⓑ Ⓒ Ⓓ Ⓔ

....

REGULAR MATH

3. Three people stop for lunch at a hot dog stand. If each person orders one item and there are three items to choose from, how many different combinations of food could be purchased? (Assume that order doesn't matter; e.g., a hot dog and two sodas are considered the same as two sodas and a hot dog.)

   (A) 6
   (B) 9
   (C) 10
   (D) 18
   (E) 27

   Ⓐ Ⓑ Ⓒ Ⓓ Ⓔ

Answers to Combinations Problems

1. (E) Every code starts with 2, so the last two digits determine the number of possibilities. The last two digits could be: 46, 48, 64, 68, 84, and 86. That makes six combinations that fit the conditions.

2. (B) Be careful not to count each handshake twice. Call the five people A, B, C, D, and E. We can pair them off like this:

    A with B, C, D, and E (four handshakes)

    B with C, D, and E (three more—note that we leave out A, since the handshake between A and B is already counted)

    C with D and E (two more)

    D with E (one more)

    The total is 4 + 3 + 2 + 1, or 10 handshakes.

3. (C) To find the number, let's call the three items they can purchase A, B, and C. The possibilities:

    All three order the same thing: AAA, BBB, CCC

    Two order the same thing: AAB, AAC, BBA, BBC, CCA, CCB

    All three order something different: ABC

    So there are ten different ways the three items could be ordered.

SIMULTANEOUS EQUATIONS

Kaplan Rules

When subtracting one equation from another, be sure to distribute the minus sign to each term. In the example to the left,

$$-p - 2q = -14$$

EXAMPLE

If $p + 2q = 14$ and $3p + q = 12$, then $p =$

(A) −2

(B) −1

(C) 1

(D) 2

(E) 3

In order to get a numerical value for each variable, you need as many different equations as there are variables to solve for. So, if you have two variables, you need two independent equations.

You could tackle this problem by solving for one variable in terms of the other, and then plugging this expression into the other equation. But the simultaneous equations that appear on the SAT can usually be handled in an easier way.

HINT: *Combine the equations—by adding or subtracting them—to cancel out all but one of the variables.*

You can't eliminate p or q by adding or subtracting the equations in their present form. But if you multiply the second equation by 2:

$$2(3p + q) = 2(12)$$
$$6p + 2q = 24$$

Now when you subtract the first equation from the second, the qs will cancel out so you can solve for p:

$$6p + 2q = 24$$
$$\underline{-[p + 2q = 14]}$$
$$5p + 0 = 10$$

If $5p = 10$, $p = 2$.

Practice Problems: Simultaneous Equations

REGULAR MATH

1. If $x + y = 8$ and $y - x = -2$, then $y =$

   (A) −2
   (B) 3
   (C) 5
   (D) 8
   (E) 10

GRID-IN

2. If $4a + 3b = 19$ and $a + 2b = 6$, then $a + b =$

REGULAR MATH

3. If $m - n = 5$ and $2m + 3n = 15$, then $m + n =$

   (A) 1
   (B) 6
   (C) 7
   (D) 10
   (E) 15

Answers to Simultaneous Equations Problems

1. (B) When you add the two equations, the xs cancel out and you find that $2y = 6$, so $y = 3$.

2. (5) Adding the two equations, you find that $5a + 5b = 25$. Dividing by 5 shows that $a + b = 5$.

3. (C) Multiply the first equation by 2, then subtract the first equation from the second to eliminate the ms and find that $5n = 5$, or $n = 1$:

$$2m + 3n = 15$$
$$\underline{-2m + 2n = -10}$$
$$5n = 5$$
$$n = 1$$

Plugging this value for n into the first equation shows that $m = 6$:

$$m - n = 5$$
$$m - 1 = 5$$
$$m = 6$$

So $m + n = 7$:

$$m + n = 6 + 1 = 7$$

Choice (C) is correct.

SYMBOLISM

You should be quite familiar with the arithmetic symbols + , – , ×, ÷, and %. Finding the value of 10 + 2, 18 – 4, 4 × 9, or 96 ÷ 16 is easy.

However, on the SAT, you may come across bizarre symbols. You may even be asked to find the value of 10 ★ 2, 5 ❋ 7, 10 ✳ 6, or 65 ♥ 2.

The SAT test makers put strange symbols in questions to confuse or unnerve you. Don't let them. The question stem always tells you what the strange symbol means. Although this type of question may look difficult, it is really an exercise in plugging in. Look at the following example:

> **Kaplan Rules**
>
> Intimidated by symbols?
>
> The test makers put symbolism on the SAT to test your ability to think. Once you get over your fear of seeing something completely unknown, you'll realize the math is usually quite easy.

EXAMPLE

If $a \star b = \sqrt{a + b}$ for all non-negative numbers, what is the value of $10 \star 6$?

(A) 0

(B) 2

(C) 4

(D) 8

(E) 16

To solve, just plug in 10 for a and 6 for b into the expression $\sqrt{a + b}$. That equals $\sqrt{10 + 6}$ or $\sqrt{16}$ or 4, choice (C).

How about a more involved symbolism question?

EXAMPLE

If a ▲ means to multiply by 3 and a ✳ means to divide by –2, what is the value of $((8✳)▲)✳$?

(A) –6

(B)   0

(C)   2

(D)   3

(E)   6

HINT: *When a symbolism problem includes parentheses, do the operations inside the parentheses first.*

First find 8✹. This means to divide 8 by –2, which is –4. Working out to the next set of parentheses, we have (–4)▲, which means to multiply –4 by 3, which is –12. Lastly, we find (–12) ✹, which means to divide –12 by –2, which is 6, choice (E).

HINT: *When two or three questions include the same symbol, expect the last question to be the most difficult, and be extra careful.*

Practice Problems: Symbolism

QC

Column A	Column B

If $x \neq 0$, let ♠ x be defined by ♠ $x = x - \dfrac{1}{x}$.

1.   –3   ♠ –3   (A) (B) (C) (D) (E)

REGULAR MATH

2. If $r \heartsuit s = r(r - s)$ for all integers r and s, then $4 \heartsuit (3 \heartsuit 5)$ equals

   (A) –8
   (B) –2
   (C) 2
   (D) 20
   (E) 40   (A) (B) (C) (D) (E)

Questions 3 and 4 refer to the following definition:

$$c \star d = \frac{c - d}{c}, \text{ where } c \neq 0.$$

3. $12 \star 3 =$

   (A) –3

   (B) $\dfrac{1}{4}$

   (C) $\dfrac{2}{3}$

   (D) $\dfrac{3}{4}$

   (E) 3   (A) (B) (C) (D) (E)

4. If $9 \bigstar 4 = 15 \bigstar k$, then $k =$

(A) 3

(B) 6

(C) $\dfrac{20}{3}$

(D) $\dfrac{25}{3}$

(E) 9

Answers to Symbolism Problems

1.　(B) Plug in −3 for x: $\spadesuit x = -3 - \dfrac{1}{-3} = -3 + \dfrac{1}{3} = -2\dfrac{2}{3}$, which is greater than −3 in Column A.

2.　(E) Start in the parentheses and work out: $(3 \heartsuit 5) = 3(3 - 5) = 3(-2) = -6; 4 \heartsuit (-6) = 4[4 - (-6)] = 4(10) = 40.$

3.　(D) Plug in 12 for c and 3 for d: $\dfrac{12 - 3}{12} = \dfrac{9}{12} = \dfrac{3}{4}.$

4.　(C) Plug in on both sides of the equation:

$$\frac{9 - 4}{9} = \frac{15 - k}{15}$$

$$\frac{5}{9} = \frac{15 - k}{15}$$

Cross-multiply and solve for k:

$$75 = 135 - 9k$$

$$-60 = -9k$$

$$\frac{-60}{-9} = k$$

$$\frac{20}{3} = k$$

SPECIAL TRIANGLES

The Specials

The test makers often put triangles on the SAT to test your knowledge of special triangles.

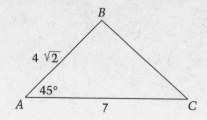

Note: Figure not drawn to scale.

EXAMPLE

In the triangle above, what is the length of side *BC*?

(A) 4

(B) 5

(C) $4\sqrt{2}$

(D) 6

(E) $5\sqrt{2}$

HINT: *Look for the special triangles in geometry problems.*

Special triangles contain a lot of information. For instance, if you know the length of one side of a 30-60-90 triangle, you can easily work out the lengths of the others. Special triangles allow you to transfer one piece of information around the whole figure.

The following are the special triangles you should look for on the SAT.

Speed Tip

Popular right triangles:

- 3-4-5

- 5-12-13

Or multiples of these, such as:

- 6-8-10

- 10-24-26

Equilateral Triangles

All interior angles are 60° and all sides are of the same length.

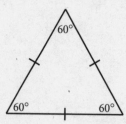

Isosceles Triangles

Two sides are of the same length and the angles facing these sides are equal.

Right Triangles

Contain a 90° angle. The sides are related by the Pythagorean theorem. $a^2 + b^2 = c^2$ where a and b are the legs and c is the hypotenuse.

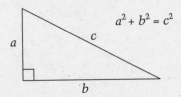

$$a^2 + b^2 = c^2$$

The "Special" Right Triangles

Many triangle problems contain "special" right triangles, whose side lengths always come in predictable ratios. If you recognize them, you won't have to use the Pythagorean theorem to find the value of a missing side length.

The 3-4-5 Right Triangle

(Be on the lookout for multiples of 3-4-5 as well.)

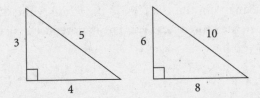

**If You Have a
Bad Memory . . .**

If you forget the triangle ratios, you can find a description of the isosceles right triangle and 30-60-90 triangle in the information box at the start of every Math section on the SAT.

The Isosceles Right Triangle

(Note the side ratio—1:1:$\sqrt{2}$.)

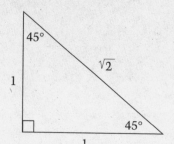

The 30-60-90 Right Triangle

(Note the side ratio—1:$\sqrt{3}$:2, and which side is opposite which angle.)

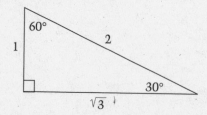

Getting back to our example, you can drop a vertical line from *B* to line *AC*. This divides the triangle into two right triangles.

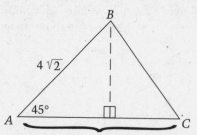

That means you know two of the angles in the triangle on the left: 90° and 45°. So this is an isosceles right triangle, with sides in the ratio of 1:1:$\sqrt{2}$. The hypotenuse here is 4$\sqrt{2}$, so both legs have length 4. Filling this in, you have:

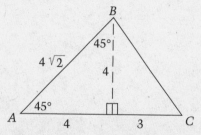

Now you can see that the legs of the smaller triangle on the right must be 4 and 3, making this a 3-4-5 right triangle, and the length of hypotenuse *BC* is 5.

Practice Problems: Special Triangles

REGULAR MATH

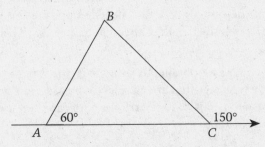

Note: Figure not drawn to scale.

1. In triangle ABC above, if $AB = 4$, then $AC =$

(A) 10
(B) 9
(C) 8
(D) 7
(E) 6

Ⓐ Ⓑ Ⓒ Ⓓ Ⓔ

QC

Column A   Column B

In the coordinate plane, point R has coordinates $(0, 0)$ and point S has coordinates $(9, 12)$.

2. The distance from   16
     R to S

Ⓐ Ⓑ Ⓒ Ⓓ Ⓔ

REGULAR MATH

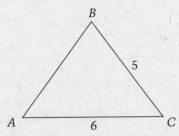

3. If the perimeter of triangle ABC above is 16, what is its area?

(A) 8
(B) 9
(C) 10
(D) 12
(E) 15

Ⓐ Ⓑ Ⓒ Ⓓ Ⓔ

Answers to Special Triangles Problems

1. (C) Angle *BCA* is supplementary to the angle marked 150°, so angle *BCA* = 180° – 150° = 30°. Since the sum of interior angles of a triangle is 180°, angle *A* + angle *B* + angle *BCA* = 180°, so angle *B* = 180° – 60° – 30° = 90°. So triangle *ABC* is a 30-60-90 right triangle, and its sides are in the ratio 1: $\sqrt{3}$: 2. The side opposite the 30°, *AB*, which we know has length 4, must be half the length of the hypotenuse, *AC*. Therefore *AC* = 8, and that's answer choice (C).

2. (B) Draw a diagram. Since *RS* isn't parallel to either axis, the way to compute its length is to create a right triangle with legs that are parallel to the axes, so their lengths are easy to find. If the triangle formed is not a special triangle, we can then use the Pythagorean theorem to find the length of *RS*.

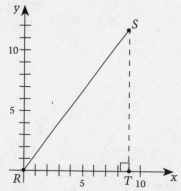

Since *S* has a *y*-coordinate of 12, it's 12 units above the *x*-axis, so the length of *ST* must be 12. And since *T* is the same number of units to the right of the *y*-axis as *S*, given by the *x*-coordinate of 9, the distance from the origin to *T* must be 9. So we have a right triangle with legs of 9 and 12. You should recognize this as a multiple of the 3-4-5 triangle. 9 = 3 × 3; 12 = 3 × 4; so the hypotenuse *RS* must be 3 × 5, or 15. That's the value of Column A, so Column B is greater.

3. (D) To find the area you need to know the base and height. If the perimeter is 16, then *AB* + *BC* + *AC* = 16; that is, *AB* = 16 – 5 – 6 = 5. Since *AB* = *BC*, this is an isosceles triangle. If you drop a line from vertex *B* to *AC*, it will divide the base in half. This divides up the triangle into two smaller right triangles:

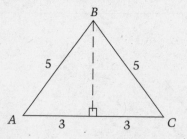

These right triangles each have one leg of 3 and a hypotenuse of 5; therefore they are 3-4-5 right triangles. So the missing leg (which is also the height of triangle *ABC*) must have length 4. We now know that the base of *ABC* is 6 and the height is 4, so the area is $\frac{1}{2}$ × 6 × 4, or 12, answer choice (D).

MULTIPLE AND ODDBALL FIGURES

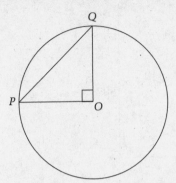

EXAMPLE

In the figure above, if the area of the circle with center O is 9π, what is the area of triangle POQ ?

(A) 4.5

(B) 6

(C) 9

(D) 3.5π

(E) 4.5π

Breaking Up Is Easy

When you see a shape that isn't a triangle, rectangle, or circle, try breaking it into familiar figures.

In a problem that combines figures, you have to look for the relationship between the figures.

HINT: *Look for pieces the figures have in common.*

For instance, if two figures share a side, information about that side will probably be the key.

In this case the figures don't share a side, but the triangle's legs are important features of the circle—they are radii. You can see that $PO = OQ = $ the radius of circle O.

The area of the circle is 9π. The area of a circle is πr^2, where $r = $ the radius. So $9\pi = \pi r^2$, $9 = r^2$, and the radius = 3. The area of a triangle is $\frac{1}{2}$ base times height. Therefore, the area of $\triangle POQ$ is $\frac{1}{2}$ (leg$_1$ $\times$ leg$_2$) $= \frac{1}{2}$ (3 $\times$ 3) $= \frac{9}{2} = 4.5$, answer choice (A).

But what if, instead of a number of familiar shapes, you are given something like this?

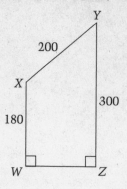

EXAMPLE

Kaplan Rules

Multiple figures are almost always made up of either several familiar shapes put together, or one familiar shape with a recognizable piece shaded or cut out of it.

What is the perimeter of quadrilateral *WXYZ* ?

(A) 680

(B) 760

(C) 840

(D) 920

(E) 1,000

Try breaking the unfamiliar shape into familiar ones. Once this is done, you can use the same techniques that you would for multiple figures. Perimeter is the sum of the lengths of the sides of a figure, so you need to find the length of *WZ*. Drawing a perpendicular line from point *X* to side *YZ* will divide the figure into a right triangle and a rectangle. Call the point of intersection *A*.

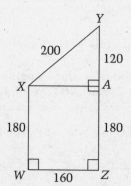

Opposite sides of a rectangle have equal length, so *WZ* = *XA* and *WX* = *ZA*. *WX* is labeled as 180, so *ZA* = 180. Since *YZ* measures 300, *AY* is 300 − 180 = 120. In right triangle *XYA*, hypotenuse *XY* = 200 and leg *AY* = 120; you should recognize this as a multiple of a 3-4-5 right triangle. The hypotenuse is 5 × 40, one leg is 3 × 40, so *XA* must be 4 × 40 or 160. (If you didn't recognize this special right triangle you could have used the Pythagorean theorem to find the length of *XA*.) Since *WZ* = *XA* = 160, the perimeter of the figure is 180 + 200 + 300 + 160 = 840, answer choice (C).

Practice Problems: Multiple and Oddball Figures

REGULAR MATH

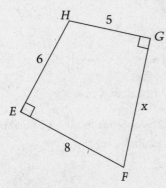

1. What is the value of x in the figure above?

(A) 4
(B) $3\sqrt{3}$
(C) $3\sqrt{5}$
(D) $5\sqrt{3}$
(E) 9

Ⓐ Ⓑ Ⓒ Ⓓ Ⓔ

....

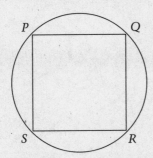

2. In the figure above, square $PQRS$ is inscribed in a circle. If the area of square $PQRS$ is 4, what is the radius of the circle?

(A) 1
(B) $\sqrt{2}$
(C) 2
(D) $2\sqrt{2}$
(E) $4\sqrt{2}$

Ⓐ Ⓑ Ⓒ Ⓓ Ⓔ

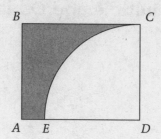

Note: Figure not drawn to scale.

3. In the figure above, the quarter circle with center *D* has a radius of 4 and rectangle *ABCD* has a perimeter of 20. What is the perimeter of the shaded region?

    (A) $20 - 8\pi$
    (B) $10 + 2\pi$
    (C) $12 + 2\pi$
    (D) $12 + 4\pi$
    (E) $4 + 8\pi$

    (A) (B) (C) (D) (E)

Answers to Multiple and Oddball Figures Problems

1. (D) Draw a straight line from point *H* to point *F*, to divide the figure into two right triangles.

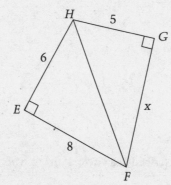

ΔEFH is a 3-4-5 right triangle with a hypotenuse of length 10. Use the Pythagorean theorem in ΔFGH to find *x*:

$$x^2 + 5^2 = 10^2$$
$$x^2 + 5^2 = 100$$
$$x^2 = 75$$
$$x = \sqrt{75}$$
$$x = \sqrt{25}\,\sqrt{3}$$
$$x = 5\,\sqrt{3}$$

2. (B) Draw in diagonal *QS* and you will notice that it is also a diameter of the circle.

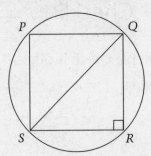

Since the area of the square is 4 its sides must each be 2. Think of the diagonal as dividing the square into two isosceles right triangles. Therefore, the diagonal $= 2\sqrt{2}$ = the diameter; the radius is half this amount, or $\sqrt{2}$.

3. (C) The perimeter of the shaded region is $BC + AB + AE +$ arc EC. The quarter circle has its center at D, and point C lies on the circle, so side DC is a radius of the circle and equals 4.

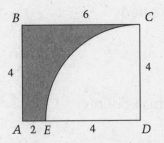

Opposite sides of a rectangle are equal, so AB is also 4. The perimeter of the rectangle is 20, and since the two short sides account for 8, the two longer sides must account for 12, making BC and AD each 6. To find AE, subtract the length of ED, another radius of length 4, from the length of AD, which is 6; $AE = 2$.

Since arc EC is a quarter circle, the length of the arc EC is $\frac{1}{4}$ of the circumference of a whole circle with radius 4: $\frac{1}{4} \times 2\pi r = \frac{1}{4} \times 8\pi = 2\pi$.

So the perimeter of the shaded region is $6 + 4 + 2 + 2\pi = 12 + 2\pi$.

Checklist

Once you've mastered a concept, check it off.

Classic Problem-Solving Techniques:

❏ Remainders

❏ Averages

❏ Ratios

❏ Rates

❏ Percents

❏ Combinations

❏ Simultaneous equations

❏ Symbolism

❏ Special triangles

❏ Multiple and oddball figures

14

Top Ten SAT Math Traps

- Study the most common SAT Math traps and how to avoid them

- Train yourself to recognize wrong and tricky answer choices

- Pick up tips and hints on how to solve problems

- Complete the Math Traps Practice Sets

It's time for us to let you in on a little secret that will allow you to breeze through the entire SAT, get into any college you want, succeed in life, and find eternal happiness.

If you believed a word of the preceding paragraph, you need to pay special attention to this chapter. This chapter presents ten common SAT traps. Traps lure you into one answer, usually one that's easy to get to. But they conceal the correct answer, which requires some thought. If you're not wary of traps on the SAT, they may trip you up. Learn to recognize common traps and you'll gain more points.

HINT: *If you see what appears to be a basic problem late in a question set, there is probably a trap.*

SAT Emergency

If you have only a week or two to prep for the SAT, here's the best way to spend your time:

- Skim the chapter, paying special attention to the "Top Ten Trap" sidebars.

- Do the first practice set on p. 164. If you miss an answer, identify the trap that caught you and study that section.

- Do the second practice set on p. 178. Identify any trap that caught you and study that section. If you get all the answers right, you're strong at avoiding traps.

Kaplan's Favorite Trap

When the hands of your watch show 12:30, how many degrees separate the hour hand from the minute hand?

The obvious answer is 180 degrees. That's a trap. (At 12:30 the hour hand doesn't point directly at the 12; it's halfway between the 12 and the 1.) The test makers hoped that you would jump to the obvious answer, without taking the time to think it through.

Over the years, the SAT has had plenty of problems like this one. Traps catch unwary students who forget to think through the problem before they answer it. How do you prevent yourself from falling for other SAT Math traps? Read this chapter.

WATCH OUT FOR TRAPS

The following ten questions have one thing in common—they all have traps. Take 12 minutes to try to work through all of them. Then check your answers on p. 168.

1. Jackie purchased a new car in 1990. Three years later she sold it to a dealer for 40 percent less than she paid for it in 1990. The dealer then added 20 percent onto the price he paid and resold it to another customer. The price the final customer paid for the car was what percent of the original price Jackie paid in 1990?

   (A)   40 percent
   (B)   60 percent
   (C)   72 percent
   (D)   80 percent
   (E)   88 percent   Ⓐ Ⓑ Ⓒ Ⓓ Ⓔ

   ....

2. In a class of 27 students, the average (arithmetic mean) score of the boys on the final exam was 83. If the average score of the 15 girls in the class was 92, what was the average of the whole class?

   (A)   86.2
   (B)   87.0
   (C)   87.5
   (D)   88.0
   (E)   88.2   Ⓐ Ⓑ Ⓒ Ⓓ Ⓔ

   ....

3. Mike's coin collection consists of quarters, dimes, and nickels. If the ratio of the number of quarters to the number of dimes is 5:2, and the ratio of the number of dimes to the number of nickels is 3:4, what is the ratio of the number of quarters to the number of nickels?

   (A) 5 to 4
   (B) 7 to 5
   (C) 10 to 6
   (D) 12 to 7
   (E) 15 to 8   Ⓐ Ⓑ Ⓒ Ⓓ Ⓔ

   ....

	Column A	Column B	
	$p > q > 1$		
4.	$p^2 - q^2$	$(p - q)^2$	Ⓐ Ⓑ Ⓒ Ⓓ Ⓔ

....

A, B, and C are points on a line such that point A is 12 units away from point B and point B is four units away from point C.

5.   The distance from   16
     point A to point C Ⓐ Ⓑ Ⓒ Ⓓ Ⓔ

6.
The area of a square with a perimeter of 14	Twice the area of a square with a perimeter of 7	(A)(B)(C)(D)(E)

....

7. If $n \neq 0$, then which of the following must be true?

   I. $n^2 > n$
   II. $2n > n$
   III. $n + 1 > n$

   (A) I only
   (B) II only
   (C) III only
   (D) I and III only
   (E) I, II, and III   (A)(B)(C)(D)(E)

....

8. At a certain restaurant, the hourly wage for a waiter is 20 percent greater than the hourly wage for a dishwasher, and the hourly wage for a dishwasher is half as much as the hourly wage for a cook's assistant. If a cook's assistant earns $8.50 an hour, how much less than a cook's assistant does a waiter earn each hour?

   (A) $2.55
   (B) $3.40
   (C) $4.25
   (D) $5.10
   (E) $5.95   (A)(B)(C)(D)(E)

....

9. A car traveled from A to B at an average speed of 40 miles per hour and then immediately traveled back from B to A at an average speed of 60 miles per hour. What was the car's average speed for the round-trip, in miles per hour?

   (A) 45
   (B) 48
   (C) 50
   (D) 52
   (E) 54   (A)(B)(C)(D)(E)

....

10. The tickets for a certain raffle are consecutively numbered. If Louis sold the tickets numbered from 75 to 148 inclusive, how many raffle tickets did he sell?

   (A) 71
   (B) 72
   (C) 73
   (D) 74
   (E) 75   (A)(B)(C)(D)(E)

HOW MATH TRAPS WORK AND HOW TO AVOID THEM

How did you do? If you got any wrong answers, unless you calculated incorrectly, chances are you got caught in a trap. The same traps occur again and again on the SAT. Learn how they work and how to avoid them. Once you can deal with traps, you'll do much better on the harder math questions.

To see how they work, let's take another look at the ten sample questions. Each contains one of the Top Ten Math Traps.

Teacher Tip

"Many students race through the section and do not read the questions carefully. If they would just slow down and make sure of what they are being asked, they would find that these problems are not so bad after all."

—Jaelithe Russ
   Kaplan Teacher
   Akron, OH

Trap 1: Percent Increase/Decrease

EXAMPLE

Jackie purchased a new car in 1990. Three years later she sold it to a dealer for 40 percent less than she paid for it in 1990. The dealer then added 20 percent onto the price he paid and resold it to another customer. The price the final customer paid for the car was what percent of the original price Jackie paid in 1990?

(A) 40 percent
(B) 60 percent
(C) 72 percent
(D) 80 percent
(E) 88 percent

Top Ten Trap #1

To get a combined percent increase or decrease, don't just add the percents.

The Wrong Answer

The increase/decrease percentage problem usually appears at the end of a section and invariably contains a trap. Most students will figure that taking away 40 percent, and then adding 20 percent gives you an overall loss of 20 percent, and pick choice (D), 80 percent, as the correct answer.

The Trap

When a quantity is increased or decreased by a percent more than once, you cannot simply add and subtract the percents to get the answer.

In this kind of percent problem:

- The first percent change is a percent of the starting amount.

- The second change is a percent of the new amount.

Avoiding the Trap

Percents can be added and subtracted only when they are percents of the same amount.

Finding the Right Answer

We know:

- The 40 percent less that Jackie got for the car is 40 percent of her original price.

- The 20 percent the dealer adds on is 20 percent of what the dealer paid, a much smaller amount.

- Adding on 20 percent of that smaller amount is not the same thing as adding back 20 percent of the original price.

So We Can Solve the Problem

- Use 100 for a starting quantity, whether or not it makes sense in the real situation. The problem asks for the relative amount of change. So you can take any starting number, and compare it with the final result. Because you're dealing with percents, 100 is the easiest number to work with.

HINT: *Pick 100 as the starting quantity and see what happens.*

- If Jackie paid $100.00 for the car, what is 40 percent less?

- In the case of $100.00, each percent equals $1.00, so she sold it for $60.00.

- If the dealer charges 20 percent more than his purchase price, he's raising the price by 20 percent of $60.00, which is $12.00 (not 20 percent of $100.00, which is $20.00).

- Therefore the dealer sold the car again for $60.00 + $12.00, or $72.00.

- Finally, what percent of the starting price ($100.00) is $72.00? It's 72 percent. So the correct answer here is choice (C).

Trap 2: Weighted Averages

EXAMPLE

In a class of 27 students, the average (arithmetic mean) score of the boys on the final exam was 83. If the average score of the 15 girls in the class was 92, what was the average of the whole class?

(A) 86.2

(B) 87.0

(C) 87.5

(D) 88.0

(E) 88.2

> **Top Ten Trap #2**
>
> Don't just average the averages.

The Wrong Answer

If you simply average 83 and 92 to come up with 87.5 as the class average, you fell for the trap.

Answer Key for Trap Exercise on pp. 164–165

1. (C)
2. (D)
3. (E)
4. (A)
5. (D)
6. (A)
7. (C)
8. (B)
9. (B)
10. (D)

The Trap

You cannot combine averages of different quantities by taking the average of those averages.

In an average problem, if one value occurs more frequently than others it is "weighted" more. Remember that the average formula calls for the sum of all the terms, divided by the total number of terms.

Avoiding the Trap

Work with the sums, not the averages.

Finding the Right Answer

If 15 of the 27 students are girls, the remaining 12 must be boys. We can't just add 83 to 92 and divide by two. In this class there are more girls than boys, and therefore the girls' test scores are "weighted" more—they contribute more to the class average. So the answer must be either (D) or (E). To find each sum, multiply each average by the number of terms it represents. After you have found the sums of the different terms, find the combined average by plugging the sums into the average formula.

$$\text{Total class average} = \frac{\text{Sum of girls' scores} + \text{Sum of boys' scores}}{\text{Total number of students}}$$

$$= \frac{(\text{\# of girls} \times \text{girls' average score}) + (\text{\# of boys} \times \text{boys' average score})}{\text{Total number of students}}$$

$$= \frac{15(92) + 12(83)}{27} = \frac{1{,}380 + 996}{27} = 88$$

So the class average is 88, answer choice (D).

Trap 3: Ratio:Ratio:Ratio

> EXAMPLE
>
> Mike's coin collection consists of quarters, dimes, and nickels. If the ratio of the number of quarters to the number of dimes is 5:2, and the ratio of the number of dimes to the number of nickels is 3:4, what is the ratio of the number of quarters to the number of nickels?
>
> (A) 5:4
>
> (B) 7:5
>
> (C) 10:6
>
> (D 12:7
>
> (E) 15:8

The Wrong Answer

If you chose 5:4 as the correct answer, you fell for the classic ratio trap.

The Trap

Parts of different ratios don't always refer to the same whole.

In the classic ratio trap, two different ratios each share a common part that is represented by two different numbers. The two ratios do not refer to the same whole, however, so they are not in proportion to each other. To solve this type of problem, restate both ratios so that the numbers representing the common part (in this case "dimes") are the same. Then all the parts will be in proportion and can be compared to each other.

Avoiding the Trap

Make sure parts of ratios refer to the same whole.

Finding the Right Answer

To find the ratio of quarters to nickels, restate both ratios so that the number of dimes is the same in both. We are given two ratios:

Quarters:dimes = 5:2   Dimes:nickels = 3:4

The number corresponding to dimes in the first ratio is 2.
The number corresponding to dimes in the second ratio is 3.
To restate the ratios, find the least common multiple of 2 and 3.
The least common multiple of 2 and 3 is 6.

> **Top Ten Trap #3**
>
> Don't take one number from one ratio and compare it to another number from another ratio.

Restate the ratios with the number of dimes as 6:

Quarters:dimes = 15:6   Dimes:nickels = 6:8

The ratios are still in their original proportions, but now they're in proportion to each other and they refer to the same whole.

The ratio of quarters to dimes to nickels is 15:6:8, so the ratio of quarters to nickels is 15:8, which is answer choice (E).

Trap 4: Expressions That Look Equal—But Aren't

> EXAMPLE

Column A	Column B

$$p > q > 1$$

$p^2 - q^2$	$(p - q)^2$

> **Top Ten Trap #4**
>
> Don't be fooled by appearances.

The Wrong Answer

If you said the expressions were equal, you'd be wrong.

The Trap

At first glance the expressions look like they're equal—but they're not.

This common SAT trap happens most often in QCs. Problems like this trap students who are too hasty, who answer on the basis of appearance, without considering the mathematical rules involved.

Avoiding the Trap

If two quantities seem obviously equal, double-check your answer, using your math knowledge and the techniques discussed in chapter 12, Quantitative Comparisons.

This is an example of the general rule that whenever an answer to a question late in a section looks obviously correct, it probably isn't.

Finding the Right Answer

In this case you can use the make-one-column-look-more-like-the-other technique discussed in chapter 12.

Factor Column A and rewrite Column B:

Column A	Column B
$(p-q)(p+q)$	$(p-q)(p-q)$

Now use the do-the-same-thing-to-both-columns technique. Both columns contain $(p-q)$. You know than $p > q$, so $p-q$ is a positive number. Therefore, you can divide both columns by $p-q$:

Column A	Column B
$p+q$	$p-q$

Since q is positive, adding q in Column A will get you more than subtracting q in Column B. Column A is greater, so the answer is (A).

This trap does not apply only to quadratics. Below are some other quantities that the hasty student might mistake as equal. Go through this list and make sure you can tell why these expressions are not equal except for special cases.

Stumped?

Pick numbers.

If $p = 3$ and $q = 2$, then

$p^2 - q^2 = 5$ and $(p-q)^2 = 1$.

Column A is bigger, so you know the answer must be either (A) or (D).

- $(x + y)^2$ does NOT equal $x^2 + y^2$

- $(2x)^2$ does NOT equal $2x^2$

- $x^{20} - x^{18}$ does NOT equal x^2

- $x^3 + x^3$ does NOT equal x^6

- $\sqrt{x} + \sqrt{x}$ does NOT equal $\sqrt{2x}$

- $\sqrt{x} - \sqrt{y}$ does NOT equal $\sqrt{x-y}$

- $\dfrac{1}{x} + \dfrac{1}{y}$ does NOT equal $\dfrac{1}{x+y}$

You could prove that any of these quantities need not be equal using the Picking Numbers technique.

Trap 5: Unspecified Order

EXAMPLE

<u>Column A</u>   <u>Column B</u>

A, *B*, and *C* are points on a line such that point *A* is 12 units away from point *B* and point *B* is 4 units away from point *C*.

The distance from   16
point *A* to point *C*

The Wrong Answer

First you should always draw a diagram to help you visualize the relationship between the points.

A ———— 12 ———— *B* — 4 — *C*

In this diagram, the distance from *A* to *C* is 16, which is the same as Column B. But choice (C) is not the right answer.

The Trap

Don't assume that there is only one arrangement of the points—in this case, alphabetical order. We are not told what the relationship between *A* and *C* is. In fact *C* could lie to the left of *B*, like so:

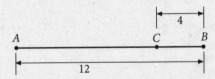

Avoiding the Trap

Don't assume points lie in the order they are given or in alphabetical order. Look for alternatives.

Finding the Right Answer

In this case, the distance from *A* to *C* is 8, which is less than Column B. Since we have two possible relationships between the columns, the answer must be (D)—you can't be certain from the data given.

Trap 6: Length:Area Ratios

EXAMPLE

Top Ten Trap #6

The ratio of areas is not the same as the ratio of lengths.

Column A

The area of a square
with a perimeter of 14

Column B

Twice the area of a square
with a perimeter of 7

The Wrong Answer
Twice the perimeter doesn't mean twice the area. Choice (C) is wrong.

The Trap
In proportional figures, the ratio of the areas is not the same as the ratio of the lengths.

Avoiding the Trap
Understand that the ratio of the areas of proportional figures is the square of the ratio of corresponding linear measures.

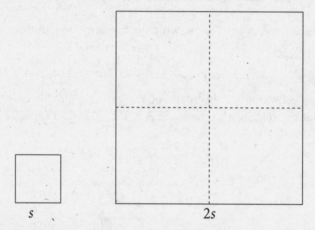

Finding the Right Answer
One way to solve this QC would be to actually compute the respective areas.

A square of perimeter 14 has side length $\frac{14}{4} = 3.5$. Its area then is $(3.5)^2 = 12.25$. On the other hand, the area of the square in Column B is $\left(\frac{7}{4}\right)^2 = (1.75)^2 = 3.0625$. Even twice that area is still less than the 12.25 in Column A. The answer is (A).

A quicker and more clever way to dodge this trap is to understand the relationship between the linear ratio and the area ratio of proportional figures. In proportional figures, the area ratio is the square of the linear ratio.

In the example above, we are given two squares with sides in a ratio of 14:7 or 2:1.

Using the rule above, we square the linear 4:1 ratio. The areas of the two figures will be in a four-to-one ratio.

The same goes for circles:

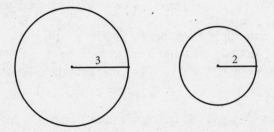

In the figure above, we are given two circles with radii in a 3:2 ratio. Using the rule above, we square the linear 3:2 ratio. The areas of the two circles will be in a 9:4 ratio.

Trap 7: Not All Numbers Are Positive Integers

EXAMPLE

If $n \neq 0$, then which of the following must be true?

    I. $n^2 > n$

    II. $2n > n$

    III. $n + 1 > n$

(A) I only

(B) II only

(C) III only

(D) I and III only

(E) I, II, and III

Top Ten Trap #7

Not all numbers are positive integers. Don't forget to consider 0, fractions, and negative numbers.

The Wrong Answer

In the example above, if you considered only positive integers greater than 1 for the value of n, you would assume that all three statements are true. However, that is not the case.

The Trap

Not all numbers are positive integers. Don't forget there are negative numbers and fractions as well. This is important because negative numbers and fractions between 0 and 1 behave very differently from positive integers.

Avoiding the Trap

When picking numbers for variables, consider fractions and negative numbers.

Finding the Right Answer

Looking at statement I, you may assume that when you square a number, you end up with a larger number as a result. For example, $4^2 = 16$, or $10^2 = 100$. However, when you square a fraction between 0 and 1, the result is quite different: $\left(\frac{1}{2}\right)^2 = \frac{1}{4} \cdot \left(\frac{1}{10}\right)^2 = \frac{1}{100}$, so you get a smaller number.

In statement II, what happens when you multiply a number by 2? $7 \times 2 = 14$; $25 \times 2 = 50$. Multiplying any positive number by 2 doubles that number, so you get a larger result. However, if you multiply a negative number by 2, your result is smaller than the original number. For example, $-3 \times 2 = -6$.

Finally, look at statement III. What happens when you add 1 to any number? Adding 1 to any number gives you a larger number as a result. For example, $5 + 1 = 6$; $\frac{1}{2} + 1 = 1\frac{1}{2}$; and $-7 + 1 = -6$.

Therefore, only statement III must be true, so choice (C) is correct. If you didn't consider fractions or negative numbers, you would have fallen into the trap and answered the question incorrectly.

HINT: *This trap appears most often in QC problems, so watch out.*

Trap 8: Hidden Instructions

| EXAMPLE |

Top Ten Trap #8

Make sure you're answering the question that's asked. Hint: underline the last phrase in the question.

At a certain restaurant, the hourly wage for a waiter is 20 percent greater than the hourly wage for a dishwasher, and the hourly wage for a dishwasher is half as much as the hourly wage for a cook's assistant. If a cook's assistant earns $8.50 an hour, how much less than a cook's assistant does a waiter earn each hour?

(A) $2.55

(B) $3.40

(C) $4.25

(D) $5.10

(E) $5.95

The Wrong Answer

To solve this problem, you must find the hourly wage of the waiter.

The cook's assistant earns $8.50 an hour. The dishwasher earns half of this—$4.25 an hour. The waiter earns 20 percent more than the dishwasher—$4.25 \times 1.2 = $5.10.

So the waiter earns $5.10 an hour, and you might reach automatically to fill in answer choice (D). But (D) is the wrong answer.

The Trap

A small step, easily overlooked, can mean the difference between a right and wrong answer.

In this case the word is *less*. After spending all this time finding the waiter's hourly wage, in their moment of triumph many students skip right over the vital last step. They overlook that the question asks not what the waiter earns, but how much less than the cook's assistant the waiter earns.

Avoiding the Trap

Make sure you answer the question that's being asked. Watch out for hidden instructions.

Finding the Right Answer

You have figured out that the waiter earns $5.10 an hour. And the cook's assistant earns $8.50 an hour. To find out how much less than the cook's assistant the waiter earns, subtract the waiter's hourly wage from the cook's assistant's hourly wage.

The correct answer is (B).

Peek-a-Boo

Hidden instructions come in many forms. Watch out for questions that give all the information in one unit (say, minutes) and ask you for the answer in another unit (say, seconds or hours). Read carefully and solve for the correct quantity.

Trap 9: Average Rates

EXAMPLE

A car traveled from *A* to *B* at an average speed of 40 miles per hour and then immediately traveled back from *B* to *A* at an average speed of 60 miles per hour. What was the car's average speed for the round-trip, in miles per hour?

(A) 45

(B) 48

(C) 50

(D) 52

(E) 54

Top Ten Trap #9

Any time it says "average rate" in the question, be alert: You usually can't just average the rates to get the right answer.

The Wrong Answer

Do you see which answer choice looks too good to be true? The temptation is simply to average 40 and 60. The answer is "obviously" 50 (C). But 50 is wrong.

The Trap

To get an average speed, you can't just average the rates.

Why is the average speed not 50 mph? Because the car spent more time traveling at 40 mph than at 60 mph. Each leg of the round trip was the same distance, but the first leg, at the slower speed, took more time.

Avoiding the Trap

You can solve almost any Average Rate problem with this general formula:

$$\text{Average Rate} = \frac{\text{Total Distance}}{\text{Total Time}}$$

Use the given information to figure out the total distance and the total time. But how can you do that when many problems don't specify the distances?

Stumped?

> Use common sense. The car spent more time at 40 mph so the answer will be less than 50—i.e., weighted more heavily towards 40 (remember weighted averages, trap #2).
>
> If you saw this much but couldn't get the answer, you could guess between (A) and (B). (More on guessing in chapter 15.)

Finding the Right Answer

In our sample above, we are told that a car went from *A* to *B* at 40 miles per hour and back from *B* to *A* at 60 miles per hour. In other words, it went half the total distance at 40 mph and half the total distance at 60 mph.

How do you use the formula:

$$\text{Average Rate} = \frac{\text{Total Distance}}{\text{Total Time}}$$

if you don't know the total distance?

HINT: *Pick a number! Pick any number you want for the total distance.*

Divide that total distance into half distances. Calculate the time needed to travel each half distance at the different rates.

HINT: *Pick a number that's easy to work with.*

A good number to pick here would be 240 miles for the total distance, because you can figure in your head the times for two 120-mile legs at 40 mph and 60 mph:

$$A \text{ to } B: \frac{120 \text{ miles}}{40 \text{ miles per hour}} = 3 \text{ hours}$$

$$B \text{ to } A: \frac{120 \text{ miles}}{60 \text{ miles per hour}} = 2 \text{ hours}$$

Total time = 5 hours

Now plug "total distance = 240 miles" and "total time = 5 hours" into the general formula:

$$\text{Average Rate} = \frac{\text{Total Distance}}{\text{Total Time}} = \frac{240 \text{ miles}}{5 \text{ hours}} = 48 \text{ miles per hour}$$

Correct answer choice: (B).

Trap 10: Counting Numbers

EXAMPLE

The tickets for a certain raffle are consecutively numbered. If Louis sold the tickets numbered from 75 to 148 inclusive, how many raffle tickets did he sell?

(A) 71

(B) 72

(C) 73

(D) 74

(E) 75

You just can't subtract the first number from the last number; you have to add one.

The Wrong Answer

If you subtract 75 from 148 and get 73 as the answer, you are wrong.

The Trap

Subtracting the first and last integers in a range will give you the difference of the two numbers. It won't give you the number of integers in that range.

Avoiding the Trap

To count the number of integers in a range, subtract and then add 1.

If you forget the rule, pick two small numbers that are close together, such as 1 and 4. Obviously, there are four integers from 1 to 4, inclusive. But if you had subtracted 1 from 4, you would have gotten 3.

In the diagram below, you can see that 3 is actually the distance between the integers, if the integers were on a number line or a ruler.

Finding the Right Answer

In the problem above, subtract 75 from 148. The result is 73. Add 1 to this difference to get the number of integers. That gives you 74. The correct answer choice is (D).

The word "inclusive" tells you to include the first and last numbers given. So, for example, "the integers from 5 to 15 inclusive" would include 5 and 15. Questions always make it clear whether you should include the outer numbers or not, since the correct answer hinges on this point.

MORE PRACTICE

Now that you can recognize the Top Ten Traps, try the following test. This time, try to identify the trap in each problem. Check your answers on page 182.

<u>Column A</u>   <u>Column B</u>

A car traveled the first half of a 100-kilometer distance at an average speed of 120 kilometers per hour, and it traveled the remaining distance at an average speed of 80 kilometers per hour.

1. The car's average speed,   100
   in kilometers per hour,
   for the 100 kilometers   Ⓐ Ⓑ Ⓒ Ⓓ Ⓔ

....

The ratio of $\frac{1}{4}$ to $\frac{2}{5}$ is equal to the ratio of $\frac{2}{5}$ to x.

2. x $\frac{3}{5}$ Ⓐ Ⓑ Ⓒ Ⓓ Ⓔ

....

3. $14 - 6$ $\sqrt{14^2 - 6^2}$ Ⓐ Ⓑ Ⓒ Ⓓ Ⓔ

....

4. $\frac{a+b}{3}$ $a + b$ Ⓐ Ⓑ Ⓒ Ⓓ Ⓔ

....

John buys 34 books at $6.00 each, and 17 at $12.00 each.

5.   The average price $9.00
      John pays per book   Ⓐ Ⓑ Ⓒ Ⓓ Ⓔ

....

On a certain highway Town X lies 50 miles away from Town Y, and Town Z lies 80 miles from Town X.

6. The number of minutes   30
   a car traveling at an
   average speed of 60
   miles per hour takes
   to travel from Town Y
      to Town Z Ⓐ Ⓑ Ⓒ Ⓓ Ⓔ

....

a, b, and c are positive numbers; $b < c$

7. $(a+b)^2$ $a^2 + c^2$ Ⓐ Ⓑ Ⓒ Ⓓ Ⓔ

Column A   Column B

8.   The area of a   The sum of the areas
      circle with a   of three circles each
      diameter of 3   with a diameter of 1   Ⓐ Ⓑ Ⓒ Ⓓ Ⓔ

....

      Jane invests her savings in a fund that adds 10 percent interest to her savings
      at the end of every year.

9.   The percent by which   31 percent
      her money has increased
         after three years   Ⓐ Ⓑ Ⓒ Ⓓ Ⓔ

....

                    $x > 1$

10. $7^{2x} - 7^x$ 7^x Ⓐ Ⓑ Ⓒ Ⓓ Ⓔ

....

11. Pump 1 can drain a 400-gallon water tank in 1.2 hours. Pump 2 can drain the same tank in 1.8
     hours. How many minutes longer than pump 1 would it take pump 2 to drain a 100-gallon tank?
     (A) 0.15
     (B) 1.2
     (C) 6
     (D) 9
     (E) 18   Ⓐ Ⓑ Ⓒ Ⓓ Ⓔ

....

12. Volumes 12 through 30 of a certain encyclopedia are located on the bottom shelf of a bookcase. If
     the volumes of the encyclopedia are numbered consecutively, how many volumes of the
     encyclopedia are on the bottom shelf?
     (A) 17
     (B) 18
     (C) 19
     (D) 29
     (E) 30   Ⓐ Ⓑ Ⓒ Ⓓ Ⓔ

....

13. A reservoir is at full capacity at the beginning of summer. By the first day of fall, the level in the
     reservoir is 30 percent below full capacity. Then during the fall a period of heavy rains raises the
     level by 30 percent. After the rains, the reservoir is at what percent of its full capacity?
     (A) 100 percent
     (B)   95 percent
     (C)   91 percent
     (D)   85 percent
     (E)   60 percent   Ⓐ Ⓑ Ⓒ Ⓓ Ⓔ

14. Two classes, one with 50 students, the other with 30, take the same exam. The combined average of both classes is 84.5. If the larger class averages 80, what is the average of the smaller class?

    (A) 87.2

    (B) 89.0

    (C) 92.0

    (D) 93.3

    (E) 94.5

15. In a pet shop, the ratio of puppies to kittens is 7:6 and the ratio of kittens to guinea pigs is 5:3. What is the ratio of puppies to guinea pigs?

    (A) 7:3

    (B) 6:5

    (C) 13:8

    (D) 21:11

    (E) 35:18

16. A typist typed the first n pages of a book, where $n > 0$, at an average rate of 12 pages per hour and typed the remaining n pages at an average rate of 20 pages per hour. What was the typist's average rate, in pages per hour, for the entire book?

    (A) $14\frac{2}{3}$

    (B) 15

    (C) 16

    (D) 17

    (E) 18

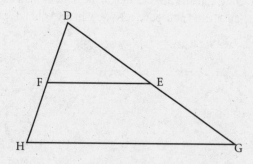

17. In triangle DGH above, $DE = EG$, $EF \parallel GH$, and the area of triangle DGH is 30. What is the area of triangle DEF?

    (A) 7.5

    (B) 15

    (C) 22.5

    (D) 60

    (E) It cannot be determined from the information given.

Checklist

Once you've mastered a concept, check it off.

How Traps Work and How to Avoid Them:

❏ The wrong way to answer the questions

❏ Avoiding the traps

❏ Finding the right answers

Kaplan's Top Ten SAT Math Traps:

❏ Percent increase/decrease

❏ Weighted averages integers

❏ Ratio:ratio:ratio

❏ Expressions that look equal— but aren't

❏ Unspecified order

❏ Length:area ratios

❏ Not all numbers are positive

❏ Hidden instructions

❏ Average rates

❏ Counting numbers

Did You Fall for the Traps?

How did you do on the practice questions? Did you spot the trap in each problem? Use the answers below to see what your weaknesses are. Each wrong answer represents one trap you need to work on. Go back and reread the section on that trap. Then try the problems again, until you answer correctly.

1. (B) Trap 9: Average rates
2. (A) Trap 3: Ratio:ratio:ratio
3. (B) Trap 4: Expressions that look equal—but aren't
4. (D) Trap 7: Not all numbers are positive integers
5. (B) Trap 2: Weighted averages
6. (D) Trap 5: Unspecified order
7. (D) Trap 4 : Expressions that look equal—but aren't
8. (A) Trap 6: Length:area ratio
9. (A) Trap 1: Percent increase/decrease
10. (A) Trap 4: Expressions that look equal—but aren't
11. (D) Trap 8: Hidden instructions
12. (C) Trap 10: Counting numbers
13. (C) Trap 1: Percent increase/decrease
14. (C) Trap 2: Weighted averages
15. (E) Trap 3: Ratio:ratio:ratio
16. (B) Trap 9: Average rates
17. (A) Trap 6: Length:area ratios

Math Guessing

- Master the five strategies for making educated guesses

- See when to eliminate unreasonable or obvious choices

- Practice eyeballing geometry diagrams

- Learn to guess with confidence on Grid-ins

Obviously, the best way to find the answer is to actually solve the problem. But if you're stuck or running out of time, guessing can be a good alternative.

The Regular Math and QC sections, like the Verbal sections, are scored to discourage random guessing. For every question you get right you earn a whole point. For every question you get wrong, you lose a fraction of a point. So if you guess at random on a number of questions, the points you gain from correct guesses are canceled out by the points you lose on incorrect guesses, for no overall gain or loss.

But you can make *educated guesses*. This raises the odds of guessing correctly, so the fractional points you lose no longer cancel out all the whole points you gain. You have just raised your score.

To make an educated guess, eliminate answer choices you know to be wrong, and guess from what's left. Of course, the more answer choices you can eliminate, the better chance you have of guessing the correct answer from what's left over.

SAT Emergency

Guessing is an important strategy for scoring points, so read this chapter carefully, even if you only have a week or two to prep for the SAT. It's a short chapter, and there are no shortcuts to learning how to guess accurately.

FIVE STRATEGIES

In the pages that follow, you'll find five strategies for guessing intelligently on all types of math problems.

Eliminate Unreasonable Answer Choices

Before you guess, think about the problem, and decide which answers don't make sense. Take as an example the following problem:

EXAMPLE

The ratio of men to women in a certain room is 13:11. If there are 429 men in the room, how many women are there?

(A)   143

(B)   363

(C)   433

(D)   507

(E)   792

Solution:

- The ratio of men to women is 13:11, so there are more men than women.

- Since there are 429 men, there must be fewer than 429 women.

- So you can eliminate choices (C), (D), and (E).

- The answer must be either (A) or (B), so guess. The correct answer is (B).

Eliminate the Obvious on Hard Questions

On the hard questions late in a set, obvious answers are usually wrong. So eliminate them when you guess. That doesn't hold true for early, easy questions, when the obvious answer could be right.

Now apply the rule. In the following difficult problem, which obvious answer should you eliminate?

Guessing Is Easy

Quick. Guess the right answer. William H. Harrison's middle name was:

- Hazel

- Hello

- Henry

- Hal

- Herbert

Except for the class clown who said Hazel, most people can safely eliminate two of the five choices. That means you've got a one-in-three chance of guessing Henry.

If you went into the SAT determined not to guess, you would have missed this great opportunity to score a point. If you can eliminate at least one answer, you should guess.

EXAMPLE

A number x is increased by 30 percent and then the result is decreased by 20 percent. What is the final result of these changes?

(A) x is increased by 10 percent

(B) x is increased by 6 percent

(C) x is increased by 4 percent

(D) x is decreased by 5 percent

(E) x is decreased by 10 percent

If you picked (A) as the obvious choice to eliminate, you'd be right. Most people would combine the decrease of 20 percent with the increase of 30 percent, getting a net increase of 10 percent. That's the easy, obvious answer, but not the correct answer. If you must guess, avoid (A). The correct answer is (C).

Eyeball Lengths, Angles, and Areas on Geometry Problems

Use diagrams that accompany geometry problems to help you eliminate wrong answer choices. First make sure that the diagram is drawn to scale. Diagrams are always drawn to scale unless there's a note like this: "Note: Figure not drawn to scale." If it's not, don't use this strategy. If it is, estimate quantities or eyeball the diagram. Then eliminate answer choices that are way too large or too small.

Length

When a geometry question asks for a length, use the given lengths to estimate the unknown length. Measure off the given length by making a nick in your pencil with your thumbnail. Then hold the pencil against the unknown length on the diagram to see how the lengths compare.

In the following problem, which answer choices can you eliminate by eyeballing?

Stuck?

- Stuck on a QC or Regular Math question? Eliminate at least one answer choice and guess.

- Stuck on a Grid-in? You won't lose points for guessing wrong on Grid-ins. So go ahead and guess.

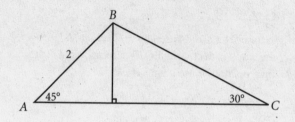

EXAMPLE

In the figure above, what is the length of *BC*?

(A) $\sqrt{2}$

(B) 2

(C) $2\sqrt{2}$

(D) 4

(E) $4\sqrt{2}$

Teacher Tip

"Many students struggle with more difficult math questions not because they don't know the math, but because they don't know where to start. That's no excuse! Don't spend forever on a single problem, but do something! Every SAT math problem is accessible—you can always do something small as a first step."

—Ed Cottrell
    Kaplan Teacher
    Houston, TX

Solution:

- *AB* is 2, so measure off this length on your pencil.

- Compare *BC* with this length.

- *BC* appears almost twice as long as *AB*, so *BC* is about 4.

- Since $\sqrt{2}$ is about 1.4, and *BC* is clearly longer than *AB*, choices (A) and (B) are too small.

- Choice (E) is much greater than 4, so eliminate that.

- Now guess between (C) and (D). The correct answer is (C).

Angles

You can also eyeball angles. To eyeball an angle, compare the angle with a familiar angle, such as a straight angle (180°), a right angle (90°), or half a right angle (45°). The corner of a piece of paper is a right angle, so use that to see if an angle is greater or less than 90°.

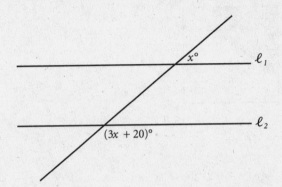

EXAMPLE

In the figure above, if $\ell_1 \parallel \ell_2$, what is the value of x?

(A) 130

(B) 100

(C) 80

(D) 50

(E) 40

Solution:

- You see that x is less than 90 degrees, so eliminate choices (A) and (B).

- Since x appears to be much less than 90 degrees, eliminate choice (C).

- Now pick between (D) and (E). In fact, the correct answer is (E).

Areas

Eyeballing an area is similar to eyeballing a length. You compare an unknown area in a diagram to an area that you do know.

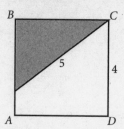

EXAMPLE

In square *ABCD* above, what is the area of the shaded region?

(A) 10

(B) 9

(C) 8

(D) 6

(E) 4

Solution:

- Since *ABCD* is a square, it has area 4^2, or 16.

- The shaded area is less than one-half the size of the square, so its area must be less than 8.

- Eliminate answer choices (A), (B), and (C). The correct answer is (D).

Eliminate Choice (D) on Some QCs

If both columns of a QC contain only concrete numbers, choice (D)—"the relationship cannot be determined"—can't be right. With no variables in either column, there must be one consistent relationship, even if you can't find it. If you don't know the answer, eliminate (D) as unreasonable and guess.

EXAMPLE

Column A	Column B
The largest prime factor of 1,224	18

Each column contains only numbers—so eliminate choice (D) and guess. If you were extra clever, you may also have seen that since 18 isn't prime, and Column A contains a prime number, the answer cannot be (C) either. The correct answer is (B).

Find the Range on Grid-Ins—then Guess

On Grid-ins, there are no answer choices to eliminate, but you won't lose points for guessing. So if you are stuck, try to estimate the general range of the answer, and guess.

Here are some examples of hard Grid-in questions.

EXAMPLE

1. If the three-digit number $11Q$ is a prime number, what digit is represented by Q?

2. The sum of five consecutive odd integers is 425. What is the greatest of these integers?

3. A triangle has one side of length 3 and another of length 7. If the length of the third side is a solution to the equation $x^2 - 2x = 63$, what is the length of the third side?

Teacher Tip

"Many students are intimidated by math problems at the end of a section because they don't know how to approach them, so they often skip them. Take your time and figure out what you can, even if you're not sure how it may lead to the correct answer. You'll be surprised at how far you get."

—Serineh Baghdasarian
Kaplan Teacher
Los Angeles, CA

Solutions:

1. Since Q is a digit, it must be one of the integers 0 through 9. Eliminate all the even digits, since they are divisible by 2. And eliminate 5, since any number ending with 5 is divisible by 5. You can also eliminate 1 and 7, because they are divisible by 3 (the digits add up to a multiple of 3). You are left with 3 and 9 to pick between. The correct answer is 3.

2. Since the integers are consecutive, they are all about the same size. So the number we are looking for is an odd number around $425 \div 5$, which is 85. The right answer is 89.

3. Even if you can't solve that quadratic, you know that one side of a triangle has to be less than the sum and greater than the difference of the other two sides. So the third side is less than $7 + 3$, or 10, and greater than $7 - 3$, or 4. Since solutions to SAT quadratics are usually integers, pick an integer from 5 to 9. If you picked 9, you'd be right.

HINT: *Read "SAT Math in a Nutshell" in the "SAT Study Aids" section.*

Checklist

Once you've mastered a concept, check it off.

Math Guessing:

❏ Eliminate unreasonable answer choices

❏ Eliminate the obvious on hard questions

❏ Eyeball lengths, angles, and areas on geometry problems

❏ Eliminate choice (D) on some QCs

❏ Find the range on Grid-ins—then guess

Ready, Set, Go!

16

Stress Management

HIGHLIGHTS

- Unearth your sources of stress and learn how to manage them

- Take stock of your strengths and weaknesses

- Imagine yourself succeeding

- Practice proper breathing and exercise techniques

- Prepare for the final countdown

The countdown has begun. Your date with THE TEST is looming on the horizon. Anxiety is on the rise. The butterflies in your stomach have gone ballistic. Perhaps you feel as if the last thing you ate has turned into a lead ball. Your thinking is getting cloudy. Maybe you think you won't be ready. Maybe you already know your stuff, but you're going into panic mode anyway. Worst of all, you're not sure of what to do about it.

Don't freak! It is possible to tame that anxiety and stress—before and during the test. We'll show you how. You won't believe how quickly and easily you can deal with that killer anxiety.

Lack of control is one of the prime causes of stress. A ton of research shows that if you don't have a sense of control over what's happening in your life you can easily end up feeling helpless and hopeless. So, just having concrete things to do and to think about—taking control—will help reduce your stress. This section shows you how to take control during the days leading up to taking the test.

SAT Emergency

If you have only a week or two to prep for the SAT, you may just want to skim this chapter. If you're feeling stressed out, take the time to read it carefully. It will help you relax!

IDENTIFY THE SOURCES OF STRESS

In the space provided, jot down (in pencil) anything you identify as a source of your test-related stress. The idea is to pin down that free-floating anxiety so that you can take control of it. Here are some common examples to get you started:

- I always freeze up on tests.

- I'm nervous about the math (or the vocabulary or reading, etc.).

- I need a good/great score to go to Acme College.

- My older brother/sister/best friend/girl- or boyfriend did really well. I *must* match their scores or do better.

Avoid Must-y Thinking

Let go of "must-y" thoughts, those notions that you must do something in a certain way—for example, "I must get a great score, or else!" or "I must meet Mom and Dad's expectations!"

- My parents, who are paying for school, will be really disappointed if I don't test well.

- I'm afraid of losing my focus and concentration.

- I'm afraid I'm not spending enough time preparing.

- I study like crazy but nothing seems to stick in my mind.

- I always run out of time and get panicky.

- I feel as though thinking is becoming like wading through thick mud.

Sources of Stress:

_____

_____

_____

_____

_____

_____

_____

_____

_____

_____

Take a few minutes to think about the things you've just written down. Then rewrite them in some sort of order. List the statements you most associate with your stress and anxiety first, and put the least disturbing items last. Chances are, the top of the list is a fairly accurate description of exactly how you react to test anxiety, both physically and mentally. The later items usually describe your fears (disappointing Mom and Dad, looking bad, etc.). As you write the list, you're forming a hierarchy of items so you can deal first with the anxiety provokers that bug you most. Very often, taking care of the major items from the top of the list goes a long way towards relieving overall testing anxiety. You probably won't have to bother with the stuff you placed last.

TAKE STOCK OF YOUR STRENGTHS AND WEAKNESSES

Take one minute to list the areas of the test that you are good at. They can be general ("algebra") or specific ("quadratic equations"). Put down as many as you can think of, and if possible, time yourself. Write for the entire time; don't stop writing until you've reached the one-minute stopping point.

Strong Test Subjects:

_____

_____

_____

_____

_____

_____

_____

Next, take one minute to list areas of the test you're not so good at, just plain bad at, have failed at, or keep failing at. Again, keep it to one minute, and continue writing until you reach the cutoff. Don't be afraid to identify and write down your weak spots! In all probability, as you do both lists you'll find you are strong in some areas and not so strong in others. Taking stock of your assets *and* liabilities lets you know the areas you don't have to worry about, and the ones that will demand extra attention and effort.

Weak Test Subjects:

_____

_____

_____

_____

_____

_____

_____

Facing your weak spots gives you some distinct advantages. It helps a lot to find out where you need to spend extra effort. Increased exposure to tough material makes it more familiar and less intimidating. (After all, we mostly fear what we don't know and are probably afraid to face.) You'll feel better about yourself because you're dealing directly with areas of the test that bring on your anxiety. You can't help feeling more confident when you know you're actively strengthening your chances of earning a higher overall test score.

Very Superstitious

Stress expert Stephen Sideroff, Ph.D., tells of a client who always stressed out before, during, and even after taking tests. Yet, she always got outstanding scores. It became obvious that she was thinking superstitiously—subconsciously believing that the great scores were a result of her worrying. She also didn't trust herself, and believed that if she didn't worry she wouldn't study hard enough. Sideroff convinced her to take a risk and work on relaxing before her next test. She did, and her test results were still as good as ever—which broke her cycle of superstitious thinking.

KAPLAN 193

Now, go back to the "good" list, and expand it for two minutes. Take the general items on that first list and make them more specific; take the specific items and expand them into more general conclusions. Naturally, if anything new comes to mind, jot it down. Focus all of your attention and effort on your strengths. Don't underestimate yourself or your abilities. Give yourself full credit. At the same time, don't list strengths you don't really have; you'll only be fooling yourself.

Expanding from general to specific might go as follows. If you listed "Verbal" as a broad topic you feel strong in, you would then narrow your focus to include areas of this subject about which you are particularly knowledgeable. Your areas of strength might include analogies, ability to decipher unfamiliar words through knowledge of Latin, ability to recognize vocabulary bridges, etc.

Whatever you know comfortably (that is, almost as well as you know the back of your hand) goes on your "good" list. Okay. You've got the picture. Now, get ready, check your starting time, and start writing down items on your expanded "good" list.

Strong Test Subjects: An Expanded List:

_____

_____

_____

_____

_____

_____

_____

_____

_____

_____

_____

_____

_____

_____

Stress Tip

Don't work in a messy or cramped area. Before you sit down to study, clear yourself a nice, open space. And, make sure you have books, paper, pencils—whatever tools you will need—within easy reach before you sit down to study.

After you've stopped, check your time. Did you find yourself going beyond the two minutes allotted? Did you write down more things than you thought you knew? Is it possible you know more than you've given yourself credit for? Could that mean you've found a number of areas in which you feel strong?

You just took an active step towards helping yourself. Notice any increased feelings of confidence? Enjoy them.

Here's another way to think about your writing exercise. Every area of strength and confidence you can identify is much like having a reserve of solid gold at Fort Knox. You'll be able to draw on your reserves as you need them. You can use your reserves to solve difficult questions, maintain confidence, and keep test stress and anxiety at a distance. The encouraging thing is that every time you recognize another area of strength, succeed at coming up with a solution, or get a good score on a test, you increase your reserves. And, there is absolutely no limit to how much self-confidence you can have or how good you can feel about yourself.

IMAGINE YOURSELF SUCCEEDING

This next little group of exercises is both physical and mental. It's a natural follow-up to what you've just accomplished with your lists.

First, get yourself into a comfortable sitting position in a quiet setting. Wear loose clothes. If you wear glasses, take them off. Then, close your eyes and breathe in a deep, satisfying breath of air. Really fill your lungs until your rib cage is fully expanded and you can't take in any more. Then, exhale the air completely. Imagine you're blowing out a candle with your last little puff of air. Do this two or three more times, filling your lungs to their maximum and emptying them totally. Keep your eyes closed, comfortably but not tightly. Let your body sink deeper into the chair as you become even more comfortable.

With your eyes shut you can notice something very interesting. You're no longer dealing with the worrisome stuff going on in the world *outside* of you. Now you can concentrate on what happens *inside* you. The more you recognize your own physical reactions to stress and anxiety, the more you can do about them. You may not realize it, but you've begun to regain a sense of being in control.

Let images begin to form on the "viewing screens" on the back of your eyelids. You're experiencing visualizations from the place in your mind that makes pictures. Allow the images to come easily and naturally; don't force them. Imagine yourself in a relaxing situation. It might be in a special place you've visited before or one you've read about. It can be a fictional location that you create in your imagination, but a real-life memory of a place or situation you know is usually better. Make it as detailed as possible and notice as much as you can.

Stay focused on the images as you sink farther back into your chair. Breathe easily and naturally. You might have the sensations of any stress or tension draining from your muscles and flowing downward, out your feet and away from you.

Teacher Tip

"I always tell my students that the best gift that Kaplan can give them is to eliminate the element of surprise, which can spell disaster. With Kaplan, students know what to expect; they always know what's coming. Remember, you are in control of the test. The test makers can dictate the questions themselves, but not how you handle them."

—Fran Longo
Kaplan Teacher
Boston, MA

Take a moment to check how you're feeling. Notice how comfortable you've become. Imagine how much easier it would be if you could take the test feeling this relaxed and in this state of ease. You've coupled the images of your special place with sensations of comfort and relaxation. You've also found a way to become relaxed simply by visualizing your own safe, special place.

Stress Tip

If you want to play music, keep it low and in the background. Music with a regular, mathematical rhythm—reggae, for example—aids the learning process. A recording of ocean waves is also soothing.

Now, close your eyes and start remembering a real-life situation in which you did well on a test. If you can't come up with one, remember a situation in which you did something (academic or otherwise) that you were really proud of—a genuine accomplishment. Make the memory as detailed as possible. Think about the sights, the sounds, the smells, even the tastes associated with this remembered experience. Remember how confident you felt as you accomplished your goal. Now start thinking about the upcoming test. Keep your thoughts and feelings in line with that successful experience. Don't make comparisons between them. Just imagine taking the upcoming test with the same feelings of confidence and relaxed control.

This exercise is a great way to bring the test down to earth. You should practice this exercise often, especially when the prospect of taking the exam starts to bum you out. The more you practice it, the more effective the exercise will be for you.

EXERCISE YOUR FRUSTRATIONS AWAY

Whether it is jogging, walking, biking, mild aerobics, pushups, or a pickup basketball game, physical exercise is a very effective way to stimulate both your mind and body and to improve your ability to think and concentrate. A surprising number of students get out of the habit of regular exercise, ironically because they're spending so much time prepping for exams. Also, sedentary people—this is a medical fact—get less oxygen to the blood and hence to the head than active people. You can live fine with a little less oxygen; you just can't think as well.

Any big test is a bit like a race. Thinking clearly at the end is just as important as having a quick mind early on. If you can't sustain your energy level in the last sections of the exam, there's too good a chance you could blow it. You need a fit body that can weather the demands any big exam puts on you. Along with a good diet and adequate sleep, exercise is an important part of keeping yourself in fighting shape and thinking clearly for the long haul.

Take a Hike, Pal

When you're in the middle of studying and hit a wall, take a short, brisk walk. Breathe deeply and swing your arms as you walk. Clear your mind. (And, don't forget to look for flowers that grow in the cracks of the sidewalk.)

There's another thing that happens when students don't make exercise an integral part of their test preparation. Like any organism in nature, you operate best if all your "energy systems" are in balance. Studying uses a lot of energy, but it's all mental. When you take a study break, do something active instead of raiding the fridge or vegging out in front of the TV. Take a five- to ten-minute activity break for every 50 or 60 minutes that you study. The physical exertion gets your body into the act, which helps to keep your mind and body in sync. Then, when you finish studying for the night and hit the sack, you won't lie there, tense and unable to sleep because your head is overtired and your body wants to pump iron or run a marathon.

One warning about exercise, however: It's not a good idea to exercise vigorously right before you go to bed. This could easily cause sleep onset problems. For the same reason, it's also not a good idea to study right up to bedtime. Make time for a "buffer period" before you go to bed: For 30 to 60 minutes, just take a hot shower, meditate, simply veg out.

THE DANGERS OF DRUGS

Using drugs (prescription or recreational) specifically to prepare for and take a big test is definitely self-defeating. (And if they're illegal drugs, you may end up with a bigger problem than the SAT on your hands.) Except for the drugs that occur naturally in your brain, every drug has major drawbacks—and a false sense of security is only one of them.

You may have heard that popping uppers helps you study by keeping you alert. If they're illegal, definitely forget about it. They wouldn't really work anyway, since amphetamines make it hard to retain information. Mild stimulants, such as coffee, cola, or over-the-counter caffeine pills can sometimes help as you study, since they keep you alert. On the down side, they can also lead to agitation, restlessness, and insomnia. Some people can drink a pot of high-octane coffee and sleep like a baby. Others have one cup and start to vibrate. It all depends on your tolerance for caffeine. Remember, a little anxiety is a good thing. The adrenaline that gets pumped into your bloodstream helps you stay alert and think more clearly. But, too much anxiety and you can't think straight at all.

Instead, go for endorphins—the "natural morphine." Endorphins have no side effects and they're free—you've already got them in your brain. It just takes some exercise to release them. Running around on the basketball court, bicycling, swimming, aerobics, power walking—these activities cause endorphins to occupy certain spots in your brain's neural synapses. In addition, exercise develops staying power and increases the oxygen transfer to your brain. Go into the test naturally.

Nutrition and Stress: The Dos and Don'ts

Do eat:

- Fruits and vegetables (raw is best, or just lightly steamed or nuked)
- Low-fat protein such as fish, skinless poultry, beans, and legumes
- Whole grains such as brown rice, whole wheat bread, and pasta

Don't eat:

- Refined sugar; sweet, high-fat snacks (simple carbohydrates like sugar make stress worse and fatty foods lower your immunity)
- Salty foods (they deplete potassium, which you need for nerve functions)

TAKE A DEEP BREATH . . .

Here's another natural route to relaxation and invigoration. It's a classic isometric exercise that you can do whenever you get stressed out—just before the test begins, even *during* the test. It's very simple and takes just a few minutes.

Close your eyes. Starting with your eyes and—*without holding your breath*—gradually tighten every muscle in your body (but not to the point of pain) in the following sequence:

1. Close your eyes tightly.
2. Squeeze your nose and mouth together so that your whole face is scrunched up. (If it makes you self-conscious to do this in the test room, skip the face-scrunching part.)
3. Pull your chin into your chest, and pull your shoulders together.
4. Tighten your arms to your body, then clench your hands into tight fists.
5. Pull in your stomach.
6. Squeeze your thighs and buttocks together, and tighten your calves.
7. Stretch your feet, then curl your toes (watch out for cramping in this part).

At this point, every muscle should be tightened. Now, relax your body, one part at a time, in *reverse order*, starting with your toes. Let the tension drop out of each muscle. The entire process might take five minutes from start to finish (maybe a couple of minutes during the test). This clenching and unclenching exercise should help you to feel very relaxed.

AND KEEP BREATHING

The Relaxation Paradox

Forcing relaxation is like asking yourself to flap your arms and fly. You can't do it, and every push and prod only gets you more frustrated. Relaxation is something you don't work at. You simply let it happen. Think about it. When was the last time you tried to force yourself to go to sleep, and it worked?

Conscious attention to breathing is an excellent way of managing test stress (or any stress, for that matter). The majority of people who get into trouble during tests take shallow breaths. They breathe using only their upper chests and shoulder muscles, and may even hold their breath for long periods of time. Conversely, the test taker who by accident or design keeps breathing normally and rhythmically is likely to be more relaxed and in better control during the entire test experience.

So, now is the time to get into the habit of relaxed breathing. Do the next exercise to learn to breathe in a natural, easy rhythm. By the way, this is another technique you can use during the test to collect your thoughts and ward off excess stress. The entire exercise should take no more than three to five minutes.

With your eyes still closed, breathe in slowly and deeply through your nose. Hold the breath for a bit, and then release it through your mouth. The key is to breathe slowly and deeply by using your diaphragm (the big band of muscle that spans your body just above your waist) to draw air in and out naturally and effortlessly. Breathing with your diaphragm encourages relaxation and helps minimize tension. Try it and notice how relaxed and comfortable you feel.

QUICK TIPS FOR THE DAYS JUST BEFORE THE EXAM

- The best test takers do less and less as the test approaches. Taper off your study schedule and take it easy on yourself. You want to be relaxed and ready on the day of the test. Give yourself time off, especially the evening before the exam. By that time, if you've studied well, everything you need to know is firmly stored in your memory banks.

- Positive self-talk can be extremely liberating and invigorating, especially as the test looms closer. Tell yourself things such as, "I choose to take this test" rather than "I have to"; "I will do well" rather than "I hope things go well"; "I can" rather than "I cannot." Be aware of negative, self-defeating thoughts and images and immediately counter any you become aware of. Replace them with affirming statements that encourage your self-esteem and confidence. Create and practice doing visualizations that build on your positive statements.

- Get your act together sooner rather than later. Have everything (including choice of clothing) laid out days in advance. Most important, know where the test will be held and the easiest, quickest way to get there. You will gain great peace of mind if you know that all the little details—gas in the car, directions, etc.—are firmly in your control before the day of the test.

- Experience the test site a few days in advance. This is very helpful if you are especially anxious. If at all possible, find out what room your part of the alphabet is assigned to, and try to sit there (by yourself) for a while. Better yet, bring some practice material and do at least a section or two, if not an entire practice test, in that room. In this case, familiarity doesn't breed contempt, it generates comfort and confidence.

- Forego any practice on the day before the test. It's in your best interest to marshal your physical and psychological resources for 24 hours or so. Even race horses are kept in the paddock and treated like princes the day before a race. Keep the upcoming test out of your consciousness; go to a movie, take a pleasant hike, or just relax. Don't eat junk food or tons of sugar. And—of course—get plenty of rest the night before. Just don't go to bed too early. It's hard to fall asleep earlier than you're used to, and you don't want to lie there thinking about the test.

HANDLING STRESS DURING THE TEST

The biggest stress monster will be the test itself. Fear not; there are methods of quelling your stress during the test.

- Keep moving forward instead of getting bogged down in a difficult question or passage. You don't have to get everything right to achieve a fine score. So, don't linger out of desperation on a question that is going nowhere even after you've spent considerable time on it. The best test takers skip difficult material temporarily in search of the easier stuff. They mark the ones that require extra time and thought. This strategy buys time and builds confidence so you can handle the tough stuff later.

- Don't be thrown if other test takers seem to be working more busily and furiously than you are. Continue to spend your time patiently but doggedly thinking through your answers; it's going to lead to higher-quality test taking and better results. Don't mistake the other people's sheer activity as signs of progress and higher scores.

- *Keep breathing!* Weak test takers tend to share one major trait: They forget to breathe properly as the test proceeds. They start holding their breath without realizing it, or they breathe erratically or arrhythmically. Improper breathing hurts confidence and accuracy. Just as important, it interferes with clear thinking.

- Some quick isometrics during the test—especially if concentration is wandering or energy is waning—can help. Try this: Put your palms together and press intensely for a few seconds. Concentrate on the tension you feel through your palms, wrists, forearms, and up into your biceps and shoulders. Then, quickly release the pressure. Feel the difference as you let go. Focus on the warm relaxation that floods through the muscles. Now you're ready to return to the task.

What Are "Signs of a Winner," Alex?

Here's some advice from a Kaplan instructor who won big on *Jeopardy!*™ In the green room before the show, he noticed that the contestants who were quiet and "within themselves" were the ones who did great on the show. The contestants who did not perform as well were the ones who were fact-cramming, talking a lot, and generally being manic before the show. Lesson: Spend the final hours leading up to the test getting sleep, meditating, and generally relaxing.

Teacher Tip

"Take care of yourself. Sounds simple, no? Sleep well, eat well, be nice to others, and drive safely before you take the test. Sick and injured people don't do well on exams!"

—Tayna Kormeili
   Kaplan Teacher
   Los Angeles, CA

• Here's another isometric that will relieve tension in both your neck and eye muscles. Slowly rotate your head from side to side, turning your head and eyes to look as far back over each shoulder as you can. Feel the muscles stretch on one side of your neck as they contract on the other. Repeat five times in each direction.

With what you've just learned here, you're armed and ready to do battle with the test. This book and your studies will give you the information you'll need to answer the questions. It's all firmly planted in your mind. You also know how to deal with any excess tension that might come along, both when you're studying for and taking the exam. You've experienced everything you need to tame your test anxiety and stress. You're going to get a great score.

17

What Do I Do Now?

HIGHLIGHTS

- Find out what to do in the time before, during, and after the test

- Improve your test mentality with confidence and the right attitude

Is it starting to feel like your whole life is a build-up to the SAT? You've known about it for years, worried about it for months, and now spent at least a few hours in solid preparation for it. As the test gets closer, you may find your anxiety is on the rise. You shouldn't worry. After the preparation you've received from this book, you're in good shape for the test.

ITINERARY

To calm any pretest jitters you may have, this chapter leads you through a sane itinerary for the last week.

The Week Before the Test

Review the checklists in the chapters. Are there major holes in your preparation? If there are, choose a few of these areas to work on—but don't overload. You can't cram for the SAT.

Take a full-length SAT. If you haven't done so already, take one or more of the practice tests in this book. Actual SATs released by ETS are available in libraries and bookstores. You could also pick up from your guidance counselor a copy of *Taking the SAT I*, a College Board publication with a practice test. All of these are good practice for the real thing.

SAT Emergency

Even if you're short on time, read this entire chapter. It tells you how to use your time wisely before, during, and after the test.

Two Days Before the Test

Do your last studying—a few more practice problems, a few more vocabulary words, and call it quits.

The Night Before the Test

Don't study. Get together the following items:

- A calculator with fresh batteries
- A watch
- A few No. 2 pencils
- Erasers
- Photo ID card
- Your admission ticket from ETS
- A snack—there are two breaks and you'll probably get hungry

Know exactly where you're going and exactly how you're getting there.

Relax the night before the test. Read a good book, take a bubble bath, watch TV. Get a good night's sleep. Go to bed at a reasonable hour and leave yourself extra time in the morning.

Teacher Tip

"A skill that's absolutely necessary for all sections of the test is concentration. Being easily distracted diminishes your ability to pick up on every subtle and not-so-subtle component of the text. Everything from construction or traffic outside to a proctor's noisy watch can distract on test day. You can train to get into the test 'zone' by practicing with a radio on, or in a busy coffee shop. This is a valuable skill not only in every section of the test, but in school as well."

—Antonette Brigidi
Kaplan Teacher
Baltimore, MD

The Morning of the Test

Eat breakfast. Make it something substantial, but not anything too heavy or greasy. Don't drink a lot of coffee if you're not used to it; bathroom breaks cut into your time.

Dress in layers so that you can adjust to the temperature of the test room.

Read something. Warm up your brain with a newspaper or a magazine. You shouldn't let the SAT be the first thing you read that day.

Be sure to get there early.

During the Test

Don't be shaken. If you find your confidence slipping, remind yourself how well you've prepared. You know the structure of the test; you know the instructions; you've studied for every question type.

Even if something goes really wrong, don't panic. If the test booklet is defective—two pages are stuck together or the ink has run—try to stay calm. Raise your hand, tell the proctor you need a new book. If you accidentally misgrid your answer page or put the answers in the wrong section, again don't panic. Raise your hand, tell the proctor. He or she might be able to arrange for you to regrid your test after it's over, when it won't cost you any time.

Don't think about which section is experimental. Remember, you never know for sure which section won't count. Besides, you can't work on any other section during that section's designated time slot.

After the Test

Once the test is over, put it out of your mind. If you don't plan to take the test again, give this book away and start thinking about more interesting things.

You might walk out of the SAT thinking that you blew it. You probably didn't.
You tend to remember the questions that stumped you, not the many that you knew. If you're really concerned, you can call ETS within 24 hours to find out about canceling your score. But there is usually no good reason to do so. Remember, you can retake the test as many times as you want, and most colleges consider only your highest scores.

If you want more help, or just want to know more about the SAT, college admissions, or Kaplan prep courses for the SAT, and ACT, give us a call at 1-800-KAP-TEST. We're here to answer your questions and to help you in any way that we can.

Good luck!

Need More Help?

Call 1-800-KAP-TEST if you have any questions about the SAT or want more information about our other books or courses. You can also check out our website at www.kaptest.com.

Practice Tests and Explanations

Practice Test One

HOW TO TAKE THIS PRACTICE TEST

Before taking this practice test, find a quiet room where you can work uninterrupted for two and a half hours. Make sure you have a comfortable desk, your calculator, and several No. 2 pencils.

Use the answer sheet provided to record your answers. (You can cut it out or photocopy it.)

Once you start this practice test, don't stop until you've finished. Remember—you can review any questions within a section, but you may not go back or forward a section.

You'll find an answer key, score conversion charts, and explanations following the test.

Good luck.

SAT Practice Test One Answer Sheet

Remove (or photocopy) this answer sheet and use it to complete the practice test.
(See answer key following the test when finished.)

Start with number 1 for each section. If a section has fewer questions than answer spaces, leave the extra spaces blank.

SECTION 1

1 Ⓐ Ⓑ Ⓒ Ⓓ Ⓔ   11 Ⓐ Ⓑ Ⓒ Ⓓ Ⓔ   21 Ⓐ Ⓑ Ⓒ Ⓓ Ⓔ   31 Ⓐ Ⓑ Ⓒ Ⓓ Ⓔ
2 Ⓐ Ⓑ Ⓒ Ⓓ Ⓔ   12 Ⓐ Ⓑ Ⓒ Ⓓ Ⓔ   22 Ⓐ Ⓑ Ⓒ Ⓓ Ⓔ   32 Ⓐ Ⓑ Ⓒ Ⓓ Ⓔ
3 Ⓐ Ⓑ Ⓒ Ⓓ Ⓔ   13 Ⓐ Ⓑ Ⓒ Ⓓ Ⓔ   23 Ⓐ Ⓑ Ⓒ Ⓓ Ⓔ   33 Ⓐ Ⓑ Ⓒ Ⓓ Ⓔ
4 Ⓐ Ⓑ Ⓒ Ⓓ Ⓔ   14 Ⓐ Ⓑ Ⓒ Ⓓ Ⓔ   24 Ⓐ Ⓑ Ⓒ Ⓓ Ⓔ   34 Ⓐ Ⓑ Ⓒ Ⓓ Ⓔ
5 Ⓐ Ⓑ Ⓒ Ⓓ Ⓔ   15 Ⓐ Ⓑ Ⓒ Ⓓ Ⓔ   25 Ⓐ Ⓑ Ⓒ Ⓓ Ⓔ   35 Ⓐ Ⓑ Ⓒ Ⓓ Ⓔ
6 Ⓐ Ⓑ Ⓒ Ⓓ Ⓔ   16 Ⓐ Ⓑ Ⓒ Ⓓ Ⓔ   26 Ⓐ Ⓑ Ⓒ Ⓓ Ⓔ   36 Ⓐ Ⓑ Ⓒ Ⓓ Ⓔ
7 Ⓐ Ⓑ Ⓒ Ⓓ Ⓔ   17 Ⓐ Ⓑ Ⓒ Ⓓ Ⓔ   27 Ⓐ Ⓑ Ⓒ Ⓓ Ⓔ   37 Ⓐ Ⓑ Ⓒ Ⓓ Ⓔ
8 Ⓐ Ⓑ Ⓒ Ⓓ Ⓔ   18 Ⓐ Ⓑ Ⓒ Ⓓ Ⓔ   28 Ⓐ Ⓑ Ⓒ Ⓓ Ⓔ   38 Ⓐ Ⓑ Ⓒ Ⓓ Ⓔ
9 Ⓐ Ⓑ Ⓒ Ⓓ Ⓔ   19 Ⓐ Ⓑ Ⓒ Ⓓ Ⓔ   29 Ⓐ Ⓑ Ⓒ Ⓓ Ⓔ   39 Ⓐ Ⓑ Ⓒ Ⓓ Ⓔ
10 Ⓐ Ⓑ Ⓒ Ⓓ Ⓔ   20 Ⓐ Ⓑ Ⓒ Ⓓ Ⓔ   30 Ⓐ Ⓑ Ⓒ Ⓓ Ⓔ   40 Ⓐ Ⓑ Ⓒ Ⓓ Ⓔ

right in section 1

wrong in section 1

SECTION 2

1 Ⓐ Ⓑ Ⓒ Ⓓ Ⓔ   11 Ⓐ Ⓑ Ⓒ Ⓓ Ⓔ   21 Ⓐ Ⓑ Ⓒ Ⓓ Ⓔ   31 Ⓐ Ⓑ Ⓒ Ⓓ Ⓔ
2 Ⓐ Ⓑ Ⓒ Ⓓ Ⓔ   12 Ⓐ Ⓑ Ⓒ Ⓓ Ⓔ   22 Ⓐ Ⓑ Ⓒ Ⓓ Ⓔ   32 Ⓐ Ⓑ Ⓒ Ⓓ Ⓔ
3 Ⓐ Ⓑ Ⓒ Ⓓ Ⓔ   13 Ⓐ Ⓑ Ⓒ Ⓓ Ⓔ   23 Ⓐ Ⓑ Ⓒ Ⓓ Ⓔ   33 Ⓐ Ⓑ Ⓒ Ⓓ Ⓔ
4 Ⓐ Ⓑ Ⓒ Ⓓ Ⓔ   14 Ⓐ Ⓑ Ⓒ Ⓓ Ⓔ   24 Ⓐ Ⓑ Ⓒ Ⓓ Ⓔ   34 Ⓐ Ⓑ Ⓒ Ⓓ Ⓔ
5 Ⓐ Ⓑ Ⓒ Ⓓ Ⓔ   15 Ⓐ Ⓑ Ⓒ Ⓓ Ⓔ   25 Ⓐ Ⓑ Ⓒ Ⓓ Ⓔ   35 Ⓐ Ⓑ Ⓒ Ⓓ Ⓔ
6 Ⓐ Ⓑ Ⓒ Ⓓ Ⓔ   16 Ⓐ Ⓑ Ⓒ Ⓓ Ⓔ   26 Ⓐ Ⓑ Ⓒ Ⓓ Ⓔ   36 Ⓐ Ⓑ Ⓒ Ⓓ Ⓔ
7 Ⓐ Ⓑ Ⓒ Ⓓ Ⓔ   17 Ⓐ Ⓑ Ⓒ Ⓓ Ⓔ   27 Ⓐ Ⓑ Ⓒ Ⓓ Ⓔ   37 Ⓐ Ⓑ Ⓒ Ⓓ Ⓔ
8 Ⓐ Ⓑ Ⓒ Ⓓ Ⓔ   18 Ⓐ Ⓑ Ⓒ Ⓓ Ⓔ   28 Ⓐ Ⓑ Ⓒ Ⓓ Ⓔ   38 Ⓐ Ⓑ Ⓒ Ⓓ Ⓔ
9 Ⓐ Ⓑ Ⓒ Ⓓ Ⓔ   19 Ⓐ Ⓑ Ⓒ Ⓓ Ⓔ   29 Ⓐ Ⓑ Ⓒ Ⓓ Ⓔ   39 Ⓐ Ⓑ Ⓒ Ⓓ Ⓔ
10 Ⓐ Ⓑ Ⓒ Ⓓ Ⓔ   20 Ⓐ Ⓑ Ⓒ Ⓓ Ⓔ   30 Ⓐ Ⓑ Ⓒ Ⓓ Ⓔ   40 Ⓐ Ⓑ Ⓒ Ⓓ Ⓔ

right in section 2

wrong in section 2

SECTION 3

1 Ⓐ Ⓑ Ⓒ Ⓓ Ⓔ   11 Ⓐ Ⓑ Ⓒ Ⓓ Ⓔ   21 Ⓐ Ⓑ Ⓒ Ⓓ Ⓔ   31 Ⓐ Ⓑ Ⓒ Ⓓ Ⓔ
2 Ⓐ Ⓑ Ⓒ Ⓓ Ⓔ   12 Ⓐ Ⓑ Ⓒ Ⓓ Ⓔ   22 Ⓐ Ⓑ Ⓒ Ⓓ Ⓔ   32 Ⓐ Ⓑ Ⓒ Ⓓ Ⓔ
3 Ⓐ Ⓑ Ⓒ Ⓓ Ⓔ   13 Ⓐ Ⓑ Ⓒ Ⓓ Ⓔ   23 Ⓐ Ⓑ Ⓒ Ⓓ Ⓔ   33 Ⓐ Ⓑ Ⓒ Ⓓ Ⓔ
4 Ⓐ Ⓑ Ⓒ Ⓓ Ⓔ   14 Ⓐ Ⓑ Ⓒ Ⓓ Ⓔ   24 Ⓐ Ⓑ Ⓒ Ⓓ Ⓔ   34 Ⓐ Ⓑ Ⓒ Ⓓ Ⓔ
5 Ⓐ Ⓑ Ⓒ Ⓓ Ⓔ   15 Ⓐ Ⓑ Ⓒ Ⓓ Ⓔ   25 Ⓐ Ⓑ Ⓒ Ⓓ Ⓔ   35 Ⓐ Ⓑ Ⓒ Ⓓ Ⓔ
6 Ⓐ Ⓑ Ⓒ Ⓓ Ⓔ   16 Ⓐ Ⓑ Ⓒ Ⓓ Ⓔ   26 Ⓐ Ⓑ Ⓒ Ⓓ Ⓔ   36 Ⓐ Ⓑ Ⓒ Ⓓ Ⓔ
7 Ⓐ Ⓑ Ⓒ Ⓓ Ⓔ   17 Ⓐ Ⓑ Ⓒ Ⓓ Ⓔ   27 Ⓐ Ⓑ Ⓒ Ⓓ Ⓔ   37 Ⓐ Ⓑ Ⓒ Ⓓ Ⓔ
8 Ⓐ Ⓑ Ⓒ Ⓓ Ⓔ   18 Ⓐ Ⓑ Ⓒ Ⓓ Ⓔ   28 Ⓐ Ⓑ Ⓒ Ⓓ Ⓔ   38 Ⓐ Ⓑ Ⓒ Ⓓ Ⓔ
9 Ⓐ Ⓑ Ⓒ Ⓓ Ⓔ   19 Ⓐ Ⓑ Ⓒ Ⓓ Ⓔ   29 Ⓐ Ⓑ Ⓒ Ⓓ Ⓔ   39 Ⓐ Ⓑ Ⓒ Ⓓ Ⓔ
10 Ⓐ Ⓑ Ⓒ Ⓓ Ⓔ   20 Ⓐ Ⓑ Ⓒ Ⓓ Ⓔ   30 Ⓐ Ⓑ Ⓒ Ⓓ Ⓔ   40 Ⓐ Ⓑ Ⓒ Ⓓ Ⓔ

right in section 3

wrong in section 3

Remove (or photocopy) this answer sheet and use it to complete the practice test.

Start with number 1 for each section. If a section has fewer questions than answer spaces, leave the extra spaces blank.

SECTION 4

1 (A) (B) (C) (D) (E)   11 (A) (B) (C) (D) (E)   21 (A) (B) (C) (D) (E)   31 (A) (B) (C) (D) (E)
2 (A) (B) (C) (D) (E)   12 (A) (B) (C) (D) (E)   22 (A) (B) (C) (D) (E)   32 (A) (B) (C) (D) (E)
3 (A) (B) (C) (D) (E)   13 (A) (B) (C) (D) (E)   23 (A) (B) (C) (D) (E)   33 (A) (B) (C) (D) (E)
4 (A) (B) (C) (D) (E)   14 (A) (B) (C) (D) (E)   24 (A) (B) (C) (D) (E)   34 (A) (B) (C) (D) (E)
5 (A) (B) (C) (D) (E)   15 (A) (B) (C) (D) (E)   25 (A) (B) (C) (D) (E)   35 (A) (B) (C) (D) (E)
6 (A) (B) (C) (D) (E)   16 (A) (B) (C) (D) (E)   26 (A) (B) (C) (D) (E)   36 (A) (B) (C) (D) (E)
7 (A) (B) (C) (D) (E)   17 (A) (B) (C) (D) (E)   27 (A) (B) (C) (D) (E)   37 (A) (B) (C) (D) (E)
8 (A) (B) (C) (D) (E)   18 (A) (B) (C) (D) (E)   28 (A) (B) (C) (D) (E)   38 (A) (B) (C) (D) (E)
9 (A) (B) (C) (D) (E)   19 (A) (B) (C) (D) (E)   29 (A) (B) (C) (D) (E)   39 (A) (B) (C) (D) (E)
10 (A) (B) (C) (D) (E)   20 (A) (B) (C) (D) (E)   30 (A) (B) (C) (D) (E)   40 (A) (B) (C) (D) (E)

right in section 4

wrong in section 4

If section 4 of your test book contains math questions that are not multiple choice, continue to item 16 below. Otherwise, continue to item 16 above.

16   17   18   19   20   21   22   23   24   25

[grid-in answer boxes with bubbles 0–9]

SECTION 5

1 (A) (B) (C) (D) (E)   11 (A) (B) (C) (D) (E)   21 (A) (B) (C) (D) (E)   31 (A) (B) (C) (D) (E)
2 (A) (B) (C) (D) (E)   12 (A) (B) (C) (D) (E)   22 (A) (B) (C) (D) (E)   32 (A) (B) (C) (D) (E)
3 (A) (B) (C) (D) (E)   13 (A) (B) (C) (D) (E)   23 (A) (B) (C) (D) (E)   33 (A) (B) (C) (D) (E)
4 (A) (B) (C) (D) (E)   14 (A) (B) (C) (D) (E)   24 (A) (B) (C) (D) (E)   34 (A) (B) (C) (D) (E)
5 (A) (B) (C) (D) (E)   15 (A) (B) (C) (D) (E)   25 (A) (B) (C) (D) (E)   35 (A) (B) (C) (D) (E)
6 (A) (B) (C) (D) (E)   16 (A) (B) (C) (D) (E)   26 (A) (B) (C) (D) (E)   36 (A) (B) (C) (D) (E)
7 (A) (B) (C) (D) (E)   17 (A) (B) (C) (D) (E)   27 (A) (B) (C) (D) (E)   37 (A) (B) (C) (D) (E)
8 (A) (B) (C) (D) (E)   18 (A) (B) (C) (D) (E)   28 (A) (B) (C) (D) (E)   38 (A) (B) (C) (D) (E)
9 (A) (B) (C) (D) (E)   19 (A) (B) (C) (D) (E)   29 (A) (B) (C) (D) (E)   39 (A) (B) (C) (D) (E)
10 (A) (B) (C) (D) (E)   20 (A) (B) (C) (D) (E)   30 (A) (B) (C) (D) (E)   40 (A) (B) (C) (D) (E)

right in section 5

wrong in section 5

SECTION 6

1 (A) (B) (C) (D) (E)   11 (A) (B) (C) (D) (E)   21 (A) (B) (C) (D) (E)   31 (A) (B) (C) (D) (E)
2 (A) (B) (C) (D) (E)   12 (A) (B) (C) (D) (E)   22 (A) (B) (C) (D) (E)   32 (A) (B) (C) (D) (E)
3 (A) (B) (C) (D) (E)   13 (A) (B) (C) (D) (E)   23 (A) (B) (C) (D) (E)   33 (A) (B) (C) (D) (E)
4 (A) (B) (C) (D) (E)   14 (A) (B) (C) (D) (E)   24 (A) (B) (C) (D) (E)   34 (A) (B) (C) (D) (E)
5 (A) (B) (C) (D) (E)   15 (A) (B) (C) (D) (E)   25 (A) (B) (C) (D) (E)   35 (A) (B) (C) (D) (E)
6 (A) (B) (C) (D) (E)   16 (A) (B) (C) (D) (E)   26 (A) (B) (C) (D) (E)   36 (A) (B) (C) (D) (E)
7 (A) (B) (C) (D) (E)   17 (A) (B) (C) (D) (E)   27 (A) (B) (C) (D) (E)   37 (A) (B) (C) (D) (E)
8 (A) (B) (C) (D) (E)   18 (A) (B) (C) (D) (E)   28 (A) (B) (C) (D) (E)   38 (A) (B) (C) (D) (E)
9 (A) (B) (C) (D) (E)   19 (A) (B) (C) (D) (E)   29 (A) (B) (C) (D) (E)   39 (A) (B) (C) (D) (E)
10 (A) (B) (C) (D) (E)   20 (A) (B) (C) (D) (E)   30 (A) (B) (C) (D) (E)   40 (A) (B) (C) (D) (E)

right in section 6

wrong in section 6

Practice Test One—Section 1

Time—30 Minutes   For each of the following questions, choose the best answer and darken the
30 Questions   corresponding oval on the answer sheet.*

Select the lettered word or set of words that best completes the sentence.

Example:

Today's small, portable computers contrast markedly with the earliest electronic computers, which were ----.

(A) effective
(B) invented
(C) useful
(D) destructive
(E) enormous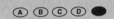

1   More insurers are limiting the sale of property insurance in coastal areas and other regions ---- natural disasters.

(A) safe from
(B) according to
(C) despite
(D) which include
(E) prone to

2   Roman legions ---- the mountain ---- of Masada for three years before they were able to seize it.

(A) dissembled . . bastion
(B) assailed . . symbol
(C) besieged . . citadel
(D) surmounted . . dwelling
(E) honed . . stronghold

3   Unlike his calmer, more easygoing colleagues, the senator was ----, ready to quarrel at the slightest provocation.

(A) whimsical
(B) irascible
(C) gregarious
(D) ineffectual
(E) benign

4   Although historians have long thought of Genghis Khan as a ---- potentate, new research has shown he was ---- by many of his subjects.

(A) tyrannical . . abhorred
(B) despotic . . revered
(C) redundant . . venerated
(D) jocular . . esteemed
(E) peremptory . . invoked

5   Jill was ---- by her employees because she often ---- them for not working hard enough.

(A) deified . . goaded
(B) loathed . . berated
(C) disregarded . . eulogized
(D) cherished . . derided
(E) execrated . . lauded

6   Reconstructing the skeletons of extinct species like dinosaurs is ---- process that requires much patience and effort by paleontologists.

(A) a nascent
(B) an aberrant
(C) a disheveled
(D) a worthless
(E) an exacting

7   Nearly ---- by disease and the destruction of their habitat, koalas are now found only in isolated parts of eucalyptus forests.

(A) dispersed
(B) compiled
(C) decimated
(D) infuriated
(E) averted

8   Deep ideological ---- and internal power struggles ---- the government.

(A) disputes . . facilitated
(B) similarities . . protracted
(C) distortions . . accelerated
(D) agreements . . stymied
(E) divisions . . paralyzed

9   Medical experts have viewed high doses of vitamins as a popular remedy whose value is, as yet, ----.

(A) medicinal
(B) prescribed
(C) recommended
(D) unproven
(E) beneficial

*The directions on the actual SAT will vary slightly.

GO ON TO THE NEXT PAGE ➡

Choose the lettered pair of words that is related in the same way as the pair in capital letters.

Example:

FLAKE : SNOW ::

(A) storm : hail
(B) drop : rain
(C) field : wheat
(D) stack : hay
(E) cloud : fog

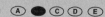

10 TROUT : FISH ::

(A) grain : sand
(B) human : mammal
(C) river : stream
(D) chicken : egg
(E) frog : toad

11 INHALE : LUNGS ::

(A) swallow : stomach
(B) attack : heart
(C) ache : head
(D) pump : blood
(E) travel : foot

12 BRAGGART : BOAST ::

(A) laggard : tarry
(B) hypocrite : speak
(C) extrovert : brood
(D) mendicant : compromise
(E) boor : gratify

13 ALLEVIATE : PAIN ::

(A) soothe : antidote
(B) depreciate : value
(C) contract : job
(D) deviate : standard
(E) officiate : safety

14 INFURIATE : ANNOY ::

(A) admire : respect
(B) indulge : lure
(C) terrify : frighten
(D) satiate : deprive
(E) vex : startle

15 MISERLY : MAGNANIMITY ::

(A) greedy : mirth
(B) transient : stupefaction
(C) admirable : fastidiousness
(D) innocent : culpability
(E) offensive : avarice

GO ON TO THE NEXT PAGE ➡

Answer the questions below based on the information in the accompanying passages.

Questions 16–23 are based on the following passage.

In this excerpt, a Nobel Prize–winning scientist discusses ways of thinking about extremely long periods of time.

There is one fact about the origin of life which is reasonably certain. Whenever and wherever it happened, it started a very long time ago, so long
Line ago that it is extremely difficult to form any
(5) realistic idea of such vast stretches of time. The shortness of human life necessarily limits the span of direct personal recollection.

Human culture has given us the illusion that our memories go further back than that. Before
(10) writing was invented, the experience of earlier generations, embodied in stories, myths, and moral precepts to guide behavior, was passed down verbally or, to a lesser extent, in pictures, carvings, and statues. Writing has made more precise and
(15) more extensive the transmission of such information and, in recent times, photography has sharpened our images of the immediate past. Even so, we have difficulty in contemplating steadily the march of history, from the beginnings of
(20) civilization to the present day, in such a way that we can truly experience the slow passage of time. Our minds are not built to deal comfortably with periods as long as hundreds or thousands of years.

Yet when we come to consider the origin of life,
(25) the time scales we must deal with make the whole span of human history seem but the blink of an eyelid. There is no simple way to adjust one's thinking to such vast stretches of time. The immensity of time passed is beyond our ready
(30) comprehension. One can only construct an impression of it from indirect and incomplete descriptions, just as a blind man laboriously builds up, by touch and sound, a picture of his immediate surroundings.

(35) The customary way to provide a convenient framework for one's thoughts is to compare the age of the universe with the length of a single earthly day. Perhaps a better comparison, along the same lines, would be to equate the age of our earth with
(40) a single week. On such a scale the age of the universe, since the Big Bang, would be about two or three weeks. The oldest macroscopic fossils (those from the start of the Cambrian Period*) would have been alive just one day ago. Modern
(45) man would have appeared in the last 10 seconds and agriculture in the last one or two. Odysseus** would have lived only half a second before the present time.

Even this comparison hardly makes the longer
(50) time scale comprehensible to us. Another alternative is to draw a linear map of time, with the different events marked on it. The problem here is to make the line long enough to show our own experience on a reasonable scale, and yet short
(55) enough for convenient reproduction and examination. But perhaps the most vivid method is to compare time to the lines of print themselves. Let us make a 200-page book equal in length to the time from the start of the Cambrian to the present;
(60) that is, about 600 million years. Then each full page will represent roughly three million years, each line about ninety thousand years and each letter or small space about fifteen hundred years. The origin of the earth would be about seven books ago and the
(65) origin of the universe (which has been dated only approximately) ten or so books before that. Almost the whole of recorded human history would be covered by the last two or three letters of the book.

If you now turn back the pages of the book, slowly
(70) reading *one letter at a time*—remember, each letter is fifteen hundred years—then this may convey to you something of the immense stretches of time we shall have to consider. On this scale the span of your own life would be less than the width of a comma.

*Cambrian: the earliest period in the Paleozoic era, beginning about 600 million years ago.
**Odysseus: the most famous Greek hero of antiquity; he is the hero of Homer's *The Odyssey*, which describes the aftermath of the Trojan War (ca. 1200 B.C.).

16 The word *span* in line 6 most nearly means

(A) rate of increase
(B) value
(C) bridge
(D) extent
(E) accuracy

GO ON TO THE NEXT PAGE ➡

17 The phrase *to a lesser extent* in line 13, indicates that, before the invention of writing, the wisdom of earlier generations was

(A) rejected by recent generations when portrayed in pictures, carvings, or statues
(B) passed down orally, or not at all
(C) transmitted more effectively by spoken word than by other means
(D) based on illusory memories that turned fact into fiction
(E) more strongly grounded in science than in the arts

18 The author most likely describes the impact of writing (lines 14–17) in order to

(A) illustrate the limitations of the human memory
(B) provide an example of how cultures transmit information
(C) indicate how primitive preliterate cultures were
(D) refute an opinion about the origin of human civilization
(E) explain the difference between historical facts and myth

19 The word *ready* in line 29 most nearly means

(A) set
(B) agreeable
(C) immediate
(D) apt
(E) willing

20 The analogy of the "blind man" (line 32) is presented primarily to show that

(A) humans are unable to comprehend long periods of time
(B) myths and legends fail to give an accurate picture of the past
(C) human history is only a fraction of the time since life began
(D) humans refuse to learn the lessons of the past
(E) long periods of time can only be understood indirectly

21 In lines 40–44, the author mentions the Big Bang and the Cambrian Period in order to demonstrate which point?

(A) The age of the earth is best understood using the time scale of a week.
(B) Agriculture was a relatively late development in human history.
(C) No fossil record exists before the Cambrian Period.
(D) Convenient time scales do not adequately represent the age of the earth.
(E) The customary framework for thinking about the age of the universe should be discarded permanently.

22 According to lines 52–56, one difficulty of using a linear representation of time is that

(A) linear representations of time do not meet accepted scientific standards of accuracy
(B) prehistoric eras overlap each other, making linear representation deceptive
(C) the more accurate the scale, the more difficult the map is to copy and study
(D) there are too many events to represent on a single line
(E) our knowledge of pre-Cambrian time is insufficient to construct an accurate linear map

23 The author of this passage discusses several kinds of time scales primarily in order to illustrate the

(A) difficulty of assigning precise dates to past events
(B) variety of choices faced by scientists investigating the origin of life
(C) evolution of efforts to comprehend the passage of history
(D) immensity of time since life began on earth
(E) development of the technology of communication

GO ON TO THE NEXT PAGE ➡

Questions 24–30 are based on the following passage.

The following excerpt is from a speech delivered in 1873 by Susan B. Anthony, a leader in the women's rights movement of the 19th century.

Friends and fellow-citizens: I stand before you tonight under indictment for the alleged crime of having voted at the last Presidential election,
Line without having a lawful right to vote. It shall be
(5) my work this evening to prove to you that in thus voting, I not only committed no crime, but, instead, simply exercised my citizen's rights, guaranteed to me and all United States citizens by the National Constitution, beyond the power of
(10) any State to deny.

The preamble of the Federal Constitution says: "We, the people of the United States, in order to form a more perfect union, establish justice, insure domestic tranquillity, provide for the common
(15) defense, promote the general welfare, and secure the blessings of liberty to ourselves and our posterity, do ordain and establish this Constitution for the United States of America."

It was we, the people; not we, the white male
(20) citizens; nor yet we, the male citizens; but we, the whole people, who formed the Union. And we formed it, not to give the blessings of liberty, but to secure them; not to the half of ourselves and the half of our posterity, but to the whole people—
(25) women as well as men. And it is a downright mockery to talk to women of their enjoyment of the blessings of liberty while they are denied the use of the only means of securing them provided by this democratic-republican government—the
(30) ballot.

For any State to make sex a qualification that must ever result in the disfranchisement* of one entire half of the people is a violation of the supreme law of the land. By it the blessings of
(35) liberty are forever withheld from women and their female posterity. To them this government had no just powers derived from the consent of the governed. To them this government is not a democracy. It is not a republic. It is an odious
(40) aristocracy; a hateful oligarchy of sex; this oligarchy of sex, which makes father, brothers, husband, sons, the oligarchs over the mother and sisters, the wife and daughters of every household —which ordains all men sovereigns, all women
(45) subjects, carries dissension, discord and rebellion into every home of the nation.

Webster, Worcester and Bouvier all define a citizen to be a person in the United States, entitled to vote and hold office.

(50) The one question left to be settled now is: Are women persons? And I hardly believe any of our opponents will have the hardihood to say they are not. Being persons, then, women are citizens; and no State has a right to make any law, or to enforce
(55) any old law, that shall abridge their privileges or immunities. Hence, every discrimination against women in the constitutions and laws of the several States is today null and void, precisely as is every one against Negroes.

*disfranchisement: to deprive of the right to vote.

24 In the first paragraph, Anthony states that her action in voting was

(A) illegal, but morally justified
(B) the result of her keen interest in national politics
(C) legal, if the Constitution is interpreted correctly
(D) an illustration of the need for a women's rights movement
(E) illegal, but worthy of leniency

25 Which best captures the meaning of the word *promote* in line 15?

(A) further
(B) organize
(C) publicize
(D) commend
(E) motivate

26 By saying "we, the people . . . the whole people, who formed the Union" (lines 19–21), Anthony means that

(A) the founders of the nation conspired to deprive women of their rights
(B) some male citizens are still being denied basic rights
(C) the role of women in the founding of the nation is generally ignored
(D) society is endangered when women are deprived of basic rights
(E) all people deserve to enjoy the rights guaranteed by the Constitution

27 By "the half of our posterity" (lines 23–24),
    Anthony means

    (A) the political legacy passed down from her era
    (B) future generations of male United States
        citizens
    (C) those who wish to enjoy the blessings of
        liberty
    (D) current and future opponents of the women's
        rights movement
    (E) future members of the democratic-republican
        government

28 In the fifth paragraph, lines 31–46, Anthony's
    argument rests mainly on the strategy of
    convincing her audience that

    (A) any state which denies women the vote
        undermines its status as a democracy
    (B) women deprived of the vote will eventually
        raise a rebellion
    (C) the nation will remain an aristocracy if the
        status of women does not change
    (D) women's rights issues should be debated in
        every home
    (E) even an aristocracy cannot survive without the
        consent of the governed

29 The word *hardihood* in line 52 could best be
    replaced by

    (A) endurance
    (B) vitality
    (C) nerve
    (D) opportunity
    (E) stupidity

30 When Anthony warns that "no State . . . shall
    abridge their privileges" (lines 54–55), she means
    that

    (A) women should be allowed to live a life of
        privilege
    (B) women on trial cannot be forced to give up
        their immunity
    (C) every state should repeal its outdated laws
    (D) governments may not deprive citizens of their
        rights
    (E) the rights granted to women must be decided
        by the people, not the state

**IF YOU FINISH BEFORE TIME IS CALLED, YOU MAY CHECK YOUR WORK ON
THIS SECTION ONLY. DO NOT TURN TO ANY OTHER SECTION IN THE TEST.** **STOP**

Practice Test One—Section 2

Time—30 Minutes

25 Questions

Solve each of the following problems, decide which is the best answer choice, and darken the corresponding oval on the answer sheet. Use available space in the test booklet for scratchwork.*

Notes:

(1) Calculator use is permitted.

(2) All numbers used are real numbers.

(3) Figures are provided for some problems. All figures are drawn to scale and lie in a plane UNLESS otherwise indicated.

Reference Information

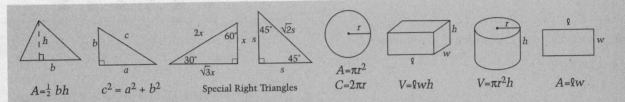

$A=\frac{1}{2}bh$ $c^2 = a^2 + b^2$ Special Right Triangles $A=\pi r^2$ $C=2\pi r$ $V=\ell wh$ $V=\pi r^2 h$ $A=\ell w$

The sum of the degree measures of the angles of a triangle is 180.
The number of degrees of arc in a circle is 360.
A straight angle has a degree measure of 180.

---

1 Which of the following must be equal to 30 percent of x ?

(A) $30x$

(B) $3x$

(C) $\frac{3x}{10}$

(D) $\frac{3x}{100}$

(E) $\frac{3x}{1000}$

2 $(2 \times 10^4) + (5 \times 10^3) + (6 \times 10^2) + (4 \times 10^1) =$

(A)   2,564
(B)   20,564
(C)   25,064
(D)   25,604
(E)   25,640

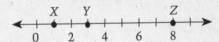

3 On the number line shown above, the length of YZ is how much greater than the length of XY ?

(A) 3
(B) 4
(C) 5
(D) 6
(E) 7

4 If $2^{x+1} = 16$, what is the value of x ?

(A) 2
(B) 3
(C) 4
(D) 5
(E) 6

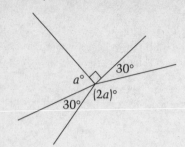

Note: Figure not drawn to scale.

5 In the figure above, what is the value of *a* ?

(A) 50
(B) 55
(C) 60
(D) 65
(E) 70

6 A machine labels 150 bottles in 20 minutes. At this rate, how many minutes does it take to label 60 bottles?

(A) 2
(B) 4
(C) 6
(D) 8
(E) 10

7 If $x - 1$ is a multiple of 3, which of the following must be the next greater multiple of 3?

(A) x
(B) $x + 2$
(C) $x + 3$
(D) $3x$
(E) $3x - 3$

8 When x is divided by 5, the remainder is 4. When x is divided by 9, the remainder is 0. Which of the following is a possible value for x ?

(A) 24
(B) 45
(C) 59
(D) 109
(E) 144

9 In triangle ABC, $AB = 6$, $BC = 12$, and $AC = x$. Which of the following cannot be a value of x ?

(A) 6
(B) 7
(C) 8
(D) 9
(E) 10

10 The average of 20, 70, and x is 40. If the average of 20, 70, x, and y is 50, then $y =$

(A) 100
(B) 80
(C) 70
(D) 60
(E) 30

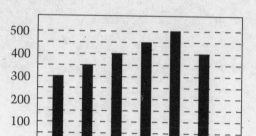

NUMBER OF BOOKS BORROWED
FROM MIDVILLE LIBRARY

11 According to the graph above, the number of books borrowed during the month of January was what fraction of the total number of books borrowed during the first six months of the year?

(A) $\frac{1}{8}$

(B) $\frac{1}{7}$

(C) $\frac{1}{6}$

(D) $\frac{3}{16}$

(E) $\frac{5}{12}$

12 If 40 percent of r is equal to s, then which of the following is equal to 10 percent of r ?

(A) $4s$

(B) $2s$

(C) $\frac{s}{2}$

(D) $\frac{s}{4}$

(E) $\frac{s}{8}$

GO ON TO THE NEXT PAGE ➡

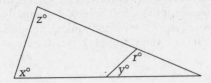

13 In the figure above, which of the following must be true?

(A) $x + r = z + y$
(B) $x + r = z - y$
(C) $x - y = z + r$
(D) $x - r = y - z$
(E) $x + y = z + r$

14 If a *prifact number* is a nonprime integer such that each factor of the integer other than 1 and the integer itself is a prime number, which of the following is a *prifact number*?

(A) 12
(B) 18
(C) 21
(D) 24
(E) 28

15 If $3x + y = 14$, and x and y are positive integers, each of the following could be the value of $x + y$ EXCEPT

(A) 12
(B) 10
(C) 8
(D) 6
(E) 4

16 A certain deck of cards contains r cards. After the cards are distributed evenly among s people, 8 cards are left over. In terms of r and s, how many cards did each person receive?

(A) $\dfrac{s}{8 - r}$

(B) $\dfrac{r - s}{8}$

(C) $\dfrac{r - 8}{s}$

(D) $s - 8r$

(E) $rs - 8$

17 If d is a positive integer, which of the following CANNOT be an integer?

(A) $\dfrac{d}{2}$

(B) $\dfrac{\sqrt{d}}{2}$

(C) $2d$

(D) $d\sqrt{2}$

(E) $d + 2$

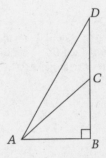

18 In the figure above, the area of triangle ABC is 6. If $BC = CD$, what is the area of triangle ACD ?

(A)   6
(B)   8
(C)   9
(D)   10
(E)   12

19 The ratio of x to y to z is 3 to 6 to 8. If $y = 24$, what is the value of $x + z$?

(A) 11
(B) 33
(C) 44
(D) 66
(E) 88

20 What is the minimum number of rectangular tiles, each 12 centimeters by 18 centimeters, needed to completely cover five flat rectangular surfaces, each 60 centimeters by 180 centimeters?

(A) 50
(B) 100
(C) 150
(D) 200
(E) 250

GO ON TO THE NEXT PAGE ➡

21 If $x + y = 11$, $y + z = 14$, and $x + z = 13$, what is the value of $x + y + z$?

(A) 16
(B) 17
(C) 18
(D) 19
(E) 20

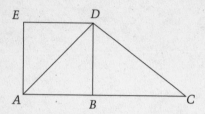

22 In the figure above, side AB of square $ABDE$ is extended to point C. If $BC = 8$ and $CD = 10$, what is the perimeter of triangle ACD ?

(A) $18 + 6\sqrt{2}$
(B) $24 + 6\sqrt{2}$
(C) $26 + 6\sqrt{2}$
(D) 30
(E) 36

23 If $r < 0$ and $(4r - 4)^2 = 36$, what is the value of r ?

(A) -2

(B) -1

(C) $-\frac{1}{2}$

(D) $-\frac{1}{4}$

(E) $-\frac{1}{8}$

24 Five liters of water were poured from tank A into tank B, and 10 liters of water were then poured from tank A into tank C. If tank A originally had 10 more liters of water than tank C, how many more liters of water does tank C now have than tank A ?

(A) 0
(B) 5
(C) 10
(D) 15
(E) 20

25 If a cube has a surface area of $36n^2$ square feet, what is its volume in cubic feet, in terms of n ?

(A) $n^3\sqrt{6}$

(B) $6n^3\sqrt{6}$

(C) $36n^3$

(D) $36n^3\sqrt{6}$

(E) $216n^3$

IF YOU FINISH BEFORE TIME IS CALLED, YOU MAY CHECK YOUR WORK ON THIS SECTION ONLY. DO NOT TURN TO ANY OTHER SECTION IN THE TEST.

STOP

Time—30 Minutes
35 Questions

For each of the following questions, choose the best answer and darken the corresponding oval on the answer sheet.

Select the lettered word or set of words that best completes the sentence.

Example:

Today's small, portable computers contrast markedly with the earliest electronic computers, which were ----.

(A) effective
(B) invented
(C) useful
(D) destructive
(E) enormous

1   The rain is so rare and the land is so ---- that few of the men who work there see much ---- in farming.

(A) plentiful . . hope
(B) barren . . difficulty
(C) productive . . profit
(D) infertile . . future
(E) dry . . danger

2   The principal declared that the students were not simply ignoring the rules, but openly ---- them.

(A) accepting
(B) redressing
(C) reviewing
(D) flouting
(E) discussing

3   Some critics believe that the ---- of modern art came with dadaism, while others insist that the movement was a ----.

(A) zenith . . sham
(B) pinnacle . . triumph
(C) decline . . disaster
(D) acceptance . . success
(E) originality . . fiasco

4   She would never have believed that her article was so ---- were it not for the ---- of correspondence that followed its publication.

(A) interesting . . dearth
(B) inflammatory . . lack
(C) controversial . . spate
(D) commonplace . . influx
(E) insignificant . . volume

5   The writings of the philosopher Descartes are ----; many readers have difficulty following his complex, intricately woven arguments.

(A) generic
(B) trenchant
(C) reflective
(D) elongated
(E) abstruse

6   The prisoner was ---- even though he presented evidence clearly proving that he was nowhere near the scene of the crime.

(A) abandoned
(B) indicted
(C) exculpated
(D) exhumed
(E) rescinded

7   Many biologists are critical of the film's ---- premise that dinosaurs might one day return.

(A) scientific
(B) tacit
(C) speculative
(D) unwitting
(E) ambiguous

8   Mozart composed music with exceptional ----; he left no rough drafts because he was able to write out his compositions in ---- form.

(A) audacity . . original
(B) facility . . finished
(C) incompetence . . ideal
(D) prestige . . orchestral
(E) independence . . concise

9   Known for their devotion, dogs were often used as symbols of ---- in Medieval and Renaissance art.

(A) resistance
(B) benevolence
(C) generosity
(D) fidelity
(E) antagonism

10 It is ---- that a people so capable of treachery and brutality should also exhibit such a tremendous capacity for heroism.

(A) unfortunate
(B) explicable
(C) paradoxical
(D) distressing
(E) appalling

GO ON TO THE NEXT PAGE ➡

Choose the lettered pair of words that is related in the same way as the pair in capital letters.

Example:

FLAKE : SNOW ::

(A) storm : hail
(B) drop : rain
(C) field : wheat
(D) stack : hay
(E) cloud : fog

11 CHARLATAN : SCRUPULOUS ::

(A) confidant : virtuous
(B) laborer : stalwart
(C) officer : mutinous
(D) dullard : irritable
(E) tyrant : just

12 GREED : ACQUIRE ::

(A) fear : disguise
(B) inertia : persuade
(C) gluttony : eat
(D) conformity : agree
(E) ignorance : speak

13 PARRY : BLOW ::

(A) counter : argument
(B) sidestep : offense
(C) defer : ruling
(D) stumble : pitfall
(E) shine : light

14 MALIGN : SLURS ::

(A) satisfy : treaties
(B) persecute : complaints
(C) torment : whispers
(D) court : debates
(E) flatter : compliments

15 LENTIL : LEGUME ::

(A) rice : cereal
(B) nutrition : food
(C) horseshoe : pony
(D) husk : corn
(E) baker : cake

16 INDULGE : APPETITE ::

(A) filter : impurity
(B) infuriate : anger
(C) coddle : emotion
(D) humor : whim
(E) liberate : freedom

17 MELLIFLUOUS : SOUND ::

(A) musical : entertainment
(B) fragrant : smell
(C) pale : color
(D) raucous : discussion
(E) auspicious : occasion

18 GUFFAW : LAUGH ::

(A) sniffle : sneeze
(B) whoop : cough
(C) yell : talk
(D) snore : sleep
(E) chuckle : sigh

19 CELESTIAL : HEAVENS ::

(A) planetary : orbit
(B) scientific : experiment
(C) nautical : ships
(D) solar : heat
(E) viscous : matter

20 ENERVATE : VITALITY ::

(A) consolidate : power
(B) energize : action
(C) daunt : courage
(D) estimate : worth
(E) admit : guilt

21 OLIGARCHY : FEW ::

(A) government : majority
(B) authority : consent
(C) constitution : country
(D) monarchy : one
(E) discrimination : minority

22 UNTRUTHFUL : MENDACIOUSNESS ::

(A) circumspect : caution
(B) timid : behavior
(C) agile : physique
(D) sensitive : patient
(E) trusting : honesty

23 INEXCUSABLE : JUSTIFY ::

(A) isolated : abandon
(B) unassailable : attack
(C) affable : like
(D) famous : admire
(E) splendid : revere

GO ON TO THE NEXT PAGE ➡

Answer the questions below based on the information in the accompanying passages.

Questions 24–35 are based on the following passage.

In the following passage, a 19th-century American writer recalls his boyhood in a small town along the Mississippi River.

My father was a justice of the peace, and I supposed he possessed the power of life and death over all men and could hang anybody that offended
Line him. This was distinction enough for me as a
(5) general thing; but the desire to be a steamboatman kept intruding, nevertheless. I first wanted to be a cabin boy, so that I could come out with a white apron on and shake a tablecloth over the side, where all my old comrades could see me. Later I
(10) thought I would rather be the deck hand who stood on the end of the stage plank with a coil of rope in his hand, because he was particularly conspicuous.

But these were only daydreams—too heavenly to be contemplated as real possibilities. By and by
(15) one of the boys went away. He was not heard of for a long time. At last he turned up as an apprentice engineer or "striker" on a steamboat. This thing shook the bottom out of all my Sunday-school teachings. That boy had been notoriously worldly
(20) and I had been just the reverse—yet he was exalted to this eminence, and I was left in obscurity and misery. There was nothing generous about this fellow in his greatness. He would always manage to have a rusty bolt to scrub while
(25) his boat was docked at our town, and he would sit on the inside guard and scrub it, where we could all see him and envy him and loathe him.

He used all sorts of steamboat technicalities in his talk, as if he were so used to them that he forgot
(30) common people could not understand them. He would speak of the "labboard" side of a horse in an easy, natural way that would make you wish he was dead. And he was always talking about "St. Looy" like an old citizen. Two or three of the boys had long
(35) been persons of consideration among us because they had been to St. Louis once and had a vague general knowledge of its wonders, but the day of their glory was over now. They lapsed into a humble silence, and learned to disappear when the
(40) ruthless "cub" engineer approached. This fellow had money, too, and hair oil, and he wore a showy brass watch chain, a leather belt, and used no suspenders. No girl could withstand his charms. He "cut out" every boy in the village. When his boat blew up at
(45) last, it diffused a tranquil contentment among us such as we had not known for months. But when he came home the next week, alive, renowned, and appeared in church all battered up and bandaged, a shining hero, stared at and wondered over by
(50) everybody, it seemed to us that the partiality of Providence for an undeserving reptile had reached a point where it was open to criticism.

This creature's career could produce but one result, and it speedily followed. Boy after boy
(55) managed to get on the river. Four sons of the chief merchant, and two sons of the county judge became pilots, the grandest position of all. But some of us could not get on the river—at least our parents would not let us.

(60) So by and by I ran away. I said I would never come home again till I was a pilot and could return in glory. But somehow I could not manage it. I went meekly aboard a few of the boats that lay packed together like sardines at the long St. Louis
(65) wharf, and very humbly inquired for the pilots, but got only a cold shoulder and short words from mates and clerks. I had to make the best of this sort of treatment for the time being, but I had comforting daydreams of a future when I should be a great and
(70) honored pilot, with plenty of money, and could kill some of these mates and clerks and pay for them.

24 The author makes the statement that "I supposed he . . . offended him" (lines 1–4) primarily to suggest the

(A) power held by a justice of the peace in a frontier town
(B) naive view that he held of his father's importance
(C) respect in which the townspeople held his father
(D) possibility of miscarriages of justice on the American frontier
(E) harsh environment in which he was brought up

25 As used in line 4, the word *distinction* most nearly means

(A) difference
(B) variation
(C) prestige
(D) desperation
(E) clarity

26 The author decides that he would rather become a deck hand than a cabin boy (lines 6–12) because

(A) the job offers higher wages
(B) he believes that the work is easier
(C) he wants to avoid seeing his older friends
(D) deck hands often go on to become pilots
(E) the job is more visible to passersby

GO ON TO THE NEXT PAGE ➡

27 The author most likely mentions his "Sunday-school teachings" in lines 18–19 in order to emphasize

(A) the influence of his early education in later life
(B) his sense of injustice at the engineer's success
(C) his disillusionment with longstanding religious beliefs
(D) his determination to become an engineer at all costs
(E) the unscrupulous nature of the engineer's character

28 The author most likely concludes that the engineer is not "generous" (line 22) because he

(A) has no respect for religious beliefs
(B) refuses to share his wages with friends
(C) flaunts his new position in public
(D) takes a pride in material possessions
(E) ignores the disappointment of other people's ambitions

29 The author most probably mentions the use of "steamboat technicalities" (lines 28–30) in order to emphasize the engineer's

(A) expertise after a few months on the job
(B) fascination for trivial information
(C) ignorance on most other subjects
(D) desire to appear sophisticated
(E) inability to communicate effectively

30 The word consideration in line 35 most nearly means

(A) generosity
(B) deliberation
(C) contemplation
(D) unselfishness
(E) reputation

31 According to the passage, the "glory" of having visited St. Louis (lines 36–38) was over because

(A) the boys' knowledge of St. Louis was much less detailed than the engineer's
(B) St. Louis had changed so much that the boys' stories were no longer accurate
(C) the boys realized that traveling to St. Louis was not a mark of sophistication
(D) the engineer's account revealed that the boys' stories were lies
(E) travel to St. Louis had become too commonplace to be envied

32 The author describes the engineer's appearance (lines 41–42) primarily in order to

(A) suggest one reason why many people found the engineer impressive
(B) convey the way steamboatmen typically dressed
(C) emphasize the inadequacy of his own wardrobe
(D) contrast the engineer's behavior with his appearance
(E) indicate his admiration for fashionable clothes

33 In lines 50–52, the author's response to the engineer's survival is one of

(A) thankfulness for what he believes is God's providence
(B) astonishment at the engineer's miraculous escape
(C) reflection on the occupational hazards of a steamboating career
(D) outrage at his rival's undeserved good fortune
(E) sympathy for the extent of the engineer's wounds

34 The major purpose of the passage is to

(A) sketch the peaceful life of a frontier town
(B) relate the events that led to a boy's first success in life
(C) portray the unsophisticated ambitions of a boy
(D) describe the characteristics of a small-town boaster
(E) give a humorous portrayal of a boy's conflicts with his parents

35 At the end of the passage, the author reflects on

(A) his new ambition to become either a mate or a clerk
(B) the wisdom of seeking a job in which advancement is easier
(C) the prospect of abandoning a hopeless search for fame
(D) the impossibility of returning home and asking his parents' pardon
(E) his determination to keep striving for success in a glorious career

IF YOU FINISH BEFORE TIME IS CALLED, YOU MAY CHECK YOUR WORK ON THIS SECTION ONLY. DO NOT TURN TO ANY OTHER SECTION IN THE TEST. **STOP**

Time—30 Minutes
25 Questions

Solve each of the following problems, decide which is the best answer choice, and darken the corresponding oval on the answer sheet. Use available space in the test booklet for scratchwork.*

Notes:

(1)   Calculator use is permitted.

(2).   All numbers used are real numbers.

(3)   Figures are provided for some problems. All figures are drawn to scale and lie in a plane UNLESS otherwise indicated.

Reference Information

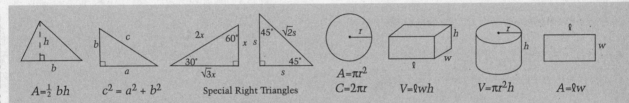

$A=\frac{1}{2}bh$ $c^2 = a^2 + b^2$ Special Right Triangles $A=\pi r^2$
$C=2\pi r$ $V=\ell wh$ $V=\pi r^2 h$ $A=\ell w$

The sum of the degree measures of the angles of a triangle is 180.
The number of degrees of arc in a circle is 360.
A straight angle has a degree measure of 180.

DIRECTIONS FOR QUANTITATIVE COMPARISON QUESTIONS

Compare the boxed quantity in Column A with the boxed quantity in Column B. Select answer choice

  A   if Column A is greater;
  B   if Column B is greater;
  C   if the columns are equal; or
  D   if more information is needed to determine the relationship.

An E response will be treated as an omission.

Notes:

1.   Some questions include information about one or both quantities. That information is centered and unboxed.
2.   A symbol that appears in both Column A and Column B stands for the same thing in both columns.
3.   All numbers used are real numbers.

EXAMPLES

	Column A	Column B	Answers
E1	3×4	$3 + 4$	● Ⓑ Ⓒ Ⓓ Ⓔ
E2	x	160	Ⓐ Ⓑ ● Ⓓ Ⓔ
E3	$x + 1$	$y - 1$	Ⓐ Ⓑ Ⓒ ● Ⓔ

(E2: figure with angles $x°$ and $20°$ on a line)

(E3: x and y are positive)

GO ON TO THE NEXT PAGE ➡

*The directions on the actual SAT will vary slightly.

Column A	Column B

1 $\frac{3}{8} + \frac{2}{5}$ | 1

2 The cost of six pens at two for 22 cents | The cost of five pens at 22 cents each

$$2a + b = 17$$
$$b - 3 = 2$$

3 a | b

4 $x - 2(y + z)$ | $x - 2y - 2z$

a, b, and c are positive integers such that $a + b + c = 150$.

5 The mean of a, b, and c | The median of a, b, and c

For all numbers x and y, let $x \circledast y = (x + y)^3$.

6 $4 \circledast 5$ | $0 \circledast 9$

Column A	Column B

7 The circumference of circle O | 30

Jimmy owns a plant he waters every other day.

8 The number of times Jimmy waters the plant during a certain week | The number of times Jimmy waters the plant during the following week

A certain line in the rectangular coordinate plane contains the points $(1, 1)$, $(3, r)$, $(s, 9)$, and $(6, 11)$.

9 r | s

$$r^2 + 4 = 21$$

10 r | 4

GO ON TO THE NEXT PAGE ➡

KAPLAN

Column A	Column B	Column A	Column B

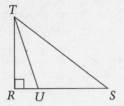

In right triangle *RST*,
RT = *US* = 6 and *RU* < 2.

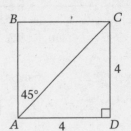

Note: Figure not drawn to scale.

11

The perimeter of *RST*	24

14

The length of *AB*	4

At a science fair, five students are semifinalists for first- and second-place prizes.

t is a positive integer.

12

The total number of ways to select the two science fair prize winners	10

15

The number of distinct prime factors of 2*t*	The number of distinct prime factors of 8*t*

$$x > 0$$
$$0 < x^2 < 1$$

13

$1 - x^2$	$1 - x$

GO ON TO THE NEXT PAGE ➡

DIRECTIONS FOR STUDENT-PRODUCED RESPONSE QUESTIONS

For each of the questions below (16–25), solve the problem and indicate your answer by darkening the ovals in the special grid. For example:

Answer: 1.25 or $\frac{5}{4}$ or 5/4

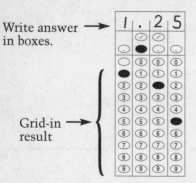

Write answer in boxes.

Grid-in result

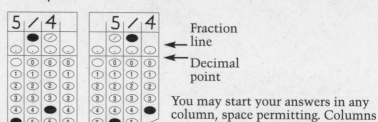

Fraction line

Decimal point

You may start your answers in any column, space permitting. Columns not needed should be left blank.

Either position is correct.

- It is recommended, though not required, that you write your answer in the boxes at the top of the columns. However, you will receive credit only for darkening the ovals correctly.

- Grid only one answer to a question, even though some problems have more than one correct answer.

- Darken no more than one oval in a column.

- No answers are negative.

- Mixed numbers cannot be gridded. For example: the number $1\frac{1}{4}$ must be gridded as 1.25 or 5/4.

(If $1\,1\,/\,4$ is gridded, it will be interpreted as $\frac{11}{4}$, not $1\frac{1}{4}$.)

- Decimal Accuracy: Decimal answers must be entered as accurately as possible. For example, if you obtain an answer such as 0.1666..., you should record the result as .166 or .167. **Less accurate values such as .16 or .17 are not acceptable.**

Acceptable ways to grid $\frac{1}{6}$ = .1666...

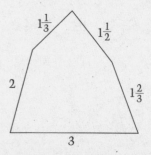

16 If $A = 2.54$ and $20B = A$, what is the value of B ?

17 What is the perimeter of the figure shown above?

GO ON TO THE NEXT PAGE ➡

18 If $\frac{h}{3}$ and $\frac{h}{4}$ are integers, and if $75 < h < 100$, what is one possible value of h ?

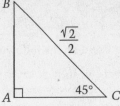

19 A retailer buys 16 shirts at \$4.50 each, and she sells all 16 shirts for \$6.75 each. If the retailer purchases more of these shirts at \$4.50 each, what is the greatest number of these shirts that she can buy with the profit she made on the 16 shirts?

23 What is the area of $\triangle ABC$ shown above?

24 If x is a factor of 8,100 and if x is an odd integer, what is the greatest possible value of x ?

20 Lines ℓ and m intersect at a point to form four angles. If one of the angles formed is 15 times as large as an adjacent angle, what is the measure, in degrees, of the smaller angle?

25 In a certain class, $\frac{1}{2}$ of the male students and $\frac{2}{3}$ of the female students speak French. If there are $\frac{3}{4}$ as many girls as boys in the class, what fraction of the entire class speaks French?

21 If $x = -4$ when $x^2 + 2xr + r^2 = 0$, what is the value of r ?

22 Let $n\ast = n^2 - n$ for all positive numbers n.

What is the value of $\frac{1}{4}\ast - \frac{1}{2}\ast$?

IF YOU FINISH BEFORE TIME IS CALLED, YOU MAY CHECK YOUR WORK ON THIS SECTION ONLY. DO NOT TURN TO ANY OTHER SECTION IN THE TEST.

STOP

KAPLAN   229

Time—15 Minutes
13 Questions Answer the questions below based on the information in the accompanying passages.

Questions 1–13 are based on the following passages.

The controversy over the authorship of Shakespeare's plays began in the 18th century and continues to this day. Here, the author of Passage 1 embraces the proposal that Francis Bacon actually wrote the plays, while the author of Passage 2 defends the traditional attribution to Shakespeare himself.

Passage 1

Anyone with more than a superficial knowledge of Shakespeare's plays must necessarily entertain some doubt concerning their true authorship. Can
Line (5) scholars honestly accept the idea that such masterworks were written by a shadowy actor with limited formal education and a social position that can most charitably be called "humble"? Obviously, the author of the plays must have traveled widely,
(10) yet there is no record that Shakespeare ever left his native England. Even more obviously, the real author had to have intimate knowledge of life within royal courts and palaces, yet Shakespeare was a commoner, with little firsthand experience of the aristocracy. No, common sense tells us that the
(15) plays must have been written by someone with substantial expertise in the law, the sciences, classics, foreign languages, and the fine arts— someone, in other words, like Shakespeare's eminent contemporary, Sir Francis Bacon.
(20) The first person to suggest that Bacon was the actual author of the plays was Reverend James Wilmot. Writing in 1785, Wilmot argued that someone of Shakespeare's educational background could hardly have produced works of such erudition
(25) and insight. But a figure like Bacon, a scientist and polymath* of legendary stature, would certainly have known about, for instance, the circulation of the blood as alluded to in *Coriolanus*. And as an aristocrat, Bacon would have possessed the
(30) familiarity with court life required to produce a *Love's Labour's Lost*.
Delia Bacon (no relation to Sir Francis) was next to make the case for Francis Bacon's authorship. In 1856, in collaboration with Nathaniel Hawthorne,
(35) she insisted that it was ridiculous to look for the creator of Hamlet among "that dirty, doggish group of players, who come into the scene [of the play Hamlet] summoned like a pack of hounds to his service." Ultimately, she concluded that the plays
(40) were actually composed by a committee consisting of Bacon, Edmund Spenser, Walter Raleigh, and several others.
Still, some might wonder why Bacon, if indeed the plays were wholly or partly his work, would

(45) not put his own name on them. But consider the political climate of England in Elizabethan times. Given that it would have been politically and personally damaging for a man of Bacon's position to associate himself with such controversial plays,
(50) it is quite understandable that Bacon would hire a lowly actor to take the credit—and the consequences.
But perhaps the most convincing evidence of all comes from the postscript of a 1624 letter sent to
(55) Bacon by Sir Tobie Matthew. "The most prodigious wit that I ever knew . . . is your lordship's name," Matthew wrote, "though he be known by another." That name, of course, was William Shakespeare.

*polymath—a person of wide and varied learning

Passage 2

Over the years, there have been an astonishing
(60) number of persons put forth as the "true author" of Shakespeare's plays. Some critics have even gone so far as to claim that only a "committee" could have possessed the abundance of talent and energy necessary to produce Shakespeare's thirty-seven
(65) plays. Among the individual figures most seriously promoted as "the real Shakespeare" is Sir Francis Bacon. Apparently, the fact that Bacon wrote most of his own work in academic Latin does nothing to deter those who would crown him the premier
(70) stylist in the English language.
Although the entire controversy reeks of scholarly gamesplaying, the issue underlying it is worth considering: how could an uneducated actor create such exquisite works? But the answer to that
(75) is easy. Shakespeare's dramatic gifts had little to do with encyclopedic knowledge, complex ideas, or a fluency with great systems of thought. Rather, Shakespeare's genius was one of common sense and perceptive intuition—a genius that grows not out of
(80) book-learning, but out of a deep understanding of human nature and a keen grasp of basic emotions, passions, and jealousies.
One of the most common arguments advanced by skeptics is that the degree of familiarity with the
(85) law exhibited in a *Hamlet* or a *Merchant of Venice* can only have been achieved by a lawyer or other man of affairs. The grasp of law evidenced in these plays, however, is not a detailed knowledge of formal law, but a more general understanding of so-
(90) called "country law." Shakespeare was a landowner —an extraordinary achievement in itself for an ill-paid Elizabethan actor—and so would have been

GO ON TO THE NEXT PAGE ➡

knowledgeable about legal matters related to the buying, selling, and renting of real estate. Evidence (95) of such a common understanding of land regulations can be found, for instance, in the gravedigging scene of *Hamlet*.

So no elaborate theories of intrigue and secret identity are necessary to explain the (100) accomplishment of William Shakespeare. Scholars who have made a career of ferreting out "alternative bards" may be reluctant to admit it, but literary genius can flower in any socioeconomic bracket. Shakespeare, in short, was Shakespeare—an (105) observation that one would have thought was obvious to everyone.

1 In line 2, *entertain* most nearly means

(A) amuse
(B) harbor
(C) occupy
(D) cherish
(E) engage

2 In Passage 1, the author draws attention to Shakespeare's social standing as a "commoner" (line 13) in order to cast doubt on the Elizabethan actor's

(A) aptitude for writing poetically
(B) knowledge of foreign places and habits
(C) ability to support himself by playwriting
(D) familiarity with life among persons of high rank
(E) understanding of the problems of government

3 *Coriolanus* and *Love's Labour's Lost* are mentioned in lines 28–31 as examples of works that

(A) only Francis Bacon could have written
(B) exhibit a deep understanding of human nature
(C) resemble works written by Francis Bacon under his own name
(D) portray a broad spectrum of Elizabethan society
(E) reveal expertise more likely held by Bacon than Shakespeare

4 In Passage 1, the quotation from Delia Bacon (lines 36–39) conveys a sense of

(A) disdain for the disreputable vulgarity of Elizabethan actors
(B) resentment at the way Shakespeare's characters were portrayed
(C) regret that conditions for Elizabethan actors were not better
(D) doubt that Shakespeare could actually have created such unsavory characters
(E) disappointment at the incompetence of Elizabethan actors

5 The author of Passage 1 maintains that Bacon did not put his own name on the plays attributed to Shakespeare because he

(A) regarded writing as an unsuitable occupation for an aristocrat
(B) wished to protect himself from the effects of controversy
(C) preferred being known as a scientist and politician rather than as a writer
(D) did not want to associate himself with lowly actors
(E) sought to avoid the attention that fame brings

6 In the first paragraph of Passage 2, the author calls into question Bacon's likely ability to

(A) write in a language with which he was unfamiliar
(B) make the transition between scientific writing and playwriting
(C) produce the poetic language evident in the plays
(D) cooperate with other members of a committee
(E) single-handedly create thirty-seven plays

7 The word *premier* in line 69 most nearly means

(A) earliest
(B) influential
(C) inaugural
(D) greatest
(E) original

GO ON TO THE NEXT PAGE ➡

8 In line 76, the word *encyclopedic* most nearly means

(A) technical
(B) comprehensive
(C) abridged
(D) disciplined
(E) specialized

9 The author of Passage 2 cites Shakespeare's status as a landowner in order to

(A) prove that Shakespeare was a success as a playwright
(B) refute the claim that Shakespeare had little knowledge of aristocratic life
(C) prove that Shakespeare didn't depend solely on acting for his living
(D) dispute the notion that Shakespeare was a commoner
(E) account for Shakespeare's apparent knowledge of the law

10 In lines 100–103, the author maintains that literary genius

(A) is not dependent on a writer's external circumstances
(B) must be based on an inborn comprehension of human nature
(C) is enhanced by the suffering that poverty brings
(D) frequently goes unrecognized among those of modest means and position
(E) can be stifled by too much book-learning and academic training

11 The author of Passage 2 would probably respond to the speculation in the fourth paragraph of Passage 1 by pointing out that

(A) Shakespeare's plays would not have seemed particularly controversial to Elizabethan audiences
(B) The extent and range of Bacon's learning has been generally exaggerated
(C) such scenarios are farfetched and unnecessary if one correctly understands Shakespeare's genius
(D) Bacon would not have had the knowledge of the lower classes required to produce the plays
(E) the claim implies that Shakespeare was disreputable when in fact he was a respectable landowner

12 The author of Passage 1 would probably respond to the skepticism expressed in lines 67–70 by making which of the following statements?

(A) The similarities between English and Latin make it plausible that one person could write well in both languages.
(B) Plays written in Latin would not have been likely to attract a wide audience in Elizabethan England.
(C) The premier stylist in the English language is more likely to have been an eminent scholar than an uneducated actor.
(D) Writing the plays in Latin would have shielded Bacon from much of the political damage he wanted to avoid.
(E) The style of the plays is notable mostly for the clarity of thought behind the lines rather than their musicality or beauty.

13 In line 105, "observation" most nearly means

(A) inspection
(B) measurement
(C) research
(D) comment
(E) memorandum

IF YOU FINISH BEFORE TIME IS CALLED, YOU MAY CHECK YOUR WORK ON THIS SECTION ONLY. DO NOT TURN TO ANY OTHER SECTION IN THE TEST. **STOP**

Time—15 Minutes

10 Questions

Solve each of the following problems, decide which is the best answer choice, and darken the corresponding oval on the answer sheet. Use available space in the test booklet for scratchwork.

Notes:

(1) Calculator use is permitted.

(2) All numbers used are real numbers.

(3) Figures are provided for some problems. All figures are drawn to scale and lie in a plane UNLESS otherwise indicated.

Reference Information

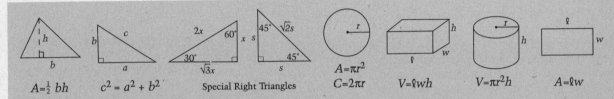

$A = \frac{1}{2}bh$ $c^2 = a^2 + b^2$ Special Right Triangles $A = \pi r^2$ $C = 2\pi r$ $V = \ell wh$ $V = \pi r^2 h$ $A = \ell w$

The sum of the degree measures of the angles of a triangle is 180.
The number of degrees of arc in a circle is 360.
A straight angle has a degree measure of 180.

---

1 If $p = -2$ and $q = 3$, then $p^3 q^2 + p^2 q =$

(A) −84
(B) −60
(C) 36
(D) 60
(E) 84

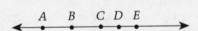

Note: Figure not drawn to scale.

2 In the figure above, B is the midpoint of AC and D is the midpoint of CE. If $AB = 5$ and $BD = 8$, what is the length of DE ?

(A) 8
(B) 6
(C) 5
(D) 4
(E) 3

N	P
2	7
4	13
6	19
8	25

3 Which of the following equations describes the relationship of each pair of numbers (N, P) in the table above?

(A) $P = N + 5$
(B) $P = 2N + 3$
(C) $P = 2N + 5$
(D) $P = 3N + 1$
(E) $P = 3N - 1$

GO ON TO THE NEXT PAGE ➡

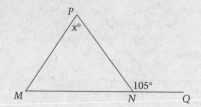

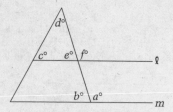

Note: Figure not drawn to scale.

4   In the figure above, *MQ* is a straight line. If
     PM = *PN*, what is the value of *x* ?

(A) 30
(B) 45
(C) 60
(D) 75
(E) 90

5   Marty has exactly five blue pens, six black pens,
     and four red pens in his knapsack. If he pulls out
     one pen at random from his knapsack, what is the
     probability that the pen is either red or black?

(A) $\frac{11}{15}$

(B) $\frac{2}{3}$

(C) $\frac{1}{2}$

(D) $\frac{1}{3}$

(E) $\frac{1}{5}$

6   Two hot dogs and a soda cost $3.25. If three hot
     dogs and a soda cost $4.50, what is the cost of two
     sodas?

(A) $0.75
(B) $1.25
(C) $1.50
(D) $2.50
(E) $3.00

7   In the figure above, if $\ell \parallel m$, which of the
     following must be equal to *a* ?

(A) $b + c$
(B) $b + e$
(C) $c + d$
(D) $d + e$
(E) $d + f$

8   A certain phone call costs 75 cents for the first
     three minutes plus 15 cents for each additional
     minute. If the call lasted *x* minutes and *x* is an
     integer greater than 3, which of the following
     expresses the cost of the call, in dollars?

(A) $0.75(3) + 0.15x$
(B) $0.75(3) + 0.15(x + 3)$
(C) $0.75 + 0.15(3 - x)$
(D) $0.75 + 0.15(x - 3)$
(E) $0.75 + 0.15x$

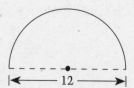

9   The figure above shows a piece of wire in the
     shape of a semicircle. If the piece of wire is bent to
     form a circle without any of the wire overlapping,
     what is the area of the circle?

(A) 6π
(B) 9π
(C) 12π
(D) 18π
(E) 36π

10   If $a^2 - a = 72$, and *b* and *n* are integers such that
     $b^n = a$, which of the following cannot be a value
     for *b* ?

(A) -8
(B) -2
(C)   2
(D)   3
(E)   9

**IF YOU FINISH BEFORE TIME IS CALLED, YOU MAY CHECK YOUR WORK ON
THIS SECTION ONLY. DO NOT TURN TO ANY OTHER SECTION IN THE TEST.**   **STOP**

ANSWER KEY ON FOLLOWING PAGE ➡

Answer Key

Section 1	Section 2	Section 3	Section 4	Section 5	Section 6
1. E	1. C	1. D	1. B	1. B	1. B
2. C	2. E	2. D	2. B	2. D	2. E
3. B	3. A	3. A	3. A	3. E	3. D
4. B	4. B	4. C	4. C	4. A	4. A
5. B	5. E	5. E	5. D	5. B	5. B
6. E	6. D	6. B	6. C	6. C	6. C
7. C	7. B	7. C	7. A	7. D	7. C
8. E	8. E	8. B	8. D	8. B	8. D
9. D	9. A	9. D	9. C	9. E	9. B
10. B	10. B	10. C	10. D	10. A	10. C
11. A	11. A	11. E	11. B	11. C	
12. A	12. D	12. C	12. A	12. C	
13. B	13. D	13. A	13. A	13. D	
14. C	14. C	14. E	14. D		
15. D	15. E	15. A	15. C		
16. D	16. C	16. D	16. .127		
17. C	17. D	17. B	17. 9.5 or 19/2		
18. B	18. A	18. C	18. 84 or 96		
19. C	19. C	19. C	19. 8		
20. E	20. E	20. C	20. 45/4, 11.2, or 11.3		
21. A	21. D	21. D	21. 4		
22. C	22. B	22. A	22. 1/16, .062, or .063		
23. D	23. C	23. B	23. 1/8 or .125		
24. C	24. D	24. B	24. 2025		
25. A	25. B	25. C	25. 4/7 or .571		
26. E		26. E			
27. B		27. B			
28. A		28. C			
29. C		29. D			
30. D		30. E			
		31. A			
		32. A			
		33. D			
		34. C			
		35. E			

KAPLAN

Compute Your Raw Score

First, check your answers against the answer key on the previous page, and count up the number right and the number wrong for each section (there are boxes on your answer sheet to record these numbers). Remember not to count omissions as wrong.

Then figure out your raw scores using the table below. The Verbal raw score is equal to the total right in the three Verbal sections minus one-fourth of the number wrong in those sections. The Math raw score is equal to the total right in the three Math sections minus one-fourth of the number wrong in the two Regular Math sections and minus one-third the number wrong in the QCs. (Remember: There is no deduction for wrong answers in the Grid-ins.) Round each raw score to the nearest whole number.

Finally, use the tables on the next page to convert each raw score to a range of scaled scores.

	NUMBER RIGHT		NUMBER WRONG	RAW SCORE
SECTION 1:	☐	−[.25 x	☐]	= ☐
SECTION 3:	☐	−[.25 x	☐]	= ☐
SECTION 5:	☐	−[.25 x	☐]	= ☐
			VERBAL RAW SCORE:	☐ (ROUNDED)
SECTION 4A: (Questions 1 to 15)	☐	−[.33 x	☐]	= ☐
SECTION 4B: (Questions 16 to 25)	☐	(No wrong-answer penalty)		= ☐
SECTION 2:	☐	−[.25 x	☐]	= ☐
SECTION 6:	☐	−[.25 x	☐]	= ☐
			MATH RAW SCORE:	☐ (ROUNDED)

Convert Your Score

Verbal

Raw	Scaled	Raw	Scaled	Raw	Scaled
−3 or		22	450	48	620
less	200	23	460	49	630
−2	230	24	470	50	640
−1	270	25	470	51	640
0	290	26	480	52	650
1	300	27	490	53	660
2	310	28	490	54	670
3	320	29	500	55	670
4	330	30	510	56	670
5	330	31	510	57	680
6	340	32	520	58	690
7	350	33	530	59	690
8	360	34	530	60	700
9	370	35	540	61	710
10	370	36	550	62	720
11	380	37	550	63	730
12	390	38	560	64	730
13	390	39	570	65	740
14	400	40	570	66	750
15	410	41	580	67	760
16	410	42	590	68	770
17	420	43	590	69	780
18	430	44	600	70	790
19	430	45	600	71 or	
20	440	46	610	more	800
21	450	47	610		

Math

Raw	Scaled	Raw	Scaled	Raw	Scaled
−1 or		19	440	40	600
less	200	20	450	41	610
0	220	21	460	42	620
1	240	22	470	43	630
2	260	23	480	44	640
3	280	24	480	45	650
4	300	25	490	46	650
5	310	26	500	47	660
6	330	27	510	48	670
7	340	28	520	49	680
8	350	29	520	50	690
9	360	30	530	51	700
10	370	31	530	52	720
11	380	32	540	53	730
12	390	33	550	54	740
13	400	34	560	55	760
14	410	35	560	56	770
15	420	36	570	57	780
16	430	37	580	58	790
17	430	38	590	59	800
18	440	39	600	60	800

Don't take these scores too literally. Practice test conditions cannot precisely mirror real test conditions. Your actual SAT scores will almost certainly vary from your practice test scores.

Your score on the practice test gives you a rough idea of your range on the actual exam. If you don't like your score, it's not too late to do something about it. Work your way way through this book again, and turn to Kaplan's *SAT Verbal Workbook* and *SAT Math Workbook* for even more help.

Practice Test One Answers and Explanations

SECTION 1

1. E

It's easy enough to understand that insurers don't like to insure property in places where natural disasters are likely to happen. The term **prone to** in (E) means "having a tendency to," so it is correct.

2. C

If it took Roman legions three years to seize Masada, we can predict that they spent a long time "surrounding or isolating" the mountain "fortress or stronghold" of Masada before they were finally able to take it. (C) is the best choice. (B) **assailed**, meaning "attacked," would make sense in the first blank, and (E) **stronghold** and (A) **bastion** would fit, too. But (A), (B), and (E)'s first-position words don't make sense when plugged in.

> besieged: surrounded with armed forces
> citadel: fortress
> assailed: attacked
> bastion: fortified area
> dissembled: concealed
> honed: sharpened

3. B

If the senator was **unlike** "his calmer, more easygoing colleagues" and "ready to quarrel at the slightest provocation," it's fair to infer that the senator was short-tempered or extremely irritable. The best choice is (B)—**irascible.**

> irascible: easily angered
> whimsical: fanciful, erratic, or unpredictable
> gregarious: sociable, friendly
> ineffectual: futile, unproductive
> benign: harmless or gentle

4. B

You don't have to know that Genghis Khan was a violent dictator to get this question right. What's important to know is that the first word of the sentence, *although*, implies that the two blanks have to contain words that contrast with each other. (B) is the best choice—although historians had thought that Genghis Khan was a **despotic** potentate, new research shows that many of his subjects nevertheless **revered** him. Although (A) **tyrannical** is synonymous with *despotic*, (A)'s second-blank choice, **abhorred,** doesn't provide the predicted contrast. Choice (C) **venerated** doesn't really contrast with **redundant**. And in (E), it doesn't make sense to say that Khan's subjects **invoked** him despite his **peremptory** reputation.

> despotic: oppressive, dictatorial
> potentate: dictator
> revered: worshiped, adored
> abhorred: hated
> venerated: highly respected
> redundant: repetitive
> jocular: jolly
> peremptory: putting an end to debate
> invoke: call upon for help

5. B

The word *because* in the middle of the sentence lets us know that the words in the blanks will be consistent in meaning, which means that they will share the same type of charge. We can predict two positive words, like "Jill was appreciated by her employees because she often forgave" the fact that they were lazy, or two negative words like "Jill was disliked by her employees because she often scolded them" for being lazy. (B) matches the latter prediction—Jill was **loathed** by her employees because she often **berated** them for not working hard enough. No other choice besides (B) contains two like charges.

> *loathed: hated*
> *berated: scolded*
> *deified: made godlike*
> *lauded: praised or celebrated*
> *derided: made fun of*
> *execrated: condemned, cursed*

6. E

If "reconstructing the skeletons of extinct species like dinosaurs . . . requires much patience and effort by paleontologists," we can predict that such an activity is a "painstaking or tough, demanding process." (E) **exacting** is our best choice.

> *exacting: requiring lots of attention and extreme accuracy*
> *nascent: introductory or starting*
> *aberrant: abnormal*

7. C

Because of disease and the destruction of their habitat, koalas are now found only in isolated parts of eucalyptus forests. The word in the blank must mean something like "killed off" or "destroyed," since things like "disease and habitat destruction" are destructive processes. (C) is our best choice—"nearly **decimated** or wiped out by disease and habitat destruction," koalas are now found only in isolated parts of eucalyptus forests. (A) **dispersed,** meaning "scattered," may have been a little tempting, but there's no reason to assume that the koalas were scattered around the forests due to "disease and habitat destruction."

> *dispersed: scattered*
> *compiled: categorized, collected, arranged*
> *averted: avoided*

8. E

Looking at the first blank first, if there were "internal power struggles" in the government, then it's likely that the government had something like "deep ideological differences or conflicts." For the second blank, we can predict that these conflicts and power struggles harmed or crippled the government. Although choice (C)'s first-blank choice, **distortions,** sounds negative, like "differences or conflicts," choices (A) and (E) make *more* sense. We can easily imagine "deep ideological **disputes**" or "deep ideological **divisions**" going hand in hand with "internal power struggles," but it's hard to imagine ideological **distortions.**

Now we can turn to (A) and (E)'s second-blank choices. (A) doesn't make sense given the context of the sentence—why would "deep ideological **disputes** and internal power struggles **facilitate** the government"? (E) is the best choice—"deep ideological **divisions** and internal power struggles **paralyzed** the government."

> *distortions: perversions, twisted versions*
> *facilitate: assist*
> *stymied: frustrated, impeded*

9. D

The terms *popular remedy* and *as yet* are key in this sentence. Large doses of vitamins are popularly thought to be good, but their effectiveness has not been proven at this time. (D) **unproven** is the correct answer. Answer choices (A), (B), (C), and (E) are wrong because they imply that medical experts understand and approve of large doses, which clearly contradicts the sentence.

10. B

A **TROUT** is a type of **FISH**, just as a **human** is a type of **mammal.**

11. A

Bridge: If you **INHALE** something, it goes into your **LUNGS.** If you **swallow** something, it goes into your **stomach.**

12. A

A **BRAGGART** is, by definition, someone who **BOAST**s. A **laggard** is, by definition, someone who **tarries.** A speaker, not a **hypocrite,** is someone who, by definition, **speaks,** so (B) is wrong.

> laggard: lingerer, one who lags behind
> extrovert: someone very outgoing
> tarry: to dawdle, be late, delay
> hypocrite: someone who pretends to be what he or she is not

13. B

To **ALLEVIATE** is to reduce **PAIN,** just as to **depreciate** is to reduce **value.** In choice (D), to **deviate** is to move away from some set **standard.** That's not the same as lowering a **standard.**

14. C

Bridge: To **INFURIATE** someone is to **ANNOY** him or her a great deal. In correct choice (C), to **terrify** someone is to **frighten** him or her a great deal.

> satiate: to satisfy

15. D

Someone **MISERLY** is not characterized by **MAGNANIMITY,** or generousness. Similarly, someone **innocent** is not characterized by **culpability.**

> transient: wandering from place to place
> stupefaction: overwhelming amazement
> fastidiousness: the quality of being painstaking or particular
> avarice: greed
> magnanimity: generosity
> culpability: guilt

The Time Passage

Next up is a fairly abstract science passage. This particular passage is perhaps a little bit harder than the ones you're going to encounter on the test—but don't be intimidated by the subject matter. Even if your passage is written by a Nobel Prize winner, it's going to contain ideas that you can relate to, and probably some ideas that you've seen before.

The topic of the passage is how difficult it is to comprehend long stretches of time. Paragraph two tells us that our minds aren't built to handle the idea of thousands of years passing. We have *some* conception of the past through the art, writing, and photography of previous generations, but the scale of longer time periods eludes us. Paragraphs four and five attempt to bridge this gap by providing a few everyday yardsticks; the time the human race has been around is compared to a few seconds in a week, or a few letters in a book. Essentially, that's all you need to take from your first reading of the passage; the details you can come back to later.

16. D

Here, in paragraph one, the author's talking about why we find it difficult to understand vast stretches of time. We're told that the "span" of what we can remember is limited because our lives are relatively short. So *span* in this context means the *amount* of time we're able to recollect—the (D) **extent.**

(A) **rate of increase,** (B) **value,** and (E) **accuracy** are all correct definitions of *span*, but they're not aspects of memory as discussed in the passage. And (C) **bridge,** the most common definition, doesn't fit at all.

HINT: *The golden rule about vocabulary questions on the Critical Reading section is that they test vocabulary IN CONTEXT. You're being asked how a particular word is used in the passage, not how it's usually defined.*

17. C

Before writing, we're told, the wisdom of generations was passed down in two ways—verbally, and "to a lesser extent," in pictures, carvings, and statues. This means that the wisdom of the past was transmitted less effectively by nonverbal means, and thus (C) **more effectively by the spoken word than by other means.**

Choices (A) and (B) *distort* this idea. Nowhere are we told that wisdom was rejected. And since spoken words *and* pictures were both used, it was obviously not an all or nothing proposition. (E) doesn't make much sense. How could there be an emphasis on science before writing existed? (D), finally, makes no sense at all—the author never says that all ancient wisdom was fiction.

18. B

This is a Little Picture question asking about the purpose of a detail. The question asks why the author discusses the impact of writing. Looking at the lines around the line reference given, we're told that writing has made the transmission of information about the past a lot more precise and extensive. Pictures and photography are also mentioned as ways in which the experience of the past has been passed down. So choice (B)'s correct here—writing is mentioned as an **example** of how cultures record knowledge about the past.

(A) is a distortion—the author is showing us something about the past, not why we remember hardly anything. He never implies any criticism of preliterate cultures, so choice (C) is out too. Choices (D) and (E) are wrong because the author never mentions them in the context referred to or in the whole passage.

19. C

Another Vocabulary-in-Context question. The word *ready* can mean several things—choices (A), (C), (D), and (E) are all possible meanings. In this context, however, it most nearly means **immediate,** choice (C). In the sentence before the cited line, the author says

"there is no simple way" to understand vast stretches of time. And in the sentence following the cited line, the author compares the way we understand time to the way a blind man "laboriously" constructs a picture of his surroundings. This implies that our understanding of time is a difficult and time-consuming task, not something we can do *readily* or **immediately.**

20. E

Another question asking about the *purpose behind* part of the author is argument. Give the context a quick scan. Once again, the author's talking about how difficult it is to understand vast stretches of time. We're told that it's like a blind man building up a sensory picture of his surroundings. This is an **indirect** process, so choice (E) is right.

Choice (C) is dealt with later in paragraph four, so you can eliminate it right away.

Choice (A) is too sweeping. The author never says that human beings are *completely* **unable to comprehend time.** (B) and (D) have nothing to do with the passage.

21. A

Inference skills are required here. What is the author's underlying point in mentioning the Big Bang and the Cambrian Period? The author *introduces* this discussion in the cited passage by saying that **a week** provides a better yardstick for the age of the earth than a day. The Big Bang and the Cambrian Period are used as examples to support this point. So (A) is right—it's the point about the time scale that the author's trying to demonstrate.

Choices (D) and (E) both distort the point in different ways. The author is not suggesting that the time scale of a day should be totally abandoned—just that the week is a better scale. The development of (B) **agriculture** is another supporting example like the Big Bang and the Cambrian Period, but it's not the author's central point here. Finally, **fossils** have nothing to do with the question at hand, so (C) is easily eliminated.

22. C

A more straightforward comprehension question this time. When we go back to the lines referred to, we're told about the problem with linear maps: When you produce one that's big enough to show us on it, the map becomes too big to study and reproduce conveniently. (C) gets the right paraphrase here. Notice especially the match up in synonyms for "convenient reproduction" and "examination."

(A), (B), and (E) aren't supported here—there's nothing about **overlapping** periods, **scientific standards,** or ignorance about **pre-Cambrian times** in the passage. (D) doesn't address the problem. The question is about getting our human experience on the map.

23. D

What's the overall point the author is trying to prove?

The Big Picture is that life started on earth so long ago that it is difficult for us to comprehend. Everything that follows is meant to illustrate this point, including the time scales. Don't let the material confuse you. The point is (D)—**the immensity of time** since the origin of **life.**

(C) is tricky to reject because it's an aspect of the larger argument, but it's not the whole point. The other wrong choices mention issues that the author hardly touches on. In paragraphs four to six, the author's *not* concerned with getting dates right (A), the question of how life actually began (B), or the (E) **development of communication.**

The Susan B. Anthony Passage

This humanities passage is from a speech by Susan B. Anthony, a 19th-century women's rights leader. Anthony admits at the outset that she was recently charged with the "crime" of voting. Her intention is to prove that her vote was no crime, but rather the exercise of her Constitutional rights, which no state should be allowed to impinge upon. This generates the passage's big idea: that Anthony—and by extension all women—should be allowed to vote. You may have found Anthony's style a little dated or confusing. Don't worry; the questions will help you focus on specific details.

24. C

The important thing here is to see what exactly Anthony is saying. The question stem is keyed to the first paragraph. In the second sentence she states that

she "not only committed no crime, but . . . simply exercised my citizen's rights, guaranteed me . . . by the National Constitution." The words *no crime* are the first important clue. You can immediately rule out (A) and (E) because they say she believes the act was illegal. The second part of the line discusses the Constitution, so (C) is clearly a restatement of her argument.

(B) and (D) both make sense, but she does not state these points in the first paragraph. Therefore, they are wrong.

25. A

The most common meaning of "promote" is to move up—to a higher position, rank, or job. This doesn't make sense, though, in the phrase "promote the general welfare." "General welfare" means the good of all people, so to (A) **further** it, makes the most sense.

(B) **organize** and (C) **publicize** both could apply to the general welfare, but not as well as (A). They refer more to promotion as you would do with a concert or sports event. (D) **commend** means "praise," which seems silly in the context given, as does (E) **motivate.**

HINT: *In Vocabulary-in-Context questions, the right answer is usually not the most common meaning of the given word. Be sure to reread the context.*

26. E

Anthony points out that no subgroup was excluded by the wording of the preamble of the Constitution. " . . . we formed it . . . to secure [the blessings of liberty,] not to the half of ourselves . . . but to . . . women as well as men." Therefore (E) is correct. **All people deserve to enjoy the rights** of **the Constitution.**

Anthony never claims that the Founding Fathers plotted to deny women their rights (A). (B) is incorrect because the author's concern is women's rights and not rights of any other group. Though **some male citizens may still be denied basic rights,** (B) goes against the gist of what is being said. (C) is like (A) in that it's a claim Anthony never makes. Finally, though (D) is a point that Anthony does make, she doesn't make it until the next paragraph.

27. B

We're still looking at the same part of the passage.

Look at the structure of the quoted sentence: "We didn't do it only for X, but for X *and* Y." *Posterity* means "future generations," which would include men and women. So the X, the "half of our posterity," refers to the posterity of those who already enjoy the blessings of liberty. In other words, men. (B) is the right choice.

(A) has nothing to do with what Anthony is discussing. Since the construction of the sentence makes it clear that the "half of our posterity" is not the whole of those who want to vote, (C) is out. There's no way of saying that one-half of the people are and will be opponents of women's rights, so (D) is wrong. And (E) wrongly suggests that in the future, one half of the country's population will be members of government.

28. A

Reread the keyed paragraph. Anthony is saying that a state that prohibits women from voting violates federal law—the Constitution. Therefore it becomes "an odious aristocracy, a hateful oligarchy." Neither of these things is a democracy. (A) is the correct answer.

Anthony mentions rebellion, but she doesn't mean the kind of violent rebellion (B) talks about. (C) is wrong because of the word *remain.* The nation is not and never has been an aristocracy. (D) plays off the same sentence as (B) does, but instead of going too far, it doesn't go far enough. Anthony wants the laws against women voting repealed; she doesn't want them merely discussed. (E) is totally wrong because at no point is Anthony arguing that an aristocracy should be preserved.

29. C

You might readily associate *hardihood* with (A) **endurance** and (B) **vitality,** but a quick check back in context shows you these aren't correct. Anthony says she doesn't believe her opponents would have the ---- to say women aren't "persons." Saying such an offensive thing would take a lot of **nerve,** choice (C). It might also take a lot of **stupidity** (E), but that's too strong a word, considering Anthony's diplomatic tone.

30. D

The stem keys you to the second to last sentence of the passage. *Abridge* means "deprive," so Anthony is saying that no state can deprive citizens of their rights. (D) states exactly this.

In (A), *privilege* means "luxury," but voting is a basic right, not a luxury. (B) comes out of nowhere; there's no discussion of courts in this passage. (C) plays off Anthony's reference to "any old law." She's not talking about *any* outdated laws in this passage; she means any law *that prohibits women from voting.* Anthony never addresses how the laws will be changed, only that they must be changed, so (E) is out.

---

antagonism: hostility

SECTION 2

1. C

Use the formula Percent × Whole = Part.

30 percent is $\frac{30}{100}$, or $\frac{3}{10}$. So $\frac{3}{10} \times x$ = part, and choice (C) is correct.

2. E

$2 \times 10^4 = 20,000$. $5 \times 10^3 = 5,000$. $6 \times 10^2 = 600$. $4 \times 10^1 = 40$. So the sum is 25,640.

3. A

Find the length of each segment, and then subtract the length of XY from the length of YZ. Y is at 3 on the number line and Z is at 8, so the length of YZ is $8 - 3 = 5$. X is at 1 on the number line and Y is at 3, so the length of XY is $3 - 1 = 2$. So the length of YZ is $5 - 2 = 3$ greater than the length of XY.

4. B

To find the value of x, you need to change 16 into a power of 2: $16 = 2^4$. Therefore, $2^{x+1} = 2^4$. So $x + 1 = 4$, or $x = 3$.

5. E

The number of degrees around a point is 360. Therefore:

$$90 + 30 + 2a + 30 + a = 360$$
$$150 + 3a = 360$$
$$3a = 210$$
$$a = 70$$

6. D

If a machine labels 150 bottles in 20 minutes, it labels 15 bottles every 2 minutes. To label 60, or 4×15, bottles would take 4×2, or 8 minutes.

7. B

To find the next multiple of 3, simply add 3 to the expression: $x - 1 + 3 = x + 2$, choice (B).

If this is unclear, pick a number for x. If $x = 4$, $4 - 1 = 3$; the next greatest multiple of 3 is 6. Plugging 4 for x into each answer choice, we find that only choice (B) gives us 6.

8. E

Since x leaves a remainder of 4 when divided by 5, it must end in either a 4 or a 9, so choice (B) can be eliminated. Since x leaves no remainder when divided by 9, it is evenly divisible by 9. Of the remaining choices only 144 is divisible by 9.

9. A

The sum of the lengths of any two sides of a triangle must be greater than the length of the third side. So $AB + AC$ must be greater than BC; $6 + x > 12$. If $x = 6$, $6 + 6 = 12$ is not greater than 12, so x cannot equal 6.

10. B

Number of terms × average = sum of the terms. For the first group, $3 \times 40 = 120$, so the sum of 20, 70, and x is 120. For the second group, $4 \times 50 = 200$, so $20 + 70 + x + y = 200$. Since the sum of the first three terms is 120, $120 + y = 200$, $y = 80$.

11. A

Looking at the graph, you can see that the number of books borrowed in January was 300. To find the total number of books borrowed during the first six months of the year, add the values of each bar: $300 + 350 + 400 + 450 + 500 + 400 = 2,400$ books. So the number of books borrowed in January is $\frac{300}{2400}$ or $\frac{1}{8}$ of the total number of books borrowed during the first six months of the year.

12. D

We're told that 40% of $r = s$. The value of 40% of r is 4 times the value of 10% of r, so 10% of $r = \frac{1}{4} \times s = \frac{s}{4}$.

An alternative method is to pick numbers. Since you're dealing with percents, let $r = 100$. 40% of $r = s$, so 40% of $100 = 40 = s$. You're asked which answer choice is equal to 10% of r; 10% of $100 = 10$. Now plug the value for s into the answer choices to see which ones give you 10:

(A) $4s = 4 \times 40 = 160$. Eliminate.

(B) $2s = 2 \times 40 = 80$. Eliminate.

(C) $\frac{s}{2} = \frac{40}{2} = 20$. Eliminate.

(D) $\frac{s}{4} = \frac{40}{4} = 10$. Works!

(E) $\frac{s}{8} = \frac{40}{8} = 5$. Eliminate.

Since (D) is the only choice that produces the desired result, it is the correct answer. But remember, when picking numbers you need to check all the answer choices; if more than one works, pick new numbers and plug them in until only one answer choice works.

13. D

The two overlapping triangles share a common angle, which we can label $p°$. Since the interior angles of any triangle add up to $180°$, we have two equations: $x + z + p = 180$ and $y + r + p = 180$. Subtracting p from both sides of each equation, we have $x + z = 180 - p$ and $y + r = 180 - p$. Since $x + z$ and $y + r$ both equal the same quantity, $x + z$ and $y + r$ must be equal to each other. Rearranging $x + z = y + r$, we get $x - r = y - z$, which matches choice (D).

14. C

Check the answer choices. If a number has even one factor (not including 1 and itself) that is not a prime number, eliminate that choice:

(A) 12: 4 is not prime. Eliminate.

(B) 18: 6 is not prime. Eliminate.

(C) 21: 3 and 7 are its only other factors, and both are prime. Correct!

(D) 24: 6 is not prime. Eliminate.

(E) 28: 4 is not prime. Eliminate.

15. E

Try different possible values for x and y, eliminating the incorrect answer choices. Since x is multiplied by 3, let's begin with the smallest positive integer value for x: 1. If $3(1) + y = 14$, then $y = 11$, and $x + y = 12$. So choice (A) is out.

If $3(2) + y = 14$, then $y = 8$, and $x + y = 10$. So choice (B) is out. If $3(3) + y = 14$, then $y = 5$, and $x + y = 8$. So choice (C) is also out. If you're really clever, you'll see at this point that answer choice (E) is impossible (which makes it the right choice). After all, the next smallest possible value of x is 4, and since x and y must both be positive integers, neither one can equal 0. (Zero is *not* positive—or negative.) So the sum of x and y must be greater than 4. (Sure enough, if $x = 4$, then $y = 2$, and $x + y = 6$, eliminating choice (D) as well.)

16. C

When the r cards are distributed, there are 8 left over, so the number of cards distributed is $r - 8$. Divide the number of cards distributed by the number of people. Since there are s people, each person gets $\frac{r-8}{s}$ cards.

Another approach is to pick numbers. Let $r = 58$ and $s = 10$; if $58 - 8$ or 50 cards were distributed evenly among 10 people, each would receive 5 cards. Plug the values you picked for r and s into the answer choices to see which ones give you 5:

(A) $\frac{s}{8-r} = \frac{10}{8-58} = -\frac{1}{5}$. Eliminate.

(B) $\frac{r-s}{8} = \frac{58-10}{8} = 6$. Eliminate.

(C) $\frac{r-8}{s} = \frac{58-8}{10} = 5$. Works!

(D) $s - 8r = 10 - (8 \times 58) = -454$. Eliminate.

(E) $rs - 8 = (58 \times 10) - 8 = 572$. Eliminate.

Since (C) is the only answer choice that gives you 5, it is the correct answer. But be sure to check all the answer choices when picking numbers.

17. D

Check each answer choice to see which doesn't work:

(A) $\dfrac{d}{2}$: If d is an even integer, say 2, then $\dfrac{d}{2} = \dfrac{2}{2} = 1$ is an integer. Eliminate.

(B) $\dfrac{\sqrt{d}}{2}$: If d is a perfect square with an even square root, say $d = 4$, then $\dfrac{\sqrt{4}}{2} = \dfrac{2}{2} = 1$ is an integer. Eliminate.

(C) $2d$: This will always produce an even integer; if $d = 3$, $2d = 2 \times 3 = 6$ is an integer. Eliminate.

(D) $d\sqrt{2}$ CANNOT produce an integer. An integer would result if $\sqrt{2}$ is multiplied by another multiple of $\sqrt{2}$, which is impossible because d is a positive integer. So (D) is correct.

Let's check (E) just to make sure.

(E) $d + 2$: This will always produce an integer; if $d = 5$, $d + 2 = 5 + 2 = 7$ is an integer. Eliminate.

18. A

The area of a triangle $= \dfrac{1}{2}$(base × height). Since the area of $\triangle ABC$ is 6, $\dfrac{1}{2}(AB \times BC) = 6$. If you consider CD as the base of $\triangle ACD$, you will notice that its height is represented by altitude AB. So the area of $\triangle ACD = \dfrac{1}{2}(CD \times AB)$. Since $CD = BC$, the area of $\triangle ACD$ can be expressed as $\dfrac{1}{2}(BC \times AB)$, which you know equals 6.

19. C

Since the ratio of x to y to z is 3:6:8, if $y = 24$ or 4×6, x and z must also be multiplied by 4 for the ratio to hold. So $x = 4 \times 3 = 12$ and $z = 4 \times 8 = 32$, and $x + z = 44$.

20. E

Each of the five surfaces is 60 by 180 centimeters, so tiles measuring 12 by 18 centimeters can be laid down in 5 rows of 10 to exactly cover one surface. There are 5 surfaces so $5 \times 5 \times 10 = 250$ tiles are needed.

21. D

If you add the 3 equations together, you find that $2x + 2y + 2z = 38$; dividing both sides by 2 shows that $x + y + z = 19$, answer choice (D).

22. B

The perimeter of triangle $ACD = AD + AB + BC + CD$. You are given the lengths of BC and CD, so you need to find the lengths of AD and AB. Angle DBC is a right angle because it is supplementary to $\angle DBA$, one of the 4 right angles of square $ABDE$. Since right triangle DBC has sides of length 8 and 10, you should recognize it as a 6-8-10 right triangle (a multiple of the 3-4-5 right triangle) and realize that $BD = 6$. (If you didn't recognize this, you could have used the Pythagorean theorem to find the length of BD.) BD is also a side of the square and since all sides of a square are equal, $AB = 6$.

So triangle DBA is an isosceles right triangle with sides in the ratio of $1:1:\sqrt{2}$. That means hypotenuse AD is equal to the length of a side times $\sqrt{2}$, so $AD = 6\sqrt{2}$. Now you can find the perimeter of triangle ACD: $6\sqrt{2} + 6 + 8 + 10 = 24 + 6\sqrt{2}$.

23. C

$(4r - 4)^2 = 36$, so $4r - 4$ could equal 6 or -6, since the result is 36 when each of these integers is squared. But the problem states that $r < 0$, so try -6. $4r - 4 = -6$, $4r = -2$, and $r = -\dfrac{2}{4} = -\dfrac{1}{2}$, answer choice (C). (If you try $4r - 4 = 6$ you'll find $r = 2\frac{1}{2}$, which cannot be correct for this question since $r < 0$.)

24. D

Tank A originally contained 10 more liters of water than tank C, so represent the initial number of liters in each tank in terms of tank A:

tank $A = a$

tank $C = a - 10$

5 liters of water are poured from A to B, and an additional 10 liters are poured from A to C. A total of 15 liters are removed from tank A so it now contains $a - 15$ liters of water. 10 liters are added to tank C so it now contains $a - 10 + 10 = a$ liters. So tank C contains 15 more liters of water than tank A.

25. B

The surface area of a cube is $6e^2$, where e = the length of an edge of the cube. Since the surface area is $36n^2$:

$$6e^2 = 36n^2$$
$$e^2 = 6n^2$$
$$e = n\sqrt{6}$$

The volume of a cube is e^3. To solve for the volume in terms of n, plug in the value for an edge that you just found: Volume $= e^3 = (n\sqrt{6})^3 = 6n^3\sqrt{6}$, answer choice (B).

SECTION 3

1. D

This is not a difficult question. The use of the word *and* tells us that we're looking for a word to fill the first blank which is consistent with "scarcity of rain"—a word like *dry*. We can, therefore, eliminate (A) and (C) at once. Since farming conditions are "bad," our second blank should express the idea that there's no point in trying to work there. By that criterion, choices (B) and (E) can be eliminated. This leaves us with (D) **future.** (D)'s first word, **infertile,** also fits perfectly, so (D) is the correct answer.

barren: not productive

2. D

The structural clue in this sentence is *not only . . . but,* which suggests that the students were doing something even worse than ignoring the rules. The only word that fits here is **flouting,** choice (D).

flouting: mocking, treating with contempt

3. A

The word *while* following the comma in the second part of the sentence tells us that there will be a contrast between what some critics believe about dadaism and what *others* "insist the movement was." The best choice is (A)—"some critics believe that the **zenith** of modern art came with dadaism, while others insist the movement was a **sham.**" Other choices have single words that would make sense in one of the blanks, but none of the pairs except (A) expresses the contrast that is implied by the sentence.

zenith: highest point
sham: hoax

4. C

In this question you are asked to make a logical connection between two parts of a sentence. It is clear that the content of the journalist's article either had no impact, in which case there was little or no response from the public, or it attracted a great deal of attention and was followed by a lot of correspondence. (C) is the correct answer. The author would never have thought her article was **controversial** were it not for the **spate** of correspondence. The other answer choices are wrong because they sound contradictory when plugged into the sentence. For example, in choice (A), if the article were **interesting,** one would expect it to be followed by a lot of correspondence—not by a **dearth,** or lack of it. In choice (D), if the article were **commonplace** (ordinary), why would an **influx** of letters follow its publication?

> *spate: a sudden flood or rush*
> *dearth: lack*
> *inflammatory: likely to arouse strong*
>   *feeling or anger*
> *influx: flow coming in*

5. E

If many readers have difficulty following Descartes's complex, intricately woven arguments, then it's likely that his writings are something like *complicated, esoteric,* or *obscure.* The best choice is (E) **abstruse.**

> *abstruse: difficult to understand*
> *generic: common, general*
> *trenchant: extremely perceptive,*
>   *insightful*

6. B

The phrase *even though* indicates contrast. So, *even though* the prisoner "presented evidence clearly proving that he was nowhere near the scene of the crime," he was **indicted** or formally charged with committing the crime.

> *exculpated: absolved, proved to be*
>   *innocent*
> *exhumed: removed from a grave*
> *rescinded: cancelled, taken back*

7. C

A *premise* is a proposition which is used as the basis for an argument—or a story. If scientists are critical of the premise for a movie, we can infer that they are so because they consider it to be unscientific, without basis in fact, or **speculative.** (C) is therefore the correct answer. (A) is wrong, because if the premise, or underlying argument, were **scientific** then it would hardly be open to criticism by scientists. (B) is wrong because there's no reason to think that the theme of the return of the dinosaurs is unexpressed in the movie.

> *tacit: silent; understood but*
> *unexpressed*

8. B

Looking at the second blank first, if Mozart "left no rough drafts," it's probably "because he was able to write out his compositions in a complete, unrevised form." So, for the second blank, (B) **finished** looks best. (E) **concise** is also possible, so let's try (B) and (E) in the first blank. We've already seen that Mozart didn't need to revise his compositions—therefore, it makes sense to say that he "composed music with exceptional *ease* or **facility.**" (E) **independence** is just too ambiguous to fit in to the context of the sentence.

> *concise: using as few words as possible,*
>   *to the point*

9. D

If dogs are "known for their devotion," then it's likely that they "were often used as symbols of *faithfulness, loyalty,* or **fidelity**" in Medieval and Renaissance art. (A) **resistance** and (E) **antagonism** are not what we're looking for, and choices (B) and (C), while positive, don't relate to the idea of *devotion.*

> *antagonism: hostility*

10. C

In this sentence we find a description of two contradictory characteristics which exist in the same group of people. On the one hand, they are brutal; on the other, they are heroic. Such an occurrence is termed a *paradox* and therefore (C) **paradoxical** is the correct answer. Choices (A), (D), and (E) are wrong; it is **unfortunate, distressing,** and **appalling** that they are brutal—but not that they are heroic.

> *paradoxical: like a riddle; opposed to common sense but true*
> *explicable: able to be explained*

11. E

A **CHARLATAN** is, by definition, not **SCRUPULOUS.** A **tyrant** is a ruler who uses power oppressively and unjustly. So a **tyrant** is, by definition, not **just.**

> *charlatan: a fraud or a quack, someone who pretends to have more knowledge or skill than he or she possesses*

12. C

GREED is the desire to **ACQUIRE** large amounts of things. **Gluttony** is the desire to **eat** large amounts, so (C) is the best answer.

(A) won't work; someone who experiences **fear** may or may not want to **disguise** himself or herself. In (B), it may be hard to **persuade** someone characterized by **inertia,** but **inertia** isn't the desire to **persuade** large amounts.

> *inertia: apathy, inactivity*

13. A

The word **BLOW** is being used to mean "a swipe or punch." To **PARRY** means "to deflect, ward off," so our bridge is "to **PARRY** a **BLOW** is to deflect it." (A) shares the same bridge—to **counter** an **argument** is to deflect it.

In choice (B), you might **sidestep** or avoid an argument or issue, but there isn't really any clear connection between **sidestep** and **offense.** In (C), to **defer** isn't to deflect or ward off a **ruling.**

> *pitfall: a trap or hidden danger*
> *defer: put off or delay*

14. E

By definition, **SLURS** are words that **MALIGN,** just as **compliments** are words that **flatter.** The other choices don't fit this bridge. For instance, in (C), **whispers** aren't necessarily words that **torment.**

15. A

A **LENTIL** is classified as a **LEGUME,** a bean or pea, in the same way that **rice** is classified as a **cereal.**

Even if you didn't know that a **LENTIL** is a **LEGUME,** you might have been able to arrive at the answer by eliminating all choices with no good bridges. For example, in (B) **food** may or may not provide **nutrition,** or nourishment.

> *husk: the outer covering of a kernel or seed*

16. D

To **INDULGE** an **APPETITE** is to satisfy it. Similarly, to **humor** a **whim** is to satisfy it.

In (A), you can **filter** out an **impurity,** but it doesn't make sense to say that to **filter** out an **impurity** is to satisfy it. (C) might have been a tempting choice, since the word **coddle** is similar to **indulge.** But **coddle** doesn't have a necessary connection to **emotion.**

> *coddle: to overindulge, pamper*

17. B

Bridge: **MELLIFLUOUS** means "sweet **SOUND**ing." **Fragrant** means "sweet **smell**ing."

In (D), a **raucous discussion** would be a harsh-sounding, noisy debate.

> *mellifluous: sweet sounding, melodious*
> *fragrant: sweet smelling*
> *raucous: harsh or grating*

18. C

By definition, a **GUFFAW** is loud, unrestrained **LAUGH**ing. In the same way, a **yell** is loud, unrestrained **talk**ing.

19. C

The word **CELESTIAL** means "having to do with the **HEAVENS**." The word **nautical** means "having to do with **ships**."

> *celestial: having to do with the heavens*
> *nautical: having to do with ships*
> *viscous: thick and gluey*

20. C

To **ENERVATE** is to lessen or decrease **VITALITY**. In (C), to **daunt** is to lessen **courage**.

You could have worked backwards by eliminating answer choices with inappropriate or weak bridges. For example, in (A), one can **consolidate power** by securing and strengthening one's position, but that bridge doesn't work with the stem words. Choice (B) has a weak bridge, too: To **energize** is to fill with energy, but that doesn't always result in **action**. If you plug the stem words into (D)'s bridge, you get, "To enervate is to assess the vitality of something." It doesn't sound sensible, so (D) is out, too. In (E) to **admit guilt** is to confess. That couldn't be true of the stem as well. By process of elimination, (C) is correct.

> *enervate: to lessen or decrease vitality*
> *daunt: to subdue or dismay*
> *energize: to fill with energy*
> *estimate: to assess the worth of something*

21. D

An **OLIGARCHY** is, by definition, a form of government in which power is held by a **FEW** people. Answer choice (D) is analogous to this: A **monarchy** is a form of government in which power is held by **one** person.

If the definition of **OLIGARCHY** posed a problem, you could again eliminate wrong answers. For instance, in choice (A), the terms **government** and **majority** are not always linked. Similarly, in (B), **authority** and **consent** don't necessarily go together. In (C), a **country** may or may not have a **constitution**.

> *oligarchy: a form of government in*
> *   which power is held by a few people*
> *monarchy: a form of government in*
> *   which power is held by one person*
> *constitution: a set of principles according*
> *   to which a nation is governed*

22. A

Bridge: Someone who is **UNTRUTHFUL** is characterized by **MENDACIOUSNESS**. Choice (A) is correct: Someone who is **circumspect** is characterized by **caution**.

What if you don't know what *mendaciousness* or *circumspect* mean? You must try to eliminate wrong answers. Remember that the stem words and the correct answer choice will have the same strong bridge. Work backwards. Does (B) have a strong bridge? A person who is **timid** exhibits a certain type of **behavior**—that's not a strong connection. Similarly, (C)'s bridge is weak: Everyone has a **physique** of some kind, not just **agile** people. Answer choices (D) and (E) can also be eliminated because they have weak bridges. That leaves us with (A).

> *mendaciousness: lying*
> *circumspect: cautious or watchful*

23. B

The bridge can be stated as: Something that is **INEXCUSABLE** is impossible to **JUSTIFY**. Likewise, in (B), something that is **unassailable** is impossible to **attack**.

> *unassailable: not open to attack or question*
> *affable: friendly and polite*
> *revere: to feel deep respect or awe for*

The Twain Passage

This excerpt from Mark Twain's *Life on the Mississippi* should be amusing and easy to read. All the humor comes from the same technique—using deadpan, matter-of-fact language to describe the exaggerated daydreams and jealousies of a boy's life.

The central point here is the author's envy of the engineer, and many of the questions focus on this. The author starts with his own glamorous ideas about steamboating, then spends most of the passage on the show-off engineer. The passage finishes with the author's own failure to find work as a pilot. The slightly old-fashioned style isn't hard to follow, but several questions focus on the author's figurative use of words.

24. B

The key word in the sentence is *supposed*. Of course, a justice of the peace *doesn't* possess unlimited power, but because of inexperience the author "supposed" he did. (B) accurately uses *naive* (inexperienced, gullible) to characterize the author's misconception. Three of the wrong choices assume that the father really *did* have unlimited powers and explain this in different ways—frontier justice (A, D), public support (C). (E) mistakenly views the boy's description of his father as an indication that the boy's childhood environment was harsh.

25. C

Distinction has several meanings, including those in (A), (B), (C), and (E). The key to its use here is context: In the previous sentence the author is talking about his naive ideas of his father's great power. **Prestige,** (C), suggesting high status and honor, fits this context; the other three don't. (D) is not a meaning of *distinction* at all.

26. E

This question asks about the literal meaning of the sentence, but inference and context help, too. The sentence explains that the author wanted the job because a deck hand was "conspicuous," or easily seen. The previous sentence stresses standing "where all my old comrades could see me," so you can deduce that the author wants to be seen and admired in what he imagines is a glamorous profession (E).

(A) and (B) invent advantages that are not mentioned, and miss the humor by suggesting common-sense economic motivations. (C) assumes that if the author could be seen by his "old comrades" in the first job, he must want *not* to be seen by them in a different job; but this is false, since he'd be "conspicuous" in the second job, too. (D) brings in an ambition—becoming a pilot—that the author doesn't develop until the end of the passage.

27. B

Again, context helps you to figure out the answer to the question. The **Sunday-school** reference is explained in the next sentence. The engineer had been "worldly"—which is what Sunday-school probably taught students not to be—and the author had been "just the reverse." In other words, the author followed his Sunday-school teachings and the engineer didn't—yet the engineer gets the glory. The underlying idea is that this was unjust, choice (B).

(A) is never mentioned. (C) takes the Sunday-school reference literally and misses the humorous tone. (D) invents an ambition that the author never mentions; his reaction is pure envy, not frustrated ambition. (E) misconstrues the reference to the engineer as "worldly"; it means he didn't take Sunday-school seriously, not that he was **unscrupulous** (dishonest or crooked).

28. C

To get this question, you need to read the sentence that follows. The engineer was not generous because he sat about where "we all could see him and envy him." The implication is that great people should be generous by not showing off or (C) **flaunting** their success.

(A) refers to the Sunday-school comment, but that was about undeserved greatness, not lack of generosity. (B) and (D) interpret *generous* in the literal sense of not caring for money, but the author is using the word figuratively. (E) relates to the author's unfulfilled desire to work on a steamboat, but the engineer is not thinking about the author, he is just showing off.

29. D

The engineer does everything for the purpose of showing off. He talks the jargon of the trade to make himself look knowledgeable, or (D) **sophisticated.**

Reading between the lines, we realize he's not an expert (A), and doesn't care about knowledge for its own sake (B). His (C) **ignorance** on other subjects is not mentioned; in fact, he has a working knowledge of St. Louis. (E) takes literally the phrase about how the engineer "forgot common people could not understand"—he couldn't **communicate effectively.** But the author says the engineer talked "as if" he forgot common people. In other words he didn't *fail* to communicate, he *chose not* to, to impress others.

30. E

The first four choices are all common meanings of *consideration,* but the context makes it clear that the figurative use in (E) is meant. The boys had "consideration" because they knew something about St. Louis, but their glory is over because the engineer knows much more. Prestige, respect, or (E) **reputation** supplies the meaning that fits. Boys are not likely to have the qualities of **generosity, deliberation, contemplation,** or **unselfishness** as a result of knowing a little about St. Louis.

31. A

The context makes it clear that the engineer had, or at least seemed to have, much more familiarity with St. Louis than the other boys with their "vague knowledge"; their "glory" is ended because he can talk rings around them about St. Louis (A).

There's no indication that (B) **St. Louis has changed,** or that the boys had been lying—their knowledge was "vague," not false (D). Reading between the lines, it's clear that travel to St. Louis was still rare enough to seem enviable (E). As for choice (C), the passage implies just the opposite.

32. A

With his "hair oil . . . showy brass watch chain, [and] leather belt," the engineer was obviously out to impress (A). The next sentence confirms that, telling us "no girl could withstand his charms."

The author never says the young man's dress is typical (B). (C) and (E) are both wrong; the emphasis here is on the engineer's charms, not the author's wardrobe or fashion ideas. (D) won't work because the engineer's behavior is as showy and superficial as his clothes.

33. D

As often in these questions, wrong choices give flat-footed, literal interpretations where the author is being humorous. (A) misunderstands the reference to Providence—the author is criticizing providence, not thanking it, because it has spared an "undeserving reptile," the engineer. So the author feels resentment, or (D) **outrage,** because the engineer's good luck seems **undeserved.**

Choice (B) sounds believable at first, but the passage doesn't emphasize the lucky escape—it focuses on people's sense that the engineer got better than he deserved. (C) and (E) are never mentioned.

34. C

The passage focuses on the author's ambition to work on a steamboat and his envy of the engineer. This makes (C) and (D) the strongest choices, so you need to decide between them. Looking at (D), the passage certainly emphasizes the engineer's **boastfulness,** but only within the framework of the author's dreams and ambitions (paragraphs one and five) and the author's reactions to the engineer. So (C) describes the *whole* passage whereas (D) describes only the long central paragraphs. In a *major purpose/major focus* question, the answer that sums up the *whole* passage will be correct.

The (A) **life** of the **town** is barely suggested. (B) is wrong because the passage's events don't end in **success**—although in reality, Mark Twain did go on to become a pilot. The author's (E) **conflict with his parents** is mentioned only briefly, toward the end of paragraph four.

35. E

The last paragraph discusses the author's failed attempts to become a pilot, and his daydreams that he will still become one, so (E) works best. Mates and clerks are mentioned as ignoring the author, but he never considers becoming either a (A) **mate or a clerk,** looking for some other job (B), giving up his aim of being a pilot (C), or asking his parents' forgiveness (D).

SECTION 4

1. B

You could find the answer by calculating the value of Column A, but there's a shortcut. You should see that both fractions in Column A are less than $\frac{1}{2}$. Therefore, their sum must be less than 1, and Column B is greater than Column A.

2. B

The cost of 6 pens at 2 for 22 cents is $\frac{22}{2}$ cents $\times$ 6, or $0.66, which is the value of Column A. The cost of 5 pens at 22 cents each is $1.10, and that's the value of Column B. So Column B is greater, and choice (B) is correct.

3. A

You can solve for b using the second equation: $b - 3 = 2$, so $b = 5$. Plug in 5 for b in the first equation and solve for a: $2a + 5 = 17$, $2a = 12$, $a = 6$. So Column A is greater than Column B, and choice (A) is correct.

4. C

Make one column look more like the other. Perform the multiplication in Column A: $x - 2(y + z)$ becomes $x - 2y - 2z$, which is the same expression as in Column B. Therefore, choice (C) is correct.

5. D

The mean (or average) of a group of terms is equal to the sum of the terms divided by the number of terms. You don't know the values of a, b, or c, but you do know that they sum to 150. So in Column A their mean is $\frac{150}{3} = 50$. The median is the middle term in a group of terms in numerical order. All you know about *a*, *b*, and *c* is that their sum is 150. It is possible that *a* = 1, *b* = 2, and *c* = 147; if so, the median would be 2 and in this case Column A would be greater. But what if *a* = *b* = *c* = 50? Then the median would be 50 and the columns would be equal. Since more than one relationship between the columns is possible, the answer must be choice (D).

6. C

Plug the values from each column into the given expression:

Column A = $(4 + 5)^3$ or $(9)^3$.

Column B = $(0 + 9)^3$ or $(9)^3$.

Since the values in both columns are equal, choice (C) is correct.

7. A

To find the circumference of circle *O*, you need to find the length of its radius. Draw a right triangle as shown below:

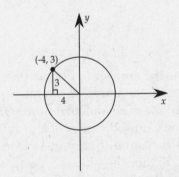

The lengths of the legs of the triangle are 4 and 3. You should recognize that this is a special 3-4-5 right triangle, so the length of the hypotenuse, which is also the radius of the circle, must be 5. Since circumference = $2\pi r$, the circumference of circle *O* = 10π. Since π is approximately 3.14, the circumference of circle *O* is greater than 30; Column A is greater than Column B.

8. D

If Jimmy waters his plant every other day, the number of times he waters it in one week depends upon whether he waters it the first day of the week or not. If he does, then he will water the plant the first, third, fifth, and seventh days for a total of 4 times that week. So Column A can be 4. Then the following week he will water it on the second, fourth, and sixth days for a total of 3 times. So Column B is 3, which makes Column A greater in this case. However, it's possible that in a given week he doesn't water the plant until the second day of the week. Then he will water it only 3 times that week and 4 times the following week. In this case, Column A is 3 and Column B is 4, making Column B greater. So Column A can be either greater than or less than Column B, and the answer must be choice (D).

9. C

To find the values of *r* and *s*, you need to find the slope of the line. Plug coordinates (1, 1) and (6, 11) into the slope formula:

$$\text{Slope} = \frac{y_2 - y_1}{x_2 - x_1}$$

$$= \frac{11 - 1}{6 - 1}$$

$$= \frac{10}{5}$$

$$= 2$$

So the slope of the line is 2.

Now find the value of *r* using coordinates (1, 1) and (3, *r*):

$$2 = \frac{r - 1}{3 - 1}$$

$$2 = \frac{r - 1}{2}$$

$$4 = r - 1$$

$$5 = r$$

Then find the value of *s* using coordinates (*s*, 9) and (6, 11):

$$2 = \frac{11 - 9}{6 - s}$$

$$2 = \frac{2}{6 - s}$$

$$12 - 2s = 2$$

$$-2s = -10$$

$$s = 5$$

The values in both columns are the same, and choice (C) is correct.

10. D

$r^2 + 4 = 21$, so $r^2 = 17$. You might think this means that r in Column A is greater than 4 in Column B, since $r^2 = 17$ while 4^2 equals only 16. But r can have a positive or negative value, since a negative squared also produces a positive. If r has a positive value, Column A is greater; if r has a negative value, Column B is greater. Since more than one relationship is possible, the answer is choice (D).

11. B

The perimeter of a triangle is equal to the sum of the lengths of its sides. You're given that $RT = US = 6$ and $RU < 2$. This means that RS must be less than 8. However, if $RS = 8$, then triangle RST would be a special right triangle with side lengths in a ratio of 3:4:5. So the length of ST would be 10, and the perimeter would be $6 + 8 + 10$, or 24. But RS is less than 8, which means the perimeter must be less than 24. Therefore, Column B is greater than Column A, and choice (B) is correct.

12. A

Think of the 5 students as A, B, C, D, and E and then systematically consider all the possible winning combinations. If A wins 1st place, then B, C, D, or E could win 2nd; if B wins 1st place, then A, C, D, or E could win 2nd; if C wins 1st place, then A, B, D, or E could win 2nd; if D wins 1st place, then A, B, C, or E could win 2nd; if E wins 1st place, then A, B, C, or D could win 2nd. This is a total of 20 different combinations, so Column A is greater than 10 in Column B.

13. A

Since x^2 is a positive fraction less than 1, its positive square root, x, must also be a fraction less than 1, which you are told is positive. When a positive fraction less than 1 is squared, the result is a positive fraction smaller than the original. Therefore, $x^2 < x$.

For example, $\left(\frac{1}{2}\right)^2 < \frac{1}{2}$, since $\left(\frac{1}{2}\right)^2 = \frac{1}{4}$. So in Column A you're subtracting a positive value from 1, and in Column B you're subtracting a larger positive value from 1, so Column A must be greater.

14. D

Do not assume that $ABCD$ is a square and that $AB = BC = AD = 4$. You know that triangle ACD is an isosceles right triangle and angle CAD is a 45° angle, which means that angle BAD is a right angle. However, no information is given about the lengths of AB and BC, or whether angles ABC and BCD are right angles. If necessary, redraw the diagram to see this. So the relationship cannot be determined and answer choice (D) is correct.

15. C

To determine the number of distinct prime factors of an integer, break the integer down into its prime factors and see how many different prime factors it has. Since you don't know the value of t, there is no way to determine how many distinct prime factors it has. This isn't a problem though—since t appears as a factor in both of the columns, we can eliminate it from each without affecting the relationship between the columns. So that leaves 2 in Column A and 8 in Column B. The only prime factor of 2 is 2, and the prime factorization of 8 is $2 \times 2 \times 2$. While 2 appears as a factor three times in Column B, there is still only one distinct prime factor in each, so the columns are equal.

16. .127

If $A = 2.54$ and $20B = A$, then $20B = 2.54$. So $B = \frac{2.54}{20}$ or .127.

17. 9.5 or 19/2

The perimeter of the figure is equal to the sum of the lengths of its sides: $2 + 1\frac{1}{3} + 1\frac{1}{2} + 1\frac{2}{3} + 3 = 9\frac{1}{2}$, which is $\frac{19}{2}$ expressed as an improper fraction, or 9.5 expressed as a decimal.

18. 84 or 96

If $\frac{h}{3}$ and $\frac{h}{4}$ are both integers, then h must be a multiple of 3×4, or 12. Since it's given that h is between 75 and 100, h must be 84 or 96.

19. 8

The profit made by the retailer on the shirts is equal to the difference between the selling price and the cost for each shirt, multiplied by the number of shirts: $(\$6.75 - \$4.50) \times 16 = \$2.25 \times 16 = \$36.00$ profit. To find the number of \$4.50 shirts that can be bought for \$36.00, you need to divide \$36.00 by \$4.50, and $\frac{36}{4.5} = 8$.

20. 45/4 or 11.2 or 11.3

Draw a diagram and label it according to the given information:

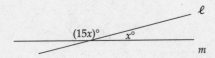

Let the smaller angle measure $x°$. Since the other angle formed is 15 times as large, label it $(15x)°$. Notice that these two angles are supplementary, that is, they add up to 180°. Therefore:

$$x + 15x = 180$$
$$16x = 180$$
$$x = \frac{45}{4}$$

So the smaller angle is $\frac{45}{4}$ degrees, which can also be gridded in decimal form as 11.2 or 11.3.

21. 4

Before you plug in -4 for x, you should factor the given equation:

$$x^2 + 2xr + r^2 = 0$$
$$(x + r)(x + r) = 0$$
$$(x + r)^2 = 0$$

Now plug in -4 for x to solve for r: $(-4 + r)^2 = 0$, $-4 + r = 0$, and $r = 4$.

22. 1/16 or .062 or .063

Plug the values into the given definition:

$$\frac{1}{4} \ast = \left(\frac{1}{4}\right)^2 - \frac{1}{4}$$
$$= \frac{1}{16} - \frac{1}{4}$$
$$= \frac{1}{16} - \frac{4}{16}$$
$$= \frac{-3}{16}$$
$$\frac{1}{2} \ast = \left(\frac{1}{2}\right)^2 - \frac{1}{2}$$
$$= \frac{1}{4} - \frac{1}{2}$$
$$= \frac{-1}{4}$$

So:

$$\frac{1}{4} \ast - \frac{1}{2} \ast = \frac{-3}{16} - \left(\frac{-1}{4}\right)$$
$$= \frac{-3}{16} - \left(-\frac{4}{16}\right)$$
$$= \frac{1}{16}$$

This can also be gridded as .062 or .063.

23. 1/8 or .125

You should recognize that right $\triangle ABC$ is a 45-45-90 triangle, with side lengths in a ratio of $1:1:\sqrt{2}$. Therefore, the length of the two equal legs AB and AC is $\frac{1}{2}$.

To find the area of the triangle, plug the values of the base and height (the lengths of the two equal legs) into the area formula:

Area of a triangle $= \frac{1}{2}(\text{base} \times \text{height})$

$$= \frac{1}{2}\left(\frac{1}{2}\right)^2$$

$$= \frac{1}{2}\left(\frac{1}{4}\right)$$

$$= \frac{1}{8}, \text{ or } .125$$

24. 2025

You're given that x is a factor of 8,100 and it's an odd integer. To find the greatest possible value of x, begin factoring 8,100 by using its smallest prime factor, 2, as one of the factors. Continue factoring out a 2 from the remaining factors until you find an odd one as shown below:

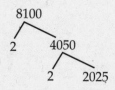

8,100

$2 \times 4,050$

$2 \times 2,025$

Since 2,025 is odd, you can stop factoring; it is the greatest odd factor of 8,100.

25. 4/7 or .571

Translate the problem into math: Let b = number of boys; let g = number of girls. So $b + g$ = total number of students in the class.

$\frac{1}{2}$ of the boys speak French, so $\frac{1}{2}b$ = the number of boys who speak French.

$\frac{2}{3}$ of the girls speak French, so $\frac{2}{3}g$ = the number of girls who speak French.

Therefore, $\frac{1}{2}b + \frac{2}{3}g$ = total French speakers.

So the fraction of the class that speaks French

$$= \frac{\frac{1}{2}b + \frac{2}{3}\left(\frac{3}{4}b\right)}{b + g}$$

Since there are $\frac{3}{4}$ as many girls as boys in the class, $g = \frac{3}{4}b$. Plug in $\frac{3}{4}b$ for g into the fraction above.

Fraction of the class that speaks French:

$$= \frac{\frac{1}{2}b + \frac{2}{3}\left(\frac{3}{4}b\right)}{b + \frac{3}{4}b}$$

$$= \frac{\frac{1}{2}b + \frac{1}{2}b}{\frac{7}{4}b}$$

$$= \frac{b}{\frac{7}{4}b}$$

$$= \frac{4}{7}, \text{ or } .571$$

SECTION 5

The Shakespeare Pair

These paired passages present two opposing arguments on a single subject, the subject here being "Who Really Wrote Shakespeare's Plays?" The author of the first passage maintains that Francis Bacon actually wrote the plays, basing that conclusion on the assertion that Shakespeare didn't have the education and social experience necessary to create such sophisticated plays. The author of the second passage takes issue with that, claiming that Shakespeare's genius grew out of a deep understanding of human nature rather than any wide learning or arcane knowledge.

1. B

A Vocabulary-in-Context question. Here we're asked the definition of the word *entertain* in line 2, where it is used in the phrase "entertain some doubt." Well, when you entertain doubt, or entertain an idea, you are holding it in your head. You are **harboring** it, in the sense of **to harbor** as "to be host to." So choice (B) is correct.

The other choices are all acceptable dictionary definitions of the verb *entertain*, but none fits the context as well as choice (B) does. (A) **amuse** is a common synonym for *entertain*, but how does one amuse doubt? (C) **occupy** and (E) **engage** are closer, but they don't fit the sentence either. One's *mind* is occupied or engaged, but the doubt itself is not occupied or engaged. Meanwhile, (D) **cherish** adds a sense of valuing the entertained thing, as if it were something desirable.

2. D

The author claims that the person who actually wrote the plays must have had "intimate knowledge of life within royal courts and palaces," but that Shakespeare was just a commoner, without that kind of "firsthand experience" of the aristocracy. He wants to cast doubt on Shakespeare's **familiarity with the life of [aristocrats],** or choice (D).

Shakespeare's ability to (A) **write poetically** and his (C) **ability to support himself as a playwright** never come up in Passage 1. The **knowledge of foreign places** mentioned in (B) does come up, but being a

commoner is not necessarily related to Shakespeare's apparent lack of travel. Choice (E) is the closest wrong choice, since the aristocracy was the **government** in Elizabethan England, but the issue is his knowledge of all aspects of aristocratic life.

3. E

Two Shakespearian plays—*Coriolanus* and *Love's Labour's Lost*—are mentioned in lines 28–31 in connection with the allegedly specialized knowledge they contain. They support the point that the educated aristocrat Bacon was a more likely author than was the undereducated commoner Shakespeare. So (E) answers the question best.

Choice (A) is a clever wrong choice, but it's too extreme. The author's not trying to prove that *only* Bacon could have written these plays, just that Bacon was far more likely than Shakespeare to have written them. The **deep understanding of human nature** mentioned in (B) is something brought up in Passage 2, not Passage 1. The author is not comparing the two plays to **works written by Bacon,** as (C) claims. And (D) is wrong since nothing about society is mentioned with regard to *Coriolanus*. Also, it's not the **broad spectrum of society** the author alludes to with regard to *Love's Labour's Lost,* but rather the knowledge of just the upper range of society.

4. A

It's clear that Ms. Bacon is looking down on actors, of which Shakespeare was one, regarding them with the **disdain** expressed in correct choice (A).

She's not **resentful** at how the **characters are portrayed,** choice (B), since she's talking about the characters themselves and what they tell us about real-life actors. Given her opinion of actors, she certainly doesn't **regret that their conditions weren't better,** choice (C). (D) is closer, but it's a distortion. She never doubts that anyone could **create such characters;** she doubts that the author of the plays could *be like* such a character. And finally, in (E), there's no evidence in the quote that Ms. Bacon thinks the actors are inept at their art, just that they are vulgar and lowly persons.

5. B

This question sends you back to paragraph 4 of Passage 1, where Bacon's preference for anonymity is explained. The author claims that, because the plays were "controversial," Bacon felt that associating himself with them would have been "politically and personally damaging." So **he wished to protect himself from the effects of controversy,** choice (B).

(A) is wrong, since Bacon did publish a lot of writing under his own name. (C) is plausible, but it's not the reason given in paragraph 4 or anywhere else in the first passage. (D) tries to confuse us by introducing the subject of **lowly actors** from the preceding paragraph. And (E) is a fabrication since we know that Bacon was already famous from his other writings.

6. C

This question takes us to the first paragraph of Passage 2, where the emphasis is on language ability. The author doubts that Bacon, a writer primarily of academic Latin, would have had the ability to produce the exalted English in which the plays were written. That makes (C) the best answer.

(A) is a distortion. Just because Bacon wrote most of his own work in another language doesn't mean that he was **unfamiliar** with English. (B)'s emphasis on the difficult switch from **scientific writing** to **writing plays** is close, but language rather than the type of writing is the focus. There's no reason to surmise that the author doubts Bacon's ability to **cooperate** on a **committee,** choice (D). Finally, (E) is wrong because there is no evidence in the first paragraph that the author has doubts about Bacon's ability to produce that amount of work.

7. D

Back to Vocabulary-in-Context. This question asks about *premier* as it is used in the phrase "premier stylist in the English language." The author definitely wants to indicate the sublime language of the plays here, so *premier* is being used in the sense of "of the first rank," or, as choice (D) has it, **greatest.** (A), (C), and (E) all play on the sense of premier as "first in sequence"(*inaugural,* by the way, means "marking the commencement or beginning"), but the author is not referring here to *when* Shakespeare wrote. He's writing about how *well*

Shakespeare wrote. On the other hand, (B) **influential** misses on two counts—first, it's not a definition of *premier* in any context, and second, the issue of influence on other writers is not brought up here.

8. B

The next Vocabulary-in-Context question concerns the adjective *encyclopedic* in line 76, where it's used to modify the noun "knowledge." The author says that Shakespeare's genius was one of common sense and perceptive intuition, not encyclopedic knowledge, which is related to great book-learning. So the knowledge described as "encyclopedic" is wide-ranging and in-depth—**comprehensive,** in other words, choice (B).

(A) **technical** is close to the sense of the context, but it's not a synonym of *encyclopedic,* so it really won't work here. (C) won't work either, since **abridged** (meaning "condensed") cannot describe the kind of exhaustive knowledge the author is describing here. And while it may take discipline to gain encyclopedic knowledge, *encyclopedic* itself cannot be defined as **disciplined,** so cut (D). Finally, (E) **specialized** isn't quite right, since it implies a narrowness of focus.

9. E

The reference to Shakespeare's status as a landowner comes in the third paragraph of Passage 2, where it is brought up to show that Shakespeare would have been "knowledgeable about legal matters related to . . . real estate." That makes (E) the best answer, "legal matters" being equivalent to **the law.**

(A) is interesting, since the author does say that owning land was quite an accomplishment for a playwright, but it has nothing to do with his knowledge of the law. (B) is off, since owning land doesn't make one automatically friendly with the highborn set. (C) is wrong, because Shakespeare's financial state is just a side issue; it's not the point of bringing up Shakespeare's landowning status. And (D) doesn't fit, since no one doubts that **Shakespeare was a commoner.**

10. A

This question directs us to lines 100–103, where the author claims that literary genius "can flower in any socioeconomic bracket." That implies that genius has little to do with a person's social and financial position—or, as correct choice (A) has it—genius doesn't depend **on a writer's external circumstances.**

(B) fails by bringing in the notion of **comprehension of human nature** from elsewhere in the passage. (C) is a common cliché, but there's no evidence here that the author felt that Shakespeare's genius was **enhanced by poverty.** In fact, this author implies that Shakespeare wasn't even all that poor. (D) may be a true statement, but recognition of genius isn't really under discussion here; it's the simple existence of genius. And (E) is a distortion; the author claims that at least one kind of genius does not *stem* from **book-learning and academic training,** but that doesn't mean that those things would **stifle** *literary genius.*

11. C

Go back to the fourth paragraph of Passage 1, where our first author claims that Bacon may have "hired a lowly actor" like Shakespeare to put his name to the plays and take the heat of controversy. How would our second author respond to this claim? The second author, remember, writes in the concluding paragraph of Passage 2 that "no elaborate theories of intrigue and secret identity are necessary to explain the accomplishment of William Shakespeare." Surely author 2 would regard the **scenario** described in Passage 1 as just this kind of **unnecessary** theory, so (C) is the best guess for how author 2 would react.

As for choice (A), author 2 may or may not agree that the plays were **controversial** in their time, so (A) won't work. (B) gets the thrust of author 2's argument wrong. Author 2 denigrates the notion that Bacon wrote the plays *not* by arguing that Bacon wasn't a great scholar, but by arguing that it didn't require a great scholar to write the plays. (D) tries to turn author 1's argument on its head. A nice idea, perhaps, but author 2 shows no hint of doing anything of the kind. And (E) brings up the notion of Shakespeare's social *respectability,* which really isn't of much concern to author 2.

12. C

What would be author 1's reaction to author 2's skepticism that Bacon, the author of Latin treatises, could be the "premier stylist in the English language"? Well, author 1's repeated assertions of Bacon's scholarly genius and Shakespeare's lack of education are both reflected in choice (C), which makes it a good bet as the correct answer.

(A)'s mention of the **similarities between Latin and English** is enough to kill this choice, since author 1 mentions no such similarities in the passage. (B) is a true statement, perhaps, but it doesn't really address the issue. (D) is fairly nonsensical, since it would weaken author 1's entire theory about why Bacon hired Shakespeare. Finally, (E) makes a good point, but again, there is no hint of this sentiment in author 1's statements.

13. D

Always check back to the passage to figure out the meaning of a Vocab-in-Context word. Here, the word "observation" refers to the phrase that "Shakespeare, in short, was Shakespeare"—a jokey comment on the author's part. None of the other choices fits the context of an informal remark, so (D) is correct here.

SECTION 6

1. B

Plug in −2 for p and 3 for q: $p^3q^2 + p^2q = (-2)^3 3^2 + (-2)^2 3 = (-8)(9) + 4(3)$, or $(-72) + 12 = -60$. (Note that a negative number raised to an *even* power becomes positive, but raised to an *odd* power stays negative.)

2. E

Keep track of the lengths you know on the diagram. *B* is the midpoint of *AC* so $AB = BC$. Since $AB = 5$, $BC = 5$. $BD = 8$, so $BC + CD = 8$. $BC = 5$, so $5 + CD = 8$, $CD = 3$. *D* is the midpoint of *CE*, so $CD = DE = 3$.

3. D

Try each answer choice until you find one that works for all of the pairs of numbers.

Choice (A), $P = N + 5$ works for 2 and 7, but not for 4 and 13.

Choice (B), $P = 2N + 3$ also works for 2 and 7, but not for 4 and 13.

Choice (C), $P = 2N + 5$, doesn't work for 2 and 7.

Choice (D), $P = 3N + 1$, works for all four pairs of numbers, so that's the answer.

4. A

$\angle PNM$ is supplementary to $\angle PNQ$, so $\angle PNM + 105° = 180°$, and $\angle PNM = 75°$. Since $PM = PN$, triangle *MPN* is an isosceles and $\angle PMN = \angle PNM = 75°$. The interior angles of a triangle sum to 180°, so $75 + 75 + x = 180$, and $x = 30$.

5. B

Probability is defined as the number of desired events divided by the total number of possible events. There are $5 + 6 + 4$, or 15 pens in the knapsack. If he pulls out 1 pen, there are 15 different pens he might pick, or 15 possible outcomes. The desired outcome is that the pen be either red or black.

The group of acceptable pens consists of $4 + 6$, or 10 pens. So the probability that one of these pens will be picked is 10 out of 15, or $\frac{10}{15}$, which we can reduce to $\frac{2}{3}$.

6. C

Pick variables for the two items and translate the given information into algebraic equations. Let $h =$ the price of a hot dog and $s =$ the price of a soda. The first statement is translated as $2h + s = \$3.25$, and the second as $3h + s = \$4.50$. If you subtract the first equation from the second, the s is eliminated so you can solve for h:

$$3h + s = \$4.50$$
$$\underline{-2h + s = \$3.25}$$
$$h \quad\quad = \$1.25$$

Plug this value for h into the first equation to solve for s:

$$2(\$1.25) + s = \$3.25$$
$$\$2.50 + s = \$3.25$$
$$s = \$0.75$$

So two sodas would cost $2 \times \$0.75 = \$1.50$.

7. C

$a = f$, since all the obtuse angles formed when two parallel lines are cut by a transversal are equal. f is an exterior angle of the small triangle containing angles c, d, and e, so it is equal to the sum of the two nonadjacent interior angles, c and d. Since $a = f$ and $f = c + d$, $a = c + d$, answer choice (C).

8. D

The first 3 minutes of the phone call cost 75 cents or 0.75 dollars. If the entire call lasted x minutes, the rest of the call lasted $x - 3$ minutes. Each minute after the first 3 cost 15 cents or $\$0.15$, so the rest of the call cost $\$0.15(x - 3)$. So the cost of the entire call is $0.75 + 0.15(x - 3)$ dollars.

If this isn't clear, pick numbers. Let $x = 5$. The first 3 minutes cost $\$0.75$ and the additional $5 - 3 = 2$ minutes are $\$0.15$ each. So the entire call costs $\$0.75 + 2(\$0.15) = \$1.05$. Plug 5 for x into all the answer choices to see which ones give you 1.05:

(A) $0.75(3) + 0.15x = 2.25 + 0.15(5) = 2.25 + 0.75 = 3.00$. Eliminate.

(B) $0.75(3) + 0.15(x + 3) = 2.25 + 0.15(5 + 3) = 2.25 + 1.20 = 3.45$. Eliminate.

(C) $0.75 + 0.15(3 - x) = 0.75 + 0.15(3 - 5) = 0.75 - 0.30 = 0.45$. Eliminate.

(D) $0.75 + 0.15(x - 3) = 0.75 + 0.15(5 - 3) = 0.75 + 0.30 = 1.05$. Works!

(E) $0.75 + 0.15(5) = 0.75 + 0.75 = 1.50$. Eliminate.

The only choice that yields the desired result is (D), so it must be correct.

9. B

Before you can find the area of the circle, you need to find the length of the wire. The wire is in the shape of a semicircle with diameter 12. Since circumference = πd, the length of a semicircle is half of that, $\frac{\pi d}{2}$. So the length of the wire is $\frac{\pi(12)}{2}$, or 6π. When this wire is bent to form a circle, the circumference of this circle will equal 6π. So the length of the circle's diameter must equal 6, and the radius must be 3. Now you can find the area of the circle:

$$\text{Area} = \pi r^2$$
$$= \pi(3)^2$$
$$= 9\pi$$

10. C

If $a^2 - a = 72$, then $a^2 - a - 72 = 0$. Factoring this quadratic equation: $(a - 9)(a + 8) = 0$. So $a - 9 = 0$ or $a + 8 = 0$, and $a = 9$ or $a = -8$. b to the nth power equals a, so b must be a root of either 9 or -8. Look through the answer choices to find the choice that is not a root of either 9 or -8:

(A) -8: $(-8)1 = -8$, so this can be a value for b.

(B) -2: $(-2)3 = -8$, so this can be a value for b.

(C) 2: $23 = 8$, *not* -8, so this *cannot* be a value for b.

(D) 3: $32 = 9$, so this can be a value for b.

(E) 9: $91 = 9$, so this can be a value for b.

So (C) is the only answer choice that cannot be a value for b.

SAT

Practice Test Two

HOW TO TAKE THIS PRACTICE TEST

Before taking this practice test, find a quiet room where you can work uninterrupted for two and a half hours. Make sure you have a comfortable desk, your calculator, and several No. 2 pencils.

Use the answer sheet provided to record your answers. (You can cut it out or photocopy it.)

Once you start this practice test, don't stop until you've finished. Remember—you can review any questions within a section, but you may not go back or forward a section.

You'll find an answer key, score conversion charts, and explanations following the test.

Good luck.

SAT Practice Test Two Answer Sheet

Remove (or photocopy) this answer sheet and use it to complete the practice test.
(See answer key following the test when finished.)

Start with number 1 for each section. If a section has fewer questions than answer spaces, leave the extra spaces blank.

SECTION 1

1 Ⓐ Ⓑ Ⓒ Ⓓ Ⓔ	11 Ⓐ Ⓑ Ⓒ Ⓓ Ⓔ	21 Ⓐ Ⓑ Ⓒ Ⓓ Ⓔ	31 Ⓐ Ⓑ Ⓒ Ⓓ Ⓔ
2 Ⓐ Ⓑ Ⓒ Ⓓ Ⓔ	12 Ⓐ Ⓑ Ⓒ Ⓓ Ⓔ	22 Ⓐ Ⓑ Ⓒ Ⓓ Ⓔ	32 Ⓐ Ⓑ Ⓒ Ⓓ Ⓔ
3 Ⓐ Ⓑ Ⓒ Ⓓ Ⓔ	13 Ⓐ Ⓑ Ⓒ Ⓓ Ⓔ	23 Ⓐ Ⓑ Ⓒ Ⓓ Ⓔ	33 Ⓐ Ⓑ Ⓒ Ⓓ Ⓔ
4 Ⓐ Ⓑ Ⓒ Ⓓ Ⓔ	14 Ⓐ Ⓑ Ⓒ Ⓓ Ⓔ	24 Ⓐ Ⓑ Ⓒ Ⓓ Ⓔ	34 Ⓐ Ⓑ Ⓒ Ⓓ Ⓔ
5 Ⓐ Ⓑ Ⓒ Ⓓ Ⓔ	15 Ⓐ Ⓑ Ⓒ Ⓓ Ⓔ	25 Ⓐ Ⓑ Ⓒ Ⓓ Ⓔ	35 Ⓐ Ⓑ Ⓒ Ⓓ Ⓔ
6 Ⓐ Ⓑ Ⓒ Ⓓ Ⓔ	16 Ⓐ Ⓑ Ⓒ Ⓓ Ⓔ	26 Ⓐ Ⓑ Ⓒ Ⓓ Ⓔ	36 Ⓐ Ⓑ Ⓒ Ⓓ Ⓔ
7 Ⓐ Ⓑ Ⓒ Ⓓ Ⓔ	17 Ⓐ Ⓑ Ⓒ Ⓓ Ⓔ	27 Ⓐ Ⓑ Ⓒ Ⓓ Ⓔ	37 Ⓐ Ⓑ Ⓒ Ⓓ Ⓔ
8 Ⓐ Ⓑ Ⓒ Ⓓ Ⓔ	18 Ⓐ Ⓑ Ⓒ Ⓓ Ⓔ	28 Ⓐ Ⓑ Ⓒ Ⓓ Ⓔ	38 Ⓐ Ⓑ Ⓒ Ⓓ Ⓔ
9 Ⓐ Ⓑ Ⓒ Ⓓ Ⓔ	19 Ⓐ Ⓑ Ⓒ Ⓓ Ⓔ	29 Ⓐ Ⓑ Ⓒ Ⓓ Ⓔ	39 Ⓐ Ⓑ Ⓒ Ⓓ Ⓔ
10 Ⓐ Ⓑ Ⓒ Ⓓ Ⓔ	20 Ⓐ Ⓑ Ⓒ Ⓓ Ⓔ	30 Ⓐ Ⓑ Ⓒ Ⓓ Ⓔ	40 Ⓐ Ⓑ Ⓒ Ⓓ Ⓔ

right in section 1

wrong in section 1

SECTION 2

1 Ⓐ Ⓑ Ⓒ Ⓓ Ⓔ	11 Ⓐ Ⓑ Ⓒ Ⓓ Ⓔ	21 Ⓐ Ⓑ Ⓒ Ⓓ Ⓔ	31 Ⓐ Ⓑ Ⓒ Ⓓ Ⓔ
2 Ⓐ Ⓑ Ⓒ Ⓓ Ⓔ	12 Ⓐ Ⓑ Ⓒ Ⓓ Ⓔ	22 Ⓐ Ⓑ Ⓒ Ⓓ Ⓔ	32 Ⓐ Ⓑ Ⓒ Ⓓ Ⓔ
3 Ⓐ Ⓑ Ⓒ Ⓓ Ⓔ	13 Ⓐ Ⓑ Ⓒ Ⓓ Ⓔ	23 Ⓐ Ⓑ Ⓒ Ⓓ Ⓔ	33 Ⓐ Ⓑ Ⓒ Ⓓ Ⓔ
4 Ⓐ Ⓑ Ⓒ Ⓓ Ⓔ	14 Ⓐ Ⓑ Ⓒ Ⓓ Ⓔ	24 Ⓐ Ⓑ Ⓒ Ⓓ Ⓔ	34 Ⓐ Ⓑ Ⓒ Ⓓ Ⓔ
5 Ⓐ Ⓑ Ⓒ Ⓓ Ⓔ	15 Ⓐ Ⓑ Ⓒ Ⓓ Ⓔ	25 Ⓐ Ⓑ Ⓒ Ⓓ Ⓔ	35 Ⓐ Ⓑ Ⓒ Ⓓ Ⓔ
6 Ⓐ Ⓑ Ⓒ Ⓓ Ⓔ	16 Ⓐ Ⓑ Ⓒ Ⓓ Ⓔ	26 Ⓐ Ⓑ Ⓒ Ⓓ Ⓔ	36 Ⓐ Ⓑ Ⓒ Ⓓ Ⓔ
7 Ⓐ Ⓑ Ⓒ Ⓓ Ⓔ	17 Ⓐ Ⓑ Ⓒ Ⓓ Ⓔ	27 Ⓐ Ⓑ Ⓒ Ⓓ Ⓔ	37 Ⓐ Ⓑ Ⓒ Ⓓ Ⓔ
8 Ⓐ Ⓑ Ⓒ Ⓓ Ⓔ	18 Ⓐ Ⓑ Ⓒ Ⓓ Ⓔ	28 Ⓐ Ⓑ Ⓒ Ⓓ Ⓔ	38 Ⓐ Ⓑ Ⓒ Ⓓ Ⓔ
9 Ⓐ Ⓑ Ⓒ Ⓓ Ⓔ	19 Ⓐ Ⓑ Ⓒ Ⓓ Ⓔ	29 Ⓐ Ⓑ Ⓒ Ⓓ Ⓔ	39 Ⓐ Ⓑ Ⓒ Ⓓ Ⓔ
10 Ⓐ Ⓑ Ⓒ Ⓓ Ⓔ	20 Ⓐ Ⓑ Ⓒ Ⓓ Ⓔ	30 Ⓐ Ⓑ Ⓒ Ⓓ Ⓔ	40 Ⓐ Ⓑ Ⓒ Ⓓ Ⓔ

right in section 2

wrong in section 2

SECTION

3

1 (A) (B) (C) (D) (E)   11 (A) (B) (C) (D) (E)   21 (A) (B) (C) (D) (E)   31 (A) (B) (C) (D) (E)
2 (A) (B) (C) (D) (E)   12 (A) (B) (C) (D) (E)   22 (A) (B) (C) (D) (E)   32 (A) (B) (C) (D) (E)
3 (A) (B) (C) (D) (E)   13 (A) (B) (C) (D) (E)   23 (A) (B) (C) (D) (E)   33 (A) (B) (C) (D) (E)
4 (A) (B) (C) (D) (E)   14 (A) (B) (C) (D) (E)   24 (A) (B) (C) (D) (E)   34 (A) (B) (C) (D) (E)
5 (A) (B) (C) (D) (E)   15 (A) (B) (C) (D) (E)   25 (A) (B) (C) (D) (E)   35 (A) (B) (C) (D) (E)
6 (A) (B) (C) (D) (E)   16 (A) (B) (C) (D) (E)   26 (A) (B) (C) (D) (E)   36 (A) (B) (C) (D) (E)
7 (A) (B) (C) (D) (E)   17 (A) (B) (C) (D) (E)   27 (A) (B) (C) (D) (E)   37 (A) (B) (C) (D) (E)
8 (A) (B) (C) (D) (E)   18 (A) (B) (C) (D) (E)   28 (A) (B) (C) (D) (E)   38 (A) (B) (C) (D) (E)
9 (A) (B) (C) (D) (E)   19 (A) (B) (C) (D) (E)   29 (A) (B) (C) (D) (E)   39 (A) (B) (C) (D) (E)
10 (A) (B) (C) (D) (E)   20 (A) (B) (C) (D) (E)   30 (A) (B) (C) (D) (E)   40 (A) (B) (C) (D) (E)

right in
section 3

wrong in
section 3

If section 3 of your test book contains math questions that are not multiple choice, continue to item 16 below. Otherwise, continue to item 16 above.

16 17 18 19 20 21 22 23 24 25

[grid-in answer grids for items 16 through 25, each with digits 0–9]

SECTION

4

1 (A) (B) (C) (D) (E)   11 (A) (B) (C) (D) (E)   21 (A) (B) (C) (D) (E)   31 (A) (B) (C) (D) (E)
2 (A) (B) (C) (D) (E)   12 (A) (B) (C) (D) (E)   22 (A) (B) (C) (D) (E)   32 (A) (B) (C) (D) (E)
3 (A) (B) (C) (D) (E)   13 (A) (B) (C) (D) (E)   23 (A) (B) (C) (D) (E)   33 (A) (B) (C) (D) (E)
4 (A) (B) (C) (D) (E)   14 (A) (B) (C) (D) (E)   24 (A) (B) (C) (D) (E)   34 (A) (B) (C) (D) (E)
5 (A) (B) (C) (D) (E)   15 (A) (B) (C) (D) (E)   25 (A) (B) (C) (D) (E)   35 (A) (B) (C) (D) (E)
6 (A) (B) (C) (D) (E)   16 (A) (B) (C) (D) (E)   26 (A) (B) (C) (D) (E)   36 (A) (B) (C) (D) (E)
7 (A) (B) (C) (D) (E)   17 (A) (B) (C) (D) (E)   27 (A) (B) (C) (D) (E)   37 (A) (B) (C) (D) (E)
8 (A) (B) (C) (D) (E)   18 (A) (B) (C) (D) (E)   28 (A) (B) (C) (D) (E)   38 (A) (B) (C) (D) (E)
9 (A) (B) (C) (D) (E)   19 (A) (B) (C) (D) (E)   29 (A) (B) (C) (D) (E)   39 (A) (B) (C) (D) (E)
10 (A) (B) (C) (D) (E)   20 (A) (B) (C) (D) (E)   30 (A) (B) (C) (D) (E)   40 (A) (B) (C) (D) (E)

right in
section 4

wrong in
section 4

Remove (or photocopy) this answer sheet and use it to complete the practive test.

Start with number 1 for each section. If a section has fewer questions than answer spaces, leave the extra spaces blank.

SECTION 5

1 Ⓐ Ⓑ Ⓒ Ⓓ Ⓔ   11 Ⓐ Ⓑ Ⓒ Ⓓ Ⓔ   21 Ⓐ Ⓑ Ⓒ Ⓓ Ⓔ   31 Ⓐ Ⓑ Ⓒ Ⓓ Ⓔ
2 Ⓐ Ⓑ Ⓒ Ⓓ Ⓔ   12 Ⓐ Ⓑ Ⓒ Ⓓ Ⓔ   22 Ⓐ Ⓑ Ⓒ Ⓓ Ⓔ   32 Ⓐ Ⓑ Ⓒ Ⓓ Ⓔ
3 Ⓐ Ⓑ Ⓒ Ⓓ Ⓔ   13 Ⓐ Ⓑ Ⓒ Ⓓ Ⓔ   23 Ⓐ Ⓑ Ⓒ Ⓓ Ⓔ   33 Ⓐ Ⓑ Ⓒ Ⓓ Ⓔ
4 Ⓐ Ⓑ Ⓒ Ⓓ Ⓔ   14 Ⓐ Ⓑ Ⓒ Ⓓ Ⓔ   24 Ⓐ Ⓑ Ⓒ Ⓓ Ⓔ   34 Ⓐ Ⓑ Ⓒ Ⓓ Ⓔ
5 Ⓐ Ⓑ Ⓒ Ⓓ Ⓔ   15 Ⓐ Ⓑ Ⓒ Ⓓ Ⓔ   25 Ⓐ Ⓑ Ⓒ Ⓓ Ⓔ   35 Ⓐ Ⓑ Ⓒ Ⓓ Ⓔ
6 Ⓐ Ⓑ Ⓒ Ⓓ Ⓔ   16 Ⓐ Ⓑ Ⓒ Ⓓ Ⓔ   26 Ⓐ Ⓑ Ⓒ Ⓓ Ⓔ   36 Ⓐ Ⓑ Ⓒ Ⓓ Ⓔ
7 Ⓐ Ⓑ Ⓒ Ⓓ Ⓔ   17 Ⓐ Ⓑ Ⓒ Ⓓ Ⓔ   27 Ⓐ Ⓑ Ⓒ Ⓓ Ⓔ   37 Ⓐ Ⓑ Ⓒ Ⓓ Ⓔ
8 Ⓐ Ⓑ Ⓒ Ⓓ Ⓔ   18 Ⓐ Ⓑ Ⓒ Ⓓ Ⓔ   28 Ⓐ Ⓑ Ⓒ Ⓓ Ⓔ   38 Ⓐ Ⓑ Ⓒ Ⓓ Ⓔ
9 Ⓐ Ⓑ Ⓒ Ⓓ Ⓔ   19 Ⓐ Ⓑ Ⓒ Ⓓ Ⓔ   29 Ⓐ Ⓑ Ⓒ Ⓓ Ⓔ   39 Ⓐ Ⓑ Ⓒ Ⓓ Ⓔ
10 Ⓐ Ⓑ Ⓒ Ⓓ Ⓔ   20 Ⓐ Ⓑ Ⓒ Ⓓ Ⓔ   30 Ⓐ Ⓑ Ⓒ Ⓓ Ⓔ   40 Ⓐ Ⓑ Ⓒ Ⓓ Ⓔ

right in section 5

wrong in section 5

SECTION 6

1 Ⓐ Ⓑ Ⓒ Ⓓ Ⓔ   11 Ⓐ Ⓑ Ⓒ Ⓓ Ⓔ   21 Ⓐ Ⓑ Ⓒ Ⓓ Ⓔ   31 Ⓐ Ⓑ Ⓒ Ⓓ Ⓔ
2 Ⓐ Ⓑ Ⓒ Ⓓ Ⓔ   12 Ⓐ Ⓑ Ⓒ Ⓓ Ⓔ   22 Ⓐ Ⓑ Ⓒ Ⓓ Ⓔ   32 Ⓐ Ⓑ Ⓒ Ⓓ Ⓔ
3 Ⓐ Ⓑ Ⓒ Ⓓ Ⓔ   13 Ⓐ Ⓑ Ⓒ Ⓓ Ⓔ   23 Ⓐ Ⓑ Ⓒ Ⓓ Ⓔ   33 Ⓐ Ⓑ Ⓒ Ⓓ Ⓔ
4 Ⓐ Ⓑ Ⓒ Ⓓ Ⓔ   14 Ⓐ Ⓑ Ⓒ Ⓓ Ⓔ   24 Ⓐ Ⓑ Ⓒ Ⓓ Ⓔ   34 Ⓐ Ⓑ Ⓒ Ⓓ Ⓔ
5 Ⓐ Ⓑ Ⓒ Ⓓ Ⓔ   15 Ⓐ Ⓑ Ⓒ Ⓓ Ⓔ   25 Ⓐ Ⓑ Ⓒ Ⓓ Ⓔ   35 Ⓐ Ⓑ Ⓒ Ⓓ Ⓔ
6 Ⓐ Ⓑ Ⓒ Ⓓ Ⓔ   16 Ⓐ Ⓑ Ⓒ Ⓓ Ⓔ   26 Ⓐ Ⓑ Ⓒ Ⓓ Ⓔ   36 Ⓐ Ⓑ Ⓒ Ⓓ Ⓔ
7 Ⓐ Ⓑ Ⓒ Ⓓ Ⓔ   17 Ⓐ Ⓑ Ⓒ Ⓓ Ⓔ   27 Ⓐ Ⓑ Ⓒ Ⓓ Ⓔ   37 Ⓐ Ⓑ Ⓒ Ⓓ Ⓔ
8 Ⓐ Ⓑ Ⓒ Ⓓ Ⓔ   18 Ⓐ Ⓑ Ⓒ Ⓓ Ⓔ   28 Ⓐ Ⓑ Ⓒ Ⓓ Ⓔ   38 Ⓐ Ⓑ Ⓒ Ⓓ Ⓔ
9 Ⓐ Ⓑ Ⓒ Ⓓ Ⓔ   19 Ⓐ Ⓑ Ⓒ Ⓓ Ⓔ   29 Ⓐ Ⓑ Ⓒ Ⓓ Ⓔ   39 Ⓐ Ⓑ Ⓒ Ⓓ Ⓔ
10 Ⓐ Ⓑ Ⓒ Ⓓ Ⓔ   20 Ⓐ Ⓑ Ⓒ Ⓓ Ⓔ   30 Ⓐ Ⓑ Ⓒ Ⓓ Ⓔ   40 Ⓐ Ⓑ Ⓒ Ⓓ Ⓔ

right in section 6

wrong in section 6

Practice Test Two—Section 1

Time—30 Minutes
25 Questions

Solve each of the following problems, decide which is the best answer choice, and darken the corresponding oval on the answer sheet. Use available space in the test booklet for scratchwork.*

Notes:

(1) Calculator use is permitted.

(2) All numbers used are real numbers.

(3) Figures are provided for some problems. All figures are drawn to scale and lie in a plane UNLESS otherwise indicated.

Reference Information

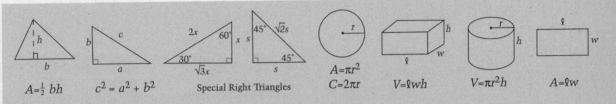

$A = \frac{1}{2} bh$ $c^2 = a^2 + b^2$ Special Right Triangles $A = \pi r^2$ $C = 2\pi r$ $V = \ell wh$ $V = \pi r^2 h$ $A = \ell w$

The sum of the degree measures of the angles of a triangle is 180.
The number of degrees of arc in a circle is 360.
A straight angle has a degree measure of 180.

1 $\left(\frac{1}{5} + \frac{1}{3} \right) \div \frac{1}{2} =$

(A) $\frac{1}{8}$

(B) $\frac{1}{4}$

(C) $\frac{4}{15}$

(D) $\frac{1}{2}$

(E) $\frac{16}{15}$

2 What is the value of $x^2 - 2x$ when $x = -2$?

(A) -8
(B) -4
(C) 0
(D) 4
(E) 8

3 Vito read 96 pages in 2 hours and 40 minutes. What was Vito's average rate of pages per hour?

(A) 24
(B) 30
(C) 36
(D) 42
(E) 48

4 For how many integer values of x will $\frac{7}{x}$ be greater than $\frac{1}{4}$ and less than $\frac{1}{3}$?

(A) 6
(B) 7
(C) 12
(D) 28
(E) Infinitely many

5 What is the average (arithmetic mean) of $2x + 5$, $5x - 6$, and $-4x + 2$?

(A) $x + \frac{1}{3}$

(B) $x + 1$

(C) $3x + \frac{1}{3}$

(D) $3x + 3$

(E) $3x + 3\frac{1}{3}$

*The directions on the actual SAT will vary slightly.

GO ON TO THE NEXT PAGE ➡

6   In a group of 25 students, 16 are female. What percent of the group is female?

(A)   16%
(B)   40%
(C)   60%
(D)   64%
(E)   75%

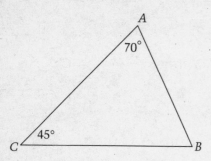

7   In the triangle above, what is the degree measure of angle B ?

(A)   45
(B)   60
(C)   65
(D)   75
(E)   80

8   For all $x \neq 0$, $\dfrac{x^2 + x^2 + x^2}{x^2} =$

(A)   3
(B) $3x$
(C) x^2
(D) x^3
(E) x^4

9   The equation $x^2 = 5x - 4$ has how many distinct real solutions?

(A)   0
(B)   1
(C)   2
(D)   3
(E)   Infinitely many

10 Which of the following sets of numbers has the property that the sum of any two numbers in the set is also a number in the set?

I.   The set of even integers
II. The set of odd integers
III. The set of prime numbers

(A)   I only
(B)   III only
(C)   I and II only
(D)   I and III only
(E)   I, II, and III

11 Martin's average (arithmetic mean) score after 4 tests is 89. What score on the 5th test would bring Martin's average up to exactly 90?

(A)   90
(B)   91
(C)   92
(D)   93
(E)   94

12 The price s of a sweater is reduced by 25% for a sale. After the sale, the reduced price is increased by 20%. Which of the following represents the final price of the sweater?

(A) $1.05s$
(B) $.95s$
(C) $.90s$
(D) $.85s$
(E) $.80s$

13 How many distinct prime factors does the number 36 have?

(A)   2
(B)   3
(C)   4
(D)   5
(E)   6

14 If the area of a triangle is 36 and its base is 9, what is the length of the altitude to that base?

(A)   2
(B)   4
(C)   6
(D)   8
(E)   12

15 Let $a\clubsuit$ be defined for all positive integers a by the equation $a\clubsuit = \dfrac{a}{4} - \dfrac{a}{6}$. If $x\clubsuit = 3$, what is the value of x ?

(A)   18
(B)   28
(C)   36
(D)   40
(E)   54

16 Joan has q quarters, d dimes, n nickels, and no other coins in her pocket. Which of the following represents the total number of coins in Joan's pocket?

(A) $q + d + n$
(B) $5q + 2d + n$
(C) $.25q + .10d + .05n$
(D) $(25 + 10 + 5)(q + d + n)$
(E) $25q + 10d + 5n$

GO ON TO THE NEXT PAGE ➡

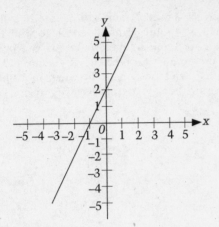

17 Which of the following is an equation for the graph above?

(A) $y = -2x + 1$
(B) $y = x + 1$
(C) $y = x + 2$
(D) $y = 2x + 1$
(E) $y = 2x + 2$

18 If an integer is divisible by 6 and by 9, then the integer must be divisible by which of the following?

    I. 12
    II. 18
    III. 36

(A) I only
(B) II only
(C) I and II only
(D) II and III only
(E) I, II, and III

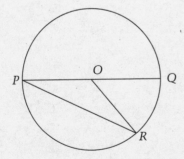

19 In the figure above, O is the center of the circle and P, O, and Q are collinear. If $\angle ROQ$ measures $50°$, what is the degree measure of $\angle RPQ$?

(A) 20
(B) 25
(C) 30
(D) 35
(E) 40

20 A wooden cube with volume 64 is sliced in half horizontally. The two halves are then glued together to form a rectangular solid which is not a cube. What is the surface area of this new solid?

(A) 128
(B) 112
(C) 96
(D) 56
(E) 48

21 A drawer contains 6 blue socks, 12 black socks, and 14 white socks. If one sock is chosen at random, what is the probability that it will be black?

(A) $\frac{1}{4}$

(B) $\frac{1}{3}$

(C) $\frac{3}{8}$

(D) $\frac{1}{2}$

(E) $\frac{5}{8}$

22 Danielle drives from her home to the store at an average speed of 40 miles per hour. She returns home along the same route at an average speed of 60 miles per hour. What is her average speed, in miles per hour, for her entire trip?

(A) 45
(B) 48
(C) 50
(D) 52
(E) 55

23 What is the area of a right triangle if the length of one leg is a and the length of the hypotenuse is c ?

(A) $\frac{ac}{2}$

(B) $\frac{ac - a^2}{2}$

(C) $\frac{a^2 + c^2}{2}$

(D) $\frac{a\sqrt{c^2 - a^2}}{2}$

(E) $\sqrt{a^2 + c^2}$

GO ON TO THE NEXT PAGE ➡

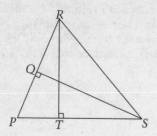

24 In △*PRS* above, *RT* is the altitude to side *PS* and *QS* is the altitude to side *PR*. If *RT* = 7, *PR* = 8, and *QS* = 9, what is the length of *PS* ?

(A) $5\frac{1}{7}$

(B) $6\frac{2}{9}$

(C) $7\frac{7}{8}$

(D) $10\frac{2}{7}$

(E) $13\frac{4}{9}$

25 There are 3 routes from Bay City to Riverville. There are 4 routes from Riverville to Straitstown. There are 3 routes from Straitstown to Frog Pond. If a driver must pass through Riverville and Straitstown exactly once, how many possible ways are there to go from Bay City to Frog Pond?

(A) 6
(B) 10
(C) 12
(D) 24
(E) 36

IF YOU FINISH BEFORE TIME IS CALLED, YOU MAY CHECK YOUR WORK ON THIS SECTION ONLY. DO NOT TURN TO ANY OTHER SECTION IN THE TEST.   **STOP**

Time—30 Minutes
35 Questions

For each of the following questions, choose the best answer and darken the corresponding oval on the answer sheet.*

Select the lettered word or set of words that best completes the sentence.

Example:

Today's small, portable computers contrast markedly with the earliest electronic computers, which were ----.

(A) effective
(B) invented
(C) useful
(D) destructive
(E) enormous

1   Finding an old movie poster that is still ---- usually proves difficult because such posters were meant to be used and then ----.

(A) recognizable . . returned
(B) relevant . . discarded
(C) intact . . destroyed
(D) immaculate . . restored
(E) displayed . . maintained

2   The Kemp's Ridley turtle, long considered one of the most ---- creatures of the sea, finally appears to be making some headway in its battle against extinction.

(A) elusive
(B) prevalent
(C) combative
(D) voracious
(E) imperiled

3   Before the invention of the tape recorder, quotes from an interview were rarely ----; journalists usually paraphrased the words of their subject.

(A) verbatim
(B) misconstrued
(C) pragmatic
(D) extensive
(E) plagiarized

4   Batchelor's reputation as ---- novelist encouraged hopes that his political thriller would offer more ---- characterizations than are usually found in the genre.

(A) a serious . . subtle
(B) a maturing . . sweeping
(C) a prolific . . accurate
(D) an accomplished . . fictional
(E) a reclusive . . authentic

5   The governor commented on the disadvantages of political ----, saying that after his extended tenure in office the voters had grown used to blaming him for everything.

(A) acumen
(B) savvy
(C) longevity
(D) decorum
(E) celebrity

6   Although normally ----, the researcher was ---- by the news that her work had not been accepted for publication.

(A) introverted . . devastated
(B) imperious . . incensed
(C) melodramatic . . electrified
(D) buoyant . . subdued
(E) reserved . . bewildered

7   The agency's failure to ---- policies that it has acknowledged are flawed is a potent demonstration of its ---- approach to correcting its problems.

(A) support . . ambiguous
(B) institute . . earnest
(C) rescind . . lackadaisical
(D) amend . . devoted
(E) chasten . . meticulous

8   The inconsistency of the educational policies adopted by various schools across the state has been greatly ---- by the rapid turnover of school superintendents.

(A) counteracted
(B) stabilized
(C) criticized
(D) exacerbated
(E) understated

9   The journalist's claim of ---- is belied by her record of contributing to the campaign funds of only one party's candidates.

(A) innocence
(B) corruption
(C) impartiality
(D) affluence
(E) loyalty

GO ON TO THE NEXT PAGE ➡

*The directions on the actual SAT will vary slightly.

10 The repeated breakdown of negotiations only
---- the view that the two sides were not truly
committed to the goal of ---- a military
confrontation.

(A) established . . escalating
(B) undermined . . avoiding
(C) distorted . . financing
(D) strengthened . . initiating
(E) reinforced . . averting

11 These are times of national budgetary ---- now
that a long era of sustained growth has been
succeeded by a period of painful ----.

(A) turmoil . . acquisition
(B) stringency . . decline
(C) expansion . . stagnation
(D) indecision . . renewal
(E) prudence . . development

12 To the ---- of those who in bygone years tiptoed
their way past poinsettia displays for fear of
causing leaves to fall, breeders have developed
more ---- versions of the flower.

(A) consternation . . amorphous
(B) dismay . . fragrant
(C) surprise . . alluring
(D) disappointment . . diversified
(E) relief . . durable

13 Aristotle espoused a ---- biological model in which
all extant species are unchanging and eternal and
no new species ever come into existence.

(A) paradoxical
(B) morbid
(C) static
(D) holistic
(E) homogeneous

GO ON TO THE NEXT PAGE ➡

Choose the lettered pair of words that is related in the same way as the pair in capital letters.

Example:

FLAKE : SNOW ::

(A) storm : hail
(B) drop : rain
(C) field : wheat
(D) stack : hay
(E) cloud : fog

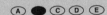

14 LABORATORY : EXPERIMENT ::

(A) garage : repair
(B) beach : sunbathe
(C) statement : formulate
(D) graveyard : inter
(E) invention : create

15 EXONERATE : BLAME ::

(A) disinfect : contamination
(B) divert : stream
(C) indict : guilt
(D) obey : order
(E) absolve : ministry

16 LOOK : SCRUTINIZE ::

(A) amble : scurry
(B) deliberate : propose
(C) read : peruse
(D) importune : plead
(E) flicker : shine

17 GULLIBLE : DUPE ::

(A) fallible : err
(B) foolhardy : confuse
(C) dejected : dishearten
(D) headstrong : coax
(E) submissive : control

18 CONVERSATION : INTERLOCUTOR ::

(A) speech : orator
(B) hearing : prosecutor
(C) game : player
(D) novel : publisher
(E) diagnosis : doctor

19 ENTOMOLOGY : INSECTS ::

(A) agriculture : cows
(B) pedagogy : education
(C) astronomy : telescope
(D) literature : character
(E) evolution : man

20 SKIRMISH : BATTLE ::

(A) misdemeanor : crime
(B) desertion : divorce
(C) fledgling : expert
(D) faculty : instructor
(E) estimate : measurement

21 FORENSIC : LITIGATION ::

(A) maritime : sea
(B) euphoria : feeling
(C) conjugal : bliss
(D) exemplary : example
(E) illusory : magic

22 FEIGN : IMPRESSION ::

(A) adapt : evolution
(B) perjure : testimony
(C) play : role
(D) impersonate : celebrity
(E) slander : reputation

23 POLEMIC : IMPARTIAL ::

(A) antidote : curative
(B) discipline : harsh
(C) heretic : persecuted
(D) defendant : guilty
(E) extrovert : retiring

GO ON TO THE NEXT PAGE ➡

Answer the questions below based on the information in the accompanying passage.

Questions 24–35 are based on the following passage.

The following passage is an excerpt from a book about wolves, written by a self-taught naturalist who studied them in the wild.

My precautions against disturbing the wolves were superfluous. It had required me a week to get their measure, but they must have taken mine at
Line our first meeting; and while there was nothing
(5) disdainful in their evident assessment of me, they managed to ignore my presence, and indeed my very existence, with a thoroughness which was somehow disconcerting.

Quite by accident I had pitched my tent within
(10) ten yards of one of the major paths used by the wolves when they were going to, or coming from, their hunting paths to the westward; and only a few hours after I had taken up my residence one of the wolves came back from a trip and discovered
(15) me and my tent.

He was at the end of a hard night's work and was clearly tired and anxious to go home to bed. He came over a small rise fifty yards from me with his head down, his eyes half-closed, and a preoccupied
(20) air about him. Far from being the preternaturally alert and suspicious beast of fiction, this wolf was so self-engrossed that he came straight on to within fifteen yards of me, and might have gone right past the tent without seeing it at all, had I not banged an
(25) elbow against the teakettle, making a resounding clank. The wolf's head came up and his eyes opened wide, but he did not stop or falter in his pace. One brief, sidelong glance was all he vouchsafed to me as he continued on his way.

(30) By the time this happened, I had learned a great deal about my wolfish neighbors, and one of the facts which had emerged was that they were not nomadic roamers, as is almost universally believed, but were settled beasts and the possessors of a large
(35) permanent estate with very definite boundaries. The territory owned by my wolf family comprised more than a hundred square miles, bounded on one side by a river but otherwise not delimited by geographical features. Nevertheless there were
(40) boundaries, clearly indicated in wolfish fashion.

Once a week, more or less, the clan made the rounds of the family lands and freshened up the boundary markers—a sort of lupine* beating of the bounds. This careful attention to property rights
(45) was perhaps made necessary by the presence of two other wolf families whose lands abutted on ours, although I never discovered any evidence of bickering or disagreements between the owners of the various adjoining estates. I suspect, therefore,
(50) that it was more of a ritual activity.

In any event, once I had become aware of this strong feeling of property among the wolves, I decided to use this knowledge to make them at least recognize my existence. One evening, after
(55) they had gone off for their regular nightly hunt, I staked out a property claim of my own, embracing perhaps three acres, with the tent at the middle, and including a hundred yard long section of the wolves' path. This took most of the night and
(60) required frequent returns to the tent to consume copious quantities of tea; but before dawn brought the hunters home the task was done and I retired, somewhat exhausted, to observe the results.

I had not long to wait. At 0814 hours, according
(65) to my wolf log, the leading male of the clan appeared over the ridge behind me, padding homeward with his usual air of preoccupation. As usual, he did not deign to look at the tent; but when he reached the point where my property line
(70) intersected the trail, he stopped as abruptly as if he had run into an invisible wall. His attitude of fatigue vanished and was replaced by one of bewilderment. Cautiously he extended his nose and sniffed at one of my marked bushes. After a minute
(75) of complete indecision he backed away a few yards and sat down. And then, finally, he looked directly at the tent and me. It was a long, considering sort of look.

Having achieved my object—that of forcing at
(80) least one of the wolves to take cognizance of my existence—I now began to wonder if, in my ignorance, I had transgressed some unknown wolf law of major importance and would have to pay for my temerity. I found myself regretting the absence
(85) of a weapon as the look I was getting became longer, more thoughtful, and still more intent. In an effort to break the impasse I loudly cleared my throat and turned my back on the wolf to indicate as clearly as possible that I found his continued
(90) scrutiny impolite, if not actually offensive.

He appeared to take the hint. Briskly, and with an air of decision, he turned his attention away from me and began a systematic tour of the area, sniffing each boundary marker once or twice, and
(95) carefully placing his mark on the outside of each clump of grass or stone. In fifteen minutes he rejoined the path at the point where it left my property and trotted off towards his home, leaving me with a good deal to occupy my thoughts.

*lupine: relating to wolves

GO ON TO THE NEXT PAGE →

24 According to the author, why were his precautions against disturbing the wolves "superfluous" (line 2)?

(A) It was several weeks before he encountered his first wolf.
(B) Other wild animals posed a greater threat to his safety.
(C) The wolves noticed him, but were not interested in harming him.
(D) He was not bothered by the wolves until he started interfering with them.
(E) The wolves were unable to detect him due to their poor eyesight.

25 The author mentions the wolves' "assessment" of him (line 5) in order to

(A) account for their strange behavior towards him
(B) convey his initial fear of being attacked
(C) emphasize his ignorance on first encountering them
(D) indicate the need for precautions against disturbing them
(E) suggest his courage in an unfamiliar situation

26 In the third paragraph, the author is primarily surprised to find that the wolf

(A) is traveling alone
(B) lacks the energy to respond
(C) is hunting at night
(D) is not more on its guard
(E) does not attack him

27 In line 17, the word *anxious* most nearly means

(A) distressed
(B) afraid
(C) eager
(D) uneasy
(E) worried

28 In line 34, the word *settled* most nearly means

(A) decided
(B) resolute
(C) stable
(D) inflexible
(E) confident

29 Lines 30–35 provide

(A) a contradiction of popular myth
(B) an explanation of a paradox
(C) a rebuttal of established facts
(D) an exception to a general rule
(E) a summary of conclusions

30 The author suggests that boundary marking was a "ritual activity" (line 50) because

(A) the wolves marked their boundaries at regular intervals
(B) no disputes over territory ever seemed to occur
(C) the boundaries were marked by geographical features
(D) the boundaries were marked at the same time each week
(E) the whole family of wolves participated in the activity

31 Which of the following discoveries would most weaken the author's thesis concerning the wolves' "strong feeling of property" (line 52)?

(A) Disputes over boundaries are a frequent occurrence.
(B) Wolf territories are typically around one hundred square miles in area.
(C) Wolf families often wander from place to place to find food.
(D) Territorial conflicts between wolves and human beings are rare.
(E) Wolves are generally alert when encountering other animals.

32 The author most likely mentions an "invisible wall" (line 71) in order to emphasize

(A) his delight in attracting the wolf's attention
(B) the wolf's annoyance at encountering a challenge
(C) the high speed at which the wolf was traveling
(D) the sudden manner in which the wolf stopped
(E) the wolf's exhaustion after a night of hunting

GO ON TO THE NEXT PAGE ➡

33 The wolf's first reaction on encountering the author's property marking is one of

(A) combativeness
(B) confusion
(C) anxiety
(D) wariness
(E) dread

34 In line 84, *temerity* means

(A) discourtesy
(B) rashness
(C) courage
(D) anger
(E) discretion

35 The author turns his back on the wolf (lines 88–90) primarily in order to

(A) demonstrate his power over the wolf
(B) bring about some change in the situation
(C) compel the wolf to recognize his existence
(D) look for a suitable weapon
(E) avoid the wolf's hypnotic gaze

IF YOU FINISH BEFORE TIME IS CALLED, YOU MAY CHECK YOUR WORK ON THIS SECTION ONLY. DO NOT TURN TO ANY OTHER SECTION IN THE TEST. **STOP**

Time—30 Minutes

25 Questions

Solve each of the following problems, decide which is the best answer choice, and darken the corresponding oval on the answer sheet. Use available space in the test booklet for scratchwork.*

Notes:

(1)   Calculator use is permitted.

(2)   All numbers used are real numbers.

(3)   Figures are provided for some problems. All figures are drawn to scale and lie in a plane UNLESS otherwise indicated.

Reference Information

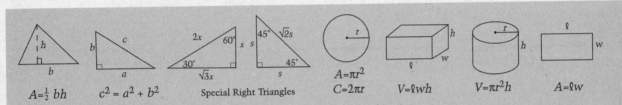

$A=\frac{1}{2}bh$ $c^2 = a^2 + b^2$ Special Right Triangles $A=\pi r^2$ $V=\ell wh$ $V=\pi r^2 h$ $A=\ell w$
                                                                                                  $C=2\pi r$

The sum of the degree measures of the angles of a triangle is 180.

The number of degrees of arc in a circle is 360.

A straight angle has a degree measure of 180.

DIRECTIONS FOR QUANTITATIVE COMPARISON QUESTIONS

Compare the boxed quantity in Column A with the boxed quantity in Column B. Select answer choice

A   if Column A is greater;
B   if Column B is greater;
C   if the columns are equal; or
D   if more information is needed to determine the relationship.

An E response will be treated as an omission.

Notes:

1.   Some questions include information about one or both quantities. That information is centered and unboxed.
2.   A symbol that appears in both Column A and Column B stands for the same thing in both columns.
3.   All numbers used are real numbers.

EXAMPLES

	Column A	Column B	Answers
E1	3×4	$3 + 4$	● Ⓑ Ⓒ Ⓓ Ⓔ
E2	x	160	Ⓐ Ⓑ ● Ⓓ Ⓔ
E3	$x + 1$	$y - 1$	Ⓐ Ⓑ Ⓒ ● Ⓔ

(E2: $x°$ / $20°$)

(E3: x and y are positive)

GO ON TO THE NEXT PAGE ➡

*The directions on the actual SAT will vary slightly.

Column A	Column B
$\frac{1}{8} + \frac{1}{10}$	$\frac{1}{9} + \frac{1}{11}$

1

$x < 1$

2

Column A	Column B
x	$\frac{1}{x}$

3

Column A	Column B
52% of 34	17

4

Column A	Column B
$3(x - 2)$	$3x - 4$

The product of two integers is 10.

5

Column A	Column B
6	The sum of the integers

x and y are nonzero integers.

6

Column A	Column B
$\frac{x^2}{y^2}$	x^2y^2

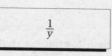

$AC = BD$

7

Column A	Column B
AB	BC

$x > 0$
$y > 1$

8

Column A	Column B
x	xy

$x > 1$

9

Column A	Column B
x^5	$(x^3)^2$

$y \neq 0$

10

Column A	Column B
$\frac{1}{y}$	$\frac{y^2}{y}$

GO ON TO THE NEXT PAGE ➡

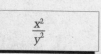

Column A	Column B	Column A	Column B

11

The number of square units in the area of a square with side 6	The number of units in the perimeter of a square with side 9

$y > 0$

14

$1 - \dfrac{y}{1+y}$	$1 - \dfrac{1}{1+y}$

Wilfredo's math test scores are the following:
88, 82, 94, 93, 85, 90, 93, 98

12

Wilfredo's mode test score	Wilfredo's median test score

$ABCD$ is a rectangle with perimeter 32.
$AB > BC$

15

The area of $ABCD$	The area of a square with perimeter 32

13

The area of the circle	The area of the rectangle

DIRECTIONS FOR STUDENT-PRODUCED RESPONSE QUESTIONS

For each of the questions below (16–25), solve the problem and indicate your answer by darkening the ovals in the special grid. For example:

Answer: 1.25 or $\frac{5}{4}$ or 5/4

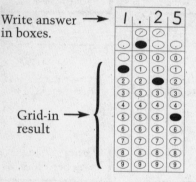

Write answer in boxes.

Grid-in result

Either position is correct.

Fraction line

Decimal point

You may start your answers in any column, space permitting. Columns not needed should be left blank.

- It is recommended, though not required, that you write your answer in the boxes at the top of the columns. However, you will receive credit only for darkening the ovals correctly.

- Grid only one answer to a question, even though some problems have more than one correct answer.

- Darken no more than one oval in a column.

- No answers are negative.

- Mixed numbers cannot be gridded. For example: the number $1\frac{1}{4}$ must be gridded as 1.25 or 5/4.

(If $\boxed{1\,1\,/\,4}$ is gridded, it will be interpreted as $\frac{11}{4}$, not $1\frac{1}{4}$.)

- <u>Decimal Accuracy:</u> Decimal answers must be entered as accurately as possible. For example, if you obtain an answer such as 0.1666..., you should record the result as .166 or .167. **Less accurate values such as .16 or .17 are not acceptable.**

Acceptable ways to grid $\frac{1}{6}$ = .1666...

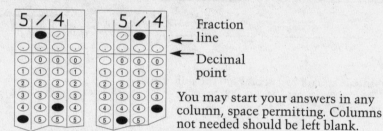

---

17 What is $\frac{1}{4}$ percent of 16?

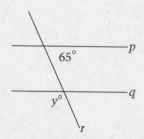

16 In the figure above, if line p is parallel to line q, what is the value of y?

GO ON TO THE NEXT PAGE ➡

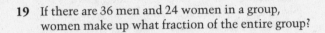

$$\frac{3}{a}, \frac{5}{a}, \frac{14}{a}$$

18 Each of the fractions above is in its simplest reduced form and a is an integer greater than 1 and less than 50. Grid in one possible value of a.

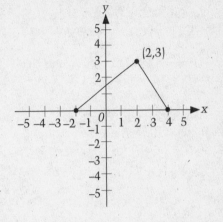

19 If there are 36 men and 24 women in a group, women make up what fraction of the entire group?

23 What is the area of the triangle in the figure above?

20 What is the value of $\frac{3s+5}{4}$ when $s = 9$?

24 A square is divided in half to form two congruent rectangles, each with perimeter 24. What is the area of the original square?

21 If the positive integer x leaves a remainder of 2 when divided by 6, what will the remainder be when $x + 8$ is divided by 6 ?

25 The formula for converting a Fahrenheit temperature reading to a Celsius temperature reading is $C = \frac{5}{9}(F - 32)$, where C is the reading in degrees Celsius and F is the reading in degrees Fahrenheit. What is the Fahrenheit equivalent to a reading of 95° Celsius?

22 Pat deposited 15% of last week's take-home pay into a savings account. If she deposited $37.50, what was last week's take-home pay?

IF YOU FINISH BEFORE TIME IS CALLED, YOU MAY CHECK YOUR WORK ON THIS SECTION ONLY. DO NOT TURN TO ANY OTHER SECTION IN THE TEST.

STOP

Time—30 Minutes
31 Questions

For each of the following questions, choose the best answer and darken the corresponding oval on the answer sheet.

Select the lettered word or set of words that best completes the sentence.

Example:

Today's small, portable computers contrast markedly with the earliest electronic computers, which were ----.

(A) effective
(B) invented
(C) useful
(D) destructive
(E) enormous

1   The band has courted controversy before in order to get attention, and the ---- lyrics on their new album demonstrate that they found the strategy ----.

(A) sedate . . plausible
(B) vacuous . . rewarding
(C) belligerent . . counterproductive
(D) scandalous . . effective
(E) provocative . . comparable

2   James Joyce regarded ---- as central to the creative process, which is evident in the numerous scribbled edits that cover even his supposedly final drafts.

(A) contrivance
(B) revision
(C) inspiration
(D) obsession
(E) disavowal

3   Fans who believe that the players' motivations are not ---- would be ---- to learn that they now charge for their signatures.

(A) self-serving . . vindicated
(B) venal . . chagrined
(C) altruistic . . unsurprised
(D) atypical . . disillusioned
(E) tainted . . gratified

4   Though the film ostensibly deals with the theme of ----, the director seems to have been more interested in its absence—in isolation and the longing for connection.

(A) reliance
(B) fraternity
(C) socialism
(D) privation
(E) levity

5   Everything the candidate said publicly was ----; he manipulated the media in order to present the image he wanted.

(A) incendiary
(B) calculated
(C) facetious
(D) scrupulous
(E) impromptu

6   Most young artists struggle, producing works that have but ---- of future greatness, but Walt Whitman's transformation into a genius was ----.

(A) glimmers . . effortless
(B) shadows . . noteworthy
(C) features . . protracted
(D) critiques . . immediate
(E) aspirations . . unforeseeable

7   Although Sub-Saharan Africa encompasses a large number of ---- cultures, its music is often considered an essentially ---- mass.

(A) disparate . . homogeneous
(B) impoverished . . inimitable
(C) warring . . concrete
(D) interwoven . . distinctive
(E) proud . . languid

8   His face was ----, his features pulled downward by the weight of heavy thoughts.

(A) morose
(B) onerous
(C) contorted
(D) ossified
(E) inscrutable

9   The unfortunate demise of the protagonist in the final scene of the movie ---- all possibility of a sequel.

(A) entertained
(B) dissembled
(C) raised
(D) exacerbated
(E) precluded

GO ON TO THE NEXT PAGE ➡

Choose the lettered pair of words that is related in the same way as the pair in capital letters.

Example:

FLAKE : SNOW ::

(A) storm : hail
(B) drop : rain
(C) field : wheat
(D) stack : hay
(E) cloud : fog

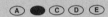

10 SCAR : INJURY ::

(A) monument : marble
(B) fever : illness
(C) dent : collision
(D) exhibition : painting
(E) blood : fistfight

11 YAWN : BOREDOM ::

(A) react : surprise
(B) pout : displeasure
(C) gasp : breath
(D) repose : sleep
(E) cheer : depression

12 ACTOR : AUDITION ::

(A) singer : debut
(B) judge : verdict
(C) architect : plan
(D) instrumentalist : solo
(E) gymnast : tryout

13 ALIENATE : ESTRANGEMENT ::

(A) discommode : inconvenience
(B) sequester : monasticism
(C) palliate : boredom
(D) orchestrate : symphony
(E) aspire : enthusiasm

14 PUNGENT : SNIFFED ::

(A) itinerant : traveled
(B) prickly : touched
(C) venomous : bitten
(D) acrid : burned
(E) belligerent : feuded

15 DISCONCERT : CONFUSION ::

(A) fear : superstition
(B) daunt : discouragement
(C) spend : extravagance
(D) remonstrate : reward
(E) stabilize : imbalance

GO ON TO THE NEXT PAGE ➡

Answer the questions below based on the information in the accompanying passages.

Questions 16–22 are based on the following passage.

The following passage is from a discussion of the origin of the Cold War between the United States and the Soviet Union.

Line
(5)

Revisionist historians maintain that it was within the power of the United States, in the years during and immediately after the Second World War, to prevent the Cold War with the Soviet Union. Revisionists suggest that the prospect of impending conflict with the Soviets could have been avoided in several ways. The U.S. could have officially recognized the new Soviet sphere of influence in Eastern Europe instead of continuing
(10) to call for self-determination in those countries. A much-needed reconstruction loan could have helped the Soviets recover from the war. The Americans could have sought to assuage Soviet fears by giving up the U.S. monopoly of the atomic
(15) bomb and turning the weapons over to an international agency (with the stipulation that future nuclear powers do the same).

This criticism of the post-war American course of action fails to take into account the political
(20) realities in America at the time, and unfairly condemns the American policy-makers who did consider each of these alternatives and found them to be unworkable. Recognition of a Soviet Eastern Europe was out of the question. Roosevelt had
(25) promised self-determination to the Eastern European countries, and the American people, having come to expect this, were furious when Stalin began to shape his spheres of influence in the region. The President was in particular acutely
(30) conscious of the millions of Polish-Americans who would be voting in the upcoming election.

Negotiations had indeed been conducted by the administration with the Soviets about a reconstruction loan, but the Congress refused to
(35) approve it unless the Soviets made enormous concessions tantamount to restructuring their system and withdrawing from Eastern Europe. This, of course, made Soviet rejection of the loan a foregone conclusion. As for giving up the bomb—
(40) the elected officials in Washington would have been in deep trouble with their constituents had that plan been carried out. Polls showed that 82 percent of the American people understood that other nations would develop bombs eventually, but that
(45) 85 percent thought that the U.S. should retain exclusive possession of the weapon. Policy-makers have to abide by certain constraints in deciding what is acceptable and what is not. They, and not historians, are in the best position to perceive those
(50) constraints and make the decisions.

(55)

Revisionist historians tend to eschew this type of political explanation of America's supposed failure to reach a peaceful settlement with the Soviets in favor of an economic reading of events. They point to the fact that in the early post-war years American businessmen and government officials cooperated to expand American foreign trade vigorously and to exploit investment opportunities in many foreign countries. In order to
(60) sustain the lucrative expansion, revisionists assert, American policy-makers were obliged to maintain an "Open Door" foreign policy, the object of which was to keep all potential trade opportunities open. Since the Soviets could jeopardize such
(65) opportunities in Eastern Europe and elsewhere, they had to be opposed. Hence, the Cold War. But if American policy-makers were simply pawns in an economic game of expansionist capitalism, as the revisionists seem to think, why do the revisionists
(70) hold them responsible for not attempting to reach an accord with the Soviets? The policy-makers, swept up by a tidal wave of capitalism, clearly had little control and little choice in the matter.

Even if American officials had been free and
(75) willing to make conciliatory gestures toward the Soviets, the Cold War would not have been prevented. Overtures of friendship would not have been reciprocated (as far as we can judge; information on the inner workings of the Kremlin
(80) during that time is scanty). Soviet expert George F. Kennan concluded that Russian hostility could not be dampened by any effort on the part of the United States. The political and ideological differences were too great, and the Soviets had too long a
(85) history of distrust of foreigners—exacerbated at the time by Stalin's rampant paranoia, which infected his government—to embark on a process of establishing trust and peace with the United States, though it was in their interest to do so.

16 The primary purpose of the passage is to

(A) explode a popular myth
(B) criticize historical figures
(C) refute an argument
(D) analyze an era
(E) reconcile opposing views

GO ON TO THE NEXT PAGE ➡

KAPLAN

17 In line 8, the word *recognized* most nearly means

(A) identified
(B) noticed
(C) acknowledged
(D) distinguished
(E) remembered

18 The author refers to the Polish-Americans
(lines 29–31) chiefly to illustrate that

(A) the president had an excellent rapport with
    ethnic minorities
(B) immigrants had fled from Eastern European
    countries to escape communism
(C) giving up the idea of East European self-
    determination would have been costly in
    political terms
(D) the Poles could enjoy self-determination only
    in America
(E) the political landscape of the United States had
    changed considerably since the President was
    elected

19 A fundamental assumption underlying the
author's argument in the second and third
paragraphs is that

(A) the Soviets were largely to blame for the
    failure of conciliatory U.S. initiatives
(B) the American public was very well-informed
    about the incipient Cold War situation
(C) none of the proposed alternatives would have
    had its intended effect
(D) the American public was overwhelmingly
    opposed to seeking peace with the Soviets
(E) the government could not have been expected
    to ignore public opinion

20 The phrase *certain constraints* in line 47 most
likely refers to

(A) the etiquette of international diplomacy
(B) the danger of leaked information about atomic
    bombs
(C) the views of the electorate
(D) the potential reaction of the enemy
(E) the difficulty of carrying out a policy initiative

21 Which statement best summarizes the revisionist
argument concerning the origin of the Cold War
(lines 51–66)?

(A) The United States started the Cold War in
    order to have a military cover for illegal trading
    activities.
(B) The Soviets were oblivious to the negative
    impact they had on the American economy.
(C) The economic advantage of recognizing Soviet
    Europe outweighed the disadvantage of an
    angry public.
(D) America could trade and invest with foreign
    countries only if it agreed to oppose the Soviet
    Union.
(E) American economic interests abroad would
    have been threatened by any Soviet expansion.

22 The question at the end of the fourth paragraph
(lines 66–71) serves to

(A) point out an inconsistency in a position
(B) outline an area that requires further research
(C) contrast two different historical
    interpretations
(D) sum up a cynical view of post-war economic
    activity
(E) restate the central issue of the passage

GO ON TO THE NEXT PAGE ➡

Questions 23–31 are based on the following passage.

James Weldon Johnson was a poet, diplomat, composer and historian of black culture who wrote around the turn of the century. In this narrative passage Johnson recalls his first experience of hearing rag-time jazz.

When I had somewhat collected my senses, I realized that in a large back room into which the main room opened, there was a young fellow
Line singing a song, accompanied on the piano by a
(5) short, thickset black man. After each verse he did some dance steps, which brought forth great applause and a shower of small coins at his feet. After the singer had responded to a rousing encore, the stout man at the piano began to run his fingers
(10) up and down the keyboard. This he did in a manner which indicated that he was a master of a good deal of technique. Then he began to play; and such playing! I stopped talking to listen. It was music of a kind I had never heard before. It was music that
(15) demanded physical response, patting of the feet, drumming of the fingers, or nodding of the head in time with the beat. The dissonant harmonies, the audacious resolutions, often consisting of an abrupt jump from one key to another, the intricate
(20) rhythms in which the accents fell in the most unexpected places, but in which the beat was never lost, produced a most curious effect . . .

This was rag-time music, then a novelty in New York, and just growing to be a rage, which has
(25) not yet subsided. It was originated in the questionable resorts about Memphis and St. Louis by Negro piano-players who knew no more of the theory of music than they did of the theory of the universe, but were guided by natural musical
(30) instinct and talent. It made its way to Chicago, where it was popular some time before it reached New York. These players often improvised simple and, at times, vulgar words to fit the melodies. This was the beginning of the rag-time song . . .

(35) American musicians, instead of investigating rag-time, attempt to ignore it, or dismiss it with a contemptuous word. But that has always been the course of scholasticism in every branch of art. Whatever new thing the *people* like is pooh-
(40) poohed; whatever is *popular* is spoken of as not worth the while. The fact is, nothing great or enduring, especially in music, has ever sprung full-fledged and unprecedented from the brain of any master; the best that he gives to the world he
(45) gathers from the hearts of the people, and runs it through the alembic* of his genius. In spite of the bans which musicians and music teachers have placed upon it, the people still demand and enjoy rag-time. One thing cannot be denied; it is music
(50) which possesses at least one strong element of greatness: it appeals universally; not only the American, but the English, the French, and even

the German people find delight in it. In fact, there is not a corner of the civilized world in which it is
(55) not known, and this proves its originality; for if it were an imitation, the people of Europe, anyhow, would not have found it a novelty . . .

I became so interested in both the music and the player that I left the table where I was sitting,
(60) and made my way through the hall into the back room, where I could see as well as hear. I talked to the piano player between the musical numbers and found out that he was just a natural musician, never having taken a lesson in his life. Not only
(65) could he play almost anything he heard, but he could accompany singers in songs he had never heard. He had, by ear alone, composed some pieces, several of which he played over for me; each of them was properly proportioned and
(70) balanced. I began to wonder what this man with such a lavish natural endowment would have done had he been trained. Perhaps he wouldn't have done anything at all; he might have become, at best, a mediocre imitator of the great masters in
(75) what they have already done to a finish, or one of the modern innovators who strive after originality by seeing how cleverly they can dodge about through the rules of harmony and at the same time avoid melody. It is certain that he would not have
(80) been so delightful as he was in rag-time.

alembic: scientific apparatus used in the process of distillation

23 In relating his initial impression of rag-time music to the reader, the narrator makes use of

(A) comparison with the improvisations of classical music
(B) reference to the audience's appreciative applause
(C) description of the music's compelling rhythmic effect
(D) evocation of poignant visual images
(E) allusion to several popular contemporary tunes

24 In the first paragraph, the narrator portrays rag-time as a type of music that

(A) would be a challenge to play for even the most proficient musician
(B) satisfied the narrator's expectations regarding the genre
(C) violated all of the accepted rules governing musical composition
(D) made up for a lack of melody with a seductive rhythm
(E) contained several surprises for the discerning listener

GO ON TO THE NEXT PAGE ➡

25 In line 26, *questionable* most nearly means

(A) disreputable
(B) ambiguous
(C) doubtful
(D) approachable
(E) unconfirmed

26 The narrator's perspective during the second and third paragraphs is that of

(A) an impartial historian of events in the recent past
(B) a mesmerized spectator of a musical spectacle
(C) a knowledgeable critic of the contemporary musical scene
(D) a commentator reflecting on a unique experience
(E) an adult reminiscing fondly about his youth

27 In lines 28–29, the reference to "the theory of the universe" serves to

(A) emphasize that rag-time at its inception was an unconventional musical form
(B) show that the originators of rag-time were wholly engrossed in their own music
(C) imply that the attainment of musical proficiency should take priority over academic pursuits
(D) suggest that those who founded rag-time could not have imagined the extent of its future influence
(E) demonstrate that level of education is not commensurate with artistic success

28 The discussion in the third paragraph of the refusal of American musicians to investigate rag-time suggests that they

(A) have little or no interest in pleasing people with their music
(B) need to be made aware of the popularity of rag-time in Europe
(C) are misguided in their conservative and condescending attitude
(D) attack rag-time for being merely an imitation of an existing style
(E) know that it would be difficult to refine rag-time as a musical form

29 Which statement best summarizes the author's argument in the third paragraph?

(A) Any type of music that is extremely popular should be considered great.
(B) The two criteria for musical greatness are popularity and originality.
(C) Music that has become popular overseas cannot be ignored by American musicians.
(D) Rag-time must be taken up by a musical master and purified to earn critical acclaim.
(E) Mass appeal in music can be a sign of greatness rather than a stigma.

30 The statement in lines 72–73 ("Perhaps he wouldn't have done anything at all") is best interpreted as conveying

(A) doubt about the depth of the piano player's skill
(B) understanding that no amount of talent can compensate for a lack of discipline
(C) cynicism about the likelihood that a man can live up to his potential
(D) a recognition that the piano player might have wasted his talent
(E) frustration at the impossibility of knowing what might have been

31 The author's view (lines 72–80) about the rag-time piano player's lack of formal training can best be summarized as which of the following?

(A) The piano player's natural talent had allowed him to develop technically to the point where formal training would have been superfluous.
(B) Formal lessons would have impaired the piano player's native ability to play and compose by ear alone.
(C) More would have been lost than gained if the piano player had been given formal lessons.
(D) The piano player's potential to be a truly innovative rag-time artist had been squandered because he had not been formally trained.
(E) Although dazzling when improvising rag-time, the piano player could never have been more than mediocre as a classical pianist.

IF YOU FINISH BEFORE TIME IS CALLED, YOU MAY CHECK YOUR WORK ON THIS SECTION ONLY. DO NOT TURN TO ANY OTHER SECTION IN THE TEST.

STOP

KAPLAN   291

Time—15 Minutes

10 Questions

Solve each of the following problems, decide which is the best answer choice, and darken the corresponding oval on the answer sheet. Use available space in the test booklet for scratchwork.

Notes:

(1) Calculator use is permitted.

(2) All numbers used are real numbers.

(3) Figures are provided for some problems. All figures are drawn to scale and lie in a plane UNLESS otherwise indicated.

Reference Information

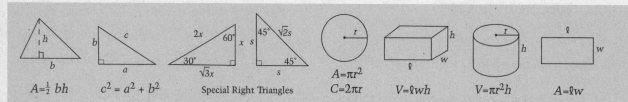

$A=\frac{1}{2}bh$ $\qquad$ $c^2 = a^2 + b^2$ $\qquad$ Special Right Triangles $\qquad$ $A=\pi r^2$ $\qquad$ $V=\ell wh$ $\qquad$ $V=\pi r^2 h$ $\qquad$ $A=\ell w$
$\qquad\qquad\qquad\qquad\qquad\qquad\qquad\qquad\qquad\qquad$ $C=2\pi r$

The sum of the degree measures of the angles of a triangle is 180.
The number of degrees of arc in a circle is 360.
A straight angle has a degree measure of 180.

---

1 For all x, $(3x + 4)(4x - 3) =$

(A) $7x + 1$
(B) $7x - 12$
(C) $12x^2 - 12$
(D) $12x^2 - 25x - 12$
(E) $12x^2 + 7x - 12$

2 In a certain set of numbers, the ratio of integers to nonintegers is 2:3. What percent of the numbers in the set are integers?

(A) 20%

(B) $33\frac{1}{3}\%$

(C) 40%

(D) 60%

(E) $66\frac{2}{3}\%$

3 If $xyz \neq 0$, which of the following is equivalent to $\frac{x^2y^3z^4}{(xyz^2)^2}$?

(A) $\frac{1}{y}$

(B) $\frac{1}{z}$

(C) y

(D) $\frac{x}{yz}$

(E) xyz

4 When the positive integer p is divided by 7, the remainder is 5. What is the remainder when $5p$ is divided by 7?

(A) 0
(B) 1
(C) 2
(D) 3
(E) 4

GO ON TO THE NEXT PAGE ➡

5 What is the *y*-intercept of the line with the equation $2x - 3y = 18$?

(A) −9
(B) −6
(C) −3
(D)   6
(E)   9

6 Jan types at an average rate of 12 pages per hour. At that rate, how long will it take Jan to type 100 pages?

(A) 8 hours and 3 minutes

(B) 8 hours and 15 minutes

(C) 8 hours and 20 minutes

(D) 8 hours and 30 minutes

(E) 8 hours and $33\frac{1}{3}$ minutes

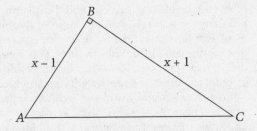

7 In the figure above, *AB* is perpendicular to *BC*. The lengths of *AB* and *BC* are given in terms of *x*. Which of the following represents the area of $\triangle ABC$ for all $x > 1$?

(A) *x*

(B) 2*x*

(C) x^2

(D) $x^2 - 1$

(E) $\dfrac{x^2 - 1}{2}$

8 If Jim and Bill have less than 15 dollars between them, and Bill has 4 dollars, which of the following could be the number of dollars that Jim has?

   I. 10
   II. 11
   III. 15

(A) I only
(B) II only
(C) I and II only
(D) II and III only
(E) I, II, and III

9 Angelo makes *x* dollars for *y* hours of work. Sarah makes the same amount of money for 1 less hour of work. Which of the following expressions represents the positive difference between the two people's hourly wage?

(A) $\dfrac{x}{y-1} - \dfrac{x}{y}$

(B) $\dfrac{x}{y} - \dfrac{x}{y-1}$

(C) $\dfrac{x}{y-1} + \dfrac{x}{y}$

(D) $\dfrac{y-1}{x} - \dfrac{y}{x}$

(E) $\dfrac{y}{x} - \dfrac{y-1}{x}$

10 Erica has 8 squares of felt, each with area 16. For a certain craft project she cuts the largest circle possible from each square of felt. What is the combined area of the excess felt left over after cutting out all the circles?

(A) $4(4 - \pi)$
(B) $8(4 - \pi)$
(C) $8(\pi - 2)$
(D) $32(4 - \pi)$
(E) $16(16 - \pi)$

IF YOU FINISH BEFORE TIME IS CALLED, YOU MAY CHECK YOUR WORK ON THIS SECTION ONLY. DO NOT TURN TO ANY OTHER SECTION IN THE TEST. **STOP**

Time—15 Minutes
12 Questions   Answer the questions below based on the information in the accompanying passages.

Questions 1–12 are based on the following passages.

These passages present two critics' perspectives on the topic of design museums.

Passage 1

City museums are places where people can learn about various cultures by studying objects of particular historical or artistic value. The
Line increasingly popular "design museums" that are
(5) opening today perform quite a different function. Unlike most city museums, the design museum displays and assesses objects that are readily available to the general public. These museums place ignored household appliances under
(10) spotlights, breaking down the barriers between commerce and creative invention.

Critics have argued that design museums are often manipulated to serve as advertisements for new industrial technology. But their role is not
(15) simply a matter of merchandising—it is the honoring of impressive, innovative products. The difference between the window of a department store and the showcase in a design museum is that the first tries to sell you something, while the
(20) second informs you of the success of the attempt.

One advantage that the design museum has over other civic museums is that design museums are places where people feel familiar with the exhibits. Unlike the average art gallery patron, design
(25) museum visitors rarely feel intimidated or disoriented. Partly this is because design museums clearly illustrate how and why mass-produced consumer objects work and look as they do, and show how design contributes to the quality of our
(30) lives. For example, an exhibit involving a particular design of chair would not simply explain how it functions as a chair. It would also demonstrate how its various features combine to produce an artistic effect or redefine our manner of performing the
(35) basic act of being seated. The purpose of such an exhibit would be to present these concepts in ways that challenge, stimulate and inform the viewer. An art gallery exhibit, on the other hand, would provide very little information about the chair and charge
(40) the visitor with understanding the exhibit on some abstract level.

Within the past decade, several new design museums have opened their doors. Each of these museums has responded in totally original ways to
(45) the public's growing interest in the field. London's Design Museum, for instance, displays a collection of mass-produced objects ranging from Zippo lighters to electric typewriters to a show of Norwegian sardine-tin labels. The options open to
(50) curators of design museums seem far less rigorous, conventionalized and pre-programmed than those applying to curators in charge of public galleries of paintings and sculpture. The humorous aspects of our society are better represented in the display of
(55) postmodern playthings or quirky Japanese vacuum cleaners in pastel colors than in an exhibition of Impressionist landscapes.

Passage 2

The short histories of some of the leading technical and design museums make clear an
(60) underlying difficulty in this area. The tendency everywhere today is to begin with present machines and technological processes and to show how they operate and the scientific principles on which they are based without paying much
(65) attention to their historical development, to say nothing of the society that produced them. Only a few of the oldest, largest and best-supported museums collect historical industrial objects. Most science centers put more emphasis on mock-
(70) ups, graphs and multimedia devices. This approach of "presentism" often leads the museum to drop all attempts at study and research; if industry is called upon to design and build the exhibits, curators may be entirely dispensed with, so that impartial
(75) and scientific study disappears, and emphasis is placed on the idea that progress automatically follows technology.

Industrialization and the machine have, of course, brought much progress; a large portion of
(80) humankind no longer works from sunup to sundown to obtain the bare necessities of life. But industrialization also creates problems—harm to the environment and ecology, neglect of social, cultural and humanistic values, depletion of
(85) resources, and even threats of human extinction. Thus progress needs to be considered critically— from a wider social and humanitarian point of view. Unfortunately, most museums of science and technology glorify machines. Displayed in
(90) pristine condition, elegantly painted or polished, they can make the observer forget the noise, dirt, danger and frustration of machine-tending. Mines, whether coal, iron or salt, are a favorite museum display but only infrequently is there even a hint of
(95) the dirt, the damp, the smell, the low headroom, or the crippling and destructive accidents that sometimes occur in industry.

GO ON TO THE NEXT PAGE ➡

Machinery also ought to be operated to be meaningful. Consequently, it should not be shown
(100) in sculptured repose but in full, often clattering, action. This kind of operation is difficult to obtain, and few museums can command the imagination, ingenuity, and manual dexterity it requires. Problems also arise in providing adequate safety
(105) devices for both the public and the machine operators. These, then, are some of the underlying problems of the technical museum—problems not solved by the usual push buttons, cranks or multimedia gimmicks. Yet attendance figures show
(110) that technical museums outdraw all the others; the public possesses lively curiosity and a real desire to understand science and technology.

1 In line 7, the word *readily* most nearly means

(A) easily
(B) willingly
(C) instantly
(D) cheaply
(E) constantly

2 In lines 14–20, the author of Passage 1 suggests that design museums are different from store windows in that

(A) design museums display more technologically advanced products
(B) store window displays are not created with as much concern to the visual quality of the display
(C) design museums are not concerned with the commercial aspects of a successful product
(D) design museums focus on highlighting the artistic qualities that help sell products
(E) the objects in store displays are more commercially successful than those in design museums

3 From lines 21–30, it can be inferred that the author believes that most museum visitors

(A) are hostile towards the concept of abstract art
(B) prefer to have a context in which to understand museum exhibits
(C) are confused when faced with complex technological exhibits
(D) are unfamiliar with the exhibits in design museums
(E) undervalue the artistic worth of household items

4 The third paragraph of Passage 1 suggests that one important difference between design museums and the art galleries is

(A) the low price of admission at design museums
(B) the amount of information presented with design museum exhibits
(C) the intelligence of the average museum visitor
(D) that art galleries feature exhibits that have artistic merit
(E) the contribution that design museums make to our quality of life

5 In line 49, the word *options* most likely refers to the ability of curators of design museums to

(A) afford large collections of exhibits
(B) attract a wide range of visitors
(C) put together unconventional collections
(D) feature rare objects that interest the public
(E) satisfy their own personal whims in planning exhibitions

6 In line 57, the author most likely mentions "Impressionist landscapes" in order to

(A) provide an example of a typical design museum exhibit
(B) compare postmodern exhibits to nineteenth-century art
(C) point out a decline in the sophistication of the museum-going public
(D) refute the notion that postmodern art is whimsical
(E) emphasize the contrast between two different types of exhibits

7 Which of the following best describes the "underlying difficulty" mentioned in line 60 of Passage 2?

(A) Design museums rarely mention the historical origin of objects they display.
(B) Industrial involvement often forces curators out of their jobs.
(C) Design museums appropriate technology that is essential for study and research.
(D) Technology almost never leads to progress.
(E) Industry places too much emphasis on impartial research.

GO ON TO THE NEXT PAGE ➡

8 The author of Passage 2 most likely mentions "harm to the environment and ecology" (lines 82–83) in order to

(A) encourage a critical response to the technological age
(B) discourage the reader from visiting technology museums
(C) describe the hazardous conditions in coal, iron and salt mines
(D) dissuade museum visitors from operating the machinery on display
(E) praise museums that present an accurate depiction of technology

9 The author uses the phrase "sculptured repose" (line 100) in order to

(A) condemn the curators of design museums for poor planning
(B) illustrate the greatest problem inherent in design museums
(C) present an idealized vision of a type of exhibit
(D) describe the unrealistic way in which machinery is generally displayed
(E) compare the shape of a machine to a work of art

10 The word *command* (line 102) most nearly means:

(A) oversee
(B) direct
(C) control
(D) summon
(E) order

11 The author of Passage 2 would probably object to the statement that design "contributes to the quality of our lives" (lines 29–30) on the grounds that

(A) technical innovation has historically posed threats to our physical and social well-being
(B) the general public would benefit more from visiting art galleries
(C) machinery that is not shown in action is meaningless to the viewer
(D) industry has made a negligible contribution to human progress
(E) few people have a genuine interest in the impact of science and technology

12 The authors of both passages would probably agree that

(A) machinery is only enjoyable to watch when it is moving
(B) most people are curious about the factors behind the design of everyday objects
(C) the public places a higher value on packaging than it does on quality
(D) the very technology that is displayed in the museums is likely to cost curators their jobs
(E) design museums are flawed because they fail to accurately portray the environmental problems that technology sometimes causes

IF YOU FINISH BEFORE TIME IS CALLED, YOU MAY CHECK YOUR WORK ON THIS SECTION ONLY. DO NOT TURN TO ANY OTHER SECTION IN THE TEST.

STOP

296 **KAPLAN**

ANSWER KEY ON FOLLOWING PAGE ➡

Answer Key

Section 1	Section 2	Section 3	Section 4	Section 5	Section 6
1. E	1. C	1. A	1. D	1. E	1. A
2. E	2. E	2. D	2. B	2. C	2. D
3. C	3. A	3. A	3. B	3. C	3. B
4. A	4. A	4. B	4. B	4. E	4. B
5. A	5. C	5. D	5. B	5. B	5. C
6. D	6. D	6. D	6. A	6. C	6. E
7. C	7. C	7. D	7. A	7. E	7. A
8. A	8. D	8. B	8. A	8. A	8. A
9. C	9. C	9. B	9. E	9. A	9. D
10. A	10. E	10. D	10. C	10. D	10. D
11. E	11. B	11. C	11. B		11. A
12. C	12. E	12. A	12. E		12. B
13. A	13. C	13. A	13. A		
14. D	14. D	14. D	14. B		
15. C	15. A	15. B	15. B		
16. A	16. C	16. 115	16. C		
17. E	17. E	17. .04	17. C		
18. B	18. C	18. 11, 13, 17,	18. C		
19. B	19. B	19, 23, 29,	19. E		
20. B	20. A	31, 37, 41,	20. C		
21. C	21. A	43, or 47	21. E		
22. B	22. B	19. 2/5 or .4	22. A		
23. D	23. E	20. 8	23. C		
24. D	24. C	21. 4	24. E		
25. E	25. A	22. 250	25. A		
	26. D	23. 9	26. C		
	27. C	24. 64	27. A		
	28. C	25. 203	28. C		
	29. A		29. E		
	30. B		30. D		
	31. C		31. C		
	32. D				
	33. B				
	34. B				
	35. B				

Compute Your Raw Score

First, check your answers against the answer key on the previous page, and count up the number right and the number wrong for each section (there are boxes on your answer sheet to record these numbers). Remember not to count omissions as wrong.

Then figure out your raw scores using the table below. The Verbal raw score is equal to the total right in the three Verbal sections minus one-fourth of the number wrong in those sections. The Math raw score is equal to the total right in the three Math sections minus one-fourth of the number wrong in the two Regular Math sections and minus one-third the number wrong in the QCs. (Remember: There is no deduction for wrong answers in the Grid-ins.) Round each raw score to the nearest whole number.

Finally, use the tables on the next page to convert each raw score to a range of scaled scores.

	NUMBER RIGHT		NUMBER WRONG		RAW SCORE
SECTION 2:	☐	−[.25 x	☐]	=	☐
SECTION 4:	☐	−[.25 x	☐]	=	☐
SECTION 6:	☐	−[.25 x	☐]	=	☐
VERBAL RAW SCORE:					☐ (ROUNDED)
SECTION 3A: (Questions 1 to 15)	☐	−[.33 x	☐]	=	☐
SECTION 3B: (Questions 16 to 25)	☐	(No.wrong − answer penalty)		=	☐
SECTION 1:	☐	−[.25 x	☐]	=	☐
SECTION 5:	☐	−[.25 x	☐]	=	☐
MATH RAW SCORE:					☐ (ROUNDED)

Convert Your Score

	Verbal							Math					
Raw	Scaled	Raw	Scaled	Raw	Scaled	Raw	Scaled	Raw	Scaled	Raw	Scaled		
−3 or		22	450	48	620	−1 or		19	440	40	600		
less	200	23	460	49	630	less	200	20	450	41	610		
−2	230	24	470	50	640	0	220	21	460	42	620		
−1	270	25	470	51	640	1	240	22	470	43	630		
0	290	26	480	52	650	2	260	23	480	44	640		
1	300	27	490	53	660	3	280	24	480	45	650		
2	310	28	490	54	670	4	300	25	490	46	650		
3	320	29	500	55	670	5	310	26	500	47	660		
4	330	30	510	56	670	6	330	27	510	48	670		
5	330	31	510	57	680	7	340	28	520	49	680		
6	340	32	520	58	690	8	350	29	520	50	690		
7	350	33	530	59	690	9	360	30	530	51	700		
8	360	34	530	60	700	10	370	31	530	52	720		
9	370	35	540	61	710	11	380	32	540	53	730		
10	370	36	550	62	720	12	390	33	550	54	740		
11	380	37	550	63	730	13	400	34	560	55	760		
12	390	38	560	64	730	14	410	35	560	56	770		
13	390	39	570	65	740	15	420	36	570	57	780		
14	400	40	570	66	750	16	430	37	580	58	790		
15	410	41	580	67	760	17	430	38	590	59	800		
16	410	42	590	68	770	18	440	39	600	60	800		
17	420	43	590	69	780								
18	430	44	600	70	790								
19	430	45	600	71 or									
20	440	46	610	more	800								
21	450	47	610										

Don't take these scores too literally. Practice test conditions cannot precisely mirror real test conditions. Your actual SAT scores will almost certainly vary from your practice test scores.

Your score on the practice test gives you a rough idea of your range on the actual exam. If you don't like your score, it's not too late to do something about it. Work your way way through this book again, and turn to Kaplan's *SAT Verbal Workbook* and *SAT Math Workbook* for even more help.

Practice Test Two Answers and Explanations

SECTION 1

1. E

Do what's in parentheses first:

$$\left(\frac{1}{5} + \frac{1}{3}\right) \div \frac{1}{2} = \left(\frac{3}{15} + \frac{5}{15}\right) \div \frac{1}{2}$$

$$= \frac{8}{15} \div \frac{1}{2}$$

Then, to divide fractions, invert the one after the division sign and multiply:

$$\frac{8}{15} \div \frac{1}{2} = \frac{8}{15} \times \frac{2}{1} = \frac{16}{15}$$

2. E

Plug in $x = -2$ and see what you get:

$$x^2 - 2x = (-2)^2 - 2(-2)$$

$$= 4 - (-4)$$

$$= 4 + 4$$

$$= 8$$

3. C

To get Vito's rate in pages per hour, take the 96 pages and divide by the time *in hours*. The time is given as "2 hours and 40 minutes." Forty minutes is $\frac{2}{3}$ of an hour, so you can express Vito's time as $2\frac{2}{3}$ hours, or $\frac{8}{3}$ hours:

$$\text{Pages per hour} = \frac{96 \text{ pages}}{\frac{8}{3} \text{ hours}}$$

$$= 96 \times \frac{3}{8} = 36$$

4. A

For $\frac{7}{x}$ to be greater than $\frac{1}{4}$, the denominator x has to be less than 4 times the numerator, or 28. And for $\frac{7}{x}$ to be less than $\frac{1}{3}$, the denominator x has to be greater than 3 times the numerator, or 21. Thus x could be any of the integers 22 through 27, of which there are 6.

5. A

To find the average of three numbers—even if they're algebraic expressions—add them up and divide by 3:

$$\text{Average} = \frac{(2x + 5) + (5x - 6) + (-4x + 2)}{3}$$

$$= \frac{3x + 1}{3}$$

$$= x + \frac{1}{3}$$

6. D

Percent times Whole equals Part:

$$(\text{Percent}) \times 25 = 16$$

$$\text{Percent} = \frac{16}{25} \times 100\% = 64\%$$

7. C

The measures of the interior angles of a triangle add up to 180, so add the two given measures and subtract the sum from 180. The difference will be the measure of the third angle:

$$45 + 70 = 115$$

$$180 - 115 = 65$$

8. A

$$\frac{x^2 + x^2 + x^2}{x^2} = \frac{3x^2}{x^2} = 3$$

9. C

To solve a quadratic equation, put it in the "$ax^2 + bx + c = 0$" form, factor the left side (if you can), and set each factor equal to 0 separately to get the two solutions. To solve $x^2 = 5x - 4$, first rewrite it as $x^2 - 5x + 4 = 0$. Then factor the left side:

$$x^2 - 5x + 4 = 0$$
$$(x - 1)(x - 4) = 0$$
$$x = 1 \text{ or } 4$$

10. A

Picking numbers is the easiest, fastest way to do this problem. Choose a pair of numbers from each set and add them together. If you are unable to prove immediately that a set does not have the property described in the question stem, you may want to choose another pair. In set I, if we add 2 and 4, we get 6. Adding 12 and 8 gives us 20. Adding −2 and 8 gives us 6. Since each sum is a member of the set of even integers, set I seems to be true. For set II, adding 3 and 5 yields 8, which is not an odd integer. Therefore, II is not true. Finally, if we add two primes, say 2 and 3, we get 5. That example is true. If we add 3 and 5, however, we get 8, and 8 is not a prime number. Therefore, only set I has the property and the answer is (A).

11. E

The best way to deal with changing averages is to use the sum. Use the old average to figure out the total of the first 4 scores:

Sum of first 4 scores = $(4)(89) = 356$

Use the new average to figure out the total he needs after the 5th score:

Sum of 5 scores = $(5)(90) = 450$

To get his sum from 356 to 450, Martin needs to score $450 - 356 = 94$.

12. C

Don't fall for the trap choice (B): You can't add or subtract percents of different wholes. Let the original price $s = 100$. Reducing s by 25% gives you a sale price of 75. This price is then increased by 20%, so the final price

is 90. Since $s = 100$, it's easy to see that this is equal to choice (C), $.90s$.

13. A

The prime factorization of 36 is $2 \times 2 \times 3 \times 3$. That factorization includes 2 distinct prime factors, 2 and 3.

14. D

The area of a triangle is equal to one-half the base times the height:

$$\text{Area} = \frac{1}{2}(\text{base})(\text{height})$$
$$36 = \frac{1}{2}(9)(\text{height})$$
$$36 = \frac{9}{2}h$$
$$h = \frac{2}{9} \times 36 = 8$$

15. C

According to the definition, $x \clubsuit = \frac{x}{4} - \frac{x}{6}$. Set that equal to 3 and solve for x:

$$\frac{x}{4} - \frac{x}{6} = 3$$
$$12\left(\frac{x}{4} - \frac{x}{6}\right) = 12(3)$$
$$3x - 2x = 36$$
$$x = 36$$

16. A

Read carefully. This question's a lot easier than you might think at first. It's asking for the total *number* of coins, not the total value. q quarters, d dimes, and n nickels add up to a total of $q + d + n$ coins.

17. E

Use the points where the line crosses the axes—$(-1, 0)$ and $(0, 2)$—to find the slope:

$$\text{Slope} = \frac{y_2 - y_1}{x_2 - x_1} = \frac{2 - 0}{0 - (-1)} = 2$$

The y-intercept is 2. Now plug $m = 2$ and $b = 2$ into the slope-intercept equation form:

$$y = mx + b$$
$$y = 2x + 2$$

18. B

An integer that's divisible by 6 has at least one 2 and one 3 in its prime factorization. An integer that's divisible by 9 has at least two 3's in its prime factorization. Therefore, an integer that's divisible by both 6 and 9 has at least one 2 and two 3's in its prime factorization. That means it's divisible by 2, 3, $2 \times 3 = 6$, $3 \times 3 = 9$, and $2 \times 3 \times 3 = 18$. It's *not* necessarily divisible by 12 or 36, each of which includes *two* 2's in its prime factorization.

You could also do this one by picking numbers. Think of a common multiple of 6 and 9 and use it to eliminate some options. $6 \times 9 = 54$ is an obvious common multiple—and it's not divisible by 12 or 36, but it is divisible by 18. The *least* common multiple of 6 and 9 is 18, which is also divisible by 18. It looks like every common multiple of 6 and 9 is also a multiple of 18.

19. B

Angles *POR* and *ROQ* are adjacent and supplementary, so the measure of $\angle ROP$ is $180° - 50° = 130°$. Now look at $\triangle POR$:

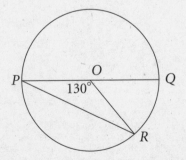

OP and *OR* are radii of the same circle, so they are equal and $\triangle POR$ is isosceles. That means $\angle P$ and $\angle R$

are equal. The two of them need to add up to 50° so that the triangle's 3 interior angles will add up to 180°. If $\angle P$ and $\angle R$ are equal and add up to 50°, then they each measure 25°.

20. B

The volume of a cube is equal to an edge cubed, so $e^3 = 64$ and each edge of the cube has length 4. If the cube is sliced horizontally in two, each of the resulting solids will have two sides of length 4, and one of length 2. So when they are glued together, the resulting figure will have one edge of length 2, one of length 4, and one of length $4 + 4$ or 8.

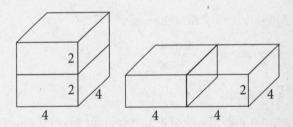

The surface area is the sum of the areas of the solid's six faces. The top and bottom each have area $8 \times 4 = 32$, the front and back each have area $8 \times 2 = 16$, and each side has area $4 \times 2 = 8$. So the surface area of the new solid is $2(32) + 2(16) + 2(8) = 64 + 32 + 16 = 112$.

21. C

Probability equals the number of favorable outcomes over the number of total outcomes. In this case, the favorable outcome is that the chosen sock will be black. Since there are 12 black socks, there are 12 favorable outcomes. The number of total outcomes is the total number of socks. $6 + 12 + 14 = 32$, so there are 32 total outcomes. The probability is $\frac{12}{32}$, which can be reduced to $\frac{3}{8}$.

22. B

This is an average rate problem, so don't just average the two rates. Instead, you have to use total distance and total time to find the average rate. First, pick a distance that is easy to use. For instance, since the speeds for the two halves of the trip are 40 and 60 miles per hour, 120 is an easy number to work with. Using 120 miles as the distance to the store, it would take $\frac{120}{40}$, or 3 hours to go to the store and $\frac{120}{60}$, or 2 hours to return. Thus, it takes 5 hours to complete a round trip of 240 miles. Now find the rate:

$$\text{Average rate} = \frac{\text{distance}}{\text{time}} = \frac{240}{5} = 48$$

23. D

You can use the 2 legs of a right triangle to get the area. Here one leg is a and you can use the Pythagorean theorem to get the other leg:

$$(\text{leg}_1)^2 + (\text{leg}_2)^2 = (\text{hypotenuse})^2$$
$$a^2 + b^2 = c^2$$
$$b^2 = c^2 - a^2$$
$$b = \sqrt{c^2 - a^2}$$

Now plug the legs a and $\sqrt{c^2 - a^2}$ into the triangle area formula:

$$\text{Area} = \frac{1}{2}(\text{base})(\text{height})$$
$$= \frac{1}{2}(\text{leg}_1)(\text{leg}_2)$$
$$= \frac{1}{2}a\sqrt{c^2 - a^2}$$
$$= \frac{a\sqrt{c^2 - a^2}}{2}$$

24. D

The area of a triangle is equal to one-half the base times the height. You can use any of the 3 sides of a triangle for the base—each side has a height to go along with it. It doesn't make any difference which base-height pair you use—a triangle has the same area no matter how you figure it. Thus one-half times PR times QS will be the same as one-half times PS times RT:

$$\frac{1}{2}(PR)(QS) = \frac{1}{2}(PS)(RT)$$
$$\frac{1}{2}(8)(9) = \frac{1}{2}(PS)(7)$$
$$(8)(9) = (PS)(7)$$
$$PS = \frac{72}{7} = 10\frac{2}{7}$$

25. E

In order to find the number of possibilities, multiply the number of possibilities in each step. In other words, there are 3 routes from Bay City to Riverville and 4 routes from Riverville to Straitstown. There are 3 more routes from Straitstown to Frogs Pond, so there are $12 \times 3 = 36$ total routes from Bay City to Frog Pond.

SECTION 2

1. C

The phrase "proves difficult" is a clue: the two missing words have to be nearly opposite in meaning. Choice (C) is correct, because few posters would be **intact** if they were meant to be **destroyed.** None of the other choices makes sense: being (A) **returned** would not stop something from being **recognizable,** being (B) **discarded** would not necessarily stop something from being **relevant,** and so on.

2. E

The phrases "long considered" and "finally" suggest contrast. The missing word is probably the opposite of "making some headway in its battle against extinction." (E) **imperiled,** "in danger," is the best answer. (A) **elusive** means "hard to find"; (B) **prevalent** means "common"; (C) **combative** means "eager to fight"; (D) **voracious** means "having a huge appetite."

3. A

The sentence sets up a contrast between the situation before the invention of the tape recorder, and the situation after. We need a word that's the opposite of "paraphrased," which means "expressed in different words." The answer is **verbatim,** "word-for-word."

4. A

The phrase "encouraged hopes" suggests that the two missing words will be somewhat related in meaning. Choice (A) is the best answer, because we expect **a serious** novelist to use **subtle** characterizations. The other choices make less sense; in fact, it's not clear what (C) **accurate** or (D) **fictional** or (E) **authentic** characterizations would be. (C) **prolific** means "highly productive"; (D) **accomplished** means "skillful, experienced"; (E) **reclusive** means "unsociable."

5. C

The missing word has to be related in meaning to "extended tenure." (C) **longevity** is the best choice. (A) **acumen** and (B) **savvy** both mean "skill" or "knowledge." (D) **decorum** means "proper behavior"; (E) **celebrity** means "fame."

6. D

The word *although* indicates contrast: the two missing words have to be opposite in meaning. This is the case with **buoyant,** "light-hearted, cheerful," and **subdued,** "quiet." In (A), **introverted** means "reserved, not outgoing." In (B), **imperious** means "commanding," and **incensed** means "angry."

7. C

The phrase "failure to" establishes the negative tone of the sentence. An agency ought to "fix" or "get rid of" flawed policies. Possible answers for the first blank are (C) **rescind** or "remove, cancel," and (D) **amend** or "fix." Failure to do this is a bad thing, so we need a negative word for the second blank. The best choice is **lackadaisical,** "careless, sloppy."

8. D

"Rapid turnover" would tend to increase "inconsistency," so we need a word that means "increased" or "worsened." **Exacerbated** means "made worse."

9. C

What claim would be "belied" or contradicted by a record of contributing to only one party? A claim of **impartiality,** of not favoring one side over the other.

10. E

"Repeated breakdown of negotiations" would tend to "support" or **reinforce** the view that the sides "were not truly committed to" "preventing" or **averting** a military confrontation. In (A) and (D), **established** and **strengthened** fit the first blank, but **escalating** and **initiating** are wrong for the second. In (B), **avoiding** fits the second blank, but **undermined** is wrong for the first.

11. B

The phrase "now that" suggests a similarity of tone between the two missing words, and the word "painful" tells us that the words will be negative. Only (B) provides a negative word for both blanks. A painful **decline** would indeed tend to cause budgetary **stringency** or tightness.

12. E

The word in the second blank has to relate in some logical way to "fear of causing leaves to fall," and the only word that does so is **durable,** "tough, not fragile." If the plant has become more **durable,** that should be a **relief** to those who were afraid of damaging it. In (A), **consternation** is "concern or worry," and **amorphous** means "shapeless."

13. C

Words like "unchanging" and "eternal" provide a definition of the missing word, (C) **static.** (D) **holistic** means "functioning as a whole," and (E) **homogeneous** means "all of one kind"; neither word implies species being unchanging and no new species coming into existence.

14. D

A **LABORATORY** is by definition a place where you **EXPERIMENT.** A **graveyard** is by definition a place where you **inter,** or bury, people. Choices (A) and (B) are wrong because you can do things in a **garage** besides **repair** things, and you can do things on a **beach** besides **sunbathe.**

15. A

To **EXONERATE** someone is to remove **BLAME** from him or her. To **disinfect** something is to remove **contamination** from it. To (B) **divert** a **stream** is to change its course; to (C) **indict** someone is to assert that person's **guilt.** Choice (E) is a bridgeless pair.

16. C

By definition, to **SCRUTINIZE** something is to **LOOK** at it very carefully. To **peruse** something is to **read** it very carefully. In (D), **importune** means the same thing as **plead.**

17. E

A **GULLIBLE** person is easy to **DUPE** or fool. A **submissive** person is easy to **control.** In (A), a **fallible** person has a tendency to **err;** this is a different bridge. Choice (B) is a bridgeless pair. In (C), a **dejected** person is already **disheartened.** In choice (D) a **headstrong** person is difficult to **coax.**

18. C

A **CONVERSATION** is carried on by two or more **INTERLOCUTOR**s, the people who participate in a conversation. A **game** is carried on by two or more **players.** The other choices have different bridges. An (A) **orator** makes a **speech** and an (E) **doctor** makes a **diagnosis.** Choices (B) and (D) have weak bridges: a **prosecutor** can take part in a **hearing,** and a **publisher** can publish a **novel.**

19. B

ENTOMOLOGY is, by definition, the study of **INSECTS. Pedagogy** is the study of **education.** In each of the other choices, there is a connection between the two words, but not the same connection as in the stem pair.

20. A

A **SKIRMISH** is, by definition, a minor **BATTLE.** A **misdemeanor** is a minor **crime.**

21. A

FORENSIC means "having to do with **LITIGATION,**" or legal procedure (you've probably heard of "forensic medicine," medical procedure used in the investigation of a crime). (A) **Maritime** means "having to do with the sea." Choice (D) may be tempting, but **exemplary** means "ideal," not "having to do with an **example.**" Choice (C) simply combines two words that are often paired, but have no necessary relation. In (B), **euphoria** is an example of a **feeling.** In (E), something **illusory** does not necessarily have to do with **magic.**

22. B

By definition, to **FEIGN** is to give a false **IMPRESSION.** To **perjure** is to give false **testimony.** In (C),

(D), and (E), the first word has connotations of false-hood, but it does not specifically mean falsifying the second word.

23. E

A **POLEMIC** is a speech or piece of writing that advo-cates a particular point of view; by definition, it is not **IMPARTIAL.** Similarly, an **extrovert,** a sociable, out-going person, is not **retiring** or shy and withdrawn. In (A), an **antidote** is **curative.** In the other choices, **dis-cipline** may or may not be **harsh,** a **heretic** may or may not be **persecuted,** and a **defendant** may or may not be **guilty.**

The Wolves Passage

This Science passage is written by a naturalist who recounts how he went into the wilderness and, through trial and error experimentation and observa-tion, learned some new and surprising things about the way wolves live. For example, wolves are a lot less suspicious and aggressive than people think they are, and contrary to popular belief, wolf families are not nomadic—they live and stay in territories with very definite boundaries.

24. C

In the first paragraph, the author explains how the wolves were aware of his presence but ignored him. That's why the author's precautions were superfluous. (C) basically paraphrases that idea: the author's pre-cautions were unnecessary because the wolves weren't interested in him. (A) doesn't work because the author never really says how long it was before he encountered the wolves. (B) is out because the author never men-tions any wild animals other than wolves. Contrary to (D), even after the author interfered with the wolves' boundaries, they never bothered him. (E) is out because it's never suggested that the wolves have poor eyesight.

25. A

The author's basic point in paragraph 1 is that he was surprised at the way the wolves behaved towards him: they sized him up quickly right at the beginning and, from then on, ignored him. He found this behavior

disconcerting, or **strange,** as (A) puts it. (B) sounds exaggerated—the author never really suggests that he was fearful of attack. With (C), the author says that he took longer to assess the wolves than they took to assess him, but his basic point is not to emphasize his own ignorance. (D) doesn't work because the wolves left the author alone—precautions weren't necessary. (E), like (B), isn't suggested—that the author thinks he has a lot of courage.

26. D

In paragraph 3 the author describes how the wolf was so preoccupied that he came within 15 yards of his tent without seeing it. It wasn't until the author made noise that the wolf suddenly became aware of its surround-ings. (D) paraphrases this idea: that the wolf was not **on its guard**—it was self-absorbed. The author expresses no surprise about the wolf traveling alone (A) or hunting at night (C). As for (B), the point is not that the wolf lacks energy—it does respond when the author startles it. (E) is out because the author doesn't really mention any fear of attack.

27. C

The first sentence of paragraph 3 describes the wolf as "anxious to go home to bed." The idea is that he was **eager** to get home (C). **Distressed** (A), **afraid** (B), **uneasy** (D), and **worried** (E) are other definitions of *anxious,* but they don't fit the idea in the sentence.

28. C

In paragraph 4, the author explains that one of the things he learned is that, contrary to popular belief, the wolves were "settled beasts" rather than "nomadic hunters." The idea, in other words, is that the wolves were **stable**—they had established homes. **Decided** (A) and **resolute** (B) are other meanings of *settled,* but they don't work in the sentence. Neither **inflexible** (D) nor **confident** (E) fits when plugged in.

29. A

The idea at the beginning of paragraph 4 is that the wolves, contrary to what people generally think, are not nomadic. (A) catches the idea: the author is coun-tering a popular myth or belief about the behavior of wolves. (B) is tricky, but there's really no paradox or ambiguity: the idea is that the wolves are NOT nomadic. (C) is tricky too, but the passage never says that the idea that wolves are nomadic is an established fact. As for (D), there's no indication that what the author observed—that the wolves live in established territories—is an exception to a general rule. (E) doesn't work because there's really no summary of any conclusions in the quoted lines. (A) is the best choice.

30. B

In the middle of paragraph 5 the author describes how the wolf family regularly made the rounds of their lands and "freshened up the boundary markers." He guessed that this was done because there were other wolves living in adjacent areas, although he never saw any sign of trouble between the neighboring wolf families. Then you get the quoted idea: since he never witnessed any disputes, he figured that it was all basically a ritual activity. (B) catches the idea. The idea that the activity was a ritual isn't related to the fact that it was repeated (A), that the boundaries were marked by geographic features (C), that they were marked at the same time each week (D)—that's never suggested, or that the whole family participated (E). The wrong choices miss the point.

31. C

One of the author's discoveries is that the wolves live in territories with clearly marked boundaries. So, contrary to what most people think, they aren't nomadic—they don't travel endlessly from place to place looking for food and sleeping in new areas. The idea in (C), if it were true, would contradict or weaken that idea. The idea in (A) would strengthen the thesis—if there were disputes over boundaries, that would suggest that the wolves are protective of their territory. The idea in (B)—the particular size of the wolves' territory—is irrelevant—it doesn't really relate to the question. (D) is tricky, but it doesn't work: the author finds that the wolves are territorial even though they actually don't have conflicts with their neighbors. The idea in (E) is irrelevant: the passage never discusses whether or not wolves are alert when encountering other animals.

32. D

The phrase "invisible wall" occurs in paragraph 7, and the point is that the wolf, who was plodding home as preoccupied as usual, was suddenly stopped in its tracks when it encountered the spot where the author had left his own markings. So the idea about the invisible wall is that the wolf was stopped suddenly (D), as if it had suddenly banged up against it. The idea of an invisible wall has nothing to do with delight in getting the wolf's attention (A), annoyance on the part of the wolf (B), high speed (C)—the wolf was "padding," not running—or exhaustion after a night of hunting (E).

33. B

In the very same sentence in paragraph 7, the author says that the wolf, upon finding the author's marks, immediately became bewildered. (B) restates that. The passage says nothing about **combativeness** (A), **anxiety** (C), **wariness** (D), or **dread** (E).

34. B

Temerity is a tough vocabulary word—it means impetuousness or **rashness** (B). But you really didn't have to know that definition to pick the right answer. All you have to do with Vocab-in-Context questions is plug in each of the answer choices, and eliminate the ones that don't fit the sentence's meaning. If you do that here, none of the other choices works. With (A), it's not that the author's being discourteous. That sounds strange. Rather, he's being too bold—only (B) makes sense. Remember, if you're stumped with any hard question, work backwards by eliminating any wrong choices you can—and then guess.

35. B

At the end of paragraph 8, the author states that he turned his back on the wolf "in an effort to break the impasse." In other words, he did it to bring about a change in the situation (B). Nothing suggests that he did it to show his power over the wolf (A); make the wolf recognize his existence (C)—the wolf already did; look for a weapon (D); or avoid the wolf's "hypnotic" gaze (E).

SECTION 3

1. A

Don't calculate. Compare piece by piece. The first fraction in Column A is greater than the first fraction in Column B, and the second fraction in Column A is greater than the second fraction in Column B. Therefore the sum in Column A is also greater.

2. D

Try a few numbers. Plugging in $\frac{1}{2}$ for x, you get $\frac{1}{2}$ in Column A, but in Column B you get 1 over $\frac{1}{2}$, which is 1 divided by $\frac{1}{2}$, which is 2. Here Column B is greater. But when you plug in a negative number, things change. Plugging in $-\frac{1}{2}$ gives you $-\frac{1}{2}$ in Column A, and 1 over $-\frac{1}{2}$, which is the same as -2, in Column B. More than one relationship exists, so the answer is (D).

3. A

Don't calculate. Compare Column A to a percent of 34 that's easy to find. Think of 52% as just a bit more than 50%, or $\frac{1}{2}$. 52% of 34, then, is just a bit more than half of 34, so it's more than 17.

4. B

Expand Column A to make it look more like Column B. Distribute the 3 and you get $3x - 6$. No matter what x is, subtracting 6 from $3x$ will leave you with less than subtracting 4 from $3x$.

5. D

There are several pairs of integers that have a product of 10. You don't need to find every pair. Just try to find a pair that has a sum greater than 6 and another pair that has a sum less than 6. An example of the former is 5 and 2. An example of the latter is -5 and -2. The answer is (D).

6. D

We know that x and y are integers that do not equal zero, but that's all we know. First instinct may tell you that Column B is larger because the squares of x and y are both positive, and the product of two positive integers is usually greater than the quotient. However, what if $y = 1$? In this case, $\frac{x^2}{y^2} = x^2y^2$. Since there is more than one possible relationship between Column A and Column B, the answer is (D).

7. D

It looks at first glance like B and C divide the segment into three equal pieces. But check the mathematics of the situation to be sure. You're given that $AC = BD$:

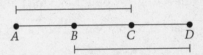

What can you deduce from that? You can subtract BC from both equal lengths and you'll end up with another equality: $AB = CD$. But what about BC? Does it have to be the same as AB and CD? No. The diagram could be resketched like this:

Now you can see that it's possible for AC and BD to be equal but for BC to be longer than AB. It's also possible for BC to be shorter:

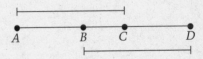

More than one relationship is possible, so the answer is (D).

8. B

If you try picking numbers, you'll find that Column B is always greater. It has to be, because $y > 1$, and multiplying a positive number x by something greater than 1 will result in something greater than x.

9. B

First figure out what the simplified form of Column B is. Since x^3 is squared, you must multiply the exponents, leaving you with x^6. Since x is greater than 1, the number gets larger as it is raised to higher powers. Since x^6 has a larger exponent than x^5, and since x is greater than 1, Column B must be greater.

10. D

First simplify Column B by dividing both the numerator and denominator by y. Thus you're left comparing $\frac{1}{y}$ in Column A to y in Column B. Don't jump to the conclusion that Column A is a fraction and Column B is an integer. It could be the other way around. If $y = 2$, then Column A is $\frac{1}{2}$ and Column B is 2. On the other hand, if $y = \frac{1}{2}$, then Column A is 2 and Column B is $\frac{1}{2}$. More than one possible relationship means that the answer is (D).

11. C

The first step in this problem is finding the values you must compare. Column A equals the area of a square with side 6, so plug 6 into the formula for the area of a square:

$A = s^2$

$A = 6^2$

$A = 36$

Now find the value of Column B by plugging 9 into the formula for the perimeter of a square:

$P = 4s$

$P = 4(9)$

$P = 36$

Since the columns are equal, the answer is (C).

12. A

The key to this problem is knowing how to find the median and mode of the scores. The mode is the value occurring most often, which is 93 for this set of scores. The median is the middle value, so the first thing you have to do is to rearrange the scores into numerical order:

82, 85, 88, 90, 93, 93, 94, 98

Now take the middle value. Since there is an even number of scores, you'll have to take the average of the two middle scores for the median. In this case, the two middle scores are 90 and 93. $90 + 93 = 183$, which when divided by 2 is 91.5. Therefore, the mode, 93, is greater than the median, 91.5, and Column A is greater than Column B.

13. A

The area of the circle is $\pi r^2 = \pi(3)^2 = 9\pi$. The area of the rectangle is 9×3. Don't think of it as 27; it's easier to compare in the form 9×3. π is more than 3, so 9π is more than 9×3.

14. D

Re-express both columns. In each case you can turn 1 into $\frac{1+y}{1+y}$. Column A, then, becomes $\frac{1+y}{1+y} - \frac{y}{1+y}$, which is equal to $\frac{1+y-y}{1+y}$, or $\frac{1}{1+y}$. Column B becomes $\frac{1+y}{1+y} - \frac{1}{1+y}$, which is equal to $\frac{1+y-1}{1+y}$, or $\frac{y}{1+y}$. Now both columns have the same positive denominator, so the larger quantity will be the one with the larger numerator. (You could think of it as multiplying both columns by the positive quantity $1 + y$.) All you have to do now is compare 1 to y. Which is bigger? You don't know. All you know is that y is positive, but because it could be less than, more than, or even equal to 1, the answer is (D).

15. B

First consider Column B. If a square has a perimeter of 32, the length of each side must be 8. Therefore the area is $8^2 = 64$. Now consider Column A. Since $AB > BC$, one dimension of the rectangle must be larger than the other. To get an idea of how the area of a rectangle changes as its dimensions change, pick numbers for the dimensions. Since the perimeter of $ABCD$ is 32, the sum of one length and one width is half of that, or 16. Pick numbers that add up to 16, but also give you a clear idea of how the area changes. To do this, pick one pair of numbers which represents something near a square and one pair which represents a very elongated rectangle. You could choose 9 and 7 for the first pair and 15 and 1 for the second, for instance. Now find the areas of the rectangles with your chosen dimensions. Multiplying the first pair gives you $9 \times 7 = 63$, while the second yields $15 \times 1 = 15$. As the dimensions get closer to the square, the area gets larger. However, a square with a certain perimeter has a greater area than any other rectangle with the same perimeter, so Column B is larger than Column A.

16. 115

Since lines p and q are parallel, we can use the rule about alternate interior angles to fill in the following:

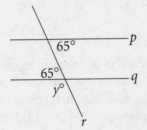

Since the angle marked $y°$ is adjacent and supplementary to a 65° angle, $y = 180 - 65 = 115$.

17. .04

Be careful. The question is not asking: "What is $\frac{1}{4}$ of 16?" It's asking: "What is $\frac{1}{4}$ *percent* of 16?" One-fourth of 1 percent is 0.25%, or 0.0025:

$$\frac{1}{4}\% \text{ of } 16 = 0.0025 \times 16 = 0.04$$

18. 11, 13, 17, 19, 23, 29, 31, 37, 41, 43, or 47

In order for each of these fractions to be in its simplest form, a would have to be a number that has no prime factors in common with 3, 5, or 14 . So just find a value between 2 and 50 that fits that description. Your best bet is to use a prime number, such as 11. That's one of 11 acceptable answers.

19. 2/5 or .4

If there are 36 men and 24 women in the group, then the total number of group members is 60. The women make up $\frac{24}{60}$ of the group. Since this fraction cannot be gridded, reduce it or turn it into a decimal. To reduce it, divide both the numerator and denominator by 12, and you end up with $\frac{2}{5}$. To turn it into a decimal, divide 60 into 24, and you end up with .4.

20. 8

To evaluate this expression when $s = 9$, simply plug 9 in for s. Substituting 9 into the expression yields:

$$\frac{3(9) + 5}{4} = \frac{27 + 5}{4} = \frac{32}{4} = 8$$

21. 4

The easiest way to get the answer here is to pick numbers. Pick a number for x that has a remainder of 2 when divided by 6, such as 8. Increase the number you picked by 8. In this case, $8 + 8 = 16$. Now divide 16 by 6, which gives you 2 remainder 4. Therefore, the answer is 4.

22. 250

Percent times Whole equals Part:

$$(15\%) \times \text{(take-home pay)} = \$37.50$$

$$(0.15) \times \text{(take-home pay)} = \$37.50$$

$$\text{take-home pay} = \frac{\$37.50}{0.15} = \$250.00$$

23. 9

The area of a triangle is equal to one-half the base times the height. Here the base (along the x-axis) is 6 and the height (perpendicular to the base—i.e., parallel to the y-axis) is 3, so the area is $\frac{1}{2}bh = \frac{1}{2}(6)(3) = 9$.

24. 64

You cannot find the area of the square without finding the length of a side, so use the information you are given about the rectangles to find the length of the square's sides. Since the rectangles have the same dimensions, we know that the side of the square must be twice the length of the shorter side of either rectangle. The side of the square must also be the longer side of either rectangle.

Call the length of a side of the square, which is also the length of a longer side of either rectangle, x. Then the shorter side of either rectangle is $\frac{x}{2}$. Now use the formula for the perimeter:

$$P = 2l + 2w$$

For either rectangle, you have

$$24 = 2x + 2\left(\frac{x}{2}\right)$$

$$24 = 2x + x$$

$$24 = 3x$$

$$8 = x$$

To find the area of the square, simply multiply 8 by 8. The answer is 64.

25. 203

This looks like a physics question, but in fact it's just a "plug-in-the-number-and-see-what-you-get" question. Be sure you plug 95 in for C (not F):

$$C = \frac{5}{9}(F - 32)$$

$$95 = \frac{5}{9}(F - 32)$$

$$\frac{9}{5} \times 95 = F - 32$$

$$F - 32 = 171$$

$$F = 171 + 32 = 203$$

SECTION 4

1. D

The word in the first blank has to be similar in meaning to "controversy": (C) **belligerent,** (D) **scandalous,** and (E) **provocative** would fit. The band wouldn't do this if they didn't find that the strategy worked, so (B) **rewarding** and (D) **effective** fit for the second blank. Only (D) fits for both blanks.

2. B

The correct answer is implied by "numerous scribbled edits that cover even his supposed final drafts." In other words, Joyce attached great importance to (B) **revision.**

3. B

The key is that the players "now charge for their signatures." Either the fans who believe that the players are not "greedy" would be "surprised" or "disappointed," or the fans who believe that the players are not "ungreedy" would be "confirmed." Choice (B) fits the former prediction.

4. B

The words *though* and *absence* indicate contrast, so the missing word has to be nearly opposite in meaning to "isolation and the longing for connection." **Fraternity**—brotherhood or fellowship—is the best choice. Choice (D) may be tempting, but the term **socialism** refers to a specific set of political and economic doctrines, not just to any sort of society.

5. B

The part of the sentence after the semicolon pretty basically defines the missing word. The word is **calculated,** consciously planned. (A) **incendiary** means "inflaming"; (C) **facetious** means "joking"; (D) **scrupulous** means "honest"; (E) **impromptu** means "unplanned."

6. A

The word *but* after the comma indicates that the word in the second blank contrasts with "struggle." (A) **effortless** and (D) **immediate** are possibilities. The word "but" before the first blank means something like "merely," so the word in the first blank has to suggest something small, like a faint prediction. **Glimmers** fits the meaning.

7. A

The word *although* indicates contrast, and the words "large number" and "mass" provide a clue to what's missing. We need something that means "different" for the first blank, and something that means "the same" for the second blank. This is basically what **disparate** and **homogeneous** mean.

8. A

We need something here that goes with "heavy thoughts." **Morose,** "gloomy," is the best choice.

9. E

The "demise" or death of the protagonist presumably "eliminated" all possibility of a sequel. That's what **precluded** means.

10. C

A **SCAR** is the mark left by an **INJURY.** A **dent** is the mark left by a **collision.** In (E), **blood** is not a permanent mark, and it is not always the result of a **fistfight.**

11. B

To **YAWN** to display **BOREDOM.** To **pout** is to display **displeasure.** One can **react** to any number of things; to **react** is not necessarily to show **surprise.**

12. E

An **ACTOR**'s tryout is called an **AUDITION.** A **gymnast**'s audition is called a **tryout.** In each of the other choices, there is a valid bridge, but not the stem bridge. In (A), a **debut** is a **singer**'s first performance.

13. A

To **ALIENATE** is to impose **ESTRANGEMENT,** making people aliens or strangers. To **discommode** is to impose **inconvenience.** In (B), **monasticism** is the life of monks and nuns; these people are usually **sequestered** or separated from other people, not everyone who is **sequestered** enters a life of **monasticism** (for example, juries are often sequestered). In (C), **palliate** is to relieve **boredom.**

14. B

Something **PUNGENT** or foul-smelling is, by definition, unpleasant to be **SNIFFED.** Something **prickly** is unpleasant to be **touched.** Something (C) **venomous** does not necessarily work by being **bitten.**

15. B

To **DISCONCERT** is to cause **CONFUSION.** To **daunt** is to cause **discouragement.** Note that (D) is a bridgeless pair.

The Cold War Passage

The author of this passage has one overarching strategy: Set up the arguments of the revisionist historians and then knock 'em down. Paragraph 1 explains the things that, according to the revisionists, could have been done to avoid the Cold War, which are 1) the U.S. could have just accepted Soviet domination in Eastern Europe, 2) the U.S. could have given them money for reconstruction, and 3) the U.S. could have given up its monopoly of the bomb. Paragraphs 2 and 3 outline the author's refutation of these arguments; he concentrates on the American political atmosphere as the main reason that the revisionists' ideas were not really workable at the time. Revisionists, he then asserts in paragraph 4, would reject this politics-based argument and claim instead that it was the economic situation that forced American policy makers to oppose the Soviets. The author of course then knocks down this new argument; it is contradictory, he says, to say that American officials were caught in an economic tide and then to blame them for not doing things differently. The author concludes in the final paragraph by stating that there was essentially no way, given the climate in the Soviet Union, that the Cold War could have been avoided.

16. C

As we noted above, the author of this passage is primarily engaged in setting up and knocking down the arguments of the revisionist historians of the Cold War. This makes (C) correct and (E) wrong (the author is definitely not interested in reconciling his view with that of the revisionists). (A) is wrong because the ideas of the revisionists are not, as far as we know, a popular myth. (B) is out because the author is defending historical figures—the policy makers—for what they did, not criticizing them. (D) is too neutral a choice for this passage; the author does engage in analysis of the era of the beginning of the Cold War, but his purpose is to do far more than just analyze events. He wants to poke holes in revisionist theories.

17. C

When revisionists say that the U.S. could have "recognized" the Soviet influence in Eastern Europe, they mean that the U.S. could have formally **acknowledged** this Soviet presence. (C) is correct.

18. C

Look back to the second half of the second paragraph. The author says there that Roosevelt could never have recognized a Soviet Eastern Europe because the American people did not like the idea of the Soviets holding sway in that region. In particular, the president would have lost the votes of the Polish Americans who, you can infer, did not want the Soviets controlling their "old country." (C) spells out this point. Each of the other choices is a misreading of the context of the sentence about the Polish American voters.

19. E

In the second and third paragraphs, the author refutes the suggestions of the revisionists primarily by saying that the policy-makers couldn't do what was necessary to avoid the Cold War because the American people were against it. The assumption the author makes is that the policy makers **could not have been expected to ignore public opinion** (E). The author never says in the second and third paragraphs that the Soviets were to blame for failed U.S. peace initiatives (A), or that none of the alternatives would work (C)—what he does say, in a later paragraph, is that if peace initiatives had not run aground due to American politics, then they would have run aground due to the Soviet climate. The author also does not say in the second and third paragraphs that the American public was **well-informed** (B) or **overwhelmingly opposed to seeking peace** (D); all we know is that they opposed Soviet influence in Eastern Europe as well as the idea of giving up the atom bomb monopoly.

20. C

This question is closely linked to the previous one. The author refers to the "certain constraints" at the end of the third paragraph, in the midst of the discussion on the impact of public opinion on the policy-makers. From context, then, you know that the constraints the author is talking about are the opinions of the people—in other words, **the views of the electorate** (C). If you didn't put the sentence about "constraints" in context, any of the other choices might have looked appealing.

21. E

This question centers on the fourth paragraph, which is where the author explains the revisionists' view that American policy makers decided to oppose the Soviet Union because Soviet expansion could jeopardize U.S. trade and investment opportunities in Eastern Europe and elsewhere. (E) captures this idea. The author says nothing about illegal trading activities (A), nor does he indicate whether or not the Soviets knew about the negative impact they could have on the American economy (B). (C) is out because the Soviet Union was not recognized by the United States, so this could not possibly have had anything to do with the origin of the Cold War. (D) is wrong because there is no evidence in the paragraph to support it.

22. A

The author poses the question in order to show that there is a problem with the revisionists' economic interpretation of the Cold War: you can't blame the policy-makers if they didn't have any control. Thus the question serves to **point out an inconsistency** (A) in the revisionists' position. (D) might be tempting since the revisionists' view is pretty cynical, but the author is questioning that view here, not summing it up.

The James Weldon Johnson Passage

Johnson, the author of this autobiographical piece, does not just describe the experience he had watching the piano-player playing rag-time; he also uses the scene as a jumping-off point from which to comment on the origin of rag-time (second paragraph), to disparage American musicians for refusing to accept rag-time (third paragraph), and to speculate on what the piano player could have amounted to under different circumstances (fourth paragraph).

23. C

The author's initial impression of rag-time can be found in the first paragraph. He emphasizes how the beat demanded a physical response and meshed with the "dissonant harmonies," etc. to produce a "curious effect." (C) is the correct answer. The only other choice that has anything to do with the first paragraph is (B). (B) is wrong because the audience is said to have applauded the singer's dance steps, not the rag-time music.

24. E

Let's go through the choices one-by-one, keeping in mind that we're focusing exclusively on the first paragraph. Although the piano player is "master of a good deal of technique," choice (A) is too extreme to be correct. We know nothing in the first paragraph of the author's expectations of rag-time, so (B) is out too. (C), (D), and (E) are different interpretations of the author's description of the piano player's playing. While it is certainly true that rag-time has dissonant harmonies and jumps from one key to another, you cannot infer from this that rag-time violates every rule of musical composition (C) or that it has no melody at all (D). (E) is correct since the narrator notes that "the accents fell in the most unexpected places."

25. A

In the context of the phrase "questionable resorts about Memphis and St. Louis," the word *questionable* means **disreputable** (A).

26. C

Choice (B) might have jumped right out at you since the narrator's perspective in paragraph 1 is that of a mesmerized spectator, but his perspective in paragraphs 2 and 3 changes. He steps back from the description of his first encounter with rag-time and begins to discuss rag-time's history, appeal, and impact on the contemporary musical scene. Therefore, (C) is the correct answer. (A) is wrong because the author is not impartial; he thinks highly of rag-time. Watching rag-time playing is not a "unique experience," which eliminates (D). As for (E), the narrator says nothing about his youth in the second and third paragraphs.

27. A

Put the reference to the "theory of the universe" in the context of the second paragraph. The author says that the players who first developed rag-time knew "no more of the theory of music than they did of the theory of the universe"—in other words, they had no formal music education—but their natural talent guided them. Since they had no conventional schooling in music, you can infer that their invention, rag-time, was **an unconventional musical form** (A).

(B) and (E) are the close wrong answers. (B) is out because the originators of rag-time could have been interested in other people's music even though they had no formal music education. (E) is wrong since it misunderstands the overall point of the paragraph; the author is not interested in making general statements about the relationship between education and artistic success. (C) is the sort of choice you can rule out by common sense; no SAT question is going to have a correct answer that downplays the importance of academics. Finally, there is no evidence that indicates (D) could be true.

28. C

The narrator argues in the third paragraph that rag-time should not be ignored or dismissed by American musicians just because it is popular. All great music, he states, comes from the hearts of the people. In other words, he is saying that the **conservative and condescending attitude** of the American musicians is misguided (C). There is no evidence in the third paragraph to support any of the other choices. (B) is perhaps the most tempting, since the author talks in the third paragraph about rag-time's popularity in Europe, but it seems as though American musicians do know about rag-time's popularity and find it distasteful.

29. E

This question is a follow-up on the previous one. As we've said, the author's argument in the third paragraph is that music should not be dismissed by serious musicians just because it happens to be popular. (E) paraphrases this idea. (A) stretches the author's argument way too far. (B) is wrong because the author does not try to establish criteria for musical greatness. (C) focuses too narrowly on the author's mention of the fact that rag-time was popular abroad. (D) is clearly wrong since rag-time gained popularity even though it had not been "taken up by a musical master."

30. D

The narrator poses to himself the question about what might have become of the piano player had he been properly trained and then answers himself by saying "perhaps he wouldn't have done anything at all." The narrator goes on to say that even if the piano player achieved some success as an imitator of the greats or as an innovator, he still would not have been as "delightful" as he was playing rag-time. Thus the statement that "perhaps he wouldn't have done anything at all" can best be interpreted as a **recognition that the piano player might have wasted his talent** (D) had he been formally trained. (A) and (B) are wrong because the narrator thinks highly of the piano player's skill even if that skill is not genius-level or particularly disciplined. (C) and (E) are both far too broad and too negative to be the correct answer.

31. C

The correct answer here is going to be a paraphrase of the idea that no matter how far the piano player would have gone if trained, he would not have been as delightful as he was as a rag-time player. (C) is the choice you're looking for. (E) is the most tempting wrong answer since the author's statements at the end of the passage can easily be misconstrued to mean that the piano player could never have been more than mediocre as a classical artist. However, "never" is too strong a word here—the narrator is not, and cannot be, as sure as that—so this choice is wrong.

SECTION 5

1. E

Use FOIL:

$$(3x + 4)(4x - 3)$$
$$= (3x \times 4x) + [3x \times (-3)] + (4 \times 4x) + [4 \times (-3)]$$
$$= 12x^2 - 9x + 16x - 12$$
$$= 12x^2 + 7x - 12$$

2. C

When you know that the given parts add up to the whole, then you can turn a part-to-part ratio into 2 part-to-whole ratios—put each term of the ratio over the sum of the terms. In this case, since all the numbers in the set must be either integers or nonintegers, the parts do add up to the whole. The sum of the terms in the ratio 2:3 is 5, so the two part-to-whole ratios are 2:5 and 3:5.

$$\frac{\text{integers}}{\text{numbers}} = \frac{2}{5} = \frac{2}{5}(100\%) = \frac{200\%}{5} = 40\%$$

3. C

Get rid of the parentheses in the denominator, and then cancel factors the numerator and denominator have in common:

$$\frac{x^2 y^3 z^4}{(xyz^2)^2} = \frac{x^2 y^3 z^4}{x^2 y^2 z^4}$$
$$= \frac{x^2}{x^2} \times \frac{y^3}{y^2} \times \frac{z^4}{z^4}$$
$$= y$$

4. E

If p divided by 7 leaves a remainder of 5, you can say that $p = 7n + 5$, where n represents some integer. Multiply both sides by 5 to get $5p = 35n + 25$. The remainder when you divide 7 into $35n$ is 0. The reminder when you divide 7 into 25 is 4, so the remainder when you divide $5p$ by 7 is $0 + 4 = 4$.

For most people this one's a lot easier to do by picking numbers. Think of an example for p and try it out. p could be 12, for example, because when you divide 12

by 7, the remainder is 5. (p could also be 19, 26, 33, or any of infinitely many more possibilities.) Now multiply your chosen p by 5: $12 \times 5 = 60$. Divide 60 by 7 and see what the remainder is: $60 \div 7 = 8$, remainder 4.

5. B

To find the y-intercept of a line from its equation, put the equation in slope-intercept form:

$$2x - 3y = 18$$
$$-3y = -2x + 18$$
$$y = \frac{2}{3}x - 6$$

In this form, the y-intercept is what comes after the x—in this case it's -6.

6. C

Set up a proportion:

$$\frac{12 \text{ pages}}{1 \text{ hour}} = \frac{100 \text{ pages}}{x \text{ hours}}$$
$$12x = 100$$
$$x = \frac{100}{12} = 8\frac{1}{3}$$

One-third of an hour is $\frac{1}{3}$ of 60 minutes, or 20 minutes. So $8\frac{1}{3}$ hours is 8 hours and 20 minutes.

7. E

With a right triangle you can use the 2 legs as the base and the height to figure out the area. Here the leg lengths are expressed algebraically. Just plug the 2 expressions in for b and h in the triangle area formula:

$$\text{Area} = \frac{1}{2}(x - 1)(x + 1)$$
$$= \frac{1}{2}(x^2 - 1) = \frac{x^2 - 1}{2}$$

8. A

The easiest way to do this problem is to subtract Bill's money from the total of the money that Jim and Bill have. Doing this gives you $15 - 4 = 11$. However, the problem states that they have LESS THAN 15 dollars. Therefore, Jim must have less than 11 dollars. Of I, II, and III, the only value that is less than 11 is I, so the answer must be (A).

To solve this problem algebraically, set up an inequality where *J* is Jim's money and *B* is Bill's money:

$$J + B < 15 \text{ where } B = 4$$
$$J + 4 < 15$$
$$J < 11$$

Again, be wary of the fact that this is an inequality, NOT an equation.

9. A

Pick numbers for *x* and *y*. For instance, say that Angelo makes 20 dollars for working 5 hours and Sarah makes 20 dollars for working 4 hours. In this case, Angelo makes $4 per hour and Sarah makes $5. The difference between their wages is $1 per hour. Now plug 20 in for *x* and 5 in for *y* in each of the answer choices. Which ones give you a result of 1? Only (A), which is the answer.

10. D

A square with area 16 has sides of length 4. Therefore the largest circle that could possibly be cut from such a square would have a diameter of 4.

Such a circle would have a radius of 2, making its area 4π. So the amount of felt left after cutting such a circle from one of the squares of felt would be $16 - 4\pi$, or $4(4 - \pi)$. There are 8 such squares, so the total area of the left over felt is $8 \times 4(4 - \pi) = 32(4 - \pi)$.

SECTION 6

The Design Museums Passages

Passage 1   The position of the author of this passage starts to become clear in the second paragraph: she likes design museums and is willing to defend them against critics. She thinks design museums are not just advertisements for new technology but places where new products can be honored. Design museums, she asserts, are comfortable for visitors because the exhibits provide a lot of information about the objects displayed—information you wouldn't get in an art gallery. Another advantage of design museums, she says, is that their curators have more freedom than do the curators of public art galleries.

Passage 2   Author 2 does not hold technical and design museums in the same high regard as author 1 does, you soon find out in this passage. Author 2 complains about several things: 1) technical museums concentrate on present technology and ignore historical study and research; 2) they glorify machines and industrialization when these things do harm as well as good; and 3) they do not (and cannot safely and imaginatively) show machinery in action. Author 2 does admit at the very end, however, that the public has shown a healthy curiosity about science and technology.

1. A

To say that something is "readily available to the general public" is to say that it is **easily** available. (A) is the correct answer.

2. D

Author 1 says that department store windows try to sell you something whereas design exhibits try to give you an appreciation of the aesthetic value of something. (D) paraphrases this idea. (A), (B), and (E) can be readily eliminated. Be careful with (C), though. Even though design museums focus on the artistic qualities of products, it does not automatically follow from this that design museums are not concerned at all with the commercial aspects of a successful product. (C) is wrong.

3. B

In the third paragraph of Passage 1, the author argues that design museums make visitors feel comfortable because the exhibits illustrate the purpose behind the look and function of the displayed object; art gallery exhibits, by contrast, provide no such information. From this argument you can infer that author 1 thinks that visitors want to be informed about the object they are viewing. This makes (B) correct. There is no evidence to support any of the other choices, all of which are misreadings of paragraph 3. (A) can be eliminated as soon as you see "hostile towards . . . abstract art." (C) and (D) contradict the author, who says that visitors are not confused by technological exhibits since they are familiar and informative. (E) is an unwarranted inference based on the author's statement that design exhibits point out the artistic qualities of the displayed items; you cannot conclude from this that most museum visitors undervalue the artistic worth of household items.

4. B

Since you just reviewed paragraph 3 for the last question, the answer to this one should jump right out at you. The difference between a design museum exhibit and an art gallery exhibit is that a design museum exhibit provides you with information about the object being displayed, whereas the art gallery exhibit does not. (B) is correct. None of the other choices has any basis in the passage.

5. C

After mentioning the collection of Zippo lighters, etc., in London's Design Museum, author 1 says that curators of design museums have options that are far less rigorous, conventionalized and pre-programmed than those open to curators of art galleries. This is a fancy way of saying that the curators of design museums have more freedom to put together unconventional collections (C). (E) is the tempting wrong answer to this question. It's wrong because it goes too far: the design curators have freedom, but not, as far as we know, the freedom to satisfy "their own personal whims."

6. E

In the very last sentence of passage 1, the author says that design museums ("the display of postmodern playthings or quirky Japanese vacuum cleaners") are better able to represent humor than art galleries ("an exhibition of Impressionist landscapes"). The author is emphasizing the contrast between design museum and art gallery exhibits (E). (B) is the trickiest wrong answer. It misses the point of the last sentence because the author is not comparing "postmodern playthings" with Impressionist art; she is comparing the different ways these two things are exhibited.

7. A

The answer to this question will be the choice that summarizes paragraph 1. Since the author spends paragraph 1 complaining that design museums ignore the historical aspect of technology, choice (A) is the best answer. (B) focuses too narrowly on the last part of the paragraph, where the author says that since industry builds the exhibits, curators may be dispensed with. This is not the underlying difficulty referred to at the beginning of the paragraph. The other choices have nothing to do with the first paragraph.

8. A

Author 2's point in the second paragraph is that industrialization and "progress" have not been all good and should be considered critically, but technology museums just glorify them. He mentions industrialization's harm to the environment and ecology to support this point and to encourage **a critical response** to technology, so (A) is correct. (B) is wrong because it's too negative even for this author. (C) is a distortion of a detail at the end of the second paragraph, while (D) is a distorted idea from the third paragraph. (E) is out because author 2 doesn't do any praising in the second paragraph.

9. D

Put the phrase in context. Author 2 says that displayed machinery should be in action, not in "sculptured repose," as is the case with the machinery in technology museums. To author 2, you can infer, the "sculptured repose" is meaningless and **unrealistic** (D). (A) is out because the author is not condemning the curators for poor planning; in fact, the author admits that displaying operating machinery would be extremely difficult. (B) can be eliminated because it's too extreme. The author never says which—if any—of the problems he discusses is the "greatest problem." (C) and (E) miss the author's point and the context in which the phrase "sculptured repose" is found.

10. D

Choices (A), (B), (C), and (E) are common synonyms for "command," but none of them works in the context of the phrase "command the imagination, ingenuity and manual dexterity it requires." Only choice (D) can do the job.

11. A

Predict the answer to the question before you go looking through the choices. You know that author 2 thinks that technology has had a lot of negative consequences, so you can assume that he would point this out in response to author 1's optimistic statement. This makes (A) the best answer. We don't know what author 2's position on art galleries is, so (B) is out. (C) comes from passage 2 but is irrelevant to the question asked in the stem. (D) and (E) contradict specific things author 2 says in the course of his passage.

12. B

In questions like this one, wrong answer choices are often statements that one author, but not both, would agree with. For example, author 2 would probably agree with choice (A) and would definitely agree with (D) and (E), but author 1 would most likely not agree with any of these three. That narrows the field to (B) and (C). (C) is a very general statement that really has no basis in either passage. (B), on the other hand, is an idea that can be found in both passages, so it is the correct answer.

Practice Test Three

HOW TO TAKE THIS PRACTICE TEST

Before taking this practice test, find a quiet room where you can work uninterrupted for two and a half hours. Make sure you have a comfortable desk, your calculator, and several No. 2 pencils.

Use the answer sheet provided to record your answers. (You can cut it out or photocopy it.)

Once you start this practice test, don't stop until you've finished. Remember—you can review any questions within a section, but you may not go back or forward a section.

You'll find an answer key, score conversion charts, and explanations following the test.

Good luck.

SAT Practice Test Three
Answer Sheet

Remove (or photocopy) this answer sheet and use it to complete the practice test.
(See answer key following the test when finished.)

Start with number 1 for each section. If a section has fewer questions than answer spaces, leave the extra spaces blank.

SECTION 1

1 Ⓐ Ⓑ Ⓒ Ⓓ Ⓔ	11 Ⓐ Ⓑ Ⓒ Ⓓ Ⓔ	21 Ⓐ Ⓑ Ⓒ Ⓓ Ⓔ	31 Ⓐ Ⓑ Ⓒ Ⓓ Ⓔ	
2 Ⓐ Ⓑ Ⓒ Ⓓ Ⓔ	12 Ⓐ Ⓑ Ⓒ Ⓓ Ⓔ	22 Ⓐ Ⓑ Ⓒ Ⓓ Ⓔ	32 Ⓐ Ⓑ Ⓒ Ⓓ Ⓔ	
3 Ⓐ Ⓑ Ⓒ Ⓓ Ⓔ	13 Ⓐ Ⓑ Ⓒ Ⓓ Ⓔ	23 Ⓐ Ⓑ Ⓒ Ⓓ Ⓔ	33 Ⓐ Ⓑ Ⓒ Ⓓ Ⓔ	# right in section 1
4 Ⓐ Ⓑ Ⓒ Ⓓ Ⓔ	14 Ⓐ Ⓑ Ⓒ Ⓓ Ⓔ	24 Ⓐ Ⓑ Ⓒ Ⓓ Ⓔ	34 Ⓐ Ⓑ Ⓒ Ⓓ Ⓔ	
5 Ⓐ Ⓑ Ⓒ Ⓓ Ⓔ	15 Ⓐ Ⓑ Ⓒ Ⓓ Ⓔ	25 Ⓐ Ⓑ Ⓒ Ⓓ Ⓔ	35 Ⓐ Ⓑ Ⓒ Ⓓ Ⓔ	
6 Ⓐ Ⓑ Ⓒ Ⓓ Ⓔ	16 Ⓐ Ⓑ Ⓒ Ⓓ Ⓔ	26 Ⓐ Ⓑ Ⓒ Ⓓ Ⓔ	36 Ⓐ Ⓑ Ⓒ Ⓓ Ⓔ	
7 Ⓐ Ⓑ Ⓒ Ⓓ Ⓔ	17 Ⓐ Ⓑ Ⓒ Ⓓ Ⓔ	27 Ⓐ Ⓑ Ⓒ Ⓓ Ⓔ	37 Ⓐ Ⓑ Ⓒ Ⓓ Ⓔ	
8 Ⓐ Ⓑ Ⓒ Ⓓ Ⓔ	18 Ⓐ Ⓑ Ⓒ Ⓓ Ⓔ	28 Ⓐ Ⓑ Ⓒ Ⓓ Ⓔ	38 Ⓐ Ⓑ Ⓒ Ⓓ Ⓔ	# wrong in section 1
9 Ⓐ Ⓑ Ⓒ Ⓓ Ⓔ	19 Ⓐ Ⓑ Ⓒ Ⓓ Ⓔ	29 Ⓐ Ⓑ Ⓒ Ⓓ Ⓔ	39 Ⓐ Ⓑ Ⓒ Ⓓ Ⓔ	
10 Ⓐ Ⓑ Ⓒ Ⓓ Ⓔ	20 Ⓐ Ⓑ Ⓒ Ⓓ Ⓔ	30 Ⓐ Ⓑ Ⓒ Ⓓ Ⓔ	40 Ⓐ Ⓑ Ⓒ Ⓓ Ⓔ	

SECTION 2

1 Ⓐ Ⓑ Ⓒ Ⓓ Ⓔ	11 Ⓐ Ⓑ Ⓒ Ⓓ Ⓔ	21 Ⓐ Ⓑ Ⓒ Ⓓ Ⓔ	31 Ⓐ Ⓑ Ⓒ Ⓓ Ⓔ	
2 Ⓐ Ⓑ Ⓒ Ⓓ Ⓔ	12 Ⓐ Ⓑ Ⓒ Ⓓ Ⓔ	22 Ⓐ Ⓑ Ⓒ Ⓓ Ⓔ	32 Ⓐ Ⓑ Ⓒ Ⓓ Ⓔ	
3 Ⓐ Ⓑ Ⓒ Ⓓ Ⓔ	13 Ⓐ Ⓑ Ⓒ Ⓓ Ⓔ	23 Ⓐ Ⓑ Ⓒ Ⓓ Ⓔ	33 Ⓐ Ⓑ Ⓒ Ⓓ Ⓔ	# right in section 2
4 Ⓐ Ⓑ Ⓒ Ⓓ Ⓔ	14 Ⓐ Ⓑ Ⓒ Ⓓ Ⓔ	24 Ⓐ Ⓑ Ⓒ Ⓓ Ⓔ	34 Ⓐ Ⓑ Ⓒ Ⓓ Ⓔ	
5 Ⓐ Ⓑ Ⓒ Ⓓ Ⓔ	15 Ⓐ Ⓑ Ⓒ Ⓓ Ⓔ	25 Ⓐ Ⓑ Ⓒ Ⓓ Ⓔ	35 Ⓐ Ⓑ Ⓒ Ⓓ Ⓔ	
6 Ⓐ Ⓑ Ⓒ Ⓓ Ⓔ	16 Ⓐ Ⓑ Ⓒ Ⓓ Ⓔ	26 Ⓐ Ⓑ Ⓒ Ⓓ Ⓔ	36 Ⓐ Ⓑ Ⓒ Ⓓ Ⓔ	
7 Ⓐ Ⓑ Ⓒ Ⓓ Ⓔ	17 Ⓐ Ⓑ Ⓒ Ⓓ Ⓔ	27 Ⓐ Ⓑ Ⓒ Ⓓ Ⓔ	37 Ⓐ Ⓑ Ⓒ Ⓓ Ⓔ	
8 Ⓐ Ⓑ Ⓒ Ⓓ Ⓔ	18 Ⓐ Ⓑ Ⓒ Ⓓ Ⓔ	28 Ⓐ Ⓑ Ⓒ Ⓓ Ⓔ	38 Ⓐ Ⓑ Ⓒ Ⓓ Ⓔ	# wrong in section 2
9 Ⓐ Ⓑ Ⓒ Ⓓ Ⓔ	19 Ⓐ Ⓑ Ⓒ Ⓓ Ⓔ	29 Ⓐ Ⓑ Ⓒ Ⓓ Ⓔ	39 Ⓐ Ⓑ Ⓒ Ⓓ Ⓔ	
10 Ⓐ Ⓑ Ⓒ Ⓓ Ⓔ	20 Ⓐ Ⓑ Ⓒ Ⓓ Ⓔ	30 Ⓐ Ⓑ Ⓒ Ⓓ Ⓔ	40 Ⓐ Ⓑ Ⓒ Ⓓ Ⓔ	

SECTION 3

1 Ⓐ Ⓑ Ⓒ Ⓓ Ⓔ	11 Ⓐ Ⓑ Ⓒ Ⓓ Ⓔ	21 Ⓐ Ⓑ Ⓒ Ⓓ Ⓔ	31 Ⓐ Ⓑ Ⓒ Ⓓ Ⓔ	
2 Ⓐ Ⓑ Ⓒ Ⓓ Ⓔ	12 Ⓐ Ⓑ Ⓒ Ⓓ Ⓔ	22 Ⓐ Ⓑ Ⓒ Ⓓ Ⓔ	32 Ⓐ Ⓑ Ⓒ Ⓓ Ⓔ	
3 Ⓐ Ⓑ Ⓒ Ⓓ Ⓔ	13 Ⓐ Ⓑ Ⓒ Ⓓ Ⓔ	23 Ⓐ Ⓑ Ⓒ Ⓓ Ⓔ	33 Ⓐ Ⓑ Ⓒ Ⓓ Ⓔ	# right in section 3
4 Ⓐ Ⓑ Ⓒ Ⓓ Ⓔ	14 Ⓐ Ⓑ Ⓒ Ⓓ Ⓔ	24 Ⓐ Ⓑ Ⓒ Ⓓ Ⓔ	34 Ⓐ Ⓑ Ⓒ Ⓓ Ⓔ	
5 Ⓐ Ⓑ Ⓒ Ⓓ Ⓔ	15 Ⓐ Ⓑ Ⓒ Ⓓ Ⓔ	25 Ⓐ Ⓑ Ⓒ Ⓓ Ⓔ	35 Ⓐ Ⓑ Ⓒ Ⓓ Ⓔ	
6 Ⓐ Ⓑ Ⓒ Ⓓ Ⓔ	16 Ⓐ Ⓑ Ⓒ Ⓓ Ⓔ	26 Ⓐ Ⓑ Ⓒ Ⓓ Ⓔ	36 Ⓐ Ⓑ Ⓒ Ⓓ Ⓔ	
7 Ⓐ Ⓑ Ⓒ Ⓓ Ⓔ	17 Ⓐ Ⓑ Ⓒ Ⓓ Ⓔ	27 Ⓐ Ⓑ Ⓒ Ⓓ Ⓔ	37 Ⓐ Ⓑ Ⓒ Ⓓ Ⓔ	
8 Ⓐ Ⓑ Ⓒ Ⓓ Ⓔ	18 Ⓐ Ⓑ Ⓒ Ⓓ Ⓔ	28 Ⓐ Ⓑ Ⓒ Ⓓ Ⓔ	38 Ⓐ Ⓑ Ⓒ Ⓓ Ⓔ	# wrong in section 3
9 Ⓐ Ⓑ Ⓒ Ⓓ Ⓔ	19 Ⓐ Ⓑ Ⓒ Ⓓ Ⓔ	29 Ⓐ Ⓑ Ⓒ Ⓓ Ⓔ	39 Ⓐ Ⓑ Ⓒ Ⓓ Ⓔ	
10 Ⓐ Ⓑ Ⓒ Ⓓ Ⓔ	20 Ⓐ Ⓑ Ⓒ Ⓓ Ⓔ	30 Ⓐ Ⓑ Ⓒ Ⓓ Ⓔ	40 Ⓐ Ⓑ Ⓒ Ⓓ Ⓔ	

Remove (or photocopy) this answer sheet and use it to complete the practice test.

Start with number 1 for each section. If a section has fewer questions than answer spaces, leave the extra spaces blank.

SECTION 4

1 (A)(B)(C)(D)(E)	11 (A)(B)(C)(D)(E)	21 (A)(B)(C)(D)(E)	31 (A)(B)(C)(D)(E)
2 (A)(B)(C)(D)(E)	12 (A)(B)(C)(D)(E)	22 (A)(B)(C)(D)(E)	32 (A)(B)(C)(D)(E)
3 (A)(B)(C)(D)(E)	13 (A)(B)(C)(D)(E)	23 (A)(B)(C)(D)(E)	33 (A)(B)(C)(D)(E)
4 (A)(B)(C)(D)(E)	14 (A)(B)(C)(D)(E)	24 (A)(B)(C)(D)(E)	34 (A)(B)(C)(D)(E)
5 (A)(B)(C)(D)(E)	15 (A)(B)(C)(D)(E)	25 (A)(B)(C)(D)(E)	35 (A)(B)(C)(D)(E)
6 (A)(B)(C)(D)(E)	16 (A)(B)(C)(D)(E)	26 (A)(B)(C)(D)(E)	36 (A)(B)(C)(D)(E)
7 (A)(B)(C)(D)(E)	17 (A)(B)(C)(D)(E)	27 (A)(B)(C)(D)(E)	37 (A)(B)(C)(D)(E)
8 (A)(B)(C)(D)(E)	18 (A)(B)(C)(D)(E)	28 (A)(B)(C)(D)(E)	38 (A)(B)(C)(D)(E)
9 (A)(B)(C)(D)(E)	19 (A)(B)(C)(D)(E)	29 (A)(B)(C)(D)(E)	39 (A)(B)(C)(D)(E)
10 (A)(B)(C)(D)(E)	20 (A)(B)(C)(D)(E)	30 (A)(B)(C)(D)(E)	40 (A)(B)(C)(D)(E)

right in section 4

wrong in section 4

If section 4 of your test book contains math questions that are not multiple choice, continue to item 16 below. Otherwise, continue to item 16 above.

16 17 18 19 20 21 22 23 24 25

[grid-in answer boxes numbered 16 through 25, each with bubbles for digits 0–9, decimal points, and fraction slashes]

SECTION 5

1 (A)(B)(C)(D)(E)	11 (A)(B)(C)(D)(E)	21 (A)(B)(C)(D)(E)	31 (A)(B)(C)(D)(E)
2 (A)(B)(C)(D)(E)	12 (A)(B)(C)(D)(E)	22 (A)(B)(C)(D)(E)	32 (A)(B)(C)(D)(E)
3 (A)(B)(C)(D)(E)	13 (A)(B)(C)(D)(E)	23 (A)(B)(C)(D)(E)	33 (A)(B)(C)(D)(E)
4 (A)(B)(C)(D)(E)	14 (A)(B)(C)(D)(E)	24 (A)(B)(C)(D)(E)	34 (A)(B)(C)(D)(E)
5 (A)(B)(C)(D)(E)	15 (A)(B)(C)(D)(E)	25 (A)(B)(C)(D)(E)	35 (A)(B)(C)(D)(E)
6 (A)(B)(C)(D)(E)	16 (A)(B)(C)(D)(E)	26 (A)(B)(C)(D)(E)	36 (A)(B)(C)(D)(E)
7 (A)(B)(C)(D)(E)	17 (A)(B)(C)(D)(E)	27 (A)(B)(C)(D)(E)	37 (A)(B)(C)(D)(E)
8 (A)(B)(C)(D)(E)	18 (A)(B)(C)(D)(E)	28 (A)(B)(C)(D)(E)	38 (A)(B)(C)(D)(E)
9 (A)(B)(C)(D)(E)	19 (A)(B)(C)(D)(E)	29 (A)(B)(C)(D)(E)	39 (A)(B)(C)(D)(E)
10 (A)(B)(C)(D)(E)	20 (A)(B)(C)(D)(E)	30 (A)(B)(C)(D)(E)	40 (A)(B)(C)(D)(E)

right in section 5

wrong in section 5

SECTION 6

1 (A)(B)(C)(D)(E)	11 (A)(B)(C)(D)(E)	21 (A)(B)(C)(D)(E)	31 (A)(B)(C)(D)(E)
2 (A)(B)(C)(D)(E)	12 (A)(B)(C)(D)(E)	22 (A)(B)(C)(D)(E)	32 (A)(B)(C)(D)(E)
3 (A)(B)(C)(D)(E)	13 (A)(B)(C)(D)(E)	23 (A)(B)(C)(D)(E)	33 (A)(B)(C)(D)(E)
4 (A)(B)(C)(D)(E)	14 (A)(B)(C)(D)(E)	24 (A)(B)(C)(D)(E)	34 (A)(B)(C)(D)(E)
5 (A)(B)(C)(D)(E)	15 (A)(B)(C)(D)(E)	25 (A)(B)(C)(D)(E)	35 (A)(B)(C)(D)(E)
6 (A)(B)(C)(D)(E)	16 (A)(B)(C)(D)(E)	26 (A)(B)(C)(D)(E)	36 (A)(B)(C)(D)(E)
7 (A)(B)(C)(D)(E)	17 (A)(B)(C)(D)(E)	27 (A)(B)(C)(D)(E)	37 (A)(B)(C)(D)(E)
8 (A)(B)(C)(D)(E)	18 (A)(B)(C)(D)(E)	28 (A)(B)(C)(D)(E)	38 (A)(B)(C)(D)(E)
9 (A)(B)(C)(D)(E)	19 (A)(B)(C)(D)(E)	29 (A)(B)(C)(D)(E)	39 (A)(B)(C)(D)(E)
10 (A)(B)(C)(D)(E)	20 (A)(B)(C)(D)(E)	30 (A)(B)(C)(D)(E)	40 (A)(B)(C)(D)(E)

right in section 6

wrong in section 6

Time—30 Minutes
30 Questions

For each of the following questions, choose the best answer and darken the corresponding oval on the answer sheet.*

Select the lettered word or set of words that best completes the sentence.

Example:

Today's small, portable computers contrast markedly with the earliest electronic computers, which were ----.

(A) effective
(B) invented
(C) useful
(D) destructive
(E) enormous

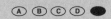

1 Despite their fierce appearance, caymans are rarely ----, and will not attack humans unless provoked.

(A) extinct
(B) timid
(C) domesticated
(D) amphibious
(E) aggressive

2 Some historians claim that the concept of courtly love is a ---- that dates from the age of chivalry, while others believe it has more ---- origins.

(A) relic . . simultaneous
(B) notion . . ancient
(C) memento . . discovered
(D) period . . documented
(E) doctrine . . amorous

3 In Shakespeare's day, ---- theater audiences would often throw fruits and vegetables at actors who failed to live up to their expectations.

(A) doting
(B) ravenous
(C) jingoistic
(D) boisterous
(E) stagnant

4 Although they physically resemble each other, the brothers could not be more ---- temperamentally; while the one is quiet and circumspect, the other is brash and ----.

(A) inimical . . timid
(B) passionate . . superficial
(C) dissimilar . . audacious
(D) different . . forgiving
(E) alike . . respectful

5 The retreat of Napoleon's army from Moscow quickly turned into a rout as French soldiers, already ---- in the snow, were ---- by Russian troops.

(A) replenishing . . ravaged
(B) pursuing . . joined
(C) sinking . . camouflaged
(D) floundering . . assaulted
(E) tottering . . upbraided

6 The Morgan Library in New York provides a ---- environment in which scholars work amidst costly tapestries, paintings, stained-glass windows, and hand-crafted furniture.

(A) realistic
(B) frugal
(C) sumptuous
(D) friendly
(E) practical

7 The lecturer's frustration was only ---- by the audience's ---- to talk during her presentation.

(A) compounded . . propensity
(B) alleviated . . invitation
(C) soothed . . authorization
(D) increased . . inability
(E) supplanted . . desire

8 The proposal to build a nuclear power plant was the most ---- issue ever to come up at a council meeting; it is astonishing, therefore, that the members' vote was unanimous.

(A) popular
(B) contentious
(C) concise
(D) exorbitant
(E) inconsequential

9 The itinerary set by their travel agent included so many stops in ---- amount of time that they received only the most ---- impressions of places visited.

(A) a limited . . lasting
(B) a brief . . cursory
(C) a generous . . favorable
(D) a sufficient . . fleeting
(E) an unnecessary . . preliminary

*The directions on the actual SAT will vary slightly.

GO ON TO THE NEXT PAGE ➡

Choose the lettered pair of words that is related in the same way as the pair in capital letters.

Example:

FLAKE : SNOW ::

(A) storm : hail
(B) drop : rain
(C) field : wheat
(D) stack : hay
(E) cloud : fog

10 STEEL : METAL ::

(A) coal : mine
(B) silk : fabric
(C) suit : card
(D) player : team
(E) carat : diamond

11 FUNNEL : CONICAL ::

(A) pipe : cylindrical
(B) solid : spherical
(C) hose : spiral
(D) line : parallel
(E) hive : hexagonal

12 FUTILE : USE ::

(A) expensive : value
(B) faint : light
(C) superficial : depth
(D) furtive : stealth
(E) educated : morals

13 SUBMISSION : KNEEL ::

(A) equilibrium : stand
(B) leisure : sit
(C) mutiny : lie
(D) disrespect : bow
(E) assent : nod

14 MOVEMENT : SYMPHONY ::

(A) note : piano
(B) projector : film
(C) act : play
(D) rhythm : poem
(E) canvas : painting

15 PURGATIVE : CLEANSING ::

(A) fixative : preparation
(B) vitamin : deficiency
(C) spice : aroma
(D) inoculation : reaction
(E) catalyst : change

GO ON TO THE NEXT PAGE ➡

KAPLAN

Answer the questions below based on the information in the accompanying passages.

Questions 16–23 are based on the following passage.

The passage below is adopted from a short story set in the wilderness of Alaska.

Day had broken cold and gray, exceedingly cold
and gray, when the man turned away from the
main Yukon trail and climbed the high earth-bank,
Line where a dim and little-traveled trail led eastward
(5) through the spruce timberland. It was a steep bank,
and he paused for breath at the top, excusing the
act to himself by looking at his watch. It was nine
o'clock. There was no hint of sun, though there
was not a cloud in the sky. It was a clear day, and
(10) yet there seemed an intangible pall over the face of
things that made the day dark. This fact did not
worry the man.
In fact, all this—the dim trail, the absence of
sun from the sky, the tremendous cold, and the
(15) strangeness and weirdness of it all—made no
impression on the man. It was not because he was
used to it. He was a newcomer in the land, and this
was his first winter. The trouble was that he was
without imagination. He was young and quick and
(20) alert in the things of life, but only in the things,
and not in the significances. It was fifty degrees
below zero, he judged. That impressed him as
being cold and uncomfortable, but it did not lead
him to meditate upon his frailty as a creature of
(25) temperature, and upon human frailty in general,
able only to live within narrow limits of heat and
cold; and from there on it did not lead him to the
conjectural field of immortality and humanity's
place in the universe. Fifty degrees below zero
(30) stood for a bite of frost that hurt and that must be
guarded against. Nothing more than that entered
his head.
He plunged in among the trees with
determination. The trail was faint. A foot of snow
(35) had fallen since the last sled had passed, and he
was glad he was traveling light. In fact, he carried
nothing but the lunch wrapped in his
handkerchief. He was surprised, however, at the
cold. It certainly was cold, he concluded, as he
(40) rubbed his numb nose and cheekbones with his
mittened hand. He was bearded, but that did not
protect the high cheekbones and the eager nose
that thrust itself aggressively into the frosty air.
At his heels walked a dog, a big native husky,
(45) gray-coated, without any visible or temperamental
difference from its close relative, the wild wolf. The
animal was depressed by the tremendous cold. It
knew that it was no time for traveling. Its instinct
told it a truer tale than was told by the man's
(50) judgment. In reality, it was not merely colder than

fifty below zero; it was colder than sixty below, than
seventy below. It was seventy-five below zero. The
dog knew nothing of thermometers. Possibly in its
brain there was no sharp consciousness of a
(55) condition of very cold such as was in the human
brain. But the brute had its instinct. It experienced a
vague but menacing apprehension that subdued it
and made it slink along at the man's heels, and that
made it question every unusual movement of the
(60) man as if expecting him to go into camp or to seek
shelter somewhere and build a fire. The dog had
learned fire, and it wanted fire, or else to burrow
under the snow and cuddle its warmth away from
the air.

16 By using the phrase "excusing the act to
himself" (lines 6–7), the author suggests that
the man
(A) is annoyed that it is already nine o'clock
in the morning
(B) distrusts his own intuitive reactions to
things
(C) finds fault with others more readily than
with himself
(D) doubts that the time of day has any real
bearing on things
(E) dislikes admitting to personal
weaknesses

17 The author identifies the man as "a
newcomer in the land" (line 17) most likely
in order to suggest that the man was
(A) excited at being in a new place with
many opportunities
(B) nervous about being alone in an
unfamiliar place
(C) lacking in knowledge and experience
about the things around him
(D) trying hard to forget something in his
past
(E) unsure about why he chose to come to
the new place

GO ON TO THE NEXT PAGE ➡

18 In lines 24–25, the phrase "a creature of temperature" refers to

(A) the man's preference for cold climates
(B) the innate human ability to judge temperature
(C) the fact that one's personality is shaped by the environment
(D) the human body's physical vulnerability in extreme climates
(E) the man's unfamiliarity with wilderness survival techniques

19 Judging from lines 18–29, the man does not see that

(A) he should appreciate the immense beauty of nature
(B) humans cannot survive in the Alaskan wilderness
(C) there is no way to accurately judge the temperature
(D) the extreme cold could potentially be fatal
(E) he has undertaken to do something which most people could not

20 The man's opinion of the temperature (lines 29–32) reveals which aspect of his character?

(A) determination to succeed against all odds
(B) lack of concern about personal welfare
(C) pragmatic approach to travel
(D) absence of insight and understanding
(E) apprehension about the extreme cold

21 In lines 46–56, by discussing the dog's reaction to the "tremendous cold," the author suggests that

(A) animal instinct can prove to be superior to human intelligence
(B) animals can judge temperature more accurately than humans can
(C) humans are ill-equipped to survive in the wilderness
(D) there is little difference between animal instinct and human judgment
(E) animals and humans have different reactions to extreme temperatures

22 The statement "the dog knew nothing of thermometers" (lines 52–53) means that

(A) dogs need not be as concerned about temperature as humans do
(B) the dog's awareness of its environment is on a different level from the man's
(C) a dog's mental faculties are not very well developed
(D) the dog's experience of humans had been rather limited
(E) the dog could not rely on the technological devices that the man could

23 Which of the following best explains why the dog would "question every unusual movement of the man" (lines 59–60)?

(A) The dog senses that it cannot rely on the man for survival.
(B) The man is beginning to be visibly affected by the cold.
(C) The dog recognizes the need for protection from the cold.
(D) The dog worries that the man intends to leave it behind.
(E) The dog understands that the man does not realize how cold it is.

GO ON TO THE NEXT PAGE ➡

Questions 24–30 are based on the following passage.

The social science passage below was adapted from an article written by a health scientist.

For people in Southeast Asian refugee families, the experience of aging in America is very different from what they had expected for their second half
Line of life. Older Southeast Asian refugees must cope
(5) with their rapidly acculturating younger family members, while taking on new roles and expectations in a foreign culture.

Many Southeast Asian immigrants find that, by American standards, they are not even considered
(10) elderly. Migration to a new culture often changes the definition of life stages. In the traditional Hmong culture of Vietnam, one can become an elder at 35 years of age when one becomes a grandparent. With grandparent status, elder Hmong
(15) can retire and expect their children to take financial responsibility for the family. Retiring at 35, of course, is not acceptable in the United States.

There is a strong influence of Confucianism in traditional Vietnamese society. Confucianism, an
(20) ancient system of moral and religious thought, fosters strong filial piety and respect for family elders. In many Southeast Asian societies, age roles are hierarchical, with strict rules for social interaction. In America, however, because older
(25) refugees lack facility with the English language and knowledge of American culture, their credibility decreases when advising younger family members about important decisions. As younger family members take on primary roles as family mediators
(30) with American institutions—schools, legal systems, and social service agencies, for example— the leadership position of elders within the family is gradually eroded.

Refugee elders must also cope with differences
(35) in gender role in the United States. Even before migration, traditional gender roles were changing in Southeast Asia. During the Vietnam War, when men of military age were away, women took responsibility for tasks normally divided along
(40) gender lines. When Vietnamese families came to this country, changes in traditional gender roles became more pronounced. There were more employment opportunities for younger refugees and middle-aged refugee women because their
(45) expectations often fit with the lower status jobs that were among the few opportunities open to refugees. Many middle-aged women and younger refugees of both sexes became family breadwinners. This was a radical change for
(50) middle-aged men, who had been the major breadwinners of the family.

Although the pattern for long-term adaptation of middle-aged and older Southeast Asian refugees is still unknown, there are indications that the
(55) outlook for women is problematic. Many older women provide household and childcare services in order to allow younger family members to hold jobs or go to school. While these women are helping younger family members to succeed in
(60) America, they themselves are often isolated at home and not learning English or other new skills, or becoming more familiar with American society. Thus, after the immigrant family passes through the early stages of meeting basic survival needs,
(65) older women may find that they are strangers in their own families as well as their new country.

24 The major purpose of the passage is to discuss

(A) the reasons why Southeast Asian people move to the United States
(B) educational challenges facing young refugees in America today
(C) problems that elderly Southeast Asian people encounter in America
(D) the influence of Confucianism in Southeast Asian cultures
(E) changing gender relationships in Southeast Asian refugee families

25 The author mentions the "traditional Hmong culture" (lines 11–12) in order to

(A) show that social expectations may vary greatly from one country to another
(B) suggest the lessening importance of traditional values in Vietnamese society
(C) indicate that modern Vietnam encompasses a number of ancient cultures
(D) illustrate the growing influence of Confucianism in Vietnamese society
(E) compare the religious beliefs of the Vietnamese to those of other Southeast Asian peoples

GO ON TO THE NEXT PAGE ➡

26 The author uses the term *family mediators* (line 29) to mean the

(A) traditional role of elders in Vietnamese families
(B) responsibilities which young refugees assume in a new country
(C) help that newly arrived refugees get from friends who migrated earlier
(D) professional help available to refugee families in U.S. communities
(E) benefits that American society derives from immigrant people

27 The word *pronounced* in line 42 most nearly means

(A) delivered
(B) noticeable
(C) famous
(D) acceptable
(E) declared

28 The phrase *radical change* (line 49) refers to the fact that

(A) older refugees find that retirement ages are very different in America
(B) women filled men's jobs during the Vietnam War
(C) education of their children is considered crucial by refugee parents
(D) refugee men are often displaced as primary income earners in their families
(E) it is difficult for young refugees of both sexes to find jobs in America

29 The author's point about the problematic long-term outlook for refugee women is made primarily through

(A) personal recollection
(B) historical discussion
(C) case study analysis
(D) philosophical commentary
(E) informed speculation

30 The author mentions which of the following problems facing elderly Southeast Asian refugees?

   I. Southeast Asian women have greater employment opportunities in their own countries than in the United States.
   II. Southeast Asians respect their elders, while Americans do not.
   III. Americans and Southeast Asians differ in their definition of when one becomes elderly.

(A) I only
(B) II only
(C) III only
(D) II and III only
(E) I, II, and III

IF YOU FINISH BEFORE TIME IS CALLED, YOU MAY CHECK YOUR WORK ON THIS SECTION ONLY. DO NOT TURN TO ANY OTHER SECTION IN THE TEST.

STOP

Time—30 Minutes
25 Questions

Solve each of the following problems, decide which is the best answer choice, and darken the corresponding oval on the answer sheet. Use available space in the test booklet for scratchwork.*

Notes:

(1) Calculator use is permitted.

(2) All numbers used are real numbers.

(3) Figures are provided for some problems. All figures are drawn to scale and lie in a plane UNLESS otherwise indicated.

Reference Information

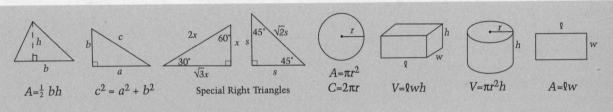

$A=\frac{1}{2}bh$ $c^2 = a^2 + b^2$ Special Right Triangles $A=\pi r^2$ $C=2\pi r$ $V=\ell wh$ $V=\pi r^2 h$ $A=\ell w$

The sum of the degree measures of the angles of a triangle is 180.
The number of degrees of arc in a circle is 360.
A straight angle has a degree measure of 180.

1   If $2(x + y) = 8 + 2y$, then $x =$

(A) 1
(B) 2
(C) 3
(D) 4
(E) 8

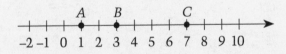

2   On the number line above, what is the distance from point B to the midpoint of AC ?

(A) 1
(B) 2
(C) 3
(D) 4
(E) 5

3   A certain machine caps 5 bottles every 2 seconds. At this rate, how many bottles will be capped in 1 minute?

(A) 10
(B) 75
(C) 150
(D) 225
(E) 300

4   If $2n + 3 = 5$, then $4n =$

(A) 1
(B) 2
(C) 4
(D) 8
(E) 16

5   If $a + b < 5$, and $a - b > 6$, which of the following pairs could be the values of a and b ?

(A) (1, 3)
(B) (3, −2)
(C) (4, −2)
(D) (4, −3)
(E) (5, −1)

*The directions on the actual SAT will vary slightly.

GO ON TO THE NEXT PAGE ➡

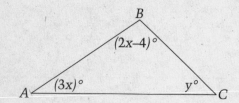

Note: Figure not drawn to scale.

6 In the triangle above, if the measure of angle B is 60 degrees, then what is the value of y ?

(A) 24
(B) 26
(C) 28
(D) 30
(E) 32

7 In a certain building, there are 10 floors and the number of rooms on each floor is R. If each room has exactly C chairs, which of the following gives the total number of chairs in the building?

(A) $10R + C$

(B) $10R + 10C$

(C) $\dfrac{10}{RC}$

(D) $10RC$

(E) $100RC$

8 If a "sump" number is defined as one in which the sum of the digits of the number is greater than the product of the digits of the same number, which of the following is a "sump" number?

(A) 123
(B) 234
(C) 332
(D) 411
(E) 521

9 If 4 percent of r is 6.2, then 20 percent of $r =$

(A) 25
(B) 26
(C) 30
(D) 31
(E) 35

10 At a certain school, if the ratio of teachers to students is 1 to 10, which of the following could be the total number of teachers and students?

(A) 100
(B) 121
(C) 144
(D) 222
(E) 1,011

11 If $x \wedge y$ is defined by the expression $(x - y)^x + (x + y)^y$, what is the value of $4 \wedge 2$?

(A) 52
(B) 44
(C) 28
(D) 20
(E) 16

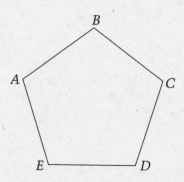

12 In pentagon $ABCDE$ shown above, each side is 1 centimeter. If a particle starts at point A and travels clockwise 723 centimeters along $ABCDE$, the particle will stop on which point?

(A) A
(B) B
(C) C
(D) D
(E) E

13 Which of the following values of s would yield the smallest value for $4 + \dfrac{1}{s}$?

(A) $\dfrac{1}{4}$

(B) $\dfrac{1}{2}$

(C) 1

(D) 2

(E) 4

GO ON TO THE NEXT PAGE ➡

14 The first and seventh terms in a sequence are 1 and 365 respectively. If each term after the first in the sequence is formed by multiplying the preceding term by 3 and subtracting 1, what is the sixth term?

(A) 40
(B) 41
(C) 121
(D) 122
(E) 123

15 If an integer is randomly chosen from the first 50 positive integers, what is the probability that an integer with a digit of 3 is selected?

(A) $\frac{7}{25}$

(B) $\frac{3}{10}$

(C) $\frac{8}{25}$

(D) $\frac{2}{5}$

(E) $\frac{3}{5}$

16 In a certain triangle, the measure of the largest angle is 40 degrees more than the measure of the middle-sized angle. If the measure of the smallest angle is 20 degrees, what is the degree measure of the largest angle?

(A) 60
(B) 80
(C) 100
(D) 120
(E) 160

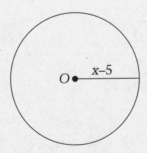

17 In the circle with center O above, for what value of x does the circle have a circumference of 20π ?

(A) 5
(B) 10
(C) 15
(D) 20
(E) 25

18 In a coordinate plane, if points $A(p, 3)$ and $B(6, p)$ lie on a line with a slope of 2, what is the value of p ?

(A) 1
(B) 2
(C) 3
(D) 4
(E) 5

19 At a fruit stand, the price of one pound of cherries is twice the price of one pound of grapes. If 32 pounds of cherries and 8 pounds of grapes were sold and sales totaled $90.00, how much more money was made on the cherries than on the grapes?

(A) $75.00
(B) $70.00
(C) $65.00
(D) $60.00
(E) $55.00

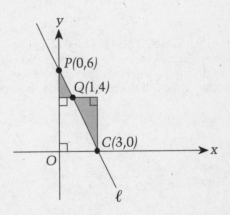

20 In the coordinate plane above, points $P(0, 6)$, $Q(1, 4)$, and $C(3, 0)$ are on line ℓ. What is the sum of the areas of the shaded triangular regions?

(A) $\frac{7}{2}$

(B) 4

(C) $\frac{9}{2}$

(D) 5

(E) $\frac{11}{2}$

GO ON TO THE NEXT PAGE ➡

21 The average (arithmetic mean) of two numbers is equal to twice the positive difference between the two numbers. If the larger number is 35, what is the small number?

(A)   3
(B)   9
(C)   15
(D)   21
(E)   27

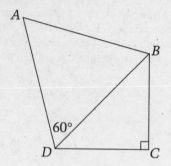

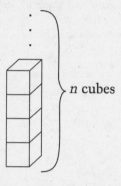

n cubes

22 In the figure above, there is a total of n cubes, each with an edge of 1 inch, stacked directly on top of each other. If $n > 1$, what is the total surface area, in square inches, of the resulting solid, in terms of n ?

(A) $2n$
(B) $2n^2 + 2$
(C) $4n + 2$
(D) $4n^2$
(E) $5n$

23 In the figure above, if $BC = DC$, and $AD = AB$, what is the value of $\frac{AB}{CD}$?

(A) $\frac{\sqrt{2}}{2}$

(B) $\sqrt{2}$

(C) $\frac{\sqrt{3}}{3}$

(D) $\sqrt{3}$

(E)   2

24 If the sum of 5 different positive integers is 100, what is greatest possible value for the median of the 5 integers?

(A)   31
(B)   32
(C)   33
(D)   34
(E)   50

25 The lengths of two sides of a triangle are $(x - 2)$ and $(x + 2)$, where $x > 2$. Which of the following ranges includes all and only the possible values of the third side y ?

(A) $0 < y < x$
(B) $0 < y < 2x$
(C) $2 < y < x$
(D) $4 < y < x$
(E) $4 < y < 2x$

IF YOU FINISH BEFORE TIME IS CALLED, YOU MAY CHECK YOUR WORK ON THIS SECTION ONLY. DO NOT TURN TO ANY OTHER SECTION IN THE TEST.

STOP

334   KAPLAN

Time—30 Minutes
35 Questions

For each of the following questions, choose the best answer and darken the corresponding oval on the answer sheet.

Select the lettered word or set of words that best completes the sentence.

Example:

Today's small, portable computers contrast markedly with the earliest electronic computers, which were ----.

(A) effective
(B) invented
(C) useful
(D) destructive
(E) enormous

1. Ozone in the upper layers of Earth's atmosphere is beneficial, ---- animal and plant life from dangerous ultraviolet radiation.

(A) reflecting
(B) withdrawing
(C) displacing
(D) thwarting
(E) protecting

2. While George Balanchine's choreography stayed within a classical context, he challenged convention by recombining ballet idioms in ---- ways.

(A) unexpected
(B) familiar
(C) redundant
(D) naive
(E) awkward

3. All of today's navel oranges are ---- of a single mutant tree that began bearing seedless fruit 200 years ago.

(A) progenitors
(B) combinations
(C) descendants
(D) conglomerations
(E) spores

4. Because he consumed ---- quantities of food and drink at feasts given in his honor, King Henry VIII was considered a ---- by his subjects.

(A) enormous . . glutton
(B) prodigious . . peer
(C) minute . . luminary
(D) unhealthy . . fraud
(E) unknown . . dolt

5. The prime minister ordered the cabinet to stay on as ---- administration until a new government could be formed.

(A) an interim
(B) a political
(C) an invalid
(D) a premature
(E) a civilian

6. Many formerly ---- peoples have moved into ---- settlements as urban areas have encroached upon their land.

(A) roving . . vulnerable
(B) despondent . . stable
(C) transitory . . covert
(D) fervid . . enduring
(E) nomadic . . permanent

7. The ---- effect of the sleeping tablets was so ---- that she still felt groggy the next day.

(A) toxic . . erratic
(B) soporific . . pronounced
(C) salubrious . . dependable
(D) pharmaceutical . . peculiar
(E) stimulating . . unreliable

8. For many years Davis had difficulty in accepting those who were in positions of authority; in fact, when he was in high school his teachers described him as a ---- student.

(A) compliant
(B) slothful
(C) conscientious
(D) model
(E) recalcitrant

9. Although the actress had lived in a large city all her life, she was such a ---- performer that she became the virtual ---- of the humble farm girl she portrayed in the play.

(A) versatile . . opposite
(B) melodramatic . . understudy
(C) natural . . nemesis
(D) consummate . . incarnation
(E) drab . . caricature

10. The chairman ---- the decision of the board members, describing it as a ---- of every worthy ideal that the organization had hitherto upheld.

(A) defended . . denial
(B) lamented . . negation
(C) criticized . . fulfillment
(D) endorsed . . renunciation
(E) applauded . . repudiation

GO ON TO THE NEXT PAGE ➡

Choose the lettered pair of words that is related in the same way as the pair in capital letters.

Example:

FLAKE : SNOW ::

(A) storm : hail
(B) drop : rain
(C) field : wheat
(D) stack : hay
(E) cloud : fog

11 MILL : FLOUR ::

(A) paddock : horses
(B) stadium : ballgame
(C) pharmacy : prescription
(D) brewery : beer
(E) pantry : food

12 STETHOSCOPE : LISTEN ::

(A) microscope : record
(B) needle : inject
(C) bandage : cut
(D) scale : reduce
(E) cough : breathe

13 BOTANIST : PLANTS ::

(A) zoologist : animals
(B) linguist : verbs
(C) philologist : stamps
(D) physicist : experiments
(E) chemist : laboratories

14 ABUNDANT : ADEQUATE ::

(A) arid : moist
(B) peaceful : boisterous
(C) timid : illegitimate
(D) overflowing : full
(E) bold : anxious

15 DOUBLE-CROSSER : BETRAY ::

(A) slowpoke : lag
(B) watchdog : dread
(C) trendsetter : pace
(D) sweetheart : hug
(E) pessimist : cooperate

16 EVADE : STRAIGHTFORWARD ::

(A) leave : inviting
(B) enliven : animated
(C) flatten : smooth
(D) boast : modest
(E) assist : helpful

17 REPREHENSIBLE : BLAME ::

(A) incomprehensible : knowledge
(B) treasonable : invasion
(C) relevant : information
(D) difficult : failure
(E) commendable : praise

18 CONCORD : AGREEMENT ::

(A) insurrection : peace
(B) chaos : order
(C) promise : force
(D) revolution : army
(E) flux : change

19 FLORAL : FLOWERS ::

(A) perennial : plants
(B) morbid : cemeteries
(C) emotional : feelings
(D) moral : stories
(E) maniacal : men

20 CALM : COMPOSURE ::

(A) scared : trouble
(B) cold : sickness
(C) congested : traffic
(D) sad : melancholy
(E) bored : gladness

21 SEQUESTER : JUROR ::

(A) quarantine : patient
(B) cloister : convent
(C) parole : prisoner
(D) graduate : pupil
(E) elect : mayor

22 HACKNEYED : ORIGINALITY ::

(A) omnipotent : power
(B) debauched : virtue
(C) fictitious : objectivity
(D) correct : judgment
(E) stubborn : resolve

23 SLAKE : THIRST ::

(A) stoke : fire
(B) starve : hunger
(C) assuage : pain
(D) endure : discomfort
(E) induce : sleep

GO ON TO THE NEXT PAGE ➡

Answer the questions below based on the information in the accompanying passages.

Questions 24–35 are based on the following passage.

In the following passage, a famous zoologist discusses the origins of the domesticated animal.

The relationship between humans and animals
dates back to the misty morning of history. The
caves of southern France and northern Spain are
Line full of wonderful depictions of animals. Early
(5) African petroglyphs depict recognizable mammals
and so does much American Indian art. But long
before art, we have evidence of the closeness of
humans and animals. The bones of dogs lie next to
those of humans in the excavated villages of
(10) northern Israel and elsewhere. This unity of death
is terribly appropriate. It marks a relationship that
is the most ancient of all, one that dates back at
least to the Mesolithic Era.* With the dog, the
hunter acquired a companion and ally very early
(15) on, before agriculture, long before the horses and
the cat. The companion animals were followed by
food animals and then by those that provided
enhanced speed and range, and those that worked
for us.
(20) How did it all come about? A dog of some kind
was almost inevitable. Consider its essence: a
social carnivore, hunting larger animals across the
broad plains it shared with our ancestors. Because
of its pack structure it is susceptible to domination
(25) by, and attachment to, a pack leader—the top dog.
Its young are born into the world dependent,
rearable without too much skill, and best of all,
they form bonds with the rearers. Dogs have a set
of appeasement behaviors that elicit affective
(30) reactions from even the most hardened and
unsophisticated humans. Puppies share with
human babies the power to transform cynics into
cooing softies. Furthermore, the animal has a sense
of smell and hearing several times more acute than
(35) our own, great advantages to a hunting companion
and intrusion detector. The dog's defense behavior
makes it an instinctive guard animal.
No wonder the dog was first and remains so
close to us. In general, however, something else
(40) was probably important in narrowing the list—the
candidates had to be camp followers or
cohabitants. When humankind ceased to be
continually nomadic, when we put down roots and
established semi-permanent habitations, hut
(45) clusters and finally villages, we created an instant,
rich food supply for guilds of opportunistic feeders.
Even today, many birds and mammals parasitize
our wastes and feed from our stores. They do so
because their wild behaviors provide the
(50) mechanisms for opportunistic exploitation. A
striking example occurred in Britain during the

1940s and '50s. In those days, milk was delivered
to the homeowners' doorstep in glass bottles with
aluminum foil caps. Rich cream topped the milk,
(55) the paradise before homogenization. A chickadee
known as the blue tit learned to puncture the cap
and drink the cream. The behavior soon spread
among the tits, and soon milk bottles were being
raided in the early morning throughout Britain. If
(60) the birds had been so specialized that they only fed
in deep forest, it never would have happened. But
these were forest-edge opportunists, pioneers
rather than conservatives. It is from animals of this
ilk that we find our allies and our foes.
(65) Returning to the question of how it all came
about, my instincts tell me that we first
domesticated those individual animals that were
orphaned by our hunting ancestors. In my years in
the tropics, I have seen many wild animals raised
(70) by simple people in their houses. The animals
were there, without thought of utility or gain,
mainly because the hunter in the family had
brought the orphaned baby back for his wife and
children. In Panama it was often a beautiful small,
(75) spotted cat that bounced friskily out of a peasant's
kitchen to play at my feet. The steps from the
home-raised wolfling to the domestic dog probably
took countless generations. I bet it started with
affection and curiosity. Only later did it become
(80) useful.
When we consider that there are more than 55
million domestic cats and 50 million dogs in this
country, and that they support an industry larger
than the total economy of medieval Europe, we
(85) must recognize the strength of the ancient bond.
Without the "aid" of goats, sheep, pigs, cattle and
horses we would never have reached our present
population densities. Our parasitization of some
species and symbiosis with others made
(90) civilization possible. That civilization, in turn, is
increasingly causing the extinction of many
animals and plant species—an ironic paradox
indeed.

*Mesolithic Era: also known as the Middle Stone Age, between 8,000 and 3,000 years B.C.

GO ON TO THE NEXT PAGE ➡

24 The author most likely describes the archeological discoveries mentioned in lines 8–10 as "terribly appropriate" because

(A) dogs were always buried next to their owners in the Mesolithic Era

(B) few animals were of religious significance in prehistoric cultures

(C) they illustrate the role of dogs on a typical hunting expedition

(D) our relationship with dogs goes back farther than with any other animal

(E) they indicate the terrible speed of natural disasters

25 According to the first paragraph, the first animals that humans had a close relationship with were those that

(A) acted as companions

(B) provided a source of food

(C) helped develop agriculture

(D) enabled humans to travel farther

(E) raided our food supply

26 According to the author, why was some kind of dog "inevitable" (line 21) as a companion animal for humans?

(A) It survived by maintaining its independence.

(B) It was stronger than other large animals.

(C) It shared its prey with our ancestors.

(D) It was friendly to other carnivores.

(E) It was suited for human domination.

27 In line 21, *essence* means

(A) history

(B) nature

(C) scent

(D) success

(E) aggression

28 Judging from lines 29–30, *affective reactions* most probably means

(A) callous decisions

(B) rational judgements

(C) emotional responses

(D) juvenile behavior

(E) cynical comments

29 The author most likely compares puppies with human babies in lines 31–33 in order to

(A) criticize an uncaring attitude towards animals

(B) point out ways in which animals dominate humans

(C) support the idea that dogs form bonds with their owners

(D) dispel some misconceptions about the innocence of puppies

(E) show how rewarding the ownership of a dog can be

30 In line 40, *the list* most likely refers to

(A) the types of birds that scavenge human food supplies

(B) the number of animals that developed relationships with humans

(C) the group of species that are able to communicate with dogs

(D) the variety of attributes that make dogs good hunters

(E) the range of animals depicted in cave paintings

31 The author most likely discusses the case of the British blue tit (lines 52–59) in order to

(A) highlight a waste of valuable food supplies

(B) indicate the quality of milk before homogenization

(C) explain how unpredictable animal behavior can be

(D) point out the disadvantages of living in rural areas

(E) provide one example of an opportunistic feeder

32 In lines 63–64, *animals of this ilk* refers to animals that are

(A) good companions

(B) forest inhabitants

(C) adaptable feeders

(D) efficient hunters

(E) persistent pests

GO ON TO THE NEXT PAGE ➡

33 The author most likely describes his experience in the tropics (lines 68–76) in order to

(A) portray the simple life led by a hunter's family
(B) show how useful animals can be in isolated places
(C) underline the effort involved in training a wild animal
(D) illustrate how the first domesticated animals were created
(E) indicate the curious nature of the domestic cat

34 In line 86, the use of "aid" in quotation marks emphasizes the point that

(A) the animals' help was involuntary
(B) population levels are dangerously high
(C) the contribution of animals is rarely recognized
(D) many animals benefited from the relationship
(E) livestock animals are not as loyal as dogs

35 Which of the following best describes the "ironic paradox" mentioned in line 92?

(A) More money is now spent on domestic animals than on animal livestock.
(B) Pet ownership will become impractical if population density continues to increase.
(C) The pet care industry in the U.S. today is larger than the total economy of medieval Europe.
(D) Many parasitical species have a beneficial effect on the human population.
(E) Human civilization is currently making extinct many of the other life forms that enabled it to grow.

IF YOU FINISH BEFORE TIME IS CALLED, YOU MAY CHECK YOUR WORK ON THIS SECTION ONLY. DO NOT TURN TO ANY OTHER SECTION IN THE TEST. **STOP**

KAPLAN 339

Time—30 Minutes
25 Questions

Solve each of the following problems, decide which is the best answer choice, and darken the corresponding oval on the answer sheet. Use available space in the test booklet for scratchwork.*

Notes:

(1)   Calculator use is permitted.

(2)   All numbers used are real numbers.

(3)   Figures are provided for some problems. All figures are drawn to scale and lie in a plane UNLESS otherwise indicated.

Reference Information

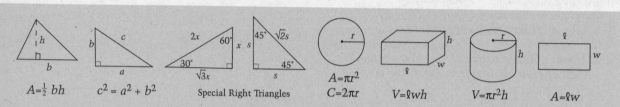

$$A = \tfrac{1}{2} bh \qquad c^2 = a^2 + b^2 \qquad \text{Special Right Triangles} \qquad \begin{matrix} A = \pi r^2 \\ C = 2\pi r \end{matrix} \qquad V = \ell wh \qquad V = \pi r^2 h \qquad A = \ell w$$

The sum of the degree measures of the angles of a triangle is 180.
The number of degrees of arc in a circle is 360.
A straight angle has a degree measure of 180.

DIRECTIONS FOR QUANTITATIVE COMPARISON QUESTIONS

Compare the boxed quantity in Column A with the boxed quantity in Column B. Select answer choice

A   if Column A is greater;
B   if Column B is greater;
C   if the columns are equal; or
D   if more information is needed to determine the relationship.

An E response will be treated as an omission.

Notes:

1.   Some questions include information about one or both quantities. That information is centered and unboxed.
2.   A symbol that appears in both Column A and Column B stands for the same thing in both columns.
3.   All numbers used are real numbers.

EXAMPLES

Column A	Column B	Answers
E1 3×4	$3 + 4$	● Ⓑ Ⓒ Ⓓ Ⓔ
E2 x	160	Ⓐ Ⓑ ● Ⓓ Ⓔ

$x°$ $20°$

x and y are positive

| E3 $x + 1$ | $y - 1$ | Ⓐ Ⓑ Ⓒ ● Ⓔ |

*The directions on the actual SAT will vary slightly.

GO ON TO THE NEXT PAGE ➡

Column A	Column B

1

$$1,000 - 3.45002$$

$$1,000 - 3.45601$$

$$x + y > 11$$
$$x < 5.5$$

2

x

y

3

$$\frac{27}{17^{17}}$$

$$\frac{27}{17^{18}}$$

4

The number of hours in 60 days

The number of seconds in 30 minutes

$$a + b = 60$$
$$b + c = 40$$
$$a > b > c > 0$$

5

The average (arithmetic mean) of a, b, and c.

50

Column A	Column B

6

The number of units of the perimeter triangle ABC

The number of square units of the area triangle ABC

$$1, 2, -3, -4, 1, 2, -3, -4\ldots$$

The sequence above begins with 1 and repeats in the pattern 1, 2, –3, –4 indefinitely.

7

The sum of the 49th and 51st terms

The sum of the 50th and 52nd terms

Kearne is twice as old as Amanda.

8

Kearne's age five years ago

Amanda's age five years from now

$$2x + y = 2$$
$$4x + y = 3$$

9

$3x$

$2y$

$$x + y = -3$$
$$x = 2y$$

10

x

y

GO ON TO THE NEXT PAGE ➡

KAPLAN 341

Column A	**Column B**

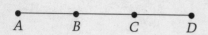

Note: Figure is not drawn to scale.

$$BD > AC$$

11

AB	CD

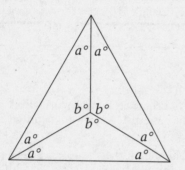

12

$b - a$	90

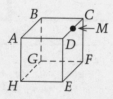

Each side of cube $ABCDEFGH$ has a length e.
M is the midpoint of segment CD.

13

The length of MH	$\frac{3}{2}e$

Column A	**Column B**

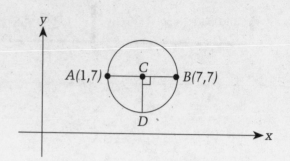

Note: Figure not drawn to scale.

C is the center of the circle.
AB is perpendicular to CD.

14

The x-coordinate of point D	The y-coordinate of point D

$$75\% \text{ of } 80 > 25\% \text{ of } x$$

15

x	200

GO ON TO THE NEXT PAGE ➡

DIRECTIONS FOR STUDENT-PRODUCED RESPONSE QUESTIONS

For each of the questions below (16–25), solve the problem and indicate your answer by darkening the ovals in the special grid. For example:

Answer: 1.25 or $\frac{5}{4}$ or 5/4

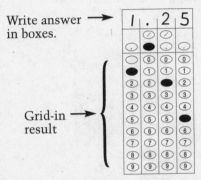

Write answer in boxes.

Grid-in result

Fraction line

Decimal point

Either position is correct.

You may start your answers in any column, space permitting. Columns not needed should be left blank.

- It is recommended, though not required, that you write your answer in the boxes at the top of the columns. However, you will receive credit only for darkening the ovals correctly.

- Grid only one answer to a question, even though some problems have more than one correct answer.

- Darken no more than one oval in a column.

- No answers are negative.

- Mixed numbers cannot be gridded. For example: the number $1\frac{1}{4}$ must be gridded as 1.25 or 5/4.

    (If ⌐ 1 1 / 4 is gridded, it will be interpreted as $\frac{11}{4}$, not $1\frac{1}{4}$.)

- Decimal Accuracy: Decimal answers must be entered as accurately as possible. For example, if you obtain an answer such as 0.1666..., you should record the result as .166 or .167. **Less accurate values such as .16 or .17 are not acceptable.**

    Acceptable ways to grid $\frac{1}{6}$ = .1666. . .

---

16 If $y = 2$, then $(5 - y)(y + 3) =$

17 At a certain car rental company, the daily rental rate for a mid-size car is $18.99. If the weekly rental rate for the same car is $123.50, how much money, in dollars, is saved by renting this car by the week instead of renting daily for seven days? (Exclude the $ sign when gridding your answer.)

GO ON TO THE NEXT PAGE ➡

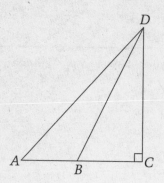

Note: Figure not drawn to scale.

18 In the figure above, $AB = 4$, $BC = 5$, and DC is 12. If point E lies somewhere between points A and B on line segment AB, what is one possible length of DE ?

19 If $\frac{3}{4}$ of a cup of a certain drink mix is needed for every 2 quarts of water, how many cups of this drink mix is needed for 10 quarts of water?

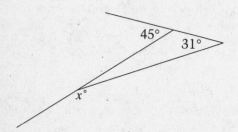

20 In the figure above, what is the value of x ?

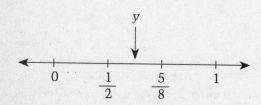

Note: Figure not drawn to scale.

21 On the number line above, what is one possible value for y ?

22 Melanie drove at an average rate of 40 miles per hour for two hours and then increased her average rate by 25% for the next 3 hours. Her average rate of speed for the 5 hours was t miles per hour. What is the value of t ?

23 At a convention of 500 dealers, each dealer sold coins or stamps or both. If 127 dealers sold both coins and stamps, and 198 dealers sold *only* stamps, how many dealers sold only coins?

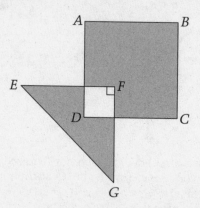

Note: Figure not drawn to scale.

24 In the figure above, square $ABCD$ and right triangle EFG overlap to form a smaller square of length 2. If $AB = EF = FG = 6$, what is the sum of the areas of the shaded regions?

$$\begin{array}{r} NR \\ + RN \\ \hline ABC \end{array}$$

25 The addition problem above is correct. If N, R, A, B, and C are different digits, what is the greatest possible value of $B + C$?

IF YOU FINISH BEFORE TIME IS CALLED, YOU MAY CHECK YOUR WORK ON THIS SECTION ONLY. DO NOT TURN TO ANY OTHER SECTION IN THE TEST.   **STOP**

Time—15 Minutes
13 Questions   Answer the questions below based on the information in the accompanying passages.

Questions 1–13 are based on the following passages.

The two excerpts below are from speeches that were made by outstanding American leaders of the nineteenth century. The first excerpt is from Thomas Jefferson's first Inaugural Address in 1801; the second was delivered by Frederick Douglass during the Fourth of July celebration in Rochester, New York, in 1852.

Passage 1

    Let us then, with courage and confidence, pursue our own federal and republican principles; our attachment to union and representative government.
(5) Kindly separated by nature and a wide ocean from the exterminating havoc of one quarter of the globe; too high-minded to endure the degradation of others, possessing a chosen country, with room enough for our descendants to the thousandth and thousandth generation, entertaining a due sense of our equal
(10) right to the use of our own faculties, to the acquisition of our own industry, to honor and confidence from our fellow-citizens, resulting not from birth, but from our actions and their sense of them, enlightened by a benign religion, professed in
(15) deed and practiced in various forms, yet all of them inculcating honesty, truth, temperance, gratitude, and the love of man...Still one thing more, fellow citizens, a wise and frugal government, which shall restrain men from injuring one another, shall leave
(20) them otherwise free to regulate their own pursuits of industry and improvement, and shall not take from the mouth of labor the bread it has earned. This is the sum of good government; and this is necessary to close the circle of our felicities.
(25)   About to enter, fellow citizens, upon the exercise of duties which comprehend everything dear and valuable to you, it is proper you should understand what I deem the essential principles of our government, and consequently, those which
(30) ought to shape its administration. I will compress them within the narrowest compass they will bear, stating the general principle, but not all its limitations. Equal and exact justice to all men, of whatever state or persuasion, religious or
(35) political...

Passage 2

    I say it with a sad sense of disparity between us. I am not included within the pale of this glorious anniversary! Your high independence only reveals the immeasurable distance between us. The
(40) blessings in which you this day rejoice are not enjoyed in common. The rich inheritance of justice, liberty, prosperity, and independence bequeathed by your fathers is shared by you, not by me. The

(45) sunlight that brought life and healing to you has brought stripes and death to me. This Fourth of July is yours, not mine. You may rejoice, I must mourn. To drag a man in fetters into the grand illuminated temple of liberty, and call upon him to join you in joyous anthems, were inhuman mockery and
(50) sacrilegious irony. Do you mean, citizens, to mock me by asking me to speak today?
    ...Fellow citizens, above your national, tumultuous joy, I hear the mournful wail of millions, whose chains, heavy and grievous
(55) yesterday, are today rendered more intolerable by the jubilant shouts that reach them. If I do forget, if I do not remember those bleeding children of sorrow this day, "may my right hand forget her cunning, and may my tongue cleave to the roof of
(60) my mouth!" To forget them, to pass lightly over their wrongs, and to chime in with the popular theme, would be treason most scandalous and shocking, and would make me a reproach before God and the world. My subject, then, fellow
(65) citizens, is "American Slavery..."
    ...Would you have me argue that man is entitled to liberty? That he is the rightful owner of his own body? You have already declared it. Must I argue the wrongfulness of slavery? Is that a question for
(70) republicans? Is it to be settled by the rules of logic and argumentation, as a matter beset with great difficulty, involving a doubtful application of the principle of justice, hard to understand?...
    ...What to the American slave is your Fourth of
(75) July? I answer, a day that reveals more to him than all other days of the year, the gross injustice and cruelty to which he is the constant victim. To him your celebration is a sham; your boasted liberty an unholy license; your national greatness, swelling
(80) vanity; your sounds of rejoicing are empty and heartless; your denunciation of tyrants, brass-fronted impudence; your shouts of liberty and equality, hollow mockery; your prayers and hymns, your sermons and thanksgivings, with all your
(85) religious parade and solemnity, are to him mere bombast, fraud, deception, impiety, and hypocrisy—a thin veil to cover up crimes which would disgrace a nation of savages. There is not a nation of the earth guilty of practices more
(90) shocking and bloody than are the people of the United States at this very hour.

GO ON TO THE NEXT PAGE ➡

1   By "our equal right . . . to honor and confidence
    from our fellow-citizens, resulting not from birth,
    but from our actions and their sense of them"
    (lines 9–14), Jefferson means that

    (A) members of all nations are welcome to come
        to America
    (B) citizens have the right to demand respect from
        each other
    (C) citizens should judge each other by their
        accomplishments rather than their ancestry
    (D) one can build trust by doing things for others
    (E) one should rely not only on one's family but
        also on other citizens

2   In line 26, the word *comprehend* most nearly
    means

    (A) include
    (B) understand
    (C) perceive
    (D) outline
    (E) realize

3   By "I will compress them within the narrowest
    compass they will bear" (lines 30–31), Jefferson
    means that

    (A) he intends to limit the role of government
    (B) those who oppose justice will be imprisoned
    (C) the general principles of government have
        boundaries
    (D) he will speak concisely about the principles of
        government
    (E) government bureaucracy has become too
        inflated

4   The word *persuasion* in line 34 most nearly means

    (A) enticement
    (B) influence
    (C) cajolery
    (D) authority
    (E) opinion

5   The statement "To drag a man . . . sacrilegious
    irony" (lines 47–50) conveys a sense of

    (A) indignation at the hypocrisy of Fourth of July
        celebrations
    (B) sorrow over the way the slaves had been
        treated
    (C) anger that slavery had not yet been abolished
    (D) disbelief that Fourth of July celebrations could
        even take place
    (E) amazement that slaves were being forced to
        join in the celebration

6   In Passage 2, the references to the "mournful wail"
    and the "jubilant shouts" (lines 53–56) serve to

    (A) remind the audience of difficulties in the past
        that have been overcome
    (B) indicate the importance of commemorating
        the Fourth of July
    (C) warn that the future of the country looks
        deceptively bright
    (D) emphasize the different outlooks of two groups
        in the country
    (E) suggest that some are faced with an unsolvable
        problem

7   In line 62, the author uses the word *treason* to
    refer to the act of

    (A) rebelling against authority
    (B) betraying the needs of a social group
    (C) renouncing one's own principles
    (D) expressing unpopular views
    (E) acting upon irrational impulses

8   The author of Passage 2 most likely describes
    "American Slavery" as "my subject" (lines 64–65)
    in order to

    (A) underline an unexpected new direction in his
        argument
    (B) indicate the broad historical scope of his
        address
    (C) emphasize his intent to discuss an apparent
        contradiction
    (D) highlight the answer to a problem facing the
        United States
    (E) underscore his eagerness to learn more about
        the topic of slavery

9   In lines 81–82 of Passage 2, the phrase *brass-
    fronted impudence* is primarily used to convey the
    author's

    (A) outrage at the contrast between political
        speeches and social reality
    (B) exasperation at the many obstacles to racial
        equality
    (C) resentment at the number of people excluded
        from July Fourth celebrations
    (D) belief that resistance to authority is ultimately
        futile
    (E) anger at the acts of tyrants throughout the
        world

GO ON TO THE NEXT PAGE ➡

10 The author of Passage 1 would most likely react to the questions at the beginning of the third paragraph of Passage 2 (lines 66–70) by commenting that

(A) a nation's political ideals are not always consistent with its actions

(B) the doctrine of equality is necessary for good government

(C) political views must be expressed through the proper democratic channels

(D) the goal of liberty for all may not be practical to attain

(E) the degradation of others must sometimes be endured

11 The author of Passage 2 would most likely react to the general principle of government in the last sentence of Passage 1 by pointing out that

(A) this general principle is hopelessly naive

(B) the real situation strongly contradicts this principle

(C) experience has proven this principle to be unattainable

(D) this principle is meaningless because it is vaguely worded

(E) the government never intended to adhere to this principle

12 Which statement is best supported by a comparison of the excerpts from the two speeches?

(A) Both excerpts denounce the degradation of some men and women in America.

(B) The purpose of both excerpts is to urge citizens to critically evaluate themselves.

(C) Both excerpts emphasize the necessity of justice for all citizens.

(D) Both excerpts argue that slavery is a violation of human rights.

(E) Both excerpts present a hopeful vision of the future.

13 The attitudes expressed in Passage 1 and Passage 2 towards equality in the United States might best be described as

(A) caution versus anger

(B) disappointment versus adulation

(C) optimism versus criticism

(D) hope versus promise

(E) indulgence versus prudence

IF YOU FINISH BEFORE TIME IS CALLED, YOU MAY CHECK YOUR WORK ON THIS SECTION ONLY. DO NOT TURN TO ANY OTHER SECTION IN THE TEST.

STOP

Time—15 Minutes
10 Questions

Solve each of the following problems, decide which is the best answer choice, and darken the corresponding oval on the answer sheet. Use available space in the test booklet for scratchwork.

Notes:

(1) Calculator use is permitted.

(2) All numbers used are real numbers.

(3) Figures are provided for some problems. All figures are drawn to scale and lie in a plane UNLESS otherwise indicated.

Reference Information

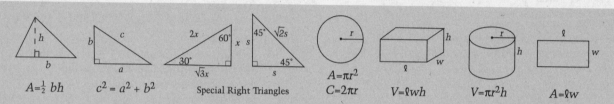

$A=\frac{1}{2}bh$ $c^2 = a^2 + b^2$ Special Right Triangles $A=\pi r^2$ $V=\ell wh$ $V=\pi r^2 h$ $A=\ell w$
$C=2\pi r$

The sum of the degree measures of the angles of a triangle is 180.
The number of degrees of arc in a circle is 360.
A straight angle has a degree measure of 180.

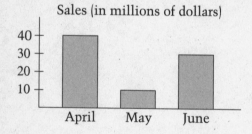

Sales (in millions of dollars)

1 According to the graph above, April sales accounted for approximately what percent of the total 2nd-quarter sales?

(A) $12\frac{1}{2}$

(B) 25

(C) $37\frac{1}{2}$

(D) 50

(E) 60

2 If xy is negative, which of the following CANNOT be negative?

(A) $y - x$
(B) $x - y$
(C) $x^2 y$
(D) xy^2
(E) $x^2 y^2$

3 If a bora = 2 fedis and 1 fedi = 3 glecks, how many boras are equal to 48 glecks?

(A) 4
(B) 8
(C) 16
(D) 48
(E) 96

GO ON TO THE NEXT PAGE ➡

4 A college class is made up of *f* freshman and *s* sophomores. If 5 freshman drop this class, the number of sophomores in the class is 3 times the number of freshman. Which of the following equations represents *s* in terms of *f* ?

(A) $s = \dfrac{f-5}{3}$

(B) $s = \dfrac{f+5}{3}$

(C) $s = 3(f-5)$

(D) $s = 3(f+5)$

(E) $s = 5(f-3)$

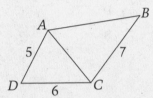

5 If the perimeter of triangle *ABC* is 4 more than the perimeter of triangle *ACD*, what is the perimeter of quadrilateral *ABCD* ?

(A) 20
(B) 22
(C) 24
(D) 25
(E) 26

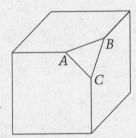

6 The figure above shows a cubed-shaped stone with edges of 3 centimeters. Points *A*, *B*, and *C* are on three different edges of the cube, each 1 centimeter away from the same vertex. A jeweler slices off the corner with a straight cut through *A*, *B*, and *C*, as shown, and slices pieces of the same size off all the other corners of the stone. What is the total number of faces on the resulting stone?

(A) seven
(B) ten
(C) twelve
(D) fourteen
(E) sixteen

7 What is the average of the first 30 positive integers?

(A) 14
(B) 14.5
(C) 15
(D) 15.5
(E) 16

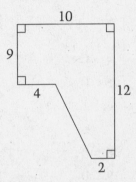

Note: Figure not drawn to scale.

8 What is the area of the figure above?

(A) 96
(B) 102
(C) 104
(D) 108
(E) 110

9 Sixty cookies were to be equally distributed to *x* campers. When 8 campers did not want the cookies, the other campers each received 2 more cookies. Which of the following equations could be used to find the number of campers *x* ?

(A) $x^2 - 8x - 240 = 0$
(B) $x^2 - 8x + 240 = 0$
(C) $x^2 + 8x - 240 = 0$
(D) $x^2 + 8x + 240 = 0$
(E) $x^2 - 4x - 120 = 0$

10 If six students are eligible for 2 scholarships worth $1,000 each how many different combinations of 2 students winning the 2 scholarships are possible?

(A) 6
(B) 9
(C) 12
(D) 15
(E) 30

IF YOU FINISH BEFORE TIME IS CALLED, YOU MAY CHECK YOUR WORK ON THIS SECTION ONLY. DO NOT TURN TO ANY OTHER SECTION IN THE TEST. STOP

Answer Key

Section 1	Section 2	Section 3	Section 4	Section 5	Section 6
1. E	1. D	1. E	1. A	1. C	1. D
2. B	2. A	2. A	2. B	2. A	2. E
3. D	3. C	3. C	3. A	3. D	3. B
4. C	4. C	4. A	4. B	4. E	4. C
5. D	5. D	5. A	5. B	5. A	5. E
6. C	6. A	6. E	6. A	6. D	6. D
7. A	7. D	7. B	7. C	7. B	7. D
8. B	8. D	8. E	8. D	8. C	8. B
9. B	9. D	9. D	9. B	9. A	9. A
10. B	10. B	10. B	10. B	10. B	10. D
11. A	11. A	11. D	11. B	11. B	
12. C	12. D	12. B	12. C	12. C	
13. E	13. E	13. A	13. C	13. C	
14. C	14. D	14. D	14. C		
15. E	15. A	15. A	15. D		
16. E	16. C	16. D	16. 15		
17. C	17. C	17. E	17. 9.43		
18. D	18. E	18. E	18. 13 < length < 15		
19. D	19. B	19. C	19. 15/4 or 3.75		
20. D	20. D	20. D	20. 166		
21. A	21. D	21. A	21. 0.5 < y < 0.625		
22. B	22. C	22. B	22. 46		
23. C	23. B	23. C	23. 175		
24. C	24. A	24. D	24. 46		
25. A	25. E	25. A	25. 11		
26. B		26. E			
27. B		27. B			
28. D		28. C			
29. E		29. C			
30. C		30. B			
		31. E			
		32. C			
		33. D			
		34. A			
		35. E			

Compute Your Raw Score

First, check your answers against the answer key on the previous page, and count up the number right and the number wrong for each section (there are boxes on your answer sheet to record these numbers). Remember not to count omissions as wrong.

Then figure out your raw scores using the table below. The Verbal raw score is equal to the total right in the three Verbal sections minus one-fourth of the number wrong in those sections. The Math raw score is equal to the total right in the three Math sections minus one-fourth of the number wrong in the two Regular Math sections and minus one-third the number wrong in the QCs. (Remember: There is no deduction for wrong answers in the Grid-ins.) Round each raw score to the nearest whole number.

Finally, use the tables on the next page to convert each raw score to a range of scaled scores.

	NUMBER RIGHT		NUMBER WRONG		RAW SCORE
SECTION 1:	☐	−[.25 x	☐]	=	☐
SECTION 3:	☐	−[.25 x	☐]	=	☐
SECTION 5:	☐	−[.25 x	☐]	=	☐

VERBAL RAW SCORE: ☐ (ROUNDED)

SECTION 4A: (Questions 1 to 15)	☐	−[.33 x	☐]	=	☐
SECTION 4B: (Questions 16 to 25)	☐	(No wrong-answer penalty)		=	☐
SECTION 2:	☐	−[.25 x	☐]	=	☐
SECTION 6:	☐	−[.25 x	☐]	=	☐

MATH RAW SCORE: ☐ (ROUNDED)

Convert Your Score

Verbal						Math					
Raw	Scaled	Raw	Scaled	Raw	Scaled	Raw	Scaled	Raw	Scaled	Raw	Scaled
−3 or less	200	22	450	48	620	−1 or less	200	19	440	40	600
−2	230	23	460	49	630	0	220	20	450	41	610
−1	270	24	470	50	640	1	240	21	460	42	620
0	290	25	470	51	640	2	260	22	470	43	630
1	300	26	480	52	650	3	280	23	480	44	640
2	310	27	490	53	660	4	300	24	480	45	650
3	320	28	490	54	670	5	310	25	490	46	650
4	330	29	500	55	670	6	330	26	500	47	660
5	330	30	510	56	670	7	340	27	510	48	670
6	340	31	510	57	680	8	350	28	520	49	680
7	350	32	520	58	690	9	360	29	520	50	690
8	360	33	530	59	690	10	370	30	530	51	700
9	370	34	530	60	700	11	380	31	530	52	720
10	370	35	540	61	710	12	390	32	540	53	730
11	380	36	550	62	720	13	400	33	550	54	740
12	390	37	550	63	730	14	410	34	560	55	760
13	390	38	560	64	730	15	420	35	560	56	770
14	400	39	570	65	740	16	430	36	570	57	780
15	410	40	570	66	750	17	430	37	580	58	790
16	410	41	580	67	760	18	440	38	590	59	800
17	420	42	590	68	770			39	600	60	800
18	430	43	590	69	780						
19	430	44	600	70	790						
20	440	45	600	71 or more	800						
21	450	46	610								
		47	610								

Don't take these scores too literally. Practice test conditions cannot precisely mirror real test conditions. Your actual SAT scores will almost certainly vary from your practice test scores.

Your score on the practice test gives you a rough idea of your range on the actual exam. If you don't like your score, it's not too late to do something about it. Work your way way through this book again, and turn to Kaplan's *SAT Verbal Workbook* and *SAT Math Workbook* for even more help.

Practice Test Three Answers and Explanations

SECTION 1

1. E

Despite is our first clue word, signaling a contrast coming up. Despite their fierce appearance, caymans are actually rarely ----, to the point at which they won't attack humans unless provoked. So for the blank we need a word that means the same as "fierce." The closest word here is choice (E), **aggressive.** Choice (B) was the exact opposite of what we wanted. Choice (C), **domesticated,** means tame, and usually refers to animals treated as house pets.

2. B

There are two different schools of thought competing in this sentence. One group believes one thing *while* another believes something else. So, clearly we want words that help create a sense of the opposition between these two viewpoints. Let's start with the second blank. One group argues that courtly love "dates from the age of chivalry." In other words, they think it's a fairly old idea, dating back from the days of knights and fair maidens. Another group thinks something else though, so they must feel it's either an even older idea or a more recent idea. A quick check through the answer choices for the second blank leads us to choice (B) **ancient. Notion,** or idea, fits quite nicely into the first blank, fitting with the word "concept" in the first half of the sentence.

3. D

Here we want a word that would describe the sort of people who might throw fruits and vegetables at those whose performance dissatisfied them. People like this are surely not **doting** (A), overindulgent or excessively fond, nor are they **ravenous** (B), or extremely hungry. If they were hungry, they'd eat the food instead of throwing it at the stage. There's nothing to imply that the audience is (C) **jingoistic,** or excessively national-

istic. However, the audience might certainly be described as (D) **boisterous,** or rowdy. (E) **stagnant** means dead or lifeless, which is illogical in the blank.

4. C

"Although" two brothers look alike, they could not be more ---- in terms of their personalities. "Not alike" or "different" or some such word must go into this first blank, something that helps convey that they look alike, but their behavior is not alike. The semicolon is our hint that the information following it will be more or less in line with what preceded it. So, *while* one is circumspect, or cautious, the other is brash, or the opposite of cautious. For this second blank, you should predict something that means the opposite of quiet, something that's sort of synonymous with brash. The best answer is choice (C), because **dissimilar** fits our prediction for the first blank, while **audacious** means bold—it's kind of a synonym for brash. (A) **inimical** is related to the word "enemy." **Inimical** means hostile.

5. D

Napoleon's army was hightailing it out of Moscow. The retreat "quickly turned into a rout," a state of wild confusion, a disastrous defeat. Why did it turn into an even bigger defeat? Probably because the French were stuck or struggling in the snow—if they were doing well traveling through snow, it's unlikely they'd end up being such big losers. Then, something was done to them by Russian troops. Well, if you know that Napoleon's army was routed by the opposing side, then it seems that we want a second-blank word that means something like "clobbered." Choices (A) and (D) come close to that prediction. **Ravage** means to violently destroy. Now, going back to the first blank, we know we want something that implies the troops were stuck or struggling in the snow. Only choice (D) fits both blanks: the retreat of Napoleon's army turned into a rout as French troops, already **floundering** in the snow, were **assaulted** by Russian soldiers. To flounder is to struggle awkwardly and stumble about. In (A), **replenishing** in the snow sounds a bit weird—**replenishing** means replacing something that was used up. In (E), **tottering** means walking unsteadily, and **upbraided** means scolded or reprimanded—a little mild-mannered for our purposes here.

6. C

The word that will fill in the blank is defined here in the sentence—we want a word that describes an environment composed of tapestries, paintings, stained glass windows, and hand-crafted furniture. A quick survey of the answer choices leads us to choice (C), because **sumptuous** means costly or lavish, particularly with regard to furnishings and decor. While you might have been tempted to think that **friendly** in choice (D) was a plausible answer, it's hard to say to sure that an environment filled with rich, arty items is a friendly environment. For some people, such surroundings might be quite intimidating. **Frugal,** in choice (B), means thrifty or careful with money, which is quite the opposite of what we wanted here.

7. A

In this question, a lecturer is frustrated by something her audience has done. This frustration was only ---- by some connection between the audience and talking. It sounds like the lecturer was frustrated by her audience's desire or tendency to talk during her presentation. Lecturers want to be heard; an audience's inability or lack of desire to talk would not frustrate a lecturer. So, for the second blank, we want something like desire—choice (A) **propensity,** or tendency, and choice (E) **desire** could work. (C) makes no sense. What's an "audience's **authorization**"? To choose between (A) and (E), let's look at the second blank. (E) **supplanted,** or replaced, is illogical. So (A)'s got to be correct. In fact, it makes the most sense: The lecturer's frustration was **compounded,** or increased, by the audience's **propensity,** or tendency, to talk.

8. B

There's something about the issue of the nuclear power plant that makes it surprising the council all voted in agreement. If it was shocking that there was agreement, the issue must have been divisive or controversial. The answer here is (B), because **contentious** means causing controversy and disagreement. **Concise** in (C) means brief and to the point, while **exorbitant** in (D) means extravagant or excessive.

9. B

So many stops in some particular amount of time led to only the most ---- impression about the places the tour visited. There's a connection between the amount of time spent visiting, and the impression of the places visited. So the two words that will fill in the blanks here must be roughly synonymous. Only choice (B) works here. There were so many stops in such a **brief** amount of time that only a **cursory** (superficial or hasty) impression of places was gained. (D)'s second word fits the blank, but (D)'s first word, **sufficient,** isn't a rough synonym and doesn't fit. In (A), many stops probably wouldn't leave a **lasting** impression. Nor would a tour at breakneck speed necessarily leave (C) a **favorable** impression on travelers.

10. B

STEEL is a type of **METAL,** just as **silk** is a type of **fabric.** In choice (E), a **carat** is a measure of the weight of a precious stone. It is not a type of **diamond.**

11. A

By definition, all **FUNNEL**s have a **CONICAL** shape. Choice (A) is correct here because **pipe**s have a **cylindrical** shape. **Solid**s are substances which have a definite size, shape and weight—in other words, **solid**s are substances which aren't liquids or gases. Not all solids are **spherical** or round in shape—there are many differently shaped **solid**s. In (C), a twisted **hose** might be **spiral** in shape, but not every **hose** is **spiral.** As for choice (D), **parallel** is not a shape of a **line,** it's the relationship between **line**s which never cross.

12. C

When something is **FUTILE,** it's hopeless; it has no **USE.** So, the answer here is (C), because something **superficial,** or shallow, has no **depth.** If you weren't quite sure what the link was, you still might have ruled out (B) and (E). After all, all **light** is not **faint.** And education and morals have little to do with each other; receiving an **education** doesn't mean you have **morals. Furtive,** in choice (D), means sneaky. Stealth describes the quality of secretive actions or movement, as in the Stealth Bomber, the radar-evading plane. Something or someone **furtive** is characterized by **stealth.**

13. E

KNEELing is a gesture of **SUBMISSION,** obedience or meekness. People may kneel in prayer, to show their reverence to a deity. Therefore, (E) is correct, because **nod**ding is a gesture of **assent,** or agreement. You need **equilibrium,** poise or balance, in order to **stand,** but **stand**ing isn't a gesture of **equilibrium.** A **mutiny,** in choice (C), is an uprising against the powers that be; this word is used most frequently to describe a mutiny of a crew on a ship against the captain or officers.

14. C

A **MOVEMENT** is, by definition, one part of a **SYMPHONY** as a whole. The right answer here is choice (C), because an **act** is one part of a **play.** If you didn't know this meaning of **MOVEMENT,** process of elimination could have led you to the right answer. A **projector,** in choice (B), is a machine you use to show a film. Could a **MOVEMENT** be a machine used to show a **SYMPHONY?** No, so (B) can be crossed out. In (E), a **canvas** might be the material that a **painting** is done on; might a **MOVEMENT** be the material a **SYMPHONY** is done on? No again; (E) can be crossed out, too. Finally, choices (A) and (D) can be eliminated because of their weak bridges. In (D), a **poem** may or may not have **rhythm.** In (A), a **note** is something you might play on a **piano;** then again, you might play it on a guitar, on a piccolo, or on many other instruments.

15. E

Perhaps the word **PURGATIVE** reminded you of the related word "purge." You may have heard "purge" in history class. Dictators are fond of purging their party or government of so-called traitors by, for example, killing them. To purge means to cleanse or rid of impurities or other undesirable elements. So, a **PURGATIVE** results in **CLEANSING.** Similarly, a **catalyst** results in **change,** so (E) is correct here. A **fixative,** in choice (A), is almost what it sounds like; it's a

substance that "fixes" something or holds it in place. Artists spray **fixative** on pastel or pencil drawings to prevent them from smearing. An **inoculation** is the injection of some sort of virus or serum meant to produce resistance to a disease.

To Build a Fire Passage

This fiction passage shouldn't pose too many problems: it's short, clear, and straightforward. If you enjoy reading fiction, be careful not to relax too much while reading the passage—you may slow down and lose time. Save pleasure reading for when you're not taking the SAT! The passage describes a man and a dog entering a little-traveled path in Alaska. A comparison is set up between the man, who "lacks imagination" and isn't alarmed by the extreme cold, and his dog who, going on instinct, is alarmed.

16. E

Review the beginning of the passage to see what "act" the man is "excusing to himself." It turns out he stopped because he was out of breath, but doesn't want to admit it (to himself, since he's alone), so he plays it off by looking at his watch. That makes choice (E) correct. He shows no reaction to what time it is (A). You may have been confused by choice (B) because the narrator (later in the passage) implies that the dog's instincts are more accurate than the man's. However, the man never shows distrust of himself (B). You're overinterpreting if you chose (C)—there's no evidence in the passage to support this inference. The point of the man's "excusing the act to himself" has nothing to do with "the time of day" (D); it has to do with him not admitting why he stopped in the first place.

17. C

Watch for the tone in the lines around the quote—it'll help you eliminate choices. For example, does the man seem at all "excited"? No, so (A) is out. He also doesn't seem "nervous" (B), although by the end of the passage there's an ominous feeling of danger in the air. (C) is right because it's a straightforward description of what's going on. There's no evidence in the passage to support choice (D). (E) is similarly wrong—there's no discussion of why the man is in the wilderness. Remember, most inferences (or "suggestions," as the question phrases it) are very mild, and are always supported by the passage.

18. D

Reread the lines the quote appears in. The man's being a "creature of temperature" is the same "frailty" that all humans have: we're "able only to live within narrow limits of heat and cold." In other words, if it's too cold, we'll freeze to death. Choice (D) is correct. "A creature of temperature" does not imply the man prefers cold climates (A), because "temperature" includes hot and cold. The author shows later in the passage how wrong the man's judgment of the temperature is, so (B) is unlikely. There's no discussion of "personality being shaped by the environment" (C). The man may or may not know wilderness survival techniques (E), but in any case, that's not what "a creature of temperature" refers to.

19. D

This question refers you to a big chunk of text, so save time by scanning the choices before you go to the passage. Choice (A) implies the wrong thing. This wilderness must be immensely beautiful, but whether the man notices it or not is not the point. The point is the judgment the man makes about the temperature. (B) overstates the case. The author isn't flatly declaring, "humans can't survive in the Alaskan wilderness." Instead, he's describing a man who is underestimating the potential danger. That makes (D) correct. Just because this character can't judge the temperature accurately doesn't mean "there's no way to accurately judge the temperature" (C). There's no evidence that "most people could not do" what this guy is doing, even though it's obviously a difficult thing (E).

20. D

All of paragraph 2 leads up to the four lines you're sent to for this question. After a discussion of the potential danger extreme temperatures pose to humans, the paragraph concludes by saying none of this entered the man's head. In other words, he lacks "insight and understanding" (D). The man thinks the cold "must be guarded against," so (B) can't be right. At the same time, (A) is too strong—the man doesn't even acknowledge that there are "odds" to succeed against.

(C) is too general. "Apprehension" in (E) means "fearfulness," which we've already seen the man lacks.

21. A

Again, you have a lot of lines to review, so save time by scanning the answer choices before you check the passage. It's in these lines that the author introduces the dog and its "instinct"—which tells it to take shelter from the cold. Correct choice (A) restates what's in lines 48–50. The dog isn't judging the temperature (B), it's just reacting to an instinct of danger. Choice (C) is an inference that goes too far—it's too general for these lines. (D) contradicts the point the author's making. (E) is partially true, but it captures only a small part of what the author suggests.

22. B

This question doesn't require too much interpretation, so don't go digging for difficult answers. The passage says that the dog "knew nothing of thermometers," but that it "had its instinct." In other words, it didn't read the temperature with a device as humans do, and it didn't need to—it knew instinctively how cold it was. The answer is (B)—the dog's awareness of its environment is different from the man's. Nothing implies that dogs "need not be concerned about temperature" (A); the point is that they perceive it differently than people do. (C) is too negative. Although the author calls the dog a "brute" at one point, it is done with respect, since the dog's instincts prove to be more valuable than the man's intelligence. (D) is too literal. And the point is not that the dog "could not rely on technological devices" (E), but that the dog has no need of them.

23. C

Reread the lines at the end of the passage to see what's going on. We've seen that the dog fears the cold, and the end of the passage describes the dog watching the man for a sign that they are heading for protection (C). Choices (A) and (E) miss the mark because the author never says that the dog recognizes the man's mistaken estimation of the cold. There is also no sign that the man is being visibly affected by the cold (B). Choice (D) invents something not found in the passage.

Elderly Asians Passage

Next you have a passage about Southeast Asian immigrants' experience of aging in America. This passage may be a little dry, but it's not complex. The discussion focuses on the problems older immigrants have when they come to America. These include: different standards of what's considered "elderly;" not getting the kind of respect they would in their homelands; dealing with different gender roles; and elderly women being isolated in the home and becoming estranged from their families. Don't worry about any more detail than this until you get to the questions.

24. C

Remember this strategy for dealing with main idea questions: look for an answer that's not too broad or too narrow, but that encompasses the whole passage. In this case, (A) is too broad. From the first paragraph, you know that the focus is more specific than "the reasons why Southeast Asian people move to the U.S." This helps you eliminate (B) as well: from the start you're told the passage is concerned with the problems of the elderly, not the young. (C) covers the whole passage, and is correct. (D) picks up on a detail—Confucianism—and expands it beyond the scope of the passage. And (E) is just one topic discussed in the passage, not the focus of it.

25. A

Review paragraph 2 to understand why the author mentions the "traditional Hmong culture." There, the author says that American and Asian cultures define "elderly" differently. In the Hmong culture, people become elders and retire at 35; obviously, in American culture, this is not the case. So Hmong culture is mentioned to illustrate the paragraph's main point—that "social expectations vary greatly from one country to another" (A). There's no mention of traditional values in Vietnamese society "lessening" (B). No other ancient cultures are mentioned in paragraph 2, so (C) is out. (D) is out because Confucianism isn't mentioned until paragraph 3. Likewise, no other Southeast Asian peoples are mentioned (E).

26. B

Go back to the line in which "family mediators" appears. This part of paragraph 3 says that younger members of immigrant families deal with schools and other institutions because they have better English language skills than older family members. So being a "family mediator" is a responsibility that young refugees assume in a new country (B). (A) might've confused you because a hasty reading of the passage makes it sound like this is a role older people used to fill—but in fact, it's not. The passage really says that in the traditional culture there are strict rules for social interaction based on age, which the new role of "family mediator" gradually erodes. The passage says nothing about getting help from friends (C) or professionals (D). The author doesn't write about the benefits American society derives from immigrant people anywhere (E).

27. B

After rereading the line that "pronounced" is in, the first thing you should do is eliminate the obvious choice. In this case, that's (E), "declared." The author uses "pronounced" to mean (B) "noticeable." Gender roles changed somewhat in Southeast Asia during the Vietnam War, but they changed even more drastically for families that emigrated to the United States. None of the other choices fits this context. The author doesn't imply that these changes became more "acceptable" (D); she implies that they happened out of necessity and says they were a "radical change."

28. D

As the discussion of question 27 touched on, the "radical change" the author refers to is the fact that women often become the main source of income in immigrant families in the U.S. This is a major change in gender roles, because in Asia men were usually the breadwinners. (D) is correct. (A) is an unlikely answer because retirement ages were discussed back in paragraph 2. (B) might've been tempting, because the Vietnam War is mentioned in paragraph 4, along with the answer. But the author says that while gender roles are changing in Southeast Asia due to the Vietnam War, the "radical change" occurs when families emigrate. Education (C) is not discussed in these lines. (E) is out because the author says there are more jobs for younger refugees, not that it's hard for young refugees to find them.

29. E

When you're not given a line reference, it makes sense to look in the passage where the previous question left off because Critical Reading questions are ordered sequentially. So that takes you to the last paragraph, which is indeed where the author makes a point about the "long-term outlook for refugee women." The author starts off by saying that although the long-term outlook is "unknown," there are "indications" about it. Now look at the choices. There's no evidence that this is a "personal recollection" (A), or a "historical discussion" (B). No specific "case" is mentioned or analyzed (C). The author isn't being "philosophical" (D); if anything, she's being as scientific as possible, given the lack of data. That leaves (E), "informed speculation." Since the author is knowledgeable about the subject matter, but has to go on "indications" to make her final point, (E) is the best answer.

30. C

Use the available combinations of Roman Numeral options to help you get through this oddball question type easily. Option I is false: the author never gives us a sense of Southeast Asian women's employment opportunities in Asia. All we know is that during the Vietnam war, women were forced to take on more traditionally male responsibilities. If anything, female refugees have greater access than do men to lower-paying jobs here. So if Option I is false, you can eliminate choices A and E. II is also false: you can't infer from the passage that Americans don't respect their elders. Since Option II is false, you can eliminate choices B and D. That leaves C—III only—as the correct choice. Double check to make sure, though, and you'll see from paragraph 2 that Americans and Asians have different notions of when one is considered old.

SECTION 2

1. D

We want the value of x. Let's begin by distributing the 2 over the terms inside the parentheses on the left side of the equation. This gives us $2x + 2y = 8 + 2y$. Subtracting $2y$ from both sides results in $2x = 8$. Dividing both sides by 2 gives us $x = 4$.

2. A

Since point A is at 1 on the number line and point C is on the 7, the distance between them is $7 - 1$, or 6. Half the distance from A to C is $\frac{1}{2}$ of 6, or 3, and 3 units from either point A or point C is 4, since $1 + 3 = 4$ and $7 - 3 = 4$. Therefore the point at 4 on the number line is the midpoint of AC, since a midpoint by definition divides a line in half. Point B is at 3 and the midpoint of AC is at 4, so the distance between them is 1, answer choice (A).

3. C

The machine caps 5 bottles every 2 seconds, and we want to know how many bottles it caps in 1 minute, or 60 seconds. Multiplying 2 seconds by 30 gives you 60 seconds. If the machine caps 5 bottles in 2 seconds, how many bottles does it cap in 30 times 2 seconds? Just 30×5, or 150 bottles, answer choice (C).

4. C

All you have to do here is solve the equation, but instead of solving it for n, you have to solve it for $4n$. If $2n + 3 = 5$, then you can subtract 3 from both sides of the equation to get $2n = 2$. Multiplying both sides of this equation by 2 gives you $4n = 4$, choice (C).

5. D

The easiest way to do this problem is just to backsolve. Since each pair of numbers in the answer choices represents possible values of a and b, just add up each a and b to see if $a + b < 5$, and subtract each b from each a to see if $a - b > 6$. If you do this, you'll find that in all 5 cases $a + b < 5$, but in only 1 case, in choice (D), is $a - b > 6$. In choice (D), $a + b = 4 + (-3) = 1$ and $a - b = 4 - (-3) = 7$.

If you think about the properties of negative and positive numbers (drawing a number line can help) you'll probably realize that the only way $a - b$ could be larger than $a + b$ is if b is a negative number, but that would only eliminate choice (A). In some problems your knowledge of math only helps you a little bit. In those cases you just have to play with the given answer choices in order to solve.

6. A

In the figure angle B is labeled $(2x - 4)°$ and in the question stem you're told that angle B measures 60°. So $2x - 4 = 60$, and $x = 32$. That means that angle A, which is labeled $(3x)°$, must measure 3×32, or 96°. Since the 3 angles of a triangle must add up to 180°, $60° + 96° + y° = 180°$, and $y = 24$.

7. D

This one is easier if you plug in numbers for C and R. Suppose R is 2. Then there would be 2 rooms on each floor, and since there are 10 floors in the building, there would be 2×10 or 20 rooms altogether. If $C = 3$, then there are 3 chairs in each room. Since there are 20 rooms and 3 chairs per room there are $20 \times 3 = 60$ chairs altogether. Which answer choices are 60 when R is 2 and C is 3? Only $10RC$, choice (D).

You don't have to plug in numbers here if you think about the units of each variable. There are 10 floors, R rooms per floor, and C chairs per room. If you multiply 10 floors by $R \frac{\text{rooms}}{\text{floor}}$, the unit "floors" will cancel out, leaving you with $10R$ rooms, and if you multiply $10R$

rooms by $C \frac{\text{chairs}}{\text{room}}$, the unit "rooms" will cancel out, leaving $10RC$ chairs in the building, again choice (D).

8. D

Here you have a strange word, *sump*, which describes a number that has a certain relationship between the sum and the product of its digits. To solve this one, just find the sum and the product of the digits for each answer choice. You're told that for a "sump" number, the sum should be greater than the product. Choice (D), 411, has a sum of 6 and a product of 4, so that's the one you're looking for.

9. D

In this question, if you think about the relationship between the information you're given and the information you have to find it becomes very easy. You're given 4% of a number and you have to find 20% of that same number. 4% of r is just a certain fraction, $\frac{4}{100}$ to be exact, times r; and 20% of r is just $\frac{20}{100}$ times r. That means that 20% of r is 5 times as great as 4% of r, since $\frac{4}{100}$ times 5 is $\frac{20}{100}$. So if you're given that 4% of r is 6.2, then 20% of r must be 5 times 6.2, or 31, choice (D).

You could also have figured out the value of r and then found 20% of that value, but this takes a bit longer. 4% of r is the same as 4% times r, or $.04r$. If $.04r = 6.2$, then $r = \frac{6.2}{.04} = 155$, and 20% of 155 is $.2 \times 155 = 31$, choice (D) again.

10. B

The ratio of teachers to students is 1 to 10, so there might be only 1 teacher and 10 students, or there might be 50 teachers and 500 students, or just about any number of teachers and students that are in the ratio 1 to 10. That means that the teachers and the students can be divided into groups of 11: one teacher and 10 students in each group. Think of it as a school with a large number of classrooms, all with 1 teacher and 10 students, for a total of 11 people in each room. So, the total number of teachers and students in the school must be a multiple of 11. If you look at the answer choices, you'll notice that 121, choice (B), is the only multiple of 11, so (B) must be correct.

11. A

Since x and y with a funny symbol between them is equal to $(x - y)^x + (x + y)^y$, to find 4 and 2 with a funny symbol between them just plug 4 in for x and 2 in for y. That gives you $(4 - 2)^4 + (4 + 2)^2$, or $2^4 + 6^2$, or $16 + 36$, or 52, answer choice (A).

12. D

If the particle travels from A to B to C to D to E and then back to A it has traveled 5 centimeters, since each side of the pentagon measures 1 centimeter. If it goes all the way around the pentagon again it's traveled another 5 centimeters, for a total of 10 centimeters. In fact, every time the particle makes a complete revolution around the pentagon (from point A back to point A again) it travels an additional 5 centimeters. So if the number of centimeters the particle has traveled is a multiple of 5, the particle must be at point A. The number 723 is 3 more than a multiple of 5. If the particle had gone 720 centimeters it would be at point A; since it has gone 3 more centimeters it must be at point D, answer choice (D).

13. E

When would $4 + \dfrac{1}{s}$ have the smallest possible value? Certainly if s, and its reciprocal $\dfrac{1}{s}$, were negative, $4 + \dfrac{1}{s}$ would be smaller than 4, since adding a negative number is like subtracting a positive number. However, none of the answer choices are negative, so $4 + \dfrac{1}{s}$ will be greater than 4. However, it will be as small as possible when $\dfrac{1}{s}$ is as small as possible. If you look at the answer choices, you can find the values for $\dfrac{1}{s}$. If $s = \dfrac{1}{4}$,

then $\dfrac{1}{s} = 4$, etc. If you do that you'll probably notice that as s gets larger its reciprocal gets smaller, so $\dfrac{1}{s}$ is smallest when s is largest, in this case when $s = 4$, choice (E).

14. D

Since you're looking for the sixth term of the sequence, let's call the sixth term x. Every term in this sequence is formed by multiplying the previous term by 3 and then subtracting 1, so the seventh term must be formed by multiplying the sixth term, x, by 3 and then subtracting 1; in other words, the seventh term is equal to $3x - 1$. Since the seventh term is 365, $365 = 3x - 1$, and you can solve for x to get $x = 122$, choice (D).

15. A

If an integer is chosen randomly from the first 50 integers the probability of choosing any particular number is 1 divided by 50, and the probability of choosing an integer with a digit of 3 is the number of integers with a digit of 3 divided by 50. The integers 3, 13, 23, 30, 31, 32, 33, 34, 35, 36, 37, 38, 39, and 43 are the only integers with 3's in them, for a total of 14 different integers, so the probability is $\dfrac{14}{50}$, or $\dfrac{7}{25}$, choice (A).

16. C

Let's call the degree measure of the largest angle x. Since the degree measure of the middle-sized angle is 40 degrees less than the degree measure of the largest angle, the degree measure of the middle-sized angle is $x - 40$. We also know that the smallest angle is 20 degrees. We know that the sum of the measures of the three interior angles of any triangle is 180 degrees. So we can write an equation for our triangle: $x + (x - 40) + 20 = 180$.

Now let's solve for x:

$$x + x - 40 + 20 = 180$$
$$2x - 20 = 180$$
$$2x = 200$$
$$x = 100$$

17. C

The diagram tells you that the radius of the circle is $x - 5$ and the question stem tells you that the circumference of the circle is 20π. Since the circumference of a circle is 2π times the radius, 20π must equal 2π times $(x - 5)$, which gives you the equation $20\pi = 2\pi(x - 5)$. Solving this equation gives you $x = 15$, answer choice (C).

18. E

The slope of a line is defined as the change in the y-coordinate divided by the change in the x-coordinate. As you go from point A to point B, the x-coordinate goes from p to 6 and the y-coordinate goes from 3 to p, so the change in the x-coordinate is $6 - p$ and the change in the y-coordinate is $p - 3$. You can make this into an equation: $\frac{p - 3}{6 - p} = 2$, and solve this equation for p. That would give you $p = 5$, choice (E). You could also plug the 5 possible values for p into the expression $\frac{p-3}{6-p}$ to see which one gives you 2 as a result. Either way, choice (E) is correct.

19. B

If C is the price of one pound of cherries and G is the price of one pound of grapes, then $C = 2G$. The total cost of 32 pounds of cherries and 8 pounds of grapes is $32C + 8G$, and is also equal to $90. You can use the equations $C = 2G$ and $32C + 8G = 90$ to solve for C and G. Plugging $2G$ for C into the equation $32C + 8G = 90$,

we have $32(2G) + 8G = 90$, $64G + 8G = 90$, $72G = 90$, and $G = \frac{90}{72} = \frac{5}{4} = 1.25$. $C = 2G$, so $C = 2(1.25) = 2.50$. Since 32 pounds of cherries and 8 pounds of grapes were sold, $2.50 \times 32 = 80$ were made on the cherries, and $1.25 \times 8 = 10$ were made on the grapes. That means that $80 - 10 = 70$ more was made on the cherries than on the grapes, answer choice (B).

20. D

In order to find the areas of the shaded triangles, you have to find the coordinates of all the vertices of the triangles. You know where points P, Q, and C are in the coordinate plane, but what about the rest of them? Well, first of all let's label all the other points that are vertices of the triangles. The triangle on top has 2 labeled vertices, P and Q. The third vertex of that triangle is on the y-axis between P and the origin. Let's call it point A. The other triangle has vertices Q, C, and an unlabeled point that is also the upper right-hand corner of the rectangle. Call that point B. Points A and B are both on the same horizontal line that point Q is on, so all 3 points must have the same y-coordinate of 4. The x-coordinate of point A is 0 since it is on the y-axis, and the x-coordinate of B must be 3, the same as point C's x-coordinate, since points B and C lie on the same vertical line. So point A's coordinates are $(0, 4)$ and point B's coordinates are $(3, 4)$. Since triangles PQA and QBC are right triangles, we just need to know the lengths of their legs in order to find their areas. In the coordinate plane, the length of a horizontal line segment is the difference of the x-coordinates of its endpoints and the length of a vertical line segment is the difference of the y-coordinates of its endpoints. So, the length of PA is $6 - 4$, or 2, and the length of AQ is $1 - 0$, or 1, so the area of triangle PQA is $\frac{1}{2} \times 2 \times 1 = 1$. The length of QB is $3 - 1$, or 2, and length of BC is $4 - 0$, or 4, so the area of triangle QBC is $\frac{1}{2} \times 2 \times 4 = 4$. The sum of those areas is $1 + 4 = 5$, answer choice (D).

21. D

Here you're told about certain properties of two numbers and that the larger of the two numbers is 35, and you're asked to find the smaller number, which we'll of course call x. The positive difference of 2 numbers is simply the larger number minus the smaller number, or in this case $35 - x$. The average of 35 and x is equal to twice the positive difference, or twice $35 - x$, or $2(35 - x)$. The average of 35 and x is just $\frac{35 + x}{2}$, so all you have to do is solve the equation $\frac{35 + x}{2} = 2(35 - x)$, and if you do that, you'll get $x = 21$, choice (D).

You could also solve this by backsolving. Starting with choice (C), if the smaller number is 15, the positive difference is $35 - 15$, or 20, and twice the positive difference is 40. Is 40 the average of 35 and 15? No, it couldn't be, since 40 is larger than both 35 and 15. That means that the smaller number must be closer to 35 than 15 is, in order to make the positive difference smaller, so let's try 21. $35 - 21$ is 14, and twice 14 is 28. The average of 21 and 35 is half of $21 + 35$, or half of 56, which is indeed 28, so again choice (D) is correct.

22. C

No matter what the value of n is, this figure will be a rectangular solid. All rectangular solids have 6 faces. You just have to figure out the area of each of the 6 faces. The face on the bottom, which is the face up against the table or whatever this stack of cubes is sitting on, is a square, and it will have an area of 1 square

inch, since the edge of each cube has a length of 1 inch. The face on the top of the stack of cubes is also a square and it will also have a surface area of 1 square inch. The other 4 faces making up the stack are identical rectangles, each with dimensions of 1 inch by n inches. So the area of one of these rectangles is $1 \times n$ or n square inches and these four identical rectangular faces have a total area of $4 \times n$ or $4n$ square inches. So the total surface area of the solid is the sum of the areas of the square top, the square bottom, and the four identical rectangular faces, which is $1 + 1 + 4n$ or $4n + 2$ square inches.

If you found that confusing, it might be easier just to pick a value for n. Suppose $n = 4$ and there are 4 cubes, as in the figure shown. Then just add up the areas of the faces of the stack in the figure, but don't forget the faces that aren't shown in the drawing. Since each face of each cube has an area of 1, in square inches, the figure shown has an area of 4 in the front plus 4 on the right side plus 4 on the left side (not shown in the drawing) plus 4 in the back (not shown in the drawing) plus 1 on the top and finally 1 on the bottom (not shown in the drawing), for a total of 18. Only choice (C) has a value of 18 when $n = 4$, so choice (C) must be correct.

23. B

Since $BC = DC$, triangle BCD is an isosceles right triangle and angles BDC and DBC each equal 45°. Since $AD = AB$, angle ABD must equal angle ADB, which is 60°. Since 2 angles of triangle ADB measure 60°, the third must also measure 60°, and triangle ADB is equilateral. That means that all 3 sides are equal. One of those sides, BD, is also the hypotenuse of isosceles right triangle BCD. That means that you can figure out the relationship between all the line segments in this figure. If the length of CD is x, then the length of BC is also x and the length of BD is $x\sqrt{2}$, using the $1:1:\sqrt{2}$ ratio of the sides of a 45–45–90 triangle. That means that AD and AB are also $x\sqrt{2}$. So $\frac{AB}{CD}$ is $\frac{x\sqrt{2}}{x}$, which reduces to $\sqrt{2}$, answer choice (B).

You could have eyeballed the diagram here. Since *AB* is clearly longer than *CD*, the ratio $\frac{AB}{CD}$ must be greater than 1, which eliminates choices (A) and (C). *AB* doesn't look anywhere near twice as large as *CD*, however, so choice (E) is also out. That narrows it down to only two answer choices, (B) and (D).

24. A

Here you're looking for the largest possible median of a group of 5 numbers, all of which are positive integers, and which sum to 100. The median of group of numbers is simply the one in the middle when the numbers are placed in ascending order. That means that 2 of the 5 numbers are greater than the median and 2 of the 5 numbers are less than the median. Since we're looking for the largest possible value for the median, let's start by looking at the largest of the 5 answer choices, choice (E). If 50 were the median, 2 other numbers would have to be greater than 50. The smallest values that those 2 numbers could have are 51 and 52. But if 3 of the 5 positive numbers are 50, 51, and 52, the sum of the 5 numbers will be greater than 100, so cross out choice (E). If choice (D), 34, is the median, then the 2 larger numbers have to be at least 35 and 36 so the sum is again too large (34 + 35 + 36 = 105). Choice (C), 33, doesn't work as the median either, since 33 + 34 + 35 = 102, so eliminate choices (D) and (C). Choice (B) looks like it might be okay, since 32 as the median gives you 33 and 34 as the smallest possible numbers larger than the median. However, the smallest possible values for the 2 numbers less than the median are 1 and 2, so if 32 is the median, the smallest values the 5 numbers could have would be 1, 2, 32, 33, and 34, which add up to 102, so forget choice (B). Choice (A) is the only one left, so it must be correct. Just to check, though, if 31 were the median, then 32 and 33 could be the larger numbers. They add up to 96, so the 2 smaller numbers could be 1 and 3, and the sum of the 5 would be 100. Choice (A) is correct.

25. E

In order to solve this problem, you have to know that the sum of the lengths of any 2 sides of a triangle must be greater than the length of the third side. If the 3 sides of a triangle have lengths $x + 2$, $x - 2$, and y, then adding up any 2 of those quantities should give you a greater value than the value of the third quantity. If you add together the 2 sides with the lengths involving x, you get $x + 2 + (x - 2) = 2x$. This value must be greater than the third side, which is y, so $2x > y$. Switching this around gives you $y < 2x$. So far we have one condition for y. The 2 sides with lengths $x + 2$ and y must add up to more than the third side, $x - 2$, so $x + 2 + y > x - 2$. Subtracting x from both sides of this inequality results in $2 + y > -2$, and subtracting 2 from both sides results in $y > -4$. The 2 sides with lengths $x - 2$ and y must add up to more than the third side, $x + 2$, so $x - 2 + y > x + 2$. Subtracting x from both sides of this inequality results in $-2 + y > 2$, and adding 2 to both sides results in $y > 4$. So the results of these 3 calculations are $y < 2x$, $y > -4$, and $y > 4$. The second result, $y > -4$, is irrelevant since if y is greater than 4, then it is automatically also greater than -4, so what is significant is that $y < 2x$ and $y > 4$. Another way of writing this is $4 < y < 2x$, answer choice (E).

SECTION 3

1. E

The key here is the word *beneficial*, or helpful. If you don't know *beneficial*, a knowledge of word roots would help you. *Beneficial* contains the root BENE, meaning good, which indicates to you that it's a positive word. Well, if in one breath we are told that the ozone layer is positive, and in the next, that it does something for plant and animal life relating to dangerous ultraviolet radiation, we know we need a fairly positive word in the blank. The only choice that fits this requirement is choice (E) **protecting**. (D), **thwarting,** means impeding or preventing.

2. A

"While" is our tip-off that this sentence will in some way contain a contrast. While George Balanchine's choreography stayed within a classical context, he challenged convention by recombining ballet idioms. (If you don't know exactly what this means, it doesn't matter—you just need to grasp that this is how he challenged convention.) He's challenging convention by recombining typical ballet moves or whatever in some ---- way. The word in the blank must mean something like unconventional. The best choice here is (A), **unexpected**. Choice (C), **redundant,** means needlessly repetitive or excessive.

3. C

All of today's navel oranges have some common relationship to a single mutant tree that produced seedless fruit 200 years ago. They must all be descended from this one mutant. So the word in the blank must mean "descended from." Choice (C), **descendants,** jumps out as the correct choice. **Progenitors,** in choice (A) is meant to fool you since it has something to do with genetics. If you break **progenitor** down, PRO means "for" or "before," while the GENUS root is related to the word "gene." So, **progenitors** are ancestors—people (or things) which are related but came before—like grandparents. **Progenitors** are the opposite of descendants. Choice (E) was another word trap—just because **spores** have something to do with plants doesn't mean this is right. A **spore** is a reproductive body found in

simpler forms of life. But you don't need to know biology to figure this one out. Just use your reasoning skills. While a seed could be a spore, it makes no sense to say that all of today's navel oranges are the actual **spores** of a 200-year-old tree. But it is more plausible that this one tree produced a number of seeds, which in turn produced more of their own seeds, and so on.

4. A

In this sentence, there's a relationship between the quantities of food and drink Henry VIII consumed, and the type of person he was seen as. Either he consumed minimal quantities of food and drink, and was considered a spartan of sorts, or he consumed large amounts, and was considered a pig. Well, choice (A) is the only one that fits either one of these predictions. A **glutton** is one who overindulges in the consumption of food and drink. This option is the only one that fits, where there's a connection between the type of person his subjects saw him as, and the amount of food and drink he scarfed up. (C)'s first word, **minute,** or very small, fits okay, but a **luminary,** a famous or important person, doesn't. Consuming small quantities of food wouldn't make someone famous. In (B), **prodigious** means either extraordinary or enormous, while a **peer** is an equal, or a member of nobility.

5. A

You want a vocabulary word that means something like "transition" or "temporary"—some word that describes a government that no longer is in power, but is staying in power just until a new government is ready to take over the reins. Choice (A), **interim,** means temporary or provisional, so this is the answer. INTER is a root you should know—it means between.

6. E

The peoples discussed in this sentence were formerly ----. But now they've lost their land. They're living in ---- settlements. So we need two adjectives that are roughly the opposite of each other. The answer here is (E). Peoples who were once **nomadic,** or roaming freely without a **permanent** home, have moved into permanent settlements as their land got swallowed up by growing cities. **Fervid,** in choice (D), means passionate.

7. B

For the first blank, we want something that describes sleeping tablets—I'd rule out (E) right away, since **stimulating** is the one word here that most definitely would not describe sleeping tablets, even those with little impact. For the second blank, we want a word that characterizes the effect of those sleeping tablets, an effect that resulted in a woman feeling groggy the day after taking them. Something like "strong" or "intense" would be good. The best choice here is (B), because **soporific** means sleep-inducing—what word could be better to describe sleeping pills? **Pronounced,** meaning unmistakable or obvious, fits closely with our prediction. **Salubrious** in choice (C) means healthful.

8. E

Here we want a vocabulary word meaning something like "unable to accept the authority of others." Choice (A), **compliant,** means the exact opposite of this; a **compliant** person is one who bends easily to the will of others. (B) **slothful** means lazy. In choice (C), **conscientious** means responsible, hardly a word to describe Davis. (E) is correct because **recalcitrant** describes someone who refuses to obey authority.

9. D

"Although" tells us that there will be some sort of contrast with the fact that the actress has lived in a large city her whole life. The contrast will be that, despite her upbringing in a city, she still manages to be successful at portraying a humble farm girl. Therefore, she must be quite a good performer—the first blank will be a positive word, describing what a good actress she is. The second blank must be a word that explains how successfully she portrays the farm girl. The best choice here is (D), because a **consummate** actress is very skilled, while an **incarnation** is the embodiment of something or someone—you'd have to be a pretty good actress to become the embodiment of the character you're playing. In choice (C), **nemesis** means enemy.

10. B

Notice the word *hitherto* in this sentence. It means "previously." The board members had previously upheld worthy ideals. This implies that they no longer

do. For the second blank, then, we need a word like *rejection*: the board's recent decision must be a rejection of the previous worthy ideals. In the first blank, we need a word to describe what the chairman was doing as he described the board's decision so negatively. So the first blank must mean something like "criticized." (C) fits in the first blank, but not in the second. Remember to try both words in the blanks! Choice (B) works with both blanks: to **lament** is to regret, while a **negation** is what it sounds like, a rejection. The chairman lamented the decision of the board, describing it as a **negation** of worthy ideals. This was the only choice with two negative words that fit the context. To **endorse,** in choice (D), is to offer one's support, while a **renunciation** is a giving up or casting off of something like values. Finally, in (E), a **repudiation** is similar to a **renunciation**—it is a denial or rejection of something or someone.

11. D

A **MILL** is, by definition, a place where **FLOUR** is made. A **brewery** is a place where **beer** is made. A **pharmacy** is a place where a **prescription** is filled; but the **prescription** itself is not made there. A pharmacist dispenses pills and other medicines; a pharmaceutical company makes the medicine.

12. B

A **STETHOSCOPE** is an instrument used for **LISTEN**ing. A **needle** is an instrument used for **inject**ing.

13. A

By definition, a **BOTANIST** is one who pursues the scientific study of **PLANTS**. And a **zoologist** is one who scientifically studies **animals.** A **philologist** is a scholar, someone who studies the role of speech in literature.

14. D

ABUNDANT means more than **ADEQUATE.** So we're looking at a question of extremes—the first word is a more extreme version of the second. **Arid,** in choice (A), describes a desert environment, not a more extreme version of **moist. Boisterous,** in (B) means loud and rowdy. The answer is (D): something **overflowing** is more than **full.**

15. A

A **DOUBLE-CROSSER** is one who **BETRAY**s, by definition. Similarly, a **slowpoke** is one who **lags,** moves slowly or falls behind.

16. D

When you **EVADE,** or avoid the truth, you are not being **STRAIGHTFORWARD.** When you **boast,** or brag, you are not being **modest,** so (D) is right here. To **enliven,** in choice (B), is what it sounds like—to put a little life or energy into something. **Animated** means spirited or lively.

17. E

A **REPREHENSIBLE** person is someone who's done something wrong. So someone **REPREHENSIBLE** deserves **BLAME.** (E) is the right answer because someone **commendable** deserves **praise.**

18. E

In this question, **CONCORD** is not referring to the site where the American Revolution began, but to a state of **AGREEMENT.** Remember, CON can mean together or with, while COR is a root you've seen in words like "discord," and means "heart." An **insurrection,** in choice (A), means an uprising, hardly a state of **peace.** The answer is (E), because **flux** is a state of **change.**

19. C

FLORAL means having to do with **FLOWERS.** (C) is right, because **emotional** means having to do with **feelings. Perennial,** in (A), means perpetual, permanent, lasting for several years. **Perennials** are plants that bloom year after year without needing to be replanted. This was an SST, a wrong answer choice from the same subject category as the stem. But it doesn't have the same bridge. Be sure to pick an answer pair because it has the same bridge as the stem, not just because it reminds you of the stem. (B) **morbid** means gloomy.

20. D

A **CALM** person possesses **COMPOSURE.** You might be familiar with the phrase "calm and composed" which describes a relaxed and poised individual. (D) is

the best answer here because a **sad** person possesses **melancholy,** or sorrow. In choice (B), don't confuse the adjective **cold** with the noun. If you have a **cold** you sort of do "possess" **sickness,** but if you *feel* **cold,** which is what this choice is referring to, you don't necessarily possess **sickness.** As for (C), there's no necessary connection between **congested** and **traffic.** While a **congested** highway might possess **traffic,** a **congested** person probably possesses sinus problems.

21. A

By definition, to **SEQUESTER** a **JUROR** is to place him or her in isolation. During trials covered extensively by the media, **JUROR**s are often **SEQUESTER**ed to prevent them from being influenced by what the rest of the world thinks about the case they're working on. The right answer is (A) because to **quarantine** a **patient** is to place them in isolation, to prevent them from spreading whatever wildly contagious disease they have. To cloister can also mean to place in isolation; it generally describes what members of religious orders do, particularly nuns. They go into seclusion at a religious site. However, you don't **cloister** a **convent,** you're cloistered within a **convent.** Choice (C) was an SST, with its reference to the world of crime and punishment.

22. B

By definition, something **HACKNEYED** lacks **ORIGINALITY.** You know what **ORIGINALITY** means—if you at least knew that **HACKNEYED** was negative, you'd be in good shape. You could get a rough idea of the stem's bridge. **Debauched** means corrupted. Someone who's **debauched** is lacking in **virtue,** so (B)'s correct.

23. C

To **SLAKE** one's **THIRST** is to satisfy or ease it. **Stoke** sounds a little like **SLAKE,** but (A)'s bridge differs from the stem's. To stoke a **fire,** in (A), is to stir it up or feed it, to make it burn longer and stronger. (B) doesn't work here either. You don't satisfy or lessen **hunger** by **starving** it. (B)'s another SST. To **assuage pain** means to ease it, and so this is the right answer. To **induce sleep** is to cause it. Drinking warm milk before bed, or reading a long, boring book, may **induce** sleep.

Domesticated Animals Passage

If you're an animal lover you might enjoy this passage. Actually, it's not a bad passage, but it's long, so be sure to keep up a good pace. You should aim at getting the main points of paragraphs and moving on. Basically, the author says that the dog was the first domesticated animal, which makes sense because of the dog's nature (it comes from a pack and likes to have a leader; puppies are cute and trainable; and it has better senses of hearing and smell than humans do, which makes it a valuable hunting companion). Then the author wonders how domestication occurred, which sends him off on a tangent about animals that "parasitize" human wastes or food stores. He speculates that domestication began because baby animals were cute—only later did domesticated animals actually become useful. He concludes that it's ironic that human civilization is destroying many species, since our learning to live with them is what made civilization possible.

24. D

The "archaeological discoveries" mentioned in the question stem are human and dog bones lying next to each other in ancient burial sites. The reason the author feels it's "terribly appropriate" that these bones are found together comes a few lines later, when he says "it marks a relationship that is the most ancient of all." (D) paraphrases that idea. You can see from this how important it is to read a few lines before and after the line reference in the stem. The author says nothing about burial habits in the Mesolithic Era (A), or the religious significance of animals in prehistoric cultures (B). He says nothing about "natural disasters" (E) either. He does mention hunting (C), but the bone finds are not "appropriate" because they "illustrate the role of dogs in hunting expeditions." (D) is the only possibility.

25. A

The end of paragraph 1 provides the answer. The author says that the dog was the first domesticated animal because it served as "a companion and an ally" (A). Only *after* domesticating animals as companions did humans domesticate "food animals" (B) and then "those that provide enhanced speed and range" (D) and then those that helped us farm (C). The key thing is to see that all these other types of domesticated animals came after animals were domesticated as companions.

26. E

The line reference takes you to the beginning of paragraph 2. The author says that having a dog as a companion animal was almost "inevitable," and then lists several reasons why. One of these is that the dog "is susceptible to domination by, and attachment to, a pack leader—the top dog." The implication is that humans formed bonds with dogs because they could dominate them (E). None of the other choices gives characteristics that make sense in answer to the question.

27. B

As with all Vocabulary-in-Context questions, you should go back to the sentence to see how the word is used. The author asks us to consider the "essence" of the dog in order to understand why it became a companion. He then lists several of the dog's characteristics that made it easy to domesticate. In other words, we're looking at the dog's "nature" (B). The only other choice that might seem to make sense in this context is (A) "history"—but what follows the line "consider its essence" is not a history; rather, it's a list of characteristics that make up the dog's nature.

28. C

This is definitely a question you need to return to the passage to answer. You're back in the second paragraph, where the author lists the characteristics that made dogs "inevitable" companions for humans. In addition to being born dependent and forming bonds with their rearers, dogs "have a set of appeasement behaviors" that elicit "affective reactions" from even the most "hardened" humans. The author goes on to talk about puppies transforming "cynics" into "cooing softies." Even if you weren't sure what "appeasement behaviors" were, you can see the gist of the author's point here: humans form bonds with dogs largely because dogs are cute and loveable. So would it make sense if "affective reactions" were "callous" (A), "rational" (B), or "cynical" (E)? No. (D) goes too far. The author isn't saying humans become childish around dogs, but that dogs arouse human emotions. (C) is the best answer.

29. C

The easiest way to understand the point of a comparison is to understand the context. What's the author saying in these lines? He's trying to show why it was inevitable that dogs became human companions. One reason is that dogs form bonds with their owners (C). That's the only reason he compares puppies with babies—to show how emotional people get about dogs. The author's point has nothing to do with "criticizing an uncaring attitude" (A), so that can't be the point of his comparing puppies and babies. The same is true for the rest of the choices, so (C) is correct.

30. B

Again, go back to the passage. Notice that the start of paragraph 3 actually refers back to the end of the *first* paragraph. Paragraph 1 ended with the author listing the dog as the first domesticated animal, followed by food animals, work animals, etc. Paragraph 2 talks about *why* the dog came first. So when paragraph 3 begins with "no wonder the dog was first," it's referring to the dog's status as the first domesticated animal. Similarly, "the list" refers to other domesticated animals, or "the number of animals that developed relationships with humans" (B). The author hasn't yet mentioned "birds that scavenge human food supplies," and when he does, he only mentions one, not many "types" (A). The passage never mentions species that are able to communicate with dogs (C), or the variety of attributes that make dogs good hunters (D). Finally, if you chose (E), you were losing track of the author's main points. Read over the first three paragraphs to see what's going on, and give a closer reading next time.

31. E

This question might seem more complicated than it really is. If you were confused by the digression the author made to talk about the blue tit, taking a look at the choices first probably would've saved you time. (A), (B), and (D) are fairly easy to eliminate—they have nothing to do with any of the author's main points. Good—now that you've eliminated three choices, you can always guess. But first let's go back to the passage. In line 46 the author mentions "opportunistic feeders." He goes on, saying "even today, many birds . . . feed from our stores." So (E) must be right;

the blue tit is an example of an opportunistic feeder. The question doesn't go any more into depth than that, so you're done.

32. C

A clear reference question. Go back to the lines you're given to see what kind of animals are being referred to. You have to read above a little to find the answer. The author has just finished describing the blue tit as an example of an opportunistic feeder. He reinforces the idea that the tit is an animal that feeds when and where it can by saying, "If all birds had been so specialized that they only fed in deep forest, it never would have happened." In other words, they are *not* so specialized—they'll eat wherever they find a food source (C). The author isn't talking here about companion animals (A). Forest inhabitants (B) is too broad. (D) is out because the birds are not hunting, they're feeding. And the point about the tits is not to give an example of "persistent pests" (E).

33. D

Go back to the passage to see in what context the author discusses his experiences in the tropics. At the beginning of paragraph 4, the author says that he thinks that the very first domesticated animals were orphaned as a result of hunting. He then tells how, in the tropics, he saw many instances of wild animals raised in homes of hunters. So his experiences illustrate his theory about how "the first domesticated animals were created" (D). None of the other choices relate to the author's argument here (or anywhere in the passage).

34. A

This one's a little tricky—if you thought so, you should've jumped ahead and come back later if you had time. Remember, reading questions don't go from easy to hard, so the next one could be easier. Check out the line "aid" is in to see what's going on. The author says that without domesticated animals—goats, sheep, pigs, cattle, and horses—we never would've achieved civilization. These animals helped or "aided" us—but they didn't have much choice in the matter. We dominated them, and then used them for food or labor. That's why "aid" is in quotes, and (A) is correct. The passage never says "population levels are dangerously high" (B). (C) is a better possibility—but it's not a point the author makes; you're inferring too much if you chose (C). It's not clear that animals benefited at all from domestication (D). (E) is really far-out, not supported by the passage.

35. E

The "ironic paradox" is found in the last four lines of the passage. The author says our living with other species—using them for food and labor—is what made our civilization possible. It is ironic then, that our civilization is presently wiping out many plant and animal species (E). Nowhere does the author say anything about (A) or (B). With (C), the author does talk about the pet care industry in the final paragraph, but not to say its size is "ironic." His point is just to show how big it is. (D) twists the author's point. It's by being parasites on other species that humans benefit, not the other way around.

SECTION 4

1. A

3.45601 is greater than 3.45002, since 3.45601 has a 6 in the thousandths' place and 3.45002 has a 0 is the thousandths' place. The number that is being subtracted from 1000 is greater in Column B than in Column A, so the result will be smaller in Column B than in Column A and choice (A) is correct.

2. B

The centered information tells you that the sum of x and y is greater than 11, and that x is less than 5.5. If x is less than 5.5, but $x + y$ is greater than 11, then y must be greater than $11 - 5.5$, or $y > 5.5$. If you try a few values for x and y you'll see that this is true. Since x is less than 5.5 and y is greater than 5.5, y is greater than x and choice (B) is correct.

3. A

The numerators of the 2 fractions are the same, so the fraction with the smaller denominator is the larger number. Since $17^{17} < 17^{18}$, choice (A) is correct.

4. B

There are 24 hours in one day, so there are 24×60 hours in 60 days. There are 60 seconds in one minute, so there are 30×60 seconds in 30 minutes. 30×60 is greater than 24×60, so choice (B) is correct.

5. B

Since $a + b = 60$ and $b + c = 40$, $a + b + b + c = 100$. The 3 variables are all positive, so $a + b + b + c$ is greater than $a + b + c$. Therefore $a + b + c < 100$. The average of a, b, and c is just $\frac{a+b+c}{3}$, and since $a + b + c < 100$, $\frac{a+b+c}{3}$ must be less than $\frac{100}{3}$, which is also less than the 50 in Column B, so the correct answer choice is (B).

6. A

You should immediately recognize that this is a 3-4-5 right triangle, so AC must measure 3. Even if you didn't you could have plugged in 4 and 5 for b and c in the Pythagorean equation $(a^2 + b^2 = c^2)$, and you would have gotten 3 for the third side. Since the sides measure 3, 4, and 5, the perimeter of the triangle is $3 + 4 + 5 = 12$. The area of the triangle is $\frac{1}{2} \times 3 \times 4 = 6$, so Column A is greater and choice (A) is correct.

7. C

This is a sequence consisting of a cycle of 4 numbers that repeats forever. The first term is 1, the second term is 2, the third term is –3, and the fourth term is –4. When it repeats the first time, the fifth term is 1, the sixth term is 2, the seventh term is –3, and the eight term is –4. It will repeat again, and the ninth term will be 1, the tenth term will be 2, the eleventh term will be –3, and the twelfth term will be –4. Notice that the number –4 is so far the fourth, eighth, and twelfth term. Since it is the fourth term in a repeating cycle of 4 numbers, its position in the sequence will always be a multiple of 4. So –4 will be the fourth, eighth, twelfth, sixteenth, twentieth, etc., terms in the sequence. This means that –4 will be the 48th term in the sequence, since 48 is a multiple of 4. If –4 is the 48th term, then the 49th term is 1, the 50th term is 2, the 51st term is –3, and the 52nd term is –4. So the sum of the 49th and 51st terms is the sum of 1 and –3, or $1 – 3$, or –2, and the sum of the 50th and 52nd terms is the sum of 2 and –4, or $2 – 4$, or –2, so the 2 columns are the same and the correct answer is (C).

8. D

If K represents Kearne's age and A represents Amanda's age, then the centered information can be translated to $K = 2A$. Then Kearne's age 5 years ago is $K – 5$, or $2A – 5$. Amanda's age 5 years from now is $A + 5$. Now you're comparing $2A – 5$ with $A + 5$. You can't really tell which is greater without knowing more about A, so the correct answer is (D). If you're not convinced, try doing the same thing to both columns. If you add 5

and then subtract A from both columns, you get A in Column A and 10 in Column B. Since you don't have any way of knowing whether or not Amanda's age is greater than 10, choice (D) must be correct.

You could also use picking numbers here. If Kearne is 40 and Amanda is 20 you have 35 in Column A and 25 in Column B and Column A is greater. Now you know that the correct answer is either (A) or (D). If Kearne is 16 and Amanda is 8, then you have 11 in Column A and 13 in Column B. Since the relationship changes for different values of K and A, choice (D) is the correct answer.

9. B

We want to compare $3x$ with $2y$. To do this, we need the values of x and y which we can find by solving the two equations in the centered information. We could solve these two equations by first solving for one variable in terms of the other in one equation and then plugging the expression for the variable we solved for into the other equation, resulting in one equation with one variable. We would then solve for this variable and then we could use either of the two original equations and the value of the variable we found to solve for the value of the other variable. However, there is a much faster way to solve for x and y in this problem. Notice that there is a y being added in each equation, so if we subtract the first equation from the second, the y's will cancel each other out:

$$4x + y = 3$$
$$\underline{-(2x + y = 2)}$$
$$2x = 1$$
$$x = \frac{1}{2}$$

Now plug $\frac{1}{2}$ for x into the first equation, $2x + y = 2$. We have $2\left(\frac{1}{2}\right) + y = 2$, $1 + y = 2$, and $y = 1$. Column A, $3x$, is $3\left(\frac{1}{2}\right) = \frac{3}{2}$, or $1\frac{1}{2}$. Column B, $2y$, is $2(1) = 2$. Column B is greater.

10. B

The second equation tells you that $x = 2y$, so substitute $2y$ for x in the first equation. Then $x + y = -3$ becomes $2y + y = -3$, or $3y = -3$, or $y = -1$. Since $x = 2y$, $x = 2 \times (-1)$, or -2. Since x is -2 and y is -1, y is greater and choice (B) is correct.

11. B

Line segment BD is the same as line segments BC and CD put together. In other words $BD = BC + CD$. For the same reason we can say that $AC = AB + BC$. Since $BD > AC$, $BC + CD > AB + BC$. You can subtract BC from both sides of that inequality to give you $CD > AB$, which tells you that Column B is greater.

12. C

Each angle of the larger triangle here measures $a° + a°$, or $2a°$. Since the sum of the angles of a triangle is $180°$, $2a° + 2a° + 2a° = 180°$, and $6a = 180$. That means that $a = 30$. The smaller triangles each have 2 angles measuring $a°$ and 1 angle measuring $b°$. Since $a = 30$, $30 + 30 + b = 180$. Therefore $60 + b = 180$ and $b = 120$. That means that $b - a = 120 - 30 = 90$. The 2 columns are equal so choice (C) is correct.

13. C

This is a tough question, as you would expect for one of the last three QC's. If you draw the line MH in the figure, you'll probably notice that there are a number of points on the cube each of which together with M and H can be three vertices of a right triangle. Whenever you have to find the length of a line segment in a complicated figure you should look for right triangles—this is often the key to solving. There are several ways to proceed from here. Probably the easiest way is to draw a line from M to A and a line from M to H. This creates a right triangle, AMH, inside the cube with MH as hypotenuse, AH as one leg and AM as the other leg. The length of AH is e, since it is an edge of the cube, so if you can figure out the length of AM, the other leg, you can figure out the length of the hypotenuse, MH, which is what you're looking for.

In order to find the length of AM you'll have to use another right triangle, ADM, on top of the cube. AM is the hypotenuse of this right triangle and AD and DM are the legs. AD is an edge of the cube so it has length e, and since M is the midpoint of CD, DM has length $\frac{e}{2}$. You can find the length of the hypotenuse using the Pythagorean theorem: $e^2 + \left(\frac{e}{2}\right)^2 = (AM)^2$, so $(AM)^2 = e^2 + \frac{e^2}{4} = \frac{5e^2}{4}$ and $AM = \frac{e\sqrt{5}}{2}$. Now back to triangle AMH. The legs have lengths e and $\frac{e\sqrt{5}}{2}$, so again using the Pythagorean theorem, $(MH)^2 = e^2 + \left(\frac{e\sqrt{5}}{2}\right)^2 = e^2 + \frac{5e^2}{4} = \frac{9e^2}{4}$. MH is then $\frac{3e}{2}$, so both columns are the same and the correct answer is choice (C).

14. C

Since points A and B have the same y-coordinate, the line segment they are on must be parallel to the x-axis, or a horizontal line segment, so point C has the same y-coordinate as A and B, 7. This line segment is also a diameter of circle C. The length of a horizontal segment in a coordinate plane is the difference in the x-coordinates of the line's endpoints, or in this case $7 - 1 = 6$. That means that circle C has a diameter of 6 and therefore a radius of 3. Since C is the center of the circle, AC is a radius and the distance from A to C is 3, so the x-coordinate of C must be $1 + 3 = 4$. The coordinates of point C are $(4, 7)$. The line segment that C and D are on is perpendicular to AB, so it must be a vertical line segment, parallel to the y-axis. So, C and D have the same x-coordinate of 4. CD is a radius of the circle and so has length 3, so the y-coordinate of D is $7 - 3 = 4$. Point D has coordinates $(4, 4)$. That means that its x- and y-coordinates are the same, and the answer is (C).

15. D

75% of 80 is the same as $\frac{3}{4}$ of 80, or 60. 25% is the same as $\frac{1}{4}$, so 25% of x is $\frac{1}{4}$ of x. If 60 is greater than $\frac{1}{4}$ of x then 4 times 60, or 240, is greater than 4 times $\frac{1}{4}$ of x, or x. If 240 is greater than x, x could be less than 200, but it could also be greater than or equal to 200, so the correct answer is (D).

16. 15

This is a simple plug-in, but make sure you write out every step so as to avoid a careless error. This is especially important in the Grid-ins. If $y = 2$, the expression $(5 - y)(y + 3)$ becomes $(5 - 2)(2 + 3)$. Remember to do the calculations inside the parentheses first. $5 - 2$ is 3 and $2 + 3$ is 5 so $(5 - 2)(2 + 3) = 3 \times 5 = 15$, so put a 15 in the grid.

17. 9.43

If the daily rate is $18.99, then the price for a week, or 7 days, is $7 \times \$18.99 = \$132.93$. Since the weekly rate is less, only $123.50, you can save $132.93 - $123.50 = $9.43 by renting at the weekly rate.

18. 13 < length < 15

The first thing to do is to put the numbers 4, 5, and 12 in the appropriate places in the figure. Now you should see that you have the lengths of 2 sides of triangle BCD. Since BCD is a right triangle, you can use the Pythagorean theorem to figure out the length of the hypotenuse, but if you've memorized the common Pythagorean triplets you don't have to do that—you'll immediately recognize that this is a 5-12-13 right triangle, and so the length of BD is 13. The length of AC is $4 + 5 = 9$, so the triangle ACD has legs of lengths 9 and 12. Again, you can use the Pythagorean theorem to find the length of the hypotenuse, but you should notice that ACD is a multiple of the 3-4-5 right triangle, and AD has length 15. If you draw in point E in the figure between A and B, you'll see that DE will be longer than BD but shorter than AD, or greater than 13 but less than 15. So, any number between 13 and 15, such as 14, is a possible answer.

19. 15/4 or 3.75

If you need $\frac{3}{4}$ of a cup of drink mix for 2 quarts of water, then you need more than $\frac{3}{4}$ of a cup of drink mix for 10 quarts of water. How much more? Since $2 \times 5 = 10$, you have 5 times as much water, so you also need 5 times as much drink mix. $5 \times \frac{3}{4} = \frac{15}{4}$, so grid in $\frac{15}{4}$ (in the form of 15/4).

20. 166

The sum of the 3 angles of the triangle must be 180°. One angle measures 31°, but you don't know the measures of the other 2 angles in the triangle. However, the interior angle of the triangle on top lies on a straight line with an angle measuring 45°, so that interior angle must measure $180° - 45° = 135°$. If 2 angles of a triangle measure 135° and 31°, then the third angle measures $180° - 135° - 31° = 14°$. The 14° angle lies on a straight line with the $x°$ angle, so $14° + x° = 180°$, and $x = 166$.

If you remembered that any exterior angle of a triangle has the same measure as the sum of the 2 opposite interior angles, you could have saved a few steps. Once you figure out that the top angle of the triangle is 135°, you know that $x° = 135° + 31°$, and therefore $x = 166$.

21. 0.5 < y < 0.625

The only thing you know about y is that it is between $\frac{1}{2}$ and $\frac{5}{8}$. $\frac{1}{2}$ is the same as $\frac{4}{8}$, so y is between $\frac{4}{8}$ and $\frac{5}{8}$. You can't grid a fraction like $\frac{4\frac{1}{2}}{8}$, but you can change $\frac{4}{8}$ to $\frac{8}{16}$ and $\frac{5}{8}$ to $\frac{10}{16}$. That gives you an obvious value for y; since y is between $\frac{8}{16}$ and $\frac{10}{16}$, it could be $\frac{9}{16}$, so that's one possible number to grid in. You could also

KAPLAN

solve this question by converting $\frac{1}{2}$ and $\frac{5}{8}$ to decimals.

If you convert $\frac{1}{2}$ to .5 and $\frac{5}{8}$ to .625, you can grid in

any number greater .5 and less than .625. For example,

you can grid in .6.

22. 46

The average rate of speed is the total distance traveled divided by the total hours traveled. Melanie drove at 40 miles per hour for 2 hours, for a total of 40 × 2 or 80 miles. If she increased her speed by 25%, then she increased her speed by 25% of 40, or 10, so her new speed was 40 + 10 = 50. So, she drove at 50 miles per hour for the next 3 hours, for a total of 50 × 3 = 150 miles. She went 80 miles and then 150 miles, for a total of 230 miles, and she drove for 2 hours and then for 3 hours, for a total of 5 hours. Her average rate for the trip was therefore 230 miles divided by 5 hours, or 46 miles per hour.

23. 175

There are 3 types of dealers at this convention—dealers who sell only stamps, dealers who sell only coins, and dealers who sell both stamps and coins. The total number of dealers is 500. You're given the number of 2 out of the 3 types of dealers—there are 127 that sell both stamps and coins, and 198 that sell only stamps. Since there are only 3 types of dealers, 127 + 198 + the number of dealers who sell only coins = 500, and so the number of dealers who sell only coins is 500 − 198 − 127 = 175.

24. 46

Since the small square has a side of length 2, the area of the square must be 2^2, or 4. The larger square has a side of length 6, so its area is 6^2, or 36. The shaded part of square *ABCD* is then 36 − 4, or 32. The triangle is a right triangle with both legs of length 6, so the area of

the triangle is $\frac{1}{2} \times 6 \times 6$, or 18. The shaded area of the triangle is then 18 − 4 = 14. The total shaded area is 32 + 14, or 46, so grid in a 46.

25. 11

If *N* and *R* added up to a number less than 10, the problem would look different, something like:

    NR
    RN
    ──
    XX

Since it doesn't look like that, *N* + *R* must be greater than 10. The best way to proceed from here is to try different pairs of numbers for *R* and *N*, and see what you get for *B* and *C* (keeping in mind that *N*, *R*, *A*, *B*, and *C* are different digits.) If you try setting either *N* or *R* equal to 9, you'll notice that you won't get different digits for all 5 variables. For example, if *R* = 9 and *N* = 7:

    79
    97
    ───
    176

Since there is always a 1 carried over into the tens' place, if *R* = 9 then the tens' column will add up to 9 + *N* + 1, or 10 + *N*. The sum 10 + *N* has the same units' digit as *N*, so *B* and *N* will be the same if *R* = 9. The same thing happens if *N* = 9, only *R* and *B* turn out to be the same. If you try the next largest combination of numbers for *N* and *R*, which is 7 and 8, *B* and *C* turn out to be 6 and 5, so *B* + *C* = 11. Any smaller values for *N* and *R* will result in smaller values for *B* and *C*, so the largest possible value of *B* + *C* is 11.

SECTION 5

The Jefferson/Douglass Passages

These two passages may seem hard because of their old-fashioned language. But the main points should be clear on a quick read-through. Jefferson emphasizes the natural and social riches of the United States (paragraph 1), supports the idea of limited government (end of paragraph 1), and states the principle of equal justice for all (paragraph 2). Douglass, speaking as an escaped slave, stresses that slaves do not have the freedoms celebrated on the Fourth of July. (If you don't remember who Douglass was, you may not catch the point of his speech until the end of paragraph 2, where it is stated directly. Always be patient—the drift of a passage often becomes clearer as you go along.) In paragraph 2, Douglass says that the case against slavery should not have to be argued, because freedom and liberty are basic American principles. In paragraph 3, he concludes that as long as slavery exists, the Fourth of July is a "sham."

Before going to the questions it can be helpful to think for a second about how the two passages relate—an important paired-passage strategy. You should come up with something like: Jefferson is stating American principles, but Douglass is saying they haven't been applied in practice. In a double passage, you'll have several questions on passage 1, followed by several on passage 2, followed by some asking for comparisons. Since answering the questions is the priority, be sure to read the first passage, do the questions that relate to it, then read the second passage and answer the rest of the questions.

1. C

In the cited lines, Jefferson is saying that Americans feel entitled to respect, or "honor and confidence," on the basis of "actions" rather than "birth." (C) is a paraphrase of this idea. Remember that the United States didn't have a hereditary aristocracy like European countries—that's what Jefferson is talking about. (A), (D), and (E) bring in ideas not mentioned in the excerpt—immigration (A), mutual help (D), family (E). (B)'s idea of demanding respect is wrong; Jefferson feels respect has to be based on actions.

2. A

In this Vocabulary-in-Context question, choice (B) might've jumped out at you. *But remember, the correct answer is probably not going to be the most common or familiar definition of the word, so don't be too hasty. Find the word in the passage and see how it's used there.* In this case, Jefferson is talking about what his duties as president involve, or "include." Choices (A). (C) and (E) give you other common synonyms for "comprehend," but they don't fit the context. (D) does not mean "comprehend."

3. D

Again, look at the context. Read the rest of the sentence in question, and the sentence before it. This should clarify that Jefferson is about to state what he believes to be the essential principles of government. Further, he's going to state them in the briefest possible way, which is what correct choice (D) says. (A) and (C) refer to Jefferson's mention of "limitations," but all Jefferson says is that he won't mention "limitations" or exceptions to the general principles. (B) is wrong because "them" in Jefferson's sentence refers to the principles of government, not to people who oppose the principles. Finally, Jefferson never mentions bureaucracy, choice (E).

4. E

Ignore the choices for the moment and look at the context: Jefferson is talking about equal justice for all, regardless of something, religious or political. This suggests that Jefferson is talking about people's beliefs, creeds, opinions, or convictions. (E) gives you the word that fits this context. (A), (B), and (C) are all vocabulary-list meanings for "persuasion," but they don't fit the context. "Authority" (D) is often seen as the opposite of persuasion; it has nothing to do with Jefferson's meaning here.

5. A

The next two questions take us through the Douglass excerpt. This one asks about paragraph 1, in which Douglass is contrasting the American celebration of independence and liberty with the bondage of slaves. The overall idea is that the celebrations are a "mockery" and an "irony" (lines 49–50) because they don't apply to everyone. In other words, they are hypocritical (A). (B) and (C) refer to emotions Douglass undoubtedly feels, but is not expressing here. (D) is an idea he never expresses at all. (E) interprets "drag a man in fetters" (chains) literally—force a slave to attend. Don't go for a simple paraphrase like this. *Go back and get the meaning in context!* Douglass is speaking figuratively; he doesn't mean he's actually being dragged to the celebration in chains.

6. D

In the cited sentence, the "millions" who are wailing are the slaves, while the "shouts" come from Fourth of July celebrants. Douglass uses this contrast to emphasize the differences between the lives and attitudes of slaves and free Americans (D). (A) and (C) twist the meaning of Douglass's mention of "yesterday" and "today" in these lines. Choice (B) goes against Douglass's overall point, which is to point out the hypocrisy of Fourth of July celebrations. And while the problem of slavery is not yet solved, Douglass doesn't imply it is "unsolvable" (E).

7. B

Always put the detail in context by rereading the surrounding lines. Here, the author's referring to the "treason" of betraying the American slaves by failing to protest during July 4th celebrations. Douglass is saying that he'd be committing "treason" to them by not speaking out. So in this example, "treason" refers to acting against the needs of a social group, i.e., the slaves. (A) and (D) may have sounded tempting as common definitions of "treason," but they don't express what the author means in this context.

8. C

A tough Little Picture question. Rereading the context, you can see that Douglass is emphasizing throughout paragraph 2 the contradiction between July 4th celebrations and the condition of the slaves. When he describes "American Slavery" as "my subject," he's highlighting this paradox, and also describing what

he's about to talk about next—literally outlining what the subject of the rest of his speech is. (A)'s wrong because the topic of slavery is not unexpected—it's what Douglass has been discussing all along. (B)'s wrong because Douglass isn't talking about slavery through the ages. (D)'s wrong because Douglass suggests no immediate answer to the problem. Finally, there's no suggestion that Douglass has to (E) learn more about his topic.

9. A

Again, put the detail in context—who or what is "impudent" here? Douglass is contrasting political speeches with the actual conditions that slaves endured, making (A) the correct answer. (B) is too general; (C) is off the point. (D) actually contradicts Douglass's explicit point of view. Finally, (E) is a distortion—according to the passage, it's the hypocritical speeches of politicians that railed against tyrants.

10. B

A tricky Compare and Contrast question. In passage 1, Jefferson deals with the themes of liberty and equality as the necessary principles of good government—he's describing these qualities as the bedrock of the Constitution. Based on passage 1, you can infer that he would respond to Douglass's questions about liberty in a similar manner—by agreeing that these are staples in any democracy. None of the other choices are consistent with any statement made in passage 1—remember, you've always got to find evidence for your answer in the passage.

11. B

The last two questions ask for comparisons. In this one, you're asked how Douglass would respond to Jefferson's stated principle, "equal and exact justice to all men." Douglass gives the answer when he says slaves do not enjoy the liberties of other Americans (paragraph 1). So he would respond that the principle is not being carried out in reality (B). (A), (C), and (E) all imply that the principle is invalid. But Douglass's argument is that a principle that is valid in general isn't being followed for African Americans. (E) is a possible response, but (B) sums up Douglass's overall point better.

12. C

Since each of the answer choices uses the word "both," you should be looking for a similarity between the speeches. Jefferson states a general principle; Douglass points out how it has been violated. The only point that both agree on is that equal justice is desirable, choice (C). Choices (A) and (D) describe Douglass's speech as a whole; (B) is implied in Douglass's final sentence—but Jefferson's speech never discusses these topics. (E), on the other hand, is true of Jefferson's speech but not Douglass's.

13. C

Summarizing each passage's point of view, you'd probably argue that Jefferson was optimistic about equality in the United States (having just established the Constitution), but that Douglass was critical of United States standards on equality 50 years later. Choice (C) picks up this contrast. None of the other choices captures the appropriate positive/negative answer required.

SECTION 6

1. D

The graph shows you the sales of all the toys for each month of the second quarter of a certain year, which is the months April, May, and June. If you look at the sales for those 3 months, you'll see that the bar for April goes up to 40, the bar for May goes up to 10, and the bar for June goes up to 30. The title on the vertical axis says "Sales (in millions of dollars)" so that's what those numbers represent: $40 million in sales for April, $10 million for May, and $30 million for June, for a total of $40 + 10 + 30 = 80$ million dollars total in sales for the 2nd quarter. The total sales were $80 million and the April sales were $40 million, and you want to know what percent of the total the April sales were. Since it says "of the total," the total, or $80 million is the whole and the $40 million is the part, so using the formula PERCENT × WHOLE = PART you get PERCENT × 80 = 40, or PERCENT $= \frac{40}{80} = \frac{1}{2} = 50\%$, answer choice (D).

2. E

If you remembered that any number squared is positive, a quick look at the answer choices would tell you that choice (E), x^2y^2, will be positive for any nonzero values of x and y. If you didn't remember that you should make a note of it, since it's a very important concept. You can also solve this one by picking numbers. If xy is negative, then either x or y is negative and the other is positive since a negative times a positive equals a negative. Picking a couple of pairs of numbers for x and y will tell you that both $x - y$ and $y - x$ can be either positive or negative depending on the exact values of x and y. x^2y can be negative if y is negative and

xy^2 can be negative if x is negative. However, any values you pick for x and y will give you a positive number for x^2y^2, so again choice (E) is correct.

3. B

Don't get confused by the strange words! They're just symbols for an unknown quantity, the same as the letters x and y, which we usually use as symbols for unknown quantities. If 1 fedi = 3 glecks, then multiplying both sides by 2 tells you that 2 fedis = 6 glecks. You're given that 1 bora = 2 fedis, so 1 bora must be equal to 6 glecks. Now that we know the relationship between boras and glecks (whatever they are), the rest is easy. 1 bora is equal to 6 glecks, so how many boras equal 48 glecks? Since $6 \times 8 = 48$, just multiply both sides of the equation 1 bora = 6 glecks by 8 to get 8 boras = 48 glecks. So, the correct answer is 8, answer choice (B).

4. C

If algebra confuses you, try picking numbers. If $f = 10$ then there are 10 freshmen in the class. If 5 freshmen drop the class then there are $10 - 5$, or 5 freshmen left in the class. The number of sophomores is 3 times the number of freshmen left, or 3 times 5, or 15. So there are 15 sophomores in the class and $s = 15$. Which of the answer choices work with $f = 10$ and $s = 15$? All you have to do is plug those numbers into the 5 choices and you'll find that only choice (C) works and is therefore correct.

To do it algebraically, just translate one step at a time. There are f freshmen in the class, but if 5 freshmen drop the class there are $f - 5$ freshmen left. The number of sophomores is 3 times the number of freshmen left, or 3 times $f - 5$, or $3(f - 5)$. So $s = 3(f - 5)$, answer choice (C).

5. E

The perimeter of triangle ABC is $AC + AB + 7$, and the perimeter of triangle ACD is $AC + 5 + 6$. You can combine that with the given information that the perimeter of triangle ABC is 4 more than the perimeter of tri-

angle ACD to get $AC + AB + 7 = AC + 5 + 6 + 4$. Adding the numbers on the right side of the equation gives you $AC + AB + 7 = AC + 15$ and subtracting 7 from both sides gives you $AC + AB = AC + 8$. If you subtract AC from both sides you get $AB = 8$. That's all you need to find the perimeter of $ABCD$, which is $5 + 6 + 7 + 8$, or 26, answer choice (E).

6. D

Notice that at each corner of the cube, a triangular face like triangular face ABC is being made. How many corners are there? There are 8 corners; 4 of the corners are on the top and 4 of them are on the bottom. After all 8 triangular faces are made, a part of each of the original 6 faces of the cube remains. The total number of faces of the resulting stone must be $6 + 8$, or 14.

7. D

We want the average of the first 30 positive integers. Whenever we want the average of a group of evenly spaced numbers, we just have to take the average of the smallest number and the largest number. If you have difficulty seeing this, consider a simpler problem. Consider the average of 1, 2, 3, and 4. The average of 1, 2, 3, and 4 is $\frac{1+2+3+4}{4} = \frac{10}{4} = \frac{5}{2} = 2\frac{1}{2}$, using the average formula: Average $= \frac{\text{Sum of the terms}}{\text{Number of terms}}$. What happens if we just take the average of the smallest number, 1, and the largest number, 4? We get $\frac{1+4}{2} = \frac{5}{2} = 2\frac{1}{2}$, which is what we got by finding the average the other way. So the average of the first 30 positive integers is just the average of 1 and 30, which is $\frac{1+30}{2} = \frac{31}{2} = 15\frac{1}{2}$. None of the answer choices is $15\frac{1}{2}$, but $15\frac{1}{2}$ is 15.5. The average is 15.5.

8. B

You may notice that the figure looks like a rectangle with a quadrilateral piece hanging off of it. That means that you can find the area of the figure by adding the area of the rectangle and the area of the quadrilateral. The quadrilateral piece can be divided into a rectangle and a triangle. It may help to draw in some dotted lines to represent this:

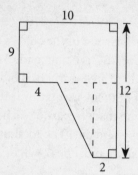

The larger rectangle on the top has length 10 and width 9. Since the vertical line segment on the right is labeled 12, the length of the part of that line that is not part of the larger rectangle must be 12 − 9, or 3, so write that on your figure. The short horizontal line in the middle of the figure has length 4, the small rectangle on the bottom has length 2, and the entire figure has a top horizontal length of 10, so the dotted horizontal line that is a leg of the right triangle must have length 10 − 4 − 2, or 4. Now we've got the lengths of all the pieces of the figure:

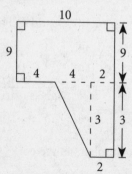

The rectangle on the top has an area of 9 × 10 = 90. The small rectangle on the bottom right has length 3 and width 2, so its area is 6, and the triangle has legs 4 and 3, so its area is also 6. The total area of the figure is 90 + 6 + 6 = 102, answer choice (B).

9. A

If 60 cookies are distributed among x campers, then each camper gets $\frac{60}{x}$ cookies. When the same number of cookies is divided among less campers, then each camper gets 2 more than $\frac{60}{x}$ cookies, or $\frac{60}{x} + 2$. This number of cookies per camper is also equal to 60 cookies divided by 8 less than the original number of campers, or $\frac{60}{x-8}$. This gives us the equation $\frac{60}{x} + 2 = \frac{60}{x-8}$. Unfortunately, this equation is not in the same form as the equations in the answer choices, so you'll have to do some algebra:

$$\frac{60}{x} + 2 = \frac{60}{x-8}$$
$$\frac{60 + 2x}{x} = \frac{60}{x-8}$$
$$(60 + 2x)(x - 8) = 60x$$
$$60x - 480 + 2x^2 - 16x = 60x$$
$$2x^2 - 16x - 480 = 0$$
$$x^2 - 8x - 240 = 0, \text{ answer choice (A)}.$$

10. D

All they're asking here is—how many different pairs can you make from a group of 6? Let's call the 6 students $A, B, C, D, E,$ and $F. A$ can be joined with the others to make the 5 pairs $AB, AC, AD, AE,$ and $AF.$ Since you've already paired A and B you don't have to do it again, so just pair B up with the rest of the group to get $BC, BD, BE,$ and $BF.$ That's 4 new pairs. C has already been matched up with A and $B,$ so the new pairs that involve C are $CD, CE,$ and $CF,$ for 3 new pairs. There are only 2 new pairs left for $D, DE,$ and $DF,$ and finally 1 more, $EF.$ So there's a total of $5 + 4 + 3 + 2 + 1 = 15,$ choice (D).

SAT
Study Aids

SAT Word List

This Word List can boost your knowledge of SAT-level words, and that can help you get more questions right. No one can predict exactly which words will show up on your SAT test. But there are certain words that the test makers favor. The more of these you know, the better.

MEMORIZING SAT WORDS

In general, the very best way to improve your vocabulary is to read. Choose challenging, college-level material. If you encounter an unknown word, put it on a flashcard or in your vocabulary notebook. If you are mainly concerned with honing your knowledge of SAT words, memorizing the words on the following list can help. Here are some techniques for memorizing words.

1. Learn words in groups. You can group words by a common root they contain (see the Root List for some examples), or you can group words together if they are related in meaning (i.e., Word Families). Memorizing words this way may help you to remember them.

2. Use flashcards. Write down new words or word groups and run through them when you have a few minutes to spare. Put one new word or word group on one side of a 3 × 5 card and put a short definition or definitions on the back.

SAT Emergency

If you're short on time, you may want to just skim through this Word List to familiarize yourself with the types of words the SAT often tests.

3. Make a vocabulary notebook. List words in one column and their definitions in another. Test yourself. Cover up the meanings, and see which words you can define from memory. Make a sample sentence using each word in context.

4. Think of hooks that lodge a new word in your mind—create visual images of words.

5. Use rhymes, pictures, songs, and any other devices that help you remember words.

To get the most out of your remaining study time, use the techniques that work for you, and stick with them.

A

ABANDON *n* (uh <u>baan</u> duhn)
total lack of inhibition
With her strict parents out of town, Kelly danced all night with *abandon*.
synonyms: exuberance, enthusiasm

ABASE *v* (uh <u>bays</u>)
to humble; disgrace
My intention was not to *abase* the comedian.
synonyms: demean, humiliate

ABASH *v* (uh <u>baash</u>)
to embarrass
My brother tries to *abash* everyone at our family reunions.
synonyms: disconcert, discomfit, faze, mortify

ABATE *v* (uh <u>bayt</u>)
to decrease, to reduce
My hunger *abated* when I saw how filthy the chef's hands were.
synonyms: dwindle, ebb, recede

ABDICATE *v* (<u>aab</u> duh kayt)
to give up a position, right, or power
With the angry mob clamoring outside the palace, the king *abdicated* his throne and fled.
synonyms: cede, relinquish, resign, quit, yield

ABERRATION *n* (aa buhr <u>ay</u> shuhn)
something different from the usual
Because of the bizarre *aberration* in the author's behavior, her publicist decided that the less the public saw of her, the better.
synonyms: anomaly, irregularity, abnormality, deviation

ABET *v* (uh <u>beht</u>)
to aid, to act as an accomplice
While Derwin robbed the bank, Marvin *abetted* his friend by pulling up the getaway car.
synonyms: help, succor, assist

ABEYANCE *n* (uh <u>bay</u> uhns)
temporary suppression or suspension
The baseball game was held in *abeyance* while it continued to rain.
synonyms: delay, deferral, postponement, dormancy, remission

ABHOR *v* (uh <u>bohr</u>)
to loathe, detest
After she repeatedly failed to learn the Pythagorean theorem, Susan began to *abhor* geometry.
synonyms: hate, contemn, abominate, execrate, despise

ABJECT *adj* (<u>aab</u> jehkt)
miserable, pitiful
When we found the *abject* creature lying on the ground, we took it inside and tended to its broken leg.
synonyms: pathetic, lamentable, sorry

ABOMININATE *v* (uh <u>bahm</u> uhn ayt)
·to loathe, hate
I *abominate* people who talk about themselves all of the time.
synonyms: abhor, contemn, despise, detest, execrate

ABORTIVE *adj* (uh <u>bohr</u> tihv)
ending without results
Her *abortive* attempt to swim the full five miles left her frustrated.
synonyms: fruitless, futile, unsuccessful

ABRIDGE *v* (uh <u>brihj</u>)
to condense, shorten
The assignment was to *abridge* a popular work of fiction.
synonyms: abbreviate, cut, prune

ABSCOND *v* (aab <u>skahnd</u>)
to leave quickly in secret
The criminal *absconded* during the night with all of his mother's money.
synonyms: slip, sneak, flee

ABSOLVE *v* (uhb <u>sahlv</u>)
to forgive, free from blame
If you are in the Queen's good graces, she may *absolve* you of your crime.
synonyms: acquit, clear, exculpate, exonerate, pardon

*ABSTAIN *v* (uhb <u>stayn</u>)
not partaking in some activity or action
During Lent, practicing Catholics *abstain* from eating meat.
synonyms: forbear, refrain

ACCEDE *v* (aak <u>seed</u>)
to express approval, to agree to
Once the mayor heard the reasonable request, she happily *acceded* to the proposal.
synonyms: consent, concur

ACCOLADE *n* (<u>aak</u> uh layd)
praise, distinction
The winner of the spelling bee enjoyed the *accolade* of the head judge.
synonyms: praise, acclaim, approbation, commendation, kudos

ACCOST *v* (uh <u>cahst</u>) (uh <u>kawst</u>)
to approach and speak to someone, often in an aggressive way
Ruby has been known to *accost* random people at the mall.
synonyms: stop, address, detain, buttonhole

ACCRETION *n* (uh <u>kree</u> shuhn)
a growth in size, an increase in amount
The committee's strong fund-raising efforts resulted in an *accretion* in scholarship money.
synonyms: buildup, accumulation

ACCRUE *v* (uh <u>kroo</u>)
to accumulate, grow by additions
In my efforts to pay for college, I was forced to *accrue* a large debt.
synonyms: augment, enlarge, expand, burgeon, wax

ACERBIC *adj* (uh <u>suhr</u> bihk)
bitter, sharp in taste or temper
Gina's *acerbic* wit and sarcasm were feared around the office.
synonyms: tart, biting, caustic, cutting

ACME *n* (<u>aak</u> mee)
highest point; summit
the highest level or degree attainable
Just when he reached the *acme* of his power, the dictator was overthrown.
synonyms: apex, peak, summit

ACQUIESCE *v* (<u>aak</u> wee ehs)
to agree; comply quietly
The princess was forced to *acquiesce* to demands that she marry a nobleman, but she was not happy about it.
synonyms: accede, consent, submit

ACRID *adj* (<u>aak</u> rihd)
harsh, bitter
The *acrid* smell of vinegar drove the children out of the kitchen.
synonyms: sharp, pungent, caustic

ACRIMONY *n* (<u>aak</u> rih moh nee)
bitterness, animosity
The *acrimony* the newly divorced couple showed towards each other made everyone feel uncomfortable.
synonyms: choler, spleen, rancor, asperity, antipathy

*ACUMEN *n* (<u>aak</u> yuh muhn) (uh <u>kyoo</u> muhn)
sharpness of insight, mind, and understanding; shrewd judgment
The investor's financial *acumen* helped him to select high-yield stocks.
synonyms: discernment, shrewdness

ACUTE *adj* (uh <u>kyoot</u>)
sharp, pointed, severe
There is an *acute* shortage of food in the city.
synonyms: intense, fierce

ADAGE *n* (<u>aa</u> dihj)
old saying or proverb
"A penny saved is a penny earned" is a popular *adage*.
synonyms: apothem, aphorism, maxim

ADAMANT *adj* (<u>aad</u> uh mihnt)
stubbornly unyielding
She was *adamant* about leaving the restaurant after the waiter was rude.
synonyms: inflexible, obdurate, inexorable

ADAPT *v* (uh <u>daapt</u>)
to accommodate; adjust
Although it may be difficult at first, we all have to *adapt* to the new computer system.
synonyms: conform, fit, reconcile

*ADEPT *adj* (uh <u>dehpt</u>)
extremely skilled
She is *adept* at computing math problems in her head.
synonyms: quick, masterful

ADHERE *v* (aad <u>heer</u>)
to cling or follow without deviation
A strict Catholic *adheres* to all the teachings of the Church.
synonyms: cleave, stick

ADJACENT *adj* (uh <u>jay</u> suhnt)
next to, close
The photocopier is down the hall, *adjacent* to the water cooler.
synonyms: neighboring, adjoining, abutting, bordering

*ADMONISH *v* (aad <u>mahn</u> ihsh)
to caution or warn gently in order to correct something
My mother *admonished* me about my poor grades.
synonyms: reprimand

ADROIT *adj* (uh <u>droyt</u>)
skillful, accomplished, highly competent
The *adroit* athlete completed even the most difficult obstacle course with ease.
synonyms: dexterous, proficient

*ADULATION *n* (<u>aaj</u> juh lay shuhn)
excessive flattery or admiration
The *adulation* she showed her professor seemed insincere; I suspected she really wanted a better grade.
synonyms: fawning, buttering up

*ADULTERATE *v* (uh <u>duhl</u> tuhr ayt)
to corrupt or make impure
The owner plans to *adulterate* his ketchup with more preservatives.
synonyms: contaminate, dilute

ADVERSARIAL *adj* (aad vuhr <u>saa</u> ree uhl)
disagreeable, hostile
The brothers' *adversarial* relationship made it impossible for them to support each other in times of need.
synonyms: antagonistic, hostile

*ADVERSITY *n* (aad <u>vuhr</u> sih tee)
hardship
Soldiers on both sides in World War I struggled to keep up their morale amid terrible *adversity*.
synonyms: suffering, distress, tribulation

ADVOCATE *v* (<u>aad</u> vuh kayt)
to urge, to recommend
I *advocate* reducing your cholesterol consumption.
synonyms: encourage, advise

AERIE *n* (<u>ayr</u> ee) (<u>eer</u> ee)
a nest built high in the air; an elevated, often secluded, dwelling
Perched high among the trees, the eagle's *aerie* was filled with eggs.
synonyms: perch, stronghold

AERODYNAMIC *n* (ayr oh die <u>naa</u> mihk)
relating to objects moving smoothly through the air
We made the paper airplane more *aerodynamic* by folding the wings at an angle.
synonyms: sleek, streamlined

*AESTHETIC *adj* (ehs theh tihk)
pertaining to beauty or art
The museum curator, with her fine *aesthetic* sense, created an exhibit that was a joy to behold.
synonyms: artistic, tasteful

AFFABLE *adj* (<u>aa</u> fuh buhl)
friendly, easy to approach
The *affable* postman was on good terms with everyone on his route.
synonyms: sociable

AFFECTED *adj* (uh <u>fehk</u> tihd)
phony, artificial
The *affected* hairdresser spouted French phrases, though she had never been to France.
synonyms: put-on, insincere, pretentious

AFFINITY *n* (uh <u>fih</u> nih tee)
fondness, liking, similarity
George felt an instant *affinity* for his new neighbor when he realized that he, too, was a Broncos fan.
synonyms: partiality, penchant, inclination

AFFLUENT *adj* (<u>aa</u> floo uhnt) (uh <u>floo</u> uhnt)
rich, abundant
Enid was able to give large sums of money to charity because she was an *affluent* women.
synonyms: wealthy, prosperous

AFFRONT *n* (uh <u>front</u>)
a personal offense, insult
Clyde took the waiter's insulting remark as an *affront* to his whole family.
synonyms: indignity, contumely, disgrace

AGENDA *n* (uh <u>jehn</u> duh)
a plan, schedule
The board put the urgent issue at the top of the *agenda* for their next meeting.
synonyms: program, protocol

AGGRANDIZE *v* (uh <u>graan</u> diez) (<u>aa</u> gruhn diez)
to make larger or greater in power
All the millionaire really wanted was to *aggrandize* his personal wealth as much as possible.
synonyms: elevate, glorify, magnify, exalt, advance

AGGREGATE *n* (<u>aa</u> grih giht)
a collective mass, the sum total
An *aggregate* of panic-stricken customers mobbed the bank, demanding their life savings.
synonyms: whole, entirety

AGGRIEVE *v* (uh <u>greev</u>)
to afflict, to distress
Elizabeth *aggrieved* her chambermaid for not performing her duties properly.
synonyms: grieve, mistreat, abuse

AGILE *adj* (<u>aa</u> giel)
well coordinated, nimble
The *agile* monkey leapt onto the table and snatched the boy's banana away in the blink of an eye.
synonyms: spry, limber, lithe

AGITATION *n* (aa gih <u>tay</u> shuhn)
commotion, excitement; uneasiness
The patient's *agitation* at the thought of undergoing the operation was obvious.
synonyms: disturbance, restlessness, anxiety, fluster, disquiet

AGNOSTIC *n* (aag <u>nah</u> stihk)
one who is not concerned with whether God exists
Although everyone one in her family was a devoted Christian, Sally was *agnostic*.
synonyms: skeptic, doubter

AGRARIAN *adj* (uh <u>grayr</u> ee uhn)
relating to farming or rural matters
She took a course in *agrarian* accounting to help her family run the farm after college.
synonyms: agricultural, rustic

ALACRITY *n* (uh <u>laak</u> crih tee)
cheerful willingness, eagerness; speed
The dog fetched with *alacrity* the stick that had been tossed for him.
synonyms: dispatch, celerity, briskness

ALCHEMY *n* (<u>aal</u> kuh mee)
medieval chemical philosophy aimed at trying to change metal into gold
Scientists of old struggled to master the secrets of *alchemy*, but they could never change metal to gold.
synonyms: hermeticism, magic, pseudo-science, occultism

ALIAS *n* (<u>ay</u> lee uhs)
assumed name
The basketball star who goes by the *alias* "Big Bad Bobby" was just arrested.
synonyms: pseudonym, sobriquet, penname, nom de guerre

ALIENATE *v* (<u>ay</u> lee uhn ayt) (<u>ayl</u> yuhn ayt)
to make hostile or distanced
Anthony made an effort to *alienate* the new kid in school because he was jealous.
synonyms: estrange, disaffected

ALIGN *v* (uh <u>lien</u>)
precisely adjust; commit to one side
Jackie always made sure to *align* her pens in her drawer.
synonyms: allied, adjusted, trued

ALLAY *v* (uh <u>lay</u>)
to lessen, ease, reduce in intensity
Trying to *allay* their fears, the nurse sat with them all night.
synonyms: alleviate, soothe

ALLEGE *v* (uh <u>lehj</u>)
to charge, claim
I don't care what they *allege* he did. It's not true!
synonyms: assert, contend, declare

ALLEGORY *n* (<u>aa</u> lih gohr ee)
symbolic representation
The novelist used the stormy ocean as an *allegory* for her life's struggles.
synonyms: symbolism, metaphor

ALLEVIATE *v* (uh <u>lee</u> vee ayt)
to relieve, improve partially
This medicine will help to *alleviate* the pain; you'll feel better for awhile.
synonyms: allay, assuage, palliate, mitigate, quell

ALLURE *v* (uh <u>lohr</u>)
to entice by charm; attract
The video arcade owner knew that by installing the coolest, most desirable new games he could *allure* the teenage crowd.
synonyms: lure, entice, draw, captivate

ALLUSION *n* (uh <u>loo</u> zhuhn)
indirect reference
He was sometimes referred to as "the Slugger," an *allusion* to his ability to hit the baseball very hard.
synonyms: intimation, suggestion

ALOOF *adj* (uh <u>loof</u>)
removed or distant
The newcomer remained *aloof* from all our activities and therefore made no new friends.
synonyms: remote, indifferent, withdrawn, unsociable

ALTERCATION *n* (awl tehr <u>kay</u> shuhn)
noisy dispute
When the cowboy knocked someone's bottle off the table, a serious *altercation* ensued.
synonyms: argument, clash, fight, quarrel

ALTRUISM *n* (<u>aal</u> troo ihz uhm)
unselfish concern for the welfare of others
The woman's *altruism* revealed itself in the way she gave out money to all who seemed needy.
synonyms: benevolence, generosity, kindness

AMALGAMATE *v* (uh <u>maal</u> guh mayt)
to mix, combine
Giant Industries will *amalgamate* with Mega Products to form Giant-Mega Products Incorporated.
synonyms: integrate, assimilate, merge, incorporate, league

*AMBIGUOUS *adj* (aam <u>bihg</u> yoo uhs)
uncertain; subject to multiple interpretations
The directions he gave were so *ambiguous* that we disagreed on which way to turn.
synonyms: equivocal, dubious

*AMBIVALENCE *n* (aam <u>bih</u> vuhl uhns)
attitude of uncertainty; conflicting emotions
Jane was filled with *ambivalence*; switching jobs would get her away from her tyrannical boss, but she'd lose her high salary and corner office.
synonyms: indecision, vacillation

*AMELIORATE *v* (uh <u>meel</u> yuhr ayt)
to make better, improve
The hospital board wanted to *ameliorate* the ER, so they hired a dozen more nurses.
synonyms: amend, better, reform

AMENABLE *adj* (uh <u>mehn</u> uh buhl)
agreeable, cooperative
Although the new director seemed rigid at first, the cast soon found her to be *amenable* to change.
synonyms: compliant, receptive

AMEND *v* (uh <u>mehnd</u>)
to improve or correct flaws in
Congress must *amend* the bill before the president will agree to sign it.
synonyms: adjust, emend, ameliorate, rectify, revise

AMENITY *n* (uh <u>mehn</u> ih tee)
pleasantness, something increasing comfort
The star was overjoyed to have access to all the *amenities* of civilized society after her stint in the jungle.
synonyms: convenience, accommodation

AMIABLE *adj* (<u>ay</u> mee uh buhl)
friendly, pleasant, likable
The new boss was an *amiable* young man with a smile for everyone.
synonyms: affable, convivial, amicable, agreeable, genial

*AMICABLE *adj* (<u>aa</u> mih kuh buhl)
friendly, agreeable
Despite their former arguments, the team was able to form an *amicable* working relationship.
synonyms: affable, convivial, amiable, genial, cordial

AMITY *n* (<u>aa</u> mih tee)
friendship, good will
Correspondence over the years contributed to a lasting *amity* between the women.
synonyms: harmony

AMORAL *adj* (ay <u>mohr</u> uhl) (ay <u>mahr</u> uhl)
outside the scope of morality
The judge found that no ruling could be handed down to the amoral child because of his age.
synonyms: dishonorable, impious, unscrupulous

*AMORPHOUS *adj* (<u>ay mohr</u> fuhs)
having no definite form
The Blob featured an *amorphous* creature that was constantly changing shape.
synonyms: shapeless, indistinct

AMPLE *adj* (<u>aam</u> puhl)
abundant, plentiful
Though our backpacks were small, we had *ample* food for the hike.
synonyms: substantial, generous

AMPLIFY *v* (<u>aam</u> pluh fie)
increase, intensify
We will need to *amplify* the music at the wedding so that everyone can dance.
synonyms: augment, escalate, magnify

AMULET *n* (<u>aam</u> yoo liht)
ornament worn as a charm against evil spirits
Though she claimed it was not because of superstition, Vivian always wore an *amulet* around her neck.
synonyms: talisman, fetish

*ANACHRONISM *n* (uh <u>naak</u> ruh nih suhm)
out of chronological order or place
The *anachronism* was the hippie at the Renaissance Festival.
synonyms: anomalous, inconsistent, inappropriate

ANALOGOUS *adj* (uh <u>naal</u> uh guhs)
drawing a likeness, parallel
In a famous argument for the existence of God, the universe is *analogous* to a mechanical watch, which is the creation of a divinely intelligent "clockmaker."
synonyms: akin, corresponding, correlative, homologous, similar

ANARCHY *n* (<u>aa</u> nuhr kee) (<u>aa</u> nahr kee)
absence of government or law; chaos
Some believe that without a strong police force, *anarchy* would quickly prevail.
synonyms: disorder, turmoil, confusion

ANATHEMA *n* (uh <u>naath</u> uh muh)
ban, curse; something shunned or disliked
Sweaty, soiled clothing was an *anathema* to the elegant Madeleine.
synonyms: execration, aversion, horror, abomination

ANCILLARY *adj* (<u>aan</u> suhl eh ree)
accessory; subordinate; helping
Because reforms were instituted at the main factory but not at its *ancillary* plants, defects continued to occur.
synonyms: adjunct, additional, auxiliary, supplemental

*ANECDOTE *n* (<u>aa</u> nihk doht)
short, usually funny account of an event
The child's grandparents entertained him for hours with *anecdotes* from their younger days.
synonyms: story, joke

ANIMATION *n* (aa nih <u>may</u> shuhn)
enthusiasm, excitement
Ben's face filled with *animation* as he described his wonderful, exciting trip to Venice.
synonyms: elation, vivacity, brio, spirit, verve

ANIMOSITY *n* (aa nih <u>mah</u> sih tee)
hatred, hostility
The deep-rooted *animosity* between them made it difficult for the cousins to work together.
synonyms: antipathy, enmity, malice, rancor, malevolence

ANNUL *v* (uh <u>nuhl</u>)
to cancel, nullify, declare void, or make legally invalid
The couple asked the court to *annul* their marriage because they realized they had made a mistake.
synonyms: abrogate, negate, undo, rescind

ANOMALY *n* (uh <u>nahm</u> uh lee)
a deviation from the common rule, something that is difficult to classify
Among the top-ten albums of the year was one *anomaly*—a compilation of polka classics.
synonyms: irregularity

*ANONYMOUS *adj* (uh <u>nahn</u> uh muhs)
of unknown authorship; lacking recognizability
After abandoning her movie career, Greta Garbo chose to live an *anonymous* life in Manhattan.
synonyms: unacknowledged, unattributed, unknown, unheralded

*ANTAGONIST *n* (uh <u>nahn</u> uh muhs)
foe, opponent, adversary
She became my antagonist after she stole my homework.
synonyms: enemy, rival

ANTECEDENT *adj* (aan tih <u>see</u> duhnt)
coming before in place or time
Though the war appeared to be over, the *antecedent* events made the soldiers wary of retreating.
synonyms: previous, prior, anterior, preceding

ANTEDILUVIAN *adj* (aan tih duh <u>loo</u> vee uhn)
ancient beyond measure
The *antediluvian* fossils were displayed in the museum.
synonyms: old, archaic, antique

ANTIPATHY *n* (aan <u>tih</u> puh thee)
dislike, hostility; extreme opposition or aversion
The *antipathy* between the French and the English regularly erupted into open warfare.
synonyms: enmity, malice, antagonism

ANTIQUATED *adj* (<u>aan</u> tih kway tihd)
too old to be fashionable or useful
Next to her coworker's brand-new model, Marisa's computer looked *antiquated*.
synonyms: outdated, obsolete

ANTITHESIS *n* (aan <u>tih</u> thih sihs)
exact opposite or direct contrast
The mean boy was often described as the *antithesis* of his sweet sister.
synonyms: contrary, reverse

APATHY *n* (<u>aa</u> pah thee)
lack of feeling or emotion
The *apathy* of voters is so great that less than half the people who are eligible to vote bother to do so.
synonyms: indifference, insouciance, disregard, unconcern

APEX *n* (<u>ay</u> pehks)
highest point, summit, zenith
Ronald Reagan was at the *apex* of his acting career when, alas, Bonzo the ape expired.
synonyms: acme, crown, peak, crest

APHORISM *n* (<u>aa</u> fuhr ihz uhm)
a short statement of a principle
The country doctor was given to such *aphorisms* as "Still waters run deep."
synonyms: adage, proverb

*APOCRYPHAL *adj* (uh <u>pahk</u> ruh fuhl)
not genuine; fictional
Sharon knew that she was telling an apocryphal story when she said there were alligators in the sewer.
synonyms: erroneous, fictitious, fraudulent, false

APOSTATE *n* (uh <u>pahs</u> tayt)
one who renounces a religious faith
So that he could divorce his wife, the king scoffed at the church doctrines and declared himself an *apostate*.
synonyms: traitor, defector, deserter

APPEASE *v* (uh <u>pees</u>)
to satisfy, placate, calm, pacify
We all sang lullabies to try to *appease* the bawling infant.
synonyms: assuage, mollify, propitiate, soothe

APPROBATION *n* (aa pruh <u>bay</u> shuhn)
praise; official approval
Billy was sure he had gained the *approbation* of his teacher when he received a glowing report card.
synonyms: acclaim, accolade, encomium, applause, homage

APPROPRIATE *v* (uh <u>proh</u> pree ayt)
to assign to a particular purpose, allocate
The mayor *appropriated* funds for the clean-up effort.
synonyms: appoint, earmark

AQUATIC *adj* (uh <u>kwah</u> tihk)
belonging or living in water
The whale, the heaviest *aquatic* creature, has most of its weight supported by water.
synonyms: watery, maritime, pelagic

ARABLE *adj* (<u>aa</u> ruh buhl)
suitable for cultivation
The overpopulated country desperately needed more *arable* farmland.
synonyms: farmable, fertile

ARBITRARY *adj* (<u>ahr</u> bih trayr ee)
depending solely on individual will; inconsistent
Because Fred didn't win a prize after his spectacular performance, the judges' decisions seemed completely *arbitrary*.
synonyms: discretional, whimsical, impulsive

ARBORETUM *n* (ahr bohr <u>ee</u> tuhm)
place where trees are displayed and studied
The professor spent more time teaching in the *arboretum* than in the classroom.
synonyms: garden, arbor

ARCANE *adj* (ahr <u>kayn</u>)
secret, obscure, known only to a few
The *arcane* rituals of the sect were passed down through many generations.
synonyms: esoteric, mysterious

ARCH *adj*
mischievous, roguish
The practical joker sized up his intended victims with an *arch* smile.
synonyms: impish, waggish, saucy, ironic

ARCHAIC *adj* (ahr <u>kay</u> ihk)
antiquated, from an earlier time; outdated
Her *archaic* Commodore computer could not run the latest software.
synonyms: antediluvian, ancient, obsolete, prehistoric

ARCHIPELAGO *n* (ahr kuh <u>pehl</u> uh goh)
a large group of islands
Between villages in the Stockholm *archipelago*, boat taxis are the only form of transportation.
synonyms: cluster, scattering

ARDENT *adj* (<u>ahr</u> dihnt)
passionate, enthusiastic, fervent
After a 25-game losing streak, even the Tar Heels' most *ardent* fans realized the team wouldn't finish first.
synonyms: intense, vehement, fervid

ARDUOUS *adj* (<u>ahr</u> jyoo uhs) (<u>aar</u> dyoo uhs)
extremely difficult, laborious
Amy thought she would pass out after completing the *arduous* trail up the mountain.
synonyms: burdensome, onerous, hard, toilsome

*ARID *adj* (aarihd)
extremely dry or lacking in interest
The *arid* farmland produced no crops.
synonyms: desert, thirsty, desiccated, parched

ARRAIGN *v* (uh <u>rayn</u>)
to call to court to answer an indictment
The DA was going to arraign the con man, but he failed to show up.
synonyms: accuse, challenge, denounce, inculpate, blame

ARROGATE *v* (<u>aa</u> ruh gayt)
to claim without justification; to claim for oneself without right
Lynn watched in astonishment as her boss *arrogated* the credit for her brilliant work on the project.
synonyms: take, presume, appropriate

ARSENAL *n* (<u>ahr</u> sih nuhl)
ammunition storehouse
The soldiers rushed to the *arsenal* to fetch more cannonballs.
synonyms: supply, depot

ARTICULATE *adj* (ahr <u>tih</u> kyoo layt)
well spoken, expressing oneself clearly
She is such an *articulate* defender of labor that unions are among her strongest supporters.
synonyms: eloquent, persuasive

ARTIFACT *n* (<u>ahr</u> tih faakt)
historical relic, item made by human craft
The archaeologist discovered hundreds of interesting *artifacts* in the ruins of the mansion.
synonyms: creation, handiwork

ARTISAN *n* (<u>ahr</u> tih zuhn) (<u>ahr</u> tih suhn)
craftsperson; expert
Artisans were among the most valued citizens of the village for their skills in tool-making.
synonyms: maker, master

ASCEND *v* (uh <u>sehnd</u>)
to rise to another level or climb; move upward
Because there was no other way to go, Mrs. Biechler had to ascend the stairs, despite her bad hip.
synonyms: elevate, escalate, hoist, lift, mount

ASCERTAIN *v* (aa suhr <u>tayn</u>)
to determine, discover, make certain of
Try as he might, the archaeologist couldn't *ascertain* the correct age of the Piltdown man's skeleton.
synonyms: verify, calculate, detect

*ASCETIC *adj* (uh <u>seh</u> tihk)
self-denying, abstinent, austere
The monk lived an *ascetic* life deep in the wilderness, which was in accordance with his faith.
synonyms: continent, temperate, abstemious

ASCRIBE *v* (uh <u>skrieb</u>)
to attribute to, assign
Aunt Fran was shocked when she heard about the negative qualities her family *ascribed* to her.
synonyms: accredit, impute, refer

ASHEN *adj* (<u>aash</u> un)
resembling ashes; deathly pale
The *ashen* look on Jesse's face made it clear he had already heard the bad news.
synonyms: blanched, pallid, pasty

ASPERSION *n* (uh <u>spuhr</u> shuhn)
false rumor, damaging report, slander
It is unfair to cast *aspersions* on someone behind his or her back.
synonyms: allegation, insinuation, reproach

ASPIRE *v* (uh <u>spier</u>)
to have great hopes; to aim at a goal
Although Matt is happy starting out in the mailroom, he will still *aspire* to own the company someday.
synonyms: intend, strive, purpose, resolve, expect

ASSAIL *v* (uh <u>sayl</u>)
to attack, assault
The foreign army will try to assail our bases, but they will not be successful in their attack.
synonyms: beset, storm, strike

ASSENT *v* (uh <u>sehnt</u>)
to agree, as to a proposal
After careful deliberation, the CEO *assented* to the proposed merger.
synonyms: accede, yield, concur

*ASSIDUOUS *adj* (uh <u>sih</u> dee uhs)
diligent, persistent attention
The chauffeur scrubbed the limousine with *assiduous* zeal, hoping to make a good impression on his employer.
synonyms: industrious, steadfast, thorough

ASSONANCE *n* (<u>aa</u> suh nehns)
resemblance in sound, especially in vowel sounds; partial rhyme
The professor pointed out how *assonance* among the words contributed to the flow of the poem.
synonyms: repetition, similarity, echo

*ASSUAGE *v* (uh <u>swayj</u>) (uh <u>swayzh</u>) (uh <u>swahzh</u>)
to make less severe; to ease, relieve
A frequently cited argument for capital punishment is the need to *assuage* the anger and grief of victims' families.
synonyms: mitigate, alleviate, ease, appease, mollify

ASTRINGENT *adj* (uh <u>strihn</u> juhnt)
harsh, severe, stern
The principal's punishments seemed overly *astringent*, but the students did not dare to complain.
synonyms: sharp, bitter, caustic

ASTUTE *adj* (uh <u>stoot</u>)
Awareness; clever intelligence
The novelist Judy Blume is an *astute* judge of human nature; her characters ring true.
synonyms: insightful, perspicacious, shrewd, perceptive, acute

*ASYLUM *n* (uh <u>sie</u> luhm)
refuge, sanctuary
Many immigrants come to America seeking *asylum* from persecution in their native lands.
synonyms: haven, shelter

ASYMMETRICAL *adj* (ay suh <u>meh</u> trih cuhl)
not corresponding in size, shape, position
The hairstylist was shocked to find that the two sides of his customer's hair were *asymmetrical*.
synonyms: askew, lopsided, uneven, misshapen

ATONE *v* (uh <u>tohn</u>)
to make amends
Many people go to church to *atone* for their wrongdoings and seek forgiveness.
synonyms: expiate, reconcile

ATROCIOUS *adj* (uh <u>troh</u> shuhs)
revolting, shockingly bad, wicked
The officer committed the *atrocious* act of slaughtering a large group of peaceful villagers.
synonyms: horrible, appalling, deplorable, direful

ATROPHY *n* (<u>aa</u> troh fee)
to waste away, wither from disuse
The atrophy in Mimi's muscles was swift once she stopped exercising.
synonyms: deteriorate, degenerate

ATTENUATE *v* (uh <u>tehn</u> yoo ayt)
to make thin or slender; weaken
The Bill of Rights was meant to *attenuate* the traditional power of government to change laws at will.
synonyms: reduce, rarefy, diminish

ATTEST *v* (uh <u>tehst</u>)
to testify, stand as proof of, bear witness
In order for Mrs. Martin to be acquitted, her husband had to attest that she was with him the night of the murder.
synonyms: corroborate, confirm, substantiate

AUDACIOUS *adj* (aw <u>day</u> shuhs)
bold, overly daring
The teens understood the consequences of their audacious behavior after they were expelled.
synonyms: adventurous, brave, reckless

AUDIBLE *adj* (<u>aw</u> dih buhl)
capable of being heard
The shy boy's voice was barely *audible* as he answered the teacher's questions.
synonyms: detectable, perceptible

AUDIT *n* (<u>aw</u> diht)
formal examination of financial records
The audit last year forced the business to declare bankruptcy.
synonyms: review, correction, verification

AUDITORY *adj* (<u>aw</u> dih tohr ee)
having to do with hearing
The auditory lessons in the Spanish class are hard for many students who are visual learners.
synonyms: aural, otic, auricular

AUGMENT *v* (awg <u>mehnt</u>)
to expand, extend
Ben tried to *augment* his salary with overtime hours as much as possible.
synonyms: enhance, compound, increase, enlarge, inflate

AUGURY *n* (<u>aw</u> gyuh ree) (<u>aw</u> guh ree)
prophecy, prediction of events
Troy hoped the rainbow was an *augury* of good things to come.
synonyms: omen, auspices, portent, harbinger, presage

AUGUST *adj* (aw <u>guhst</u>)
dignified, grandiose
The *august* view of the Grand Teton summit took my breath away.
synonyms: grand, majestic, admirable, awesome

*AUSPICIOUS *adj* (aw <u>spih</u> shuhs)
having favorable prospects, promising
Tamika thought that having lunch with the boss was an *auspicious* start to her new job.
synonyms: encouraging, propitious, hopeful, positive

AUSTERE *adj* (aw <u>steer</u>)
stern, strict, unadorned
The austere speaker was like a machine because she simply spewed out facts.
synonyms: dour, bare, ascetic

AUTHORITARIAN *adj* (aw thohr ih <u>tehr</u> ee uhn)
extremely strict, desiring submission from others
The *authoritarian* manager alienated his employees by canceling Halloween, one of their favorite holidays.
synonyms: despotic, autocratic, imperious, tyrannical

*AUTOCRAT *n* (<u>aw</u> toh kraat)
a dictator
Mussolini has been described as an *autocrat* who tolerated no opposition.
synonyms: tyrant, despot

AUTONOMOUS *adj* (aw <u>tah</u> nuh muhs)
separate, independent
Mary's autonomous lifestyle was mainly a consequence of her parent's jet-setting ways.
synonyms: sovereign, self-governed, free

AVARICE *n* (<u>aa</u> vuhr ihs)
greed
Rebecca's *avarice* motivated her to stuff the $100 bill in her pocket instead of returning it to the man who had dropped it.
synonyms: cupidity, rapacity

AVENGE *v* (uh <u>vehnj</u>)
to retaliate, take revenge for an injury or crime
Sonny swore to avenge his loss in the elections because of ballot stuffing.
synonyms: punish, redress, repay

AVER *v* (uh <u>vuhr</u>)
to declare to be true, to affirm
"Yes, he was holding a gun," the witness *averred*.
synonyms: assert, attest

AVERSION *n* (uh <u>vuhr</u> zhuhn)
intense dislike
Laura took an instant *aversion* to Mike because he made milk come out of his nose.
synonyms: antagonism, antipathy, abhorrence, repulsion, repugnance

AVERT *v* (uh <u>vuhrt</u>)
to turn away; avoid
The queasy medical school student had to *avert* her eyes when the operation began.
synonyms: deter, forestall, preclude, deflect, parry

AVIARY *n* (<u>ay</u> vee eh ree)
large enclosure housing birds
The tourists brought their cameras to the city's famous *aviary*, hoping to capture its exotic birds on film.
synonyms: birdhouse, zoo

AWRY *adv* (uh <u>rie</u>)
crooked, askew, amiss
Something must have gone *awry* in the computer system because some of my files are missing.
synonyms: aslant, wrong

AXIOM *n* (<u>aak</u> see uhm)
premise, postulate, self-evident truth
Halle lived her life based on the *axioms* her grandmother had passed on to her.
synonyms: adage, apothegm, aphorism, maxim, rule

B

BALEFUL *adj* (<u>bayl</u> fuhl)
harmful, with evil intentions
The sullen teenager gave his nagging mother a *baleful* look.
synonyms: dark, sinister

BALK *v* (bawk)
to stop short and refuse to go on
When the horse *balked* at jumping over the high fence, the rider was thrown off.
synonyms: flinch, shirk from

BALM *n* (bahm)
soothing, healing influence
I always carry lip balm when I am in cold weather so my lips don't crack.
synonyms: succor, comfort, palliative, anodyne, salve

BAN *v* (baan)
to forbid, outlaw
After smashing dozens of cups and saucers, the owner of the café decided to *ban* Joe.
synonyms: bar, interdict, prohibit, proscribe, disallow

BANAL *adj* (buh <u>naal</u>) (<u>bay</u> nuhl) (buh n<u>ahl</u>)
trite, overly common
He used *banal* phrases like "Have a nice day," or "Another day, another dollar."
synonyms: hackneyed, shopworn, inane

BANE *n* (bayn)
something causing death, destruction, or ruin
Speeches were the *bane* of Jenny's existence; she hated having to stand up in front of a crowd.
synonyms: undoer, curse, scourge, poison

BANTER *n* (<u>baan</u> tuhr)
playful conversation
The eligible man's cheerful *banter* was misinterpreted as flirtation by the woman who adored him.
synonyms: chatter, palaver, prattle

BASTION *n* (<u>baas</u> chyuhn) (<u>baas</u> tee uhn)
fortification, stronghold
The club was well known as a *bastion* of conservative values in the liberal city.
synonyms: bulwark, defense, haven

BAWDY *adj* (<u>baw</u> dee)
obscene, lewd
Bawdy poetry often refers to bodily functions.
synonyms: vulgar, risqué, rude, coarse

BAY *v*
to bark, especially in a deep, prolonged way
The dog *bayed* all night, much to the annoyance of the neighbors.
synonyms: howl, ululate, wail, keen

BEGUILE *v* (buh <u>giel</u>)
to deceive, mislead; charm
The Sirens' attempt to beguile him had worked, for Odysseus was ready to abandon his men and family.
synonyms: lure, inveigle, coax, cajole, cozen

BEHEMOTH *n* (buh <u>hee</u> muhth)
something of monstrous size or power; huge creature
The budget became such a *behemoth* that observers believed the film would never make a profit.
synonyms: giant, mammoth

BELABOR *v* (bih <u>lay</u> buhr)
to insist repeatedly or harp on
I understand completely; you do not need to *belabor* the point.
synonyms: dwell upon, lambaste

BELEAGUER *v* (bih <u>lee</u> guhr)
to harass, plague
Mickey vowed to *beleaguer* his parents until they gave in to his request for a Nintendo.
synonyms: beset, besiege

BELFRY *n* (<u>behl</u> free)
bell tower, room in which a bell is hung
The town was shocked when a bag of money was found stashed in the old *belfry* of the church.
synonyms: steeple, spire

BELIE *v* (bih <u>lie</u>)
to misrepresent; expose as false
The first lady's attempts to belie the press with her carefree attitude worked like a charm.
synonyms: distort, refute

BELITTLE *v* (buh <u>lih</u> tuhl)
to represent as unimportant, to make slight remarks
Carla thought it was cool to belittle her sister until she was grounded by her parents.
synonyms: minimize, denigrate, deprecate

BELLICOSE *adj* (<u>beh</u> lih cohs)
warlike, aggressive
Immediately after defeating one of his enemies, the *bellicose* chieftain declared war on another.
synonyms: belligerent, hostile, combative, pugnacious

BELLIGERENT *adj* (buh <u>lih</u> juhr uhnt)
hostile, tending to fight
The clerk realized that it would be fruitless to try to subdue the *belligerent* customer by himself.
synonyms: bellicose, aggressive, combative, pugnacious

BENEFACTOR *n* (<u>behn</u> uh faak torh)
someone giving aid or money
A mysterious *benefactor* paid all of Robin's bills, making it possible for her to send her kids to college.
synonyms: contributor, backer, donor, patron

*BENEVOLENT *adj* (buh <u>neh</u> vuh luhnt)
kind, compassionate
The children played happily under the *benevolent* eye of their teacher.
synonyms: charitable, altruistic, beneficent, generous, good

BENIGHTED *adj* (bih <u>nie</u> tihd)
unenlightened
Ben scoffed at the crowd that he believed consisted entirely of *benighted* individuals.
synonyms: ignorant, unschooled, illiterate

BENIGN *adj* (bih <u>nien</u>)
kindly, gentle, or harmless
The weather person was wrong about the storm; the weather is extremely benign today.
synonyms: innocuous, mild, safe

BEQUEATH *v* (bih <u>kweeth</u>) (bih <u>kweeth</u>)
to give, as in a will; to hand down
Grandpa wants to *bequeath* the house to his daughter and the car to his son.
synonyms: pass on, transmit, bestow

*BERATE *v* (bih <u>rayt</u>)
to scold harshly
When my manager found out I had handled the situation so insensitively, he *berated* me.
synonyms: criticize

BESEECH *v* (bih <u>seech</u>)
to beg, plead, implore
Mindy had messed up the relationship so much that her only option was to beseech him to forgive her.
synonyms: petition, supplicate, entreat

BEST *v* (behst)
to get the better of, beat
The North *bested* the South in America's Civil War.
synonyms: defeat, trounce, vanquish, rout, worst

BESTIAL *adj* (<u>behs</u> chuhl) (<u>bees</u> chuhl)
beastly, animal-like
The *bestial* nature of the growl in the dark made the campers shake with fright.
synonyms: brutish, inhuman, savage

BESTOW *v* (bih <u>stoh</u>)
to give as a gift
The students were so grateful to their teacher for helping them with their test that they wanted to bestow her with gifts.
synonyms: award, endow, donate, confer, present

BEVY *n* (<u>beh</u> vee)
group
As predicted, a *bevy* of teenagers surrounded the rock star's limousine.
synonyms: band, gang, bunch, pack, troop

BIAS *n* (<u>bie</u> uhs)
prejudice, slant
Racial *bias* in employment is illegal in the United States.
synonyms: inclination, penchant, bent, partiality, discrimination

BIBLIOGRAPHY *n* (bihb lee <u>ahg</u> ruh fee)
list of books
Please include a *bibliography* at the end of your paper so I can identify your sources.
synonyms: index, source list, reading list

BILK *v* (bihlk)
to cheat, defraud
Though the lawyer seemed honest, the woman feared he would try to *bilk* her out of her money.
synonyms: swindle, dupe, fleece

BIPED *n* (<u>bie</u> pehd)
two-footed animal
Human beings are *bipeds*, whereas horses are quadrupeds.
synonyms: upright, two-legs

BLANCH *v* (blaanch)
to pale; take the color out of
The murderess *blanched* when the man she thought she had killed walked into the room.
synonyms: fade, lighten, bleach

BLANDISH *v* (<u>blaan</u> dihsh)
to coax with flattery
I was going to *blandish* the bouncer until he let us into the club.
synonyms: cajole, charm, seduce, wheedle

BLASPHEMOUS *adj* (<u>blaas</u> fuh muhs)
cursing, profane, irreverent
The politician's offhanded biblical references seemed *blasphemous*, given the context of the orderly meeting.
synonyms: foul-mouthed

BLATANT *adj* (<u>blay</u> tnt)
completely obvious and conspicuous, especially in an offensive, crass manner
Such *blatant* advertising with the bounds of the school drew protest from parents.
synonyms: obvious, flagrant

BLIGHT *v* (bliet)
to afflict, destroy
The farmers feared that the night's frost would *blight* the potato crops entirely.
synonyms: damage, plague

BLITHELY *adv* (<u>blieth</u> lee)
merrily, lightheartedly cheerful; without appropriate thought
Wanting to redecorate the office, she *blithely* assumed her co-workers wouldn't mind and moved the furniture in the space.
synonyms: in a carefree manner

*BOISTEROUS *adj* (boy stuhr uhs) (boy struhs)
rowdy, loud, unrestrained
The *boisterous* football fans rioted in the streets until the police restrained them.
synonyms: clamorous, uproarious

*BOMBASTIC *adj* (bahm baast ihk)
high-sounding but meaningless; ostentatiously lofty in style
Mussolini's speeches were mostly *bombastic*; his outrageous claims had no basis in fact.
synonyms: grandiose, inflated

BONANZA *n* (buh naan zuh)
extremely large amount; something profitable
Judi was overjoyed at the unexpected *bonanza* of winning the lottery.
synonyms: windfall, boon

BOON *n*
blessing, something to be thankful for
Dirk realized that his new coworker's computer skills would be a real *boon* to the company.
synonyms: windfall, favor, treasure, benefit

BOOR *n* (bohr)
crude person, one lacking manners or taste
"That utter *boor* ruined my recital with his constant guffawing!" wailed the pianist.
synonyms: lout, clod, oaf, vulgarian, yahoo

BOTANIST *n* (baht ihn ihst)
scientist who studies plants
The *botanist* spent endless hours studying the orchids that fascinated her.
synonyms: biologist, herbalist

BOURGEOIS *adj* (boor zhwaa) (boo zhwaa) (buh zhwaa)
middle-class; tendency toward materialism
The *bourgeois* family was horrified when the lower-class family moved in next door.
synonyms: capitalist, conventional

BOVINE *adj* (boh vien)
relating to cows; having qualities characteristic of a cow, such as sluggishness or dullness
His *bovine* demeanor did nothing to engage me.
synonyms: dull, placid

BRAZEN *adj* (bray zuhn)
bold, loud, impudent; of or like brass
Kenny's brazen attitude got him kicked off the basketball team.
synonyms: audacious, brash, contumelious, insolent

BREACH *v* (breech)
to break or violate
Even if Ed wanted to leave the fraternity, he had no right to breach the code of silence like that.
synonyms: gap, lapse, rift, contravention, dereliction

BROACH *v* (brohch)
to mention or suggest for the first time
Sandy wanted to go to college away from home, but he didn't know how to *broach* the topic with his parents.
synonyms: introduce, propose

BROOD *v*
to think gloomily about
As John *brooded* over past insults, he grew angrier and angrier.
synonyms: incubate, cover, ponder, worry, obsess

BRUSQUE *adj* (bruhsk)
rough and abrupt in manner
The bank teller's *brusque* treatment of his customers soon evoked several complaints.
synonyms: blunt, curt, gruff, rude, tactless

BUCOLIC *adj* (byoo kah lihk)
pastoral, rural
My aunt likes the hustle and bustle of the city, but my uncle prefers a more *bucolic* setting.
synonyms: rustic, country

BUFFOON *n* (buh foon)
clown or fool
The boy was known as a *buffoon*, so he wasn't taken seriously as a candidate for class president.
synonyms: jester, laughingstock

BURGEON *v* (buhr juhn)
to sprout or flourish
We will need major subway expansion if the city continues to *burgeon* like it is.
synonyms: blossom, thrive, expand, grow, proliferate

BURNISH *v* (buhr nihsh)
to polish, to make smooth and bright
Mr. Frumpkin loved to stand in the sun and *burnish* his luxury car.
synonyms: shine, buff

BUSTLE *n* (buh suhl)
commotion, energetic activity
The *bustle* of the crowd made Andrea remember how much she hated Christmas shopping.
synonyms: flurry, ado, tumult

BUTTRESS *v* (buh trihs)
to reinforce or support
The construction workers attempted to *buttress* the ceiling with pillars.
synonyms: bolster, brace, prop, strengthen

C

CACHE *n* (caash)
a hiding place; stockpile
It's good to have a *cache* where you can stash your cash.
synonyms: hoard, reserve

*CACOPHONY *n* (kuh <u>kah</u> fuh nee)
a jarring, unpleasant noise
As I walked into the open-air market after my nap, a *cacophony* of sounds surrounded me.
synonyms: clatter, racket

CAJOLE *v* (kuh <u>johl</u>)
to flatter, coax, persuade
The spoiled girl could *cajole* her father into buying her anything.
synonyms: blandish, wheedle

CALAMITY *n* (kuh <u>laam</u> ih tee)
state of despair, misfortune
The *calamity* of the accident was almost too much for Maurine to bear.
synonyms: disaster, cataclysm

CALLOUS *adj* (<u>kaa</u> luhs)
thick-skinned, insensitive
The callous football players laughed at the girl who fell down the stairs.
synonyms: impervious, indifferent, stony, unmoved, unfeeling

CALLOW *adj* (<u>kaa</u> loh)
immature, lacking sophistication
The young and *callow* fans hung on every word the talk show host said.
synonyms: ingenuous, naïve, artless

CALUMNY *n* (<u>kaa</u> luhm nee)
noun (<u>kaa</u> luhm nee)
a false and malicious accusation; misrepresentation
The unscrupulous politician used *calumny* to bring down his opponent in the senatorial race.
synonyms: libel, defamation, slander

*CAMARADERIE *n* (kahm <u>rah</u> duhr ee)
unity among a group
After coming to London, Shakespeare enjoyed the *camaraderie* of his fellow actors.
synonyms: friendship, fellowship, espirit de corps, conviviality

CANDOR *n* (<u>kaan</u> dohr)
honest expression
The *candor* of his confession impressed his parents, so they gave him a lighter punishment.
synonyms: frankness, sincerity, bluntness

CANNY *adj* (<u>kaa</u> nee)
smart; founded on common sense
The executive's *canny* business sense saved the company from bankruptcy.
synonyms: percipient, perspicacious, astute, shrewd

CANONIZE *v* (<u>kaa</u> nuhn iez)
to declare a person a saint; raise to highest honors
Discrimination may be the reason certain authors have not been *canonized* by the literary establishment.
synonyms: exult, elevate, ennoble, glorify

*CAPACIOUS *adj* (kuh <u>pay</u> shuhs)
large, roomy; extensive
We wondered how many hundreds of stores occupied the *capacious* mall.
synonyms: ample, commodious

CAPITULATE *v* (kuh <u>pih</u> choo layt)
to submit completely, surrender
After atom bombs devastated Hiroshima and Nagasaki, the Japanese had little choice but to *capitulate*.
synonyms: yield, succumb, acquiesce

CAPRICIOUS *adj* (kuh <u>pree</u> shuhs) (kuh <u>prih</u> shuhs)
impulsive, whimsical, without much thought
Queen Elizabeth I was quite *capricious*; her courtiers could never be sure what would catch her fancy.
synonyms: erratic, fickle, flighty, inconstant, wayward

CARICATURE *n* (<u>kaa</u> rih kah chuhr)
exaggerated portrait, cartoon
Although often unflattering, it was a great honor to have your caricature done by the famous cartoonist.
synonyms: burlesque, travesty, lampoon

*CARNIVOROUS *adj* (kahr <u>nih</u> vuhr uhs)
consumption of animal flesh
Dogs, as *carnivorous* animals, generally do not do well on purely vegetarian diets.
synonyms: predatory, flesh-eating

CARTOGRAPHY *n* (kahr <u>tahg</u> ruh fee)
science or art of making maps
Shawn's interest in *cartography* may stem from the extensive traveling he did as a child.
synonyms: charting, surveying, topography

CASTIGATE *v* (<u>kaa</u> stih gayt)
to punish, chastise, criticize severely
Authorities in Singapore harshly *castigate* perpetrators of what would be considered minor crimes in the United States.
synonyms: discipline, lambaste

CATALYST *n* (<u>kaa</u> tuh lihst)
something that provokes or speeds up significant change, especially without being affected by the consequences
Technology has been a *catalyst* for the expansion of alternative education, such as home schooling and online courses.
synonyms: accelerator

CATHARSIS *n* (kuh <u>thahr</u> sihs)
purification, cleansing
Plays can be more satisfying if they end in some sort of emotional *catharsis* for the characters involved.
synonyms: purgation, release

CATHOLIC *adj* (<u>kaa</u> thuh lihk) (<u>kaa</u> thlihk)
universal; broad and comprehensive
Hot tea with honey is a *catholic* remedy for a sore throat.
synonyms: extensive, general

CAUCUS *n* (<u>kaw</u> kuhs)
a closed committee within a political party; a private committee meeting
The president met with the delegated *caucus* to discuss the national crisis.
synonyms: assembly, convention

CAUSTIC *adj* (<u>kah</u> stihk)
biting, sarcastic
Writer Dorothy Parker gained her reputation for *caustic* wit, and her tombstone is inscribed with a fittingly clever "Excuse my dust."
synonyms: sardonic, incisive

CEDE *v* (seed)
to surrender possession of something
Argentina *ceded* the Falkland Islands to Britain after a brief war.
synonyms: resign, yield, relinquish

CELEBRITY *n* (suh <u>leh</u> brih tee)
fame, widespread acclaim
Some stars find that the price of *celebrity* is too high when they are stalked by crazed fans.
synonyms: eminence, distinction, note, prestige, renown

CELERITY *n* (seh <u>leh</u> rih tee)
speed, haste
The celebrity ran past his fans with great *celerity*.
synonyms: swiftness, briskness

*CENSURE *v* (<u>sehn</u> shuhr)
to criticize, find fault
People are quick to censure alleged criminals without knowing the facts.
synonyms: denounce pillory, vilify, indict, condemn

CERTITUDE *n* (<u>suhr</u> tih tood)
assurance, freedom from doubt
assurance, freedom from doubt
The witness' *certitude* about the night in question had a big impact on the jury.
synonyms: certainty, conviction

CESSATION *n* (seh <u>say</u> shuhn)
a temporary or complete halt
The *cessation* of hostilities ensured that soldiers were able to spend the holidays with their families.
synonyms: arrest, termination

CHAGRIN *n* (shuh grihn)
shame, embarrassment, humiliation
No doubt, the president felt a good deal of *chagrin* after vomiting on his host at the state banquet.
synonyms: mortification, discomfiture

CHAMPION *v* (chaam pee uhn)
to defend or support
Ursula continued to *champion* the rights of the prisoner, even after it was proven beyond a doubt that he was guilty.
synonyms: advocate, promote

CHAOS *n* (kay ahs)
extreme disorder
Because of all the *chaos* in his office, he couldn't find the proposal he was supposed to present.
synonyms: incoherent, random, disorganized

CHARLATAN *n* (shahr luh tihn)
quack, fake
Many believe that Chiropractors are more or less charlatans.
synonyms: imposter, fraud, humbug

CHARY *adj* (chahr ee)
watchful, cautious, extremely shy
Mindful of the fate of the Titanic, the captain was *chary* of navigating the iceberg-filled sea.
synonyms: wary, careful

CHASTE *adj* (chayst)
pure, virginal
It is important in the Baptist church for girls to behave in a *chaste* manner.
synonyms: celibate, virtuous

CHASTISE *v* (chaa stiez)
to punish, discipline, scold
Bruno was quick to *chastise* his peers for having different beliefs than his.
synonyms: castigate, penalize

CHERUBIC *adj* (chuh roo bihk) (chehr uh bihk)
innocent, resembling a cherub
Her *cherubic* appearance made people think she was sweet, although the opposite was true.
synonyms: angelic, babyish

CHICANERY *n* (shih kayn ree) (shi kay nuh ree) ("ch" can replace "sh")
artful trickery, fraud, or deception
Used car salesmen often use *chicanery* to sell their beat-up old cars.
synonyms: deceit, duplicity, dishonesty

CHIDE *v* (chied)
to scold, express disapproval
Florence *chided* her poodle for eating the birthday cake she had baked for her friend.
synonyms: chasten, chastise, admonish, reprimand, reprove

CHIMERICAL *adj* (kie <u>mehr</u> ih kuhl) (kie <u>meer</u> ih kuhl)
fanciful; imaginary, impossible
The inventor's plans seemed *chimerical* to the conservative businessman from whom he was asking for financial support.
synonyms: illusory, unreal

CHOLERIC *adj* (<u>kah</u> luhr ihk)
easily angered, short-tempered
The *choleric* principal raged at the students who had come late to school.
synonyms: irritable, surly, wrathful, irate

CHORTLE *v* (<u>chohr</u> tuhl)
to chuckle
I used to love to hear my Grandfather *chortle* while reading the Sunday comics.
synonyms: laugh, chuckle, snort

*CIRCUITOUS *adj* (suhr <u>kyoo</u> ih tuhs)
indirect, roundabout
The venue was only a short walk from the train station, but a roadblock meant I had to take a *circuitous* route.
synonyms: lengthy, devious

CIRCUMLOCUTION *n* (suhr kuhm loh <u>kyoo</u> shuhn)
roundabout, lengthy way of saying something
He avoided discussing the real issues with endless *circumlocutions*.
synonyms: wordiness, evasion

CIRCUMSPECT *adj* (suhr kuhm <u>spehkt</u>)
cautious, wary
His failures have made Jack far more *circumspect* in his exploits than he used to be.
synonyms: prudent, careful, chary

CIRCUMVENT *v* (suhr kuhm <u>vehnt</u>)
to go around; avoid
Laura was able to *circumvent* the hospital's regulations, slipping into her mother's room long after visiting hours were over.
synonyms: evade, sidestep

CIVIL *adj* (<u>sih</u> vuhl)
polite
Police officers are almost always *civil* to the general public, although cases of police brutality do occur.
synonyms: courteous, communal

*CLAIRVOYANT *adj* (klayr <u>voy</u> uhnt)
psychic; extremely persceptive
My *clairvoyant* aunt claimed to have communicated with the ghost of Abraham Lincoln.
synonyms: prophetic, oracular

*CLAMOR *n* (<u>klaa</u> muhr)
noisy outcry
The *clamor* of children playing outside made it impossible for me to study.
synonyms: din, cacophony, racket, uproar

*CLANDESTINE *adj* (klaan <u>dehs</u> tien)
secretive, concealed for a darker purpose
The double agent paid many *clandestine* visits to the president's office in the dead of night.
synonyms: covert, underground

CLAUSTROPHOBIA *n* (klaw struh <u>foh</u> bee uh)
fear of small, confined places
Isaac's *claustrophobia* made it impossible for him to join his friends in exploring the cave.
synonyms: anxiety, discomfort

CLEAVE *v* (kleev)
to split or separate or to stick, cling, adhere
Brent *cleaved* the log in two in one mighty blow.
synonyms: sunder, dissever; cohere, bond

CLEMENCY *n* (<u>kleh</u> muhn see)
merciful leniency
Kyle begged for *clemency*, claiming that he had been under the influence of his allergy medication when he robbed the bank.
synonyms: indulgence, pardon

CLOD *n* (klahd)
a chunk of earth or clay; a bumbling person
Poor Claude has no more brains than a *clod*.
synonyms: lump, nugget, dolt, oaf, dullard

CLOISTER *v* (<u>kloy</u> stuhr)
to confine, seclude
The Montagues *cloistered* their wayward daughter in a convent, hoping to keep her out of trouble.
synonyms: isolate, sequester

*CLOYING *adj* (<u>kloy</u> ing)
sickly sweet, excessive
When Dave and Liz got together their *cloying* affection towards one another often made their friends ill.
synonyms: excessive, fulsome

COAGULATE *v* (koh <u>aag</u> yuh layt)
to clot; to cause to thicken
Hemophiliacs can bleed to death from a minor cut because their blood does not *coagulate*.
synonyms: jell, congeal

COALESCE *v* (koh uh <u>lehs</u>)
to grow together or cause to unite as one
The different factions of the organization want to *coalesce* to form one united front against their opponents.
synonyms: combine, merge

CODDLE *v* (<u>kah</u> duhl)
to baby, treat indulgently
The strict grandmother frowned disapprovingly as her daughter *coddled* the whining infant.
synonyms: pamper, spoil, cosset

COERCE *v* (koh <u>ehrs</u>)
to compel by force or intimidation
The mayor was willing to *coerce* the voters to get his way by threatening to raise taxes.
synonyms: domineer, constrain

*COGENT *adj* (<u>koh</u> juhnt)
logically forceful; compelling, convincing
Swayed by the *cogent* argument of the defense, the jury had no choice but to acquit the defendant.
synonyms: persuasive, winning

COGNITION *n* (kahg <u>nih</u> shuhn)
mental process by which knowledge is acquired
If scientists completely understood the processes of *cognition*, education could be revolutionized.
synonyms: awareness, perception, reasoning, judgment, intuition

COHABIT *v* (koh <u>haa</u> biht)
to live together
Ron's parents didn't approve of his plan to *cohabit* with his girlfriend in the city.
synonyms: room, couple, pair up

COHERENT *adj* (koh <u>heer</u> uhnt)
intelligible, lucid, understandable
Cathy was so tired that her speech was barely *coherent*.
synonyms: orderly, logical, consistent

*COLLABORATE *v* (kuh <u>laab</u> uh rayt)
to cooperate, work together
To make movies, you must be prepared to *collaborate* with other artists of different temperaments.
synonyms: cooperate, collude, conspire, co-author

COLLOQUIAL *adj* (kuh <u>loh</u> kwee uhl)
characteristic of informal speech
The book was written in a *colloquial* style so it would be user-friendlier.
synonyms: conversational, idiomatic

COLLUSION *n* (kuh <u>loo</u> zhuhn)
collaboration, complicity, conspiracy
It came to light that the police chief and the mafia had a *collusion* in running the numbers racket.
synonyms: intrigue, machination, connivance

COMELINESS *n* (<u>kuhm</u> lee nihs)
physical grace and beauty
Ann's *comeliness* made her perfect for the role of Sleeping Beauty.
synonyms: attractiveness, seemliness

COMMENSURATE *adj* (kuh <u>mehn</u> suhr ayt)
proportional
Steve was given a salary *commensurate* with his experience.
synonyms: corresponding, comparable

COMMODIOUS *adj* (kuh <u>moh</u> dee uhs)
roomy, spacious
Jesse was able to stretch out fully in the *commodious* bathtub.
synonyms: capacious, extensive, ample

COMMUTE *v* (kuh <u>myoot</u>)
to change a penalty to a less severe one
In exchange for cooperating with detectives on another case, the criminal had his charges *commuted*.
synonyms: exchange, mitigate

COMPENSATE *v* (<u>kah</u> pehn sayt)
to repay or reimburse
The moving company *compensated* me for the furniture they broke while moving my stuff to the new house.
synonyms: indemnify, recompense, balance

*COMPLACENT *adj* (kuhm <u>play</u> sihnt)
self-satisfied, smug
Alfred always shows a *complacent* smile whenever he wins the spelling bee.
synonyms: contented, unconcerned

COMPLEMENT *v* (<u>kahm</u> pluh muhnt)
to complete, perfect
Gina's pink sweater was a good *complement* to her red hair.
synonyms: harmonize, enhance, supplement

*COMPLIANT *adj* (kuhm <u>plie</u> uhnt)
adj (kuhm <u>plie</u> uhnt)
submissive, yielding
The boss was unused to an assistant who spoke her mind, but he grew to respect the fact that she wasn't *compliant*.
synonyms: malleable, bending

COMPLICITY *n* (kuhm <u>plih</u> sih tee)
knowing partnership in wrongdoing
The two boys exchanged a look of sly *complicity* when their father shouted "Who broke the window?"
synonyms: involvement, collaboration, cahoots

*COMPROMISE *v* (<u>kahm</u> pruh miez)
to concede something, take the middle ground
One teacher wanted to fail the student but the other wanted to give her an A, so they decided to *compromise* and give her a C.
synonyms: settle, mediate, negotiate

COMPULSIVE *adj* (kuhm <u>puhl</u> sihv)
obsessive, fanatic
Reggie told his boss that he had once climbed Mount Everest with a yak on his back because he is a *compulsive* liar.
synonyms: driven, pathological

COMPUNCTION *n* (kuhm <u>puhnk</u> shuhn)
feeling of uneasiness caused by guilt or regret
It is often said that psychopaths have no consciences, suffering little *compunction* for the pain
they cause.
synonyms: dubiety, qualm, scruple

CONCEDE *v* (kuhn <u>seed</u>)
to yield, admit
Ralph had to *concede* to his wife; he should have checked the gas before driving into the wilderness.
synonyms: grant, acknowledge, recognize

CONCILIATE *v* (kuhn <u>sih</u> lee ayt)
To become agreeable; to appease
Fred wanted to *conciliate* after he fought with Marge, so he bought her flowers.
synonyms: diplomatic, friendly, generous

CONCORD *n* (<u>kahn</u> kohrd)
agreement
The sisters are now in *concord* about the car they had to share.
synonyms: accord, concurrence

CONCUR *v* (kuhn <u>kuhr</u>)
to agree
When Jamal proposed that the staff devote more time to quality control, everyone *concurred*, and the
change was made.
synonyms: assent, accede, acquiesce, consent

*CONDESCENDING *adj* (kahn dih <u>sehn</u> ding)
possessing an attitude of superiority
His *condescending* attitude towards non-Ivy League trained scholars annoyed many of his colleagues.
synonyms: patronizing, superior, smug, supercilious

*CONDITIONAL *adj* (kuhn <u>dih</u> shuhn uhl)
depending on a condition
His employment by the law firm was *conditional* upon his being able to pass the bar exam.
synonyms: provisional, dependent, contingent, tentative

CONDONE *v* (kuhn <u>dohn</u>)
to pardon or forgive; overlook, justify, or excuse a fault
"We cannot *condone* your behavior," said Raj's parents after he missed his curfew. "You're grounded."
synonyms: defend, vindicate, dismiss

CONFISCATE *v* (<u>kahn</u> fih skayt)
to appropriate, seize
After the FBI agents *confiscated* the heroin shipment, they arrested the drug dealers.
synonyms: commandeer, arrogate, expropriate

CONFLAGRATION *n* (kahn fluh <u>gray</u> shuhn)
big, destructive fire
After the *conflagration* had finally died down, the city center was nothing but a mass of
blackened embers.
synonyms: blaze, inferno

*CONFORMIST n (kuhn <u>fohr</u> mihst)
person who complies with accepted rules and customs
Many people were considered to be conformists in the xenophobic, button-down world of the 1950s.
synonyms: orthodox, conventional, mainstream, conservative

CONFOUND v (kuhn <u>fownd</u>)
to baffle, perplex
Sarah didn't mean to *confound* her students when she wrote the equation on the board.
synonyms: overwhelm, confuse, disconcert, entangle, muddle

CONGEAL v (kuhn <u>jeel</u>)
to become thick or solid; to make rigid
The ice in the cooler made the butter *congeal*, forming a sticky mass.
synonyms: jell, coagulate, clot

CONGENIAL adj (kuhn <u>jee</u> nee uhl) (kuhn <u>jeen</u> yuhl)
similar in tastes and habits; having a pleasant disposition
Couples with *congenial* personalities stay together longer than couples who are polar opposites.
synonyms: affable, pleasurable, amiable, personable, agreeable

*CONGREGATION n (kahn gruh <u>gay</u> shuhn)
a crowd of people, an assembly
After he moved the *congregation* with his tearful confession, they agreed to absolve him of his misdeeds.
synonyms: group, gathering, fold, multitude

CONJECTURE n (kuhn <u>jehk</u> shuhr)
inference, prediction
The actor refused to comment, forcing gossip columnists to make *conjectures* on his love life.
synonyms: postulation, hypothesis, supposition, surmise

CONJUGAL adj (<u>kahn</u> juh guhl)
pertaining to marriage
Larry terminated all *conjugal* relations with his wife without warning.
synonyms: connubial, matrimonial, spousal, marital

CONNIVE v (kuh <u>niev</u>)
to conspire, scheme
The schoolmaster accused Mary of trying to *connive* her way onto the cheer squad.
synonyms: collude, plot, contrive

CONSCIENTIOUS adj (kahn shee <u>ehn</u> shuhs)
governed by conscience; careful and thorough
Harrison was always *conscientious* about writing in his diary, never missing a day if he could help it.
synonyms: principled, scrupulous, assiduous

CONSECRATE v (<u>kahn</u> suh krayt)
to declare sacred; dedicate to a worship
The priest *consecrated* the clothing of the saint, and it was placed in the church to be.
synonyms: sanctify, devote

CONSOLATION *n* (kahn suh <u>lay</u> shuhn)
something providing comfort or solace for a loss or hardship
The millions she inherited were little *consolation* to the grief-stricken widow.
synonyms: condolence, solace

CONSOLIDATE *v* (kuhn <u>sahl</u> ih dayt)
to combine, incorporate
The author was asked to *consolidate* various articles she had previously published into one book.
synonyms: merge, amalgamate, pool

CONSONANT *adj* (<u>kahn</u> suh nuhnt)
consistent with, in agreement with
The pitiful raise Ingrid received was consonant with the low opinion her manager had of
her performance.
synonyms: accordant, compatible, congruous

CONSTITUENT *n* (kuhn <u>stih</u> choo uhnt)
component, part; citizen, voter
A machine will not function properly if one of its *constituents* is defective.
synonyms: element, factor

CONSTRAINT *n* (kuhn <u>straynt</u>)
something that restricts or confines within prescribed bounds
Given the *constraints* of the budget, it was impossible to accomplish my goals.
synonyms: limitation, check

CONSTRUE *v* (kuhn <u>stroo</u>)
to explain or interpret
"I wasn't sure how to *construe* that last remark he made," said Delia, "but I suspect it was an insult."
synonyms: analyze, translate

CONSUMMATE *adj* (<u>kahn</u> suh muht) (<u>kahn</u> soo miht)
accomplished, complete, perfect
The skater delivered a *consummate* performance and won the gold.
synonyms: thorough, exhaustive, ideal, flawless

*CONTEMPTUOUS *adj* (kuhn <u>tehmp</u> choo uhs)
scornful; expressing contempt
The diners were intimidated by the waiter's *contemptuous* manner.
synonyms: derisive, disdainful, supercilious

CONTENTIOUS *adj* (kuhn <u>tehn</u> shuhs)
quarrelsome, disagreeable, belligerent
The *contentious* gentleman in the bar ridiculed anything anyone said.
synonyms: argumentative, fractious, litigious

CONTINENCE *n* (<u>kahn</u> tih nihns)
self-control, self-restraint
Lucy exhibited impressive *continence* in steering clear of fattening foods, and she lost 50 pounds.
synonyms: moderation, discipline

CONTRAVENE *v* (kahn truh <u>veen</u>)
to contradict, deny, act contrary to
The watchman *contravened* his official instructions by leaving his post for an hour.
synonyms: violate, transgress, disobey

CONTRITE *adj* (kuhn <u>triet</u>)
deeply sorrowful and repentant for a wrong
After three residents were mugged in the lobby while the watchman was away from his post, he felt very *contrite*.
synonyms: regretful, apologetic, remorseful

*CONUNDRUM *n* (kuh <u>nuhn</u> druhm)
riddle, puzzle, or problem with no solution
The old man puzzled over the *conundrum* for hours, but he eventually gave up in disgust.
synonyms: enigma, mystery, paradox, poser

CONVALESCE *v* (kahn vuhl <u>ehs</u>)
to gradually recovery after an illness
After her bout with malaria, Tatiana needed to *convalesce* for a whole month.
synonyms: heal, recuperate

CONVENE *v* (kuhn <u>veen</u>)
to meet, come together, assemble
The members of the board *convene* at least once a week.
synonyms: sit, congregate, muster, gather

CONVENTIONAL *adj* (kuhn <u>vehn</u> shuhn uhl)
typical, customary, commonplace
Conventional wisdom today says that a good job requires a college education.
synonyms: traditional, usual, normal

*CONVERGENCE *n* (kuhn <u>vehr</u> juhns)
the state of separate elements joining or coming together
A *convergence* of factors led to the tragic unfolding of World War I.
synonyms: union, concurrence, coincidence

CONVOKE *v* (kuhn <u>vohk</u>)
to call together, summon
The president has to *convoke* a group of experts to advise him on how to deal with a crisis.
synonyms: assemble, convene, gather

CONVOLUTED *adj* (kahn vuh <u>loo</u> tehd)
twisted, complicated, involved
Although many people read *A Brief History of Time*, few could follow its *convoluted* ideas and theories.
synonyms: intricate, elaborate, baroque

COPIOUS *adj* (<u>koh</u> pee uhs)
abundant, plentiful
The hostess had prepared *copious* amounts of food for the banquet.
synonyms: ample, abounding

CORPOREAL *adj* (kohr <u>pohr</u> ee uhl)
having to do with the body; tangible, material
Makiko realized that the supposed ghost was *corporeal* in nature when it bumped into a chair.
synonyms: somatic, concrete, physical

CORPULENCE *n* (<u>kohr</u> pyuh luhns)
obesity, bulkiness
Egbert's *corpulence* increased because he didn't get any exercise.
synonyms: stoutness, rotundity, portliness, plumpness

*CORROBORATE *v* (kuh <u>rahb</u> uhr ayt)
to confirm, verify
All the DA needed were fingerprints to *corroborate* the witness's testimony that he saw the defendant in the victim's apartment.
synonyms: confirm, prove, substantiate, warrant

COSMOPOLITAN *adj* (kahz muh <u>pah</u> lih tuhn)
sophisticated, worldwide experience
Diplomats are usually more *cosmopolitan* than people who have never left the towns they were born in.
synonyms: worldly, urbane, civilized

COTERIE *n* (<u>koh</u> tuh ree)
an intimate group of persons with a similar purpose
Judith invited a *coterie* of fellow stamp enthusiasts to a stamp-trading party.
synonyms: clique, set

COUNTENANCE *n* (<u>kown</u> tuh nuhns)
to favor, support
The babysitter showed no *countenance* when the kids started a food fight.
synonyms: condone, approve, tolerate

COVEN *n* (<u>kuh</u> vihn)
group of witches or people with similar interests
The *coven* cackled as they brewed a potion that would turn the prince into a frog.
synonyms: circle, coterie, cult

COVERT *adj* (koh <u>vuhrt</u>)
secretive, not openly shown
The *covert* military operation wasn't disclosed until weeks later after it was determined to be a success.
synonyms: veiled

COVET *v* (<u>kuh</u> viht)
to desire strongly something possessed by another
Harold *coveted* his neighbor's new Mercedes Benz because he did not have enough money to buy his own.
synonyms: envy, crave

CRASS *adj* (kraas)
crude, unrefined
Miss Manner watched in horror as her *crass* date belched loudly and snapped his fingers at the waiter.
synonyms: coarse, boorish

CRAVEN *adj* (<u>kray</u> vuhn)
lacking courage
The *craven* lion cringed in the corner of his cage, terrified of the mouse.
synonyms: faint-hearted, timid, spineless

CREDIBLE *adj* (<u>kreh</u> duh buhl)
plausible, believable
With such a *credible* witness testifying against his client, the lawyer's chances of winning the case were small.
synonyms: possible, reliable

CREDULOUS *adj* (<u>kreh</u> juh luhs)
gullible, trusting
Although some four-year-olds believe in the Easter Bunny, only the most *credulous* nine-year-olds do.
synonyms: uncritical, naïve

CREED *n* (kreed)
statement of belief or principle
It was a basic tenet of the old man's *creed* that killing was indefensible.
synonyms: tenet, credo, doctrine, dogma, precept

CRYPTIC *adj* (<u>krihp</u> tihk)
Having hidden meaning; mysterious
Sherlock Holmes was concerned by the *cryptic* message left on his doorstep.
synonyms: recondite, inscrutable, enigmatic

CUISINE *n* (kwih <u>zeen</u>)
characteristic style of cooking
French *cuisine* is delicious but fattening.
synonyms: food, fare

CULL *v* (kuhl)
to select, weed out
You should *cull* the words you need to study from all the flash cards.
synonyms: pick, extract

CULMINATION *n* (kuhl mih <u>nay</u> shuhn)
climax, final stage
Fireworks marked the *culmination* of the festivities.
synonyms: fulfillment, consummation, acme, apex, zenith

CULPABLE *adj* (<u>kuhl</u> puh buhl)
guilty, responsible for wrong
The CEO is *culpable* for the bankruptcy of the company; he was, after all, in charge of it.
synonyms: blameworthy, answerable

*CUMULATIVE *adj* (<u>kyoom</u> yuh luh tihv)
increasing, collective
The new employee didn't mind her job at first, but the daily petty indignities had a *cumulative* demoralizing effect.
synonyms: added up, gradual

CUPIDITY *n* (kyoo <u>pih</u> dih tee)
greed; strong desire
The thief stared at the shining jewels with *cupidity* in his gleaming eyes.
synonyms: avarice, rapacity, covetousness

CURMUDGEON *n* (kuhr <u>muh</u> juhn)
cranky person, usually old
Tom was a notorious *curmudgeon* who snapped at anyone who disturbed him for any reason.
synonyms: grouch, crab, coot

CURSORY *adj* (<u>kuhr</u> suh ree)
hastily done, superficial
The copy editor gave the article a *cursory* once-over, missing dozens of errors.
synonyms: shallow, careless

CURT *adj* (kuhrt)
abrupt, short with words
The grouchy shop assistant was *curt* with one of her customers, which resulted in a reprimand from her manager.
synonyms: terse, rude

CURTAIL *v* (kuhr <u>tayl</u>)
to shorten; cutoff
I had to *curtail* my vacation in the Bahamas after I ran out of money.
synonyms: crop, lop, truncate, trim, prune

CYNIC *n* (<u>sih</u> nihk)
person who distrusts the motives of others
Have we become a nation of *cynics* who have lost faith in our own system of government?
synonyms: skeptic, scoffer, doubter

D

DAINTY *adj* (<u>dayn</u> tee)
delicate, sweet
The slim, *dainty* girl made a perfect ballerina.
synonyms: fine, graceful

DAUNT *v* (dawnt)
to discourage, intimidate
She tried hard not to let the enormity of the situation *daunt* her.
synonyms: demoralize, dishearten, consternate, cow

DEARTH *n* (duhrth)
a lack, scarcity, insufficiency
The *dearth* of supplies in our city made it difficult to survive the blizzard.
synonyms: absence, shortage

DEBASE *v* (dih <u>bays</u>)
to degrade or lower in quality or stature
The president's deceitful actions *debased* the stature of his office.
synonyms: demean, denigrate, defile, adulterate

DEBAUCH *v* (dih <u>bahch</u>)
to corrupt, seduce from virtue or duty; indulge
The other players tried hard to *debauch* the rookie, but he held fast to team rules.
synonyms: carouse, riot, debase, defile

DEBILITATE *v* (dih <u>bih</u> lih tayt)
to weaken, enfeeble
Debilitated by the flu, the postman was barely able to finish his rounds.
synonyms: devitalize, enervate, exhaust, drain, sap

DEBUNK *v* (dih <u>buhnk</u>)
to discredit, disprove
It was the teacher's mission in life to *debunk* the myth that girls are bad at math.
synonyms: belie, controvert, contradict, confute, explode

DEBUTANTE *n* (<u>dehb</u> yoo tahnt)
young woman making debut in high society
The *debutante* spent hours dressing for her very first ball, hoping to catch the eye of an eligible bachélor.
synonyms: maiden, lady

DECLIVITY *n* (dih <u>klih</u> vih tee)
downward slope
Because the village was situated on the *declivity* of a hill, it never flooded.
synonyms: decline, descent, grade, slant, tilt

*DECOROUS *adj* (<u>deh</u> kuhr uhs) (deh <u>kohr</u> uhs)
proper, tasteful, socially correct
The countess trained her daughters in the finer points of *decorous* behavior, hoping they would make a good impression when she presented them at Court.
synonyms: polite, courteous, appropriate, comme il faut

DECRY *v* (dih <u>crie</u>)
to belittle, openly condemn
Governments all over the world *decry* the dictator's vicious massacre of the helpless peasants.
synonyms: deride, disparage, depreciate, derogate, minimize

DEFACE *v* (dih <u>fays</u>)
to mar the appearance of, vandalize
After the wall was torn down, the students began to *deface* the statues of Communist leaders of former Eastern bloc.
synonyms: spoil, impair, disfigure

DEFAMATORY *adj* (dih <u>faam</u> uh tohr ee)
injurious to the reputation
The tabloid was sued for making *defamatory* statements about the celebrity.
synonyms: libelous, slanderous

DEFERENTIAL *adj* (dehf uh <u>rehn</u> shuhl)
respectful and polite in a submissive way
The young law clerk showed the Supreme Court justice very *deferential* treatment.
synonyms: courteous, obsequious

DEFILE *v* (dih <u>fiel</u>)
to dirty, spoil; to disgrace, dishonor
The natives became enraged after the insensitive explorer *defiled* their temple by spitting in it.
synonyms: debase, degrade, corrupt, desecrate, besmear

DEFORM *v* (dih <u>fohrm</u>)
to disfigure, spoil
Betty shrieked at the sight of her husband about to deform the birthday cake she had worked all day on.
synonyms: contort, twist, mar, misshape

DEFT *adj* (dehft)
skillful, dexterous
It was a pleasure to watch the *deft* carpenter as he repaired the furniture.
synonyms: adept, adroit, nimble, proficient, expert

DEFUNCT *adj* (dih <u>fuhnkt</u>)
no longer existing, dead, extinct
That factory, which used to produce bowler hats, has been *defunct* for many years.
synonyms: gone, vanished, deceased, departed, extinguished

DELECTABLE *adj* (dih <u>lehkt</u> uh buhl)
appetizing, delicious
"That cake was simply *delectable*!" cooed Mrs. Vanderbilt, congratulating the chef.
synonyms: tasty, savory, succulent, palatable

DELEGATE *v* (<u>deh</u> lih gayt)
to give powers to another
After learning to *delegate* more work to his assistants, the manager reduced his stress level significantly.
synonyms: assign, entrust, commit, appoint, authorize

*DELETERIOUS *adj* (dehl ih <u>teer</u> ee uhs)
subtly or unexpectedly harmful
If only we had known the clocks were defective before putting them on the market, it wouldn't have been quite so *deleterious* to our reputation.
synonyms: injurious, adverse, inimical, hurtful

*DELINEATION *n* (dih lihn ee <u>ay</u> shuhn)
depiction, representation
Mrs. Baxter was very satisfied with the artist's *delineation* of her new mansion.
synonyms: portrayal, illustration, picture, portraiture, figuration

DELUGE *v* (<u>dehl</u> yooj) (<u>dehl</u> yoozh) (<u>day</u> looj) (<u>day</u> loozh) (dih <u>looj</u>) (dih <u>loozh</u>)
to submerge, overwhelm
The popular actor was deluged with fan mail.
synonyms: engulf, immerse, inundate, whelm, swamp

*DEMAGOGUE *n* (<u>deh</u> muh gahg) (<u>deh</u> muh gawg)
a leader, rabble-rouser, usually appealing to emotion or prejudice
Hitler began his political career as a *demagogue*, giving fiery speeches in beer halls.
synonyms: agitator, inciter, instigator

DEMEAN *v* (dih <u>meen</u>)
to degrade, humiliate, humble
The editor felt that it would *demean* the newspaper to publish letters containing obscenities.
synonyms: abase, desecrate, defile, lower, diminish

DEMOTE *v* (dih <u>moht</u>)
to reduce to a lower grade or rank
The army will *demote* any soldier who disobeys orders.
synonyms: degrade, downgrade, diminish, humble, diminish

DEMUR *v* (dih <u>muhr</u>)
to express doubts or objections
When scientific authorities claimed that all the planets revolved around the Earth, Galileo, with his superior understanding of the situation, was forced to *demur*.
synonyms: protest, remonstrate, kick, expostulate, dissent

DENIGRATE *v* (<u>deh</u> nih grayt)
to slur or blacken someone's reputation
The people still loved the coach, despite his media's attempts to *denigrate* his character.
synonyms: malign, belittle, disparage, vilify, slander

DENOUNCE *v* (dih <u>nowns</u>)
to accuse, blame
After Stella *denounced* her coworkers for stealing pencils from the office, she was promoted.
synonyms: censure, criticize, condemn, vilify, brand

DEPICT *v* (dih <u>pihkt</u>)
to describe, represent
Official royal portraits generally *depict* their subjects in a flattering light.
synonyms: portray, render, delineate, limn, picture

DEPLETE *v* (dih <u>pleet</u>)
to use up, exhaust
If we do not do something about the pollution problem, we will completely *deplete* the ozone layer.
synonyms: consume, dissipate, sap, devour

DEPLORE *v* (dih <u>plohr</u>)
to express or feel grief of; regret strongly
I deplore the fact that my relationship with my boyfriend is over.
synonyms: bemoan, lament, complain

DEPLOY *v* (dih <u>ploy</u>)
to spread out strategically over an area
The general *deployed* his troops over the region, overwhelming the enemy through sheer numbers.
synonyms: position, distribute, array

DEPOSE *v* (dih pohs)
to remove from a high position, as from a throne
The king spent the rest of his life in exile after his countrymen moved to *depose* him.
synonyms: unseat, dethrone, topple, overthrow, displace

DEPRAVITY *n* (dih praav ih tee)
sinfulness, moral corruption
The *depravity* of the actor's Hollywood lifestyle shocked his traditional parents.
synonyms: decadence, debauchery, enormity, corruption, degradation

DEPRECATE *v* (dehp rih kayt)
to belittle, disparage
Ernest *deprecated* his own contribution instead of praising the efforts of his coworkers.
synonyms: minimize, denigrate, discount

DERIDE *v* (dih ried)
to laugh at contemptuously, to make fun of
As soon as Jorge heard the others *deriding* Anthony, he came to his defense.
synonyms: ridicule

DERIVATIVE *adj* (dih rihv uh tihv)
copied or adapted; not original
The TV show was so obviously *derivative* of *Seinfeld* that viewers who prize originality were not
interested in watching it.
synonyms: secondhand, parroted, apish

DESECRATE *v* (dehs ih krayt)
to abuse something sacred
The archaeologist tried to convince the tourists not the *desecrate* the shrine, but they did anyway.
synonyms: defile, profane, violate, degrade

DESICCATE *v* (deh sih kayt)
to dry completely, dehydrate
After a few weeks of lying on the desert's baking sands, the cow's carcass began to *desiccate*.
synonyms: parch, evaporate, exsiccate

DESIST *v* (dih sihst) (dih zihst)
to stop doing something
The old man was ordered to *desist* from breeding rats in his apartment by the manager.
synonyms: cease, abort, discontinue, end, quit

DESPONDENT *adj* (dih spahn duhnt)
feeling discouraged and dejected
Mr. Baker was lonely and *despondent* after his wife's death.
synonyms: sad, depressed, desolate, dejected, forlorn

DESPOT *n* (dehs puht) (dehs paht)
tyrannical ruler
The *despot* executed half the nobles in his court on a whim.
synonyms: authoritarian, autocrat, dictator, totalitarian

DESTITUTE *adj* (<u>dehs</u> tih toot) (dehs tih <u>tyoot</u>)
very poor, poverty-stricken
After the stock market crash, there were a lot of *destitute* people looking for hope.
synonyms: insolvent, impecunious, penurious, needy, broke

DETER *adj* (dih <u>tuhr</u>)
to discourage; prevent from happening
Some sociologists claim that the death penalty does not really *deter* criminals from committing crimes.
synonyms: avert, forestall, preclude

DETRIMENTAL *adj* (deht ruh <u>mehn</u> tuhl)
causing harm or injury
It is generally acknowledged that cigarette smoking is a *detrimental* habit.
synonyms: adverse, deleterious, inimical, destructive, hurtful

DEVIATE *v* (<u>dee</u> vee ayt)
to stray, wander
As long as you don't *deviate* from the trail, you should be fine out there in the wilderness.
synonyms: diverge, dissent, digress, disagree, divert

DEVOID *adj* (dih <u>voyd</u>)
being without
Roger is utterly *devoid* of tact; did you hear him tell that off-color joke at the funeral?
synonyms: destitute, empty, vacant, null, bare

DEVOUT *adj* (dih <u>vowt</u>)
Devoted, as to religion
Priests and nuns are known to be *devout* people.
synonyms: pious, observant, sincere, earnest, reverent

DEXTEROUS *adj* (<u>dehk</u> stuhr uhs) (<u>dehk</u> struhs)
skilled physically or mentally
The gymnast who won the contest was far more *dexterous* than the other competitors.
synonyms: deft, adroit, skilled, nimble, adept

DIALECT *n* (<u>die</u> uh lehkt)
regional style of speaking
Jay has lost his original southern *dialect* completely; he sounds like he was born in New York City.
synonyms: argot, idiom, patois, jargon, vernacular

*DIAPHANOUS *adj* (die <u>aaf</u> uh nuhs)
allowing light to show through; delicate
These *diaphanous* curtains do nothing to block out the sunlight.
synonyms: sheer, transparent, gauzy, tenuous, translucent

DIATRIBE *n* (<u>die</u> uh trieb)
bitter verbal attack
During the CEO's lengthy *diatribe*, the board members managed to remain calm and self-controlled.
synonyms: tirade, jeremiad, fulmination, harangue, philippic

DICHOTOMY *n* (die <u>kah</u> tuh mee)
division into two parts; contradictory qualities
There was a marked *dichotomy* in the company between management and labor.
synonyms: split, distinction, bifurcation, opposition

DICTUM *n* (<u>dihk</u> tuhm)
authoritative statement
'You have time to lean, you have time to clean,' was the *dictum* our boss made us live by.
synonyms: adage, apothegm, aphorism, decree, edict

DIDACTIC *adj* (die <u>daak</u> tihk)
excessively instructive
The father was overly *didactic* with his children, turning every activity into a lesson.
synonyms: educational, improving, moralistic

DIFFIDENCE *n* (<u>dih</u> fih duhns) (<u>dih</u> fih dehns)
shyness, lack of confidence
Steve's *diffidence* during the job interview stemmed from his nervous nature and lack of experience.
synonyms: timidity, reticence

DIFFUSE *adj* (dih <u>fyooz</u>)
to spread out widely, to scatter freely, to disseminate
They turned on the fan, but all that did was *diffuse* the cigarette smoke throughout the room.
synonyms: disperse, soften

*DIGRESS *v* (die <u>grehs</u>)
to turn aside, especially from the main point; to stray from the subject
The professor repeatedly *digressed* from the topic, boring his students.
synonyms: deviate, wander

DILAPIDATED *adj* (dih <u>laap</u> ih dayt ihd)
in disrepair, run down
Rather than get discouraged, the architect saw great potential in the *dilapidated* house.
synonyms: decayed, fallen into partial ruin

DILATE *v* (die <u>layt</u>) (<u>die</u> layt)
to enlarge, swell, extend
When you enter a darkened room, the pupils of your eyes *dilate* to let in more light.
synonyms: expand, spread, expatiate

DILATORY *adj* (<u>dihl</u> uh tohr ee)
slow, tending to delay
The congressman used *dilatory* measures to delay the passage of the bill.
synonyms: sluggish, tardy, unhurried

*DILIGENT *adj* (dihl uh guhnt)
characterized by steady and earnest application of effort
He was a *diligent* detective who gave up on a case only after all his leads had been exhausted.
synonyms: dogged, persistent, assiduous, industrious

DIMINUTIVE *adj* (dih <u>mihn</u> yuh tihv)
small
Napoleon made up for his *diminutive* stature with his aggressive personality, terrifying his courtiers.
synonyms: short, tiny, wee, minuscule

DIRGE *n* (duhrj)
funeral hymn
The deceased's relatives wept as the mournful *dirge* was played on the funeral home's organ.
synonyms: elegy, threnody, lament

DISARRAY *n* (dihs uh <u>ray</u>)
clutter, disorder
Johnny's room fell into *disarray* after his mother decided to stop cleaning it up for him.
synonyms: chaos, confusion, muddle, jumble, disorganization

DISBURSE *v* (dihs <u>buhrs</u>)
to pay out
The government *disbursed* millions of dollars to reform elementary schools.
synonyms: spend, allot, apportion, dispense, distribute

DISCERN *v* (dihs <u>uhrn</u>)
to perceive something obscure
It is easy to *discern* the difference between real butter and butter-flavored topping.
synonyms: descry, observe, recognize, glimpse, distinguish

DISCLOSE *v* (dihs <u>klohs</u>)
to open up, divulge
The CIA agent was forced to *disclose* top secrets to the enemy.
synonyms: confide, reveal, impart

*DISCORDANT *adj* (dihs <u>kohr</u> duhnt)
disagreeing; at variance
The feelings about the child's education were becoming more and more *discordant*.
synonyms: dissonant, inharmonious, cacophonous

*DISCREDIT *v* (dihs <u>kreh</u> diht)
to disbelieve, claim as false
Henry was upset when a member of his squad tried to *discredit* his coaching methods.
synonyms: shame, repudiate

DISCREPANCY *n* (dih <u>skrehp</u> uhn see)
difference between
The obvious *discrepancy* between the appearance of the man and the photo in his passport led officials to believe that the passport was a fake.
synonyms: contradiction, divergence, incongruity, disparity, incompatibility

DISCRETIONARY *adj* (dih <u>skrehsh</u> uh nehr ee)
subject to one's own judgment
Ambassadors have some *discretionary* powers, although they must bow to the authority of the secretary of state.
synonyms: elective, optional, voluntary, unforced

*DISDAIN *v* (dihs <u>dayn</u>)
to regard with scorn and contempt
The gorgeous contestant *disdained* her competitors, certain that she would win the Miss America crown.
synonyms: despise, scout, snub, spurn

DISHEVELED *adj* (dih <u>shehv</u> uhld)
untidy, disarranged, unkempt
After his car broke down and he had to walk to work through the rain, Pete was quite *disheveled*.
synonyms: disordered, messy, rumpled

*DISINTERESTED *adj* (dihs <u>ihn</u> trih stihd) (dihs <u>ihn</u> tuh reh stihd)
fair-minded, unbiased
A fair trial is made possible by the selection of *disinterested* jurors.
synonyms: impartial, unprejudiced

DISPARAGE *v* (dih <u>spaar</u> ihj)
to belittle, speak disrespectfully about
Gregorio loved to *disparage* his brother's dancing skills.
synonyms: denigrate, derogate, ridicule, deride

DISPARITY *n* (dih <u>spaar</u> ih tee)
contrast, dissimilarity
There was a marked *disparity* between his high opinion of himself and the low opinion others had of him.
synonyms: discrepancy, contradiction, divergence, incongruity, incompatibility

DISPASSIONATE *adj* (dihs <u>paash</u> ih niht)
unaffected by bias or strong emotions; not personally or emotionally involved in something
Ideally, photographers should be *dispassionate* observers of what goes on in the world.
synonyms: disinterested, impartial

DISPEL *v* (dihs <u>pehl</u>)
to drive out or scatter
Arnie's heroic rescue of the family from the flames was enough to *dispel* any doubts that he could be a good fireman.
synonyms: disband, disperse

DISPERSE *v* (dihs <u>puhrs</u>)
to break up, scatter
The workers *dispersed* after receiving their paychecks, many of them heading for the local bar.
synonyms: dissipate, disintegrate, dispel

DISREPUTE *n* (dihs rih <u>pyoot</u>)
disgrace, dishonor
The law firm fell into *disrepute* after it was revealed that one of its lawyers was guilty of jury tampering.
synonyms: ignominy, infamy, obloquy, odium, opprobrium

*DISSEMBLE *v* (dihs <u>sehm</u> buhl)
to pretend, disguise one's motives
The villain could *dissemble* to the police no longer; he finally had to confess to the forgery.
synonyms: feign, conceal, cloak, camouflage

*DISSEMINATE *v* (dih <u>sehm</u> uh nayt)
to spread far and wide
The wire service *disseminates* information so rapidly that events get reported shortly after they happen.
synonyms: circulate, diffuse, disperse

DISSIPATE *v* (<u>dihs</u> uh payt)
to scatter; to pursue pleasure to excess
The fog gradually began to *dissipate*, revealing all the ships docked in the harbor.
synonyms: carouse, squander, disperse, consume, dissolve

DISSONANT *adj* (<u>dihs</u> uh nuhnt)
harsh and unpleasant sounding
The screeching of the opera singer was completely *dissonant* to the ears of her audience.
synonyms: discordant, harsh, inharmonious

DISSUADE *v* (dih <u>swayd</u>)
to persuade someone to alter original intentions
I tried to *dissuade* him from climbing Everest without an oxygen tank, but he refused to listen.
synonyms: discourage, deter

DISTEND *v* (dih <u>stehnd</u>)
to swell, inflate, bloat
Her stomach was distended after she gorged on the six-course meal.
synonyms: broaden, bulge

DISTRAUGHT *adj* (dih <u>strawt</u>)
very worried and distressed
The *distraught* mother searched desperately for her missing children.
synonyms: despondent, agitated, mad, insane, abstracted

DITHER *v* (<u>dihth</u> uhr)
to act confusedly or without clear purpose
Ellen *dithered* around her apartment, uncertain how to tackle the family crisis.
synonyms: hesitate, waver, waffle, vacillate, falter

DIURNAL *adj* (die <u>uhr</u> nuhl)
existing during the day
Diurnal creatures tend to become inactive during the night.
synonyms: daylight, daytime

*DIVERGENT *adj* (die <u>vuhr</u> juht) (dih <u>vuhr</u> juht)
separating, moving in different directions from a particular point
We get along even though we have very *divergent* interests.
synonyms: deviating, different, anomalous

DIVINE *v* (dih <u>vien</u>)
to foretell or know by inspiration
The fortune-teller *divined* from the pattern of the tea leaves that her customer would marry five times.
synonyms: predict, intuit, auger, foresee, presage

*DIVISIVE *adj* (dih <u>vie</u> sihv) (dih <u>vih</u> sihv) (dih <u>vih</u> zihv)
creating disunity or conflict
The bully used *divisive* tactics to pit his enemies against each other.
synonyms: controversial, sensitive, disruptive

DOCILE *adj* (<u>dah</u> suhl) (<u>dah</u> siel)
tame, willing to be taught
Wolves are not as *docile* as dogs, which is why they are not recommended as house pets.
synonyms: domesticated, mild, tractable, obedient

DOCTRINAIRE *adj* (dahk truh <u>nayr</u>)
rigidly devoted to theories without regard for practicality; dogmatic
The professor's manner of teaching was considered *doctrinaire* for such a liberal school.
synonyms: inflexible, dictatorial

DOGGED *adj* (<u>daw</u> guhd)
stubbornly persevering
The police inspector's *dogged* determination helped him catch the thief.
synonyms: tenacious, obstinate

*DOGMATIC *adj* (dahg <u>maat</u> ihk) (dawg <u>maat</u> ihk)
rigidly fixed in opinion, opinionated
The dictator was *dogmatic*; he, and only he, was right.
synonyms: inflexible, doctrinaire, authoritative, obstinate

DOLEFUL *adj* (<u>dohl</u> fuhl)
sad, mournful
Looking into the *doleful* eyes of the lonely pony, the girl yearned to take him home.
synonyms: dejected, woeful

DOMINEER *v* (dahm uh <u>neer</u>)
to rule over something in a tyrannical way
The powerful man *domineered* over his timid wife and children.
synonyms: rule, govern, reign

DORMANT *adj* (<u>dohr</u> muhnt)
at rest, inactive, in suspended animation
The volcano seemed *dormant*, but a devastating eruption was brewing deep in the earth beneath it.
synonyms: quiescent, potential, latent

DOTE *v* (doht)
to lavish attention, loving to excess
Tony's father always *doted* on him in front of his friends, much to Tony's dismay.
synonyms: affectionate, adoring, cherishing, tender

DOUR *adj* (<u>doo</u> uhr) (<u>dow</u> uhr)
sullen and gloomy; stern and severe
The *dour* hotel concierge demanded payment for the room in advance.
synonyms: austere, strict, grave

DOWRY *n* (<u>dow</u> ree)
money or property given by a bride to her husband
Because her parents could offer a large *dowry*, Sonal had her pick of husbands.
synonyms: dower, hope chest, bride-price

DRAW *v*
pull, drag, attract
An ox can *draw* a heavier plow than a horse can.
synonyms: haul, tow, tug, lure, entice

DRIVEL *n* (<u>drih</u> vuhl)
stupid talk; slobber
"I don't want to hear any more of that *drivel*," the wife shouted at her guilty husband.
synonyms: palaver, prattle, nonsense, claptrap, drool

DROLL *adj* (drohl)
amusing in a wry, subtle way
Although the play couldn't be described as hilarious, it was certainly *droll*.
synonyms: witty, comic, funny, entertaining, risible

DULCET *adj* (<u>duhl</u> suht)
pleasant sounding, soothing to the ear
The *dulcet* tone of her voice lulled me to sleep.
synonyms: melodious, agreeable, sweet, harmonious

DUPE *v* (doop)
to deceive, trick; (*n*)fool, pawn
Bugs Bunny was able to *dupe* Elmer Fudd by dressing up as a lady rabbit.
synonyms: hoodwink, cozen, beguile, gull

DUPLICITY *n* (doo <u>plih</u> sih tee)
deception, dishonesty, double-dealing
Diplomatic relations between the two superpowers were outwardly friendly, yet characterized by *duplicity*.
synonyms: perfidy, infidelity, disloyalty, treachery, guile

DURESS *n* (duhr <u>ehs</u>)
threat of force or intimidation; imprisonment
Under *duress*, the political dissident revealed the names of others in his organization to the secret police.
synonyms: coercion, constraint, pressure, compulsion

DYSPEPTIC *adj* (dihs <u>pehp</u> tihk)
suffering from indigestion; gloomy and irritable
The *dyspeptic* young man cast a gloom over the party the minute he walked in.
synonyms: morose, solemn, melancholy, sour, acerb

E

EBB *n* (ehb)
reflux of the tide
Melissa enjoyed watching the *ebb* from her beachside balcony.
synonyms: retreat, subside, abate, wane, withdraw

EBULLIENT *adj* (<u>ih</u> byool yuhnt) (<u>ih</u> buhl yuhnt)
exhilarated, full of enthusiasm and high spirits
The *ebullient* child exhausted the baby-sitter, who lacked the energy to keep up with her.
synonyms: ardent, avid, zestful, bubbly

ECLECTIC *adj* (ih <u>klehk</u> tihk) (eh <u>klehk</u> tihk)
selecting from various sources
Budapest's architecture is an *eclectic* mix of eastern and western styles.
synonyms: catholic, selective, broad

*ECSTATIC *adj* (ehk <u>staa</u> tihk) (ihk <u>staa</u> tihk)
joyful
Mortimer's parents were *ecstatic* when they learned of his 1600 SAT score.
synonyms: blissful, rapturous, delighted, exultant, jubilant

EDICT *n* (<u>ee</u> dihkt)
law, command, official public order
Pedestrians often disobey the *edict* that they should not jaywalk.
synonyms: decree, fiat, ukase, dictum, directive

EDIFICE *n* (<u>eh</u> duh fuhs)
large structure
The towering *edifice* dominated the city skyline.
synonyms: structure, construction, skyscraper

EDIFY *v* (<u>eh</u> duh fie)
to instruct morally and spiritually
The guru was paid to *edify* the actress in the ways of Buddhism.
synonyms: teach, enlighten, guide, educate

EFFACE *v* (ih <u>fays</u>) (eh <u>fays</u>)
to erase or make indistinct
Benjamin attempted to *efface* all traces of his troubled past by assuming a new identity.
synonyms: expunge, obliterate

EFFERVESCENT *adj* (eh fuhr <u>vehs</u> uhnt)
bubbly, lively
Tina's *effervescent* personality made her perfect for the job of game show host.
synonyms: excited, spirited

EFFICACIOUS *adj* (eff uh <u>kay</u> shuhs)
effective, efficient
Penicillin was one of the most *efficacious* drugs on the market when it was first introduced; it completely eliminated almost all bacterial infections for which it was administered.
synonyms: effectual, potent

EFFIGY *n* (<u>eh</u> fuh jee)
stuffed doll; likeness of a person
The anti-American militants burned Uncle Sam in *effigy* during their demonstration.
synonyms: figure, dummy, image

EFFRONTERY *n* (ih <u>fruhnt</u> uhr ee) (eh <u>fruhnt</u> uhr ee)
impudent boldness; audacity
The receptionist had the *effrontery* to laugh out loud when the CEO tripped over a computer wire and fell flat on his face.
synonyms: presumption, brashness, temerity, nerve, gall

EFFUSIVE *adj* (ih <u>fyoo</u> sihv) (eh <u>fyoo</u> sihv) (eh <u>fyoo</u> zihv)
expressing emotion without restraint
The teacher was *effusive* in her praise of Brian for his brilliant essay.
synonyms: gushy, profuse, overflowing

EGOCENTRIC *adj* (ee goh <u>sehn</u> trihk)
acting as if things are centered around oneself
Craig was so *egocentric* that he didn't even notice that his comments were hurting Pat's feelings.
synonyms: conceited, narcissistic, selfish, egotistic, egomaniacal

*EGREGIOUS *adj* (ih <u>gree</u> juhs)
conspicuously bad
The English text book contained several *egregious* errors; for example, "grammar" was misspelled as "gramer" throughout.
synonyms: blatant, flagrant, glaring, gross, rank

ELATION *n* (ih <u>lay</u> shuhn)
exhilaration, joy
The actress was filled with *elation* when she heard that she had been awarded the Emmy.
synonyms: happiness, gladness, bliss, felicity, euphoria

ELEGY *n* (<u>eh</u> luh jee)
a mournful poem, usually about the dead
A memorable *elegy* was read aloud for the spiritual leader.
synonyms: memorial, lament

ELICIT *v* (ih <u>lih</u> siht)
to draw out, provoke
The tough policeman was not able to *elicit* the confession he wanted from the murder suspect.
synonyms: evoke, educe, wring, extract, tap

ELOQUENCE *n* (<u>eh</u> luh kwuhns)
persuasive and effective speech
The Gettysburg Address is moving because of its lofty sentiments as well as its *eloquence*.
synonyms: expressiveness, fluency

ELUCIDATE *v* (ih <u>loo</u> suh dayt)
to explain, clarify
The teacher *elucidated* the reasons why she had failed the student to his parents.
synonyms: explicate, illuminate, define, interpret

*ELUDE *v* (ih <u>lood</u>)
to avoid cleverly, to escape the perception of
Somehow, the runaway *eluded* detection for weeks.
synonyms: evade, dodge

EMACIATE *v* (ih <u>may</u> shee ay tihd)
to cause to lose weight, make feeble
The deli owner helped to *emaciate* the homeless man by refusing to give him the day-old bread.
synonyms: meager

EMANCIPATE *v* (ih <u>maan</u> suh payt)
to set free, liberate
After the slaves were *emancipated*, many of them moved to eastern cities in search of new opportunities.
synonyms: deliver, manumit, release

*EMBELLISH *v* (ehm <u>behl</u> ihsh)
to ornament; make attractive with decoration or details; add details to a statement
Sanjev's story is too short; she needs to *embellish* it with more details.
synonyms: grace, adorn, embroider, elaborate

EMBEZZLE *v* (ehm <u>behz</u> uhl)
to steal money in violation of a trust
The accountant *embezzled* millions of dollars from the company before management discovered what he was up to.
synonyms: misappropriate, peculate, steal, pirate, expropriate

EMBROIL *v* (ehm <u>broyl</u>)
to involve in; cause to fall into disorder
Lawyers became *embroiled* in the dispute when it became obvious that no compromise could be reached without them.
synonyms: implicate, ensnare, entangle

EMINENT *adj* (<u>ehm</u> uh nuhnt)
celebrated, distinguished; outstanding, towering
They were amazed that such an *eminent* scholar could have made such an obvious error.
synonyms: noted, famous, prominent, important, illustrious

*EMPATHY *n* (<u>ehm</u> puh thee)
identification with another's feelings
Having taught English herself, Julie felt a strong *empathy* for the troubled English teacher in the film.
synonyms: sensitivity, compassion, sympathy, commiseration

*EMULATE *v* (<u>ehm</u> yuh layt)
to strive to equal or excel, to imitate
Children often *emulate* their parents.
synonyms: follow, mimic

ENCOMPASS *v* (ehn <u>kuhm</u> puhs)
to include, cover, take in
The president's ambitious plan *encompassed* many aims.
synonyms: surround, enclose, envelop, constitute, include

ENCUMBER *v* (ehn <u>kuhm</u> buhr)
to weigh down, to burden
She often felt *encumbered* by the distractions of the city, so she sought a quieter place in the country.
synonyms: to hamper the activity of

ENDEMIC *adj* (ehn <u>deh</u> mihk)
belonging to a particular area, inherent
The health department determined that the outbreak was *endemic* to the small village, so they quarantined the inhabitants before the virus could spread.
synonyms: native, indigenous, local

*ENERVATE *v* (<u>ehn</u> uhr vayt)
to weaken, sap strength from
The guerrillas hoped that a series of surprise attacks would *enervate* the regular army.
synonyms: deplete, debilitate, drain, exhaust

ENGENDER *v* (ehn <u>gehn</u> duhr)
to produce, cause, bring about
His fear of clowns was *engendered* when he saw one in a horror movie.
synonyms: procreate, propagate, originate, generate

*ENHANCE *v* (ehn <u>haans</u>)
to improve, bring to a greater level of intensity
The Olympics Committee bars the use of any drugs that can *enhance* an athlete's performance.
synonyms: heighten, intensify, amplify, improve

ENIGMATIC *adj* (eh nihg <u>mah</u> tihk)
puzzling, inexplicable
Because he spoke in riddles and dressed in robes, his peers considered the artist's behavior *enigmatic*.
synonyms: mysterious, cryptic, baffling

ENJOIN *v* (ehn <u>joyn</u>)
to direct or impose with urgent appeal, to order with emphasis; to forbid
Patel is *enjoined* by his culture from eating the flesh of a cow, which is sacred in India.
synonyms: instruct, charge

ENMITY *n* (<u>ehn</u> muh tee)
hostility, antagonism, ill-will
After McDonald was killed by McDuff, the *enmity* between their families continued for hundreds of years.
synonyms: animosity, antipathy, rancor, animus

ENNUI *n* (ahn <u>wee</u>) (<u>ahn</u> wee)
boredom, lack of interest and energy
Many teenagers are filled with *ennui* whenever their parents start to go on about "the good old days."
synonyms: tedium, listlessness, world-weariness

ENORMITY *n* (ih <u>nohr</u> muh tee)
state of being gigantic or terrible
The manager underestimated the *enormity* of the problem and did not act quickly to solve it, which resulted in disaster.
synonyms: outrageousness, atrociousness

ENTAIL *v* (ehn <u>tayl</u>) (ihn <u>tayl</u>)
to involve as a necessary result, necessitate
The reforms you are suggesting would *entail* massive changes in the way we do things around here.
synonyms: demand, require

*ENTHRALL *v* (ehn <u>thrahl</u>)
to captivate, enchant, enslave
The children were *enthralled* by the spectacular circus show.
synonyms: bewitch, fascinate, enrapture, transfix, mesmerize

ENTREAT *v* (ehn <u>treet</u>)
to plead, beg
I *entreat* you to just tell me what the problem is instead of bottling it up inside.
synonyms: beseech, implore, importune, request, petition

ENUNCIATE *v* (ih <u>nuhn</u> see ayt) (ee <u>nuhn</u> see ayt)
to pronounce clearly
Subway conductors must learn to *enunciate* clearly so that passengers can understand them.
synonyms: articulate, state, utter

*EPHEMERAL *adj* (ih <u>fehm</u> uhr uhl)
momentary, transient, fleeting
The lives of mayflies seem *ephemeral* to us because the average life span is a matter of hours.
synonyms: transitory, fugitive, evanescent, momentary

EPICURE *n* (<u>eh</u> pih kyoor) (<u>eh</u> pih kyuhr)
person with refined taste in food and wine
Restaurant critics are the epitome of *epicures*.
synonyms: gourmet, gourmand, connoisseur, gastronome

EPIGRAM *n* (<u>eh</u> puh graam)
short, witty saying or poem
The poet was renowned for his skill in making up amusing *epigrams*.
synonyms: maxim, adage, saw, aphorism

*EPILOGUE *n* (<u>eh</u> puh lahg)
concluding section of a literary work
In the *epilogue* of the novel, the author described the ultimate fate of its characters.
synonyms: afterward, finale

EPITOME *n* (ih <u>piht</u> uh mee)
representative of an entire group; embodiment
The host was the *epitome* of graciousness, making all of his guests feel perfectly comfortable.
synonyms: paragon, exemplar, prototype, quintessence, abstract

EQUANIMITY *n* (ee kwuh <u>nihm</u> ih tee) (ehk wuh <u>nihm</u> ih tee)
calmness, composure
Kelly took the news that she had been fired with outward *equanimity*, although she was crying inside.
synonyms: coolness, poise, sang-froid, aplomb, serenity

EQUINE *adj* (<u>ehk</u> wien) (<u>ee</u> kwien)
relating to horses
Many donkeys have *equine* characteristics, although they are not horses.
synonyms: horsy, asinine, mulish

*EQUIVOCAL *adj* (ih <u>kwihv</u> uh kuhl)
ambiguous, open to more than one interpretation
Poems are inherently *equivocal*, and there is no point in trying to assign a definitive meaning to them.
synonyms: doubtful, misleading, uncertain

EQUIVOCATE *v* (ih <u>kwihv</u> uh kayt)
to avoid committing oneself in what one says, to be deliberately unclear
Not wanting to implicate himself in the crime, the suspect *equivocated* for hours.
synonyms: lie, mislead

*ERADICATE *v* (ih <u>raad</u> ih kayt)
to erase or wipe out
It is unlikely that our society will ever *eradicate* poverty, although the general standard of living has significantly improved in recent decades.
synonyms: uproot, abolish, eliminate, annihilate

*ERRATIC *adj* (ih <u>raat</u> ihk)
inconsistent, irregular
Ezra's friends were often puzzled by his *erratic* behavior.
synonyms: eccentric, capricious, unstable, unpredictable

*ERUDITE *adj* (<u>ehr</u> yuh diet) (<u>ehr</u> uh diet)
learned, scholarly
The annual meeting of professors brought together the most *erudite*, respected individuals in the field.
synonyms: knowledgeable, cultured, well-read, educated, literate

ESCHEW *v* (ehs <u>choo</u>)
to shun; to avoid (as something wrong or distasteful)
The filmmaker *eschewed* artifical light for her actors, resulting in a stark movie style.

*ESOTERIC *adj* (eh suh <u>tehr</u> ihk)
understood by or designed for only a few
Only a handful of experts are knowledgeable about the *esoteric* world of particle physics.
synonyms: mysterious, arcane, occult, recondite, secret

ESPOUSE *v* (ih <u>spowz</u>)
to take up and support as a cause; to marry
Because of his religious beliefs, the preacher could not *espouse* the use of capital punishment.
synonyms: champion, adopt

SAT Word List

ESTRANGE *v* (ih <u>straynj</u>)
to alienate, keep at a distance
Having *estranged* himself from his family for many years, Alan had not heard that his parents
had divorced.
synonyms: disaffect, separate, divorce

ETHEREAL *adj* (ih <u>theer</u> ee uhl)
not earthly, spiritual, delicate
Her delicate, *ethereal* beauty made her a popular model for pre-Raphaelite artists.
synonyms: intangible, diaphanous, airy, gossamer, sheer

*EULOGY *n* (<u>yoo</u> luh jee)
high praise, often in a public speech
His best friend gave the *eulogy*, outlining his many achievements and talents.
synonyms: tribute, commendation, encomium, panegyric, salute

EUPHEMISM *n* (<u>yoo</u> fum ih zuhm)
an inoffensive and agreeable expression that is substituted for one that is considered offensive
The funeral director preferred to use the *euphemism* "passed away" instead of the word "dead."

EUPHONY *n* (<u>yoo</u> fuh nee)
pleasant, harmonious sound
To their loving parents, the children's orchestra performance sounded like *euphony*, although an
outside observer probably would have called it a cacophony of hideous sounds.
synonyms: harmony, melody, music, sweetness

EUPHORIA *n* (yoo <u>fohr</u> ee uh)
feeling of well-being or happiness
Euphoria overwhelmed her when she discovered that she had scored a perfect 1600 on her SAT.
synonyms: elation, bliss, joy, delight, exhilaration

EVADE *v* (ih <u>vayd</u>)
to avoid, dodge
He *evaded* answering my question by pretending not to hear me and changing the subject.
synonyms: escape, shun, escape, elude, circumvent

*EVANESCENT *adj* (eh vuh <u>nehs</u> uhnt)
momentary, tendency toward vanishing
It is lucky that eclipses are *evanescent*, or the world would never see sunlight.
synonyms: transient, ephemeral, fleeting, fugitive

EVOKE *v* (ih <u>vohk</u>)
to inspire memories; to produce a reaction
The sight of the old elm tree *evoked* memories of the tree house she had built as a little girl.
synonyms: educe, elicit, conjure, occasion

EXACERBATE *v* (ihg <u>zaas</u> uhr bayt)
to aggravate, intensify the bad qualities of
It is unwise to take aspirin to relieve heartburn; instead of providing relief, the drug will only *exacerbate*
the problem.
synonyms: worsen, escalate, deepen

*EXASPERATION *n* (ihg zaas puhr <u>ay</u> shuhn)
irritation·
The catcher couldn't hide his *exasperation* after the pitcher refused to listen to his advice and threw a series of pitches that resulted in home runs for the opposing team.
synonyms: frustration, annoyance, vexation, pique

EXCERPT *n* (<u>ehk</u> suhrpt)
selection from a book or play
If you want to reprint an *excerpt* from that play, you'll have to get permission from the author.
synonyms: extract, portion, quotation

EXCOMMUNICATE *v* (ehks kuh <u>myoo</u> nih kayt)
to bar from membership in the church
The king was *excommunicated* from the Church when he decided to divorce his wife and remarry.
synonyms: exclude, ostracize, expel

EXCRUCIATING *adj* (ihks kroo shee ayt ing)
agonizing, intensely painful
Although it's a minor injury, stubbing your toe can be very *excruciating*.
synonyms: torturous, acute, fierce

EXCULPATE *v* (<u>ehk</u> skuhl payt) (ihk <u>skuhl</u> payt)
to clear of blame or fault, vindicate
The adversarial legal system is intended to convict those who are guilty and to *exculpate* those who are innocent.
synonyms: exonerate, acquit

EXECRABLE *adj* (<u>ehk</u> sih kruh buhl)
utterly detestable, abhorrent
The stew tasted utterly *execrable* after the cook accidentally dumped a pound of salt into it.
synonyms: hateful, inferior, awful, terrible, horrible

*EXEMPLARY *adj* (ihg <u>zehm</u> pluhr ee)
excellent, an especially good example of something
The manager was pleased to find that the new employee's work was *exemplary*.
synonyms: commendable, meritorious, ideal, superlative, admirable

EXHILARATION *n* (ihg zihl uh <u>ray</u> shuhn)
state of being energetic or filled with happiness
Fred was filled with *exhilaration* after he learned that he had won the lottery.
synonyms: elation, euphoria, exuberance, delight, ebullience

EXHORT *v* (ihg <u>zohrt</u>)
to urge or incite by strong appeals
Rob's friends *exhorted* him to beware of ice on the roads when he insisted on driving home in the middle of a snowstorm.
synonyms: press, prod, provoke, convince, inspire

EXHUME *v* (ihg <u>zoom</u>) (ihg <u>zyoom</u>) (ihk <u>syoom</u>) (ehks <u>hyoom</u>)
to remove from a grave; uncover a secret
The murder victim's body was *exhumed*, but no new evidence was discovered.
synonyms: disinter, unearth

EXIGENT *adj* (<u>ehk</u> suh juhnt)
urgent; excessively demanding
The patient's *exigent* wound was rapidly losing blood.
synonyms: pressing, imperative, compelling, critical, crucial

EXONERATE *v* (ihg <u>zahn</u> uh rayt)
to clear of blame, absolve
The fugitive was *exonerated* when another criminal confessed to committing the crime.
synonyms: exculpate, acquit, vindicate

EXORBITANT *adj* (ig <u>zor</u> bih tuhnt)
extravagant, greater than reasonable
After the harvest was destroyed by freezing temperatures, shops charged *exorbitant* prices for oranges.
synonyms: excessive, immoderate, inordinate, extreme

EXOTIC *adj* (ihg <u>zah</u> tihk)
foreign; romantic, excitingly strange
The atmosphere of the restaurant was *exotic*, but the food was ordinary.
synonyms: alien, fantastic

EXPATRIATE *n* (ehks <u>pay</u> tree iht) (ehks <u>pay</u> tree ayt)(ihk <u>spee</u> dee uhnt)
one who lives outside one's native land
He spent much of his adult life as an *expatriate*, only returning to his own country for his retirement.
synonyms: emigrant, exile, refugee

EXPEDIENT *adj* (ihk <u>spee</u> dee uhnt)
convenient, efficient, practical
It was considered more *expedient* to send the fruit directly to the retailer instead of through
a middleman.
synonyms: appropriate, useful, sensible

EXPIATE *v* (<u>ehk</u> spee ayt)
to atone for, make amends for
The nun had to *expiate* her sins by scrubbing the floor of the convent on her hands and knees.
synonyms: answer, compensate, pay

EXPIRE *v* (ehk <u>spier</u>)
to come to an end; die; breathe out
Because her driver's license was about to *expire*, she had to go and exchange it for a new one.
synonyms: terminate, exhale

EXPLICIT *adj* (ehk <u>splih</u> siht)
clearly defined, specific; forthright in expression
The owners of the house left a list of *explicit* instructions detailing their house-sitter's duties.
synonyms: express, categorical, definite, unequivocal

EXPONENT *n* (ihk <u>spoh</u> nuhnt) (<u>ehk</u> spoh nuhnt)
one who champions or advocates
The vice president was an enthusiastic *exponent* of computer technology.
synonyms: supporter, representative

EXPOUND *v* (ihk <u>spownd</u>)
to explain or describe in detail
The teacher *expounded* on the theory of relativity for hours.
synonyms: elucidate, elaborate

EXPUNGE *v* (ihk <u>spuhnj</u>)
to erase, eliminate completely
The parents' association *expunged* the questionable texts from the children's reading list.
synonyms: delete, obliterate

EXPURGATE *v* (<u>ehk</u> spuhr gayt)
to censor
Government propagandists *expurgated* all negative references to the dictator from the film.
synonyms: cut, bowdlerize, sanitize

EXTEMPORANEOUS *adj* (ihk stehm puh <u>ray</u> nee uhs)
unrehearsed, on the spur of the moment
Jan gave an *extemporaneous* performance of a *Monty Python* skit at her surprise birthday party.
synonyms: impromptu, spontaneous, unprepared, ad-lib

*EXTENUATE *v* (ihk <u>stehn</u> yoo ayt)
to lessen the seriousness, strength, or effect of
Ronnie wasn't trying to *extenuate* the car accident when he laughed at his friend in the neck brace.
synonyms: palliate, mitigate, lighten, excuse

EXTINCTION *n* (ihk <u>stingk</u> shuhn)
end of a living thing or species
The dodo was hunted to *extinction* by man many years ago.
synonyms: extermination, eradication, annihilation, elimination, destruction

EXTOL *v* (ihk <u>stohl</u>)
to praise
The salesman *extolled* the virtues of the used car he was trying to convince the customer to buy.
synonyms: acclaim, commend, laud, exalt, eulogize

EXTORT *v* (ihk <u>stohrt</u>)
to obtain something by threats or force
The president's ex-wife *extorted* many valuables from him, threatening to reveal his political secrets if he did not do as she wished.
synonyms: wring, coerce, blackmail, bludgeon, bully

EXTRANEOUS *adj* (ihk <u>stray</u> nee uhs)
irrelevant, unrelated, unnecessary
When none of the committee members acknowledged that she had even spoken, June realized that her presence at the meeting was completely *extraneous*.
synonyms: immaterial, impertinent, extrinsic, foreign, alien

EXTRICATE *v* (<u>ehk</u> strih kayt)
to free from, disentangle
The fly was unable to *extricate* itself from the flypaper.
synonyms: disengage, untangle, release, disencumber

EXTRINSIC *adj* (ihk <u>strihn</u> sihk) (ihk <u>strihn</u> zihk)
external, unessential; originating from the outside
"Though they are interesting to note," the meeting manager claimed, "those facts are *extrinsic* to the matter under discussion."
synonyms: extraneous, foreign

EXUBERANT *adj* (ihg <u>zoo</u> buhr uhnt)
lively, happy, full of good spirits
The *exuberant* puppy jumped up and licked the face of its master, happy to see him home again.
synonyms: blithe, cheery, elated, joyous, ecstatic

F

FAÇADE *n* (fuh <u>sahd</u>)
face, front; mask, superficial appearance
The drug dealers conducted business from a small bodega to maintain a *facade* of respectability.
synonyms: pretense, cloak, guise, semblance, surface

*FACILE *adj* (<u>faa</u> suhl)
easily accomplished; seeming to lack sincerity or depth; arrived at without due effort
Given the complexity of the problem, it seemed a rather *facile* solution.
synonyms: effortless, superficial

FACILITATE *v* (fuh <u>sihl</u> ih tayt)
to aid, assist
The organizers tried to *facilitate* the social interaction of the delegates by giving everyone name tags.
synonyms: expedite, ease, simplify

FALLACIOUS *adj* (fuh <u>lay</u> shuhs)
tending to deceive or mislead; based on a fallacy
The *fallacious* statement "the Earth is flat" misled people for many years.
synonyms: false, erroneous

FALLOW *n* (<u>faa</u> loh)
dormant, unused
This field should lie *fallow* for a year so the soil does not become completely depleted.
synonyms: unseeded, inactive, idle

FANATICISM *n* (fuh <u>naat</u> ih sih zuhm)
extreme devotion to a cause
The storm troopers' *fanaticism* in their devotion to the Emperor was so great that they would readily have sacrificed their lives for him.
synonyms: zeal, mania, obsession

FARCICAL *adj* (<u>fahr</u> sih kuhl)
absurd, ludicrous
"The idea that I would burn down my own house is completely *farcical*," sneered the arson suspect.
synonyms: laughable, foolish, risible

FASTIDIOUS *adj* (faa <u>stihd</u> ee uhs) (fuh <u>stihd</u> ee uhs)
careful with details
Brett was normally so *fastidious* that Rachel was astonished to find his desk littered with clutter.
synonyms: meticulous, painstaking, scrupulous, punctilious, precise

FATHOM *v* (<u>faath</u> uhm)
to measure the depth of, gauge
The marine scientists used their sophisticated equipment to attempt to *fathom* the depth of the underwater canyon.
synonyms: sound, comprehend

FATUOUS *adj* (<u>faach</u> oo uhs)
stupid; foolishly self-satisfied
Ted's *fatuous* comments always embarrassed his keen-witted wife at parties.
synonyms: silly, absurd, preposterous, ridiculous, ludicrous

FAWN *v*
to flatter excessively, seek the favor of
The understudy *fawned* over the director in hopes of being cast in the part on a permanent basis.
synonyms: kowtow, toady, grovel, truckle, apple-polish

FAZE *v* (fayz)
to bother, upset, disconcert
Strangely, the news that his car had been stolen did not *faze* Nathan, although his wife was hysterical.
synonyms: discomfit, rattle, chagrin

FEASIBLE *adj* (<u>fee</u> zuh buhl)
possible, capable of being done
It was decided that the idea of giving away free fur coats was not *feasible*, and it was abandoned.
synonyms: workable, practicable, viable, doable

FECKLESS *adj* (<u>fehk</u> lihs)
ineffective, worthless
Anja took on the responsibility of caring for her aged mother, realizing that her *feckless* sister was not up to the task.
synonyms: incompetent

FECUND *adj* (<u>fee</u> kuhn) (<u>fehk</u> uhnd)
fertile, fruitful, productive
The *fecund* couple yielded a total of twenty children.
synonyms: prolific, flourishing

FEIGN *v* (fayn)
to pretend, to give a false appearance of
Though she had discovered they were planning a party, she *feigned* surprise so as not to spoil the festivities.
synonyms: fake

FEISTY *adj* (<u>fie</u> stee)
excitable, easily drawn into quarrels
The *feisty* old lady alienated her neighbors with her habit of picking fights with anyone who crossed her.
synonyms: spirited, plucky, frisky, spunky, touchy

FERVID *adj* (<u>fuhr</u> vihd)
passionate, intense, zealous
The fans of Maria Callas were particularly *fervid*, doing anything to catch a glimpse of the great singer.
synonyms: vehement, ardent, enthusiastic, avid, eager

FETID *adj* (<u>feh</u> tihd)
foul-smelling, putrid
The *fetid* stench from the outhouse caused Laura to wrinkle her nose in disgust.
synonyms: noisome, stinky, funky, malodorous, rank

FETTER *v* (<u>feh</u> tuhr)
to bind, chain, confine
The sheriff decided to *fetter* the three prisoners together to prevent escape.
synonyms: shackle, manacle, handcuff, curb, tether

FIASCO *n* (fee <u>aa</u> skoh) (fee <u>ah</u> skoh)
disaster, utter failure
After the soloist turned up drunk, it was hardly surprising that the concert proved to be an utter *fiasco*.
synonyms: calamity, misfortune, blow

FICTIVE *adj* (<u>fihk</u> tihv)
fictional, relating to imaginative creation
She found she was more producing when writing *fictive* stories rather than autobiography.
synonyms: not genuine

FIDELITY *n* (fih <u>dehl</u> ih tee) (fie <u>dehl</u> ih tee)
loyalty
A traitor is someone whose *fidelity* is questioned.
synonyms: allegiance, fealty, faithfulness

FILCH *v* (fihlch)
to steal
The pickpocket managed to *filch* ten wallets in the rush hour crowd.
synonyms: purloin, pilfer, misappropriate, plunder, pocket

FINICKY *adj* (<u>fihn</u> ih kee)
fussy, difficult to please
The *finicky* child rejected every dish on the menu to the exasperation of his parents.
synonyms: fastidious, finical, persnickety

FLACCID *adj* (<u>flaa</u> sihd)
limp, flabby, weak
The woman jiggled her *flaccid* arms in disgust, resolving to begin lifting weights as soon as possible.
synonyms: soft, floppy

FLAG *v* (flaag)
to decline in vigor, strength, or interest
The marathon runner slowed down as his strength *flagged*.
synonyms: wane, subside, ebb, dwindle, slacken

FLAGRANT *adj* (<u>flay</u> gruhnt)
outrageous, conspicuous
His *flagrant* disregard for the rules has resulted in his dismissal from the job.
synonyms: glaring, egregious, blatant, gross, rank

FLAMBOYANT *adj* (flaam <u>boy</u> uhnt)
flashy, garish; exciting, dazzling
Reginald's *flamboyant* clothing made him stick out like a sore thumb at his conservative office.
synonyms: ornate, florid, ostentatious, loud, gaudy

FLAUNT *v* (flawnt)
to show off
Rhonda *flaunted* her engagement ring all over the office.
synonyms: parade, flourish, vaunt, exhibit, display

FLORA *n* (<u>flohr</u> uh)
plants
The local *flora* of the Kenyan savannah includes the baobab tree.
synonyms: vegetation, botany, verdure, herbage

*FLORID *adj* (<u>flohr</u> ihd) (<u>flahr</u> ihd)
gaudy, extremely ornate; ruddy, flushed
The palace had been decorated in an excessively *florid* style; every surface had been carved and gilded.
synonyms: ornate, flamboyant, ostentatious, loud, garish

FLOUNDER *v* (<u>flown</u> duhr)
to falter, waver; to muddle, struggle
The previously glib defendant began to *flounder* when the prosecutor found a hole in his story.
synonyms: blunder, stumble, bumble, lurch, lumber

FLUCTUATE *v* (<u>fluhk</u> choo ayt)
to alternate, waver
Certain stock prices *fluctuate* so much that it is risky to invest in them.
synonyms: swing, oscillate, vary, undulate

FODDER *n* (<u>fohd</u> uhr)
raw material, as for artistic creation; readily abundant ideas or images
The governor's hilarious blunder was good *fodder* for the comedian.

FOIBLE *n* (<u>foy</u> buhl)
minor weakness or character flaw
Her habit of licking out the centers of Oreo cookies is a *foible*, not a serious character flaw.
synonyms: fault, failing, frailty, vice, blemish

FOIL v (foyl)
to defeat, frustrate
James Bond *foiled* the villain's evil plot to take over the world.
synonyms: thwart, balk, check, baffle

FOMENT *v* (foh mehnt)
to arouse or incite
The protesters tried to *foment* feeling against the war through their speeches and demonstrations.
synonyms: instigate, abet, promote

*FOOLHARDY *adj* (fool hahr dee)
recklessly bold
The driver was *foolhardy* enough to try to cross the tracks in front of the oncoming train.
synonyms: reckless, rash, precipitate, temerarious

FORBEARANCE *n* (fohr baar uhns)
patience, restraint, leniency
In light of the fact that he was new on the job, Collette decided to exercise *forbearance* with her assistant's numerous errors.
synonyms: resignation, long-suffering, tolerance

FORD *v* (fohrd)
to cross a body of water by wading
Because of the recent torrential rains, the cowboys were unable to *ford* the swollen river.
synonyms: traverse, wade

FORECLOSE *v* (fohr klohs)
to rule out; to seize debtor's property for lack of payments
The bank *foreclosed* on the Smith family farm, forcing the entire family to drive to California in search of work.
synonyms: repossess, bar

FORESTALL *v* (fohr stahl)
to prevent, delay; anticipate
The landlord *forestalled* Bob's attempt to avoid paying the rent by waiting for him outside his door.
synonyms: preclude, avert, obviate, deter, hinder

FORLORN *adj* (fohr lohrn)
dreary, deserted; unhappy; hopeless, despairing
Ying couldn't help but have forlorn feelings at hearing of her boyfriend's cheating.
synonyms: despondent, dejected, downcast, depressed, desolate

*FORMIDABLE *adj* (fohr mih duh buhl) (fohr mih duh buhl)
fearsome, daunting; tending to inspire awe or wonder
The wrestler was not very big, but his skill and speed made him a *formidable* opponent.
synonyms: overpowering

FORSAKE *v* (fohr sayk)
to abandon, withdraw from
It is common for criminals on Death Row to feel that everyone they know will *forsake* them.
synonyms: desert, renounce, leave, quit

FORTE *n* (<u>fohr</u> tay)
strong point, something a person does well
Because math was Dan's *forte*, his friends always asked him to calculate the bill whenever they went out to dinner together.
synonyms: métier, specialty

*FORTITUDE *n* (<u>fohr</u> tih tood)
strength of mind that allows one to encounter adversity with courage
Months in the trenches exacted great *fortitude* of the soldiers.
synonyms: endurance, courage

*FORTUITOUS *adj* (fohr <u>too</u> ih tuhs)
by chance, especially by favorable chance
After a *fortuitous* run-in with an agent, Roxy won a recording contract.
synonyms: accidental

FOSTER *v* (<u>fah</u> stuhr) (<u>faw</u> stuhr)
to nourish, cultivate, promote
The record agent *fostered* the development of his clients by sending them to singing lessons.
synonyms: nurture, nurse, advance, further

FOUNDER *v* (fown duhr)
to fall helplessly; sink
After colliding with the jagged rock, the ship *foundered*, forcing the crew to abandon it.
synonyms: miscarry, immerse, plunge

FRACAS *n* (<u>fraak</u> uhs) (<u>fray</u> kuhs)
noisy dispute
When the bandits discovered that the gambler was cheating them at cards, a violent *fracas* ensued.
synonyms: brawl, broil, donnybrook, fray, melee

FRACTIOUS *adj* (<u>fraak</u> shuhs)
unruly, rebellious
The general had a hard time maintaining discipline among his *fractious* troops.
synonyms: peevish, cranky, quarrelsome, contentious

FRAUDULENT *adj* (<u>fraw</u> juh luhnt)
deceitful, dishonest, unethical
The factory engaged in *fraudulent* practices, producing radios with no internal components.
synonyms: false, bogus, counterfeit, spurious

FRAUGHT *adj* (frawt)
full of, accompanied by
The sea voyage was *fraught* with peril; the crew had to contend with storms, sharks, and scurvy on board.
synonyms: filled, charged, loaded, replete

FRENETIC *adj* (fruh <u>neht</u> ihk)
frantic, frenzied
The employee's *frenetic* schedule left him little time to socialize.
synonyms: feverish

FRIVOLOUS *adj* (<u>frihv</u> uh luhs)
petty, trivial; flippant, silly
The biggest problem in the world for the *frivolous* debutante was that her ribbon was the wrong color.
synonyms: frothy, light, vapid

*FRUGAL *adj* (<u>froo</u> guhl)
thrifty, miserly
Every day he ate a *frugal* lunch consisting of one hard-boiled egg and one slice of dry toast.
synonyms: sparing, economical, cheap, parsimonious, stingy

FURTIVE *adj* (<u>fuhr</u> tihv)
secret, stealthy
Glenn was *furtive* when he peered out of the corner of his eye at the stunningly beautiful model.
synonyms: covert, clandestine, surreptitious, underhand, shifty

G

GALL *n* (gahl)
bitterness; careless nerve; (*v*)to exasperate and irritate
I cannot believe she had the *gall* to show up at my party after what she said. She really *galls* me!
synonyms: temerity, audacity, effrontery, rancor

GARGANTUAN *adj* (gahr <u>gaan</u> choo uhn)
giant, tremendous
Cleaning a teenager's room can often be a *gargantuan* task.
synonyms: enormous, immense, huge, gigantic, colossal

GARNER *v* (<u>gahr</u> nuhr)
to gather and store
The director managed to *garner* financial backing from several different sources for his next project.
synonyms: reap, glean, harvest, amass, acquire

GARRULOUS *adj* (<u>gaar</u> uh luhs) (<u>gaar</u> yuh luhs)
very talkative
The *garrulous* parakeet distracted its owner while he was studying.
synonyms: loquacious, voluble, verbose, chatty, prolix

GAUNT *adj* (gawnt)
thin and bony
The actress's *gaunt* frame led the press to speculate that she was anorexic.
synonyms: lean, spare, skinny, scrawny, lank

GENRE *n* (<u>zhahn</u> ruh)
type, class, category
My sister loves mysteries, but I can't stand that *genre* of books.
synonyms: ilk, variety, sort

GERMINATE *v* (<u>juhr</u> muhn ayt)
to begin to grow (as with a seed or idea)
Three weeks after planting, the seeds will *germinate*.
synonyms: sprout, emerge, materialize

GESTATION *n* (jeh <u>stay</u> shuhn)
growth process from conception to birth
The longer the *gestation* period of an organism, the more developed the baby is at birth.
synonyms: pregnancy, gravidity, development

GIBE *v* (jieb)
to make heckling, taunting remarks
Tina *gibed* at her brothers mercilessly as they attempted to pitch the tent.
synonyms: ridicule, mock, twit, deride, jeer

GIRTH *n* (gihrth)
distance around something
The young boy marveled at the *girth* of his pregnant cat's stomach.
synonyms: breadth, width, size, measure

GLIB *adj* (glihb)
fluent in an insincere manner; offhand, casual
The slimy politician managed to continue gaining supporters because he was a *glib* speaker.
synonyms: easy, superficial

GLOWER *v* (<u>glow</u> uhr)
to glare, stare angrily and intensely
The cranky waitress *glowered* at the indecisive customer.
synonyms: frown, lower, scowl

GLUTTONY *n* (<u>gluht</u> nee)
eating and drinking to excess
It took days for the guests to recover their appetites after the *gluttony* that had taken place at the party.
synonyms: voracity, rapacity, gormandizing, crapulence

GNARL *v* (nahrl)
to make knotted, deform
The old oak became *gnarled* after withstanding the force of powerful winds for centuries.
synonyms: twist, contort

GOAD *v* (gohd)
to prod or urge
Denise *goaded* her sister Leigh into running the marathon with her.
synonyms: impel, incite, stimulate, provoke, rouse

GRADATION *n* (gray <u>day</u> shuhn)
process occurring by regular degrees or stages; variation in color
The paint store offers so many different *gradations* of red that it's impossible to choose among them.
synonyms: nuance, shade, step, subtlety

GRANDILOQUENCE *n* (graan <u>dihl</u> uh kwuhns)
pompous talk; fancy but meaningless language
The headmistress was notorious for her *grandiloquence* at the lectern and her ostentatious clothes.
synonyms: bravado, pretension

*GRANDIOSE *adj* (<u>graan</u> dee ohs) (graan <u>dee</u> ohs)
magnificent and imposing; exaggerated and pretentious
The house had a *grandiose* facade that disguised its humble and simple interior.
synonyms: stately, majestic, august, pompous

GRATUITOUS *adj* (gruh <u>too</u> uh tuhs) (gruh <u>tyoo</u> uh tuhs)
free, voluntary; unnecessary and unjustified
Matt's snubbing of his old friend seemed *gratuitous* because there had been no bad blood between the two of them previously.
synonyms: complimentary, gratis, unwarranted

*GREGARIOUS *adj* (greh <u>gayr</u> ee uhs)
outgoing, sociable
Unlike her introverted friends, Susan was very *gregarious*.
synonyms: convivial, friendly

GRIEVOUS *adj* (<u>gree</u> vuhs)
causing grief or sorrow; serious and distressing
Maude and Bertha sobbed loudly throughout the *grievous* event.
synonyms: dire, grave, dolorous, mournful

GRIMACE *n* (<u>grih</u> muhs) (grih <u>mays</u>)
facial expression showing pain or disgust
The count wore a *grimace* when his wife spilled a carafe of wine on the king.
synonyms: scowl, leer, glare

GROTTO *n* (<u>grah</u> toh)
a small cave
Alone on the island, Philoctetes sought shelter in a *grotto*.
synonyms: cavern, recess, burrow

GROVEL *v* (<u>grah</u> vuhl)
to humble oneself in a demeaning way
Thor *groveled* to his ex-girlfriend, hoping she would take him back.
synonyms: cringe, fawn, kowtow, toady, bootlick

*GUILE *n* (<u>gie</u> uhl)
trickery, deception
Greg used considerable *guile* to acquire his rent-controlled apartment, even claiming to be a Vietnam Vet.
synonyms: cunning, artifice, wiliness, duplicity

GULLIBLE *adj* (<u>guh</u> luh buhl)
easily deceived
The *gullible* landlord believed Rich's story that he was only going away for a few days, despite the moving boxes that littered the apartment.
synonyms: trustful, naïve, ingenuous

H

*HACKNEYED *adj* (<u>haak</u> need)
worn out by overuse
We always mock my father for his *hackneyed* expressions and dated hairstyle.
synonyms: trite, shopworn, stale, banal

HALLOWED *adj* (<u>haa</u> lohd)
holy; treated as sacred
The Constitution is a *hallowed* document in the United States.
synonyms: sanctified, consecrated, venerated, sacrosanct, blessed

HAPLESS *adj* (<u>haap</u> luhs)
unfortunate, having bad luck
I wish someone would give that poor, *hapless* soul some food and shelter.
synonyms: ill-fated, ill-starred, luckless, unlucky, jinxed

HARBINGER *n* (<u>haar</u> buhn juhr)
precursor, someone who symbolizes something to come
The groundhog's is the *harbinger* for the beginning of spring.
synonyms: forerunner, presage, omen, herald,

HARDY *adj* (<u>hahr</u> dee)
robust, vigorous
Heidi was a strong, *hardy* girl who beat up her older brothers on a daily basis.
synonyms: healthy, hale, fit, strong, courageous

HARROW *v* (<u>haa</u> roh)
to torment, terrify
We stayed up all night listening to Dave and Will try to *harrow* us with stories of their adventures on the sea.
synonyms: agonizing, dismaying, upsetting, disturbing, frightful

*HAUGHTY *adj* (<u>haw</u> tee) (<u>hah</u> tee)
arrogant and condescending
The teacher resented Sally's *haughty* attitude and gave her a D for the semester.
synonyms: proud, disdainful, supercilious, scornful, vainglorious

HEATHEN *n* (<u>hee</u> *th*uhn)
pagan; uncivilized and irreligious
The missionaries considered it their duty to convert as many of the heathens as possible.
synonyms: idolater, polytheist, unbeliever

HECTIC *adj* (<u>hehk</u> tihk)
hasty, hurried, confused
Breakfast at their house was always a *hectic* affair, with ten children running around and screaming.
synonyms: feverish, frantic, frenetic

*HEDONIST *n* (<u>hee</u> duhn ihst)
one who pursues pleasure as a goal
Michelle, an admitted *hedonist*, lays on the couch eating cookies every Saturday.
synonyms: pleasure-seeker, glutton

HEGEMONY *n* (hih <u>jeh</u> muh nee)
the domination of one state or group over its allies
When Germany claimed *hegemony* over Russia, Stalin was outraged.
synonyms: power, authority

HEINOUS *adj* (<u>hay</u> nuhs)
shocking, wicked, terrible
Nobody could believe the *heinous* crime the baby-sitter had committed.
synonyms: reprehensible, abominable, monstrous, appalling, dreadful

HEMORRHAGE *v* (<u>hehm</u> rihj) (<u>heh</u> muh rih)
to bleed heavily; (*n*) heavy bleeding
The girl applied a bandage to her wound so it wouldn't *hemorrhage*.
synonyms: seep, discharge, gush

HERETICAL *adj* (huh <u>reh</u> tih kuhl)
departing from accepted beliefs or standards, oppositional
At the onset of the Inquisition, the *heretical* priest was forced to flee the country.
synonyms: unorthodox

HERMETIC *adj* (huhr <u>meh</u> tihk)
tightly sealed
The *hermetic* seal of the jar proved impossible to break.
synonyms: airtight, watertight, impervious

HETEROGENEOUS *adj* (heh tuh ruh <u>jee</u> nee uhs) (he truh-) (-nyuhs)
composed of unlike parts, different, diverse
The United Nations is by nature a *heterogeneous* body.
synonyms: miscellaneous, mixed, varied, motley, assorted

HIATUS *n* (hie <u>ay</u> tuhs)
a gap or interruption in space, time, or continuity
After a long *hiatus* in Greece, the philosophy professor returned to university.
synonyms: break

HOARY *adj* (<u>hohr</u> ee) (<u>haw</u> ree)
very old; whitish or gray from age
The old man's *hoary* beard contrasted starkly to the new stubble of his teenage grandson.
synonyms: antediluvian, antique, vintage, ancient, venerable

HOMAGE *n* (<u>ah</u> mihj) (<u>hah</u> mihj)
public honor and respect
Upon arriving at the village, the warriors paid *homage* to its chief.
synonyms: acclaim, kudos, panegyric, tribute, encomium

HOMILY *n* (<u>hah</u> muh lee)
sermonlike speech
The congregation slept as the preacher delivered his *homily*.
synonyms: lecture, admonition, oration

HOMOGENEOUS *adj* (huh <u>mah</u> juhn uhs)
composed of identical parts
Finland was a very *homogenous* country until immigrants began to settle there several decades ago.
synonyms: uniform, unmixed

HONE *v* (hohn)
to sharpen
You might want to *hone* your writing skills before filling out college applications.
synonyms: edge, file, strop, whet, perfect

HONOR *v* (<u>ah</u> nuhr)
to praise, glorify, pay tribute to
Those who had risked their lives to defend everyone's civil rights were *honored* at the ceremony.
synonyms: homage, reverence, veneration, deference

HUMANE *adj* (hyoo <u>mayn</u>)
merciful, kindly
A *humane* man, the camp commander made sure to treat all the prisoners of war fairly.
synonyms: compassionate, humanitarian, kind

HUSBAND *v* (<u>huhz</u> buhnd)
to manage economically; to use sparingly
The cyclist paced herself at the start of the race, knowing that if she *husbanded* her resources she'd have the strength to break out of the pack later on.
synonyms: conserve

HYGIENIC *adj* (hie <u>jehn</u> ihk)
clean, sanitary
A century or two ago, it was realized that surgery should be performed under *hygienic* conditions.
synonyms: unpolluted, decontaminated

HYPERBOLE *n* (hie <u>puhr</u> boh lee)
purposeful exaggeration for effect
When the mayor claimed his town was one of the seven wonders of the world, outsiders classified his statement as a *hyperbole*.
synonyms: inflation, magnification, embellishment

HYPOCHONDRIA *n* (hie puh <u>kahn</u> dree uh)
unfounded belief that one is often ill
Dr. Pradesh groaned when he saw Mr. Crupp on his appointment list yet again; the man was a classic victim of *hypochondria*.
synonyms: valetudinarianism, neurosis

*HYPOCRITE *n* (<u>hih</u> puh kriht)
one who puts on a false appearance of virtue; one who criticizes a flaw he in fact possesses
What a *hypocrite*: He criticizes those who wear fur but then he buys for himself a leather shearling coat.
synonyms: pretender, deceiver

*HYPOTHETICAL *adj* (hie puh <u>theh</u> tih kuhl)
theoretical, speculative
The official claimed that his radical proposal to close half the city hospitals was only *hypothetical*.
synonyms: abstract, academic, suppositional

I

ICONOCLAST *n* (ie <u>kahn</u> uh klaast)
one who attacks traditional beliefs
His lack of regard for traditional beliefs soon established him as an *iconoclast*.
synonyms: rebel, dissident, nonconformist

*IDEALISM *n* (ie <u>deel</u> ihz uhm) (ie <u>dee</u> uh lih zuhm)
pursuit of noble goals
"I admire his *idealism*, but how does Bola think he can support ten orphans?" complained his sister.
synonyms: impracticality, quixoticism, romanticism

IDIOSYNCRASY *n* (ih dee uh <u>sihn</u> kruh see)
peculiarity of temperament, eccentricity
His numerous *idiosyncrasies* included a fondness for wearing bright green shoes with mauve socks.
synonyms: quirk, oddity, humor

IGNOBLE *adj* (ihg <u>noh</u> buhl)
having low moral standards, not noble in character; mean
The photographer was paid a princely sum for the picture of the self-proclaimed ethicist in the *ignoble* act of pick-pocketing.
synonyms: lowly, vulgar

IGNOMINIOUS *adj* (ihg nuh <u>mih</u> nee uhs)
disgraceful and dishonorable
He was humiliated by his *ignominious* dismissal.
synonyms: despicable, degrading, debasing

ILK *n* (ihlk)
type or kind
"I try not to associate with men of his *ilk*," sniffed the respectable old lady.
synonyms: sort, nature, character, variety, class

ILLICIT *adj* (ihl <u>lih</u> suht)
illegal, improper
The mafia is heavily involved in *illicit* activities such as racketeering and drugs.
synonyms: unlawful, criminal, prohibited, forbidden

ILLUSORY *adj* (ih <u>loo</u> suhr ee) (ih <u>loos</u> ree)
producing illusion, deceptive
The desert explorer was devastated to discover that the lake he thought he had seen was in fact *illusory*.
synonyms: false, imaginary

ILLUSTRIOUS *adj* (ih <u>luhs</u> tree uhs)
famous, renowned
The *illustrious* composer produced masterpiece after masterpiece, entrancing her fans.
synonyms: noted, celebrated, eminent, famed, notable

IMBUE *v* (ihm <u>byoo</u>)
to infuse; dye, wet, moisten
Marcia struggled to *imbue* her children with decent values, a difficult task in this day and age.
synonyms: charge, freight, impregnate, permeate, pervade

IMMACULATE *adj* (ih <u>maa</u> kyuh luht)
spotless; free from error
After I cleaned my apartment for hours, it was finally *immaculate*.
synonyms: clean, pure, unstained

IMMERSE *v* (ih <u>muhrs</u>)
to bathe, dip; to engross, preoccupy
The Japanese snow monkey *immersed* itself in the hot spring.
synonyms: douse, dunk, submerge, engage, absorb

IMMUNE *adj* (ih <u>myoon</u>)
exempt; protected from harm or disease; unresponsive to
After you get chicken pox once, you are *immune* to the disease.
synonyms: impervious, shielded

IMMUTABLE *adj* (ihm <u>myoot</u> uh buhl)
unchangeable, invariable
Poverty was an *immutable* fact of life for the unfortunate Wood family; every moneymaking scheme they tried failed.
synonyms: fixed, stationary, permanent, steady

IMPAIR *v* (ihm <u>payr</u>)
to damage, injure
After embroidering in poor light for decades, Doris's vision became *impaired*.
synonyms: harm, hurt, mar, spoil

IMPASSE *n* (<u>ihm</u> paas) (ihm <u>pass</u>)
blocked path, dilemma with no solution
The rock slide produced an *impasse*, so no one could proceed further on the road.
synonyms: cul-de-sac, deadlock, stalemate

IMPASSIVE *adj* (ihm <u>paas</u> ihv)
absent of any external sign of emotion, expressionless
Given his *impassive* expression, it was hard to tell whether he approved of my plan.
synonyms: apathetic, unemotional

IMPECCABLE *adj* (ihm <u>pehk</u> uh buhl)
flawless, without fault
The dress rehearsal was *impeccable*; nothing needed to be changed before the actual performance.
synonyms: perfect, consummate

IMPECUNIOUS *adj* (ihm pih <u>kyoo</u> nyuhs) (ihm pih <u>kyoo</u> nee uhs)
poor, having no money
After the stock market crashed, many former millionaires found themselves *impecunious*.
synonyms: indigent, needy, penniless, impoverished, destitute

IMPEDIMENT *n* (ihm <u>pehd</u> uh muhnt)
barrier, obstacle; speech disorder
Sarah's speech *impediment* made it difficult to understand what she was saying.
synonyms: obstruction, hindrance, block, hurdle

IMPERATIVE *adj* (ihm <u>pehr</u> uh tihv)
essential; mandatory
It's *imperative* that you follow the instructions of the crew in the event of a crash or chaos will result.
synonyms: peremptory, urgent, pressing

IMPERIOUS *adj* (ihm <u>pihr</u> ee uhs)
commanding, domineering; urgent
Though the king had been a kind leader, his daughter was *imperious* and demanding during her rule.
synonyms: authoritarian

IMPERTINENT *adj* (ihm <u>puhr</u> tuh nuhnt)
rude
The *impertinent* boy stuck his tongue out at the policeman.
synonyms: improper, forward, bold, impolite, discourteous

IMPERVIOUS *adj* (ihm <u>puhr</u> vee uhs)
impossible to penetrate; incapable of being affected
A good raincoat should be *impervious* to moisture.
synonyms: immune, callous

*IMPETUOUS *adj* (ihm <u>peh</u> choo uhs) (ihm <u>pehch</u> wuhs)
quick to act without thinking
The *impetuous* day trader rushed to sell his stocks at the first hint of trouble and lost $300,000.
synonyms: impulsive, passionate

IMPIOUS *adj* (ihm <u>pie</u> uhs) (<u>ihm</u> pee uhs)
not devout in religion
The nun cut herself off from her *impious* family after she entered the convent.
synonyms: irreverent, profane, immoral

IMPLACABLE *adj* (ihm <u>play</u> kuh buhl) (ihm <u>plaa</u> kuh buhl)
inflexible; not capable of being changed or pacified
The *implacable* teasing was hard for the child to take.
synonyms: merciless, relentless

IMPLICATE *v* (<u>ihm</u> pluh kayt)
to involve in a crime, incriminate
In an effort to save himself, the criminal *implicated* his friends in the murder.
synonyms: embroil, ensnare, incriminate

IMPLICIT *adj* (ihm <u>plih</u> siht)
implied, not directly expressed
Jake's desire to terminate his relationship was *implicit* in his request that Sheila return his keys.
synonyms: tacit, inferred, unstated, understood

IMPORTUNATE *adj* (ihm <u>pohr</u> chuh niht)
troublesomely urgent; extremely persistent in request or demand
Her *importunate* appeal for a job caused me to grant her an interview.
synonyms: insistent, obstinate

IMPOSE *v* (ihm <u>pohz</u>)
to inflict, force upon
The patriarch *imposed* his will upon his daughter, refusing to allow her to marry the butler.
synonyms: dictate, decree, demand, ordain, prescribe

IMPOUND *v* (ihm <u>pownd</u>)
to seize and confine
The car was *impounded* when the Hendersons could not keep up with the payments for it.
synonyms: confiscate, retain

IMPOVERISH *v* (ihm <u>pah</u> vuhr ihsh) (ihm <u>pahv</u> rihsh)
to make poor or bankrupt
Though he had more money than he could count, Bruce tried to *impoverish* his neighbors by suing them.
synonyms: beggar, ruin, pauperize, deplete, drain

IMPRECATION *n* (ihm prih <u>kay</u> shuhn)
a curse
Spouting violent *imprecations*, Hank searched for the person who had vandalized his truck.
synonyms: damnation

IMPREGNABLE *adj* (ihm <u>prehg</u> nuh buhl)
totally safe from attack, able to resist defeat
The fortress was *impregnable*, that is, until the defenders allowed the Trojan Horse to enter its gates.
synonyms: unassailable, invincible, secure, inviolable, invulnerable

IMPROMPTU *adj* (ihm <u>prahmp</u> too) (ihm <u>prahmp</u> tyoo)
spontaneous, without rehearsal
The president was fine when he had a teleprompter, but he spoke gibberish whenever he had to make *impromptu* comments.
synonyms: extemporaneous, offhand, unprepared, ad-lib

IMPUDENT *adj* (<u>ihm</u> pyuh duhnt)
marked by cocky boldness or disregard for others
Considering the judge had been lenient in her sentence, it was *impudent* of the defendant to refer to her by her first name.
synonyms: arrogant, insolent

IMPUGN *v* (ihm <u>pyoon</u>)
to call into question; to attack verbally
"How dare you *impugn* my motives?" protested the lawyer, on being accused of ambulance chasing.
synonyms: challenge, dispute

IMPULSE *n* (<u>ihm</u> puhls)
sudden tendency, inclination
On *impulse*, Sarah bought a leather jacket for her boyfriend, although she couldn't really afford it.
synonyms: urge, whim

IMPULSIVE *adj* (ihm <u>puhl</u> sihv)
spontaneous, unpredictable
Last Christmas she was on her way to London, but at the last minute her *impulsive* side took over, and she canceled the trip and went to Hawaii instead.
synonyms: instinctive, involuntary, automatic, rash, impetuous

*IMPUTE *v* (ihm <u>pyoot</u>)
to lay the responsibility or blame for, often unjustly
It seemed unfair to *impute* the accident on me, especially since they were the ones who ran the red light.
synonyms: ascribe, attribute, pin on

INADVERTENT *adj* (ihn uhd <u>vuhr</u> tnt)
unintentional
It was *inadvertent* when she gave him a black eye; his face was in the way of her fist.
synonyms: accidental, involuntary

*INANE *adj* (ih <u>nayn</u>)
foolish, silly, lacking significance
The talk show host desperately tried to make the star's *inane* comments seem more interesting.
synonyms: empty, banal, vacuous

*INARTICULATE *adj* (ihn ahr <u>tihk</u> yuh liht)
tongue-tied, unable to speak clearly
He was *inarticulate* with rage, so he could not voice his objection clearly.
synonyms: speechless, incomprehensible, unintelligible

INAUGURATE *v* (ih <u>naw</u> gyuh rayt) (ih <u>naw</u> guh rayt)
to begin or start officially; to induct into office
The president was *inaugurated* in a lavish ceremony attended by thousands.
synonyms: initiate, institute, invest, ordain

INCANDESCENT *adj* (ihn kahn <u>dehs</u> uhnt)
shining brightly
The *incandescent* glow of the moon made it a night I'll never forget.
synonyms: brilliant, radiant

INCARCERATION *n* (ihn <u>kahr</u> suhr ayt)
imprisonment
To avoid *incarceration*, the swindler struck a plea bargain with the district attorney's office.
synonyms: confinement, internment, jailing

INCENDIARY *n* (ihn <u>sehn</u> dee ehr ee)
combustible, flammable, burning easily
Gasoline is so *incendiary* that cigarette smoking is forbidden at gas stations.
synonyms: inflammable, explosive

INCENSE *v* (ihn <u>sehns</u>)
to infuriate, enrage
The general became thoroughly *incensed* when his subordinates failed to follow his orders.
synonyms: madden, exasperate, outrage

INCEPTION *n* (ihn <u>sehp</u> shuhn)
beginning
Even from its *inception*, those who were involved in the plan knew that it probably wouldn't succeed.
synonyms: origin, source, root, commencement

INCESSANT *adj* (ihn <u>sehs</u> uhnt)
continuous, never ceasing
Otis's wife was *incessant* when she nagged him about the way he sat watching TV all day instead of looking for a job.
synonyms: constant, interminable, relentless, unending, unremitting

INCHOATE *adj* (ihn <u>koh</u> iht)
being only partly in existence; imperfectly formed
For every page of the crisp writing that made it into the final book, Jessie has 10 pages of *inchoate* rambling that made up the first draft.
synonyms: formless, undefined

INCIPIENT *adj* (ihn <u>sihp</u> ee uhnt)
beginning to exist or appear; in an initial stage
The *incipient* idea seemed brilliant, but they knew it needed much more development.
synonyms: developing, basic

INCISIVE *adj* (ihn <u>sie</u> sihv)
perceptive, penetrating
The psychologist's *incisive* analysis of her patient's childhood helped him to understand his own behavior.
synonyms: clear, sharp, biting, trenchant, crisp

INCLINATION *n* (ihn cluh <u>nay</u> shuhn)
tendency towards
Her natural *inclination* was to refuse Max's invitation to dinner.
synonyms: leaning, trend, preference, disposition, propensity

INCOMPATIBLE *adj* (ihn kuhm <u>paat</u> uh buhl)
opposed in nature, not able to live or work together
Some people on the left feel that unrestricted global capitalism is *incompatible* with democracy.
synonyms: irreconcilable, unsuited, inconsistent

*INCONSEQUENTIAL *adj* (ihn kahn sih <u>kwehn</u> shuhl)
unimportant, trivial
The king dismissed the concerns of his horrified advisers as *inconsequential* and decided to go ahead with his marriage to the beautiful young woman, despite rumors that she was criminally insane.
synonyms: irrelevant, extraneous, immaterial, insignificant

INCONTROVERTIBLE *adj* (ihn kahn truh <u>vuhr</u> tuh buhl)
unquestionable, beyond dispute
The fact that Harvard would be too expensive for Lisa without scholarship money was *incontrovertible*.
synonyms: irrefutable, indisputable

INCORRIGIBLE *adj* (ihn <u>kohr</u> ih juh buhl)
incapable of being corrected or amended; difficult to control or manage
"You're *incorrigible*," yelled the frustrated mother to her son, in the middle of his third tantrum of the day.
synonyms: delinquent, unfixable

INCREDULOUS *adj* (ihn <u>krehj</u> uh luhs)
unwilling to accept what is true, skeptical
The Lasky children were *incredulous* when their parents sat them down and told them the facts of life.
synonyms: doubtful, disbelieving

INCULCATE *v* (ihn <u>kuhl</u> kayt) (<u>ihn</u> kuhl kayt)
to teach, impress in the mind
Most parents blithely *inculcate* their children with their religious beliefs instead of allowing their children to select their own faith.
synonyms: instill, indoctrinate, preach, implant

INCUMBENT *n* (ihn <u>kuhm</u> buhnt)
holding a specified office, often political
Incumbents often have an advantage over unknown parties in political races.
synonyms: sitting, acting

INDEFATIGABLE *adj* (ihn dih <u>faat</u> ih guh buhl)
never tired
Theresa seemed *indefatigable*, barely sweating after a 10-mile run.
synonyms: unflagging, weariless, inexhaustible

INDEFENSIBLE *adj* (ihn dih <u>fehn</u> suh buhl)
inexcusable, unforgivable
"Your lying and sneaking around is *indefensible*; I never want to see you again!" Amelia shouted at her boyfriend.
synonyms: unpardonable, unjustifiable, untenable, unendurable

INDELIBLE *adj* (ihn <u>dehl</u> uh buhl)
permanent, not erasable
Rita was enraged when her infant daughter drew pictures on the wall in *indelible* ink.
synonyms: ineffaceable, inexpugnable, permanent

INDICT *v* (ihn <u>diet</u>)
to accuse formally, charge with a crime
The Mafioso was *indicted* for tax evasion because the FBI could not prove any of his other crimes.
synonyms: incriminate, inculpate, arraign, denounce, impeach

*INDIFFERENT *adj* (ihn <u>dihf</u> ruhnt) (ihn <u>dihf</u> uhr uhnt)
uncaring, unbiased
John H. Holmes remarked, "The universe is not hostile, nor yet is it friendly. It is simply *indifferent*."
synonyms: unconcerned, uncurious, detached, uninterested, apathetic

INDIGENOUS *adj* (ihn <u>dihj</u> uh nuhs)
native, occurring naturally in an area
Palm trees are *indigenous* to Florida, unlike penguins.
synonyms: intrinsic, innate, endemic, autochthonous, aboriginal

INDIGENT *adj* (<u>ihn</u> dih juhnt)
very poor
Because the suspect was *indigent*, the state paid for his legal representation.
synonyms: needy, impecunious, impoverished, destitute, penniless

*INDIGNANT *adj* (ihn <u>dihg</u> nuhnt)
angry, incensed, offended
The innocent passerby was *indignant* when the police treated him as a suspect in the crime.
synonyms: furious, irate, mad, wrathful, ireful

INDOLENT *adj* (<u>ihn</u> duh luhnt)
habitually lazy, idle
Her *indolent* ways got her fired from many jobs.
synonyms: slothful, languid, lethargic, sluggish, fainéant

INDUBITABLE *adj* (ihn <u>doo</u> bih tuh buhl) (ihn <u>dyoo</u> bih tuh buhl)
unquestionable
His *indubitable* cooking skills made it all the more astonishing when his Thanksgiving dinner tasted awful.
synonyms: certain, apparent, unassailable

INDUCE *v* (ih <u>doos</u>) (ihn <u>dyoos</u>)
to persuade; bring about
Tom attempted to *induce* his girlfriend to go skydiving with him, but she refused.
synonyms: prevail, convince, lead, effect, occasion

INDUCT *v* (ihn <u>duhkt</u>)
to place ceremoniously, admit
The pitcher was proud to be *inducted* into the Baseball Hall of Fame.
synonyms: install, inaugurate, initiate

INDULGE *v* (ihn <u>duhlj</u>)
to give in to a craving or desire
Jenny *indulged* herself with a weekend at a luxurious spa.
synonyms: humor, gratify, allow, pamper

INEBRIATE *v* (ihn <u>ee</u> bree ay tihd)
to make drunk, intoxicate
The best man slurred his words during his speech at the wedding after he *inebriated* himself with whiskey.
synonyms: exhilarated, stupefied

INEPT *adj* (ih <u>ehpt</u>)
clumsy, awkward
He was so *inept* in the garden that he dug up roses and fertilized weeds.
synonyms: maladroit, gauche, ungainly

INERT *adj* (ihn <u>uhrt</u>)
unable to move, tending to inactivity
In the heat of the desert afternoon, lizards lie *inert*.
synonyms: sluggish, lethargic, inactive, idle, dormant

*INEVITABLE *adj* (ihn <u>ehv</u> ih tuh buhl)
certain, unavoidable
With all the obstacles in their path, it was perhaps *inevitable* that their affair should end unhappily.
synonyms: inescapable, sure, predictable

*INEXORABLE *adj* (ihn <u>ehk</u> suhr uh buhl)
inflexible, unyielding
The *inexorable* force of the twister swept away their house.
synonyms: adamant, obdurate, relentless

INFALLIBLE *adj* (ihn <u>faal</u> uh buhl)
incapable of making a mistake
I considered my mother to be *infallible* until she got fired from her job when I was 10.
synonyms: certain, guaranteed

INFAMY *n* (<u>ihn</u> fuh mee)
reputation for bad deeds
The corrupt mayor's *infamy* was legendary in the city.
synonyms: disgrace, dishonor, shame, ignominy, odium

INFATUATE *v* (ihn <u>faach</u> oo ayt)
To become strongly or foolishly attached to, inspired with foolish passion, or overly in love
After seeing her picture in a fashion magazine, Lester became completely *infatuated* with the beautiful model.
synonyms: besotted, enthralled, smitten, enamored, entranced

INFILTRATE *v* (<u>ihn</u> fihl trayt) (ihn <u>fihl</u> trayt)
to pass secretly into enemy territory
The spy *infiltrated* the CIA, gaining access to highly classified information.
synonyms: insinuate, penetrate

INFINITESIMAL *adj* (ihn fihn ih <u>tehs</u> uh muhl)
extremely tiny
Infinitesimal specks of dust marred the camera lens, blotching the pictures that were taken through it.
synonyms: minute, microscopic

INFIRMITY *n* (ihn <u>fuhr</u> mih tee)
disease, ailment
Plagued by an *infirmity*, the old man rarely left his bed during his final years.
synonyms: weakness, frailty, infirmity, illness, affliction

INFRINGE *v* (ihn <u>frihnj</u>)
to encroach, trespass; to transgress, violate
Koca-Cola was sued by Coca-Cola because they *infringed* on their copyright.
synonyms: contravene, appropriate, overstep

INGENIOUS *adj* (ih <u>jeen</u> yuhs)
original, clever, inventive
Luther found an *ingenious* way to solve the complex math problem.
synonyms: shrewd, cunning, imaginative

*INGENUOUS *adj* (ihn <u>jehn</u> yoo uhs)
straightforward, open; naive and unsophisticated
She was so *ingenuous* that her friends feared her innocence would be exploited when she visited the big city.
synonyms: simple, natural, unaffected, artless, candid

INGRATE *n* (<u>ihn</u> grayt)
ungrateful person
When none of her relatives thanked her for the fruit cakes she had sent them, Doris condemned them all as *ingrates*.
synonyms: churl, cad

INGRATIATE *v* (ihn <u>gray</u> shee ayt)
to gain favor with another by deliberate effort, to seek to please somebody so as to gain an advantage
The new intern tried to *ingratiate* herself with the managers so that they might consider her for a future job.
synonyms: flatter, curry favor

INHIBIT *v* (ihn <u>hihb</u> iht)
to hold back, prevent, restrain
Paulette was *inhibited* in telling Rod that she resented him borrowing money and never paying her back.
synonyms: curb, check, bridle, suppress

INIMICAL *adj* (ih <u>nihm</u> ih kuhl)
hostile, unfriendly
Even though a cease-fire had been in place for months, the two sides were still *inimical* to each other.
synonyms: injurious, harmful, adverse, antagonistic

INIQUITY *n* (ih <u>nihk</u> wih tee)
sin, evil act
"I promise to close every den of *iniquity* in this town!" thundered the conservative new mayor.
synonyms: immorality, injustice, wickedness, vice, enormity

INJUNCTION *n* (ihn <u>juhnk</u> shuhn)
command, order
The Catholic religion has an *injunction* against the use of birth control.
synonyms: directive, behest, mandate, edict, decree

INKLING *n* (<u>ingk</u> ling)
hint; vague idea
Niles had had no *inkling* that he was about to be promoted and was shocked when his manager gave him the news.
synonyms: indication, notion, clue, glimmer, intimation

INNATE *adj* (ih <u>nayt</u>) (<u>ihn</u> ayt)
natural, inborn
Her *innate* level-headedness will help her to withstand the enormous pressure she's under.
synonyms: congenital, inherent, essential, intrinsic

INNOCUOUS *adj* (ih <u>nahk</u> yoo uhs)
harmless; inoffensive
Some snakes are poisonous, but most species are *innocuous* and pose no danger to humans.
synonyms: benign, safe, insipid

INNOVATE *v* (<u>ihn</u> uh vayt)
to invent, modernize, revolutionize
Esprit *innovated* a popular new suit design, transforming the fashion industry.
synonyms: begin, introduce, author, create, devise

INNUENDO *n* (ihn yoo <u>ehn</u> doh)
indirect and subtle criticism, insinuation
Through hints and *innuendo*, the yellow journalist managed to ruin *The Star*'s reputation while ensuring that he could not be sued for slander.
synonyms: implication, aspersion, imputation, reflection, intimation

INNUMERABLE *adj* (ih <u>noo</u> muhr uh buhl) (ih <u>nyoo</u> muhr uh buhl)
too many to be counted
There are *innumerable* stars in the universe.
synonyms: incalculable, immeasurable, infinite, innumerable, inestimable

INQUEST *n* (<u>ihn</u> kwehst)
an investigation, an inquiry
The police chief ordered an *inquest* to determine what went wrong.

INSCRUTABLE *adj* (ihn <u>skroo</u> tuh buhl)
impossible to understand fully
Based on the judge's *inscrutable* face, the defense had no clue as to what the jurors' verdict would be.
synonyms: mysterious, impenetrable, cryptic, enigmatic

INSENSATE *adj* (ihn <u>sehn</u> sayt) (ihn <u>sehn</u> siht)
lacking sensibility and understanding, foolish
The shock of the accident left him *insensate*, but after some time, the numbness subsided and he was able to tell the officer what had happened.
synonyms: unfeeling, callous

INSIDIOUS *adj* (ihn <u>sihd</u> ee uhs)
treacherous, devious
Iago's *insidious* comments about Desdemona fuelled Othello's feelings of jealousy regarding his wife.
synonyms: deceitful, perfidious, alluring

INSINUATE *v* (ihn <u>sihn</u> yoo ayt)
to suggest, say indirectly, imply
Brenda *insinuated* that Deirdre's brother had stolen her watch without accusing him outright.
synonyms: hint, intimate

INSIPID *adj* (ihn <u>sihp</u> ihd)
bland, lacking flavor; lacking excitement
The critic claimed that the *insipid* soup lacked any type of spice.
synonyms: lackluster, dull, flat, weak

INSOLENT *adj* (<u>ihn</u> suh luhnt)
insultingly arrogant, overbearing
After having spoken with three *insolent* customer service representatives, Shelly was relieved when the fourth one sympathized with her complaint.
synonyms: offensive, rude

INSTIGATE *v* (<u>ihn</u> stih gayt)
to incite, urge, agitate
The man who had *instigated* the rebellion escaped, although all his followers were arrested.
synonyms: foment, goad, spark

*INSULAR *adj* (<u>ihn</u> suh luhr) (<u>ihn</u> syuh luhr)
characteristic of an isolated people, especially having a narrow viewpoint
It was a shock for Kendra to go from her small high school, with her *insular* group of friends, to a huge college with students from all over the country.
synonyms: provincial, narrow-minded

INSUPERABLE *adj* (ihn <u>soo</u> puhr uh buhl)
incapable of being surmounted or overcome
Insuperable as though our problems may seem, I'm confident we'll come out ahead.
synonyms: unconquerable

INSURGENT *adj* (ihn <u>suhr</u> juhnt)
rebellious, insubordinate
The *insurgent* crew staged a mutiny and threw the captain overboard.
synonyms: revolutionary, seditious

INSURRECTION *n* (ihn suh <u>rehk</u> shuhn)
rebellion
After the Emperor's troops crushed the *insurrection*, its leaders fled the country.
synonyms: revolution, revolt, mutiny, uprising

INTANGIBLE *adj* (ihn <u>taan</u> juh buhl)
not perceptible to the touch, not material
Falstaff rejects honor because it is *intangible*; it is merely a word, and a word is merely air.
synonyms: impalpable, imponderable, illusory, abstract

*INTEGRITY n (ihn <u>tehg</u> rih tee)
decency, honesty, wholeness
After my older brother brought shame to our family name by being a troublemaker, I tried my best restore our family's *integrity*.
synonyms: honor, probity, rectitude, virtue

INTER *v* (ihn <u>tuhr</u>)
to bury
After giving the masses one last chance to pay their respects, the leader's body was *interred*.

INTERMITTENT *adj* (ihn tuhr <u>mih</u> tnt)
starting and stopping
The flow of traffic was *intermittent* on the highway, but the commuters were thankful that it hadn't stopped completely.
synonyms: periodic, sporadic, occasional, discontinuous

INTERROGATE *v* (ihn <u>tehr</u> uh gayt)
to question formally
The secret police *interrogated* the suspected rebel for days, demanding the names of his co-conspirators.
synonyms: examine, catechize

INTERSECT *v* (ihn tuhr <u>sehkt</u>)
to divide by passing through or across
The busy freeway *intersected* the country road.
synonyms: cross, overlap, meet

INTERSPERSE *v* (ihn tuhr <u>spuhrs</u>)
to distribute among, mix with
The farmer *interspersed* the mushrooms among the bushes and clumps of moss in the shady forest.
synonyms: commingle, intermix

INTIMATION *n* (<u>ihn</u> tuh may shuhn)
a subtle and indirect hint
Abby chose to ignore Babu's *intimation* that she wasn't as good a swimmer as she claimed.
synonyms: suggestion, insinuation

INTRACTABLE *adj* (ihn <u>traak</u> tuh buhl)
not easily managed or manipulated
Intractable for hours, the wild horse eventually allowed the rider to mount.
synonyms: stubborn, unruly

*INTRANSIGENT *adj* (ihn <u>traan</u> suh juhnt) (ihn <u>traan</u> zuh juhnt)
uncompromising, refusing to abandon an extreme position
His *intransigent* positions on social issues cost him the election.
synonyms: obstinate, unyielding

*INTREPID *adj* (ihn <u>trehp</u> ihd)
fearless, resolutely courageous
Despite freezing winds, the *intrepid* hiker completed his ascent.
synonyms: brave

INTRINSIC *adj* (ihn <u>trihn</u> zihk) (ihn <u>trihn</u> sihk)
inherent, internal
The *intrinsic* value of this diamond is already considerable, and its elegant setting makes it truly priceless.
synonyms: fundamental, essential, innate

INTROSPECTIVE *adj* (ihn truh <u>spehk</u> tihv)
contemplating one's own thoughts and feelings
The *introspective* young man toured the countryside on his own, writing poetry based on his reflections.
synonyms: thoughtful, reflective, meditative

INTROVERT *n* (ihn truh vuhrt)
someone given to self-analysis; shy person
Janet's a real *introvert*; she rarely pays wants to be involved in what the people around her are doing.
synonyms: contemplative, loner, narcissist

*INTUITIVE *adj* (ihn <u>too</u> ih tihv)
instinctive, untaught
Some people seem to have an *intuitive* grasp of higher mathematics, whereas others study endlessly without success.
synonyms: visceral

INUNDATE *v* (<u>ihn</u> uhn dayt)
to cover with a flood; to overwhelm as if with a flood
The box office was *inundated* with requests for tickets to the award-winning play.
synonyms: swamp, drown

INURE *v* (ihn <u>yoor</u>)
to harden; accustom; become used to
Eventually, Hassad became *inured* to the sirens that went off every night and could sleep through them.
synonyms: habituate, familiarize, condition

INVALIDATE *v* (ihn <u>vaal</u> ih dayt)
to negate or nullify
The judge *invalidated* Niko's driver's license after he was caught speeding in a school zone.
synonyms: abrogate, cancel, rescind, void, annul

INVECTIVE *n* (ihn <u>vehk</u> tihv)
Abusive language
A stream of *invectives* poured from Mrs. Pratt's mouth as she watched the vandals smash her ceramic frog.
synonyms: vituperation, denunciation, revilement

INVETERATE *adj* (ihn <u>veht</u> uhr iht)
firmly established, especially with respect to a habit or attitude
An *inveterate* risk-taker, Lori tried her luck at bungee-jumping.
synonyms: habitual, chronic

INVIDIOUS *adj* (ihn <u>vihd</u> ee uhs)
envious; obnoxious
It is cruel and *invidious* for parents to play favorites with their children.
synonyms: resentful, discriminatory, insulting, jaundiced

INVINCIBLE *adj* (ihn <u>vihn</u> suh buhl)
invulnerable, unbeatable
At the height of his career, John Elway was considered practically *invincible*.
synonyms: unconquerable, insuperable

INVOKE *v* (ihn <u>vohk</u>)
to call upon, request help
Baxter *invoked* the financial assistance of all his relatives when his business ran into serious trouble.
synonyms: summon, solicit, conjure, evoke

IOTA *n* (ie <u>oh</u> tuh)
very tiny amount
"If I even got one *iota* of respect from you, I'd be satisfied," raged the father at his insolent son.
synonyms: bit, atom, crumb, morsel, mote

IRASCIBLE *adj* (ih <u>raas</u> uh buhl)
easily angered, hot-tempered
One of the most *irascible* barbarians of all time, Attila the Hun ravaged much of Europe during
his time.
synonyms: irritable, crabby

*IRONIC *adj* (ie <u>rahn</u> ihk)
poignantly contrary or incongruous to what was expected
It was *ironic* to learn that shy Wendy from high school grew up to be the loud-mouth host of the daily
talk show.

IRREVERENT *adj* (ih <u>rehv</u> uhr uhnt)
disrespectful in a gentle or humorous way
Kevin's *irreverent* attitude toward the principal annoyed the teacher but amused the other children.
synonyms: cheeky, satiric

IRREVOCABLE *adj* (ih <u>rehv</u> uh kuh buhl)
conclusive, irreversible
Once he had pushed the red button, the president's decision to launch a missile was *irrevocable*.
synonyms: permanent, indelible, irreparable

ITINERANT *adj* (ie <u>tihn</u> uhr uhnt)
wandering from place to place; unsettled
The *itinerant* tomcat came back to the Johansson homestead every two months.
synonyms: nomadic, vagrant

ITINERARY *n* (ie <u>tihn</u> uh reh ree)
route of a traveler's journey
The travel agent provided her customer with a detailed *itinerary* of his journey.
synonyms: plan, record, guidebook

J

JADED *adj* (<u>jay</u> dihd)
to tire by excess or overuse; slightly cynical
While the naive girls stared at the spectacle in awe, the *jaded* matrons dozed in their chairs.
synonyms: wearied, jaundiced, sated, callous, blasé

JARGON *n* (<u>jahr</u> guhn)
nonsensical talk; specialized language
You need to master technical *jargon* in order to communicate successfully with engineers.
synonyms: dialect, cant, argot, idiom, slang

JETTISON *v* (<u>jeht</u> ih zuhn) (<u>jeht</u> ih suhn)
to discard, to get rid of as unnecessary or encumbering
The sinking ship *jettisoned* its cargo in a desperate attempt to reduce its weight.
synonyms: eject, dump

JINGOISM *n* (<u>jing</u> goh ihz uhm)
belligerent support of one's country
The president's *jingoism* made him declare war on other countries at the slightest provocation.
synonyms: chauvinism, nationalism

JOCULAR *adj* (<u>jahk</u> yuh luhr)
playful, humorous
The *jocular* old man entertained his grandchildren for hours.
synonyms: comical, amusing

*JUBILATION *n* (joo bih <u>lay</u> shuhn)
joy, celebration, exultation
When victory over Europe was declared on May 14, 1945, New Yorkers poured into Times Square in an act of spontaneous *jubilation*.
synonyms: euphoria, exultation, exuberance, celebration

JUDICIOUS *adj* (joo <u>dih</u> shuhs)
sensible, showing good judgment
The wise and distinguished judge was well known for having a *judicious* temperament.
synonyms: prudent, sagacious, sapient, circumspect

JUNCTURE *n* (<u>juhnk</u> chuhr)
point of time, especially where two things are joined
At this *juncture*, I think it would be a good idea for us to take a coffee break.
synonyms: confluence, convergence, crossroads, moment, crisis

JUXTAPOSITION *n* (juk stuh puh <u>zihsh</u> uhn)
side-by-side placement
The porcelain dog was placed in *juxtaposition* with the straw dog house on the mantelpiece.
synonyms: comparison, contrast

K

KEEN *adj*
having a sharp edge; intellectually sharp, perceptive
With her *keen* intelligence, she figured out the puzzle in seconds flat.
synonyms: acute, quick, canny

KERNEL *n* (<u>kuhr</u> nuhl)
innermost, essential part; seed grain, often in a shell
The parrot cracked the hard shell of the seed in order to get at its delicious *kernel*.
synonyms: core, marrow, pith, heart

KINDLE *v* (<u>kihn</u> duhl)
to set fire to or ignite; excite or inspire
With only damp wood to work with, Tilda had great difficulty trying to *kindle* the camp fire.
synonyms: light, spark, arouse, awaken

KINETIC *adj* (kih <u>neh</u> tihk)
relating to motion; characterized by movement
The *kinetic* sculpture moved back and forth, startling the museum visitors.
synonyms: mobile, active, dynamic

KNELL *n* (nehl)
sound of a funeral bell; omen of death or failure
When the townspeople heard the *knell* from the church belfry, they knew that their mayor had died.
synonyms: toll, chime, peal

KUDOS *n* (<u>koo</u> dohz)
fame, glory, honor
The actress happily accepted *kudos* from the press for her stunning performance in the film.
synonyms: acclaim, praise, encomium, accolade, homage

L

LABYRINTH *n* (<u>laab</u> uh rihnth)
maze
When Peichi finally reached the center of the *labyrinth*, she realized that she had no idea how to get back to its entrance.
synonyms: entanglement, mesh, web

LACERATION *n* (laa suh ray shuhn)
cut or wound
The chopping knife slipped and slashed Frank's arm, making a deep *laceration*.
synonyms: gash, tear

LACHRYMOSE *adj* (<u>laak</u> ruh mohs)
tearful
Heather always became *lachrymose* when it was time to bid her daughter good-bye.
synonyms: weeping, teary

LACKADAISICAL *adj* (laak uh <u>day</u> zih kuhl)
idle, lazy; apathetic, indifferent
The clerk yawned openly in the customer's face, not bothering to hide his *lackadaisical* attitude.
synonyms: languorous, indolent, listless, blasé, fainéant

LACONIC *adj* (luh <u>kah</u> nihk)
using few words
She was a *laconic* poet who built her reputation on simplistic ideas.
synonyms: terse, concise, pithy, succinct

LAMENT *v* (luh <u>mehnt</u>)
to deplore, grieve
The children continued to *lament* the death of the goldfish weeks after its demise.
synonyms: mourn, sorrow, regret, bewail

LAMPOON *v* (laam <u>poon</u>)
to ridicule with satire
The mayor hated being *lampooned* by the press for his efforts to improve people's politeness.
synonyms: tease

LANGUID *adj* (<u>laang</u> gwihd)
lacking energy, indifferent, slow
The *languid* cat cleaned its fur, ignoring the vicious, snarling dog chained a few feet away from it.
synonyms: weak, listless, lackadaisical, sluggish, fainéant

LAP *v* (laap)
to drink using the tongue; to wash against
The dog eagerly *lapped* up all the water in its bowl, thirsty after barking nonstop for two hours.
synonyms: lick, lave, bathe, slosh, smack

LARCENY *n* (<u>laar</u> suh nee)
theft of property
The crime of stealing a wallet can be categorized as petty *larceny*.
synonyms: robbery, burglary, stealing

LARGESS *n* (laar <u>jehs</u>)
generous giving (as of money) to others who may seem inferior
She'd always relied on her parent's *largess*, but after graduation, she had to get a job.

LARYNX *n* (<u>laar</u> ingks)
organ containing vocal cords
The opera singer's *larynx* was damaged in the accident, spelling doom for her career.
synonyms: voice box, Adam's apple

LASSITUDE *n* (<u>laas</u> ih tood)
lethargy, sluggishness
The defeated French army plunged into a state of depressed *lassitude* as they trudged home
from Russia.
synonyms: weariness, listlessness, torpor, stupor

LATENT *adj* (<u>lay</u> tnt)
present but hidden; potential
Milton's *latent* paranoia began to emerge as he was put under more and more stress at the office.
synonyms: dormant, quiescent

LAUDABLE *adj* (<u>law</u> duh buhl)
deserving of praise
Kristin's dedication is *laudable*, but she doesn't have the necessary skills to be a good paralegal.
synonyms: commendable, admirable

LAX *adj* (laaks)
not rigid, loose; negligent
Because our delivery boy is *lax*, the newspaper often arrives sopping wet.
synonyms: careless, imprecise

LECHEROUS *adj* (<u>lehch</u> uh ruhs)
lewd, lustful
The school board censored the movie because of its portrayal of the *lecherous* criminal.
synonyms: lascivious, promiscuous

LEERY *adj* (<u>lihr</u> ree)
suspicious
After being swindled once, Ruth became *leery* of strangers trying to sell things to her.
synonyms: distrustful, wary, guarded

LEGIBLE *adj* (<u>leh</u> juh buhl)
readable
Gordon's chicken-scratch handwriting was barely *legible*.
synonyms: plain, clear

LENIENT *adj* (<u>lee</u> nee uhnt) (<u>leen</u> yuhnt)
easygoing, permissive
When the pitcher was fined only $50 for punching the batter, fans felt the punishment was too *lenient*.
synonyms: merciful, generous, indulgent, lax, tolerant

LETHARGY *n* (<u>lehth</u> uhr jee)
indifferent inactivity
The worker sank into a state of *lethargy*, letting dozens of defective toys pass him by on the
assembly line.
synonyms: lassitude, torpor, stupor, languor, sluggishness

LEVITY *n* (<u>leh</u> vih tee)
an inappropriate lack of seriousness, overly casual
The joke added needed *levity* to the otherwise serious meeting.
synonyms: amusement, humor

LIBERAL *adj* (<u>lihb</u> uh ruhl) (<u>lihb</u> ruhl)
tolerant, broad-minded; generous, lavish
Kate's *liberal* parents trusted her and allowed her to manage her own affairs to a large extent.
synonyms: progressive, latitudinarian, permissive, bounteous, munificent

LIBERTINE *n* (<u>lihb</u> uhr teen)
a free thinker, usually used disparagingly; one without moral restraint
The *libertine* took pleasure in gambling away his family's money.
synonyms: hedonist

LICENTIOUS *adj* (lie <u>sehn</u> shuhs)
immoral; unrestrained by society
Religious citizens were outraged by the *licentious* exploits of the free-spirited artists living in town.
synonyms: wanton, lewd

LIMPID *adj* (<u>lim</u> pihd)
clear, transparent
Shelley could see all the way to the bottom through the pond's *limpid* water.
synonyms: lucid, pellucid, serene

LIONIZE *v* (<u>lie</u> uhn iez)
to treat as a celebrity
After the success of his novel, the author was *lionized* by the press.
synonyms: regale, honor, feast, ply

LISSOME *adj* (<u>lihs</u> uhm)
easily flexed, limber, agile
The *lissome* yoga instructor twisted herself into shapes that her students could only dream of.
synonyms: supple, lithe, graceful

LISTLESS *adj* (<u>lihst</u> lihs)
lacking energy and enthusiasm
Listless and depressed after breaking up with his girlfriend, Nick spent his days moping on the couch.
synonyms: lethargic, sluggish, languid, fainéant, indolent

LITERATE *adj* (<u>liht</u> uhr iht)
able to read and write; well-read and educated
The only *literate* man in the village, Abraham was asked to read his neighbors' letters to them.
synonyms: erudite, scholarly, lettered, learned, cultured

*LITHE *adj* (lie*th*)
moving and bending with ease; marked by effortless grace
The dancer's *lithe* movements proved her to be a rising star in the ballet corps.
synonyms: flexible, limber

LIVID *adj* (<u>lih</u> vihd)
discolored from a bruise; pale; reddened with anger
Irving was *livid* when he discovered that someone had spilled grape juice all over his cashmere coat.
synonyms: furious, ashen, pallid, black-and-blue

LOATHE *v* (loh*th*)
to abhor, despise, hate
Sarah *loathed* the subject so much that she could barely stand to hear about her friend's girlfriend at all.
synonyms: abominate, execrate, detest, contemn

***LOBBYIST** *n* (lahb bee ihst)
person who seeks to influence political events
As a *lobbyist* for the insurance industry, he worked to defeat attempts to overhaul the healthcare system.
synonyms: courtier, influence peddler, agent

LOITER *v* (loy tuhr)
to stand around idly
The teenagers *loitered* on the corner, waiting for something to happen.
synonyms: linger, delay, dawdle

***LONGEVITY** *n* (lawn jehv ih tee)
long life
One Australian veteran of World War One had extraordinary *longevity*, dying in 2001 at the age of 107.
synonyms: duration, continuance

LOQUACIOUS *adj* (loh kway shuhs)
talkative
She was naturally *loquacious*, which was always a challenge when she was in a library or movie theater.
synonyms: chatty

LUCID *adj* (loo sihd)
clear and easily understood
Explanations should be written in a *lucid* manner so that people can understand them.
synonyms: intelligible, translucent, transparent, sane, rational

LUDICROUS *adj* (loo dih kruhs)
laughable, ridiculous
The scientist thought his colleague's claims were *ludicrous*, but he kept quiet because he didn't want to offend his old friend.
synonyms: hilarious, absurd, foolish, silly, preposterous

LUGUBRIOUS *adj* (loo goo bree uhs)
sorrowful, mournful; dismal
Irish wakes are a rousing departure from the *lugubrious* funeral services most people are accustomed to.
synonyms: gloomy, funereal, somber, melancholy, woeful

LUMBER *v* (luhm buhr)
to move slowly and awkwardly
The bear *lumbered* towards the garbage, drooling at the prospect of the Big Mac leftovers he smelled.
synonyms: stumble, lurch, hulk, galumph

LUMINARY *n* (loo muh nehr ee)
bright object; celebrity; source of inspiration
Logan's father was a *luminary* of the New York theater world, and many sought his advice.
synonyms: hero, lion, dignitary, light

LUMINOUS *adj* (<u>loo</u> muhn uhs)
bright, brilliant, glowing
The *luminous* moon shone right through the curtains into the bedroom.
synonyms: radiant, incandescent, effulgent, illuminated

LURID *adj* (<u>loor</u> ihd)
harshly shocking, sensational; glowing
The politician nearly had a heart attack when he saw the *lurid* headlines about his past indiscretions.
synonyms: ghastly, garish, gruesome, grisly, macabre

LURK *v* (luhrk)
to prowl, sneak
The burglar *lurked* in the bushes until the Jeffersons had left the house and then broke in.
synonyms: hide, stalk, creep, skulk, slink

LUSCIOUS *adj* (<u>luhsh</u> uhs)
tasty
These *luscious* strawberries are the best I've ever tasted!
synonyms: delectable, scrumptious, toothsome, seductive

LUXURIANCE *n* (luhg <u>zhoor</u> ee uhs) (luhk <u>shoor</u> ee uhs)
elegance, lavishness
The *luxuriance* of the couches made them an obvious choice for the palace sitting room.
synonyms: richness, abundance, profusion

M

MACABRE *adj* (muh <u>kaa</u> bruh) (muh <u>kaa</u> buhr)
having death as a subject; dwelling on the gruesome
Martin enjoyed *macabre* tales about werewolves and vampires.
synonyms: ghastly, grim

MACHINATION *n* (mahk uh <u>nay</u> shuhn)
plot or scheme
Tired of his enemies' endless *machinations* to remove him from the throne, the king had them executed.
synonyms: conspiracy, intrigue, design, cabal

MAELSTROM *n* (<u>mayl</u> struhm)
whirlpool; turmoil; agitated state of mind
The transportation system of the city had collapsed in the *maelstrom* of war.
synonyms: eddy, Charybdis, turbulence

MAGNANIMOUS *adj* (maag <u>naan</u> uh muhs)
generous, noble in spirit
Although he seemed mean at first, Uncle Frank turned out to be a very *magnanimous* fellow.
synonyms: unselfish, forgiving

MAGNATE *n* (<u>maag</u> nayt) (<u>maag</u> niht)
powerful or influential person
The entertainment *magnate* bought two cable TV stations to add to his collection of magazines and publishing houses.
synonyms: potentate, tycoon, nabob, dignitary, luminary

MALADROIT *adj* (maal uh <u>droyt</u>)
clumsy, tactless
"So, when is your baby due?" said the *maladroit* guest to his overweight but not pregnant hostess.
synonyms: awkward, inept, gauche, ungainly

MALADY *n* (<u>maal</u> uh dee)
illness
Elizabeth visited the doctor many times, but he could not identify her mysterious *malady*.
synonyms: disease, disorder, ailment, affliction, infirmity

MALAISE *n* (maa <u>layz</u>) (maa <u>lehz</u>)
a feeling of unease or depression
Jimmy Carter spoke of a "national *malaise*," and was subsequently criticized for being too negative.
synonyms: discomfort, unhappiness

MALCONTENT *n* (<u>maal</u> kuhn tehnt)
discontented person, one who holds a grudge
Dinah had always been a *malcontent*, so no one was surprised when she complained about the new carpet in the lobby.
synonyms: rebel, pessimist, defeatist, cynic, troublemaker

MALEDICTION *n* (maal ih <u>dihk</u> shun)
a curse, a wish of evil upon another
The frog prince looked for a princess to kiss him and put an end to the witch's *malediction*.

MALEFACTOR *n* (<u>maal</u> uh faak tuhr)
evil-doer; culprit
Many organizations are still trying to bring Nazi *malefactors* to justice.
synonyms: criminal, offender, felon

MALEVOLENT *adj* (muh <u>lehv</u> uh luhnt)
exhibiting ill will; wishing harm to others
The *malevolent* gossiper spread false rumors with frequency.
synonyms: malicious, hateful

MALICE *n* (<u>maal</u> ihs)
animosity, spite, hatred
Kendra felt such *malice* towards the insurance company that she celebrated when it went bankrupt.
synonyms: malevolence, cruelty, enmity, rancor, hostility

MALINGER *v* (muh <u>ling</u> guhr)
to evade responsibility by pretending to be ill
Many young men attempted to *malinger* when their draft number was called to avoid the war.
synonyms: shirk, fake

MALODOROUS *adj* (maal <u>oh</u> duhr uhs)
foul smelling, strongly offensive
The *malodorous* beggar, who had not bathed in many months, could barely stand his own smell.
synonyms: fetid, noisome, stinky, funky, rank

MANDATORY *adj* (<u>maan</u> duh tawr ee)
necessary, required
It is *mandatory* for all subway employees to wear blue uniforms while on the job.
synonyms: obligatory, compulsory, inevitable

MANNERED *adj* (<u>maan</u> uhrd)
artificial or stilted in character
The portrait is an example of the *mannered* style that was favored in that era.
synonyms: affected, unnatural

MANUAL *adj* (<u>maan</u> yoo uhl)
hand-operated; physical
When the power lines went down, the secretary dug out his old *manual* typewriter to type his letters.
synonyms: mechanical, physical, blue-collar

MAR *v* (mahr)
to damage, deface; spoil
Telephone poles *mar* the natural beauty of the countryside.
synonyms: injure, impair, disfigure, blemish, scar

MARGINAL *adj* (<u>mahr</u> jihn uhl)
barely sufficient
Because her skills were *marginal*, Edith was not a valued employee and was paid a very low salary.
synonyms: peripheral, liminal, sub-par

MARITIME *adj* (<u>maar</u> ih tiem)
relating to the sea or sailing
At the *maritime* museum, historic ships and sailing equipment are displayed.
synonyms: nautical, marine, naval

MARTIAL *adj* (<u>mahr</u> shuhl)
warlike, pertaining to the military
Experts in *martial* arts know how to physically defend themselves if anyone attacks them.
synonyms: soldierly, combative

MARTINET *n* (mahr tihn <u>eht</u>)
strict disciplinarian, one who rigidly follows rules
A complete *martinet*, the official insisted that Pete fill out all the forms again even though he was already familiar with his case.
synonyms: tyrant, stickler, dictator

MARTYR *n* (<u>mahr</u> tuhr)
person dying for his or her beliefs
Joan of Arc became a famous *martyr* after she was burned at the stake for her beliefs.
synonyms: saint, sufferer

MASOCHIST *n* (<u>maas</u> uhk ihst)
one who enjoys being subjected to pain or humiliation
Only a *masochist* would volunteer to take on this nightmarish project.

MASQUERADE *n* (maas kuh <u>rayd</u>)
disguise; action that conceals the truth
I dressed up as President Nixon for last year's *masquerade* party.
synonyms: pretense, charade, façade

MATERIALISM *n* (muh <u>tihr</u> ee uh lihz uhm)
preoccupation with material things
The couple's *materialism* revealed itself in the way they had to buy the most up-to-date model of every consumer item.
synonyms: worldliness, greed, hedonism

*MAUDLIN *adj* (<u>mawd</u> lihn)
overly sentimental
The mother's death should have been a touching scene, but the movie's treatment of it was so *maudlin* that, instead of making the audience cry, it made them cringe.
synonyms: mawkish, bathetic, saccharine, weepy

*MAVERICK *n* (<u>maav</u> rihk) (<u>maav</u> uh rihk)
an independent individual who does not go along with a group
The senator was a *maverick* who was willing to vote against his own party's position.
synonyms: nonconformist

MAWKISH *adj* (<u>maw</u> kihsh)
sickeningly sentimental
The poet hoped to charm his girlfriend with his flowery poem, but its *mawkish* tone sickened her instead.
synonyms: maudlin

MEANDER *v* (mee <u>aan</u> duhr)
to wander aimlessly
Mervyn *meandered* through the mall trying to find something for mother's day.
synonyms: ramble, roam, rove, range, stray

MEDDLER *n* (<u>mehd</u> luhr)
person interfering in others' affairs
Mickey is a real *meddler*, always sticking his nose in where it doesn't belong.
synonyms: interloper, busybody, tamperer

MEDIEVAL *adj* (<u>mehd</u> luhr)
relating to the Middle Ages (about A.D. 500-1500)
In *medieval* times, countless Europeans died of diseases because medicine was not very far advanced.
synonyms: obsolete, unenlightened

MELANCHOLY *adj* (<u>mehl</u> uhn kahl ee)
sadness, depression
The gloomy, rainy weather gave James a *melancholy* demeanor.
synonyms: dejection, despondency, woe, sorrow

MENDACIOUS *adj* (mehn <u>day</u> shuhs)
dishonest
So many of her stories were *mendacious* that I decided she must be a pathological liar.
synonyms: lying, untruthful deceitful, false

MENDICANT *n* (<u>mehn</u> dih kuhnt)
beggar
"Please, sir, can you spare a dime?" begged the *mendicant* as the businessman walked past.
synonyms: pauper, panhandler

MENTOR *n* (<u>mehn</u> tawr) (<u>mehn</u> tuhr)
experienced teacher and wise adviser
After being accepted at several colleges, Luisa asked her *mentor* which one she should choose.
synonyms: counselor, guide, master, guru

*MERCENARY *n* (<u>muhr</u> suhn ehr ee)
soldier for hire in foreign countries; (*adj*)motivated only by greed
Because his own army was so small, the dictator was forced to hire foreign *mercenaries* to protect him.
synonyms: hireling; venal, materialistic, avaricious

*MERCURIAL *adj* (muhr <u>kyoor</u> ee uhl)
quick, shrewd, and unpredictable
Her *mercurial* personality made it difficult to guess how she would react to the bad news.
synonyms: clever, crafty, volatile, whimsical

MERETRICIOUS *adj* (mehr ih <u>trihsh</u> uhs)
gaudy, falsely attractive
The casino's *meretricious* decor horrified the cultivated interior designer.
synonyms: flashy, loud, tawdry, insincere, specious

MERITORIOUS *adj* (mehr ih <u>tawr</u> ee uhs)
deserving reward or praise
The student's performance in all subjects was so *meritorious* that I'm sure she'll be awarded a scholarship.
synonyms: admirable, creditable, laudable, exemplary, commendable

METAMORPHOSIS *n* (meht uh <u>mohr</u> fuh sihs)
change, transformation
The *metamorphosis* of a caterpillar into a butterfly is a fascinating process.
synonyms: transfiguration, mutation, alteration, translation, transmogrification

METAPHOR *n* (<u>meht</u> uh fohr) (<u>meht</u> uh fuhr)
figure of speech comparing two different things
The *metaphor* "a sea of troubles" suggests a lot of troubles by comparing their number to the vastness of the sea.
synonyms: analogy, symbol, allegory, simile

METICULOUS *adj* (mih <u>tihk</u> yuh luhs)
extremely careful, fastidious, painstaking
To find all the clues at the crime scene, the *meticulous* investigators examined every inch of the area.
synonyms: scrupulous, punctilious, precise, finicky, fussy

METTLE *n* (<u>meht</u> l)
courageousness; endurance
The helicopter pilot showed her *mettle* as she landed in the battlefield to rescue the wounded soldiers.
synonyms: fortitude, spirit, character

MIGRATORY *adj* (<u>mie</u> gruh tawr ee)
wandering from place to place with the seasons
The *migratory* geese flew in from Canada at around the same time every year.
synonyms: roving, nomadic

MILITATE *v* (<u>mihl</u> ih tayt)
to operate against, work against
Lenin *militated* against the tsar for years before he overthrew him and established the Soviet Union.
synonyms: influence, affect, change

*MIMIC *v* (<u>mih</u> mihk)
to imitate or copy
The viceroy butterfly, which is edible, *mimics* the monarch butterfly to protect itself from predators.
synonyms: ape, simulate, impersonate

MINUSCULE *adj* (<u>mihn</u> ih skyool)
very small
Dave needed a magnifying glass to read the *miniscule* print on the lease.
synonyms: tiny, diminutive, infinitesimal

MIRTH *n* (muhrth)
frivolity, gaiety, laughter
Vera's hilarious jokes contributed to the general *mirth* at the dinner party.
synonyms: merriment, jollity, hilarity, glee

MISANTHROPE *n* (<u>mihs</u> ahn throhp)
a person who hates or distrusts mankind
Scrooge was such a *misanthrope* that even the sight of children singing made him angry.
synonyms: curmudgeon

MISCONSTRUE *v* (mihs kuhn <u>stroo</u>)
to misunderstand, fail to discover
Because I don't want what I've said to be *misconstrued*, I'll distribute transcripts of my speech to all of you.
synonyms: misinterpret, misread

MISERLY *adj* (<u>mie</u> zuhr lee)
extremely stingy
Although Scrooge was a rich man, he was prevented from helping others who were in need because he was *miserly*.
synonyms: greed, avarice

MISGIVING *n* (mihs <u>gihv</u> ing)
apprehension, doubt, sense of foreboding
Jews had serious *misgivings* about Hitler's intentions towards them, and they fled Germany in large numbers.
synonyms: distrust, presentiment, qualm, disquiet

MISNOMER *n* (mihs <u>noh</u> muhr)
an error in naming a person or place
Iceland is a *misnomer* since it isn't really icy; the name means "island."
synonyms: error, misapplication

MISSIVE *n* (<u>mihs</u> ihv)
a written note or letter
Priscilla spent hours composing a romantic *missive* for Elvis.
synonyms: message

*MITIGATE *v* (<u>miht</u> ih gayt)
to make less severe, make milder
A judge may *mitigate* a sentence if it's decided that the crime was committed out of necessity.
synonyms: relieve, alleviate

*MODERATE *v* (<u>mahd</u> uhr iht)
to make less excessive, restrain
The engineer *moderated* the flow of electricity to the house after its fuses blew repeatedly.
synonyms: lessen, abate, qualify, temper, mitigate

MOLLIFY *v* (<u>mahl</u> uh fie)
to soothe in temper or disposition
A small raise and increased break time *mollified* the unhappy staff, at least for the moment.
synonyms: pacify, appease

MOLLUSK *n* (<u>mahl</u> uhsk)
sea animal with soft body
Mollusks often develop hard shells in order to protect their soft, vulnerable bodies.
synonyms: clam, slug, snail, squid, conch

MOLT *v* (muhlt)
to shed hair, skin, or an outer layer periodically
The snake *molted* its skin and left it behind in a crumpled mass.
synonyms: cast, defoliate, desquamate

MONASTIC *adj* (muh <u>naas</u> tihk)
extremely plain or secluded, as in a monastery
The philosopher retired to his *monastic* lodgings to contemplate life free from any worldly distraction.
synonyms: contemplative, disciplined, regimented, self-abnegating, austere

MONOLOGUE *n* (<u>mahn</u> uh lahg)
dramatic speech performed by one actor
The only way to take a good look into Hamlet's personality is by analyzing his thoughts when he is alone in his *monologues*.
synonyms: soliloquy, address, oration, lecture, solo

MONOTONY *n* (muh <u>naht</u> nee)
tedium, dull sameness
Morris quit his job because he was bored by the *monotony* of his daily routine.
synonyms: sameness, repetitiousness, boredom, ennui

MONTAGE *n* (mahn <u>tahzh</u>)
composite picture
The artist created a *montage* of photographs, newspaper articles, and everyday objects in her work
of art.
synonyms: collage, juxtaposition, superimposition

MOOT *n*
debatable; deprived of practical significance
Charles couldn't decide what to get Alison for her birthday, but after they broke up the issue
became *moot*.
synonyms: arguable, open, inconclusive, doubtful

MORBID *adj* (<u>mohr</u> bihd)
gruesome; relating to disease; abnormally gloomy
Mrs. Fletcher had a *morbid* fascination with her dead cat, displaying photos of it everywhere.
synonyms: pathological, unhealthy, unwholesome, grisly, macabre

MORES *n* (<u>mawr</u> ayz)
fixed customs or manners; moral attitudes
In keeping with the *mores* of ancient Roman society, Nero held a celebration every weekend.
synonyms: conventions, practices

*MOROSE *adj* (muh <u>rohs</u>) (maw <u>rohs</u>)
gloomy, sullen
After hearing that the internship had been given to someone else, Lenny was *morose* for days.
synonyms: pessimistic, dour

MOTE *n* (moht)
a small particle, speck
Monica's eye watered, irritated by a *mote* of dust.
synonyms: bit, shred

MOTLEY *adj* (<u>maht</u> lee)
many colored; composed of diverse parts
The club was made up of a *motley* crew of people from the office.
synonyms: miscellaneous, heterogeneous, mixed, varied, assorted

MULTIFARIOUS *adj* (muhl tuh <u>faar</u> ee uhs)
diverse
Ken opened the hotel room window, letting in the *multifarious* noises of the great city.

*MUNDANE *adj* (muhn <u>dayn</u>)
worldly; commonplace
The plot of that thriller was completely *mundane*; as usual, the film ended in a huge explosion.
synonyms: secular, ordinary

MUNIFICENT *adj* (myoo <u>nihf</u> ih suhnt)
Generous, lavish
The *munificent* millionaire donated ten million dollars to the hospital.
synonyms: liberal, bountiful

MUTABILITY *n* (myoo tuh <u>bihl</u> uh tee)
the quality of being capable of change, in form or character; susceptibility of change
The actress lacked the *mutability* needed to perform in the improvisational play.
synonyms: inconstancy, variation

MYOPIC *adj* (mie <u>ahp</u> ihk) (mie <u>oh</u> pihk)
lacking foresight, having a narrow view or long-range perspective
Not wanting to spend a lot of money up front, the *myopic* business owner would likely suffer the consequences later.
synonyms: short-sighted, unthinking

MYRIAD *n* (<u>mihr</u> ee uhd)
immense number, multitude
Naomi moved to the city to take advantage of the *myriad* modeling contacts there.
synonyms: crowd, army, legion, mass

N

NADIR *n* (<u>nay</u> dihr)
lowest point
As Lou waited in line to audition for the diaper commercial, he realized he had reached the *nadir* of his acting career.
synonyms: bottom, depth, pit

NAÏVE *adj* (nah <u>eev</u>)
innocent, lacking in worldly experience
Inexperienced writers often are *naïve* and assume that big words make them sound smarter.
synonyms: ingenuous, unsophisticated, artless, credulous

*NARCISSIST *n* (<u>nahr</u> sih sihst)
someone who is completely self-absorbed
Nancy was a *narcissist*; whenever she entered a room, she immediately sought out the nearest mirror.
synonyms: egotist, egomaniac

NASCENT *adj* (<u>nay</u> sehnt)
starting to develop, coming into existence
The advertising campaign was still in a *nascent* stage, and nothing had been finalized yet.
synonyms: emerging, incipient, inchoate, embryonic

NEBULOUS *adj* (<u>neh</u> <u>byoo</u> luhs)
vague, undefined
The candidate's *nebulous* plans to fight crime made many voters skeptical.
synonyms: hazy, unclear

NEFARIOUS *adj* (nih <u>fahr</u> ee uhs)
intensely wicked or vicious
Nefarious deeds are never far from an evil-doer's mind.
synonyms: malevolent, sinister

NEGLIGENT *adj* (<u>nehg</u> lih jehnt)
careless, inattentive
The court determined that Mr. Glass had been *negligent* in failing to keep his vicious dog chained up.
synonyms: derelict, lax, remiss, slack, casual

NEGLIGIBLE *adj* (<u>nehg</u> lih jih buhl)
not worth considering
It's obvious from our *negligible* dropout rate that our students love our program.
synonyms: trivial, trifling, nugatory, insignificant

NEOPHYTE *n* (<u>nee</u> oh fiet)
novice, beginner
A relative *neophyte* at bowling, Seth rolled all of his balls into the gutter.
synonyms: apprentice, tyro, greenhorn

NETTLE *v* (<u>neh</u> tuhl)
to irritate
I don't particularly like having blue hair—I just do it to *nettle* my parents.
synonyms: vex, annoy

NICHE *n* (nihch)
recess in a wall; best position for something
Removing the alligators from their *niche* will destroy the species.
synonyms: alcove, cranny, crevice, place, station

NIHILISM *n* (<u>nie</u> hihl iz uhm)
belief that traditional values and beliefs are unfounded and that existence is useless; belief that
conditions in the social organization are so bad as to make destruction desirable
Robert's *nihilism* expressed itself in his lack of concern with the norms of moral society.
synonyms: skepticism, terrorism

NOCTURNAL *adj* (nok <u>tuhr</u> nuhl)
pertaining to night; active at night
Bats are *nocturnal* creatures, sleeping all day and emerging only at night.
synonyms: nightly, night-time

*NOISOME *adj* (<u>noy</u> suhm)
stinking, putrid
A dead mouse trapped in your walls produces a *noisome* odor.
synonyms: foul, disgusting, malodorous

NOMADIC *adj* (noh <u>maa</u> dihk)
moving from place to place
The *nomadic* Berber tribe travels from place to place, searching for grasslands for their herds.
synonyms: itinerant, vagabond, roving

NOMINAL *adj* (<u>nah</u> mihn uhl)
existing in name only; negligible
A *nominal* but far from devout Catholic, she rarely ever went to church.
synonyms: titular, minimal

*NONCHALANT *adj* (nahn chuh <u>lahnt</u>)
appearing casual, detached, cool
Although very excited to meet her favorite musician, Nora was acting *nonchalant*.
synonyms: composed, unruffled, cavalier, blasé

NOTORIETY *n* (noh tohr <u>ie eh</u> tee)
unfavorable fame
Wayne realized from the silence that greeted him as he entered the bar that his *notoriety* preceded him.
synonyms: infamy, disrepute, disgrace, dishonor, opprobrium

*NOVEL *adj* (<u>nah</u> vuhl)
new and not resembling anything formerly known
Piercing any part of the body other than the earlobes was *novel* in the 1950s, but now it is
quite common.
synonyms: original, innovative

*NOVICE *n* (<u>nah</u> vihs)
apprentice, beginner
Although Jen is only a *novice* at sailing, she shows great potential.
synonyms: neophyte, tyro, greenhorn

NOXIOUS *adj* (nahk shuhs)
harmful, unwholesome
The workers wore face masks to avoid breathing in the *noxious* chemical fumes.
synonyms: unhealthy, poisonous, toxic, corrupting

NUANCE *n* (<u>noo</u> ahns)
A subtle expression of meaning or quality
The scholars argued for hours over tiny *nuances* in the interpretation of the last line of the poem.
synonyms: gradation, subtlety, tone

NULLIFY *v* (<u>nuh</u> lih fie)
to make legally invalid; to counteract the effect of
Crystal *nullified* her contract with her publisher when she received a better offer from
another company.
synonyms: neutralize, negate, cancel, undo

O

*OBDURATE *adj* (<u>ahb</u> duhr uht)
stubbornly persistent, resistant to persuasion
The president was *obdurate* on the matter, and no amount of public protest could change his mind.
synonyms: inflexible, inexorable, adamant

OBFUSCATE *v* (<u>ahb</u> fyoo skayt)
to confuse, make obscure
Benny always *obfuscates* the discussion by bringing in irrelevant facts.
synonyms: shadow, complicate

OBLIQUE *adj* (oh <u>bleek</u>)
indirect, evasive; misleading, devious
Usually open and friendly, Allie has been behaving in a curiously *oblique* manner lately.
synonyms: slanted, tangential, glancing

OBLIVIOUS *adj* (oh <u>blih</u> vee uhs)
unaware, inattentive
Gandhi calmly made his way through the crowd, seemingly *oblivious* to the angry rioters around him.
synonyms: unmindful, forgetful, indifferent, heedless

OBSCURE *adj* (uhb <u>skyoor</u>)
dim, unclear; not well known
The speaker's style was so *obscure* that the audience was confused by his main point rather
than enlightened.
synonyms: dark, faint, remote, dim, minor

*OBSEQUIOUS *adj* (uhb <u>see kwee</u> uhs)
overly submissive or attentive
The *obsequious* new employee complimented her supervisor's tie and agreed with him on every issue.
synonyms: fawning, servile, compliant, groveling, unctuous

OBSOLETE *adj* (<u>ahb</u> soh leet)
no longer in use
Black-and-white television is now almost completely *obsolete*.
synonyms: outmoded, passé, old-fashioned, antiquated, dated

*OBSTINATE *adj* (<u>ahb</u> stih nuht)
unreasonably persistent
The *obstinate* journalist would not reveal his source, and thus, was jailed for 30 days.
synonyms: stubborn, headstrong

OBTUSE *adj* (uhb <u>toos</u>)
insensitive, stupid, dull
Alfred was too *obtuse* to realize that the sum of the angles of a triangle is 180 degrees.
synonyms: slow, dense, blunt

OBVIATE *v* (<u>ahb</u> vee ayt)
to make unnecessary; to anticipate and prevent
The river was shallow enough for the riders to wade across, which *obviated* the need for a bridge.
synonyms: preclude, avert, forestall, deter

OCCLUDE *v* (uh k<u>lood</u>)
to shut, block
A shadow is thrown across the Earth's surface during a solar eclipse when the light from the sun is
occluded by the moon.
synonyms: close, obstruct

ODIOUS *adj* (<u>oh</u> dee uhs)
hateful, contemptible
While most people consider studying vocabulary an *odious* task, there are a few who find it enjoyable.
synonyms: detestable, obnoxious, offensive, repellent, loathsome

OFFICIOUS *adj* (uh <u>fihsh</u> uhs)
too helpful, meddlesome
The *officious* waiter butted into the couple's conversation, advising them on how to take out a mortgage.
synonyms: eager, unwanted, intrusive

*OMINOUS *adj* (<u>ah</u> mihn uhs)
menacing, threatening, indicating misfortune
The sky filled with *ominous* dark clouds before the storm.
synonyms: inauspicious, unpropitious, sinister, dire, baleful

OMNISCIENT *adj* (ahm <u>nih</u> shehnt)
having infinite knowledge, all-seeing
Christians believe that because God is *omniscient*, they cannot hide their sins from Him.
synonyms: all-knowing, divine

ONEROUS *adj* (<u>oh</u> neh ruhs)
burdensome
The assignment was so difficult to manage that it proved *onerous* to the team in charge of it.
synonyms: oppressive, arduous, rigorous, demanding, exacting

OPALESCENT *adj* (oh pahl <u>eh</u> sehnt)
iridescent, displaying colors
The infant, fascinated by the *opalescent* stone, stared at it for hours on end.
synonyms: pearly, shimmering

OPAQUE *adj* (oh <u>payk</u>)
impervious to light; difficult to understand
The heavy buildup of dirt and grime on the windows almost made them *opaque*.
synonyms: impenetrable, obscure, dense

OPINE *v* (oh <u>pien</u>)
to express an opinion
At the "Let's Chat Talk Show," the audience member *opined* that the guest was in the wrong.
synonyms: point out, voice

OPPORTUNE *adj* (ah pohr <u>toon</u>)
appropriate, favorable
Her investment in plastics, made just before the invention of plastic bags, was *opportune*.
synonyms: seasonable, timely, advantageous

*OPULENCE *n* (<u>ah</u> pyoo lehns)
wealth
Livingston considered his BMW to be a symbol of both *opulence* and style.
synonyms: affluence, prosperity, luxury

ORACLE *n* (<u>or</u> ah kuhl)
person who foresees the future and gives advice
Opal decided to consult an *oracle* when she could not make the decision on her own.
synonyms: prophet, fortuneteller

*ORATION *n* (or <u>ay</u> shuhn)
lecture, formal speech
The class valedictorian gave an impressive *oration* on graduation day.
synonyms: discourse, declamation, sermon, address, homily

ORNITHOLOGIST *n* (or nih <u>thah</u> loh jihst)
scientist who studies birds
The team of *ornithologists* devoted their research to the study of extinct species such as dodo birds.
synonyms: birdman, bird watcher

OSCILLATE *v* (<u>ah</u> sihl ayt)
to swing back and forth like a pendulum; to vary between opposing beliefs or feelings
The move meant a new house in a lovely neighborhood, but she missed her friends, so she *oscillated* between joy and sadness.
synonyms: fluctuate, vary

OSSIFY *v* (<u>ah</u> sih fie)
to change into bone; to become hardened or set in a rigidly conventional pattern
The forensics expert ascertained the body's age based on the degree to which the facial structure had *ossified*.

OSTENSIBLE *adj* (ah <u>stehn</u> sih buhl)
apparent
The *ostensible* reason for his visit was to borrow a book, but he secretly wanted to chat with lovely Wanda.
synonyms: represented, supposed, surface

*OSTENTATIOUS *adj* (ah stehn <u>tay</u> shuhs)
showy
The billionaire's 200-room palace was considered by many to be an *ostentatious* display of wealth.
synonyms: pretentious, flamboyant, gaudy, ornate, fulsome

OSTRACIZE *v* (<u>ahs</u> truh size)
to exclude from a group by common consent
Feeling *ostracized* from her friends, Tabitha couldn't figure out what she had done. synonyms: isolate, excommunicate

OUST v (owst)
to remove from position by force; eject
After President Nixon so offensively lied to the country during Watergate, he was *ousted* from office.
synonyms: dismiss, evict

OVERWROUGHT *adj* (oh vuhr <u>rawt</u>)
agitated, overdone
The lawyer's *overwrought* voice on the phone made her clients worry about the outcome of their case.
synonyms: nervous, excited, elaborate, ornate

P

PACIFY *v* (<u>paa</u> suh fie)
to restore calm, bring peace
Nothing the king offered could *pacify* the angry princess, so he finally locked her in the dungeon.
synonyms: mollify, conciliate, appease, placate

PALATIAL *adj* (puh <u>lay</u> shuhl)
relating to a palace; magnificent
After living in a cramped studio apartment for years, Alicia thought the modest one bedroom looked downright *palatial*.
synonyms: grand, stately

PALLIATE *v* (<u>paa</u> lee ayt)
to make less serious, ease
The alleged crime was so vicious that the defense lawyer could not *palliate* it for the jury.
synonyms: extenuate, mitigate, alleviate, assuage

*PALLID *adj* (<u>paa</u> lihd)
lacking color or liveliness
The old drugstore's *pallid* window could not compete with Wal-Mart's extravagant display next door.
synonyms: pale, wan, ashen, blanched, ghostly

PALPABLE *adj* (<u>paalp</u> uh buhl)
capable of being touched or felt; easily perceived
The tension was *palpable* as I walked into the room.
synonyms: readily detected, tangible

PALTRY *adj* (<u>pol</u> tree)
pitifully small or worthless
Bernardo paid the ragged boy the *paltry* sum of 25 cents to carry his luggage all the way to the hotel.
synonyms: trifling, petty

PANACEA *n* (paan uh <u>see</u> uh)
cure-all
Some claim that vitamin C is a *panacea* for all sorts of illnesses, but I have my doubts.
synonyms: elixir, miracle drug, sovereign remedy

PANACHE *n* (puh <u>nahsh</u>)
flamboyance or dash in style and action
Leah has such *panache* when planning parties, even when they're last-minute affairs.
synonyms: flair

PANDEMIC *adj* (paan <u>deh</u> mihk)
occurring over a wide geographic area and affecting a large portion of the population
Pandemic alarm spread throughout Colombia after the devastating earthquake.
synonyms: general, extensive

PANEGYRIC *n* (paan uh <u>geer</u> ihk)
elaborate praise; formal hymn of praise
The director's *panegyric* for the donor who kept his charity going was heart-warming.
synonyms: compliment, homage

PARADIGM *n* (<u>paar</u> uh diem)
an outstandingly clear or typical example
The new restaurant owner used the fast-food giant as a *paradigm* for expansion into new locales.
synonyms: model

PARADOX *n* (<u>paar</u> uh dahks)
contradiction, incongruity; dilemma, puzzle
It is a *paradox* that those most in need of medical attention are often those least able to obtain it.
synonyms: conundrum, riddle

PARAGON *n* (<u>paar</u> uh gon)
a model of excellence or perfection
She's the *paragon* of what a judge should be: honest, intelligent, and just.
synonyms: ideal, paradigm

PARAMOUNT *adj* (<u>paar</u> uh mownt)
supreme, of chief importance
It's of *paramount* importance that we make it back to camp before the storm hits.
synonyms: primary, dominant

PARAPHRASE *v* (<u>paar</u> uh frays)
to reword, usually in simpler terms
In trying to *paraphrase* the poet, she lost the eloquence of his style and the complexity of his message.
synonyms: restatement, clarification

PARASITE *n* (<u>paar</u> uh siet)
person or animal that lives at another's expense
Joe saw his older sister as a *parasite* because she was always asking for a handout.
synonyms: leech, sycophant

*PARCHED *adj*
extremely thirsty; shriveled
The *parched* traveler searched desperately for a water source.
synonyms: dehydrated, desiccated, scorched

PARE *v* (payr)
to trim off excess, reduce
The cook's hands were sore after she *pared* hundreds of potatoes for the banquet.
synonyms: peel, clip

PARIAH *n* (puh <u>rie</u> ah)
an outcast
Once he betrayed those in his community, he was banished and lived the life of a *pariah*.

PARITY *n* (<u>paa</u> ruh tee)
equality
Mrs. Lutskaya tried to maintain *parity* between her children, although each claimed she gave the other preferential treatment.
synonyms: equivalence, par, evenness

PAROCHIAL *adj* (puh <u>ro</u> kee uhl)
of limited scope or outlook, provincial
It was obvious that Victor's *parochial* mentality would clash with Ivonne's liberal open-mindedness.
synonyms: narrow, restricted, insular

PARODY *n* (<u>paa</u> ruh dee)
humorous imitation
Shana's new play is a thinly veiled *parody* of the corruption in the White House.
synonyms: caricature, burlesque, travesty, lampoon, satire

PARRY *v* (<u>paa</u> ree)
to ward off or evade, especially by a quick-witted answer
Kari *parried* every question the army officers fired at her, much to their frustration.
synonyms: evade, avoid, repel

PARSIMONY *n* (<u>pahr</u> sih moh nee)
stinginess
Ethel gained a reputation for *parsimony* when she refused to pay for her daughter's college education.
synonyms: frugality, economy, meanness, miserliness

PARTISAN *adj* (<u>pahr</u> tih zaan)
biased in favor of
Though we claim to have a non*partisan* democratic system, it is clear that decisions always boil down to party lines.
synonyms: factional, devoted, supporting

PASTICHE *n* (pah <u>steesh</u>)
piece of literature or music imitating other works
The playwright's clever *pastiche* of the well-known Bible story had the audience rolling in the aisles.
synonyms: spoof, medley

PATENT *adj* (<u>paa</u> tehnt)
obvious, evident
Moe could no longer stand Frank's *patent* fawning over the boss and so confronted him.
synonyms: unconcealed, clear

PATERNITY *n* (puh <u>tuhr</u> nih tee)
fatherhood; descent from father's ancestors
In this week's episode, the soap opera star refuses to reveal the *paternity* of her child.
synonyms: siring, begetting, origin, authorship

*PATHETIC *adj* (puh <u>theh</u> tihk)
pitiful
Mark Twain expressed his compassion for people in general by saying, "Everything human is *pathetic*."
synonyms: piteous, lamentable, abject

PATHOGENIC *adj* (paa thoh <u>jehn</u> ihk)
causing disease
Bina's research on the origins of *pathogenic* microorganisms should help stop the spread of disease.
synonyms: noxious, infecting

PATRICIAN *n* (puh <u>trih</u> shuhn)
aristocratic
Though he really couldn't afford an expensive lifestyle, Claudius had *patrician* tastes.
synonyms: high-class

PATRONIZE *v* (<u>pay</u> troh niez)
to act as patron of, to adopt an air of condescension toward; to buy from
LuAnn *patronized* the students, treating them like simpletons, which they deeply resented.
synonyms: condescend

PAUCITY *n* (<u>paw</u> suh tee)
scarcity, lack
Because of the relative *paucity* of bananas in the country, their price was very high.
synonyms: dearth, shortage, deficiency

PAUPER *n* (<u>paw</u> puhr)
very poor person
A common theme in movies is the ascension of a *pauper* up the ranks of society to financial success.
synonyms: beggar, bankrupt, indigent, starveling

PECCADILLO *n* (pehk uh <u>dih</u> loh)
minor sin or offense
Gabriel tends to harp on his brother's *peccadillos* and never lets him live them down.
synonyms: fault, failing, lapse, misstep

PEDANT *n* (<u>peh</u> daant)
uninspired, boring academic
The professor's tedious commentary on the subject soon gained her a reputation as a *pedant*.
synonyms: scholar, schoolmaster, pedagogue

PEDESTRIAN *adj* (puh <u>deh</u> stree uhn)
commonplace
Although the restaurant's prices were high, critics considered its food little more than *pedestrian*.
synonyms: undistinguished, ordinary, dull, mediocre, lackluster

PEDIATRICIAN *n* (pee dee uh <u>trih</u> shuhn)
doctor specializing in children and their ailments
Although she was first attracted to family medicine, she became a *pediatrician* because she loved working with children.
synonyms: children's doctor, family physician

PEER *n*
contemporary, equal standing
Adults often blame their children's inappropriate actions on pressure from their *peers*.
synonyms: fellow, coeval, colleague

PEERLESS *adj* (<u>peer</u> luhs)
unequaled
Hannah's hard work and dedication to this fund-raiser have been *peerless*.
synonyms: incomparable, superlative

PEJORATIVE *n* (<u>peh</u> jaw ruh tihv)
having bad connotations; disparaging
The teacher scolded Mark for his unduly *pejorative* comments about his classmate's presentation.
synonyms: belittling, dismissive, insulting

PENANCE *n* (<u>peh</u> nihns)
voluntary suffering to repent for a wrong
The aging pirate wanted to do *penance* for his crimes of days gone by.
synonyms: atonement, reparation, chastening, reconciliation

PENCHANT *n* (<u>pehn</u> chuhnt)
an inclination, a definite liking
After Daniel visited the Grand Canyon, he developed a *penchant* for travel.
synonyms: leaning, predilection

PENITENT *adj* (<u>peh</u> nih tehnt)
expressing sorrow for sins or offenses, repentant
Claiming the murderer did not feel *penitent*, the victim's family felt his pardon should be denied.
synonyms: remorseful, apologetic

PENSIVE *adj* (<u>pehn</u> sihv)
thoughtful
Drew was a *pensive* boy who often spent time alone writing poetry.
synonyms: contemplative, reflective, meditative

PENURY *n* (<u>pehn</u> yuh ree)
an oppressive lack of resources (as money), severe poverty
Once a famous actor, he eventually died in *penury* and anonymity.
synonyms: destitution, impoverishment

*PERFIDIOUS *adj* (puhr <u>fih</u> dee uhs)
faithless, disloyal, untrustworthy
The actress's *perfidious* companion revealed all of her intimate secrets to the gossip columnist.
synonyms: treacherous, devious, deceitful

PERFUNCTORY *adj* (puhr <u>fuhnk</u> tor ee)
done in a routine way; indifferent
The machinelike bank teller processed the transaction and gave the waiting customer a *perfunctory* smile.
synonyms: halfhearted, tepid, careless

PERIPATETIC *adj* (peh ruh puh <u>teh</u> tihk)
moving from place to place
Morty claims that his *peripatetic* hot-dog stand enables him to travel all over the city.
synonyms: itinerant, nomadic, vagabond

PERJURE *v* (puhr juhr)
to tell a lie under oath
Benson *perjured* himself to protect his son, claiming that he had spent the evening with him when in fact he had not.
synonyms: forswear, falsify

PERMEABLE *adj* (puhr mee uh buhl)
penetrable
Karen discovered that her raincoat was *permeable* when she got drenched while wearing it.
synonyms: pervious, porous

PERNICIOUS *adj* (puhr nih shuhs)
very harmful
The Claytons considered Rocky, a convicted felon, to be a *pernicious* influence on their son.
synonyms: deadly, destructive, evil, wicked, pestilent

PERPETUAL *adj* (puhr peht chyoo uhl)
endless, lasting
Although objects may appear solid, the electrons that make up matter are actually in *perpetual* motion.
synonyms: continuous, constant, ceaseless, eternal, perennial

*PERSEVERANCE *n* (pehr suh veer ihns)
resolve, determination
With great *perseverance*, Percy took the SAT over and over again until he scored over 1400.
synonyms: persistence, tenacity, pertinacity, steadfastness

PERSPICACIOUS *adj* (puhr spuh kay shuhs)
shrewd, astute, keen-witted
Inspector Poirot used his *perspicacious* mind to solve mysteries.
synonyms: sagacious, insightful, intelligent

PERTINENT *adj* (pur tih nehnt)
applicable, appropriate
The supervisor felt that his employee's complaints were *pertinent* and mentioned them in the meeting.
synonyms: relevant, germane, material, apposite, apropos

PERTURB *v* (puhr tuhrb)
disturb
Grandpa sleeps so soundly that we won't be able to *perturb* him.
synonyms: bother, annoy, distress, confuse, upset

PERUSAL *v* (puh roo zuhl)
close examination
When you fly, your carry-on luggage is always subject to the *perusal* of customs officials.
synonyms: examination, scrutiny

PERVERT *v* (puhr vuhrt)
to cause to change in immoral way; to misuse
Charlene objected when the opposing lawyer seemed to *pervert* the truth.
synonyms: corrupt, debase, debauch, deprave, vitiate

PESTILENCE *n* (peh stihl ehns)
epidemic, plague
The country went into national crisis when it was plagued by both *pestilence* and floods at the same time.
synonyms: contagion, scourge, sickness, disease, illness

PETULANCE *n* (peh chu luhns)
rudeness, peevishness
The child's *petulance* annoyed the teacher, who liked her young students to be cheerful and cooperative.
synonyms: irritability, querulousness, testiness, fretfulness

PHALANX *n* (fay laanks)
a compact or close-knit body of people, animals, or things
A *phalanx* of guards stood outside the prime minister's home day and night.
synonyms: mass, legion

PHILANTHROPY *n* (fihl aan throh pee)
love of humanity; generosity to worthy causes
The Metropolitan Museum of Art owes much of its collection to the *philanthropy* of private collectors who willed their estates to it.
synonyms: charity, benevolence

PHILISTINE *n* (fihl uh steen)
a person who is guided by materialism and is disdainful of intellectual or artistic values
The *philistine* never even glanced at the rare violin in his collection but instead kept an eye on its value and sold it at a profit.

PHLEGMATIC *adj* (flehg maa tihk)
having a sluggish, unemotional temperament
His writing was energetic but his *phlegmatic* personality wasn't suited for television, so he turned down the interview.
synonyms: matter-of-fact, undemonstrative

PHOBIA *n* (foh bee uh)
exaggerated, illogical fear
Talia claims her *phobia* of spiders stems from the time she was bitten by one in third grade.
synonyms: dislike, aversion

PIETY *n* (pie eh tee)
devoutness
The nun's *piety* inspired Anne to start going to church again.
synonyms: devotion, reverence

PILFER *v* (pihl fuhr)
to steal
Marianne did not *pilfer* the money for herself but rather for her sick brother who needed medicine.
synonyms: purloin, filch, arrogate, poach, embezzle

PILLAGE *v* (<u>pihl</u> ihj)
to loot, especially during a war
The invading soldiers *pillaged* the town for food and valuables.
synonyms: sack, plunder, despoil, ravage

PINNACLE *n* (<u>pih</u> nuh kuhl)
peak, highest point of development
The whole show was excellent, but the *pinnacle* was when the skater did a backwards flip.
synonyms: summit, acme, apex, zenith, climax

PIOUS *adj* (<u>pie</u> uhs)
dedicated, devout, extremely religious
Saul, a *pious* man, walks to the synagogue on the Sabbath and prays daily.
synonyms: observant, reverent, sanctimonious

PIQUE *v* (peek)
to arouse anger or resentment in; provoke
His continual insensitivity *piqued* my anger.
synonyms: irritate, rouse

PITHY *adj* (<u>pih</u> thee)
profound, substantial; concise, succinct, to the point
Martha's *pithy* comments during the interview must have been impressive because she got the job.
synonyms: brief, compact, terse, laconic

PLACATE *v* (<u>play</u> cayt)
to soothe or pacify
The burglar tried to *placate* the snarling Doberman by saying, "Nice doggy," and offering it a treat.
synonyms: mollify, conciliate, appease

*PLACID *adj* (<u>plaa</u> sihd)
calm
Looking at Aparna's *placid* expression, no one could tell that she was inwardly seething with rage.
synonyms: tranquil, serene, peaceful, complacent

PLAGIARIST *n* (<u>play</u> juhr ihst)
one who steals words or ideas
The notable scientist lost his job when he was exposed as a *plagiarist*; years before, he had copied a paper from a magazine.
synonyms: pirate, thief, infringer

PLAINTIVE *adj* (<u>playn</u> tihv)
expressive of suffering or woe, melancholy
The *plaintive* cries from the girl trapped in the tree were heard by all.
synonyms: mournful, sorrowful

PLATITUDE *n* (<u>plaa</u> tuh tood)
overused and trite remark
Instead of the usual *platitudes*, the comedian gave a memorable and inspiring speech to the graduating class.
synonyms: cliché

PLEBEIAN *adj* (plee <u>bee</u> uhn)
crude or coarse; characteristic of commoners
After five weeks of rigorous studying, the graduate settled in for a weekend of *plebeian* socializing and television watching.
synonyms: unrefined, conventional

PLENITUDE *n* (<u>plehn</u> uh tood)
abundance, plenty
Every Thanksgiving, our family gives thanks for our *plenitude* of good fortune.
synonyms: profusion, bounteousness, copiousness

PLETHORA *n* (<u>pleh</u> thor uh)
excess, overabundance
Assuming that more was better, the defendant offered the judge a *plethora* of excuses.
synonyms: superfluity, surplus, glut, surfeit

PLIANT *adj* (<u>plie</u> uhnt)
pliable, yielding
Only those with extremely *pliant* limbs are able to perform complex yoga moves.
synonyms: malleable, adaptable, complacent

PLUCKY *adj* (<u>pluh</u> kee)
courageous, spunky
The *plucky* young nurse dove into the foxhole, determined to help the wounded soldier.
synonyms: brave

PLUMMET *v* (<u>pluh</u> meht)
to fall, plunge
Marvin screamed as he watched his new Ferrari *plummet* into the depths of the ravine.
synonyms: topple, precipitate, drop, dive, hurtle

PODIUM *n* (<u>poh</u> dee uhm)
platform or lectern for orchestra conductors or speakers
The audience could see Tara shaking as she walked up to the *podium* to conduct the piece.
synonyms: dais, rostrum

*POIGNANT *adj* (<u>poy</u> nyaant)
emotionally moving
Maria's speech in honor of her deceased friend was so *poignant* that there was not a dry eye at the funeral.
synonyms: stirring, touching, pathetic, affecting, piquant

POLARIZE *v* (<u>poh</u> luhr iez)
to tend towards opposite extremes
The leaders feared the conflict would *polarize* the group into separate camps.
synonyms: split, separate

POLEMIC *n* (puh <u>leh</u> mihk)
controversy, argument; verbal attack
The candidate's *polemic* against his opponent was vicious and small-minded rather than well reasoned and convincing.
synonyms: refutation, denunciation

POLITIC *adj* (<u>pah</u> lih tihk)
shrewd and crafty in managing or dealing with things
She was wise to curb her tongue and was able to explain her problem to the judge in a respectful and
politic manner.
synonyms: tactful

POLYGLOT *n* (<u>pah</u> lee glaht)
a speaker of many languages
Ling's extensive travels have helped her to become a true *polyglot*.

PONDEROUS *adj* (<u>pahn</u> duhr uhs)
weighty, heavy, large
We steeled ourselves before attempting to lift the *ponderous* bureau.
synonyms: hefty, massive, cumbersome, unwieldy

PONTIFICATE *v* (pahn <u>tih</u> fih kayt)
to speak in a pretentious manner
She *pontificated* about the virtues of being rich until we all left the room in disgust.
synonyms: preach, lecture, orate, declaim, sermonize

PORE *v* (pohr)
to read studiously or attentively
I've *pored* over this text, yet I still can't understand it.
synonyms: fix attention on

POROUS *adj* (<u>pohr</u> uhs)
full of holes, permeable to liquids
Unfortunately, the tent was more *porous* than we thought, and the rain soaked us to the bone.
synonyms: penetrable, spongy, pervious

PORTENTOUS *adj* (pohr <u>tehn</u> tuhs)
foreshadowing, ominous; eliciting amazement and wonder
Everyone thought the rays of light were *portentous* until they realized a nine-year-old was playing a joke
on them.
synonyms: premonitory

PORTLY *adj* (<u>pohrt</u> lee)
stout, dignified
The *portly* man wearily put on the Santa suit and set out for the mall.
synonyms: fleshy, corpulent, plump, rotund, fat

POSIT *v* (<u>pah</u> siht)
to assume as real or conceded; propose as an explanation
Before proving the math formula, we needed to *posit* that *x* and *y* were real numbers.
synonyms: suggest

POSTERIOR *adj* (pah <u>stih</u> ree ohr)
located behind or to the rear
The veterinarian injected the antibiotics into the *posterior* part of the animal.
synonyms: caudal, dorsal, aft, hindmost, rearward

POSTERITY *n* (pah <u>steh</u> ruh tee)
future generations; all of a person's descendants
Nadine saved all of her soccer trophies for *posterity*.
synonyms: progeny, offspring, line, lineage, heritage

POTABLE *adj* (<u>poh</u> tuh buhl)
suitable for drinking
Though the water was *potable*, it tasted terrible.
synonyms: unpolluted

POTENTATE *n* (<u>poh</u> tehn tayt)
a ruler; one who wields great power
Alex was much kinder before he assumed the role of *potentate*.
synonyms: leader, dominator

PRAGMATIC *adj* (praag <u>maa</u> tihk)
practical; moved by facts rather than abstract ideals
While daydreaming gamblers think they can get rich by frequenting casinos, *pragmatic* gamblers realize
that the odds are heavily stacked against them.
synonyms: prudent, wise, sensible, expedient, politic

PRATTLE *n* (<u>praa</u> tuhl)
meaningless, foolish talk
Her husband's mindless *prattle* drove Hilary insane; sometimes she wished he would just shut up.
synonyms: chatter, babble, gibberish, drivel, blather

*PRECARIOUS *adj* (prih <u>caa</u> ree uhs)
lacking in security or stability; dependent on chance or uncertain conditions
Given the *precarious* circumstances, I chose to opt out of the deal completely.
synonyms: doubtful, chancy

PRECIPICE *n* (<u>prehs</u> ih pihs)
edge, steep overhang
The hikers stood at the *precipice*, staring down over the steep cliff.
synonyms: crag, cliff, brink

PRECIPITATE *adj* (preh <u>sih</u> puh tayt)
sudden and unexpected
Since the couple wed after knowing each other only a month, many expected their *precipitate* marriage
to end in divorce.
synonyms: abrupt, impetuous, headlong, reckless, rash

PRECIPITOUSLY *adv* (pree <u>sih</u> puh tuhs lee)
steeply; hastily
At the sight of the approaching helicopters, Private Johnson *precipitously* shot a flare into the air.
synonyms: impetuously, recklessly

PRECLUDE *v* (prih <u>clood</u>)
to rule out
The seriousness of the damage to the car *precluded* any attempt to repair it; it had to be scrapped.
synonyms: prevent, avert, obviate, forestall, deter

*PRECOCIOUS *adj* (prih <u>coh</u> shuhs)
unusually advanced at an early age
The fact that Beatrice got married at age eighteen did not come as much of a shock, as she had always been *precocious*.
synonyms: premature, developed

PRECURSOR *n* (pree <u>kuhr</u> sohr)
forerunner, predecessor
It is amazing to compare today's sleek, advanced computers with their bulky, slow *precursors*.
synonyms: herald, vanguard

PREDATOR *n* (<u>preh</u> dih tohr)
one that preys on others, destroyer, plunderer
The lioness is a skilled *predator*, stalking her prey silently until it is close enough to go for the kill.
synonyms: carnivore, pillager, attacker

PREDILECTION *n* (preh dih <u>lehk</u> shuhn)
preference, liking
The old woman's *predilection* for candy was evident from the chocolate bar wrappers strewn all over her apartment.
synonyms: bias, leaning, partiality, penchant, proclivity

PREFACE *n* (<u>preh</u> fuhs)
introduction to a book; introductory remarks to a speech
Yumiko was thrilled that the famous Oprah Winfrey would be writing the *preface* to her book.
synonyms: foreword, preamble, prelude, prologue

PREMONITION *n* (preh moh <u>nih</u> shuhn)
forewarning; presentiment
Mrs. Famuyiwa had a *premonition* that if her son were to marry this woman, he would suffer a terrible fate.
synonyms: foreboding, prediction, hunch, intimation, intuition

PREPOSTEROUS *adj* (prih <u>pah</u> stehr uhs)
absurd, illogical
Hamish's *preposterous* plan to save the environment by burning all the cities to the ground made him an object of ridicule.
synonyms: ridiculous, ludicrous, nonsensical, outlandish, incredible

PRESAGE *n* (<u>preh</u> sihj)
something that foreshadows; a feeling of what will happen in the future
The demolition of the Berlin Wall was a *presage* to the fall of the Soviet Union.
synonyms: premonition

PRESCIENT *adj* (<u>preh</u> shuhnt)
having foresight
Jonah's decision to sell the apartment seemed to be a *prescient* one, as its value soon dropped by half.
synonyms: premonitory, augural, divinatory, mantic, oracular

PRESCRIBE *v* (pri <u>scrieb</u>)
to set down a rule; to recommend a treatment
The doctor *prescribed* valium to the nervous patient, not realizing how addictive the drug was.
synonyms: enjoin, order, dictate, decree, impose

PRESUMPTUOUS *adj* (pree <u>suhmp</u> chyoo uhs)
rude, improperly bold
"I don't want to be *presumptuous*, but why on earth did you choose red wallpaper?" said Cecile to her hosts.
synonyms: brash, familiar, sassy, impertinent

PREVALENT *adj* (<u>preh</u> vuh lehnt)
Widespread
The teacher struggled to counteract the *prevalent* belief in the school that girls could give boys cooties.
synonyms: rife, current, popular, common

PREVARICATE *v* (prih <u>vaar</u> uh cayt)
to lie, evade the truth
Rather than admit that he had overslept again, the employee *prevaricated*, claiming that traffic had made him late.
synonyms: equivocate, fib, palter, hedge, fabricate

PRIMEVAL *adj* (priem <u>ee</u> vuhl)
ancient, primitive
The archaeologist claimed that the skeleton was of *primeval* origin, though in fact it was the remains of a modern-day monkey.
synonyms: primordial, original

PRIMORDIAL *adj* (prie mohr dee uhl)
original, existing from the beginning
The first organisms were formed eons ago from *primordial* ooze.
synonyms: primeval, ancient, primitive, archaic, antediluvian

PRISTINE *adj* (prih steen)
untouched, uncorrupted
Because measures had been taken to prevent looting, the archeological site was still *pristine* when researchers arrived.
synonyms: pure, clean

PRIVATION *n* (prih vay shuhn)
lack of usual necessities or comforts
The convict endured total *privation* while locked up in solitary confinement for a month.
synonyms: forfeiture, loss, deprivation, poverty

PROBITY *n* (proh buh tee)
honesty, high-mindedness
The conscientious witness responded with the utmost *probity* to all the questions posed to her.
synonyms: integrity, uprightness, honor, rectitude, virtue

PROCLIVITY *n* (proh clih vuh tee)
tendency, inclination
His *proclivity* for speeding got him into trouble with the highway patrol on many occasions.
synonyms: propensity, predisposition, predilection, partiality, penchant

*PROCRASTINATE *v* (proh craa stuhn ayt)
to postpone continually and unjustifiably
Don't *procrastinate*; do your homework now!
synonyms: delay, stall, postpone

PROCURE *v* (proh kyoor)
to obtain
I was able to *procure* tickets to the premiere of the new Star Wars movie
synonyms: acquire, secure, get, gain

*PRODIGAL *adj* (prah dih guhl)
recklessly extravagant, wasteful
The *prodigal* expenditures on the military budget during a time of peace created a stir in the Cabinet.
synonyms: lavish

PRODIGIOUS *adj* (pruh dih juhs)
vast, enormous, extraordinary
The musician's *prodigious* talent made her famous all over the world.
synonyms: huge, gigantic, impressive, marvelous

PROFANE *adj* (proh fayn)
impure; contrary to religion; sacrilegious.
His *profane* comments caused him to be banished from the temple for life.
synonyms: secular, uninitiated, vulgar, coarse, blasphemous

PROFICIENT *adj* (proh fihsh ehnt)
expert, skilled in a certain subject
The mechanic was *proficient* at repairing cars, but his horrible temper made it difficult for him to keep jobs for long.
synonyms: adept, skillful, deft, experienced, accomplished

PROFLIGATE *adj* (praa flih guht)
corrupt, degenerate
Some historians claim that it was the Romans' decadent, *profligate* behavior that led to the decline of the Roman Empire.
synonyms: dissolute, wasteful, extravagant, improvident, prodigal

PROFUSE *adj* (pruh fyoos)
lavish, extravagant
Although Janet was angry with Bart for forgetting her birthday, his *profuse* apologies made her forgive him.
synonyms: plentiful, copious, abundant, riotous, prodigal

PROGENITOR *n* (proh jehn uh tuhr)
an ancestor in the direct line, forefather; founder
Though his parents had been born here, his *progenitors* were from India.
synonyms: inventor

PROGENY *n* (prah guh nee)
offspring, children
The old photograph showed Great Grandma Wells surrounded by her husband and all their *progeny*.
synonyms: heirs, issue, descendents, posterity

PROLIFERATE *v* (proh lih fuhr ayt)
to grow by rapid production of new parts; increase in number
The cancer cells *proliferated* so quickly that even the doctor was surprised.
synonyms: multiply

*PROLIFIC *adj* (proh lih fihk)
productive, fertile
Stephen King, a *prolific* writer, seems to come out with a new book every six months.
synonyms: fecund, fruitful, bountiful

PROLOGUE *n* (proh lahg)
introductory section of a literary work or play
In the novel's *prologue*, the narrator of the story is introduced.
synonyms: foreword, preamble, prelude, preface

PROMULGATE *v* (prah muhl gayt)
to make known by open declaration, proclaim
The publicist *promulgated* the idea that the celebrity had indeed gotten married.
synonyms: announce, broadcast

PROPAGATE *v* (prah puh gayt)
to spread or proliferate; to breed
She was able to *propagate* the situation with just one lie.
synonyms: distribute, circulate, disseminate, reproduce, procreate

PROPENSITY *n* (pruh pehn suh tee)
a natural inclination or preference
She has a *propensity* for lashing out at others when stressed, so we leave her alone when she's had a rough day.
synonyms: tendency

PROPITIOUS *adj* (pruh pih shuhs)
favorable, advantageous
"I realize that I should have brought this up at a more *propitious* moment, but I don't love you," said the bride to the groom in the middle of their marriage vows.
synonyms: auspicious, benign, conducive

PROPONENT *n* (pruh poh nuhnt)
advocate, defender, supporter
A devoted *proponent* of animal rights, Rose was constantly bringing home stray dogs and cats.
synonyms: champion, backer, partisan, promoter

*PROSAIC *adj* (proh <u>say</u> ihk)
relating to prose; dull, commonplace
Simon's *prosaic* style bored his writing teacher to tears, and she dreaded having to mark his essays.
synonyms: matter-of-fact, straightforward, unimaginative, pedestrian

PROSCRIBE *v* (proh <u>skrieb</u>)
to condemn or forbid as harmful or unlawful
Consumption of alcohol was *proscribed* in the country's constitution, but the ban was eventually lifted.
synonyms: prohibit, ban

PROSELYTIZE *v* (prah suhl uh tiez)
to convert to a particular belief or religion
The Jehovah's Witnesses went from door to door in the neighborhood to *proselytize* their message.
synonyms: missionize, preach, sway, move, convince

*PROSPERITY *n* (prah <u>speh</u> ruh tee)
wealth or success
This is a time of unparalleled *prosperity* for some Americans, whereas others are still struggling to make ends meet.
synonyms: affluence, abundance, opulence

PROSTRATE *adj* (<u>prah</u> strayt)
lying face downward in adoration or submission
Lying *prostrate* awaiting the Pope, a car splashed me with water.
synonyms: submissive

*PROTAGONIST *n* (proh <u>taa</u> gahn ihst)
main character in a play or story, hero
In dramatic tragedy, the *protagonist* often brings about his own downfall.
synonyms: principal, lead, star

PROTOCOL *n* (<u>proh</u> toh cahl)
ceremony and manners observed by diplomats
Diplomats must strive to observe the correct *protocol* in their dealings with foreign heads of state.
synonyms: etiquette, propriety, decorum, courtesy, agenda

PROTRACT *v* (proh <u>traakt</u>)
to prolong, draw out, extend
Since every member of the committee had to have his say, they *protracted* the meeting.
synonyms: lengthen, elongate, stretch

PROVINCIAL *adj* (pruh <u>vihn</u> shuhl)
limited in outlook, narrow, unsophisticated
Having grown up in the city, Anita sneered at the *provincial* attitudes of her country cousins.
synonyms: unpolished, unrefined

*PROVOCATIVE *adj* (proh vah kah tihv)
tending to provoke a response, e.g., anger or disagreement
The mayor tried to close down the museum after it displayed *provocative* art works.
synonyms: controversial, stimulating, contentious

PROWESS *n* (prow ihs)
bravery, skill
She credited her athletic *prowess* to daily practice and intense concentration.
synonyms: ability, strength, courage, daring

PRUDE *n* (prood)
one who is excessively proper or modest
The performance was admired by all except the *prude* in the front row, who fainted during the first sex scene.
synonyms: prig, puritan

PRUDENT *adj* (<u>proo</u> dehnt)
careful, cautious
Considering the small size of our army, it would not be *prudent* for us to attack right now.
synonyms: circumspect, politic, pragmatic, judicious, sensible

PRURIENT *adj* (<u>proo</u> ree uhnt)
lustful, exhibiting lewd desires
The drunken sailor gave many *prurient* looks.
synonyms: lascivious, lecherous, licentious, salacious, wanton

PRY *v* (prie)
to intrude into; force open
I hesitated to ask Fern what had made her cry because I didn't want to *pry* into her personal life.
synonyms: snoop, nose, spy, eavesdrop, probe

PSEUDONYM *n* (<u>soo</u> deh nihm)
a fictitious name, used particularly by writers to conceal identity
Though George Eliot sounds as though it's a male name, it was the *pseudonym* that Marian Evans used when she published her classic novel *Middlemarch*.
synonym: pen name

PUERILE *adj* (<u>pyoo</u> ruhl)
childish, immature, silly
Olivia's boyfriend's *puerile* antics are really annoying; sometimes he acts like a five-year-old!
synonyms: juvenile, infantile, jejune

PUGILISM *n* (<u>pyoo</u> juhl ih suhm)
boxing
Pugilism has been defended as a positive outlet for aggressive impulses.
synonyms: sparring, fighting

PUGNACIOUS *adj* (pug <u>nay</u> shus)
quarrelsome, eager and ready to fight
The serene 80-year-old used to be a *pugnacious* troublemaker in her youth, but she's softer now.
synonyms: belligerent, bellicose, contentious

PULCHRITUDE *n* (<u>puhl</u> kruh tood)
beauty
The mortals gazed in admiration at Venus, stunned by her incredible *pulchritude*.
synonyms: loveliness, prettiness, handsomeness, comeliness, gorgeousness

PULVERIZE *v* (<u>puhl</u> vuhr iez)
to pound, crush, or grind into powder; destroy
The polar bear's awesome strength was such that a single blow from its paw would *pulverize* a human.
synonyms: demolish, raze, wreck, annihilate

PUMMEL *v* (<u>puh</u> muhl)
to pound, beat
The parents feared that the gorilla would *pummel* their precious baby, but instead, it brought him
to safety.
synonyms: baste, buffet, hammer, thrash, batter

PUNGENT *adj* (<u>puhn</u> juhnt)
strong or sharp in smell or taste
The smoke from the burning tires was extremely *pungent*.
synonyms: acrid, penetrating, biting, caustic, piquant

PUNITIVE *adj* (<u>pyoo</u> nuh tihv)
having to do with punishment
The teacher banished Jack from the classroom as a *punitive* measure, but the boy was actually overjoyed
to be missing class.
synonyms: corrective, penal, disciplinary

PURGE *v* (puhrj)
to cleanse or free from impurities
Joe likes to *purge* his body of toxins because he always feels healthy and refreshed.
synonyms: purify, eliminate, rid

PURLOIN *v* (<u>puhr</u> loyn)
to steal
The amateur detective Dupin found the *purloined* letter for which the police had searched in vain.
synonyms: pilfer, embezzle

PURPORT *v* (puhr <u>pohrt</u>)
to profess, suppose, claim
Brad *purported* to be an opera lover, but he fell asleep at every performance he attended.
synonyms: pretend, purpose

Q

QUAGMIRE *n* (kwaag mier)
marsh; difficult situation
Kevin realized that he needed help to get himself out of this *quagmire*.
synonyms: swamp, bog, fen, mire, morass

QUALIFY *v* (kwah luh fie)
to provide with needed skills; modify, limit
Stacey needed to shave a full minute off her record in order to *qualify* for the Olympic finals.
synonyms: pass, differentiate, discriminate, distinguish

QUANDARY *n* (kwahn dree)
dilemma, difficulty
Bill found himself in quite a *quandary* when he realized that he had promised to give the job to two different applicants.
synonyms: predicament, plight, jam, fix

QUARANTINE *v* (kwahr uhn teen)
Isolate; to prevent spread of disease
When cholera hit the village, it was *quarantined* to prevent the disease from spreading any further.
synonyms: sequester, ostracize

QUELL *v* (kwehl)
to crush or subdue
The dictator dispatched troops to *quell* the rebellion.
synonyms: suppress, pacify, quiet, quash, stifle

*QUERULOUS *adj* (kwehl)
inclined to complain, irritable
Curtis' complaint letter received prompt attention after the company labeled him a *querulous* potential troublemaker.
synonyms: peevish, whiny, sniveling, puling

QUERY *n* (kweh ree)
Question
When the congressman refused to answer her *query*, the journalist repeated it in a louder voice.
synonyms: inquiry, interrogation

QUIBBLE *v* (kwih buhl)
to argue about insignificant and irrelevant details
Ignoring the widening crack in the dam, the engineers *quibbled* over whose turn it was to make coffee.
synonyms: carp, cavil, niggle, nitpick, pettifog

QUIESCENCE *n* (kwie eh sihns)
inactivity, stillness
Bears typically fall into a state of *quiescence* when they hibernate during the winter months.
synonyms: calm, repose, dormancy, idleness

QUINTESSENCE *n* (kwihn teh sihns)
most typical example; concentrated essence
As far as I'm concerned, Julio Iglesias is the *quintessence* of Spanish manliness.
synonyms: paragon, epitome, heart, root

QUIXOTIC *adj* (kwihk sah tihk)
overly idealistic, impractical
The practical Danuta was skeptical of her roommate's *quixotic* plans to build a roller coaster in their yard.
synonyms: romantic, unrealistic, capricious, impulsive

QUOTIDIAN *adj* (kwo tih dee uhn)
occurring daily; commonplace
The sight of people singing on the street is so *quotidian* in New York that passersby rarely react to it.
synonyms: everyday, normal, usual

R

RACONTEUR *n* (raa cahn <u>tuhr</u>)
witty, skillful storyteller
The *raconteur* kept all the passengers entertained with his stories during the six-hour flight.
synonyms: anecdotalist, monologist

RAIL *v* (rayl)
to scold with bitter or abusive language
When the teacher assigned twice as much homework as usual, his students *railed* against such an impossible workload.
synonyms: upbraid, berate, revile, vituperate

RALLY *v*
to assemble; recover, recuperate
Martina's neighbors *rallied* to her side after the fire destroyed her home, collecting donations for her.
synonyms: muster, gather, convene, heal, convalesce

RAMSHACKLE *adj* (<u>raam</u> shaa kuhl)
likely to collapse
The homeless man lived in a *ramshackle* cabin that had long been abandoned by its previous owners.
synonyms: rickety, dilapidated, decrepit

RANCID *adj* (<u>raan</u> sihd)
spoiled, rotten
The dead mouse was discovered after Brendan complained about the *rancid* odor emanating from behind the refrigerator.
synonyms: rank, repugnant, nasty, putrid

*RANCOR *n* (<u>raan</u> kuhr)
bitter hatred
Having been teased mercilessly for years, Herb became filled with *rancor* toward those who had humiliated him.
synonyms: deep-seated ill will

RANT *v*
to harangue, rave, forcefully scold
The teenager barely listened as her father *ranted* on and on about her disrespectful behavior.
synonyms: fulminate, thunder, yell, inveigh

RAPPORT *n* (rah pohr)
relationship of trust and respect
Initially, they disliked one another, but working together eventually forged a *rapport* between the two men.
synonyms: affinity, camaraderie, sympathy

RAPT *adj* (raapt)
deeply absorbed
The story was so well performed that the usually rowdy children were *rapt* until the final word.
synonyms: engrossed, immersed

RAREFY *v* (<u>rayr</u> uh fie)
to make rare, thin, or less dense
The atmosphere *rarefies* as altitude increases, so the air atop a mountain is too thin to breathe.
synonyms: attenuate, prune

RASH *adj*
careless, hasty, reckless
Lewis was *rash* to jump to the conclusion that the employee was completely incompetent after she made a small error.
synonyms: precipitate, foolhardy, impulsive

RATIFY *v* (<u>raa</u> tih fie)
to approve formally, confirm
The Senate *ratified* the treaty after only a brief debate, much to the delight of its supporters.
synonyms: endorse, sanction, certify, accredit

RAUCOUS *adj* (<u>raw</u> cuhs)
harsh sounding; boisterous
The grade school cafeteria was a *raucous* place at lunchtime.
synonyms: noisy, cacophonous, grating

RAVAGE *v* (<u>raa</u> vehj)
to destroy, devastate
Floods periodically *ravaged* the small town, but life was so pleasant there that residents refused to relocate.
synonyms: pillage, sack, ruin, despoil, desolate

RAVENOUS *adj* (<u>raa</u> vehn uhs)
extremely hungry
The refugee had not had a bite of food for days and was *ravenous*.
synonyms: voracious, gluttonous, rapacious, predatory, famished

RAVINE *n* (ruh <u>veen</u>)
deep, narrow gorge
Police officers scoured the crime scene for days before finding the murder weapon buried in a *ravine*.
synonyms: gully, canyon, gulch, arroyo

RAZE *v* (rayz)
to tear down, demolish
The house had been *razed*; where it once stood, there was nothing but splinters and bricks.
synonyms: level, destroy

REACTIONARY *adj* (ree <u>aak</u> shuhn <u>ayr</u> ee)
marked by extreme conservatism, especially in politics
The former radical hippie had turned into quite a *reactionary*, and the press tried to expose her as a hypocrite.
synonyms: ultraconservative, right-wing, orthodox

REBUFF *n* (ree <u>buhf</u>)
blunt rejection
The princess coldly gave her suitor's marriage proposal a *rebuff*, turning her back on him and walking away.
synonyms: repulse, refusal, check, setback

REBUKE *v* (ree <u>byook</u>)
to reprimand, scold
Sergeants often *rebuke* newly enlisted soldiers to teach them discipline.
synonyms: admonish, reprove, reproach, chide

REBUT *v* (ree <u>buht</u>)
to refute by evidence or argument
The moderator was careful to allow sufficient time for callers to *rebut* claims made by her guest speakers.
synonyms: counter, retort, disprove, confute, contradict

*RECALCITRANT *adj* (ree <u>kaal</u> sih truhnt)
resisting authority or control
The *recalcitrant* mule refused to go down the treacherous path, however hard its master pulled at its reins.
synonyms: stubborn, defiant, unruly, headstrong, willful

RECANT *v* (ree <u>kant</u>)
to retract a statement, opinion, etcetera
The statement was so damning that the politician had no hopes of recovering his credibility, even though he tried to *recant* the words.
synonyms: disavow, disclaim, disown, renounce, repudiate

RECAPITULATE *v* (<u>ree</u> kuh <u>pihch</u> yoo layt)
to review by a brief summary
After the long-winded president had finished his speech, his assistant *recapitulated* for the press the points he had made.
synonyms: synopsize, condense, digest

*RECLUSIVE *adj* (ree <u>kloo</u> sihv)
shut off from the world
Anthony's *reclusive* tendencies led him to leave the city and move into a lonely cabin in Montana.
synonyms: isolated, hermit-like, solitary, asocial

*RECONCILIATION *n* (<u>reh</u> kuhn sihl ee <u>ay</u> shuhn)
the act of agreement after a quarrel, the resolution of a dispute
Reconciliation can only come about through a good-faith effort by all of the former warring factions.
synonyms: rapprochement, settlement, accord

RECTITUDE *n* (<u>rehk</u> tih tood)
moral uprightness
Young women used to be shipped off to finishing schools to teach them proper manners and *rectitude*.
synonyms: honesty, honor, integrity, probity, righteousness

REDRESS *n* (<u>rih</u> drehs)
relief from wrong or injury
Seeking *redress* for the injuries she had received in the accident, Doreen sued the driver of the truck that had hit her.
synonyms: reparation, amends, restitution, indemnity, quittance

REDUNDANCY *n* (rih <u>duhn</u> duhn see)
unnecessary repetition
Let's delete a few paragraphs to cut down on the *redundancy* in this section of the book.
synonyms: duplication, superfluity, tautology, pleonasm, wordiness

*REFRACT *v* (rih <u>fraakt</u>)
to deflect sound or light
The crystal *refracted* the rays of sunlight so they formed a beautiful pattern on the wall.
synonyms: bend, slant

*REFURBISH *v* (rih <u>fuhr</u> bihsh)
to renovate
This old house is charming, but it's kind of shabby, and I definitely need to *refurbish* it.
synonyms: freshen, remodel, restore, clean, overhaul

*REFUTE *v* (rih <u>fyoot</u>)
to contradict, discredit.
She made such a persuasive argument that nobody could *refute* it.
synonyms: deny

REGIMEN *n* (<u>reh</u> juh mihn)
government rule; systematic plan
His marathon training *regimen* dictated that he had to run 10 miles every morning.
synonyms: control, procedure, system, course

REGRESS *v* (rih <u>grehs</u>)
to move backward; revert to an earlier form or state
Elderly people who suffer from senility often *regress* to the early years of their childhood.
synonyms: backslide, deteriorate, relapse, revert, degenerate

REHABILITATE *v* (ree huh <u>bih</u> luh tayt)
to restore to good health or condition; re-establish a person's good reputation
The star checked herself into a clinic to *rehabilitate* herself from her drug addiction.
synonyms: reinstate, reform

REITERATE *v* (ree <u>ih</u> tuhr ayt)
to say or do again, repeat
The teacher was forced to *reiterate* the instructions because the class hadn't been listening the first time.
synonyms: echo, iterate, rehash, restate, retell

REJOINDER *n* (rih <u>joyn</u> duhr)
response
Patrick tried desperately to think of a clever *rejoinder* to Marcy's joke, but he couldn't.
synonyms: retort, riposte

RELEGATE *v* (<u>reh</u> luh gayt)
to send into exile, banish; assign
Because he hadn't scored any goals during the season, Abe was *relegated* to the bench for the championship game.
synonyms: consign, classify, refer

RELINQUISH *v* (rih <u>lihn</u> kwihsh)
to renounce or surrender something
The toddler was forced to *relinquish* the toy when the girl who owned it asked for it back.
synonyms: yield, resign, abandon, cede, waive

RELISH *v* (<u>reh</u> lihsh)
to enjoy greatly
Cameron *relished* the tasty sandwich, but he didn't like the pickle that came with it.
synonyms: savor, love, fancy

REMINISCENCE *n* (reh muh <u>nhis</u> ehns)
remembrance of past events
The old timer's *reminiscence* of his childhood was of a time when there were no cars.
synonyms: memory, recollection, recall

REMISSION *n* (rih <u>mih</u> shuhn)
a lessening of intensity or degree
The doctor told me that the disease had gone into *remission*.
synonyms: abatement, subsiding

REMOTE *adj* (rih <u>moht</u>)
distant, isolated
The island was so *remote* that Chan's cell phone wouldn't operate on it.
synonyms: far, removed, aloof

REMUNERATION *n* (rih <u>myoo</u> nuh ray shuhn)
payment for goods or services or to recompense for losses
You can't expect people to do this kind of boring work without some form of *remuneration*.
synonyms: recompense, pay

RENEGADE *n* (<u>reh</u> nih gayd)
traitor, person abandoning a cause
The *renegades* plotted in secret to overthrow the government.
synonyms: deserter, rebel, apostate, turncoat, defector

RENEGE *v* (rih <u>nehg</u>)
to go back on one's word
Hitler *reneged* on his promise that he would never attack the Soviet Union when his troops invaded the country during World War II.
synonyms: break, violate

RENOUNCE *v* (rih <u>nowns</u>)
to give up or reject a right, title, person, et cetera (or etc.)
Edward *renounced* his right to the British throne to marry the divorcé, Mrs. Simpson.
synonyms: relinquish, disown, yield, resign, abandon

*RENOVATE *v* (<u>reh</u> nuh vayt)
to renew, modernize
The city *renovated* the run-down neighborhood and transformed it into a center of commerce.
synonyms: restore, revive, refurbish

RENOWN *n* (rih <u>nown</u>)
fame, widespread acclaim
Having spent her whole childhood banging on things, Jane grew up to be a drummer of great *renown*.
synonyms: eminence, distinction, prestige, standing, celebrity

REPAST *n* (<u>rih</u> paast)
meal or mealtime
Ravi prepared a delicious *repast* of chicken tikka and naan.
synonyms: feast, banquet

REPEAL *v* (rih <u>peel</u>)
to revoke or formally withdraw (often a law)
The U.S. government *repealed* Prohibition when they realized that the law was not functioning as it had been intended.
synonyms: rescind, nullify, annul, cancel, negate

REPEL *v* (rih <u>pehl</u>)
to rebuff, repulse; disgust, offend
So far, the castle defenders have managed to *repel* the attackers, but they will not be able to hold out much longer.
synonyms: reject, spurn, parry, nauseate, revolt

REPENT *v* (rih <u>pehnt</u>)
to regret a past action
"If you don't *repent* your sins, you will rot in hell!" shouted the evangelical preacher.
synonyms: rue, atone, apologize

REPENTANT *adj* (rih <u>pehnt</u> ehnt)
apologetic, guilty, remorseful
After stealing from the church collection box, Ralph was *repentant* and confessed his sin to the priest.
synonyms: contrite, regretful, penitent, shamefaced, sorry

REPLETE *adj* (rih <u>pleet</u>)
abundantly supplied, complete
The gigantic supermarket was *replete* with consumer products of every kind.
synonyms: abounding, full

REPLICATE *v* (<u>reh</u> pluh cayt)
to duplicate, repeat
If we're going to *replicate* last year's profit margins, we're going to have to work really, really hard.
synonyms: copy, reproduce, clone

REPOSE *n* (rih <u>pohz</u>)
relaxation, leisure
After working hard every day in the busy city, Mike finds his *repose* on weekends playing golf with friends.
synonyms: calmness, tranquility

REPREHENSIBLE *adj* (reh pree <u>hehn</u> suh buhl)
blameworthy, disreputable
Lowell was thrown out of the bar because of his *reprehensible* behavior toward the other patrons.
synonyms: culpable, deplorable

REPRISE *n* (rih <u>priez</u>)
repetition, especially of a piece of music
The soloist ended her aria with a *reprise* of its beautiful refrain.
synonyms: recurrence, return, resumption

REPROBATE *n* (reh <u>pruh</u> bayt)
morally unprincipled person
If you ignore your society's accepted moral code, you will be considered a *reprobate*.
synonyms: sinner, knave, scoundrel, rogue, rake

REPROVE *v* (rih <u>proov</u>)
to criticize or correct, usually in a gentle manner
Mrs. Hernandez *reproved* her daughter for staying out late and not calling.
synonyms: rebuke, admonish, reprimand

REPUDIATE *v* (rih <u>pyoo</u> dee ayt)
to reject as having no authority
The old woman's claim that she was Russian royalty was *repudiated* when DNA tests showed she was not related to them.
synonyms: disown, abjure, forswear, renounce, disclaim

REPULSE *v* (rih <u>puhls</u>)
repel, fend off; sicken, disgust
He thinks women can't resist him, when in actuality many of them are *repulsed* by his arrogance.
synonyms: rebuff, reject, parry, nauseate

REQUITE *v* (rih <u>kwiet</u>)
to return or repay
Thanks for offering to lend me $1,000, but I know I'll never be able to *requite* your generosity.
synonyms: reciprocate, compensate

RESCIND *v* (rih <u>sihnd</u>)
to repeal, cancel
After the celebrity was involved in a scandal, the car company *rescinded* its offer of an endorsement contract.
synonyms: void, annul, revoke

RESIDUE *n* (<u>reh</u> suh doo)
remainder, leftover, remnant
The fire burned everything, leaving only a *residue* of ash and charred debris.
synonyms: rest, balance, leavings, lees, dregs

*RESILIENT *adj* (rih <u>sihl</u> yuhnt)
able to recover quickly after illness or bad luck; able to bounce back to shape
Psychologists say that being *resilient* in life is one of the keys to success and happiness.
synonyms: flexible, elastic

*RESOLUTE *adj* (<u>reh</u> suh <u>loot</u>)
marked by firm determination
Louise was *resolute*: She would get into medical school no matter what.
synonyms: firm, unwavering, intent

RESOLVE *n* (rih <u>sahlv</u>)
determination, firmness of purpose
I admire your *resolve*, but is it really a good idea to go through with the marathon in this bad weather?
synonyms: resolution, decisiveness, drive, enterprise

RESONATE *v* (<u>reh</u> sih nayt)
to echo
The cries of the bald eagle *resonated* throughout the canyon.
synonyms: resound, reverberate

RESPIRE *v* (rih <u>spier</u>)
to breathe
Humans need oxygen to *respire*.
synonyms: inhale, exhale

RESPITE *n* (<u>reh</u> spiet)
interval of relief
The brief *respite* was over; once again, Bo's phone was ringing off the hook with customer complaints.
synonyms: rest, pause, intermission, recess, suspension

RESPLENDENT *adj* (rih <u>splehn</u> duhnt)
splendid, brilliant
The bride looked *resplendent* in her gown and sparkling tiara.
synonyms: dazzling, bright

RESTIVE *adj* (<u>reh</u> stihv)
impatient, uneasy, restless
The passengers became *restive* after having to wait in line for hours and began to shout complaints at the airline staff.
synonyms: anxious, agitated, fretful

RESUSCITATE *v* (rih <u>suh</u> suh tayt)
to revive, bring back to life
The doctor managed to *resuscitate* the heart attack victim one minute after he had stopped breathing.
synonyms: restore, revivify, resurrect

RETAIN *v* (rih <u>tayn</u>)
to hold, keep possession of
Britain had to give up most of its colonies, but it *retained* control over Hong Kong until very recently.
synonyms: withhold, reserve, maintain, remember

*RESTRAINED *adj* (rih <u>straynd</u>)
controlled, repressed, restricted
I was *restrained* by good etiquette from telling him what I really thought.
synonyms: hampered, bridled, curbed, checked

RETICENT *adj* (<u>reh</u> tih suhnt)
not speaking freely; reserved
Physically small and *reticent*, Joan Didion often went unnoticed by those upon whom she was reporting.
synonyms: silent, taciturn, secretive, restrained

RETORT *n* (rih <u>tohrt</u>)
cutting response
It was only after Lance had left the room that Vera came up with the perfect *retort* to his insulting remark.
synonyms: rejoinder, riposte, comeback

RETRACT *v* (rih <u>traakt</u>)
to draw in or take back
After Lance had *retracted* his insulting remark, Vera decided to forgive him.
synonyms: disavow, recede, retreat, retrogress

RETRENCH *v* (rih <u>trehnch</u>)
to regroup, reorganize
After their humiliating defeat, the troops *retrenched* back at the base to decide what to do next.
synonyms: economize, reduce, remove, delete, omit

RETRIEVE *v* (rih <u>treev</u>)
to bring, fetch; reclaim
The eager Labrador *retrieved* the frisbee from the lake.
synonyms: recover, regain, recoup, fetch

RETROGRADE *adj* (<u>reh</u> troh grayd)
having a backward motion or direction
The *retrograde* motion of the comet puzzled the astronomers, who had expected it to move forward.
synonyms: inverted, reversed

REVELRY *n* (<u>reh</u> vuhl ree)
boisterous festivity
An atmosphere of *revelry* filled the school after its basketball team's surprising victory.
synonyms: merrymaking, cavorting, frolic, gaiety, jollity

*REVERE *v* (rih <u>veer</u>)
to worship, regard with awe
All the nuns in the convent *revered* their wise Mother Superior.
synonyms: venerate, adore, idolize, admire

REVERT *v* (rih <u>vuhrt</u>)
to backslide, regress
Just when Liz thought he was finally becoming more mature, Kyle *reverted* to his childish ways.
synonyms: return, recur, recrudesce, degenerate, deteriorate

REVILE *v* (rih <u>viel</u>)
to criticize with harsh language, verbally abuse
The artist's new installation was *reviled* by critics who weren't used to the departure from his usual work.
synonyms: vituperate, scold, assail

REVOKE *v* (rih <u>vohk</u>)
to annul, cancel, call back
Jonas's green card was *revoked* when it was proven that he had illegally worked outside the country.
synonyms: void, withdraw, reverse, lift, rescind

REVULSION *n* (rih <u>vuhl</u> shuhn)
strong feeling of repugnance or dislike
Rebecca was filled with *revulsion* at the stench that the rotten melon slices in her fridge gave off.
synonyms: disgust, loathing, abhorrence, repugnance, aversion

RHAPSODY *n* (<u>raap</u> suh dee)
emotional literary or musical work
The rock group Queen played on a long musical tradition with their song "Bohemian *Rhapsody*."
synonyms: dithyramb, impromptu, paean

RHETORIC *n* (<u>reh</u> tuhr ihk)
the art of speaking or writing effectively; skill in the effective use of speech
Lincoln's talent for *rhetoric* was evident in his beautifully expressed Gettysburg Address.
synonyms: eloquence, articulateness

RHYTHM *n* (<u>rih</u> thuhm)
regular pattern or variation of sounds and stresses
Darren, who had no sense of *rhythm*, was a terrible dancer.
synonyms: meter, cadence, measure, beat, pulse

RIBALD *adj* (<u>rih</u> buhld)
humorous in a vulgar way
The court jester's *ribald* brand of humor delighted the rather uncouth king.
synonyms: lewd, coarse, indelicate, obscene, gross

RIDDLE *v* (<u>rih</u> duhl)
to make many holes in; permeate
The helicopter was *riddled* with bullet holes after its flight into the combat zone.
synonyms: perforate, honeycomb, prick, punch, pierce

RIFE *adj* (rief)
abundant prevalent especially to an increasing degree; filled with
The essay was so *rife* with grammatical errors that it had to be rewritten.
synonyms: numerous, prevailing

RISQUÉ *adj* (rih <u>skay</u>)
bordering on being inappropriate or indecent
Some of the more conservative audience members found the *risqué* variety act offensive.
synonyms: indelicate, improper, ribald

ROBUST *adj* (roh <u>buhst</u>)
strong and healthy; hardy
Many of those around her fell ill, but the *robust* Sharon remained healthy throughout the flu epidemic.
synonyms: vigorous, sturdy, sound, well, hale

ROTUND *adj* (roh <u>tuhnd</u>)
round in shape; fat
The *rotund* matron spent her days baking cookies and then eating a good share of them herself.
synonyms: plumb, portly, stout, corpulent, obese

RUE *v* (roo)
to regret
I *rue* the day I agreed to take care of that evil little cat.
synonyms: deplore, repent

RUMINATE *v* (<u>roo</u> muh nayt)
to contemplate, reflect upon
The scholars spent days at the retreat trying to *ruminate* on the complexities of the geopolitical situation.
synonyms: ponder, meditate, deliberate, mull, muse

RUSTIC *adj* (<u>ruh</u> stihk)
Rural
The *rustic* cabin was an ideal setting for a vacation in the country.
synonyms: bucolic, pastoral

S

SACCHARINE *adj* (<u>saa</u> kuh rihn)
excessively sweet or sentimental
Geoffrey's *saccharine* poems nauseated Lucy, and she wished he'd stop sending them.
synonyms: maudlin, fulsome

SACROSANCT *adj* (<u>saa</u> kroh saankt)
extremely sacred; beyond criticism.
Many people considered Mother Teresa to be *sacrosanct* and would not tolerate any criticism of her.
synonyms: holy, inviolable, off-limits

*SAGACIOUS *adj* (suh <u>gay</u> shuhs)
shrewd
Owls have a reputation for being *sagacious*, perhaps because of their big eyes, which resemble glasses.
synonyms: astute, perspicacious, wise, judicious, sage

SALIENT *adj* (<u>say</u> lee uhnt)
prominent, of notable significance
His most *salient* characteristic is his tendency to dominate every conversation.
synonyms: noticeable, marked, outstanding

SALLOW *adj* (<u>saa</u> loh)
sickly yellow in color
Due to the long hours she spent working in the sweatshop, Bertha's skin looked *sallow* and unhealthy.
synonyms: ashen, green, pasty, peaked, wan

SALUBRIOUS *adj* (suh <u>loo</u> bree uhs)
healthful
Rundown and sickly, Rita hoped that the fresh mountain air would have a *salubrious* effect on her health.
synonyms: curative, medicinal, tonic, therapeutic, bracing

SALUTATION *n* (saal yoo <u>tay</u> shuhn)
greeting
Many people keep in touch by exchanging Christmas *salutations* once a year.
synonyms: salute, regards, welcome, hello

SANCTION *n* (<u>saank</u> shuhn)
permission, support; law; penalty
"The court cannot *sanction* this type of criminal behavior, and it must stop," declared the stern judge.
synonyms: authorization, consent, leave, license, approval

SANCTUARY *n* (<u>saank</u> choo eh ree)
haven, retreat
Seeking *sanctuary* from the bloodthirsty crowd that wanted to burn her at the stake, the accused witch banged on the gate of the convent.
synonyms: refuge, asylum, shelter

SANGUINE *adj* (<u>saan</u> gwuhn)
ruddy; cheerfully optimistic
A *sanguine* person thinks the glass is half full, whereas a depressed person thinks it's half empty.
synonyms: confident, positive, hopeful, rosy, rubicund

SARDONIC *adj* (sahr <u>dah</u> nihk)
cynical, scornfully mocking
Denise was offended by the *sardonic* way in which her date made fun of her ideas and opinions.
synonyms: sarcastic, acerbic, caustic, satirical, snide

SATIATE *v* (<u>say</u> shee ayt)
to satisfy (as a need or desire) fully or to excess
After years of journeying around the world with nothing but backpacks, the friends had finally *satiated* their desire to travel.
synonyms: gorge

SAUNTER *v* (<u>sawn</u> tuhr)
to amble; walk in a leisurely manner
The plainclothes policeman *sauntered* casually down the street, hoping he would not attract attention.
synonyms: stroll, ramble

SAVANT *n* (suh <u>vahnt</u>)
a person of learning; especially one with knowledge in a special field
The *savant* so impressed us with his knowledge that we asked him to come speak at our school.
synonyms: scholar

SAVORY *adj* (<u>say</u> vuhr ee)
agreeable in taste or smell
The banquet guests consumed the *savory* treats with pleasure.
synonyms: appetizing, pungent, piquant, delectable, succulent

SCABBARD *n* (<u>skaa</u> buhrd)
sheath for sword or dagger
The knight drew his sword from its *scabbard* and prepared to attack the villain.
synonyms: sheath, holster, hanger

SCALE *v* (skayl)
to climb to the top of
The army recruits *scaled* the wall as fast as they could and raced to the end of the obstacle course.
synonyms: ascend, mount

SCATHING *adj* (<u>skay</u> thing)
harshly critical; painfully hot
After the *scathing* criticism her book of poems received, Alicia swore off poetry writing for good.
synonyms: denunciatory, injurious, blistering, excoriating

SCENARIO *n* (suh <u>naa</u> ree oh)
plot outline; possible situation
I think this triangle drama between you, your husband, and the hairdresser would make an interesting *scenario* for a play.
synonyms: treatment, synopsis, screenplay

SCINTILLA *n* (sihn <u>tihl</u> uh)
trace amount
This poison is so powerful that no more of a *scintilla* of it is needed to kill a horse.
synonyms: iota, spark, speck, atom, mote

SCINTILLATE *v* (<u>sihn</u> tuhl ayt)
to sparkle, flash
The society hostess was famous for her great wit and her ability to *scintillate*.
synonyms: gleam, glisten, glitter, shimmer, twinkle

SCOFF *v* (skahf)
to deride, ridicule
The toddler *scoffed* at the notion that cows could jump over the moon; he was too smart to believe that.
synonyms: mock, scorn, taunt, twit, flout

SCORE *v* (skohr)
to make a notch or scratch
The prisoner *scored* a mark in the door for every day he passed in captivity.
synonyms: furrow, scrape, groove, chase, rule

SCRUPULOUS *adj* (<u>skroop</u> yuh luhs)
acting in strict regard for what is considered proper; punctiliously exact
After the storm had destroyed their antique lamp, the Millers worked to repair it with *scrupulous* care.
synonyms: painstaking, meticulous

*SCRUTINY *n* (<u>skroot</u> nee)
careful observation
The prehistoric fossils were given careful *scrutiny* by a team of scientists.
synonyms: examination, study, surveillance

SCURRILOUS *adj* (<u>skuh</u> ruh luhs)
vulgar, low, indecent
The decadent aristocrat took part in *scurrilous* activities every night, unbeknownst to his family.
synonyms: coarse, abusive, foul-mouthed

SECEDE *v* (sih <u>seed</u>)
to withdraw formally from an organization
When the U.N. recognized the independence of Platvia's former colony, the country angrily *seceded* from the organization.
synonyms: quit, resign, leave, splinter off, pull out

SECLUDED *adj* (sih <u>kloo</u> dehd)
isolated and remote
The hermit lived in a *secluded* cottage, far from the other villagers.
synonyms: solitary, sequestered, out-of-the-way

SECULAR *adj* (<u>seh</u> kyoo luhr)
not specifically pertaining to religion, relating to the world
Although his favorite book was the Bible, the archbishop also read *secular* works such as mysteries.
synonyms: temporal, material

SEDATIVE *n* (<u>seh</u> duh tihv)
something, such as a drug, that sedates or makes drowsy
Laudanum, a liquid made from opium, was once sold legally as a *sedative*.
synonyms: tranquilizer, calmative, anodyne, soporific, narcotic

SEDENTARY *adj* (<u>seh</u> dehn tehry)
inactive, stationary; sluggish
Americans, who often work in *sedentary* office jobs, are becoming more overweight and out of shape.
synonyms: fixed, motionless, inactive, deskbound, idle

SEDITION *n* (sih <u>dih</u> shuhn)
behavior that promotes rebellion or civil disorder against the state
Li was arrested for *sedition* after he gave a fiery speech in the main square.
synonyms: insurrection, conspiracy

SEMINAL *adj* (<u>seh</u> muhn uhl)
influential in an original way, providing a basis for further development; creative
The scientist's discovery proved to be *seminal* in the area of quantum physics.
synonyms: original, generative

SENTENTIOUS *adj* (sehn <u>tehn</u> shuhs)
having a moralizing tone
The pastor gave a *sententious* lecture to the group of teenagers on their questionable morals.
synonyms: terse, pithy, aphoristic, pompous, moralistic

SENTIENT *adj* (<u>sehn</u> shuhnt)
aware, conscious, able to perceive
The anesthetic didn't work, and I was still *sentient* when the surgeon made her cut, so the operation was agony for me.
synonyms: thinking, feeling, intelligent

SEQUESTER *v* (suh <u>kweh</u> stuhr)
to set apart, seclude
When juries are *sequestered*, it can take days, even weeks, to come up with a verdict.
synonyms: segregate, isolate

SERAPHIC *adj* (seh <u>rah</u> fihk)
angelic, sweet
Selena's *seraphic* appearance belied her nasty, bitter personality.
synonyms: heavenly, cherubic

SERENITY *n* (suh <u>reh</u> nuh tee)
calm, peacefulness
Lisette's meditation helps her to achieve true *serenity*.
synonyms: tranquility, equanimity, composure, sang-froid, contentment

SERPENTINE *adj* (<u>suhr</u> puhn teen)
serpent-like; twisting, winding
The princess fled down the seemingly endless *serpentine* staircase of the castle keep.
synonyms: sinuous, snaky, curvilinear, vermicular

SERVILE *adj* (<u>suhr</u> viel)
submissive, obedient
As the wealthy widow screamed in rage at him, the *servile* butler apologized profusely for his mistake.
synonyms: slavish, subservient

SHARD *n* (shahrd)
piece of broken glass or pottery
Barbara picked up the *shards* of the broken vase and attempted to glue them back together.
synonyms: fragment, sliver, scrap, potsherd

SHIRK *v* (shuhrk)
to avoid a task due to laziness or fear
The garbage man *shirked* his responsibilities by picking up the trash on only half of the streets he was supposed to cover.
synonyms: neglect, loaf, skip, skulk, escape

SHROUD *v* (shrowd)
to wrap up; to hide from sight
The top of the mountain was *shrouded* by thick clouds.
synonyms: blanket, obscure, conceal, cloak, envelop

SIMIAN *adj* (<u>sih</u> mee uhn)
apelike; relating to apes
Early man was more *simian* in appearance than is modern man.
synonyms: anthropoid, primate

SIMPER *v* (<u>sihm</u> puhr)
to smile foolishly
The spoiled girl *simpered* as her mother praised her extravagantly to the guests at the party.
synonyms: smirk, grin

SINECURE *n* (<u>sien</u> ih kyoor)
a well-paying job or office that requires little or no work
The corrupt mayor made sure to set up all his relatives in *sinecures* within the administration.

SINGE *v* (sihnj)
to burn slightly, scorch
Martha *singed* the hairs on her arm while cooking food over the gas flame.
synonyms: sear, toast, parch, char

SINUOUS *adj* (<u>sihn</u> yoo uhs)
winding; intricate, complex
Thick, *sinuous* vines wound around the trunk of the tree.
synonyms: supple, lithe, devious, serpentine, curvilinear

*SKEPTICAL *adj*
doubtful, questioning
Although her parents still tried to make her believe that Santa Claus existed, the girl was *skeptical*.
synonyms: disbelieving, incredulous, cynical

SKULK *v* (skuhlk)
to move in a stealthy or cautious manner; sneak
The private detective *skulked* behind a tree, waiting for the suspect to emerge from the motel room.
synonyms: lurk, shirk, hide, evade, prowl

SLIGHT *v* (sliet)
to treat as unimportant; insult
Pete *slighted* his old friend Matt by not inviting him to his annual Super Bowl party.
synonyms: scant, belittle, snub, neglect

SLOTH *n* (slawth)
sluggish, lazy
The formerly dynamic CEO sank into *sloth* upon retiring, staying in bed until 3 in the afternoon.
synonyms: indolence, idleness

SLOUGH *v* (sluhf)
to discard or shed
The rattlesnake *sloughed* off its old skin and slithered away, shiny and new looking.
synonyms: molt, cast

SLOVENLY *adj* (<u>slah</u> vuhn lee)
untidy, messy
The cook's clothes were so stained and *slovenly* that no restaurant would hire him.
synonyms: negligent, slipshod, sloppy, unkempt

SMELT *v* (smehlt)
to melt metal in order to refine it
We could make jewelry out of this silver ore, but it would look more elegant if we *smelted* it first.
synonyms: purify, extract

SNIPPET *n* (<u>snih</u> piht)
tiny part, tidbit
From the brief *snippet* of conversation she overheard, Ida realized that her job was in danger.
synonyms: bit, scrap, morsel, section, slice

SOBRIETY *n* (suh <u>brie</u> eh tee)
state of being serious or sober
Wendell's witty comments alleviated the *sobriety* of the budget conference.
synonyms: gravity, moderation, temperance

SOBRIQUET *n* (soh brih keht)
nickname
One of Ronald Reagan's *sobriquets* was "The Gipper."
synonyms: alias, pseudonym

SODDEN *adj* (<u>sah</u> dehn)
thoroughly soaked; saturated
My shoes were thoroughly *sodden* after trekking through the damp Irish bog.
synonyms: soggy, wet, drenched, steeped, waterlogged

SOJOURN *n* (<u>soh</u> juhrn)
a temporary stay, visit
After graduating from college, Iliani embarked on a *sojourn* to China.

SOLACE *n* (<u>sah</u> lihs)
comfort in distress; consolation
Upset as she was by her poodle's death, Florence took *solace* in the fact that he had died happy.
synonyms: succor, balm, cheer, condolence, assuagement

SOLICITOUS *adj* (suh <u>lih</u> sih tuhs)
anxious, concerned; full of desire, eager
Overjoyed to see the pop idol in her very presence, the *solicitous* store owner stood ready to serve.
synonyms: considerate, attentive

SOLIDARITY *n* (sah lih <u>daar</u> ih tee)
unity based on common aims or interests
The company's owner felt a certain *solidarity* with the striking workers because of his own
humble origins.
synonyms: union, fellowship, sympathy, concurrence, accord

SOLILOQUY *n* (suh <u>lih</u> luh kwee)
literary or dramatic speech by one character, not addressed to others
Rachel's *soliloquy* gave the audience more insight into her thoughts than the other characters in the
play had.
synonyms: monologue, solo

SOMBER *adj* (<u>sahm</u> buhr)
dark and gloomy; melancholy, dismal
Everyone at the funeral was wearing dark, *somber* clothes except for the little girl in the flowered dress.
synonyms: serious, grave, mournful, lugubrious, funereal

SOMNOLENT *adj* (<u>sahm</u> nuh luhnt)
drowsy, sleepy; inducing sleep
Carter was *somnolent* after taking a couple of sleeping pills.
synonyms: slumberous, sluggish, soporific, somniferous

SONOROUS *adj* (sah <u>nuhr</u> uhs)
producing a full, rich sound
The *sonorous* blaring of the foghorn woke Lily up at 4:30 in the morning.
synonyms: resonant, vibrant, orotund

SOPHOMORIC *adj* (sahf <u>mohr</u> ihk)
exhibiting great immaturity and lack of judgment
After Sean's *sophomoric* behavior, he was grounded for weeks.
synonyms: juvenile

SOPORIFIC *adj* (sahp uhr <u>ihf</u> ihk)
sleepy or tending to cause sleep
The movie proved to be so *soporific* that soon loud snores were heard throughout the theater.
synonyms: somnolent, narcotic, somniferous, drowsy

SORDID *adj* (<u>sohr</u> dihd)
filthy; contemptible and corrupt
The details of the mayor's affair were so *sordid* that many people were too disgusted to read them.
synonyms: dirty, foul, squalid, wretched, degraded

SOVEREIGN *adj* (<u>sah</u> vuhrn)
having supreme power
The king did not take kindly to those who refused to recognize his *sovereign* power.
synonyms: royal, regal, monarchical, autonomous, independent

*SPARSE *adj* (spahrs)
thinly spread out; barely populated
He had a thick head of hair when he was young, but as he grew older, it grew *sparse*.
synonyms: meager, spare, skimpy, scant

SPARTAN *adj* (<u>spahr</u> tihn)
highly self-disciplined; frugal, austere
When he was in training, the athlete preferred to live in a *spartan* room, so he could shut out all distractions.
synonyms: restrained, simple

SPAWN *v*
to generate, produce
The frog *spawned* hundreds of tadpoles.
synonyms: engender, procreate

SPEARHEAD *v* (<u>speer</u> hehd)
to be the leader or driving force
Susan B. Anthony and her associates *spearheaded* the feminist movement in the 19th century.
synonyms: lead, impel, drive

*SPONTANEOUS *adj* (spahn <u>tay</u> nee uhs)
on the spur of the moment, impulsive
Jean made the *spontaneous* decision to go to the movies instead of visiting her in-laws as she had planned.
synonyms: instinctive, involuntary, automatic, extemporaneous, impromptu

SPORADIC *adj* (spuhr <u>aa</u> dihk)
infrequent, irregular
Because he was *sporadic* in following the diet, he lapsed into his old bad eating habits.
synonyms: periodic, intermittent, occasional, fitful, discontinuous

SPORTIVE *adj* (<u>spohr</u> tihv)
frolicsome, playful
The lakeside vacation meant more *sportive* opportunities for the kids than the wine tour through France.
synonyms: frisky, merry

SPRIGHTLY *adj* (<u>spriet</u> lee)
lively, animated, energetic
He was quite *sprightly* and active for a 98-year-old.
synonyms: spirited, brisk, vivacious, perky

*SPURIOUS *adj* (<u>spyoor</u> ee uhs)
lacking authenticity; counterfeit, false
Quoting from a *spurious* bible, the cult leader declared that all property should be signed over to him.
synonyms: fraudulent, ersatz, fake, phony, mock

SPURN *v* (spuhrn)
to reject or refuse contemptuously; scorn
When Harvey proposed to Harriet, she *spurned* him: she'd always considered him an idiot.
synonyms: disdain, snub, ostracize, ignore, cut

*SQUALID *adj* (<u>skwa</u> lihd)
filthy and degraded as the result of neglect or poverty
The *squalid* living conditions in the building outraged the new tenants.
synonyms: unclean, foul

SQUANDER *v* (<u>skwan</u> duhr)
to waste
While I've been saving for a piano, my friend Sean *squandered* all his earnings on lottery tickets.
synonyms: dissipate, fritter, misspend

STACCATO *adj* (stuh <u>kah</u> toh)
marked by abrupt, clear-cut sounds
The *staccato* sounds of the coded radio transmissions filled the ship's cabin.
synonyms: short, disconnected

*STAGNANT *adj* (<u>staag</u> nuhnt)
immobile, stale
That *stagnant* pond is a perfect breeding ground for mosquitoes; we should drain it.
synonyms: motionless, foul, inactive, sluggish, dull

STAID *adj* (stayd)
self-restrained to the point of dullness
The lively young girl felt bored in the company of her *staid*, conservative date.
synonyms: sedate, sober, serious, grave, solemn

STALK *v* (stahk)
to hunt, pursue
The rock star put a restraining order on the insane woman who had *stalked* him for many years.
synonyms: track, shadow, trail, dog, hound

STAND *n*
group of trees
The Iroquois warriors hid in a *stand* of trees, waiting to ambush the approaching British soldiers.
synonyms: growth, cluster, clump

STARK *adj* (stahrk)
bare, empty, vacant
Nancy bought posters to liven up her *stark* new apartment, although she couldn't afford furniture.
synonyms: austere, barren, bleak, grim, dismal

STASIS *n* (stay sihs)
a state of static balance or equilibrium; stagnation
The rusty, ivy-covered World War II tank had obviously been in *stasis* for years.
synonyms: inertia, standstill

STEADFAST *adj* (stehd faast)
unwavering, loyal
When everyone else abandoned Nathaniel, his son Wingate remained *steadfast*.
synonyms: faithful, true, constant, fast, staunch

STIFLE *v* (stie fuhl)
to smother or suffocate; suppress.
Much as she longed to express her anger at the dictator, Maria *stifled* her protests for fear of being arrested.
synonyms: repress, strangle, throttle

STIGMA *n* (stihg mah)
mark of disgrace or inferiority
In *The Scarlet Letter*, Hester Prynne was required to wear the letter "A" on her clothes as a public *stigma* for her adultery.
synonyms: stain, blot, brand, taint

STINT *v* (stihnt)
to be sparing or frugal; to restrict with respect to a share or allowance
Don't *stint* on the mayonnaise, because I don't like my sandwich too dry.
synonyms: skimp, scrimp

STIPEND *n* (stie pehnd)
allowance; fixed amount of money paid regularly
Unable to survive on her small *stipend* from the university, Joyce was forced to take out loans.
synonyms: salary, reward, wage, emolument, endowment

STOCKADE *n* (stahk <u>ayd</u>)
enclosed area forming defensive wall.
As the enemy approached, the soldiers took their defensive positions behind the *stockade*.
synonyms: palisade, fence, rampart, fort, jail

*STOIC *adj* (<u>stoh</u> ihk)
indifferent to or unaffected by emotions
While most of the mourners wept, the dead woman's husband kept up a *stoic*, unemotional facade.
synonyms: impassive, stolid

STOLID *adj* (<u>stah</u> lihd)
having or showing little emotion
The prisoner appeared *stolid* and unaffected by the judge's harsh sentence.
synonyms: impassive, stoic

STRATAGEM *n* (<u>straa</u> tuh guhm)
trick designed to deceive an enemy
The Trojan Horse must be one of the most successful military *stratagems* used throughout history.
synonyms: artifice, ruse, while, feint, maneuver

STRATIFY *v* (<u>straa</u> tuh fie)
to arrange or divide into layers
Schliemann *stratified* the numerous layers of Troy, an archeological dig that remains legendary.
synonyms: grade, separate

STRIDENT *adj* (<u>strie</u> dehnt)
loud, harsh, unpleasantly noisy
The traveler's *strident* manner annoyed the flight attendant, but she managed to keep her cool.
synonyms: grating, shrill, discordant

STRINGENT *adj* (<u>strihn</u> guhnt)
imposing severe, rigorous standards
Many people found it difficult to live up to the *stringent* moral standards imposed by the Puritans.
synonyms: restricted, tight, demanding

STUNTED *adj* (<u>stuhn</u> tehd)
having arrested growth or development
The bonsai tree's growth is intentionally *stunted* by the Japanese gardeners who cultivate it.
synonyms: little, petite, dwarfish, undersized, runty

STUPEFY *v* (<u>stoo</u> puh fie)
to dull the senses of; stun, astonish
The stag, *stupefied* by the bright glare of the headlights, stood right in the middle of the highway.
synonyms: daze, bemuse, benumb, amaze

STYMIE *v* (<u>stie</u> mee)
to block or thwart
The police effort to capture the bank robber was *stymied* when he escaped through a rear window.
synonyms: stump, foil

SUAVE *adj* (swahv)
smoothly gracious or polite; blandly ingratiating
Nina was a *suave* young woman who knew exactly how to act in any situation.
synonyms: urbane, diplomatic, politic

SUBJUGATE *v* (<u>suhb</u> juh gayt)
to conquer, subdue; enslave
The Romans *subjugated* many of the peoples they fought against.
synonyms: defeat, vanquish, enthrall, yoke

SUBLIME *adj* (suh <u>bliem</u>)
awe-inspiring; of high spiritual or moral value
The music was so *sublime* that it transformed the rude surroundings into a special place.
synonyms: noble, majestic, supreme, ideal

SUBLIMINAL *adj* (suh <u>blihm</u> uh nuhl)
subconscious; imperceptible
Subliminal messages flash by so quickly on the TV screen that viewers are not consciously aware that they have seen them.
synonyms: unperceived, unconscious

SUBSEQUENT *adj* (<u>suhb</u> suh kwehnt)
following in time or order
Elizabeth heard people discussing what a good president she would make, and her *subsequent* thoughts were about how wonderful it would be to be president.
synonyms: succeeding, next, afterward

*SUBSTANTIATE *v* (suhb <u>staan</u> shee ayt)
to validate or prove
I certainly hope you're ready to *substantiate* that heinous allegation against my client
synonyms: verify, confirm, corroborate, authenticate

SUBTERFUGE *n* (<u>suhb</u> tuhr fyooj)
trick or tactic used to avoid something
Spies who are not skilled in the art of *subterfuge* are generally exposed before too long.
synonyms: stratagem, ruse

SUBTERRANEAN *adj* (<u>suhb</u> tuh <u>ray</u> nee uhn)
hidden, secret; underground
Subterranean tracks were created for the trains after it was decided they had run out of room above ground.
synonyms: buried, concealed, sunken

*SUBTLE *adj* (<u>suh</u> tuhl)
hard to detect or describe; perceptive
The pickpocket was so *subtle* that his victims did not even realize they had been robbed until hours later.
synonyms: elusive, abstruse, clever, devious, insinuating

SUBVERT *v* (suhb <u>vurht</u>)
to undermine or corrupt
The traitor intended to *subvert* loyal citizens of the crown with the revolutionary propaganda he distributed.
synonyms: sabotage, ruin, overthrow, topple

SUCCINCT *adj* (suh <u>sihnkt</u>)
terse, brief, concise
She was sought after by many talk shows because her remarks were always *succinct* and to the point.
synonyms: laconic, pithy

SUCCULENT *adj* (<u>suh</u> kyoo lihnt)
juicy; full of vitality or freshness
The famished businessman dug into the *succulent* porterhouse steak with relish.
synonyms: delectable, moist, luscious

SULLEN *adj* (<u>suh</u> luhn)
brooding, gloomy
The *sullen* child sat in the corner by herself, refusing to play with her classmates.
synonyms: morose, sulky, somber, glum

SULLY *v* (<u>suh</u> lee)
to tarnish, taint
With the help of a public-relations firm, he was able to restore his *sullied* reputation.
synonyms: defile, besmirch

SUMPTUOUS *adj* (<u>suhm</u> choo uhs)
lavish, splendid
The banquet was a *sumptuous* affair, including a seven-course meal and quarts of champagne.
synonyms: elaborate, luxurious

SUPERCILIOUS *adj* (soo puhr <u>sihl</u> ee uhs)
arrogant, haughty, overbearing, condescending
She was a shallow and scornful society woman with a *supercilious* manner.
synonyms: proud, disdainful, patronizing

*SUPERFICIAL *adj* (soo puhr <u>fihsh</u> uhl)
hasty; shallow and phony
The politician was friendly, but in a *superficial*, unconvincing kind of way.
synonyms: surface, cursory, trivial

*SUPERFLUOUS *adj* (soo <u>puhr</u> floo uhs)
extra, more than necessary
The extra recommendations Jake included in his application were *superfluous*, as only one was required.
synonyms: excess, surplus

SUPERSEDE *v* (<u>soo</u> puhr <u>seed</u>)
to cause to be set aside; to force out of use as inferior, replace
Her computer was still running version 2.0 of the software, which had long since been *superseded* by at least three more versions.
synonyms: supplant

SUPPLANT *v* (suh <u>plaant</u>)
to replace (another) by force, to take the place of
The overthrow of the government meant a new leader to *supplant* the tyrannical former one.
synonyms: displace, supersede

SUPPLE *adj* (<u>suh</u> puhl)
flexible, pliant
The *supple* stalks of bamboo swayed back and forth in the wind.
synonyms: limber, elastic, lithe

SUPPLICANT *n* (<u>suh</u> plih kehnt)
one who asks humbly and earnestly
Alf is normally a cocky fellow, but he transformed himself into a *supplicant* when he begged the banker for a loan.
synonyms: petitioner, appellant, applicant, suitor, suppliant

*SUPPRESS *v* (suh <u>prehs</u>)
to hold back, restrain
The students struggled to *suppress* their laughter when the pompous professor fell on his duff.
synonyms: subdue, stifle, muffle, quell, curb

SURFEIT *n* (<u>suhr</u> fiht)
excessive amount
Because of the *surfeit* of pigs, pork prices have never been lower.
synonyms: glut, superfluity, plethora, repletion, surplus

SURLY *adj* (<u>suhr</u> lee)
rude and bad-tempered
When asked to clean the windshield, the *surly* gas station attendant tossed a dirty rag at the customer and walked away.
synonyms: gruff, testy, grumpy

SURMISE *v* (suhr <u>miez</u>)
to make an educated guess
From his torn pants and bloody nose, I *surmised* that he had been in a fight.
synonyms: conjecture, guess, speculate, infer

SURMOUNT *v* (suhr <u>mownt</u>)
to conquer, overcome
The blind woman *surmounted* great obstacles to become a well-known trial lawyer.
synonyms: clear, hurdle, leap

SURPASS *v* (suhr <u>paas</u>)
to do better than, be superior to
Ursula is a pretty girl, but her gorgeous sister *surpasses* her in beauty.
synonyms: transcend, exceed, excel, outdo

SURPLUS *n* (<u>suhr</u> pluhs)
an excess
The supermarket donated its *surplus* of fruit to a local homeless shelter.
synonyms: glut, superfluity, plethora, repletion, surfeit

*SURREPTITIOUS *adj* (<u>suh</u> rehp <u>tih</u> shuhs)
characterized by secrecy
The queen knew nothing of the *surreptitious* plots being hatched against her at court.
synonyms: clandestine, covert, furtive

SUSCEPTIBLE *adj* (suh <u>sehp</u> tuh buhl)
vulnerable, unprotected
Because of her weakened state, Valerie was *susceptible* to infection.
synonyms: sensitive, impressionable, prone, subject

SUSPEND *v* (suh <u>spehnd</u>)
to defer, interrupt; dangle, hang
Construction of the building was *suspended* when an ancient Native American burial ground was discovered at the site.
synonyms: cease, disrupt, halt, discontinue, terminate

SUSTAIN *v* (suh <u>stayn</u>)
to support, uphold; endure, undergo
If we can *sustain* our efforts a little longer, I'm sure our plan will succeed in the end.
synonyms: maintain, prop, encourage, withstand, confirm

SYBARITE *n* (<u>sih</u> buh riet)
a person devoted to pleasure and luxury
A confirmed *sybarite*, the nobleman fainted at the thought of having to leave his palace and live in a small cottage.

SYCOPHANT *n* (<u>sie</u> kuh fuhnt)
a self-serving flatterer, yes-man
Dreading criticism, the actor surrounded himself with admirers and *sycophants*.
synonyms: toady, lickspittle, fawner, bootlicker

SYLLABUS *n* (<u>sihl</u> uh buhs)
an outline of a course
Ko looked at the course *syllabus* to figure out how much work he would be expected to do each week.
synonyms: summary, schedule

SYMBIOSIS *n* (<u>sihm</u> bie <u>oh</u> sihs)
cooperation, mutual helpfulness
The rhino and the tick-eating bird live in *symbiosis*; the rhino gives the bird food in the form of ticks, and the bird rids the rhino of parasites.
synonyms: association, interdependence

SYNOPSIS *n* (sih <u>nahp</u> sihs)
plot summary
Oren wrote a one-page *synopsis* of a 55-page book.
synonyms: outline, abstract, compendium, digest, epitome

SYNTHESIS *n* (<u>sihn</u> thuh sihs)
blend, combination
The methods used in the experiment were a *synthesis* of techniques taken from biology and medicine.
synonyms: mixture, compound

T

TACIT *adj* (<u>taa</u> siht)
silently understood or implied
Although not a word had been said, everyone in the room knew that a *tacit* agreement had been made about which course of action to take.
synonyms: implicit, unspoken

TACITURN *adj* (<u>taa</u> sih tuhrn)
uncommunicative, not inclined to speak much
The clerk's *taciturn* nature earned him the nickname "Silent Sammy."
synonyms: reticent, reserved, secretive, uncommunicative, tightlipped

*TACTILE *adj* (<u>taak</u> tiel)
producing a sensation of touch
The Museum of Natural History displays objects for people to touch so that they have a *tactile* understanding of how different peoples and animals lived.
synonyms: perceptible, tangible

TAINT *v* (taynt)
to spoil or infect; to stain honor
"I will not allow you to *taint* my reputation!" stormed the politician when the blackmailer threatened to expose his corruption.
synonyms: contaminate, befoul, poison, pollute, besmirch

TALON *n* (<u>taa</u> luhn)
claw of an animal, especially a bird of prey
A vulture holds its prey in its *talons* while it dismembers it with its beak.
synonyms: nail, claw

TANG *n*
sharp flavor or odor
After being smoked together with the herring, the bacon had a distinctly fishy *tang*.
synonyms: relish, savor, piquancy, bite

TANGENTIAL *adj* (taan <u>jehn</u> shuhl)
digressing, diverting
Your argument is interesting, but it's *tangential* to the matter at hand, so I suggest we get back to the point.
synonyms: peripheral, digressive, extraneous, irrelevant, inconsequential

TANGIBLE *adj* (<u>taan</u> juh buhl)
able to be sensed, perceptible, measurable
The storming of the castle didn't bring the soldiers *tangible* rewards, but it brought them great honor.
synonyms: palpable, real, concrete, factual, corporeal

TARNISHED *adj* (<u>tahr</u> nihshd)
corroded, discolored; discredited, disgraced
The antique silver plate was so *tarnished* that Nestor had to polish it for hours before using it
synonyms: tainted, sullied, marred, soiled, blackened

TAWDRY *adj* (<u>taw</u> dree)
gaudy, cheap, showy
The performer changed into her *tawdry*, spangled costume and stepped out onto the stage to do her show.
synonyms: flashy, loud, meretricious

TEMPER *v* (<u>tehm</u> puhr)
to restrain, moderate
The atmosphere at the dinner was *tempered* by the soft jazz in the background.
synonyms: qualify, allay, strengthen, muffle

TEMPERANCE *n* (<u>tehm</u> puhr uhns)
restraint, self-control, moderation
The strict, religious community frowned on newcomers who did not behave with *temperance*.
synonyms: abstinence, sobriety, continence

TEMPESTUOUS *adj* (tehm <u>pehs</u> tyoo uhs)
stormy, turbulent
Our camping trip was cut short when the sun shower we were expecting turned into a *tempestuous* downpour.
synonyms: tumultuous, blustery

TENABLE *adj* (<u>tehn</u> uh buhl)
defensible, reasonable
Greg burned down his own house so that his ex-wife could not live in it, a scarcely *tenable* action in light of the fact that this also left his children homeless.
synonyms: maintainable, rational

*TENACIOUS *adj* (tuh <u>nay</u> shuhs)
tending to persist or cling; persistent in adhering to something valued or habitual
For years, against all odds, women *tenaciously* fought for the right to vote.
synonyms: stubborn, dogged, obstinate

TENET *n* (<u>teh</u> niht)
a principle, belief, or doctrine accepted by members of a group
One of the *tenets* of Islam is that it is not acceptable to eat pork.
synonyms: canon

TENUOUS *adj* (<u>tehn</u> yoo uhs)
having little substance or strength; flimsy, weak
Francine's already *tenuous* connection to her cousins was broken when they moved away and left no forwarding address.
synonyms: thin, shaky

TEPID *adj* (<u>teh</u> pihd)
lukewarm; showing little enthusiasm
Roxanne refused to take a bath in the *tepid* water, fearing that she would catch a cold.
synonyms: halfhearted, perfunctory

TERRESTRIAL *adj* (tuh <u>reh</u> stree uhl)
earthly; down-to-earth, commonplace
Many "extraterrestrial" objects turn out to be *terrestrial* in origin, as when flying saucers turn out
to be normal airplanes.
synonyms: mundane, earthbound, tellurian, sublunary, terrene

*TERSE *adj* (tuhrs)
concise, brief, free of extra words.
Her *terse* style of writing was widely praised by the editors, who had been used to seeing
long-winded material.
synonyms: succinct, brusque

TETHER *v* (<u>teh</u> thuhr)
to bind, tie
Rich *tethered* his boat to the pole during the severe storm.
synonyms: fasten, restrict, rope, chain, leash

THEOCRACY *n* (thee <u>ah</u> kruh see)
government by priests representing a god
Under the leadership of Ayatollah Khomeini, who claimed to represent Allah, Iran could be
characterized as a *theocracy*.
synonyms: thearchy, hierarchy, priest-riddenness

THWART *v* (thwahrt)
to block or prevent from happening; frustrate, defeat the hopes or aspirations of
Thwarted in its attempt to get at the bananas inside the box, the chimp began to squeal.
synonyms: oppose, foil, frustrate

TIMOROUS *adj* (<u>tih</u> muhr uhs)
timid, shy, full of apprehension
A *timorous* woman, Lois relied on her children to act for her whenever aggressive behavior was
called for.
synonyms: fearful, anxious, frightened

TIRADE *n* (<u>tie</u> rayd)
long, violent speech; verbal assault
Observers were shocked at the manager's *tirade* over such a minor mistake.
synonyms: diatribe, fulmination, harangue, jeremiad, philippic

TITAN *n* (<u>tie</u> taan)
person of colossal stature or achievement
Despite his odd personal habits, it can't be denied that Howard Hughes was a *titan* of industry.
synonyms: giant, colossus

TOADY *n* (<u>toh</u> dee)
one who flatters in the hope of gaining favors
The king was surrounded by *toadies* who rushed to agree with whatever outrageous thing he said.
synonyms: sycophant, parasite

TOME *n* (tohm)
book, usually large and academic
The teacher was forced to refer to various *tomes* to find the answer to the advanced student's question.
synonyms: volume, codex

TORPID *adj* (<u>tohr</u> pihd)
lethargic; unable to move; dormant
After surgery, the patient was *torpid* until the anesthesia wore off.
synonyms: benumbed, hibernating, apathetic, inactive, inert

TORRID *adj* (<u>tawr</u> ihd)
burning hot; passionate
The *torrid* weather dried out the rice paddies and ruined the entire crop
synonyms: parched, scorching, sweltering, ardent

TORTUOUS *adj* (<u>tohr</u> choo uhs)
having many twists and turns; highly complex
To reach the remote inn, the travelers had to negotiate a *tortuous* path.
synonyms: winding, circuitous

TOTTERING *adj* (<u>tah</u> tuhr ing)
barely standing
The *tottering* old man still managed to make his way to the corner shop every day to buy his favorite candy bar.
synonyms: unsteady, wobbly, swaying, reeling, staggering

TOXIN *n* (<u>tahk</u> sihn)
a poison
It's essential to keep all *toxins* away from children and animals, as they might eat them unwittingly.
synonyms: bane, venom

TRACTABLE *adj* (<u>traak</u> tuh buhl)
obedient, yielding
Though it was exhausted, the *tractable* workhorse obediently dragged the carriage through the mud.
synonyms: governable, compliant, acquiescent, docile, malleable

TRANSCEND *v* (traan <u>sehnd</u>)
to rise above, go beyond
Yoga helps me to *transcend* the petty frustrations of everyday life and to achieve true spirituality.
synonyms: surpass, excel, exceed, outdo, outstrip

TRANSFIX *v* (traans <u>fihks</u>)
to pierce; to fix fast; to render motionless
The rabbit was *transfixed* with fear of the oncoming car.
synonyms: impale, hypnotize, spellbind, stun, mesmerize

TRANSGRESS *v* (traans <u>grehs</u>)
to trespass, violate a law
After *transgressing* against every parking law in the city, Marvin had accumulated over 300 tickets.
synonyms: overstep, sin, disobey, offend

TRANSIENT adj (<u>traan</u> see uhnt)
passing with time, temporary, short-lived
The reporter lived a *transient* life, staying in one place only long enough to cover the current story.
synonyms: brief, transitory

TRANSITORY adj (<u>traan</u> sih <u>tohr</u> ee)
short-lived, existing only briefly
The actress' popularity proved *transitory* when her play folded within the month.
synonyms: transient, ephemeral, momentary

TRANSMUTE *v* (traans <u>myoot</u>)
to change in appearance or shape
In a series of stages, the caterpillar *transmuted* into a beautiful butterfly.
synonyms: transform, convert, metamorphose, transfigure, transmogrify

TRANSPIRE *v* (traan <u>spie</u> uhr)
to happen, occur; become known
It later *transpired* that a faulty gearshift had been responsible for the horrible accident.
synonyms: befall, betide

TRAVESTY *n* (<u>traa</u> vuh stee)
parody, exaggerated imitation, caricature
When the pickpocket was sentenced to life in prison, many observers called it a *travesty* of justice.
synonyms: burlesque, satire, lampoon, mockery, sham

TREACHERY *n* (<u>treh</u> chuhr ee)
betrayal of trust, deceit
For conspiring with his country's enemies, Benedict Arnold has become a byword for *treachery*.
synonyms: perfidy, treason, disloyalty, falseness, infidelity

TREMULOUS *adj* (<u>treh</u> myoo luhs)
trembling, timid; easily shaken
The *tremulous* kitten had been separated from her mother.
synonyms: shaking, timorous, anxious

TRENCHANT *adj* (<u>trehn</u> chuhnt)
acute, sharp, incisive; forceful, effective
Dan's *trenchant* observations in class made him the professor's favorite student.
synonyms: keen, biting, cutting, caustic

TREPIDATION *n* (treh pih <u>day</u> shuhn)
fear and anxiety
Mike approached the door of the principal's office with *trepidation*.
synonyms: alarm, dread, apprehension, fright, dread

TRIFLING *adj* (<u>trie</u> fling)
of slight worth, trivial, insignificant
That little glitch in the computer program is a *trifling* error; in general, it works really well.
synonyms: paltry, petty, picayune, frivolous, idle

TRITE *adj* (triet)
shallow, superficial
Lindsay's graduation speech was the same *trite* nonsense we've heard hundreds of times in the past.
synonyms: hackneyed, stale, banal, shopworn, threadbare

TROUNCE *v* (trowns)
to beat severely, defeat
The inexperienced young boxer was *trounced* in a matter of minutes.
synonyms: vanquish, conquer

TROUPE *n* (troop)
group of actors
This acting *troupe* is famous for its staging of Shakespeare's romantic comedies.
synonyms: company, band, ensemble, cast

TRUNCATE *v* (truhnk ayt)
to cut off, shorten by cutting
The mayor *truncated* his standard lengthy speech when he realized that the audience was not in the mood to listen to it.
synonyms: curtail, crop, lop

TRYST *n* (trihst)
agreement between lovers to meet; rendezvous
The knight arranged a secret *tryst* with the nobleman's wife deep in the forest.
synonyms: assignation, date, engagement, appointment

TUMULT *n* (tuh muhlt)
state of confusion; agitation
The *tumult* of the demonstrators drowned out the police chief's speech.
synonyms: disturbance, turmoil, din, commotion, chaos

TURBULENCE *n* (tuhr byoo luhns)
commotion, disorder
The plane shook violently as it passed through the pocket of *turbulence*.
synonyms: disturbance, agitation, riot, tumult, uproar

TURGID *adj* (tuhr jihd)
swollen as from a fluid, bloated
In the process of osmosis, water passes through the walls of *turgid* cells, ensuring that they never contain too much water.
synonyms: distended

TURPITUDE *n* (tuhr pih tood)
inherent vileness, foulness, depravity
John's mother told him that burping at the table was *turpitude* and to never do it again.
synonyms: baseness, immorality, wickedness

TYRO *n* (tie roh)
beginner, novice
An obvious *tyro* at salsa, Millicent received no invitations to dance.
synonyms: fledgling, neophyte, apprentice, greenhorn, tenderfoot

U

UBIQUITOUS *adj*
being everywhere simultaneously
Burger King franchises, which are *ubiquitous* in the United States, are common in foreign countries as well.
synonyms: omnipresent, inescapable

UMBRAGE *n* (<u>uhm</u> brihj)
offense, resentment
The businessman took *umbrage* at the security guard's accusation that he had shoplifted a packet of gum.
synonyms: dudgeon, pique, ire, asperity, rancor

UNCONSCIONABLE *adj* (uhn <u>kahn</u> shuhn uh buhl)
unscrupulous; shockingly unfair or unjust
After she promised me the project, the fact that she gave it to someone else is *unconscionable*.
synonyms: dishonorable, indefensible

UNCTUOUS *adj* (<u>ungk</u> choo uhs)
greasy, oily; smug and falsely earnest
The *unctuous* salesman showered the rich customers with exaggerated compliments.
synonyms: fulsome, smarmy, phony

*UNDERMINE *v* (<u>uhn</u> duhr mien)
to sabotage, thwart
Rumors of his infidelities *undermined* the star's marriage, and it eventually ended in divorce.
synonyms: weaken, sap, undercut, subvert, impair

UNDULATING *adj* (<u>uhn</u> dyoo lay ting)
moving in waves
The tourists hiked up and down the *undulating* hills of the lush countryside.
synonyms: surging, pulsating

UNEQUIVOCAL *adj* (uhn ee <u>kwih</u> vih kuhl)
absolute, certain
The jury's verdict was *unequivocal*: the sadistic murderer would be locked up for life.
synonyms: clear, unambiguous, express, categorical, explicit

UNIFORM *adj* (<u>yoo</u> nuh fohrm)
consistent and unchanging; identical
We need to come up with a *uniform* look for our customer-service employees so that they can easily be identified as such.
synonyms: unvarying, steady, even, homogeneous, constant

UNKEMPT *adj* (uhn <u>kehmpt</u>)
uncombed, messy in appearance
Sam's long hair seemed *unkempt* to his grandmother, and she told him he looked like a bum.
synonyms: disorderly, untidy, slovenly, ungroomed

UNSCRUPULOUS *adj* (uhn <u>skroo</u> pyoo luhs)
Dishonest
The *unscrupulous* cafe owner watered down his soft drinks so that he could make a bigger profit on them.
synonyms: unethical, dishonorable, amoral, base, unprincipled

UNWITTING *adj* (uhn <u>wih</u> ting)
unconscious; unintentional
Sarah gave an *unwitting* testimony against her best friend on trial for shoplifting.
synonyms: unaware, oblivious, inadvertent

UPBRAID *v* (uhp <u>brayd</u>)
to scold sharply
The teacher *upbraided* the student for scrawling graffiti all over the walls of the school.
synonyms: berate, tax, reproach, rebuke, chide

UPROARIOUS *adj* (uhp <u>rohr</u> ee uhs)
loud and forceful
The *uproarious* soccer fans made a huge racket as they filed out of the stadium after the match.
synonyms: clamorous, boisterous, hilarious

URBANE *adj* (uhr <u>bayn</u>)
courteous, refined, suave
The *urbane* teenager sneered at the mannerisms of his country-bumpkin cousin.
synonyms: cosmopolitan, debonair, elegant, soigné, polite

USURP *v* (yoo <u>suhrp</u>)
to seize by force
The power-hungry vice-principal threatened to *usurp* the principal's power
synonyms: arrogate, preempt, assume, appropriate

USURY *n* (<u>yoo</u> zuh ree)
the practice of lending money at exorbitant rates
The moneylender was convicted of *usury* when it was discovered that he charged 50 percent interest on all his loans.
synonyms: loan-sharking, interest

UTILITARIAN *adj* (yoo tih lih <u>teh</u> ree uhn)
efficient, functional, useful
The suitcase was undeniably *utilitarian* with its convenient compartments of different sizes, but it was also ugly.
synonyms: practical, pragmatic

UTOPIA *n* (yoo <u>toh</u> pee uh)
perfect place
Wilson's idea of *utopia* was a beautiful, sunny beach on a tropical island.
synonyms: paradise, Eden, heaven, cloudland

V

VACILLATE *v* (<u>vaa</u> sihl ayt)
to waver, show indecision
The customer held up the line as he *vacillated* between ordering chocolate or coffee ice cream.
synonyms: sway, oscillate, hesitate, falter, waffle

VACUOUS *adj* (<u>vaa</u> kyoo uhs)
empty, void; lacking intelligence, purposeless
The congresswoman's *vacuous* speech angered the voters, who were tired of hearing empty platitudes.
synonyms: stupid, inane, vacant, idle

VAGRANT *n* (<u>vay</u> gruhnt)
poor person with no home
Unable to afford a room for the night, the *vagrant* huddled in a sheltered doorway.
synonyms: wanderer, rover, derelict, vagabond, tramp

VALIDATE *v* (<u>vaal</u> ih dayt)
to authorize, certify, confirm
The Disney employee *validated* my guest pass so that I was able to enter Disney World for free.
synonyms: corroborate, substantiate, authenticate, verify, accredit

VANQUISH *v* (<u>vaan</u> kwihsh)
to conquer, defeat
Napoleon was *vanquished* by the English at the Battle of Waterloo.
synonyms: subjugate, overcome, subdue, suppress, trounce

VAPID *adj* (<u>vaa</u> pihd)
tasteless, dull
Todd found his blind date *vapid* and boring; he couldn't wait to get away from her.
synonyms: insipid, vacuous, inane

VARIEGATED *adj* (<u>vaar</u> ee uh <u>gayt</u> ehd)
varied; marked with different colors
The *variegated* foliage of the jungle allows it to support thousands of different animal species.
synonyms: diversified

VAUNTED *adj* (<u>vawnt</u> ehd)
boasted about, bragged about
The much-*vaunted* new computer program turned out to have so many bugs that it had to be recalled.
synonyms: acclaimed, celebrated

VEHEMENTLY *adv* (<u>vee</u> ih mehnt lee)
marked by extreme intensity of emotions or convictions
She *vehemently* opposed the closing of the neighborhood garden, and was even arrested for protesting when the bulldozers came.
synonyms: vociferously, unequivocally

VENDETTA *n* (vehn <u>deh</u> tuh)
prolonged feud marked by bitter hostility
The *vendetta* between the Montagues and the Capulets resulted in the death of Romeo and Juliet.
synonyms: feud, rivalry, contention

VENERABLE *adj* (<u>veh</u> nehr uh buhl)
respected because of age
All of the villagers sought the *venerable* old woman's advice whenever they had a problem.
synonyms: respectable, distinguished, elderly

VENERATION *n* (veh nehr <u>ay</u> shuhn)
adoration, honor, respect
In traditional Confucian society, the young treat their elders with *veneration*, deferring to the elders' wisdom.
synonyms: homage, reverence, deference, esteem

VENT *v* (vehnt)
to express, say out loud
Bob *vented* his frustrations at his malfunctioning computer by throwing coffee at it, which only served to make the problem worse.
synonyms: utter, voice, air, discharge, release

VERACITY *n* (vuhr <u>aa</u> sih tee)
accuracy, truth
She had a reputation for *veracity*, so everyone believed her version of the story.
synonyms: truthfulness, reliability

VERBATIM *adv* (vuhr <u>bay</u> tuhm)
word for word
A court stenographer's job is to take down testimony in a court case *verbatim*, making no changes whatsoever in what is said.
synonyms: literally, exactly, unaltered

VERBOSE *adj* (vuhr <u>bohs</u>)
wordy
The DNA analyst's answer was so *verbose* that the jury had trouble grasping his point.
synonyms: loquacious, garrulous

VERDANT *adj* (<u>vuhr</u> dnt)
green with vegetation; inexperienced
He wandered deep into the *verdant* woods in search of mushrooms and other edible flora.
synonyms: grassy, leafy, wooded

VERNACULAR *n* (vuhr <u>naa</u> kyoo luhr)
everyday language used by ordinary people; specialized language of a profession
Preeti could not understand the *vernacular* of the south, where she had recently moved.
synonyms: dialect, patois, lingo

VERNAL *adj* (<u>vuhr</u> nuhl)
related to spring; fresh
Bea basked in the balmy *vernal* breezes, happy that winter was coming to an end.
synonyms: springlike, youthful

VERSATILE *adj* (<u>vuhr</u> suh tuhl)
adaptable, all-purpose
This *versatile* little gadget can be used to dice vegetables, open cans, and whip cream!
synonyms: flexible, protean, multipurpose

VESTIGE *n* (<u>veh</u> stihj)
a trace, remnant
Vestiges of the former tenant still remained in the apartment, though he hadn't lived there for years.
synonyms: relic, remains, sign

VEX *v* (vehks)
to irritate, annoy; confuse, puzzle
The old man, who loved his peace and quiet, was *vexed* by his neighbor's loud music.
synonyms: bother, plague, afflict, irritate, irk

VIABLE *adj* (<u>vie</u> uh buhl)
workable, able to succeed or grow
I don't think your plan to increase sales by sending free samples to every household in the city is *viable*.
synonyms: doable, possible, feasible

VICARIOUSLY *adv* (vie <u>kaar</u> ee uhs lee)
felt or undergone as if one were taking part in the experience or feelings of another
She lived *vicariously* through the characters in the adventure books she was always reading.

VICISSITUDE *n* (vih <u>sih</u> sih tood)
a change or variation; ups and downs
Investors must be prepared for *vicissitudes* of the stock market.
synonyms: mutability, inconstancy

VIE *v*
to compete, contend
The two wrestlers *vied* for the title of champion in the final match of the competition.
synonyms: strive, rival, vie, emulate

VIGILANT *adj* (<u>vih</u> juh lehnt)
attentive, watchful
Air traffic controllers must be *vigilant* to ensure that planes do not collide with one another.
synonyms: alert, aware, careful, wary, guarded

VILIFY *v* (<u>vih</u> lih fie)
to slander, defame
As gossip columnists often *vilify* celebrities, they're usually held in low regard.
synonyms: malign

VIM *n* (vihm)
vitality and energy
The *vim* with which she worked so early in the day explained why she was so productive.
synonyms: power, force

*VINDICATE *v* (<u>vihn</u> dih kayt)
to clear of blame; support a claim
Tess felt *vindicated* when her prediction about the impending tornado came true.
synonyms: justify, exonerate

VINDICTIVE *adj* (vihn <u>dihk</u> tihv)
disposed to seek revenge
After her husband left her for a young model, the *vindictive* ex-wife plotted to destroy
their relationship.
synonyms: spiteful, vengeful, unforgiving

VIRILE *adj* (<u>vih</u> ruhl)
manly, having qualities of an adult male
John Wayne tended to play *virile*, tough roles rather than effeminate, sensitive roles.
synonyms: male, masculine, manful, potent

*VIRTUOSO *n* (vihr choo <u>oh</u> soh)
someone with masterly skill; expert musician
He is a *virtuoso* conductor and has performed in all the most prestigious concert halls.
synonyms: master, genius

VIRULENT *adj* (<u>veer</u> yuh luhnt)
extremely poisonous; malignant; hateful
Alarmed at the *virulent* press he was receiving, the militant activist decided to go underground.
synonyms: infectious, toxic

VISCOUS *adj* (<u>vih</u> shuhs)
thick, syrupy, and sticky
The *viscous* sap trickled slowly down the trunk of the tree.
synonyms: gelatinous, gummy

VITRIOLIC *adj* (vih tree <u>ah</u> lihk)
burning, caustic; sharp, bitter
Given the chance to critique his enemy's new book, the spiteful critic wrote an unusually *vitriolic*
review of it for the New York *Times*.
synonyms: scathing, acerbic

VITUPERATE *v* (vih <u>too</u> puhr ayt)
to abuse verbally, berate
Vituperating someone is never a constructive way to effect change.
synonyms: scold, reproach, castigate

VIVACIOUS *adj* (vie <u>vay</u> shuhs)
lively, spirited
She was *vivacious* and outgoing, always ready to try something new.
synonyms: animated, energetic

VOCIFEROUS *adj* (voh <u>sih</u> fuhr uhs)
loud, noisy
Amid the *vociferous* protests of the members of parliament, the prime minister continued his speech.
synonyms: vocal, boisterous

VOLITION *n* (vuh <u>lih</u> shuhn)
free choice, free will; act of choosing
Dorio gave up her property of her own *volition*; no one pressured her into anything.
synonyms: decision, autonomy

VOLLEY *n* (<u>vah</u> lee)
a flight of missiles; round of gunshots
The troops fired a *volley* of bullets at the enemy, but they couldn't be sure how many hit their target.
synonyms: discharge, barrage

VOLUBLE *adj* (<u>vahl</u> yuh buhl)
talkative, speaking easily, glib
The *voluble* man and his reserved wife proved the old saying that opposites attract.
synonyms: loquacious, verbose

VORACIOUS *adj* (vohr <u>ay</u> shuhs)
having a great appetite
The *voracious* farming family consumed a huge meal after a long day of heavy labor.
synonyms: ravenous, greedy, rapacious

VULNERABLE *adj* (<u>vuhl</u> nuhr uh buhl)
defenseless, unprotected; innocent, naïve
The child whisked the *vulnerable* little duckling out of the raging whirlpool just in time.
synonyms: susceptible, endangered

W

WAIVE *v* (wayv)
to refrain from enforcing a rule; to give up a legal right
Veronique *waived* her right to half of her ex-husband's property, ridding herself of everything that
would remind her of him.
synonyms: relinquish, surrender

WAG *n* (waag)
a humorous or droll person
Peter was quite a *wag*, with a clever remark for any occasion.
synonyms: wit, joker, humorist, jester

WALLOW *v* (<u>wah</u> loh)
to indulge oneself excessively, luxuriate
He *wallowed* in the luxurious waterbed, sighing contentedly
synonyms: revel, bask, delight, rejoice, roll

WAN *adj* (wahn)
sickly pale
The sick child had a *wan* face, in contrast to her rosy-cheeked sister.
synonyms: ashen, sickly

WANE *v* (wayn)
to decrease gradually
The moon *wanes* throughout the month; it will soon be no more than a slim crescent.
synonyms: dwindle, flag, fade, shrink, diminish

WANTON *adj* (wahn tuhn)
undisciplined, unrestrained, reckless
The townspeople were outraged by the *wanton* display of disrespect when they discovered the statue of
the town founder covered in graffiti.
synonyms: capricious, lewd, licentious

WARRANTY *n* (wahr uhn tee)
a guarantee of a product's soundness
I can't believe that the *warranty* on this radio ran out two days before it broke! Now I won't be able to
get my money back!
synonyms: indemnity, surety, underwriting, contract, covenant

*WARY *adj* (way ree)
careful, cautious
The dog was *wary* of Bola at first, only gradually letting its guard down and wagging its tail when he
came home at night.
synonyms: watchful, vigilant, alert, guarded, suspicious

WAX *v* (waaks)
to increase gradually, to begin to be
The moon was *waxing*, and would soon be full.
synonyms: enlarge, expand

WHET *v* (weht)
to sharpen, stimulate
The delicious odors wafting from the kitchen *whet* Jack's appetite, and he couldn't wait to eat.
synonyms: hone, edge, strop, grind

WHIMSICAL *adj* (wihm sih cuhl)
playful or fanciful idea
The ballet was *whimsical*, delighting the children with its imaginative characters and unpredictable sets.
synonyms: capricious, erratic, chameleonic, fickle, mutable

WILY *adj* (wie lee)
clever, deceptive
Yet again, the *wily* coyote managed to elude the ranchers who wanted to capture it.
synonyms: cunning, tricky, crafty

WINSOME *adj* (<u>wihn</u> suhm)
charming, happily engaging
Dawn gave the customs officers a *winsome* smile, and they let her pass without searching her bags.
synonyms: attractive, delightful

WIZENED *adj* (<u>wih</u> zuhnd)
withered, shriveled, wrinkled
The *wizened* old man was told that the plastic surgery necessary to make him look young again would cost more money than he could imagine.
synonyms: wasted, atrophied, gnarled, mummified, desiccated

WORST *v* (wuhrst)
to gain the advantage over, defeat
The North *worsted* the South in America's Civil War.
synonyms: beat, vanquish

WRATH *n* (raath)
anger, rage
In the Middle Ages, famine and plague were usually interpreted as signs of God's *wrath*.
synonyms: fury, ire, resentment

WRY *adj* (rie)
bent or twisted in shape or condition; dryly humorous
Every time she teased him, she shot her friends a *wry* smile.
synonyms askew, sardonic

X

XENOPHOBIA *n* (zee noh <u>foh</u> bee uh)
a fear or hatred of foreigners or strangers
Countries in which *xenophobia* is prevalent often have more restrictive immigration policies than countries that are more open to foreign influences.
synonyms: prejudice, bigotry, chauvinism

Y

YOKE *v* (yohk)
to join together
As soon as the farmer had *yoked* his oxen together, he began to plow the fields.
synonyms: pair, harness, bind

Z

ZEALOT *n* (<u>zeh</u> luht)
someone passionately devoted to a cause
The religious *zealot* had no time for those who failed to share his strong beliefs.
synonyms: fanatic, enthusiast, militant, radical

ZENITH *n* (<u>zee</u> nihth)
the point of culmination; peak
The diva considered her appearance at the Metropolitan Opera to be the *zenith* of her career.
synonyms: acme, pinnacle

ZEPHYR *n* (<u>zeh</u> fuhr)
a gentle breeze; something airy or unsubstantial
The *zephyr* from the ocean made the intense heat on the beach bearable for the sunbathers.
synonyms: breath, draft

ZOOLOGY *n* (zoo <u>ah</u> luh jee)
the study of animals
The *zoology* professor spent much of his career studying the social interaction of chimpanzees.

SAT Root List

Knowing roots can help you in two ways. First, instead of learning one word at a time, you can learn a whole group of words that contain a certain root. They'll be related in meaning, so if you remember one, it will be easier for you to remember others. Second, roots can often help you decode an unknown SAT word. If you recognize a familiar root, you could get a good enough idea of the word to answer the question.

❑ A, AN—not, without
amoral, atrophy, asymmetrical, anarchy, anesthetic, anonymity, anomaly

❑ AB, A—from, away, apart
abnormal, abdicate, aberration, abhor, abject, abjure, ablution, abnegate, abortive, abrogate, abscond, absolve, abstemious, abstruse, annul, avert, aversion

❑ AC, ACR—sharp, sour
acid, acerbic, exacerbate, acute, acuity, acumen, acrid, acrimony

❑ AD, A—to, towards
adhere, adjacent, adjunct, admonish, adroit, adumbrate, advent, abeyance, abet, accede, accretion, acquiesce, affluent, aggrandize, aggregate, alleviate, alliteration, allude, allure, ascribe, aspersion, aspire, assail, assonance, attest

❑ ALI, ALTR—another
alias, alienate, inalienable, altruism

❑ AM, AMI—love
amorous, amicable, amiable, amity

❑ AMBI, AMPHI—both
ambiguous, ambivalent, ambidextrous, amphibious

❑ AMBL, AMBUL—walk
amble, ambulatory, perambulator, somnambulist

❑ ANIM—mind, spirit, breath
animal, animosity, unanimous, magnanimous

❑ ANN, ENN—year
annual, annuity, superannuated, biennial, perennial

❑ ANTE, ANT—before
antecedent, antediluvian, antebellum, antepenultimate, anterior, antiquity, antiquated, anticipate

❑ ANTHROP—human
anthropology, anthropomorphic, misanthrope, philanthropy

SAT Emergency

If you don't have much time, just skim through this Root List to familiarize yourself with the component part of commonly tested SAT words.

❑ ANTI, ANT—against, opposite
antidote, antipathy, antithesis, antacid, antagonist, antonym

❑ AUD—hear
audio, audience, audition, auditory, audible

❑ AUTO—self
autobiography, autocrat, autonomous

❑ BELLI, BELL—war
belligerent, bellicose, antebellum, rebellion

❑ BENE, BEN—good
benevolent, benefactor, beneficent, benign

❑ BI—two
bicycle, bisect, bilateral, bilingual, biped

❑ BIBLIO—book
Bible, bibliography, bibliophile

❑ BIO—life
biography, biology, amphibious, symbiotic, macrobiotics

❑ BURS—money, purse
reimburse, disburse, bursar

❑ CAD, CAS, CID—happen, fall
accident, cadence, cascade, deciduous

❑ CAP, CIP—head
captain, decapitate, capitulate, precipitous, precipitate, recapitulate

❑ CARN—flesh
carnal, carnage, carnival, carnivorous, incarnate

❑ CAP, CAPT, CEPT, CIP—take, hold, seize
capable, capacious, captivate, deception, intercept, precept, inception, anticipate, emancipation, incipient, percipient

❑ CED, CESS—yield, go
cease, cessation, incessant, cede, precede, accede, recede, antecedent, intercede, secede, cession

❑ CHROM—color
chrome, chromatic, monochrome

❑ CHRON—time
chronology, chronic, anachronism

❑ CIDE—murder
suicide, homicide, regicide, patricide

❑ CIRCUM—around
circumference, circumlocution, circumnavigate, circumscribe, circumspect, circumvent

❑ CLIN, CLIV—slope
incline, declivity, proclivity

❑ CLUD, CLUS, CLAUS, CLOIS—shut, close
conclude, reclusive, claustrophobia, cloister, preclude, occlude

❑ CO, COM, CON—with, together
coeducation, coagulate, coalesce, coerce, cogent, cognate, collateral, colloquial, colloquy, commensurate, commodious, compassion, compatriot, complacent, compliant, complicity, compunction, concerto, conciliatory, concord, concur, condone, conflagration, congeal, congenial, congenital, conglomerate, conjugal, conjure, conscientious, consecrate, consensus, consonant, constrained, contentious, contrite, contusion, convalescence, convene, convivial, convoke, convoluted, congress

❑ COGN, GNO—know
recognize, cognition, cognizance, incognito, diagnosis, agnostic, prognosis, gnostic, ignorant

❑ CONTRA—against
controversy, incontrovertible, contravene

❑ CORP—body
corpse, corporeal, corpulence

❑ COSMO, COSM—world
cosmopolitan, cosmos, microcosm, macrocosm

❑ CRAC, CRAT—rule, power
democracy, bureaucracy, theocracy, autocrat, aristocrat, technocrat

❑ CRED—trust, believe
incredible, credulous, credence

❑ CRESC, CRET—grow
crescent, crescendo, accretion

❑ CULP—blame, fault
culprit, culpable, inculpate, exculpate

❑ CURR, CURS—run
current, concur, cursory, precursor, incursion

❑ DE—down, out, apart
depart, debase, debilitate, declivity, decry, deface, defamatory, defunct, delegate, demarcation, demean, demur, deplete, deplore, depravity, deprecate, deride, derivative, desist, detest, devoid

❑ DEC—ten, tenth
decade, decimal, decathlon, decimate

❑ DEMO, DEM—people
democrat, demographics, demagogue, epidemic, pandemic, endemic

❑ DI, DIURN—day
diary, quotidian, diurnal

❑ DIA—across
diagonal, diatribe, diaphanous

❑ DIC, DICT—speak
abdicate, diction, interdict, predict, indict, verdict

❑ DIS, DIF, DI—not, apart, away
disaffected, disband, disbar, disburse, discern, discordant, discredit, discursive, disheveled, disparage, disparate, dispassionate, dispirit, dissemble, disseminate, dissension, dissipate, dissonant, dissuade, distend, differentiate, diffidence, diffuse, digress, divert

❑ DOC, DOCT—teach
docile, doctrine, doctrinaire

❑ DOL—pain
condolence, doleful, dolorous, indolent

❑ DUC, DUCT—lead
seduce, induce, conduct, viaduct, induct

❑ EGO—self
ego, egoist, egocentric

❑ EN, EM—in, into
enter, entice, encumber, endemic, ensconce, enthrall, entreat, embellish, embezzle, embroil, empathy

❑ ERR—wander
erratic, aberration, errant

❑ EU—well, good
eulogy, euphemism, euphony, euphoria, eurythmics, euthanasia

❑ EX, E—out, out of
exit, exacerbate, excerpt, excommunicate, exculpate, execrable, exhume, exonerate, exorbitant, exorcise, expatriate, expedient, expiate, expunge, expurgate, extenuate, extort, extremity, extricate, extrinsic, exult, evoke, evict, evince, elicit, egress, egregious

❑ FAC, FIC, FECT, FY, FEA—make, do
factory, facility, benefactor, malefactor, fiction, fictive, beneficent, affect, confection, refectory, magnify, unify, rectify, vilify, feasible

❑ FAL, FALS—deceive
infallible, fallacious, false

❑ FERV—boil
fervent, fervid, effervescent

❑ FID—faith, trust
confident, diffidence, perfidious, fidelity

❑ FLU, FLUX—flow
fluent, affluent, confluence, effluvia, superfluous, flux

❑ FORE—before
forecast, foreboding, forestall

❑ FRAG, FRAC—break
fragment, fracture, diffract, fractious, refract

❑ FUS—pour
profuse, infusion, effusive, diffuse

❑ GEN—birth, class, kin
generation, congenital, homogeneous, heterogeneous, ingenious, engender, progenitor, progeny

❑ GRAD, GRESS—step
graduate, gradual, retrograde, centigrade, degrade, gradation, gradient, progress, congress, digress, transgress, ingress, egress

❑ GRAPH, GRAM—writing
biography, bibliography, epigraph, grammar, epigram

❑ GRAT—pleasing
grateful, gratitude, gratis, ingrate, congratulate, gratuitous, gratuity

❑ GRAV, GRIEV—heavy
grave, gravity, aggravate, grieve, aggrieve, grievous

❑ GREG—crowd, flock
segregate, gregarious, egregious, congregate, aggregate

❑ HABIT, HIBIT—have, hold
habit, cohabit, habitat, inhibit

❑ HAP—by chance
happen, haphazard, hapless, mishap

❑ HELIO, HELI—sun
heliocentric, heliotrope, aphelion, perihelion, helium

❑ HETERO—other
heterosexual, heterogeneous, heterodox

❑ HOL—whole
holocaust, catholic, holistic

❑ HOMO—same
homosexual, homogenize, homogeneous, homonym

❑ HOMO—man
homo sapiens, homicide, bonhomie

❑ HYDR—water
hydrant, hydrate, dehydration

❑ HYPER—too much, excess
hyperactive, hyperbole, hyperventilate

❑ HYPO—too little, under
hypodermic, hypothermia, hypochondria, hypothesis, hypothetical

❑ IN, IG, IL, IM, IR—not
incorrigible, indefatigable, indelible, indubitable, inept, inert, inexorable, insatiable, insentient, insolvent, insomnia, interminable, intractable, incessant, inextricable, infallible, infamy, innumerable, inoperable, insipid, intemperate, intrepid, inviolable, ignorant, ignominious, ignoble, illicit, illimitable, immaculate, immutable, impasse, impeccable, impecunious, impertinent, implacable, impotent, impregnable, improvident, impassioned, impervious, irregular

❑ IN, IL, IM, IR—in, on, into
invade, inaugurate, incandescent, incarcerate, incense, indenture, induct, ingratiate, introvert, incarnate, inception, incisive, infer, infusion, ingress, innate, inquest, inscribe, insinuate, inter, illustrate, imbue, immerse, implicate, irrigate, irritate

❑ INTER—between, among
intercede, intercept, interdiction, interject, interlocutor, interloper, intermediary, intermittent, interpolate, interpose, interregnum, interrogate, intersect, intervene

❑ INTRA, INTR—within
intrastate, intravenous, intramural, intrinsic

❑ IT, ITER—between, among
transit, itinerant, transitory, reiterate

❑ JECT, JET—throw
eject, interject, abject, trajectory, jettison

❑ JOUR—day
journal, adjourn, sojourn

❑ JUD—judge
judge, judicious, prejudice, adjudicate

❑ JUNCT, JUG—join
junction, adjunct, injunction, conjugal, subjugate

❑ JUR—swear, law
jury, abjure, adjure, conjure, perjure, jurisprudence

❑ LAT—side
lateral, collateral, unilateral, bilateral, quadrilateral

❑ LAV, LAU, LU—wash
lavatory, laundry, ablution, antediluvian

❑ LEG, LEC, LEX—read, speak
legible, lecture, lexicon

❑ LEV—light
elevate, levitate, levity, alleviate

❑ LIBER—free
liberty, liberal, libertarian, libertine

❑ LIG, LECT—choose, gather
eligible, elect, select

❑ LIG, LI, LY—bind
ligament, oblige, religion, liable, liaison, lien, ally

❑ LING, LANG—tongue
lingo, language, linguistics, bilingual

❑ LITER—letter
literate, alliteration, literal

❑ LITH—stone
monolith, lithograph, megalith

❑ LOQU, LOC, LOG—speech, thought
eloquent, loquacious, colloquial, colloquy,
soliloquy, circumlocution, interlocutor,
monologue, dialogue, eulogy, philology,
neologism

❑ LUC, LUM—light
lucid, elucidate, pellucid, translucent, illuminate

❑ LUD, LUS—play
ludicrous, allude, delusion, allusion, illusory

❑ MACRO—great
macrocosm, macrobiotics

❑ MAG, MAJ, MAS, MAX—great
magnify, magnanimous, magnate, magni-
tude, majesty, master, maximum

❑ MAL—bad
malady, maladroit, malevolent, malodorous

❑ MAN—hand
manual, manuscript, emancipate, manifest,
manumission

❑ MAR—sea
submarine, marine, maritime

❑ MATER, MATR—mother
maternal, matron, matrilineal

❑ MEDI—middle
intermediary, medieval, mediate

❑ MEGA—great
megaphone, megalomania, megaton,
megalith

❑ MEM, MEN—remember
memory, memento, memorabilia, reminisce

❑ METER, METR, MENS—measure
meter, thermometer, perimeter,
metronome, commensurate

❑ MICRO—small
microscope, microorganism, microcosm,
microbe

❑ MIS—wrong, bad, hate
misunderstand, misanthrope, misappre-
hension, misconstrue, misnomer, mishap

❑ MIT, MISS—send
transmit, emit, missive

❑ MOLL—soft
mollify, emollient, mollusk

❑ MON, MONIT—warn
admonish, monitor, premonition

❑ MONO—one
monologue, monotonous, monogamy,
monolith, monochrome

❑ MOR—custom, manner
moral, mores, morose

❑ MOR, MORT—dead
morbid, moribund, mortal, amortize

❑ MORPH—shape
amorphous, anthropomorphic, metamorphosis, morphology

❑ MOV, MOT, MOB, MOM—move
remove, motion, mobile, momentum,
momentous

❑ MUT—change
mutate, mutability, immutable, commute

❑ NAT, NASC—born
native, nativity, natal, neonate, innate, cognate, nascent, renascent, renaissance

❑ NAU, NAV—ship, sailor
nautical, nauseous, navy, circumnavigate

❑ NEG—not, deny
negative, abnegate, renege

❑ NEO—new
neoclassical, neophyte, neologism, neonate

❑ NIHIL—none, nothing
annihilation, nihilism

❑ NOM, NYM—name
nominate, nomenclature, nominal, cog-
nomen, misnomer, ignominious, antonym,
homonym, pseudonym, synonym,
anonymity

❑ NOX, NIC, NEC, NOC—harm
obnoxious, noxious, pernicious,
internecine, innocuous

❑ NOV—new
novelty, innovation, novitiate

❑ NUMER—number
numeral, numerous, innumerable, enumerate

❑ OB—against
obstruct, obdurate, obfuscate, obnoxious, obsequious, obstinate, obstreperous, obtrusive

❑ OMNI—all
omnipresent, omnipotent, omniscient, omnivorous

❑ ONER—burden
onerous, exonerate

❑ OPER—work
operate, cooperate, inoperable

❑ PAC—peace
pacify, pacifist, pacific

❑ PALP—feel
palpable, palpitation

❑ PAN—all
panorama, panacea, panegyric, pandemic, panoply

❑ PATER, PATR—father
paternal, paternity, patriot, compatriot, expatriate, patrimony, patricide, patrician

❑ PATH, PASS—feel, suffer
sympathy, antipathy, empathy, apathy, pathos, impassioned

❑ PEC—money
pecuniary, impecunious, peculation

❑ PED, POD—foot
pedestrian, pediment, expedient, biped, quadruped, tripod

❑ PEL, PULS—drive
compel, compelling, expel, propel, compulsion

❑ PEN—almost
peninsula, penultimate, penumbra

❑ PEND, PENS—hang
pendant, pendulous, compendium, suspense, propensity

❑ PER—through, by, for, throughout
perambulator, percipient, perfunctory, permeable, perspicacious, pertinacious, perturbation, perusal, perennial, peregrinate

❑ PER—against, destruction
perfidious, pernicious, perjure

❑ PERI—around
perimeter, periphery, perihelion, peripatetic

❑ PET—seek, go towards
petition, impetus, impetuous, petulant, centripetal

❑ PHIL—love
philosopher, philanderer, philanthropy, bibliophile, philology

❑ PHOB—fear
phobia, claustrophobia, xenophobia

❑ PHON—sound
phonograph, megaphone, euphony, phonetics, phonics

❑ PLAC—calm, please
placate, implacable, placid, complacent

❑ PON, POS—put, place
postpone, proponent, exponent, preposition, posit, interpose, juxtaposition, depose

❑ PORT—carry
portable, deportment, rapport

❑ POT—drink
potion, potable

❑ POT—power
potential, potent, impotent, potentate, omnipotence

❑ PRE—before
precede, precipitate, preclude, precocious, precursor, predilection, predisposition, preponderance, prepossessing, presage, prescient, prejudice, predict, premonition, preposition

❑ PRIM, PRI—first
prime, primary, primal, primeval, primordial, pristine

❑ PRO—ahead, forth
proceed, proclivity, procrastinator, profane, profuse, progenitor, progeny, prognosis, prologue, promontory, propel, proponent, propose, proscribe, protestation, provoke

❑ PROTO—first
prototype, protagonist, protocol

❏ PROX, PROP—near
approximate, propinquity, proximity

❏ PSEUDO—false
pseudoscientific, pseudonym

❏ PYR—fire
pyre, pyrotechnics, pyromania

❏ QUAD, QUAR, QUAT—four
quadrilateral, quadrant, quadruped, quarter, quarantine, quaternary

❏ QUES, QUER, QUIS, QUIR—question
quest, inquest, query, querulous, inquisitive, inquiry

❏ QUIE—quiet
disquiet, acquiesce, quiescent, requiem

❏ QUINT, QUIN—five
quintuplets, quintessence

❏ RADI, RAMI—branch
radius, radiate, radiant, eradicate, ramification

❏ RECT, REG—straight, rule
rectangle, rectitude, rectify, regular

❏ REG—king, rule
regal, regent, interregnum

❏ RETRO—backward
retrospective, retroactive, retrograde

❏ RID, RIS—laugh
ridiculous, deride, derision

❏ ROG—ask
interrogate, derogatory, abrogate, arrogate, arrogant

❏ RUD—rough, crude
rude, erudite, rudimentary

❏ RUPT—break
disrupt, interrupt, rupture

❏ SACR, SANCT—holy
sacred, sacrilege, consecrate, sanctify, sanction, sacrosanct

❏ SCRIB, SCRIPT, SCRIV—write
scribe, ascribe, circumscribe, inscribe, proscribe, script, manuscript, scrivener

❏ SE—apart, away
separate, segregate, secede, sedition

❏ SEC, SECT, SEG—cut
sector, dissect, bisect, intersect, segment, secant

❏ SED, SID—sit
sedate, sedentary, supersede, reside, residence, assiduous, insidious

❏ SEM—seed, sow
seminar, seminal, disseminate

❏ SEN—old
senior, senile, senescent

❏ SENT, SENS—feel, think
sentiment, nonsense, assent, sentient, consensus, sensual

❏ SEQU, SECU—follow
sequence, sequel, subsequent, obsequious, obsequy, non sequitur, consecutive

❏ SIM, SEM—similar, same
similar, verisimilitude, semblance, dissemble

❏ SIGN—mark, sign
signal, designation, assignation

❏ SIN—curve
sine curve, sinuous, insinuate

❏ SOL—sun
solar, parasol, solarium, solstice

❏ SOL—alone
solo, solitude, soliloquy, solipsism

❏ SOMN—sleep
insomnia, somnolent, somnambulist

❏ SON—sound
sonic, consonance, dissonance, assonance, sonorous, resonate

❏ SOPH—wisdom
philosopher, sophistry, sophisticated, sophomoric

❏ SPEC, SPIC—see, look
spectator, circumspect, retrospective, perspective, perspicacious, perspicuous

❏ SPER—hope
prosper, prosperous, despair, desperate

❏ SPERS, SPAR—scatter
disperse, sparse, aspersion, disparate

❑ SPIR—breathe
respire, inspire, spiritual, aspire, transpire

❑ STRICT, STRING—bind
strict, stricture, constrict, stringent, astringent

❑ STRUCT, STRU—build
structure, obstruct, construe

❑ SUB—under
subconscious, subjugate, subliminal, subpoena, subsequent, subterranean, subvert

❑ SUMM—highest
summit, summary, consummate

❑ SUPER, SUR—above
supervise, supercilious, supersede, superannuated, superfluous, insurmountable, surfeit

❑ SURGE, SURRECT—rise
surge, resurgent, insurgent, insurrection

❑ SYN, SYM—together
synthesis, sympathy, synonym, syncopation, synopsis, symposium, symbiosis

❑ TACIT, TIC—silent
tacit, taciturn, reticent

❑ TACT, TAG, TANG—touch
tact, tactile, contagious, tangent, tangential, tangible

❑ TEN, TIN, TAIN—hold, twist
detention, tenable, tenacious, pertinacious, retinue, retain

❑ TEND, TENS, TENT—stretch
intend, distend, tension, tensile, ostensible, contentious

❑ TERM—end
terminal, terminus, terminate, interminable

❑ TERR—earth, land
terrain, terrestrial, extraterrestrial, subterranean

❑ TEST—witness
testify, attest, testimonial, testament, detest, protestation

❑ THE—god
atheist, theology, apotheosis, theocracy

❑ THERM—heat
thermometer, thermal, thermonuclear, hypothermia

❑ TIM—fear, frightened
timid, intimidate, timorous

❑ TOP—place
topic, topography, utopia

❑ TORT—twist
distort, extort, tortuous

❑ TORP—stiff, numb
torpedo, torpid, torpor

❑ TOX—poison
toxic, toxin, intoxication

❑ TRACT—draw
tractor, intractable, protract

❑ TRANS—across, over, through, beyond
transport, transgress, transient, transitory, translucent, transmutation

❑ TREM, TREP—shake
tremble, tremor, tremulous, trepidation, intrepid

❑ TURB—shake
disturb, turbulent, perturbation

❑ UMBR—shadow
umbrella, umbrage, adumbrate, penumbra

❑ UNI, UN—one
unify, unilateral, unanimous

❑ URB—city
urban, suburban, urbane

❑ VAC—empty
vacant, evacuate, vacuous

❑ VAL, VAIL—value, strength
valid, valor, ambivalent, convalescence, avail, prevail, countervail

❑ VEN, VENT—come
convene, contravene, intervene, venue, convention, circumvent, advent, adventitious

❑ VER—true
verify, verity, verisimilitude, veracious, aver, verdict

❑ VERB—word
verbal, verbose, verbiage, verbatim

❏ VERT, VERS—turn
avert, convert, pervert, revert, incontrovertible, divert, subvert, versatile, aversion

❏ VICT, VINC—conquer
victory, conviction, evict, evince, invincible

❏ VID, VIS—see
evident, vision, visage, supervise

❏ VIL—base, mean
vile, vilify, revile

❏ VIV, VIT—life
vivid, vital, convivial, vivacious

❏ VOC, VOK, VOW—call, voice
vocal, equivocate, vociferous, convoke,
evoke, invoke, avow

❏ VOL—wish
voluntary, malevolent, benevolent, volition

❏ VOLV, VOLUT—turn, roll
revolve, evolve, convoluted

❏ VOR—eat
devour, carnivore, omnivorous, voracious

SAT Word Families List

□ **Talkative**
  garrulous
  glib
  loquacious
  raconteur
  verbose
  voluble

□ **Secret/Hidden**
  abscond
  alias
  arcane
  clandestine
  covert
  cryptic
  enigma
  furtive
  incognito
  inconspicuous
  lurk
  obscure
  skulk
  subterranean
  surreptitious

□ **Not Talkative**
  concise
  curt
  laconic
  pithy
  reticent
  succinct
  taciturn

□ **Praise**
  accolade
  adulation
  commend
  eulogize
  exalt
  extol
  laud
  lionize
  plaudit
  revere

SAT Emergency

If you're short on time, you may want to just skim these Word Families. Learning words in groups is good way to maximize your limited study time.

❑ **Criticize/Scold**
admonish
berate
castigate
censure
chastise
defame
denigrate
disdain
disparage
excoriate
malign
obloquy
rail
rebuke
reproach
reprimand
reprove
revile
upbraid
vilify

❑ **Stubborn**
intractable
mulish
obdurate
obstinate
pertinacious
recalcitrant
refractory
tenacious

❑ **Lazy/Lacking Energy**
indolent
lackadaisical
laggard
languid
lassitude
lethargic
listless
loiter
phlegmatic
sluggard
somnolent
torpid

❑ **Cowardly**
craven
diffident
pusillanimous
timid
timorous

❑ **Inexperienced**
callow
fledgling
infantile
ingenuous
neophyte
novice
tyro

❑ **Obedient**
amenable
assent
compliant
deferential
docile
pliant
submissive
tractable

❑ **Haughty/Pretentious**
affected
aloof
bombastic
grandiloquent
grandiose
magniloquent
mannered
ostentatious
pontificate
supercilious

❑ **Friendly**
affable
amiable
amicable
bonhomie
convivial
gregarious

❑ **Lucky**
auspicious
fortuitous
opportune
serendipity
windfall

❑ **Soothe**
allay
alleviate
anodyne
assuage
liniment
mitigate
mollify
pacify
palliate
placate

❑ **Hostility/Hatred**
abhor
anathema
animosity
antagonism
antipathy
aversion
contentious
deplore
odious
rancor

❑ **Stupid**
buffoon
dolt
dupe
fatuous
imbecile
inane
insipid
obtuse
simpleton
vacuous
vapid

❑ **Subservient**
fawn
grovel
obsequious
servile
subjection
sycophant
toady

❑ **Argumentative**
adversarial
bellicose
belligerent
fractious
irascible
obstreperous
pugnacious
quibble

❑ **Cautious**
chary
circumspect
discretion
leery
prudent
wary

❑ **Impermanent**
ephemeral
evanescent
fleeting
transient
transitory

❑ **Ability/Intelligence**
acumen
adept
adroit
agile
astute
cogent
deft
dexterous
erudite
literate
lithe
lucidity
sagacious
trenchant

❑ **Kind/Generous**
altruistic
beneficent
benevolent
bestow
largess
liberal
magnanimous
munificent
philanthropic

D

SAT Math in a Nutshell

The math on the SAT covers a lot of ground—from arithmetic to algebra to geometry.

Don't let yourself be intimidated. We've highlighted the 100 most important concepts that you'll need for SAT Math and listed them in this chapter.

You've probably been taught most of these in school already, so this list is a great way to refresh your memory.

A MATH STUDY PLAN

Use this list to remind yourself of the key areas you'll need to know. Do four concepts a day, and you'll be ready within a month. If a concept continually causes you trouble, circle it and refer back to it as you try to do the questions.

Need more help? The math reference list comes from Kaplan's *SAT Math Workbook*. For more help with the Math section of the SAT, the workbook is a great place to start.

SAT Emergency

Even if you have only a week or two to prepare for the SAT, you should read through this entire chapter—it's essential and helpful to review the major math concepts.

NUMBER PROPERTIES

1. Integer/Noninteger

Integers are **whole numbers**; they include negative whole numbers and zero.

2. Rational/Irrational Numbers

A rational number is a number that can be expressed as **a ratio of two integers**. **Irrational numbers** are real numbers—they have locations on the number line; they just **can't be expressed precisely as fractions or decimals**. For the purposes of the SAT, the most important **irrational numbers** are $\sqrt{2}$, $\sqrt{3}$, and π.

3. Adding/Subtracting Signed Numbers

To **add a positive and a negative**, first ignore the signs and find the positive difference between the number parts. Then attach the sign of the original number with the larger number part. For example, to add 23 and –34, first we ignore the minus sign and find the positive difference between 23 and 34—that's 11. Then we attach the sign of the number with the larger number part—in this case it's the minus sign from the –34. So, 23 + (–34) = –11.

Make **subtraction** situations simpler by turning them into addition. For example, think of –17 – (–21) as –17 + (+21).

To **add or subtract a string of positives and negatives**, first turn everything into addition. Then combine the positives and negatives so that the string is reduced to the sum of a single positive number and a single negative number.

4. Multiplying/Dividing Signed Numbers

To multiply and/or divide positives and negatives, treat the number parts as usual and **attach a minus sign if there were originally an odd number of negatives**. For example, to multiply –2, –3, and –5, first multiply the number parts: $2 \times 3 \times 5 = 30$. Then go back and note that there were three—an odd number—negatives, so the product is negative: $(-2) \times (-3) \times (-5) = -30$.

5. PEMDAS

When performing multiple operations, remember **PEMDAS**, which means **Parentheses** first, then **Exponents**, then **Multiplication and Division** (left to right), and lastly, **Addition and Subtraction** (left to

right). In the expression $9 - 2 \times (5 - 3)^2 + 6 \div 3$, begin with the parentheses: $(5 - 3) = 2$. Then do the exponent: $2^2 = 4$. Now the expression is: $9 - 2 \times 4 + 6 \div 3$. Next do the multiplication and division to get: $9 - 8 + 2$, which equals 3. If you have difficulty remembering PEMDAS, use this sentence to recall it: **P**lease **E**xcuse **M**y **D**ear **A**unt **S**ally.

6. Counting Consecutive Integers

To count consecutive integers, **subtract the smallest from the largest and add 1**. To count the integers from 13 through 31, subtract: $31 - 13 = 18$. Then add 1: $18 + 1 = 19$.

DIVISIBILITY

7. Factor/Multiple

The factors of integer n are the positive integers that divide into n with no remainder. The multiples of n are the integers that n divides into with no remainder. For example, 6 is a factor of 12, and 24 is a multiple of 12. 12 is both a factor and a multiple of itself, since $12 \times 1 = 12$ and $12 \div 1 = 12$.

8. Prime Factorization

To find the prime factorization of an integer, just keep breaking it up into factors until **all the factors are prime**. To find the prime factorization of 36, for example, you could begin by breaking it into 4×9: $36 = 4 \times 9 = 2 \times 2 \times 3 \times 3$.

9. Relative Primes

Relative primes are integers that have no common factor other than 1. To determine whether two integers are relative primes, break them both down to their prime factorizations. For example: $35 = 5 \times 7$, and $54 = 2 \times 3 \times 3 \times 3$. They have **no prime factors in common**, so 35 and 54 are relative primes.

10. Common Multiple

A common multiple is a number that is a multiple of two or more integers. You can always get a common multiple of two integers by **multiplying** them, but, unless the two numbers are relative primes, the product will not be the *least* common multiple. For example, to find a common multiple for 12 and 15, you could just multiply: $12 \times 15 = 180$.

11. Least Common Multiple (LCM)

To find the least common multiple, check out the **multiples of the larger integer** until you find one that's **also a multiple of the smaller**. To find the LCM of 12 and 15, begin by taking the multiples of 15: 15 is not divisible by 12; 30 is not; nor is 45. But the next multiple of 15, 60, *is* divisible by 12, so it's the LCM.

12. Greatest Common Factor (GCF)

To find the greatest common factor, break down both integers into their prime factorizations and multiply **all the prime factors they have in common**. $36 = 2 \times 2 \times 3 \times 3$, and $48 = 2 \times 2 \times 2 \times 2 \times 3$. What they have in common is two 2s and one 3, so the GCF is $2 \times 2 \times 3 = 12$.

13. Even/Odd

To predict whether a sum, difference, or product will be even or odd, just **take simple numbers such as 1 and 2 and see what happens**. There are rules—"odd times even is even," for example—but there's no need to memorize them. What happens with one set of numbers generally happens with all similar sets.

14. Multiples of 2 and 4

An integer is divisible by 2 (which is even) if the **last digit is even**. An integer is divisible by 4 if the **last two digits form a multiple of 4**. The last digit of 562 is 2, which is even, so 562 is a multiple of 2. The last two digits form 62, which is *not* divisible by 4, so 562 is not a multiple of 4. The integer 512, however is divisible by four because the last two digits form 12, which is a multiple of 4.

15. Multiples of 3 and 9

An integer is divisible by 3 if the **sum of its digits is divisible by 3**. An integer is divisible by 9 if the **sum of its digits is divisible by 9**. The sum of the digits in 957 is 21, which is divisible by 3 but not by 9, so 957 is divisible by 3 but not by 9.

16. Multiples of 5 and 10

An integer is divisible by 5 if the **last digit is 5 or 0**. An integer is divisible by 10 if the **last digit is 0**. The last digit of 665 is 5, so 665 is a multiple of 5 but *not* a multiple of 10.

17. Remainders

The remainder is the **whole number left over after division**. 487 is 2 more than 485, which is a multiple of 5, so when 487 is divided by 5, the remainder will be 2.

FRACTIONS AND DECIMALS

18. Reducing Fractions

To reduce a fraction to lowest terms, **factor out and cancel** all factors the numerator and denominator have in common.

$$\frac{28}{36} = \frac{4 \times 7}{4 \times 9} = \frac{7}{9}$$

19. Adding/Subtracting Fractions

To add or subtract fractions, first find a **common denominator**, then add or subtract the numerators.

$$\frac{2}{15} + \frac{3}{10} = \frac{4}{30} + \frac{9}{30} = \frac{4+9}{30} = \frac{13}{30}$$

20. Multiplying Fractions

To multiply fractions, **multiply** the numerators and **multiply** the denominators.

$$\frac{5}{7} \times \frac{3}{4} = \frac{5 \times 3}{7 \times 4} = \frac{15}{28}$$

21. Dividing Fractions

To divide fractions, **invert** the second one and **multiply**.

$$\frac{1}{2} \div \frac{3}{5} = \frac{1}{2} \times \frac{5}{3} = \frac{1 \times 5}{2 \times 3} = \frac{5}{6}$$

22. Converting a Mixed Number to an Improper Fraction

To convert a mixed number to an improper fraction, **multiply** the whole number part by the denominator, then **add** the numerator. The result is the new numerator (over the same denominator). To convert $7\frac{1}{3}$, first multiply 7 by 3, then add 1, to get the new numerator of 22. Put that over the same denominator, 3, to get $\frac{22}{3}$.

23. Converting an Improper Fraction to a Mixed Number

To convert an improper fraction to a mixed number, divide the denominator into the numerator to get a **whole number quotient with a remainder**. The quotient becomes the whole number part of the mixed number, and the remainder becomes the new numerator—with the same denominator. For example, to convert $\frac{108}{5}$, first divide 5 into 108, which yields 21 with a remainder of 3. Therefore, $\frac{108}{5} = 21\frac{3}{5}$.

24. Reciprocal

To find the reciprocal of a fraction, **switch the numerator and the denominator**. The reciprocal of $\frac{3}{7}$ is $\frac{7}{3}$. The reciprocal of 5 is $\frac{1}{5}$. The product of reciprocals is 1.

25. Comparing Fractions

One way to compare fractions is to **re-express them with a common denominator**. $\frac{3}{4} = \frac{21}{28}$ and $\frac{5}{7} = \frac{20}{28}$. $\frac{21}{28}$ is greater than $\frac{20}{28}$, so $\frac{3}{4}$ is greater than $\frac{5}{7}$. Another way to compare fractions is to **convert them both to decimals**. $\frac{3}{4}$ converts to .75 , and $\frac{5}{7}$ converts to approximately .714.

26. Converting Fractions to Decimals

To convert a fraction to a decimal, **divide the bottom into the top**. To convert $\frac{5}{8}$, divide 8 into 5, yielding .625.

27. Converting Decimals to Fractions

To convert a decimal to a fraction, set the decimal over 1 and **multiply the numerator and denominator by ten raised to the number of digits to the right of the decimal point**. For instance, to convert .625 to a fraction, you would multiply $\frac{.625}{1}$ by $\frac{10^3}{10^3}$, or $\frac{1000}{1000}$. Then simplify: $\frac{625}{1000} = \frac{5 \times 125}{8 \times 125} = \frac{5}{8}$.

28. Repeating Decimal

To find a particular digit in a repeating decimal, note the **number of digits in the cluster that repeats**. If there are 2 digits in that cluster, then every second digit is the same. If there are three digits in that cluster, then every third digit is the same. And so on. For example, the decimal equivalent of $\frac{1}{27}$ is .037037037..., which is best written $.\overline{037}$. There are three digits in the repeating cluster, so every third digit is the same: 7. To find the 50th digit, look for the multiple of three just less than 50—that's 48. The 48th digit is 7, and with the 49th digit the pattern repeats with 0. The 50th digit is 3.

29. Identifying the Parts and the Whole

The key to solving most fractions and percents story problems is to identify the part and the whole. Usually you'll find the **part** associated with the verb *is/are* and the **whole** associated with the word *of*. In the sentence, "Half of the boys are blonds," the whole is the boys ("of the boys"), and the part is the blonds ("are blonds").

PERCENTS

30. Percent Formula

Whether you need to find the part, the whole, or the percent, use the same formula:

Part = Percent × Whole

Example: What is 12% of 25?
Setup: Part = .12 × 25

Example: 15 is 3% of what number?
Setup: 15 = .03 × Whole

Example: 45 is what percent of 9?
Setup: 45 = Percent × 9

31. Percent Increase and Decrease

To increase a number by a percent, **add the percent to 100 percent**, convert to a decimal, and multiply. To increase 40 by 25 percent, add 25 percent to 100 percent, convert 125 percent to 1.25, and multiply by 40. $1.25 × 40 = 50$.

32. Finding the Original Whole

To find the **original whole before a percent increase or decrease, set up an equation**. Think of the result of a 15 percent increase over x as $1.15x$.

Example: After a 5 percent increase, the population was 59,346. What was the population before the increase?
Setup: $1.05x = 59,346$

33. Combined Percent Increase and Decrease

To determine the combined effect of multiple percent increases and/or decreases, **start with 100 and see what happens**.

Example: A price went up 10 percent one year, and the new price went up 20 percent the next year. What was the combined percent increase?
Setup: First year: 100 + (10 percent of 100) = 110. Second year: 110 + (20 percent of 110) = 132. That's a combined 32 percent increase.

RATIOS, PROPORTIONS, AND RATES

34. Setting up a Ratio

To find a ratio, put the number associated with the word *of* on top and the quantity associated with the word *to* on the bottom and reduce. The ratio of 20 oranges to 12 apples is $\frac{20}{12}$, which reduces to $\frac{5}{3}$.

35. Part-to-Part Ratios and Part-to-Whole Ratios

If the parts add up to the whole, a part-to-part ratio can be turned into two part-to-whole ratios by putting **each number in the original ratio over the sum of the numbers.** If the ratio of males to females is 1 to 2, then the males-to-people ratio is $\frac{1}{1+2} = \frac{1}{3}$ and the females-to-people ratio is $\frac{2}{1+2} = \frac{2}{3}$. In other words, $\frac{2}{3}$ of all the people are female.

36. Solving a Proportion

To solve a proportion, **cross-multiply:**

$$\frac{x}{5} = \frac{3}{4}$$
$$4x = 3 × 5$$
$$x = \frac{15}{4} = 3.75$$

37. Rate

To solve a rates problem, **use the units** to keep things straight.

Example: If snow is falling at the rate of one foot every four hours, how many inches of snow will fall in seven hours?

Setup:
$$\frac{1 \text{ foot}}{4 \text{ hours}} = \frac{x \text{ inches}}{7 \text{ hours}}$$

$$\frac{12 \text{ inches}}{4 \text{ hours}} = \frac{x \text{ inches}}{7 \text{ hours}}$$

$$4x = 12 × 7$$
$$x = 21$$

38. Average Rate

Average rate is *not* simply the average of the rates.

$$\text{Average } A \text{ per } B = \frac{\text{Total } A}{\text{Total } B}$$

$$\text{Average Speed} = \frac{\text{Total distance}}{\text{Total time}}$$

To find the average speed for 120 miles at 40 mph and 120 miles at 60 mph, **don't just average the two speeds**. First figure out the total distance and the total time. The total distance is 120 + 120 = 240 miles. The times are two hours for the first leg and three hours for the second leg, or five hours total. The average speed, then, is $\frac{240}{5}$ = 48 miles per hour.

AVERAGES

39. Average Formula

To find the average of a set of numbers, **add them up and divide by the number of numbers**.

$$\text{Average} = \frac{\text{Sum of the terms}}{\text{Number of terms}}$$

To find the average of the five numbers 12, 15, 23, 40, and 40, first add them: 12 + 15 + 23 + 40 + 40 = 130. Then divide the sum by 5: 130 ÷ 5 = 26.

40. Average of Evenly Spaced Numbers

To find the average of evenly spaced numbers, just **average the smallest and the largest**. The average of all the integers from 13 through 77 is the same as the average of 13 and 77:

$$\frac{13 + 77}{2} = \frac{90}{2} = 45$$

41. Using the Average to Find the Sum

Sum = (Average) × (Number of terms)

If the average of ten numbers is 50, then they add up to 10 × 50, or 500.

42. Finding the Missing Number

To find a missing number when you're given the average, **use the sum**. If the average of four numbers is 7, then the sum of those four numbers is 4 × 7, or 28.

Suppose that three of the numbers are 3, 5, and 8. These three numbers add up to 16 of that 28, which leaves 12 for the fourth number.

43. Median

The median of a set of numbers is the **value that falls in the middle of the set**. If you have five test scores, and they are 88, 86, 57, 94, and 73, you must first list the scores in increasing or decreasing order: 57, 73, 86, 88, 94.

The median is the middle number, or 86. If there is an even number of values in a set (six test scores, for instance), simply take the average of the two middle numbers.

44. Mode

The mode of a set of numbers is the **value that appears most often**. If your test scores were 88, 57, 68, 85, 99, 93, 93, 84, and 81, the mode of the scores would be 93 because it appears more often than any other score. If there is a tie for the most common value in a set, the set has more than one mode.

POSSIBILITIES AND PROBABILITY

45. Counting the Possibilities

The fundamental counting principle: If there are *m* **ways** one event can happen and *n* **ways** a second event can happen, then there are *m* × *n* **ways** for the two events to happen. For example, with five shirts and seven pairs of pants to choose from, you can put together 5 × 7 = 35 different outfits.

46. Probability

$$\text{Probability} = \frac{\text{Favorable outcomes}}{\text{Total possible outcomes}}$$

For example, if you have 12 shirts in a drawer and nine of them are white, the probability of picking a white shirt at random is $\frac{9}{12} = \frac{3}{4}$. This probability can also be expressed as .75 or 75 percent.

POWERS AND ROOTS

47. Multiplying and Dividing Powers

To multiply powers with the same base, **add the exponents and keep the same base:**

$$x^3 \times x^4 = x^{3+4} = x^7$$

To divide powers with the same base, **subtract the exponents and keep the same base:**

$$y^{13} \div y^8 = y^{13-8} = y^5$$

48. Raising Powers to Powers

To raise a power to a power, **multiply the exponents**:

$$(x^3)^4 = x^{3 \times 4} = x^{12}$$

49. Simplifying Square Roots

To simplify a square root, **factor out the perfect squares** under the radical, unsquare them and put the result in front.

$$\sqrt{12} = \sqrt{4 \times 3} = \sqrt{4} \times \sqrt{3} = 2\sqrt{3}$$

50. Adding and Subtracting Roots

You can add or subtract radical expressions **when the part under the radicals is the same:**

$$2\sqrt{3} + 3\sqrt{3} = 5\sqrt{3}$$

Don't try to add or subtract when the radical parts are different. There's not much you can do with an expression like:

$$3\sqrt{5} + 3\sqrt{7}$$

51. Multiplying and Dividing Roots

The product of square roots is equal to the **square root of the product:**

$$\sqrt{3} \times \sqrt{5} = \sqrt{3 \times 5} = \sqrt{15}$$

The quotient of square roots is equal to the **square root of the quotient:**

$$\frac{\sqrt{6}}{\sqrt{3}} = \sqrt{\frac{6}{3}} = \sqrt{2}$$

ALGEBRAIC EXPRESSIONS

52. Evaluating an Expression

To evaluate an algebraic expression, **plug in** the given values for the unknowns and calculate according to **PEMDAS**. To find the value of $x^2 + 5x - 6$ when $x = -2$, plug in -2 for x: $(-2)^2 + 5(-2) - 6 = 4 - 10 - 6 = -12$.

53. Adding and Subtracting Monomials

To combine like terms, **keep the variable part unchanged while adding or subtracting the coefficients:**

$$2a + 3a = (2 + 3)a = 5a$$

54. Adding and Subtracting Polynomials

To add or subtract polynomials, **combine like terms**.

$$(3x^2 + 5x - 7) - (x^2 + 12) =$$
$$(3x^2 - x^2) + 5x + (-7 - 12) =$$
$$2x^2 + 5x - 19$$

55. Multiplying Monomials

To multiply monomials, **multiply the coefficients and the variables separately:**

$$2a \times 3a = (2 \times 3)(a \times a) = 6a^2$$

56. Multiplying Binomials—FOIL

To multiply binomials, use **FOIL**. To multiply $(x + 3)$ by $(x + 4)$, first multiply the **F**irst terms: $x \times x = x^2$. Next the **O**uter terms: $x \times 4 = 4x$. Then the **I**nner terms: $3 \times x = 3x$. And finally the **L**ast terms: $3 \times 4 = 12$. Then add and combine like terms:

$$x^2 + 4x + 3x + 12 = x^2 + 7x + 12$$

57. Multiplying Other Polynomials

FOIL works only when you want to multiply two binomials. If you want to multiply polynomials with more than two terms, make sure you **multiply each term in the first polynomial by each term in the second.**

$$(x^2 + 3x + 4)(x + 5) =$$
$$x^2(x + 5) + 3x(x + 5) + 4(x + 5) =$$
$$x^3 + 5x^2 + 3x^2 + 15x + 4x + 20 =$$
$$x^3 + 8x^2 + 19x + 20$$

After multiplying two polynomials together, the number of terms in your expression before simplifying should equal the number of terms in one polynomial multiplied by the number of terms in the second. In the example above, you should have $3 \times 2 = 6$ terms in the product before you simplify like terms.

FACTORING ALGEBRAIC EXPRESSIONS

58. Factoring out a Common Divisor

A factor common to all terms of a polynomial can be **factored out**. Each of the three terms in the polynomial $3x^3 + 12x^2 - 6x$ contains a factor of $3x$. Pulling out the common factor yields $3x(x^2 + 4x - 2)$.

59. Factoring the Difference of Squares

One of the test maker's favorite factorables is the **difference of squares**.

$$a^2 - b^2 = (a - b)(a + b)$$

$x^2 - 9$, for example, factors to $(x - 3)(x + 3)$.

60. Factoring the Square of a Binomial

Learn to recognize polynomials that are squares of binomials:

$$a^2 + 2ab + b^2 = (a + b)^2$$
$$a^2 - 2ab + b^2 = (a - b)^2$$

For example, $4x^2 + 12x + 9$ factors to $(2x + 3)^2$, and $n^2 - 10n + 25$ factors to $(n - 5)^2$.

61. Factoring Other Polynomials—FOIL in Reverse

To factor a quadratic expression, **think about what binomials you could use FOIL on to get that quadratic expression**. To factor $x^2 - 5x + 6$, think about what First terms will produce x^2, what Last terms will produce $+6$, and what Outer and Inner terms will produce $-5x$. Some common sense—and a little trial and error—lead you to $(x - 2)(x - 3)$.

62. Simplifying an Algebraic Fraction

Simplifying an algebraic fraction is a lot like simplifying a numerical fraction. The general idea is to **find factors common to the numerator and denominator and cancel them**. Thus, simplifying an algebraic fraction begins with factoring.

For example, to simplify $\frac{x^2 - x - 12}{x^2 - 9}$, first factor the numerator and denominator:

$$\frac{x^2 - x - 12}{x^2 - 9} = \frac{(x - 4)(x + 3)}{(x - 3)(x + 3)}$$

Canceling $x + 3$ from the numerator and denominator leaves you with $\frac{x - 4}{x - 3}$.

SOLVING EQUATIONS

63. Solving a Linear Equation

To solve an equation, do whatever is necessary to both sides to **isolate the variable**. To solve the equation $5x - 12 = -2x + 9$, first get all the xs on one side by adding $2x$ to both sides: $7x - 12 = 9$. Then add 12 to both sides: $7x = 21$. Then divide both sides by 7: $x = 3$.

64. Solving "in Terms of"

To solve an equation for one variable **in terms of** another means to **isolate the one variable on one side of the equation**, leaving an expression containing the other variable on the other side of the equation. To solve the equation $3x - 10y = -5x + 6y$ for x in terms of y, isolate x:

$$3x - 10y = -5x + 6y$$
$$3x + 5x = 6y + 10y$$
$$8x = 16y$$
$$x = 2y$$

65. Translating from English into Algebra

To translate from English into algebra, **look for the key words and systematically turn phrases into algebraic expressions and sentences into equations**. Be careful about order, especially when subtraction is called for.

Example: The charge for a phone call is r cents for the first three minutes and s cents for each minute thereafter. What is the cost, in cents, of a phone call lasting exactly t minutes? ($t > 3$)

Setup: The charge begins with r, and then something more is added, depending on the length of the call. The amount added is s times the number of minutes past three minutes. If the total number of minutes is t, then the number of minutes past three is $t - 3$. So the charge is $r + s(t - 3)$.

66. Solving a Quadratic Equation

To solve a quadratic equation, put it in the "$ax^2 + bx + c = 0$" form, **factor** the left side (if you can), and set each factor equal to 0 separately to get the two solutions. To solve $x^2 + 12 = 7x$, first rewrite it as $x^2 - 7x + 12 = 0$. Then factor the left side:

$$(x - 3)(x - 4) = 0$$
$$x - 3 = 0 \text{ or } x - 4 = 0$$
$$x = 3 \text{ or } 4$$

67. Solving a System of Equations

You can solve for two variables only if you have two distinct equations. Two forms of the same equation will not be adequate. **Combine the equations** in such a way that **one of the variables cancels out**. To solve the two equations $4x + 3y = 8$ and $x + y = 3$, multiply both sides of the second equation by -3 to get: $-3x - 3y = -9$. Now add the two equations; the $3y$ and the $-3y$ cancel out, leaving: $x = -1$. Plug that back into either one of the original equations and you'll find that $y = 4$.

68. Solving an Inequality

To solve an inequality, do whatever is necessary to both sides to **isolate the variable**. Just remember that when you **multiply or divide both sides by a negative number**, you must **reverse the sign**. To solve $-5x + 7 < -3$, subtract 7 from both sides to get: $-5x < -10$. Now divide both sides by -5, remembering to reverse the sign: $x > 2$.

COORDINATE GEOMETRY

69. Finding the Distance Between Two Points

To find the distance between points, use the **Pythagorean theorem or special right triangles**. The difference between the xs is one leg and the difference between the ys is the other.

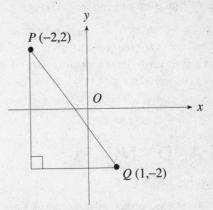

In the figure above, PQ is the hypotenuse of a 3-4-5 triangle, so $PQ = 5$.

You can also use the **distance formula**:

$$d = \sqrt{(x_1 - x_2)^2 + (y_1 - y_2)^2}$$

To find the distance between $R(3, 6)$ and $S(5, -2)$:

$$d = \sqrt{(3 - 5)^2 + [6 - (-2)]^2}$$
$$= \sqrt{(-2)^2 + (8)^2}$$
$$= \sqrt{68} = 2\sqrt{17}$$

70. Using Two Points to Find the Slope

$$\text{Slope} = \frac{\text{Change in } y}{\text{Change in } x} = \frac{\text{Rise}}{\text{Run}}$$

The slope of the line that contains the points $A(2, 3)$ and $B(0, -1)$ is:

$$\frac{y_A - y_B}{x_A - x_B} = \frac{3 - (-1)}{2 - 0} = \frac{4}{2} = 2$$

71. Using an Equation to Find the Slope

To find the slope of a line from an equation, put the equation into the **slope-intercept** form:

$$y = mx + b$$

The **slope is** m. To find the slope of the equation $3x + 2y = 4$, rearrange it:

$$3x + 2y = 4$$
$$2y = -3x + 4$$
$$y = -\frac{3}{2}x + 2$$

The slope is $-\frac{3}{2}$.

72. Using an Equation to Find an Intercept

To find the y-intercept, you can either put the equation into $y = mx + b$ (slope-intercept) form—in which case b **is the y-intercept**—or you can just **plug $x = 0$** into the equation and **solve for y**. To find the x-intercept, **plug $y = 0$** into the equation and **solve for x**.

LINES AND ANGLES

73. Intersecting Lines

When two lines intersect, **adjacent angles are supplementary and vertical angles are equal**.

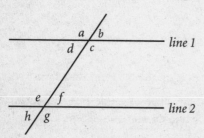

In the figure above, the angles marked $a°$ and $b°$ are adjacent and supplementary, so $a + b = 180$. Furthermore, the angles marked $a°$ and $60°$ are vertical and equal, so $a = 60$.

74. Parallel Lines and Transversals

A transversal across parallel lines forms **four equal acute angles and four equal obtuse angles**.

In the figure above, line 1 is parallel to line 2. Angles a, c, e, and g are obtuse, so they are all equal. Angles b, d, f, and h are acute, so they are all equal.

Furthermore, **any of the acute angles is supplementary to any of the obtuse angles**. Angles a and h are supplementary, as are b and e, c and f, and so on.

TRIANGLES—GENERAL

75. Interior Angles of a Triangle

The three angles of any triangle add up to 180°.

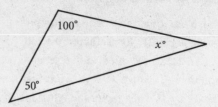

In the figure above, $x + 50 + 100 = 180$, so $x = 30$.

76. Exterior Angles of a Triangle

An exterior angle of a triangle is equal to the **sum of the remote interior angles**.

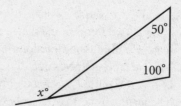

In the figure above, the exterior angle labeled $x°$ is equal to the sum of the remote angles: $x = 50 + 100 = 150$.

The three exterior angles of a triangle add up to 360°.

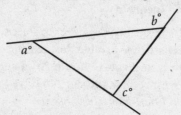

In the figure above, $a + b + c = 360$.

77. Similar Triangles

Similar triangles have the same shape; **corresponding angles are equal and corresponding sides are proportional.**

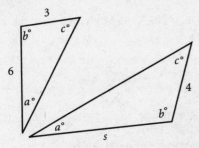

The triangles above are similar because they have the same angles. The 3 corresponds to the 4 and the 6 corresponds to the *s*.

$$\frac{3}{4} = \frac{6}{s}$$

$$3s = 24$$

$$s = 8$$

78. Area of a Triangle

$$\text{Area of Triangle} = \frac{1}{2}(\text{base})(\text{height})$$

The height is the perpendicular distance between the side that's chosen as the base and the opposite vertex.

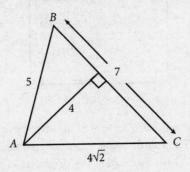

In the triangle above, 4 is the height when the 7 is chosen as the base.

$$\text{Area} = \frac{1}{2}bh = \frac{1}{2}(7)(4) = 14$$

79. Triangle Inequality Theorem

The length of one side of a triangle must be **greater than the difference and less than the sum** of the lengths of the other two sides. For example, if it is given that the length of one side is 3 and the length of another side is 7, then you know that the length of the third side must be greater than $7 - 3 = 4$ and less than $7 + 3 = 10$.

80. Isosceles Triangles

An isosceles triangle is a triangle that has **two equal sides**. Not only are two sides equal, but the angles opposite the equal sides, called base angles, are also equal.

81. Equilateral Triangles

Equilateral triangles are triangles in which **all three sides are equal**. Since all the sides are equal, all the angles are also equal. All three angles in an equilateral triangle measure 60 degrees, regardless of the lengths of sides.

RIGHT TRIANGLES

82. Pythagorean Theorem

For all right triangles:

$$(\text{leg}_1)^2 + (\text{leg}_2)^2 = (\text{hypotenuse})^2$$

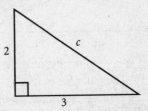

If one leg is 2 and the other leg is 3, then:

$$2^2 + 3^2 = c^2$$
$$c^2 = 4 + 9$$
$$c = \sqrt{13}$$

83. The 3-4-5 Triangle

If a right triangle's leg-to-leg ratio is 3:4, or if the leg-to-hypotenuse ratio is 3:5 or 4:5, it's a 3-4-5 triangle and you don't need to use the Pythagorean theorem to find the third side. Just figure out what multiple of 3-4-5 it is.

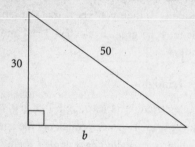

In the right triangle shown, one leg is 30 and the hypotenuse is 50. This is 10 times 3-4-5. The other leg is 40.

84. The 5-12-13 Triangle

If a right triangle's leg-to-leg ratio is 5:12, or if the leg-to-hypotenuse ratio is 5:13 or 12:13, then it's a 5-12-13 triangle. You don't need to use the Pythagorean theorem to find the third side. Just figure out what multiple of 5-12-13 it is.

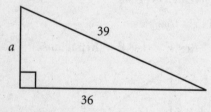

Here one leg is 36 and the hypotenuse is 39. This is 3 times 5-12-13. The other leg is 15.

85. The 30-60-90 Triangle

The sides of a 30-60-90 triangle are in a ratio of $x : x\sqrt{3} : 2x$; the Pythagorean theorem is not necessary.

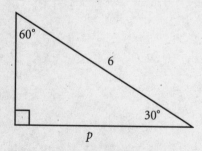

If the hypotenuse is 6, then the shorter leg is half that, or 3; and then the longer leg is equal to the short leg times $\sqrt{3}$, or $3\sqrt{3}$.

86. The 45-45-90 Triangle

The sides of a 45-45-90 triangle are in a ratio of $x : x : x\sqrt{2}$.

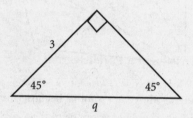

If one leg is 3, then the other leg is also 3, and the hypotenuse is equal to a leg times $\sqrt{2}$, or $3\sqrt{2}$.

OTHER POLYGONS

87. Characteristics of a Rectangle

A rectangle is a **four-sided figure with four right angles**. Opposite sides are equal. Diagonals are equal.

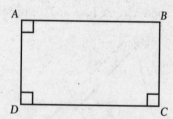

Quadrilateral *ABCD* above is shown to have three right angles. The fourth angle therefore also measures 90°, and *ABCD* is a rectangle. The perimeter of a rectangle is equal to the sum of the lengths of the four sides, which is equivalent to 2(length + width).

88. Area of a Rectangle

Area of Rectangle = Length × Width

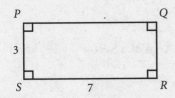

The area of a 7-by-3 rectangle is $7 \times 3 = 21$.

89. Characteristics of a Parallelogram

A parallelogram has **two pairs of parallel sides**. Opposite sides are equal. Opposite angles are equal. Consecutive angles add up to 180˚.

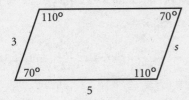

In the figure above, s is the length of the side opposite the 3, so $s = 3$.

90. Area of a Parallelogram

Area of Parallelogram = base × height

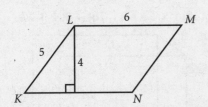

In parallelogram *KLMN* above, 4 is the height when *LM* or *KN* is used as the base. Base × height = $6 \times 4 = 24$.

91. Characteristics of a Square

A square is a **rectangle with four equal sides**.

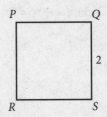

If *PQRS* is a square, all sides are the same length as *QR*. The perimeter of a square is equal to four times the length of one side.

92. Area of a Square

Area of Square = (Side)²

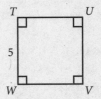

The square above, with sides of length 5, has an area of $5^2 = 25$.

93. Interior Angles of a Polygon

The **sum of the measures of the interior angles of a polygon** $= (n - 2) \times 180$, where n is the number of sides.

Sum of the Angles = $(n - 2) \times 180$

The eight angles of an octagon, for example, add up to $(8 - 2) \times 180 = 1,080$.

CIRCLES

94. Circumference of a Circle

$$\text{Circumference} = 2\pi r$$

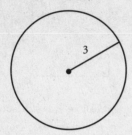

In the circle above, the radius is 3, and so the circumference is $2\pi(3) = 6\pi$.

95. Length of an Arc

An **arc** is a piece of the circumference. If n is the degree measure of the arc's central angle, then the formula is:

$$\text{Length of an Arc} = \left(\frac{n}{360}\right)(2\pi r)$$

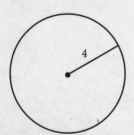

In the figure above, the radius is 5 and the measure of the central angle is 72°. The arc length is $\frac{72}{360}$ or $\frac{1}{5}$ of the circumference:

$$\left(\frac{72}{360}\right)(2\pi)(5) = \left(\frac{1}{5}\right)(10\pi) = 2\pi$$

96. Area of a Circle

$$\text{Area of a Circle} = \pi r^2$$

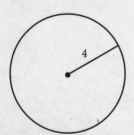

The area of the circle is $\pi(4)^2 = 16\pi$.

97. Area of a Sector

A **sector** is a piece of the area of a circle. If n is the degree measure of the sector's central angle, then the formula is:

$$\text{Area of a Sector} = \left(\frac{n}{360}\right)(\pi r^2)$$

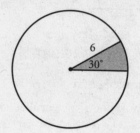

In the figure above, the radius is 6 and the measure of the sector's central angle is 30°. The sector has $\frac{30}{360}$ or $\frac{1}{12}$ of the area of the circle:

$$\left(\frac{30}{360}\right)(\pi)(6^2) = \left(\frac{1}{12}\right)(36\pi) = 3\pi$$

SOLIDS

98. Surface Area of a Rectangular Solid

The surface of a rectangular solid consists of three pairs of identical faces. To find the surface area, find the area of each face and add them up. If the length is l, the width is w, and the height is h, the formula is:

$$\text{Surface Area} = 2lw + 2wh + 2lh$$

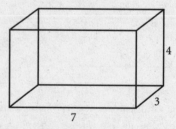

The surface area of the box above is: $2 \times 7 \times 3 + 2 \times 3 \times 4 + 2 \times 7 \times 4 = 42 + 24 + 56 = 122$

99. Volume of a Rectangular Solid

Volume of a Rectangular Solid = *lwh*

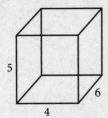

The volume of a 4-by-5-by-6 box is

$$4 \times 5 \times 6 = 120$$

A cube is a rectangular solid with length, width, and height all equal. If e is the length of an edge of a cube, the volume formula is:

Volume of a Cube = e^3

The volume of this cube is $2^3 = 8$.

100. Volume of a Cylinder

Volume of a Cylinder = $\pi r^2 h$

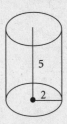

In the cylinder above, $r = 2$, $h = 5$, so:

$$\text{Volume} = \pi(2^2)(5) = 20\pi$$

How Did We Do? Grade Us.

Thank you for choosing a Kaplan book. Your comments and suggestions are very useful to us. Please answer the following questions to assist us in our continued development of high-quality resources to meet your needs. Or go online and complete our interactive survey form at **kaplansurveys.com/books**.

The title of the Kaplan book I read was: _____

My name is: _____

My address is: _____

_____

My e-mail address is: _____

What overall grade would you give this book?   Ⓐ   Ⓑ   Ⓒ   Ⓓ   Ⓕ

How relevant was the information to your goals?   Ⓐ   Ⓑ   Ⓒ   Ⓓ   Ⓕ

How comprehensive was the information in this book?   Ⓐ   Ⓑ   Ⓒ   Ⓓ   Ⓕ

How accurate was the information in this book?   Ⓐ   Ⓑ   Ⓒ   Ⓓ   Ⓕ

How easy was the book to use?   Ⓐ   Ⓑ   Ⓒ   Ⓓ   Ⓕ

How appealing was the book's design?   Ⓐ   Ⓑ   Ⓒ   Ⓓ   Ⓕ

What were the book's strong points? _____

How could this book be improved? _____

Is there anything that we left out that you wanted to know more about?

Would you recommend this book to others?   ☐ YES   ☐ NO

Other comments: _____

_____

_____

Do we have permission to quote you?   ☐ YES   ☐ NO

Thank you for your help.
Please tear out this page and mail it to:

Managing Editor
Kaplan, Inc.
1440 Broadway, 8th floor
New York, NY 10018

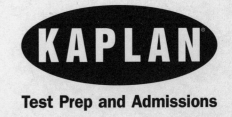

Thanks!

Need help preparing for the SAT?

We've got some recommended reading.

Guides for students taking the SAT on or before January 22, 2005

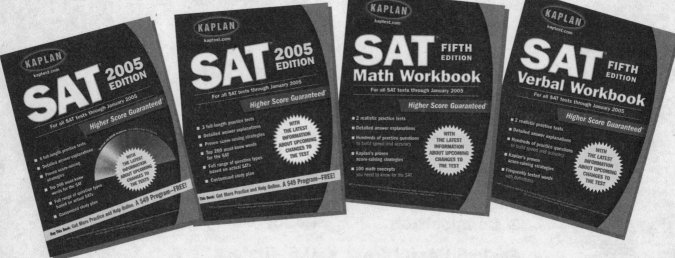

Guides for students taking the SAT beginning in March 2005

KAPLAN

Test Prep and Admissions

Published by Simon & Schuster

Ask for Kaplan wherever books are sold.